In an effort to **go green**, Oxford University Press is providing a **Sampler Edition** of *Patterns of World History*, Third Edition. This **Sampler** includes chapters 15–23, the full table of contents and front matter, and the index. By using less paper in this **Sampler**, we're saving more trees. By providing the full text in a digital format, we lessen carbon emissions with reduced shipping. The cost savings from these green initiatives will help fund our mission to support Oxford University's objective of excellence in research, scholarship, and education.

If you are considering the text for adoption and would like to see more, you can **view the complete text via eBook or receive a full printed copy** of the text. Simply contact your Oxford University Press representative or call 800.280.0280 to request a copy.

Less paper = more trees saved

eBook = no carbon emission from shipping

Cost savings = more money to fund OUP's mission

Patterns of World History, Third Edition, offers a distinct framework for understanding the global past through the study of origins, interactions, and adaptations.

New to This Edition

- A **streamlined narrative**, focusing even more on key concepts
- Fully **revised and updated chapters** throughout, with recent developments and new scholarship
- **Dashboard**, a learning management system that offers numerous assessment options and a variety of interactive content organized by chapter

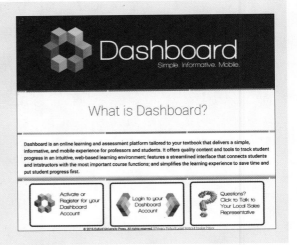

Dashboard
Simple. Informative. Mobile.

What is Dashboard?

Dashboard is an online learning and assessment platform tailored to your textbook that delivers a simple, informative, and mobile experience for professors and students. It offers quality content and tools to track student progress in an intuitive, web-based learning environment; features a streamlined interface that connects students and instructors with the most important course functions; and simplifies the learning experience to save time and put student progress first.

Activate or Register for your Dashboard Account

Login to your Dashboard Account

Questions? Click to Talk to Your Local Sales Representative

Patterns Up Close

Social Networking

As we have seen, the Tunisian revolution sparked a wave of revolts across North Africa and the Middle East in what has come to be called the Arab Spring. What makes these movements unique, however, is that they were organized and carried out by means of *social networking sites* (SNSs) like Twitter, Facebook, and YouTube, supported by cell phones and other modern communication technologies. But what are the origins of these devices, and how have they developed into such important tools of political and social revolution?

Patterns Up Close boxes in each chapter highlight a particular innovation that demonstrates the patterns approach in action

Primary sources at the end of each chapter enhance student engagement with key topics

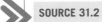 **SOURCE 31.2**

Vladimir Putin, Address to the Duma concerning the annexation of Crimea

March 19, 2014

Vladimir Putin, the former KGB officer who has dominated Russian political life since 2000, delivered this remarkable oration after annexing the Crimea region from the nation of Ukraine in March 2014. This move came after a protest movement had driven the pro-Russian president of Ukraine out of office, and as tensions between ethnic Ukrainians and ethnic Russians in the country had erupted into violence in several Ukrainian cities. Once a referendum was held in the Crimean Peninsula about whether to remain within Ukraine or to be united to Russia, Putin, believing that "the numbers speak for themselves," authorized the annexation of the region as Russian territory. In this speech, justifying his country's move against a fellow former Soviet Socialist Republic, Putin appealed to both recent and distant history—and, perhaps, signaled his further intentions for the future.

Source: http://rt.com/politics/official-word/vladimir-putin-crimea-address-658/

Turkish Citizen with His Daughter. A Turkish father and daughter during mass demonstrations in support of Turkish President Recep Erdoğan after the failed military coup of July 15, 2016. A referendum in April 2017 gave the presidency sweeping new executive powers, allowing Erdoğan to consolidate his position.

The text is complemented by a robust art program with over 400 photos and nearly 200 maps

Chapter-by-chapter Changes to the Third Edition

Part One

- Chapter 1 includes three major changes: a discussion of the new stone tool finds in Kenya, dated to 3.3 million years ago; revisions to our understanding of the Neanderthals, on the basis of the new Bruniquel Cave finds; and revisions to our understanding of the human settlement of the Americas, resulting from new genetic studies (2015–2016)

- Chapter 2 clarifies the conceptual transition from nature spirituality to what is commonly called polytheism

- Chapter 3 updates the material on ancient India and the Harappans

- In Chapter 5, the "Patterns Up Close" feature adds the results of a new 2016 genetic study on corn

Part Two

- The title of Chapter 7 has been changed to "Interaction and Adaptation in Western Eurasia: Persia, Greece, and Rome" to emphasize the interactions among these cultural zones

- Chapter 8 contains a revised section on Jainism

- Chapter 9 adds a survey of the contemporary debate about the "Han Synthesis"

Part Three

- Chapter 10 offers clearer discussions of the Arab conquests of the Middle East, North Africa, and Iberia during the 600s and early 700s and of the composition of Islamic salvation history in the 800s, including the biography of the prophet Muhammad. It also provides improved coverage of Byzantium, with a discussion of iconoclasm and the split between Catholicism and Greek Orthodoxy in 1054.

- Chapter 12 focuses more strongly on the Mongol interval and adds specificity to the discussion of Neo-Confucian philosophy. A new title, "Sultanates, Song, and the Mongol Super Empire: Contrasting Patterns in India, China, and Inner Asia, 600–1600 CE," reflects the increased coverage of the Mongols.

Part Four

- Chapter 17 eliminates considerable detail from the presentation of the European religious wars and broadens the focus in the English case to include the War of the Three Kingdoms

- Chapter 21 updates the discussion of the Chinese rural economy and the debate about the High-Level Equilibrium Trap. It also improves the discussion of Qing concepts of multicultural empire.

Part Five

- Chapter 22 reformulates the basic concepts of modern nationalism, now distinguishing between the patterns of constitutionalism and ethnic nationalism as keys for the understanding of political modernity. It also presents the process of Italian ethnic nationalist unification more clearly.

- Chapter 23 is completely reorganized, emphasizing the significance of the Paraguayan War of 1864–1870

- Chapter 24 describes the role of the Hakkas in the Taiping movement more clearly

- Chapter 26 strongly emphasizes the importance of the steam engine in the Industrial Revolution and reconceptualizes the nineteenth-century class structure in the emerging industrial societies

- Chapter 27 more sharply defines the pattern of the New Imperialism during the nineteenth century

Part Six

- Chapter 29 updates the "Patterns Up Close" feature on the Non-Aligned Movement

- Chapter 30 offers improved coverage of the Lebanese civil war, the Iranian Islamic Revolution, the U.S. Vietnam War, and the Brazilian economic miracle

- Chapter 31 includes new material on the travails of the Arab Spring; the new military regime in Egypt; the "Islamic State" of Iraq and Syria; the failed coup d'état in Turkey; and the new populist anti-globalism, complete with "Brexit" in Europe and Donald J. Trump's electoral victory in the United States. An updated "Patterns Up Close" essay on information technology discusses the misuse of IT by terrorists.

Cutting-edge digital tools

Dashboard (www.oup.com/us/dashboard)

Simple, informative, and mobile, **Dashboard** is an online learning and assessment platform tailored to your textbook that delivers a simple, informative, and mobile experience for professors and students.
Dashboard:

> » Offers quality content and tools to track student progress in an intuitive, web-based learning environment

> » Features a streamlined interface that connects students and instructors with the most important course functions

> » Simplifies the learning experience to save time and put student progress first

What is Dashboard?

Dashboard is an online learning and assessment platform tailored to your textbook that delivers a simple, informative, and mobile experience for professors and students. It offers quality content and tools to track student progress in an intuitive, web-based learning environment; features a streamlined interface that connects students and intstructors with the most important course functions; and simplifies the learning experience to save time and put student progress first.

Activate or Register for your Dashboard Account

Login to your Dashboard Account

Questions? Click to Talk to Your Local Sales Representative

What makes Dashboard different from other Learning Platforms?

We wanted to develop a platform that would really justify the term "learning solution" without the unnecessary complexity these "solutions" often create. We therefore asked *you*, the academic community, what you believe to be the most important factors in creating the ideal online platform to accompany an adopted textbook.

> **You answered: It should be *simple* to set up for my course and easy for my students to learn and use.**

We've created Dashboard to be just that. The site navigation has been designed to be streamlined, intuitive, and as clear as possible. The platform is supported and administered by OUP, so you can focus on teaching rather than IT support. Once you have access to Dashboard, you and your students can start using it immediately. You can customize the content as little or as much as you like. We expect users to master the site in under 15 minutes.

Dashboard for *Patterns of World History,* Third Edition, includes:

- An **embedded e-book** that integrates multimedia content, providing a dynamic learning space for both students and instructors

Each chapter in *Patterns of World History* includes:

Image analysis

Map analysis, interactive timelines, and interactive concept maps

Audio flashcards

Document analysis

Many chapters also include ▷ Video analysis

- Aligned according to Bloom's Taxonomy, the three sets of **quizzes** per chapter provide both low-stakes and medium-stakes testing:

    ≫ **Quiz 1 tests basic concepts and terminologies**

    ≫ **Quiz 2 provides questions that test both basic facts and ability to apply concepts**

    ≫ **Quiz 3 tests ability to evaluate and analyze key concepts**

- The **complete set of questions from the test bank** (1,500 questions) provides, for each chapter, approximately forty multiple-choice, short-answer, true-or-false, and fill-in-the-blank questions and approximately ten essay questions

"I can't imagine a better book than this. It makes teaching a balanced course so much easier and provides substantial resources for students."

—Marika Snider, *Miami University*

Additional Resources to enhance the learning experience

Ancillary Resource Center (ARC): The ARC is a convenient, instructor-focused single destination for resources to accompany *Patterns of World History*, Third Edition. Available to adopters of this text, this online resource center includes:

>> An **Instructor's Resource Manual** featuring, for each chapter:

- A detailed chapter outline, suggested lecture topics, learning objectives, map quizzes, geography exercises, classroom activities, "Patterns Up Close" activities, "Seeing Patterns and Making Connections" activities, "Against the Grain" exercises, biographical sketches, and suggested web resources and digital media files

- Approximately forty multiple-choice, short-answer, true-or-false, and fill-in-the-blank questions, and approximately ten essay questions

>> **PowerPoints and a Computerized Test Bank** offering:

- PowerPoint slides and JPEG and PDF files for all of the maps and photos in the text, an additional 400 map files from *The Oxford Atlas of World History*, and approximately 1,000 additional PowerPoint slides from OUP's Image Bank Library, organized by themes and topics in world history

- Approximately 1,500 questions that can be customized by the instructor

>> The **Oxford World History Video Library** including:

- Ten brief (2–3 minutes) videos on such key topics in world history as the Maya, the Golden Age of Islam, Genghis Khan, Cortés, the Haitian Revolution, the steam engine, the Atomic Age, and other important subjects. These are ideal as lecture-launchers or as online viewing assignments.

Companion Website (www.oup.com/us/vonsivers): Includes quizzes, flashcards, web links, and note-taking guides.

"I really value the broad scope of *Patterns of World History*. I also like the patterns between cultures and historical development; they place everything within a wide context."

—AnnaMarie Vallis, *California State University, Fresno*

Sources in Patterns of World History: **Vol. 1: To 1600** (978-0-19-939972-7) **and Vol. 2: Since 1400** (978-0-19-939973-4): Each volume includes approximately seventy-five to ninety text and visual sources in world history, organized by the chapter organization of *Patterns of World History*. Each source is accompanied by a headnote and reading questions. **Only $5** when packaged with the text.

Mapping Patterns of World History: **Vol. 1: To 1600** (978-0-19-985638-1) **and Vol. 2: Since 1400** (978-0-19-985639-8): Each volume includes approximately fifty full-color maps, each accompanied by a brief headnote, as well as blank outline maps and Concept Map exercises. **FREE** when packaged with the text.

Now Playing: Learning World History Through Film (978-0-19-998957-7): **FREE** when packaged with the text.

The Oxford Map Companion: One Hundred Sources in World History (978-0-19-976563-8): **Save 20%** when packaged with the text.

Patterns of World History, with Sources, Third Edition, is available in these volumes:

Volume One: To 1600 (Chapters 1–18) *with Sources*
eBook: 978-0-19-069363-3
Loose-leaf: 978-0-19-069369-5
Softcover: 978-0-19-069360-2

Volume Two: From 1400 (Chapters 15–31) *with Sources*
eBook: 978-0-19-069364-0
Loose-leaf: 978-0-19-069370-1
Softcover: 978-0-19-069361-9

Brief Edition

For those who prefer a shorter text, *Patterns of World History*, Third Edition, is also available in a **Brief Third Edition**. Approximately **twenty-five percent shorter** than the highly acclaimed comprehensive text, this **Brief Third Edition** features a **streamlined and tightened narrative**. With prices starting at **$24.95 per split volume**, the **Brief Third Edition** is one of the least expensive full-color world history textbooks available. It is also available as an **embedded eBook** with OUP's online learning and assessment platform, **Dashboard**.

Volume One: To 1600 (Chapters 1–18) *Brief Third Edition*

eBook: 978-0-19-069734-1
Loose-leaf: 978-0-19-069737-2
Softcover: 978-0-19-069731-0

Volume Two: From 1400 (Chapters 15–31) *Brief Third Edition*

eBook: 978-0-19-069735-8
Loose-leaf: 978-0-19-069738-9
Softcover: 978-0-19-069732-7

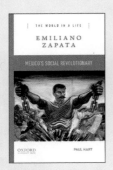

Available September 2017
Paul Hart, *Emiliano Zapata: Mexico's Social Revolutionary*

The World in a Life Series

Series Editor: Bonnie G. Smith, *Rutgers University*

Package any title from the **The World in a Life** series with *Patterns of World History* for FREE!*

* Each additional title is only $5.

Patterns of
World History

Patterns of World History

Volume Two from 1400

Third Edition

Peter von Sivers
University of Utah

Charles A. Desnoyers
La Salle University

George B. Stow
La Salle University

New York   Oxford
OXFORD UNIVERSITY PRESS

Oxford University Press is a department of the University of Oxford.
It furthers the University's objective of excellence in research,
scholarship, and education by publishing worldwide. Oxford is a
registered trade mark of Oxford University Press in the UK and
certain other countries.

Published in the United States of America by Oxford University Press
198 Madison Avenue, New York, NY 10016, United States of America.

For titles covered by Section 112 of the US Higher Education
Opportunity Act, please visit www.oup.com/us/he for the
latest information about pricing and alternate formats.

Library of Congress Cataloging-in-Publication Data
Names: Von Sivers, Peter, author. | Desnoyers, Charles, 1952- author. | Stow,
    George B., author. | Perry, Jonathan Scott, author.
Title: Patterns of world history, with sources / Peter von Sivers, University
    of Utah; Charles A. Desnoyers, La Salle University; George B. Stow, La
    Salle University; with the assistance of Jonathan S. Perry, University of
    South Florida, Sarasota-Manatee.
Description: Third edition. | New York, NY : Oxford University Press, 2017. |
    Includes bibliographical references and index.
Identifiers: LCCN 2017005347 (print) | LCCN 2017006181 (ebook) | ISBN
    9780190693602 (pbk. : alk. paper) | ISBN 9780190693619 (pbk. : alk. paper) |
    ISBN 9780190693626 (pbk. : alk. paper) | ISBN 9780190693633 (updf) |
    ISBN 9780190693640 (updf) | ISBN 9780190693657 (updf)
Subjects: LCSH: World history--Textbooks. | World history—Sources.
Classification: LCC D21 .V67 2017 (print) | LCC D21 (ebook) | DDC 909—dc23 LC record available
    at https://lccn.loc.gov/2017005347

9 8 7 6 5 4 3 2 1
Printed by LSC Communications, United States of America

—*I hear and I forget; I see and I remember; I do and I understand*
(Chinese proverb) 我听见我忘记;我看见我记住;我做我了解

Brief Contents

vii

Contents

PART THREE

The Formation of Religious Civilizations
600–1450 CE

Chapter 15
600–1550 CE

The Rise of Empires in the Americas

> PATTERNS OF EVIDENCE: **Sources for Chapter 15**

Features:

Patterns Up Close:

Against the Grain:

PART FOUR

Interactions across the Globe
1450–1750

Chapter 16
1450–1650

Western European Expansion and the Ottoman–Habsburg Struggle

The Renaissance, New Sciences, and Religious Wars in Europe

New Patterns in New Worlds: Colonialism and Indigenous Responses in the Americas

Features:

Patterns Up Close:
Voodoo and Other New
World Slave Religions   584

Against the Grain:
Oglethorpe's Free Colony 590

Features:

Patterns Up Close:
Akbar's Attempt at Religious
Synthesis   602

Against the Grain:
Sikhism in Transition 618

Chapter 21
1500–1800

Regulating the "Inner" and "Outer" Domains: China and Japan

> PATTERNS OF EVIDENCE: **Sources for Chapter 21**

PART FIVE

The Origins of Modernity
1750–1900

Chapter 22
1750–1871

Patterns of Nation-States and Culture in the Atlantic World

Chapter 23
1790–1917

Creoles and Caudillos: Latin America in the Nineteenth Century

Chapter 24
1750–1910

The Challenge of Modernity: East Asia

Features:

Patterns Up Close:
Military Transformations and the New Imperialism   826

Against the Grain:
An Anti-Imperial Perspective   846

PART SIX

From Three Modernities to One
1914–PRESENT

Features:

Patterns Up Close:
The Harlem Renaissance and the African Diaspora   860

Against the Grain:
Righteous among the Nations   886

Features:

Patterns Up Close:
Social Networking   984

Against the Grain:
North Korea, Lone Holdout
against the World   993

Maps

Studying with Maps

MAPS

World history cannot be fully understood without a clear comprehension of the chronologies and parameters within which different empires, states, and peoples have changed over time. Maps facilitate this understanding by illuminating the significance of time, space, and geography in shaping the patterns of world history.

Global Locator

Many of the maps in *Patterns of World History* include *global locators* that show the area being depicted in a larger context.

Projection

A map *projection* portrays all or part of the earth, which is spherical, on a flat surface. All maps, therefore, include some distortion. The projections in *Patterns of World History* show the earth at global, continental, regional, and local scales.

Topography

Many maps in *Patterns of World History* show *relief*—the contours of the land. Topography is an important element in studying maps because the physical terrain has played a critical role in shaping human history.

Scale Bar

Every map in *Patterns of World History* includes a *scale* that shows distances in both miles and kilometers, and in some instances in feet as well.

Map Key

Maps use symbols to show the location of features and to convey information. Each symbol is explained in the map's *key*.

One map in each chapter is accompanied by an icon that indicates that the map can be analyzed in an interactive fashion (see pages xxv–xxvi).

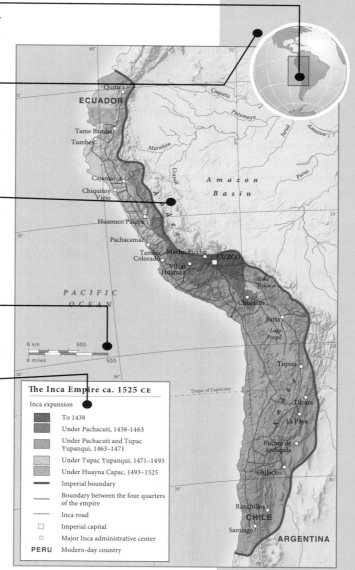

The Inca Empire ca. 1525 CE

Inca expansion

- To 1438
- Under Pachacuti, 1438–1463
- Under Pachacuti and Tupac Yupanqui, 1463–1471
- Under Tupac Yupanqui, 1471–1493
- Under Huayna Capac, 1493–1525
- Imperial boundary
- Boundary between the four quarters of the empire
- Inca road
- □ Imperial capital
- ○ Major Inca administrative center
- **PERU** Modern-day country

Preface

The response to the first two editions of *Patterns of World History* has been extraordinarily gratifying to those of us involved in its development. The diversity of schools that have adopted the book—community colleges as well as state universities; small liberal arts schools as well as large private universities—suggests to us that its central premise of exploring *patterns* in world history is both adaptable to a variety of pedagogical environments and congenial to a wide body of instructors. Indeed, from the responses to the book we have received thus far, we expect that the level of writing, timeliness and completeness of the material, and analytical approach will serve it well as the discipline of world history continues to mature. These key strengths are enhanced in the third edition of *Patterns* by constructive, dynamic suggestions from the broad range of students and instructors who are using the book.

It is widely agreed that world history is more than simply the sum of all national histories. Likewise, *Patterns of World History*, Third Edition, is more than an unbroken sequence of dates, battles, rulers, and their activities, and it is more than the study of isolated stories of change over time. Rather, in this textbook we endeavor to present in a clear and engaging way how world history "works." Instead of merely offering a narrative history of the appearance of this or that innovation, we present an analysis of the process by which an innovation in one part of the world is diffused and carried to the rest of the globe. Instead of focusing on the memorization of people, places, and events, we strive to present important facts in context and draw meaningful connections, analyzing whatever patterns we find and drawing conclusions where we can. In short, we seek to examine the interlocking mechanisms and animating forces of world history, without neglecting the human agency behind them.

The *Patterns* Approach

Our approach in this book is, as the title suggests, to look for patterns in world history. We should say at the outset that we do not mean to select certain categories into which we attempt to stuff the historical events we choose to emphasize, nor do we claim that all world history is reducible to such patterns, nor do we mean to suggest that the nature of the patterns determines the outcome of historical events. We see them instead as broad, flexible organizational frameworks around which to build the structure of a world history in such a way that the enormous sweep and content of the past can be viewed in a comprehensible narrative, with sound analysis and ample scope for debate and discussion. In this sense, we view them much like the armatures in clay sculptures, giving support and structure to the final figure but not necessarily preordaining its ultimate shape.

From its origins, human culture grew through interactions and adaptations on all the continents except Antarctica. A voluminous scholarship on all regions of the world has thus been accumulated, which those working in the field have to attempt to master if their explanations and arguments are to sound even remotely persuasive. The sheer volume and complexity of the sources, however, mean that even the knowledge and expertise of the best scholars are going to be incomplete. Moreover, the humility with which all historians must approach their material contains within it the realization that no historical explanation is ever fully satisfactory or final: As a driving force in the historical process, creative human agency moves events in directions that are never fully predictable, even if they follow broad patterns. Learning to discern patterns in this process not only helps novice historians to appreciate the complex challenges (and rewards) of historical inquiry; it also develops critical thinking abilities in all students.

As we move through the second decade of the twenty-first century, world historians have long since left behind the "West plus the rest" approach that marked the field's early years, together with economic and geographical reductionism, in the search for a new balance between comprehensive cultural and institutional examinations on the one hand and those highlighting human agency on the other. All too often, however, this is reflected in texts that seek broad coverage at the expense of analysis, thus resulting in a kind of "world history lite." Our aim is therefore to simplify the study of the world—to make it accessible to the student—without making world history itself simplistic.

Patterns of World History, Third Edition, proposes the teaching of world history from the perspective of the relationship between continuity and change. What we advocate in this book is a distinct intellectual framework for this relationship and the role of innovation and historical change through patterns of origins, interactions, and adaptations. Each small or large technical or cultural innovation originated in one geographical center or independently in several different centers. As people in the centers interacted with their neighbors, the neighbors adapted to, and in many cases were transformed by, the innovations. By "adaptation" we include the entire spectrum of human responses, ranging from outright rejection to creative borrowing and, at times, forced acceptance.

Small technical innovations often went through the pattern of origin, interaction, and adaptation across the world without arousing much attention, even though they had major consequences. For example, the horse collar, which originated in the last centuries BCE in China and allowed for the replacement of oxen with stronger horses, gradually improved the productivity of agriculture in eleventh-century western Europe. More sweeping intellectual–cultural innovations, by contrast, such as the spread of universal religions like Buddhism, Christianity, and Islam and the rise of science, have often had profound consequences—in some cases leading to conflicts lasting centuries—and affect us even today.

Sometimes change was effected by commodities that to us seem rather ordinary. Take sugar, for example: It originated in Southeast Asia and was traded and grown in the Mediterranean, where its cultivation on plantations created the model for expansion into the vast slave system of the Atlantic basin from the fifteenth through the nineteenth centuries, forever altering the histories of four continents. What would our diets look like today without sugar? Its history continues to unfold as we debate its merits and health risks and it supports huge multinational agribusinesses.

Or take a more obscure commodity: opium. Opium had been used medicinally for centuries in regions all over the world. But the advent of tobacco traded from the Americas to the Philippines to China, and the encouragement of Dutch traders in the region, created an environment in which the drug was smoked for the first time. Enterprising rogue British merchants, eager to find a way to crack closed Chinese markets for other goods, began to smuggle it in from India. The market grew, the price went down, addiction spread, and Britain and China ultimately went to war over China's attempts to eliminate the traffic. Here, we have an example of an item generating interactions on a worldwide scale, with impacts on everything from politics to economics, culture, and even the environment. The legacies of the trade still weigh heavily on two of the rising powers of the recent decades: China and India. And opium and its derivatives, like morphine and heroin, continue to bring relief as well as suffering on a colossal scale to hundreds of millions of people.

What, then, do we gain by studying world history through the use of such patterns? First, if we consider innovation to be a driving force of history, it helps to satisfy an intrinsic human curiosity about origins— our own and others. Perhaps more importantly, seeing patterns of various kinds in historical development brings to light connections and linkages among peoples, cultures, and regions—as in the aforementioned examples—that might not otherwise present themselves.

Second, such patterns can also reveal differences among cultures that other approaches to world history tend to neglect. For example, the differences between the civilizations of the Eastern and Western Hemispheres are generally highlighted in world history texts, but the broad commonalities of human groups creating agriculturally based cities and states in widely separated areas also show deep parallels in their patterns of origins, interactions, and adaptations. Such comparisons are at the center of our approach.

Third, this kind of analysis offers insights into how an individual innovation was subsequently developed and diffused across space and time—that is, the patterns by which the new eventually becomes a necessity in our daily lives. Through all of this we gain a deeper appreciation of the unfolding of global history from its origins in small, isolated areas to the vast networks of global interconnectedness in our present world.

Finally, our use of a broad-based understanding of continuity, change, and innovation allows us to restore culture in all its individual and institutionalized aspects—spiritual, artistic, intellectual, scientific—to its rightful place alongside technology, environment, politics, and socioeconomic conditions. That is, understanding innovation in this way allows this text to help illuminate the full range of human ingenuity over time and space in a comprehensive, evenhanded, and open-ended fashion.

Options for Teaching with *Patterns of World History*, Third Edition

In response to requests from teachers who adopted the previous editions, *Patterns of World History* includes a selection of primary-text and visual sources after every chapter. This section, called "Patterns of Evidence," enhances student engagement with key chapter patterns through contemporaneous voices and perspectives. Each source is accompanied by a concise introduction to provide chronological and geographical context; "Working with Sources" questions after each selection prompt students to make critical connections between the source and the main chapter narrative.

For the convenience of instructors teaching a course over two 15-week semesters, both versions of *Patterns* are limited to 31 chapters. For the sake of continuity and to accommodate the many different ways schools divide the midpoint of their world history sequence, Chapters 15–18 overlap in both volumes; in Volume 2, Chapter 15 is given as a "prelude" to Part Four. Those using a trimester system will also find divisions made in convenient places, with Chapter 10 coming at the beginning of Part Two and Chapter 22 at the beginning of Part Five. Finally, a Brief Edition of *Patterns* is also available. The Brief Edition is 25 percent shorter in length and does not include end-of-chapter primary sources..

Patterns of Change and Six Periods of World History

Similarly, *Patterns* is adaptable to both chronological and thematic styles of instruction. We divide the history of the world into six major time periods and recognize for each period one or two main patterns of innovation, their spread through interaction, and their

adoption by others. Obviously, lesser patterns are identified as well, many of which are of more limited regional interactive and adaptive impact. We wish to stress again that these are broad categories of analysis and that there is nothing reductive or deterministic in our aims or choices. Nevertheless, we believe the patterns we have chosen help to make the historical process more intelligible, providing a series of lenses that can help to focus the otherwise confusing facts and disparate details that comprise world history.

Part One (Prehistory–600 BCE): Origins of human civilization—tool making and symbol creating—in Africa as well as the origins of agriculture, urbanism, and state formation in the three agrarian centers of the Middle East, India, and China.

Part Two (600 BCE–600 CE): Emergence of the axial-age thinkers and their visions of a transcendent god or first principle in Eurasia; elevation of these visions to the status of state religions in empires and kingdoms, in the process forming multiethnic and multilinguistic polities.

Part Three (600–1450): Disintegration of classical empires and formation of religious civilizations in Eurasia, with the emergence of religiously unified regions divided by commonwealths of multiple states.

Part Four (1450–1750): Rise of new empires; interaction, both hostile and peaceful, among the religious civilizations and new empires across all continents of the world. Origins of the New Science in Europe, based on the use of mathematics for the investigation of nature.

Part Five (1750–1900): Origins of scientific–industrial "modernity," simultaneous with the emergence of constitutional and ethnic nation-states, in the West (Europe and North America); interaction of the West with Asia and Africa, resulting in complex adaptations, both coerced as well as voluntary, on the part of the latter.

Part Six (1900–Present): Division of early Western modernity into the three competing visions: communism, supremacist nationalism, and capitalism. After two horrific world wars and the triumph of nation-state formation across the world, capitalism remains as the last surviving version of modernity. Capitalism is then reinvigorated by the increasing use of social networking tools, which popularizes both "traditional" religious and cultural ideas and constitutionalism in authoritarian states.

Chapter Organization and Structure

Each part of the book addresses the role of change and innovation on a broad scale in a particular time and/or region, and each chapter contains different levels of exploration to examine the principal features of particular cultural or national areas and how each affects, and is affected by, the patterns of origins, interactions, and adaptations:

- *Geography and the Environment*: The relationship between human beings and the geography and environment of the places they inhabit is among the most basic factors in understanding human societies. In this chapter segment, therefore, the topics under investigation involve the natural environment of a particular region and the general conditions affecting change and innovation. Climatic conditions, earthquakes, tsunamis, volcanic eruptions, outbreaks of disease, and so forth all have obvious effects on how humans react to the challenge of survival. The initial portions of chapters introducing new regions for study therefore include environmental and geographical overviews, which are revisited and expanded in later chapters as necessary. The larger issues of how decisive the impact of geography on the development of human societies is—as in the commonly asked question "Is geography destiny?"—are also examined here.
- *Political Developments:* In this segment, we ponder such questions as how rulers and their supporters wield political and military power. How do different political traditions develop in different areas? How do states expand, and why? How do different political arrangements attempt to strike a balance between the rulers and the ruled? How and why are political innovations transmitted to other societies? Why do societies accept or reject

such innovations from the outside? Are there discernible patterns in the development of kingdoms or empires or nation-states?
- *Economic and Social Developments*: The relationship between economics and the structures and workings of societies has long been regarded as crucial by historians and social scientists. But what patterns, if any, emerge in how these relationships develop and function among different cultures? This segment explores such questions as the following: What role does economics play in the dynamics of change and continuity? What, for example, happens in agrarian societies when merchant classes develop? How does the accumulation of wealth lead to social hierarchy? What forms do these hierarchies take? How do societies formally and informally try to regulate wealth and poverty? How are economic conditions reflected in family life and gender relations? Are there patterns that reflect the varying social positions of men and women that are characteristic of certain economic and social institutions? How are these in turn affected by different cultural practices?
- *Intellectual, Religious, and Cultural Aspects*: Finally, we consider it vital to include an examination dealing in some depth with the way people understood their existence and life during each period. Clearly, intellectual innovation—the generation of new ideas—lies at the heart of the changes we have singled out as pivotal in the patterns of origins, interactions, and adaptations that form the heart of this text. Beyond this, those areas concerned with the search for and construction of meaning—particularly religion, the arts, philosophy, and science—not only reflect shifting perspectives but also, in many cases, play a leading role in determining the course of events within each form of society. All of these facets of intellectual life are in turn manifested in new perspectives and representations in the cultural life of a society.

Features

- **Seeing Patterns/Thinking Through Patterns:** "Seeing Patterns" and "Thinking Through Patterns" use a question–discussion format in each chapter to pose several broad questions ("Seeing Patterns") as advance organizers for key themes, which are then matched up with short essays at the end ("Thinking Through Patterns") that examine these same questions in a sophisticated yet student-friendly fashion.

- **Patterns Up Close:** Since students frequently apprehend macro-level patterns better when they see their contours brought into sharper relief, "Patterns Up Close" essays in each chapter highlight a particular innovation that demonstrates origins, interactions, and adaptations in action. Spanning technological, social, political, intellectual, economic, and environmental developments, the "Patterns Up Close" essays combine text, visuals, and graphics to consider everything from the pepper trade to the guillotine.
- **Against the Grain:** These brief essays consider counterpoints to the main patterns examined in each chapter. Topics range from visionaries who challenged dominant religious patterns, to women who resisted various forms of patriarchy, to agitators who fought for social and economic justice.
- **Marginal Glossary:** To avoid the necessity of having to flip pages back and forth, definitions of key terms are set directly in the margin at the point where they are first introduced.

Today, more than ever, students and instructors are confronted by a vast welter of information on every conceivable subject. Beyond the ever-expanding print media, the Internet and the Web have opened hitherto unimaginable amounts of data to us. Despite such unprecedented access, however, all of us are too frequently overwhelmed by this undifferentiated—and all too often indigestible—mass. Nowhere is this more true than in world history, by definition the field within the historical profession with the broadest scope. Therefore, we think that an effort at synthesis—of narrative and analysis structured around a clear, accessible, widely applicable theme—is needed, an effort that seeks to explain critical patterns of the world's past behind the billions of bits of information accessible at the stroke of a key on a computer keyboard. We hope this text, in tracing the lines of transformative ideas and things that left their patterns deeply imprinted into the canvas of world history, will provide such a synthesis.

Changes to the Third Edition

Streamlined narrative and sharpened focus To facilitate accessibility, we have shortened the text wherever possible. This reduction has not come at the expense of discarding essential topics. Instead, we have tightened the narrative, focusing even more on key concepts and (with the guidance of reviewers) discarding extraneous examples. We are profoundly grateful to the reviewers who pointed out errors and conceptual shortcomings. Factual accuracy and terminological precision are extremely important to us.

Updated scholarship All chapters were revised and updated, in accordance with recent developments and new scholarship. Here is a chapter-by-chapter overview that highlights the changes we made in the third edition:

- **Part One** Chapter 1 includes three major changes: a discussion of the new stone tool finds in Kenya, dated to 3.3 million years ago; revisions to our understanding of the Neanderthals, on the basis of the new Bruniquel Cave finds; and revisions to our understanding of the human settlement of the Americas, resulting from new genetic studies (2015–2016). Chapter 2 clarifies the conceptual transition from nature spirituality to what is commonly called polytheism. Chapter 3 updates the material on ancient India and Harappans, and the "Patterns Up Close" in Chapter 5 adds the results of a new 2016 genetic study on corn.
- **Part Two** The title of Chapter 7 has been changed to "Interaction and Adaptation in Western Eurasia: Persia, Greece, and Rome" to more emphatically show the interactions among these cultural zones. Chapter 8 contains a revised section on Jainism, and Chapter 9 adds a survey of the contemporary debate about the "Han Synthesis."
- **Part Three** Chapter 10 offers clearer discussions of the Arab conquests of the Middle East, North Africa, and Iberia during the 600s and early 700s as well as of the composition of Islamic salvation history in the 800s, including the biography of the Prophet Muhammad. The coverage of

Byzantium is improved with a discussion of icon-oclasm and the split between Catholicism and Greek Orthodoxy in 1054. Chapter 12 focuses more strongly on the Mongol interval and adds specificity to the discussion of Neo-Confucian philosophy. The coverage of the Mongols has been increased in Chapter 12, and the new chapter title, "Contrasting Patterns in India, China, and Inner Asia," reflects these changes.

- **Part Four** In Chapter 17 we eliminated considerable detail from the presentation of the European religious wars and broadened the focus in the English case to include the War of the Three Kingdoms. Chapter 21 updates the discussion of the Chinese rural economy and the debate about the High Level Equilibrium Trap. It also improves the discussion of Qing concepts of multicultural empire.
- **Part Five** In Chapter 22 the basic concepts of modern nationalism are reformulated: We now distinguish between the patterns of constitutionalism and ethnic nationalism as keys for the understanding of political modernity. In addition, the process of Italian ethnic nationalist unification is presented more clearly. Chapter 23 is completely reorganized, emphasizing in addition the significance of the Paraguayan War of 1864–1870. In Chapter 24, the role of the Hakkas in the Taiping movement is described more clearly. Chapter 26 emphasizes the importance of the steam engine in the Industrial Revolution more strongly and reconceptualizes the nineteenth-century class structure in the emerging industrial societies. Chapter 27 defines more sharply the pattern of the New Imperialism during the nineteenth century.
- **Part Six** Chapter 29 updates the "Patterns Up Close" feature on the Non-Aligned Movement. In Chapter 30 we shortened the text so as to create room for an improved coverage of the Lebanese civil war, the Iranian Islamic Revolution, the US Vietnam War, and the Brazilian economic miracle. In Chapter 31, we similarly removed text and replaced it with paragraphs on the travails of the Arab Spring, the new military regime in Egypt, the "Islamic State" of Iraq and Syria, the failed coup d'état in Turkey, as well as the new populist anti-globalism, complete with "Brexit" in Europe

and Donald J. Trump's electoral victory in the United States. The "Patterns Up Close" essay on information technology was updated to include IT's misuse by terrorists.

Ensuring Student Success

Oxford University Press offers instructors and students a comprehensive ancillary package for qualified adopters

- **Dashboard:** Simple, informative, and mobile, Dashboard is an online learning and assessment platform tailored to your textbook that delivers a simple, informative, and mobile experience for professors and students. It offers quality content and tools to track student progress in an intuitive, web-based learning environment; features a streamlined interface that connects students and instructors with the most important course functions; and simplifies the learning experience to save time and put student progress first. Dashboard for *Patterns of World History,* Third Edition, includes:
- An embedded e-book that integrates multimedia content, providing a dynamic learning space for both students and instructors. Each chapter in *Patterns of World History* includes:

image analysis

document analysis

map analysis, interactive timelines, and interactive concept maps

Many chapters also include video analysis

audio flashcards

- Three sets of quizzes per chapter for both low stakes and high stakes testing. The quizzes are aligned according to Bloom's Taxonomy: quiz

1 tests basic concepts and terminologies; quiz 2 provides questions that test both basic facts and ability to apply concepts; quiz 3 tests ability to evaluate and analyze key concepts.

- The complete set of questions from the testbank (1,500 questions), that provide for each chapter, approximately 40 multiple-choice, short-answer, true-or-false, and fill-in-the-blank as well as approximately 10 essay questions.

For more information about Dashboard, contact your Oxford University Press Representative or call 800.280.0280.

- **Ancillary Resource Center (ARC):** This online resource center, available to adopters of *Patterns of World History*, includes:
- **Instructor's Resource Manual:** Includes, for each chapter, a detailed chapter outline, suggested lecture topics, learning objectives, map quizzes, geography exercises, classroom activities, "Patterns Up Close" activities, "Seeing Patterns and Making Connections" activities, "Against the Grain" exercises, biographical sketches, and suggested Web resources and digital media files. Also includes for each chapter approximately 40 multiple-choice, short-answer, true-or-false, and fill-in-the-blank as well as approximately 10 essay questions.
- **Oxford World History Video Library:** Includes short, two- to three-minute videos that offer overviews of such key topics as the the Golden Age of Islam, Genghis Khan, the steam engine, and the atomic age.
- **PowerPoints:** Includes PowerPoint slides and JPEG and PDF files for all the maps and photos in the text, an additional 400 map files from *The Oxford Atlas of World History*, and approximately 1000 additional PowerPoint-based slides from OUP's Image Bank Library, organized by themes and topics in world history.
- **Computerized testbank:** Includes approximately 1,500 questions that can be customized by the instructor.
- **Course cartridges** containing student and instructor resources are available for the most commonly used course management systems.

Additional Learning Resources

- *Sources in Patterns of World History:* **Volume 1: To 1600:** Includes approximately 75 text and visual sources in world history, organized by the chapter organization of *Patterns of World History*. Each source is accompanied by a headnote and reading questions.
- *Sources in Patterns of World History:* **Volume 2: Since 1400:** Includes approximately 90 text and visual sources in world history, organized by the chapter organization of *Patterns of World History*. Each source is accompanied by a headnote and reading questions.
- *Mapping Patterns of World History,* **Volume 1: To 1600:** Includes approximately 50 full-color maps, each accompanied by a brief headnote, as well as blank outline maps and Concept Map exercises.
- *Mapping Patterns of World History,* **Volume 2: Since 1400:** Includes approximately 50 full-color maps, each accompanied by a brief headnote, as well as blank outline maps and Concept Map exercises.
- *Now Playing: Learning World History Through Film:* Designed specifically to accompany Patterns of World History, this free supplement examines thirty-two films to show how key themes in world history play out in a variety of time periods and contexts.
- **Open Access Companion Website (www .oup.com/us/vonsivers):** Includes quizzes, notetaking guides, and flashcards.
- **E-book for Patterns of World History:** E-books of all the volumes, at a significant discount, are available for purchase at www.redshelf.com or www.vitalsource.com.

Bundling Options

Patterns of World History can be bundled at a significant discount with any of the titles in the popular Very Short Introductions, World in a Life, or Oxford World's Classics series, as well as other titles from the Higher Education division world history catalog (www.oup.com/us/catalog/he). Please contact your OUP representative for details.

Patterns of World History, Brief Third Edition

A brief edition of *Patterns of World History* based on the same content as this volume is available. Please contact your local Oxford University Press representative for additional information.

Acknowledgments

Throughout the course of writing, revising, and preparing *Patterns of World History* for publication we have benefited from the guidance and professionalism accorded us by all levels of the staff at Oxford University Press. John Challice, vice president and publisher, had faith in the inherent worth of our project from the outset and provided the initial impetus to move forward. Meg Botteon guided us through the revisions and added a final polish, often helping us with substantive suggestions. Katherine Schnakenberg carried out the thankless task of assembling the manuscript and did so with generosity and good cheer, helping us with many details in the final manuscript. Keith Faivre steered us through the intricacies of production with the stoicism of a saint.

Most of all, we owe a special debt of gratitude to Charles Cavaliere, our editor. Charles took on the daunting task of directing the literary enterprise at a critical point in the book's career. He pushed this project to its successful completion, accelerated its schedule, and used a combination of flattery and hard-nosed tactics to make sure we stayed the course. His greatest contribution, however, is in the way he refined our original vision for the book with several important adjustments that clarified its latent possibilities. From the maps to the photos to the special features, Charles's high standards and concern for detail are evident on every page.

Developing a book like *Patterns of World History* is an ambitious project, a collaborative venture in which authors and editors benefit from the feedback provided by a team of outside readers and consultants. We gratefully acknowledge the advice that the many reviewers, focus group participants, and class testers (including their students) shared with us along the way. We tried to implement all of the excellent suggestions. We owe a special debt of thanks to Evan R. Ward, who provided invaluable guidance for the revision of the coverage of Latin America and the Caribbean in Part 5, and to Jonathan S. Perry, who deftly assembled the documents. Of course, any errors of fact or interpretation that remain are solely our own.

Reviewers of the Third Edition

Kevin Eoff, Palo Verde College

Christina Firpo, CalPoly University

Aaron Hagler, Troy University

Ephraim Harel, Montgomery College, Rockville

Michael Markus, Alabama State University

Scott Merriman, Troy University

Curtis Morgan, Lord Fairfax Community College

Joanna Neilson, Lincoln Memorial University

Jahan Salehi, Central Piedmont Community College

William Skiles, California State University, San Marcos

Marika Snider, Miami University

Daniel Stephen, Colorado State University

Jason Tatlock, Armstrong State University

Michael Thensted, Mississippi Gulf Coast Community College

Walter Ward, University of Alabama at Birmingham

Paul Tenkotte, Northern Kentucky University

Daniel R. Pavese, Wor-Wic Community College

and one anonymous reviewer.

Please let us know your experiences with *Patterns of World History* so that we may improve it in future editions. We welcome your comments and suggestions.

Peter von Sivers
pv4910@xmission.com

Charles A. Desnoyers
desnoyer@lasalle.edu

George B. Stow
gbsgeorge@aol.com

Note on Dates and Spellings

In keeping with widespread practice among world historians, we use "BCE" and "CE" to date events and the phrase "years ago" to describe developments from the remote past.

The transliteration of Middle Eastern words has been adjusted as much as possible to the English alphabet. Therefore, long vowels are not emphasized. The consonants specific to Arabic (alif, dhal, ha, sad, dad, ta, za, 'ayn, ghayn, and qaf) are either not indicated or rendered with common English letters. A similar procedure is followed for Farsi. Turkish words follow the alphabet reform of 1929, which adds the following letters to the Western alphabet or modifies their pronunciation: c (pronounced "j"), ç (pronounced "tsh"), ğ (not pronounced but lengthening of preceding vowel), ı ("i" without dot, pronunciation close to short e), i/İ ("i" with dot, including in caps), ö (no English equivalent), ş ("sh"), and ü (no English equivalent). The spelling of common contemporary Middle Eastern and Islamic terms follows daily press usage (which, however, is not completely uniform). Examples are "al-Qaeda," "Quran," and "Sharia."

The system used in rendering the sounds of Mandarin Chinese—the northern Chinese dialect that has become in effect the national spoken language in China and Taiwan—into English in this book is *hanyu pinyin*, usually given as simply pinyin. This is the official romanization system of the People's Republic of China and has also become the standard outside of Taiwan, Republic of China. Most syllables are pronounced as they would be in English, with the exception of the letter q, which has an aspirated "ch" sound; ch itself has a less aspirated "ch" sound. *Zh* carries a hard "j" and j a soft, English-style "j." Some syllables also are pronounced—particularly in the regions around Beijing—with a retroflex r so that the syllable *shi*, for example, carries a pronunciation closer to "shir." Finally, the letter r in the *pinyin* system has no direct English equivalent, but an approximation may be had by combining the sounds of "r" and "j."

Japanese terms have been romanized according to a modification of the Hepburn system. The letter g is always hard; vowels are handled as they are in Italian—*e*, for example, carries a sound like "ay." We have not, however, included diacritical markings to indicate long vowel sounds for *u* or *o*. Where necessary, these have been indicated in the pronunciation guides.

For Korean terms, we have used a variation of the McCune-Reischauer system, which remains the standard romanization scheme for Korean words used in English academic writing, but eliminated any diacritical markings. Here again, the vowel sounds are pronounced more or less like those of Italian and the consonants, like those of English.

For Vietnamese words, we have used standard renditions based on the modern Quoc Ngu ("national language") system in use in Vietnam today. The system was developed by Jesuit missionaries and is based on the Portuguese alphabet. Once more, we have avoided diacritical marks, and the reader should follow the pronunciation guides for approximations of Vietnamese terms.

Latin American terms (Spanish, Nahua, or Quechua) generally follow local usage, including accents, except where they are Anglicized, per the *Oxford English Dictionary*. Thus, the Spanish-Quechua word "Tiahuanacu" becomes the Anglicized word "Tiwanaku."

We use the terms "Native American" and "Indian" interchangeably to refer to the peoples of the Americas in the pre-Columbian period and "Amerindian" in our coverage of Latin America since independence.

In keeping with widely recognized practice among paleontologists and other scholars of the deep past, we use the term "hominins" in Chapter 1 to emphasize their greater remoteness from apes and proximity to modern humans.

Phonetic spellings often follow the first appearance of a non-English word whose pronunciation may be unclear to the reader. We have followed the rules for capitalization per *The Chicago Manual of Style*.

About the Authors

Peter von Sivers is associate professor of Middle Eastern history at the University of Utah. He has previously taught at UCLA, Northwestern University, the University of Paris VII (Vincennes), and the University of Munich. He has also served as chair of the Joint Committee of the Near and Middle East, Social Science Research Council, New York, 1982–1985; editor of the *International Journal of Middle East Studies*, 1985–1989; member of the board of directors of the Middle East Studies Association of North America, 1987–1990; and chair of the SAT II World History Test Development Community of the Educational Testing Service, Princeton, NJ, 1991–1994. His publications include *Caliphate, Kingdom, and Decline: The Political Theory of Ibn Khaldun* (1968), several edited books, and three dozen peer-reviewed chapters and articles on Middle Eastern and North African history, as well as world history. He received his Dr. phil. from the University of Munich.

Charles A. Desnoyers is professor of history and director of Asian Studies at La Salle University in Philadelphia. He has previously taught at Temple University, Villanova University, and Pennsylvania State University. In addition to serving as History Department chair from 1999–2007, he was a founder and long-time director of the Greater Philadelphia Asian Studies Consortium, and president (2011–2012) of the Mid-Atlantic Region Association for Asian Studies. He has served as a reader, table leader, and question writer for the AP European and World History exams. He served as editor of the organization's *Bulletin* from 1995–2001. In addition to numerous articles in peer-reviewed and general publications, his work includes *Patterns of Modern Chinese History* (2016, Oxford University Press) and *A Journey to the East: Li Gui's "A New Account of a Trip Around the Globe"* (2004, University of Michigan Press). He received his PhD from Temple University.

George B. Stow is professor of ancient and medieval history and director of the graduate program in history at La Salle University, Philadelphia. His teaching experience embraces a variety of undergraduate and graduate courses in ancient Greece and Rome, medieval England, and world history, and he has been awarded the Lindback Distinguished Teaching Award. Professor Stow is a member of the Medieval Academy of America and a Fellow of the Royal Historical Society. He is the recipient of a National Defense Education Act Title IV Fellowship, a Woodrow Wilson Foundation Fellowship, and research grants from the American Philosophical Society and La Salle University. His publications include a critical edition of a fourteenth-century monastic chronicle, *Historia Vitae et Regni Ricardi Secundi* (University of Pennsylvania Press, 1977), as well as numerous articles and reviews in scholarly journals including *Speculum*, *The English Historical Review*, the *Journal of Medieval History*, the *American Historical Review*, and several others. He received his PhD from the University of Illinois.

Patterns of
World History

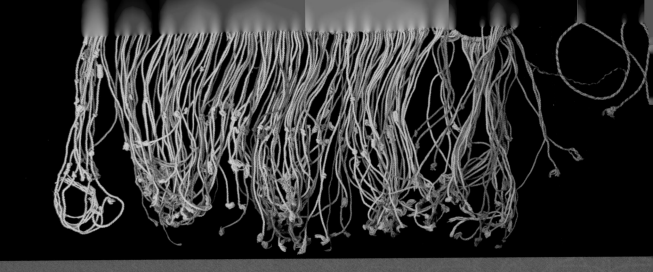

The Rise of Empires in the Americas

Just outside Lima, in a sandy and dry ravine 3 miles to the east of the city, is the shantytown of Túpac Amaru, named after the last Inca ruler, who died in 1572. People fleeing the Maoist Shining Path guerillas in the highlands southeast of Lima settled here during the 1980s. Archaeologists had known for years that the site was an ancient burial place called Puruchuco (Quechua "Feathered Helmet") but could not prevent the influx of settlers. By the late 1990s, the temporary shantytown had become an established settlement with masonry houses, streets, and a school. Dwellers were anxious to acquire title to their properties, introduce urban services and utilities, and clean up the ground contaminated in many places by raw sewage. However, residents realized that archaeologists had to be called in before the shantytown could be officially recognized. Túpac Amaru was facing an increasingly familiar dilemma in the developing world, pitting modern needs against the wish to know the past through discovering and (if possible) preserving its last traces.

During emergency excavations from 1999 to 2001, the archaeologist Guillermo Cock, together with Túpac Amaru residents hired as field assistants, unearthed one of the most astounding treasures in the history of American archaeology. The team discovered some 2,200 mummies, most of them bundled up in blankets and perfectly preserved with their hair, skin, eyes, and genitals intact. Many bundles also contained rich burial

ABOVE: This kind of knotted string assembly (a *quipu*) was used in the Andes from ca. 2500 BCE onward for the recording of taxes, population figures, calendar dates, troop numbers, and other data.

gifts, including jewelry, corn, potatoes, peanuts, peppers, and coca leaves. Forty bundles had false heads made of cotton cloth, some topped with wigs, making the bundles look like oversized persons.

Scholars hope that in a few years, when all of the mummies have been unwrapped, answers can be given as to the social characteristics of the buried people. Were they members of an Inca colony planted into one of the empire's provinces? Or were they locals under their own lord, recognizing Inca overlordship? Were they specialized laborers, such as weavers, who produced cloth tributes for the Incas? Were children and women sacrificed to accompany the cotton king in his journey to the afterlife? Had assimilation between the conquerors and conquered begun? These questions are difficult to answer as so much about the Inca Empire that ruled the Andes from 1438 to 1533 remains unknown. Yet the questions are exciting precisely because they could not have been posed prior to the discovery of these mummies.

Seeing Patterns

≫ Within the patterns of state formation basic to the Americas, which types of states emerged in Mesoamerica and the Andes during the period 600–1550? What characterized these states?

≫ Why did the Tiwanaku and Wari states have ruling classes but no dynasties and central bureaucracies? How were these patterns expressed in the territorial organization of these states?

≫ What patterns of urban life characterized the cities of Tenochtitlán and Cuzco, the capitals of the Aztec and Inca Empires? In which ways were these cities similar to those of Eurasia and Africa?

The Inca Empire and its contemporary the Aztec Empire (1427–1521) grew out of political, economic, and cultural patterns that began to form around 600 CE in Mesoamerica and the Andes (see Chapter 5). At that time, kingdoms had emerged out of polities in two small areas of Mesoamerica, the southern Yucatán Peninsula and the Mexican Basin. After 600, kingdom formation became more general across Mesoamerica and arose for the first time in the Andes. These kingdoms were states with military ruling classes that used new types of weapons and could conquer larger territories than was possible prior to the 600s. Military competition prepared the way for the origin of empires—multireligious, multilinguistic, and multiethnic states encompassing many thousands of square miles. Even though empires arrived later in the Americas than in Eurasia, they demonstrate that humans, once they had adopted agriculture, followed remarkably similar patterns of social and political formation across the world.

The Legacy of Teotihuacán and the Toltecs in Mesoamerica

As discussed in Chapter 5, the city-state of Teotihuacán had dominated northern Mesoamerica from 200 BCE to the late 500s CE. It fell into ruin probably as the result of an internal uprising against an overbearing ruling class. After its collapse, the surrounding towns and villages, as well as half a dozen other cities in and around the Mexican Basin, perpetuated the cultural legacy of Teotihuacán for centuries. Employing this legacy, the conquering state of the Toltecs unified a major part of the region for a short period from 900 to 1180. At the same time, after an internal crisis, the southern Maya kingdoms on the Yucatán Peninsula reached their late flowering, together with the northern state of Chichén Itzá.

Militarism in the Mexican Basin

After the ruling class of Teotihuacán disintegrated at the end of the sixth century, the newly independent local lords and their supporters in the small successor states of Mesoamerica continued Teotihuacán's cultural heritage. This heritage was defined by Teotihuacán's temple style, ceramics, textiles, and religious customs, especially the cult of the feathered serpent god Quetzalcoatl [ket-sal-COA]. The Toltecs, migrants from the north, militarized the Teotihuacán legacy and transformed it into a program of conquest.

Ceremonial Centers and Chiefdoms   In the three centuries after the end of the city-state of Teotihuacán, the local population declined from some 200,000 to about 30,000. Although largely ruined, the ceremonial center continued to attract pilgrims, but other places around the Mexican Basin and beyond rose in importance. The semi-arid region to the northwest of the valley had an extensive mining industry, with many mine shafts extending a mile or more into the mountains. The region produced a variety of gemstones. Independent after 600, inhabitants built ceremonial centers and small states of their own, trading their gemstones to their neighbors in all directions.

To the north were the Pueblo cultures in today's southwestern United States. These cultures were based on sophisticated irrigated farming systems and are known for their distinctive painted pottery styles. They flourished between 700 and 1500 in the canyons of what are today the states of New Mexico, Arizona, southwestern Colorado, and southeastern Utah. In turn, these cultures might have been in contact with the Mississippi cultures, among which the ceremonial center and city of Cahokia (650–1400) near modern St. Louis is the best-known site. An obsidian scraper from the Pachuca region north of the Mexican Basin found in Spiro Mounds, Oklahoma, attests to at least occasional contacts between Mesoamerica and the Mississippi culture (see Map 15.1).

To the south, in western Mesoamerica, ceremonial centers and chiefdoms flourished on the basis of metallurgy, which arrived through Ecuadoran seaborne merchants ca. 600–800. The Ecuadorans received their copper from Peru, in return for seashells found in the warm waters off the coast of Ecuador as well as farther north. Copper, too soft for agricultural implements or military weapons, served mostly in households and as jewelry for the rich. A number of small, fortified hilltop states also flourished in the south. Their inhabitants built moats and ramparts to protect these states. More than in other Mesoamerican states, the ruling classes were embroiled in fierce wars during 600–900, images of which are depicted in stone reliefs of gruesome battle scenes.

The Toltec Conquering State   Early after the collapse of Teotihuacán, crafts-people and farmers migrated some 60 miles north to Tula, a place on a ridge in the highlands watered by two tributaries of a river flowing into the Gulf of Mexico. They founded a small ceremonial center and town with workshops known for the high quality of the scrapers, knives, and spear points fabricated from the local Pachuca obsidian. Around 900, new migrants arrived from northwest Mexico as well as from the Gulf Coast. The northerners spoke Nahuatl [NA-hua], the language of the later Aztecs, and after taking possession of Tula, they made it their ancestral city.

The integration of the new arrivals was apparently not peaceful, since it resulted in the abandonment of the temple and the departure of a defeated party of Tulans.

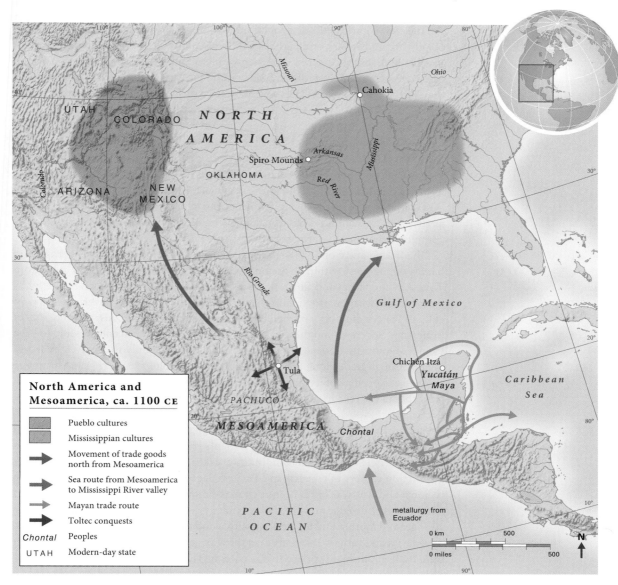

MAP 15.1 **North America and Mesoamerica, ca. 1100.**

This abandonment may well have been enshrined in the myth of Tolpiltzin, a priest-king of the feathered serpent god Quetzalcoatl, who after his departure to the east would one day return to restore the cult to its rightful center. Later, Spaniards used the myth to justify their rule in the Americas (see Chapter 18).

interactive timeline

600 End of city-state of Teotihuacán in Mexican Basin	**600–900** Late Maya kingdoms in Yucatán Peninsula	**850–1000** City-state of Chichén Itzá in northern Yucatán Peninsula	**1427–1521** Aztec Empire in Mesoamerica
600–1100 Conquering state of Tiwanaku in Andes (southern Peru/Bolivia)	**700–1000** Conquering state of Wari in Andes (central Bolivia)	**900–1170** Toltec conquering state, north of Mexican Basin	**1438–1533** Inca Empire in Andes

The new Tula of 900 developed quickly into a large city with a new temple, 60,000 urban dwellers, and perhaps another 60,000 farmers on surrounding lands. It was the first city-centered state to give pictorial prominence to the sacrifice of captured warriors. As it evolved, Tula became the capital of the conquering state of the Toltecs, which imprinted its warrior culture on large parts of Mesoamerica from around 900 to 1180 (see Map 15.1).

The Toltecs introduced two innovations in weaponry that improved the effectiveness of hand-to-hand combat. First, there was the new weapon of a short (1.5-foot) sword made of hardwood with inlaid obsidian edges, which could slash as well as crush, in contrast to the obsidian-spiked clubs that had been the primary weapons in earlier times. Second, warriors wore obsidian daggers with wooden handles inside a band on the left arm, replacing simpler obsidian blades, which were difficult to use as they had no handles. Traditional dart throwers and slings for stone projectiles completed the offensive armament of the warriors.

The Toltec army of 13,000–26,000 soldiers was sufficiently large to engage in battles of conquest within an area of 4 days' march (roughly 40 miles) away from Tula. Any target beyond this range was beyond their capabilities, given the logistics of armor, weapons, food rations, narrow dirt roads, and uneven terrain—and, of course, Toltecs did not have the benefit of wheeled vehicles. Thus, the only way of projecting power beyond the range of 40 miles was to establish colonies and to have troops accompany traders, each of which could then supply themselves by foraging or through trade along the way. As a result, the Toltec state projected its power through the prestige of its large military, rather than through a full-scale administrative scheme with the imposition of governors, tributes, and taxes.

Trade   Apart from demonstrating military might, the Toltecs pursued the establishment of a large trade network. Merchants parlayed Tula's obsidian production into a trade network that radiated southward into the cacao, vanilla, and bird-feather production centers of Chiapas and Guatemala; to the north into gemstone mining regions; and westward into centers of metal mining. Metallurgy advanced around 1200 with the development of the technology of bronze casting. Bronze axes were stronger and more useful for working with wood than copper axes. Bronze bells produced a greater variety of sounds than those of copper. As ornamental objects, both were trade goods highly prized by the elites in Tula.

The Late Toltec Era   Toltec military power declined in the course of the twelfth century when the taxable grain yield around the city diminished, because of either prolonged droughts or a depletion of the topsoil on the terraces, or a combination of the two. Sometime around 1180, a new wave of foraging peoples from the northwest invaded, attacking with bows and arrows and using hit-and-run tactics against Toltec communication lines. The disruptions caused an internal revolt, which brought down the ceremonial center and its palaces. By 1200, Tula was a city with a burned-out center, like Teotihuacán six centuries earlier, and Mesoamerica relapsed into a period of small-state coexistence like that of the pre-600 period.

Late Maya States in Yucatán

Teotihuacán's demise at the end of the sixth century was paralleled by a realignment of the balance of power among the Maya kingdoms in the southern Yucatán lowlands of Mesoamerica. This realignment, accompanied by extensive warfare, was resolved by around 650. A period of late flowering spanned the next two centuries, followed by a shift of power from the southern to the northern part of the peninsula.

The Southern Kingdoms   At its height during the fourth and fifth centuries, Teotihuacán in the Mexican Basin had interjected itself into the delicate balance of power existing among the Maya kingdoms of southern Yucatán. Alliances among the states shifted, and prolonged wars of conquest racked the lowlands, destroying several older states. A dozen new kingdoms emerged and established a new balance of power among themselves. After a lengthy hiatus, Maya culture entered its final period (650–900).

Mayan ceremonial ball game scene, Late Classic Period

The most striking phenomenon of the final period in the southern, rain-forest–covered lowlands and adjacent highlands were massive new programs of agricultural expansion and ceremonial monument construction. Agriculture was expanded again through cutting down the rain forest on hillsides and terracing the hills for soil retention. The largest kingdoms grew to 50,000–60,000 inhabitants and reached astounding rural population densities of about 1,000 persons per square mile. (In comparison, England's most densely populated counties just prior to its agricultural expansion after 1700 were Middlesex and Surrey, with 221 and 207 persons per square mile, respectively.) Although the late Maya states were geographically small, they were administratively the most centralized polities ever created in indigenous American history.

The late Maya states did not last long. In spite of all efforts, the usually torrential downpours of the rainy season gradually washed the topsoil from the newly built hillside terraces. The topsoil, accumulating as alluvium in the flatlands, was initially quite fertile, but from around 800 onward it became more and more depleted of nutrients. In addition, in many wetlands, farmers found it difficult to prevent clay from forming over the alluvium and hardening in the process. Malnutrition resulting from the shrinking agricultural surface began to reduce the labor force. Ruling classes had to make do with fewer workers and smaller agricultural surpluses. In the end, even the ruling classes suffered, with members killing each other for what remained of these surpluses. By about 900, the Maya kingdoms in southern Yucatán had shriveled to the size of chiefdoms with small towns and villages.

Mayan city-state of Palenque

Chichén Itzá in the North   A few small Maya states on the periphery survived. The most prominent among them was Chichén Itzá [chee-CHEN eat-SA] in the northern lowlands, which flourished from about 850 to 1000. At first glance the region would appear to be less than hospitable to a successful state. The climate in the north was much drier than that in the south. The surface was rocky or covered with thin topsoil, supporting mostly grass, scrub vegetation, and isolated forests. In many places, where the soil was too saline, agriculture was impossible, and the production of salt was the only source of income. There were no rivers, but many sinkholes in the porous limestone underneath the soil held water. Countless cisterns to hold additional amounts of water for year-round use were cut into the limestone and plastered to prevent seepage. This water, carried in jars to the surface, supported an intensive garden agriculture, productive enough to sustain entire towns and city-states.

Chichén Itzá was founded during the phase of renewed urbanization in 650. It was built near two major sinkholes and several salt flats. The population was composed

Chacmool (Offering Table) at the Entrance to the Temple of Warriors, Chichén Itzá. Chacmools originated here and spread to numerous places in Mesoamerica, as far north as Tenochtitlán and Tula. Offerings to the gods included food, tobacco, feathers, and incense. Offerings might have included also human sacrifices. The table in the form of a prostrate human figure is in itself symbolic of sacrifice.

of local Maya as well as the Maya-speaking Chontal from the Gulf Coast farther west. Groups among these people engaged in long-distance trade, both overland and in boats along the coast. Since trade in the most lucrative goods (such as cacao, vanilla, jade, copper, bronze, turquoise, and obsidian) required contact with people well outside even the farthest political reach of either Teotihuacán or Tula, merchants (*pochtecas* [potsh-TAY-cas]) traveled in armed caravans. These merchant groups enjoyed considerable freedom and even sponsorship by the ruling classes of the states of Mesoamerica.

Chontal traders adopted Toltec culture, and when they based themselves in Chichén Itzá around 850 they superimposed their adopted culture over that of the original Maya. How the city was ruled is only vaguely understood, but there is some evidence that there were two partially integrated ruling factions, possibly descended from the Chontal and local Maya, sharing in the governance of the city. At the very end of the period of Teotihuacán, Maya, and Toltec cultural expansion, the three cultures finally merged on the Yucatán Peninsula, albeit in only one geographically marginal place. This merger did not last long: Already around 1000 the ruling-class factions left the city-state for unknown reasons. As a result, the city-state diminished in size and power to town level.

The Legacy of Tiwanaku and Wari in the Andes

Mesoamerica and the Andes, from the time of chiefdom formation in 2500 BCE in Caral-Supé onward, shared the tradition of regional temple pilgrimages. In the Andes, the chiefdoms remained mostly coastal, with some inland extensions along valleys of the Andes. Around 600 CE, the two conquering states of Tiwanaku in the highlands of what are today southern Peru and Bolivia and Wari in central Peru emerged. Both states encompassed tens of thousands of inhabitants and represented a major step in the formation of larger, militarily organized polities.

The Expanding State of Tiwanaku

Tiwanaku was a political and cultural power center in the south-central Andes during the period 600–1100. It began as a ceremonial center with surrounding villages and gradually developed into a state dominating the region around Lake Titicaca. At its apogee it was an expanding state, planting colonies in regions far from the lake and conveying its culture through trade to peoples even beyond the colonies.

Agriculture on the High Plain The Andes consist of two parallel mountain chains stretching along the west coast of South America. For the most part, these chains are close together, divided by small plains, valleys, and lower mountains. In southeastern Peru and western Bolivia an intermountain plain, 12,500 feet above sea level, extends as wide as 125 miles. At its northern end lies Lake Titicaca, subdivided into a larger and deeper northern basin and a smaller, shallower, swampy, and reed-covered southern basin. Five major and 20 smaller rivers coming from the eastern Andes chain feed Lake Titicaca, which has one outlet at its southern end, a river flowing into Lake Poopó [po-POH], a salt lake 150 miles south. The Lake Titicaca region, located above the tree line, receives winter rains sufficient for agriculture and grazing, whereas the southern plain around Lake Poopó is too dry to sustain more than steppes.

In spite of its elevation, the region around Lake Titicaca offered nearly everything necessary for an advanced urbanization process. The lake's freshwater supported fish and resources such as reeds from the swamps, which served for the construction of boats and roofs. Corn flourished only in the lower elevations of the Andes and had to be imported, together with the corn-derived *chicha*, a beer-like drink. Instead of corn, the food staples were potatoes and quinoa. The grasslands of the upper hills served as pastures for llama and alpaca herds. Llamas were used as transportation animals, and alpacas provided wool. The meat of both animals—preserved for winter through drying—was a major protein source. Although frost was an ever-present danger in Tiwanaku, nutrition was quite diversified.

Tiwanaku, Kalassaya Gate.
Within the Temple of the Sun, this gate is aligned with the sun's equinoxes and was used for festive rituals. Note the precise stone work, which the Incas later developed further.

Farmers grew their crops on hillside terraces, where runoff water could be channeled, or on raised fields close to the lake. The raised-field system, which farmers had adopted through interaction with the peoples of the Maya lowlands, consisted of a grid of narrow strips of earth, separated from each other by channels. Mud from the channels, heaped onto the strips, replenished their fertility. A wooden foot plow, perhaps with a bronze blade, seems to have been the main farming implement, although hard archaeological proof is still elusive. By 500, the combined sustenance from fishing, hunting, farming, and herding supported dozens of villages and, by 700, the city of Tiwanaku and its 20,000 inhabitants.

Coordinated with the calendar as well as life-cycle events (such as initiation rituals), ceremonial feasts brought together elite lineages and clients, or ordinary craftspeople and villagers. Elites and clients cohered through **reciprocity**—that is, communal labor for the construction of the ceremonial centers and elaborate feasting, in which elite wealth was expended for the ceremonial leveling of status differences. Until shortly before the end of the state, it does not appear that this reciprocity gave way to more forcible ways of allocating labor through conscription or taxation.

Reciprocity: In its basic form, an informal agreement among people according to which a gift or an invitation has to be returned after a reasonable amount of time; in the pre-Columbian Americas, an arrangement of feasts instead of taxes shared by ruling classes and subjects in a state.

Expansion and Colonization   Like Tiwanaku, the core region around the southern basin of Lake Titicaca housed a set of related but competing elite–client hierarchies. Ruling clans with intermediate leaders and ordinary farmers in the villages comprised a state capable of imposing military power beyond the center. But counterbalancing clans at the head of similar hierarchies prevented the rise of dynasties that would command permanent, unified central administrations and military forces.

The projection of power over the northern lake, therefore, was not primarily of a military nature: The prevalent form of Tiwanaku authority was the outstanding prestige of its ceremonial center. This center attracted pilgrims not merely from the northern lake but also from more distant regions. Pilgrims partaking in Tiwanaku feasting ceremonies can be considered extensions of the reciprocity and clientage system of the ruling classes and, hence, of Tiwanaku power.

But there were also armed trading caravans and the foundation of colonies in the western valleys of the Andes, where military force played a role. Merchants accompanied by warriors and llama drivers crossed multiple polities in order to exchange textiles and ceramics for basalt cores in the south, metal ingots and obsidian cores in the north, and coca leaves and other psychotropic substances in the east, often hundreds of miles away. Settler colonies were additional forms of power projection, especially those established in the Moquegua [mow-KAY-gah] valley 200 miles, or 10–12 days of walking, to the west. Here, at some 2,800 feet above sea level, Tiwanaku emigrants established villages, which sent some of their corn or beer to the capital in return for salt, as well as stone and obsidian tools. Although overall less militarily inclined than the Mesoamerican states of the same time period, Tiwanaku wielded a visible influence over southern Peru (see Map 15.2).

The Expanding City-State of Wari

Little is known about early settlements in central Peru, some 450 miles, or 3–4 weeks of foot travel, north from Tiwanaku. The state of Wari emerged around 600 from a number of small polities organized around ceremonial centers. Expansion to the south put Wari into direct contact with Tiwanaku. The two states came to some form of mutual accommodation, and it appears that neither embarked on an outright conquest of the other. Their military postures remained limited to their regional spheres of influence.

Origins and Expansion   Wari was centered on the Ayacucho valley, a narrow plain in the highlands of northern Peru. Here, the land between the two chains of the Andes is mountainous, interspersed with valleys and rivers flowing to the Pacific or the Amazon. The elevation of 8,000 feet in the Ayacucho valley allowed for the cultivation of potatoes as well as corn and cotton. In the course of the seventh century, Wari grew into a city of 30,000 inhabitants and brought a number of neighboring cities under its control. It also pushed for an enlargement of the agricultural base through the expansion of terrace farming. Like Tiwanaku, Wari eventually became the center of a developed urbanism and a diversified agriculture.

In addition to maintaining control over the cities in its vicinity, Wari employed architects who constructed new towns. These planned centers included plazas, housing for laborers, and halls for feasting. Outside the core area, Wari elites established colonies between 100 and 450 miles away. It appears that Wari exercised much stronger political control over the chiefs of its core region than Tiwanaku and was more active in founding colonies.

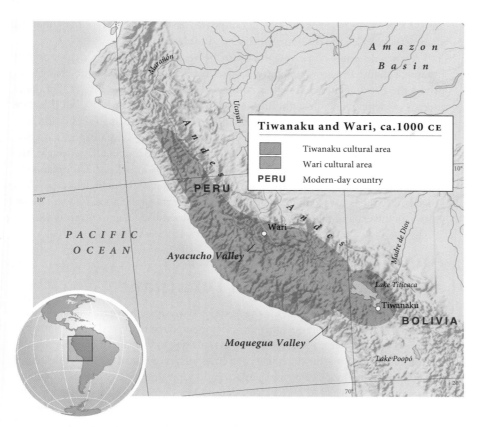

MAP 15.2 **Tiwanaku and Wari, ca. 1000.**

The Wari–Tiwanaku Frontier   Early on, Wari established a colony upstream in the Moquegua valley near southern Peru's west coast, some 100 miles southeast. The settlers built extensive terraces and canals together with protective walls and settlements on mountain peaks. This building activity coincided with the establishment by Tiwanaku of downstream farming colonies. It is possible that there was considerable tension with Tiwanaku during the initial period (650–800) over the division of water between the two colonies. But during 800–1000 the two agricultural communities developed closer ties, with indications that the two local elites engaged in a peaceful sharing of the water resources and common feasting activities. Very likely, the Moquegua valley was politically so far on the periphery of both states that neither had the means to impose itself on the other.

In its evolution, Wari was an expanding state very similar to Tiwanaku. Both were governed by elite clans under leaders who derived their strength from reciprocal patron–client organizations binding leaders to farmers and craftspeople. Extensive feasts strengthened the bond. Something must have happened to erode this bond, however, since there is evidence of increased internal tension after 950 in the two states. Groups arose which defaced sculptures, destroyed portals, and burned down edifices. Somehow, crowds previously happy to uphold elite control in return for participation in the lavish feasts must have become angry at these elites, their ceremonies, and the temple sculptures (which show traces of breakage). Scholars have argued that it was perhaps the fragility of power based on an increasingly unequal sharing that caused the rift between elites and subjects.

Why would elites allow reciprocity to be weakened to such a degree that it became a sham? Previous generations of scholars argued that climatic change deprived the elites of the wherewithal to throw large feasts. In the case of Tiwanaku there is evidence that a drought hit the high plain beginning in 1040, but this date is clearly a century too late for an explanation. A more convincing explanation suggests environmental degradation as the result of agricultural expansion. Land that was only marginally suitable for agriculture was exhausted and could no longer sustain a vastly increased population, as with the late Maya kingdoms. Unfortunately, there is still too little evidence to extend the environmental argument from the Maya kingdoms to the Andes highland and sierra. An ultimate explanation for the disintegration of the expanding states of Tiwanaku and Wari thus remains currently elusive.

American Empires: Aztec and Inca Origins and Dominance

Expanding and conquering states in the Andes and Mesoamerica gave way in the early fifteenth century to empires. At this time, demographic growth and the evolution of militarism in the Americas reached a point of transition to the pattern of imperial political formation. Conquering states had been cities with ceremonial centers, which dominated agricultural hinterlands and projected their prestige or power across regions. By contrast, the Aztec (1427–1521) and Inca (1438–1533) Empires in Mesoamerica and the Andes were states with capitals and ceremonial centers, vastly larger tributary hinterlands, and armies capable of engaging in campaigns at distances twice (or more) as far as previous states could. As in Eurasia, they were centralized multireligious, multiethnic, and multilinguistic polities: empires in every sense of the word.

The Aztec Empire of Mesoamerica

Forming part of the Uto-Aztecan–speaking group of Native Americans in the Great Basin of the American Southwest, the ancestors of the Aztecs left Tula and arrived at the Mexican Basin at an unknown time and they did so probably as migrants in search of a better life. They found this life eventually as conquerors of the Basin, the site of today's Mexico City (after the drainage of most of the valley). In the course of the fifteenth century they conquered an empire that eventually encompassed Mesoamerica from the Pacific to the Gulf of Mexico and from the middle of modern northern Mexico to the Isthmus of Panama.

Settlement in the Mexican Valley   Once arrived in the Mexican Basin, the Aztecs traced their beginnings to a founding myth. According to this myth, the first Aztec was one of seven brothers born on an island in a lake or in a mountain cave 150 leagues (450 miles) northwest of the Mexican Basin. The distance, recorded by Spaniards in the sixteenth century, can be interpreted as corresponding to a mountain in the modern state of Guanajuato [goo-wa-na-hoo-WA-to]. This Aztec ancestor and his descendants migrated south as foragers dressed in skins and lacking agriculture and urban civilization. Their hunter–warrior patron god Huitzilpochtli [hoo-it-zil-POSHT-lee] guided them to a promised land of plenty.

The Founding of Tenochtitlán

After settling for a while in Tula (claimed later as a place of heritage), their god urged the foragers to move on to the Mexican Basin. Here, an eagle perched on a cactus commanded the Aztecs to settle and build a temple to their god. In this temple, they were to nourish him with the sacrificial blood of humans captured in war. Like many peoples in Eurasia as well as the contemporary Incas, the Aztecs contrasted their later empire and its glory with a myth of humble beginnings and long periods of wandering toward an eventual promised land.

The historical record in the Mexican Basin becomes clearer in the fourteenth century. In the course of this period, the Aztecs appeared as clients of two Toltec-descended overlords in city-states on the southwestern shore. Here, they created two islands, founded a city with a ceremonial center, engaged in farming, and rendered military service to their overlords. Thanks to successes on the battlefield, Aztec leaders were able to marry into the elites of the neighboring city-states and gained the right to have their own ruler presiding over a council of leading members of the elite and priests. Toward the end of the fourteenth century, an emerging Aztec elite was firmly integrated with the ruling classes of many of the two dozen or so city-states in and around the valley.

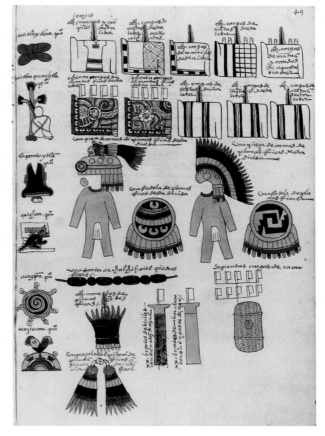

List of Tributes Owed to the Aztecs. The list includes quantities of cotton and wool textiles, clothes, headgear with feathers, and basketry. The Aztecs did not continue the complex syllabic script of the Maya but used instead images, including persons with speech bubbles, for communication. Spanish administrators and monks who copied the Aztec manuscripts added their own explanations to keep track of Native American tributes.

image analysis

The Rise of the Empire   After the successful rebellion in 1428 of a triple alliance among the Aztec city-state and two other vassal states against the reigning city-state in the Mexican Basin the Aztec leader Itzcóatl [its-CO-aw] (r. 1428–1440) emerged as the dominant figure. Itzcóatl and his three successors, together with the rulers of the two allied states, expanded their city-states on the two islands and the shore through conquests into a full-fledged empire. Tenochtitlán, the Aztec city on one of the islands, became the capital of what became an empire that consisted of a set of six "inner provinces" in the Mexican Basin. Local elites were left in place, but they were required to attend ceremonies in Tenochtitlán, bring and receive gifts, leave their sons as hostages, and intermarry with the elites of the triple alliance. Commoner farmers on the periphery of the cities had to provide tributes in the form of foodstuffs and labor services, making the imperial core self-sufficient.

After the middle of the fifteenth century, the triple alliance conquered a set of 55 city-states outside the valley as "outer provinces." It created an imperial polity from the Pacific to the Gulf, from Tarasco, 200 miles to the northwest, to Oaxaca, over 500 miles to the south (see Map 15.3). This state was now far more centralized than the preceding Teotihuacán and Toltec city-states. In this empire, local ruling families with their ceremonial centers and gods were generally left in place, but commoners had to produce tributes in the form of raw materials or lightweight processed and manufactured goods.

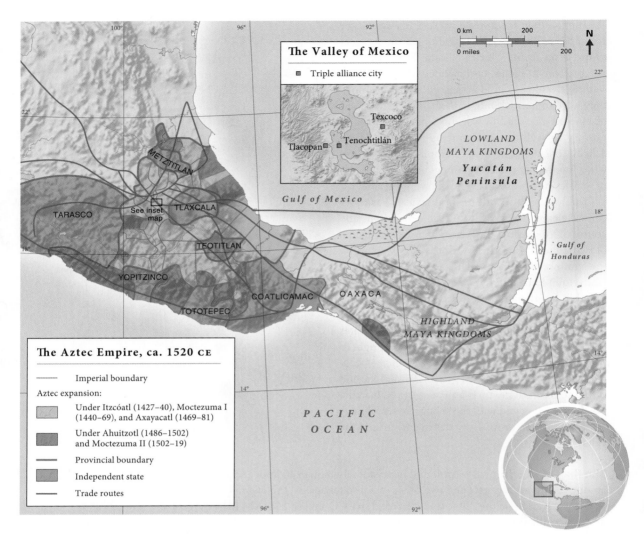

MAP 15.3 **The Aztec Empire, ca. 1520.**

In some provinces, Aztec governors replaced the rulers; in most others, Aztec tribute collectors (supported by troops) held local rulers in check and supervised the transportation of the tributes by porters to the valley. Reciprocity, once of central importance in Mesoamerica, continued on a grand scale but was now clearly subordinate to military considerations.

The resulting multiethnic, multireligious, and multilinguistic empire of eventually some 19 million inhabitants was still a work in progress in the early sixteenth century when the Spanish arrived. Right in the middle of the empire, just 50 miles east of the Mexican Basin, the large state of Tlaxcala [tlash-KAH-lah], Nahuatl-speaking like the Aztecs, held out in opposition, together with a number of enemy states on the periphery. Although the ruling elites of the triple alliance did everything to expand, even inviting enemy rulers to their festivities in order to secure their loyalty through gestures of reciprocity, pockets of anti-Aztec states survived and eventually became crucial allies of the Spanish, providing the latter's tiny military forces with a critical mass of fighters.

Some outer provinces possessed strategic importance, with Aztec colonies implanted to prepare for eventual conquest of remaining enemies of the empire. The most relentlessly pursued policy of continued expansion of Aztec central control was the threat of warfare, for the purpose of capturing rebels or enemies as prisoners of war to be sacrificed to the gods in the ceremonial centers. This fear-inducing tactic—or "power propaganda"—was an integral innovation in the imperialism of the Aztecs.

The Military Forces   The triple alliance ruled a Nahuatl-speaking population of some 1.5 million inhabitants in the core provinces of the Mexican Basin. This number yielded a maximum of a quarter of a million potential soldiers, taking into consideration that most soldiers were farmers with agricultural obligations. From this large number of adult males, the Aztecs assembled units of 8,000 troops each, which they increased as the need arose. Initially, the army was recruited from among the elite of the Aztecs and their allies. But toward the middle of the fifteenth century, Aztec rulers set up a military school system for the sons of the elite plus those commoners who were to become priests. A parallel school system for the sons of commoners, aged 15–20 years, also included military training. After graduation, recruits began as porters, carrying supplies for the combat troops—an Aztec innovation which considerably enlarged the marching range of armies on campaign. Soldiers rose in the army hierarchy on the basis of merit, particularly as demonstrated by their success in the capture of enemies for future sacrifice.

The Aztecs inherited the weaponry and armor of the Toltecs but also made some important innovations. The bow and arrow, which arrived from northwest Mexico at the end of Toltec rule, became a standard weapon in Aztec armies. In addition, perhaps as late as the fifteenth century, the Aztecs developed the 3-foot obsidian-spiked broadsword, derived from the Toltec short sword, in order to enhance the latter's slashing force. As a result, clubs, maces, and axes declined in importance in the Aztec arsenal. Thrusting spears, dart throwers, and slings continued to be used as standard weapons. Body armor, consisting of quilted, sleeveless cotton shirts, thick cotton helmets, and round wooden or cane shields, was adopted from the Toltecs. With the arrival of the Aztecs, the Americas had acquired the heaviest infantry weaponry in their history, reflective of the intensity of militarism in their society—a militarism which was also typical of the earlier empires of the beginning Iron Age in the Middle East.

Aztec Weapons. Aztec weapons were well-crafted hardwood implements with serrated obsidian edges, capable of cutting through metal, including iron. As slashing weapons they were highly effective in close combat.

The Inca Empire of the Andes

After the disintegration of Tiwanaku and Wari around 1100, the central Andes returned to the traditional politics of local chiefdoms in small city-states with ceremonial centers and agricultural hinterlands. The best-known city-state was Chimú on the Peruvian coast, with its capital of Chan Chan numbering 30,000 inhabitants. Tiwanaku cultural traditions, however, remained dominant and were expressed in religious ceremonies, textile motifs, and ceramic styles.

Given the fierce competition among the ceremonial centers for pilgrims, insecurity was rampant during the period 1100–1400. Occasional charismatic military leaders projected military force and pacified the land. After a gestation period during the fourteenth century, the southern Peruvian city-state of Cuzco with its Inca elite emerged in the early fifteenth century at the head of a highly militaristic conquering polity. Within another century, the Incas had established an empire, called Tawantinsuyu [ta-wan-tin-SOO-yuh] (Quechua "Four Regions"), symbolizing its geographical expanse. It stretched from Ecuador in the north to central Chile in the south, with extensions into the tropical upper Amazon region and western Argentinean steppes (see Map 15.4).

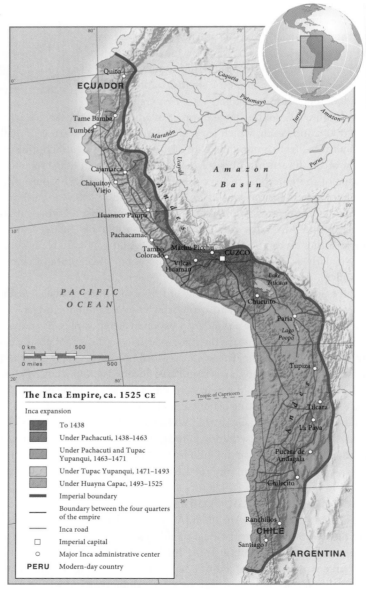

map analysis

MAP **15.4** The Inca Empire, ca. 1525.

As in the case of the Aztecs, the founding myth of the Incas involves a cave, an island, and a promised land of rich agriculture. In one version, the creator god Viracocha [vee-rah-KO-chah] summoned four brothers and four sisters from caves 7 leagues (21 miles) from Cuzco to the south, pairing them as couples and promising them a land of plenty. They would find this land when a golden rod, to be used on their wanderings, would get stuck in the soil. Alternatively, the sun god Inti [IN-tee] did the pairing of the couples on an island in Lake Titicaca and thereby bestowed the glory of Tiwanaku on them, before sending them with the golden rod to their promised land. Cuzco, where the rod plunged into the fertile soil, was settled land, however, and a war ensued in which the Incas drove out the existing farmers.

In the fourteenth century, Cuzco became a serious contender in the city-state competition. Like Wari, Cuzco was located at a highland elevation of 11,300 feet between the two Andes chains of southern Peru, roughly one-third of the way from Lake Titicaca north to Wari. Eight rulers (*curacas* [koo-RA-kas]) are said to have succeeded each other in the consolidation of Cuzco as a regional power. Although their names are recorded, events are hazy and dates are missing altogether. Firm historical terrain is reached with the ninth ruler, Pachacuti (r. 1438–1471). The history of the Incas from 1438 onward is known much better, primarily because of the memories of the grandchildren of the fifteenth-century Inca conquerors, recorded by the Spanish who defeated them in their conquest.

Imperial Expansion   The system of reciprocity that characterized earlier Mesoamerican and Andean history continued under the Incas but was also, as in the case of Aztecs, decisively cast in the mold of power-enforced unilateralism. *Ayllu* [AY-yoo], the Quechua term for a household with an ancestral lineage, implied mutual obligations among groups of households, neighborhoods, villages, and city-states. To negotiate these obligations, Inca society—from households to provinces—was divided into two halves with roughly equal reciprocities. At the elite level, there were two sets of reciprocities, the first within two main branches of the elite and the second between the two branches of the elite and the subjects. The most important social expression of reciprocity remained the feast. In the Incan Empire, the state collected considerably more from the subject *ayllus* than Tiwanaku and Wari had done, but whether it returned comparable amounts through feasts and celebrations was a matter of contention, often leading to armed rebellion.

The earliest conquests under Pachacuti were toward the near south around Lake Titicaca, as well as the agriculturally rich lands north of the former Wari state. Thereafter, in the later fifteenth century, the Incas expanded 1,300 miles northward to southern Ecuador and 1,500 miles southward to Chile. The final provinces, added in the early sixteenth century, were in northern Ecuador as well as on the eastern slopes of the Andes, from the upper Amazon to western Argentina. The capital, Cuzco, which counted some 100,000 inhabitants in the early sixteenth century, was laid out in a cross-shaped grid of four streets leading out into the suburbs. Symbolically, as indicated by the empire's Quechua name, the capital reached out to the four regions of the empire—coast, north, south, and Amazon rain forest.

Administration   Ethnic Inca governors administered the four regions, which were subdivided into a total of some 80 provinces, each again with an Inca

***Mit'a*:** Innovation of the Incas in which subjects were obligated to deliver a portion of their harvests, animal products, and domestically produced goods to nearby storehouses for use by Inca officials and troops. The *mit'a* also provided laborers for construction projects as well as workers on state farms or mines.

subgovernor. Most provinces were composites of former city-states, which remained under their local elites but had to accept a unique decimal system of population organization imposed by the Inca rulers. According to this system, members of the local elites commanded 10,000, 1,000, 100, and 10 household heads for the purpose of recruiting the manpower for the ***mit'a*** [MIT-ah] ("to take a turn," in reference to service obligations rotating among the subjects). The services, which subjects owed the empire as a form of taxes, were in farming, herding, manufacturing, military service, and portage. In its structure it was not unlike the Ming and Qing Chinese systems of local organization called *baojia* (see Chapter 12).

The *mit'a* was perhaps the single most important innovation the Incas contributed to the history of the Americas. In contrast to the Aztecs, who shipped taxes in kind to their capital by boat, the Incas had no efficient means of transportation for long distances. The only way to make use of the taxes in kind was to store them locally. The Incas built tens of thousands of storehouses everywhere in their empire, requiring subjects to deliver a portion of their harvests, animal products, and domestically produced goods under *mit'a* obligations to the nearest storehouse in their vicinity. These supplies were available to officials and troops and enabled the Incas to conduct military campaigns far from Cuzco without the need for foraging among local farmers. In addition, it was through the *mit'a* that quotas of laborers were raised for the construction of inns, roads, ceremonial centers, palaces, terraces, and irrigation canals, often far away from the urban center. Finally, the *mit'a* provided laborers for mines, quarries, state and temple farms, and colonies. No form of labor or service went untaxed.

***Quipu*:** Knotted string assembly, used in the Andes from ca. 2500 BCE onward for the recording of taxes, population figures, calendar dates, troop numbers, and other data.

To keep track of *mit'a* obligations, officials passed bundles of knotted cord (***quipu***, or *khipu* [KEE-poo], "knot") upward from level to level in the imperial administration. The numbers of knots on each cord in the bundles contained information on population figures and service obligations. As discussed in Chapter 5, the use of *quipus* was widespread in the Andes long before the Inca and can be considered as the Andean equivalent of a communication system. The only innovation contributed by the Incas seems to have been the massive scale on which these cord bundles were generated and employed. Some 700 have been preserved. Unfortunately, all modern attempts to decipher them have so far failed, and thus it is impossible to accurately outline the full picture of Inca service allocations.

Military Organization   Perhaps the most important *mit'a* obligation which subject households owed to the Inca in the conquest phase of the empire was the service of young, able-bodied men in the military. Married men 25–30 years old were foot soldiers, often accompanied by wives and children; unmarried men 18–25 years of age served as porters or messengers. As in the Aztec Empire, administrators made sure that enough laborers remained in the villages to take care of their other obligations of farming, herding, transporting, and manufacturing. Sources report armies in the range of 35,000–140,000. Intermediate commanders came from the local and regional elites, and the top commanders were members of the two upper and lower Inca ruling elites.

Inca weaponry was comparable to that of the Aztecs, consisting of bows and arrows, dart throwers, slings, clubs with spiked bronze heads, wooden broadswords, bronze axes, and bronze-tipped javelins. Using Bolivian tin, Inca smiths were able to make a much harder and more useful bronze than was possible with earlier techniques. The Incas lacked the Aztec obsidian-serrated swords but used a snare (which

Inca Roads. Inca roads were paths reserved for runners and the military. They were built on beds of rocks and rubble and connected strategic points in the most direct line possible.

the Aztecs did not possess) with attached stone or bronze weights to entangle the enemy's legs. Protective armor consisted of quilted cotton shirts, copper breastplates, cane helmets, and shields. Of course, these types of weapons and armor were also widely found among the enemies of the Incas. The advantage enjoyed by the Incas, however, resulted from the sheer massiveness of their weapons and supplies, procured from craftspeople through the *mit'a* and stored in strategically located armories.

During the second half of the fifteenth century the Incas turned from conquest to consolidation. Faced at that time with a number of rebellions, they deemphasized the decimal draft and recruited longer-serving troops from among a smaller number of select, trusted peoples. These troops garrisoned the forts distributed throughout the empire. They also were part of the settler colonies implanted in rebellious provinces and in border regions. The fiercest resistance came from the people of the former Tiwanaku state and from the northeast Peruvian provinces, areas with long state traditions of their own. Since elite infighting also became more pronounced toward the end of the fifteenth century, personal guards recruited from non-Inca populations and numbering up to 7,000 soldiers accompanied many leading ruling-class members. The professionalization of the Inca army, however, lagged behind that of the Aztecs, since the Incas did not have military academies open to their subjects.

Communications   Although they lacked the military professionalization of the Aztecs, the Incas created an imperial communication and logistics structure that was unparalleled in the Americas. Early on, the Incas systematically improved on the road network that they inherited from Tiwanaku, Wari, and other states. Two parallel trunk roads extended from Cuzco nearly the entire length of the empire in both southerly and northerly directions. One followed the coast and western slopes of the western Andes chain; the other led through the mountain lands, valleys, and high plains between the western and eastern Andes chains. In numerous places, additional highways connected the two trunk roads. Suspension bridges made of thick ropes crossed gorges, while rafts were used for crossing rivers. The roads, 3–12 feet wide, crossed the terrain as directly as possible, often requiring extensive grounding, paving, staircasing, and tunneling. In many places, the 25,000-mile road network still exists today, attesting to the engineering prowess of the Incas.

The roads were reserved for troops, officials, and runners carrying messages. For their convenience, every 15 miles, or at the end of a slow 1-day journey, an inn provided accommodation. Larger armies stopped at barracks-like constructions or pitched tents on select campgrounds. Like the Romans, and despite the fact that they did not have wheeled transport, the Incas were well aware of how crucial paved and well-supplied roads were for infantry soldiers.

Aqueduct from the Western Hills to Tenochtitlán. This aqueduct, still standing today, provided fresh water to the palace and mansions of the center of the island, to be used as drinking water and for washing.

Imperial Society and Culture

As Mesoamerica and the Andes entered their imperial age, cosmopolitan capitals with monumental ceremonial centers and palaces emerged. The sizes of both capitals and monuments were visual expressions of the exalted power that the rulers claimed. Almost daily ceremonies and rituals, accompanied by feasts, further underscored the authority of rulers. These ceremonies and rituals expressed the American spiritual and polytheistic heritage but were modified to impress on enemies and subjects alike the irresistible might of the empires.

Imperial Capitals: Tenochtitlán and Cuzco

In the fifteenth century, the Aztec and Inca capitals were among the largest cities of the world, encompassing between 100,000 and 200,000 inhabitants. Both cities maintained their high degree of urbanism through a complex command system of labor, services, and goods. Although their monumental architecture followed different artistic traditions, both emphasized platforms and sanctuaries atop large pyramid-like structures as symbols of elevated power as well as closeness to the astral gods, especially those associated with the sun and Venus.

Tenochtitlán as an Urban Metropolis   More than half of the approximately 1.5 million people living during the fifteenth century in the Mexican Basin were urban dwellers, including elites, priests, administrators, military officers, merchants, traders, craftspeople, messengers, servants, and laborers. Such an extraordinary concentration of urban citizens was unique in the agrarian world prior to the industrialization of Europe (beginning around 1800), when cities usually held no more than 10 percent of the total population (see Map 15.5).

The center of Tenochtitlán, on the southern island, was a large platform where the Aztec settlers had driven pilings into marshy ground and heaped rocks and rubble. In an enclosure on this platform were the main pyramid, with temples to the Aztec gods on top, and a series of smaller ceremonial centers. Adjacent to these centers on the platform were a food market and a series of palaces of the ruling elite, which included guest quarters, administrative offices, storage facilities for tributes, kitchens, the high court for the elite and the court of appeals for commoners, the low court for civil cases, workshops for craftspeople, the prison, and councils for teachers and the military. Large numbers of Aztecs and visitors assembled each day to pay respect to the ruler and to trade in the market in preparation for assemblies and feasts.

In 1473, the southern island was merged with the northern island to form a single unit. At the center of the northern island was a platform that contained the principal market of the combined islands. This daily market attracted as many as 40,000 farmers, craftspeople, traders, porters, and laborers. The sophistication of the market was comparable to that of any market in Eurasia during the fifteenth century.

A number of causeways crossed the capital and linked it with the lakeshore. People also traveled inside the city on a number of main and branch canals. Dikes with sluices on the east side regulated both the water level and the salinity of the

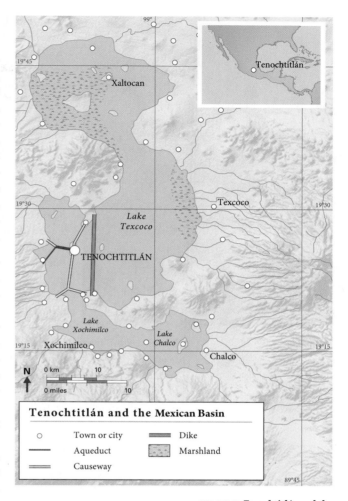

MAP **15.5 Tenochtitlán and the Valley of Mexico.**

Cuzco Stone Masonry. Inspired by the masonry of the people of Tiwanaku, the Inca built imposing structures with much larger blocks of limestone or granite. To cut the blocks, masons used copper and bronze chisels, making use of natural fissures in the stone.

Chinampas: Mesoamerican agricultural practice by which farmers grew crops on small, human-made islands in Lake Texcoco.

lake around the islands. The runoff during the summer rainy season from the southwestern mountains provided fresh water to dilute the lake's salinity, and the eastern dikes kept out salt water from the rest of the lake. Potable water arrived from the shore via an aqueduct on one of the western causeways. This aqueduct served mostly the ceremonial center and palace precinct, but branches brought potable water to a number of elite residences nearby as well. Professional water carriers took fresh water from the aqueduct to commoners in the various quarters of the city; professional waste removers collected human waste from urban residences and took it to farmers for fertilizer. In short, Tenochtitlán possessed a fully developed urban infrastructure.

The two city centers—the pyramid and palaces in the south and the market in the north—were surrounded by dozens of residential city quarters. Built on a layer of firm ground, many of these quarters were inhabited by craftspeople of a shared profession, who practiced their crafts in their residences. As discussed earlier in this chapter, merchants occupied a privileged position between the elite and the commoners. As militarily trained organizers of large caravans of porters, the merchants also provided the Aztec capital with luxury goods. Depending on their social rank, craftspeople occupied residences of larger or smaller size, usually grouped into compounds of related families. The rooms of the houses surrounded a central patio on which most of the household activities took place—an architectural preference common to Mesoamerica and the Andes, as well as the Middle East and Mediterranean.

Residents of quarters farther away from the center were farmers. In these quarters, making up nearly two-thirds of Tenochtitlán's surface, families engaged in intensive farming. Here, a grid of canals encased small, rectangular islands devoted to housing compounds and/or farming. People moved within these barrios by boat. Since the Mexican Basin received year-round rains that were often insufficient for dry farming, a raised-field system prevailed, whereby farmers dredged the canals, heaped the fertile mud on top of the rectangular islands, called **chinampas,** and added water from the canals and waste from their households or brought by boat from the urban neighborhoods. In contrast to the luxurious palaces of the elite, housing for farmers consisted of plastered huts made of cane, wood, and reeds. As in all agrarian societies, farmers—subject to high taxes or rents—were among the poorest folk.

On the surface of the *chinampas*, farmers grew corn, beans, squash, amaranth, and peppers. These seed plants were supplemented by *maguey* [mag-AY], a large succulent agave. This evergreen plant grew in poor soils; had a large root system, which helped in stabilizing the ground; and produced fiber useful for weaving and pulp useful for making *pulque* [POOL-kay], a fermented drink. To plant these crops in the soft soil, a digging stick, slightly broadened at one end, was sufficient. Regular watering made multicropping of seed plants possible. Trees, planted at the edges, protected the *chinampas* against water erosion.

Ownership of the *chinampas* was vested in clans, which, under neighborhood leaders, were responsible for the allocation of land and adjudication of disputes as well as the payment of taxes in kind to the elite. But there were also members of the elite who, as absentee owners, possessed estates and employed managers to collect rents from the farmers. Whether there was a trend from taxes to rents (that is, from a central tax authority to a decentralized landowner class) is unknown. Given the high productivity of raised-field farming, which was similar to that of the Eurasian agrarian–urban centers, such a trend would not have been surprising.

Cuzco as a Ceremonial–Administrative City   The site of the Inca city of Cuzco was an elongated triangle formed by the confluence of two rivers. At one end, opposite the confluence, was a hill with a number of structures, including the imperial armory and a temple dedicated to the sun god. Enormous, zigzagging walls followed the contours of the hill. The walls were built with stone blocks weighing up to 100 tons and cut so precisely that no mortar was needed, a technique which the Incas adopted from Tiwanaku.

Below, on the plain leading to the confluence, the city was laid out in a grid pattern. The residents of the city, all belonging to the upper and lower Inca ruling class, lived in adobe houses arranged in a block-and-courtyard pattern similar to that of Wari. Several squares and temples within the city served as ceremonial centers. One plaza contained a platform, with the imperial throne and a pillar placed symbolically atop what the Incas considered the earth's center or navel. The Coricancha [co-ri-CAN-tsha], the city's main temple, stood near the confluence of the rivers. This temple was a walled compound comprising six buildings set around a courtyard. Chambers in these buildings contained the Inca gods and goddesses as well as the divine statues or sacred objects confiscated from the provinces. Each year priests of the empire's ceremonial centers sent one such sacred object to the Coricancha, to demonstrate their obedience to the central Inca temple (see Map 15.6).

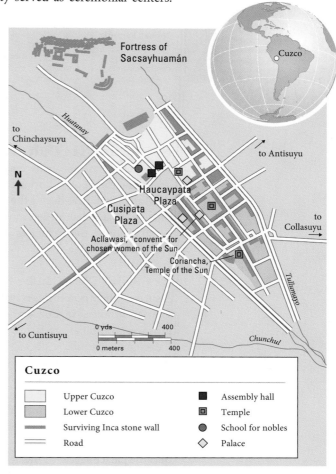

Across the rivers, in separate suburbs, were settlements for commoners with markets and storehouses. They were surrounded by fields, terraces, and irrigation canals. In the fields, interspersed stone pillars and shrines were aligned on sight lines radiating from the Coricancha, tying the countryside closely to the urban center. These alignments were reminiscent of the Nazca lines drawn half a millennium earlier in southern Peru (Chapter 9). Farther away were imperial estates with unfree laborers from outside the *mit'a* system and its reciprocal feasting. In contrast to the Aztec elite, which allowed meritorious generals to rise in the hierarchy, the Inca elite remained exclusionary, allowing no commoners to reside in Cuzco.

MAP **15.6 Cuzco.**

Patterns Up Close | Human Sacrifice and Propaganda

In the first millennium CE, Mesoamerica and the Andes evolved from their early religious spirituality to polytheism. The spiritual heritage, however, remained a strong undercurrent. Both American regions engaged in human as well as animal and agricultural sacrifices. Rulers appeased the gods also through self-sacrifice—that is, the piercing of tongue and penis, as was the case among the Olmecs (1400–400 BCE) and Mayas (600 BCE–900 CE). The feathered serpent god Quetzalcoatl was the Mesoamerican deity of self-sacrifice, revered in the city-states of Teotihuacán (200 BCE–570 CE) and Tula (ca. 900 CE). Under the Toltecs and the Aztecs, this god receded into the background, in favor of warrior gods such as Tezcatlipoca and Huitzilpochtli. The survival of traditional blood rituals within polytheism was a pattern that distinguished the early American empires from their Eurasian counterparts.

Whether human sacrifices were prolific under Aztec and Inca imperialism is questionable. About the same number of human victims were excavated at the Feathered Serpent Temple of Teotihuacán and at the Templo Mayor of Tenochtitlán: 137 versus 126 skeletons. These numbers are minuscule in comparison to the

52.

Human Sacrifice. Human sacrifice among the pre-Columbian Mesoamericans and Andeans was based on the concept of a shared life spirit or mind, symbolized by the life substance of blood. In the American spiritual-polytheistic conceptualization, the gods sacrificed their blood, or themselves altogether, during creation; rulers pierced their earlobes, tongues, or penises for blood sacrifices; and war captives lost their lives when their hearts were sacrificed.

Power and Its Cultural Expressions

Ruling elites, as repeatedly emphasized in this chapter, put a strong emphasis on displaying their power during the period 600–1500. This was particularly true with the Aztecs and Incas during the fifteenth century. Among these displays were human sacrifices, mausoleums, and mummy burials. Although all three involved changes in social relations, these changes were accommodated in the existing overall religious culture.

Inca Ruling-Class Gender Relations   The ruling classes in the Inca Empire displayed their power in several ways. Among the examples were the "Houses of Chosen Women" in Cuzco and provincial colonies. The greatest honor for Inca girls was to enter at age 10–12 into the service of these houses. An inspector from Cuzco made regular visits to the villages of the empire to select attractive young girls for the service. The girls were marched to the capital or the colonies, where they were divided according to beauty, skills, and social standing. These houses had female instructors who provided the girls with a 4-year education in cooking, beer making, weaving, and officiating in the rituals and ceremonies of the Inca religion. After their graduation, the young women became virgin temple priestesses, were given in marriage to non-Incas honored for service to the ruler, or became palace servants, musicians, or concubines of the Inca elite. The collection of this girl tribute was separate from the reciprocity system. As such, it was an impression created by the Spanish conquerors and encourage doubts about the magnitude of human sacrifices in temple ceremonies. It appears that even though the Aztec and Inca ruling classes were focused on war, the ritual of human sacrifice was not as pervasive as has been widely assumed.

Could it be that there was no significant increase in human sacrifice under the Aztecs and Incas, as the self-serving Spanish conquerors alleged? Were there perhaps, instead, imperial propaganda machines in the Aztec and Inca Empires, employed in the service of conquest and consolidation—similar to those of the Assyrians and Mongols in Eurasia—who sought to intimidate their enemies? In this case, the Aztec and Inca Empires would not be exceptional barbaric aberrations in world history. Instead, they would be but two typical examples of the general world-historical pattern of competitive militaristic states during the early agrarian era using propaganda to further their imperial power.

Questions

- In examining the question of whether empires such as the Inca and the Aztec employed human sacrifice for propaganda purposes, can this practice be considered an adaptation that evolved out of earlier rituals, such as royal bloodletting?

- If the Aztec and the Inca did indeed employ human sacrifice for propaganda purposes, what does this say about the ability of these two empires to use cultural and religious practices to consolidate their power?

act of assigning gender roles in an emerging social hierarchy defined by power inequalities.

Traditionally, gender roles were less strictly divided than in Eurasia. The horticultural form of agriculture in Mesoamerica and the Andes gave males fewer opportunities to accumulate wealth and power than plow agriculture did in Eurasia. Hoes and foot plows distinguished men and women from each other less than plows and teams of oxen or horses did. Nevertheless, it comes as no surprise that the gradual agrarian–urban diversification of society, even if it was slower in the Americas than in Eurasia, proceeded along similar paths of increasing male power concentration in villages, ceremonial centers, temple cities, conquering states, and empires. Emphasizing gender differences, therefore, should be viewed as a characteristic phenomenon arising in imperial contexts.

Inca Mummy Veneration   Other houses in Cuzco were ghostly residences in which scores of attendants and servants catered to what were believed to be the earthly needs of deceased, mummified Inca emperors and their principal wives. During the mummification process attendants removed the cadaver's internal organs, placed them in special containers, and desiccated the bodies until they were completely mummified. Servants dressed the mummies (*mallquis* [MAY-kees]) in their finest clothing and placed them back into their residences amid their possessions, as if they had never died. The mummies received daily meals and were carried around by their retinues for visits to their mummified relatives. On special occasions, mummies were lined up according to rank on Cuzco's main plaza to participate in ceremonies and processions. In this way, they remained fully integrated into the daily life of the elite.

"Ghost residences" with mummies can be considered an outgrowth of the old Andean custom of mummification. This custom was widely practiced among the elites of the ceremonial centers, who, however, generally placed their ancestors in temple tombs, shrines, or caves. Mummies were also buried in cemeteries, sometimes collectively in bundles with false heads made of cotton. Preserving the living spaces of the deceased obviously required considerable wealth—wealth provided only by imperial regimes for their elites.

As a general phenomenon in Andean society, of course, mummies were a crucial ingredient in the religious heritage, in which strong spiritual elements survived underneath the polytheistic overlay of astral gods. In the spiritual tradition, body and spirit cohabit more or less loosely. In a trance, a diviner's mind can travel, enter the minds of other people and animals, or make room for other people's minds. Similarly, in death a person's spirit, while no longer in the body, remains nearby and therefore still needs daily nourishment in order not to be driven away. Hence, even though non-Incan Andean societies removed the dead from their daily living spaces, descendants had to visit tombs regularly with food and beer or provide buried mummies with ample victuals.

The expenses for the upkeep of the mummy households were the responsibility of the deceased emperor's bloodline, headed by a surviving brother. As heirs of the emperor's estate, the members of the bloodline formed a powerful clan within the ruling class. The new emperor was excluded from this estate and had to acquire his own new one in the course of his rule, a mechanism evidently designed to intensify his imperial ambitions for conquest. In the early sixteenth century, however, when it became logistically difficult to expand much beyond the enormous territory already accumulated in the Andes, this ingenious mechanism of keeping the upper and lower rungs of the ruling class united became counterproductive. Emperors lacking resources had to contend with brothers richly endowed with inherited wealth and ready to engage in dynastic warfare—as actually occurred shortly before the arrival of the Spanish (1529–1532).

❯ Putting It All Together

interactive concept map

During the short time of their existence, the Aztec and Inca Empires unleashed extraordinary creative energies. Sculptors, painters, and (after the arrival of the Spanish) writers recorded the traditions as well as the innovations of the fifteenth century. Aztec painters produced codices, or illustrated manuscripts, that present the divine pantheons, myths, calendars, ceremonial activities, chants, poetry, and administrative activities of their societies in exquisite and colorful detail. They fashioned these codices using bark paper, smoothing it with plaster, and connecting the pages accordion-style. Today, a handful of these codices survive, preserved in Mexican and European libraries.

The Aztec and Inca Empires were polities that illustrate how humans not in contact with the rest of the world and living within an environment that was different from that of Eurasia and Africa in many respects developed patterns of innovation that were remarkably similar. On the basis of an agriculture that produced ample surpluses, humans made the same choices as their cousins in Eurasia and Africa. Specifically, in the period 600–1500, they created temple-centered city-states, just like their Sumerian and Hindu counterparts. Their military states were not unlike the Chinese warring states. And, finally, their empires—although just beginning to flourish in the Bronze Age—were comparable to those of the New Kingdom Egyptians or Assyrians. The Americas had their own unique variations of these larger historical patterns, to be sure; but they nevertheless displayed the same humanity as found elsewhere.

Review and Relate

Thinking Through Patterns

Examine the ways historians approach the big questions of this chapter.

The basic pattern of state formation in the Americas was similar to that of Eurasia and Africa. Historically, it began with the transition from foraging to agriculture and settled village life. As the population increased, villages under elders became chiefdoms, which in turn became city-states with temples. As in Eurasia and Africa, American city-states often became conquering states, beginning with the Maya kingdoms and Teotihuacán. Both, however, remained small. Military states, in which ruling classes sought to expand territories, such as Tula and, to a lesser degree, Tiwanaku and Wari, were characteristic for the early part of the period 600–1550. The successors of these—the Aztec and Inca Empires—were multiethnic, multilinguistic, and multireligious polities that dominated Mesoamerica and the Andes for about a century, before the Spanish conquest brought them to a premature end.

>> Within the patterns of state formation basic to the Americas, which types of states emerged in Mesoamerica and the Andes during the period 600–1550? What characterized these states?

The states of Tiwanaku and Wari had more or less cohesive ruling classes but no dynasties of rulers and centralized bureaucracies. These ruling classes and their subjects—corn and potato farmers—were integrated with each other through systems of reciprocity—that is, military protection in return for foodstuffs. They customarily renewed the bonds of reciprocity in common feasts. After one or two centuries, however, tensions arose, either between stronger and weaker branches of the ruling classes or between rulers and subjects over questions of obligations and justice. When these tensions erupted into internal warfare, the states disintegrated, often in conjunction with environmental degradation and climate change.

>> Why did the Tiwanaku and Wari states have ruling classes but no dynasties and central bureaucracies? How were these patterns expressed in the territorial organization of these states?

Tenochtitlán and Cuzco, the capitals of the Aztec and Inca Empires, were two urban centers organized around temples and associated residences of the ruling dynasties and their priestly classes. They also contained large city quarters inhabited

>> What patterns of urban life characterized the cities of

Tenochtitlán and Cuzco, the capitals of the Aztec and Inca Empires? In which ways were these cities similar to those of Eurasia and Africa?

by craftspeople specializing in the production of woven textiles, pottery, leather goods, and weapons. Large central markets provided for the exchange of foodstuffs, crafts, and imported luxury goods. Armed caravans of merchants and porters transported the luxury goods, such as cacao, feathers, obsidian, and turquoise, across hundreds of miles. Tenochtitlán had an aqueduct for the supply of drinking water, and Cuzco was traversed by a river. Both capitals had agricultural suburbs in which farmers used irrigation for the production of the basic food staples.

| Against the Grain

Consider this as a counterpoint to the main patterns examined in this chapter.

Amazon Rain-Forest Civilizations

- Which is more important: to save the rain forest or uncover its archaeological past? Can the two objectives be combined?

- Compare the Amazonian earthworks to those of Benin in Africa during the same period (Chapter 14). Which similarities and differences can you discover?

For many years, prevailing scholarly opinion held that the vast Amazonian river basin, covered by dense rain forest, was too inhospitable to allow for more than small numbers of widely dispersed foragers to subsist. Even farmers, living in more densely populated villages, could not possibly have founded complex, stratified societies. Slash-and-burn agriculture, the common form of farming on poor tropical soils even today, by definition prevented the advance of urban life: After exhausting the soil in a given area, whole villages had to pack up and move.

Beginning in the 1990s, however, a few scholars realized that this belief was erroneous. Modern farmers, increasingly encroaching on the rain forest, made these scholars aware of two hitherto neglected features. First, these farmers often advanced into stretches of forest and savanna on top of what is called in Portuguese *terra preta*—black soil so fertile that it did not require fertilizers for years. Second, as they slashed and burned the rain forest and savanna with their modern tools, the farmers exposed monumental earthworks that had previously escaped attention under the cover of vegetation. The two features were actually connected. *Terra preta* was the result of centuries of patient soil enrichment by indigenous people who were also the builders of the earthworks. Instead of slashing and burning, these people had engaged in "slashing and charring"—that is, turning the trees into longer-lasting nutrient-rich charcoal rather than less fertile and quickly depleted ash.

Since the early 2000s, scholars have documented large-scale settlements in areas along the southern tributaries to the Amazon, describing large village clusters with central plazas, fortification walls, bridges, causeways, and waterworks. One such cluster is located on the upper Xingu, a tributary of the lower Amazon. A set of two clusters is situated near the upper reaches of the Purus, a tributary of the upper Amazon. One occupies a fertile floodplain, the other the less fertile highlands farther away from the river. In the Purus region, researchers employing aerial photography revealed a huge area home to perhaps 60,000 inhabitants during a period around the late thirteenth century. This area is adjacent to the farthest northeastern extension of the Inca Empire into the Amazon, with fortresses being excavated by Finnish teams. Thus, when the Incas expanded into the rain forest, they clearly did so to incorporate flourishing, advanced societies into their empire. Thanks to scholars who challenged the orthodoxy of the "empty rain forest," we are rediscovering the Amazonian past.

Key Terms

audio flashcards

Chinampas 448	*Mit'a* 444
Reciprocity 435	*Quipu* 444

For additional resources, please go to
www.oup.com/us/vonsivers.
Please see the Further Resources section at the back of the book for additional readings and suggested websites.

Sources for Chapter 15

| SOURCE 15.1 | The Temple of the Jaguars, Chichén Itzá |

ca. 850–1000 CE

Chichén Itzá was founded during a period of renewed urbanization in the Mayan states around 650, and a remarkable state flourished in its vicinity between 850 and 1000. The population was composed of local Maya, as well as Maya-speaking peoples from the Gulf of Mexico coast. It owed its prosperity to long-distance trade, both overland and in boats along the coast. Around 1000, the ruling-class factions abandoned Chichén Itzá for unknown reasons, and the city-state dwindled in size to the level of a town.

Source: Dreamstime/©Alexandre Fagundes De Fagundes (top); Shutterstock/Danilo Ascione (bottom).

>> Working
with Sources

1. What does the construction of this monument suggest about the social structure of Chichén Itzá at its height?

2. What might have been the significance of the jaguars? Why would the temple have been decorated in such an elaborate fashion?

SOURCE 15.2 Skeletons in a Wari royal tomb site, El Castillo de Huarmey, Peru

ca. 600–1000 CE

In 2013, 63 skeletons were discovered in a tomb at El Castillo de Huarmey, about 175 miles north of Lima, in what would seem to be the first imperial tomb of the Wari culture discovered in modern times. Most of the bodies were female, and wrapped in bundles in a seated position typical of Wari burials. Three of the women appear to have been Wari queens, as they were buried with gold and silver jewelry and brilliantly painted ceramics. However, six of the skeletons were not wrapped in the textiles, but instead positioned on top of the burials. Archaeologists have concluded that these people may have been sacrificed for the benefit of the others.

Source: REUTERS/Enrique Castro-Mendivil.

> **Working
> with Sources**

1. How do the burial practices of Wari culture compare with those of other civilizations in Mesoamerica and the Andes?

2. What might this tomb suggest about the roles and expectations of women in Wari culture?

SOURCE 15.3　Bernal Díaz, *The Conquest of New Spain*

ca. 1568

In the course of the fifteenth century, the Aztecs established an empire centered in the Mexican Basin (surrounding present-day Mexico City, after the drainage of most of the valley) but encompassing Mesoamerica from the Pacific to the Gulf of Mexico. The resulting state, far more centralized than the preceding Teotihuacán and Toltec city-states, commanded a large extent of territory and thrived on the trade in raw materials that were brought in from both coasts of their empire. Bernal Díaz, born in 1492 in Spain, would join the Spaniards in the "conquest" of Mexico, but he also left behind vivid eyewitness accounts of occupied Aztec society in the sixteenth century. Among them is this description of the market in Tlatelolco, one of the central cities at the heart of Aztec imperial power.

Caciques: Nobles.

Our Captain and those of us who had horses went to Tlatelolco mounted, and the majority of our men were fully equipped. On reaching the market-place, escorted by the many **Caciques** whom Montezuma had assigned to us, we were astounded at the great number of people and the quantities of merchandise, and at the orderliness and good arrangements that prevailed, for we had never seen such a thing before. The chieftains who accompanied us pointed everything out. Every kind of merchandise was kept separate and had its fixed place marked for it.

Let us begin with the dealers in gold, silver, and precious stones, feathers, cloaks, and embroidered goods, and male and female slaves who are also sold there. They bring as many slaves to be sold in that market as the Portuguese bring Negroes from Guinea. Some are brought there attached to long poles by means of collars round their necks to prevent them from escaping, but others are left loose. Next there were those who sold coarser cloth, and cotton goods and fabrics made of twisted thread, and there were chocolate merchants with their chocolate. In this way you could see every kind of merchandise to be

---

Source: Bernal Díaz del Castillo, *The Conquest of New Spain*, trans. J. M. Cohen (Baltimore: Penguin, 1963), 232–234.

found anywhere in New Spain, laid out in the same way as goods are laid out in my own district of Medina del Campo, a centre for fairs, where each line of stalls has its own particular sort. So it was in this great market. There were those who sold sisal cloth and ropes and the sandals they wear on their feet, which are made from the same plant. All these were kept in one part of the market, in the place assigned to them, and in another part were skins of tigers and lions, otters, jackals, and deer, badgers, mountain cats, and other wild animals, some tanned and some untanned, and other classes of merchandise.

. . .

Then there were the sellers of pitch-pine for torches, and other things of that kind, and I must also mention, with all apologies, that they sold many canoe-loads of human excrement, which they keep in the creeks near the market. This was for the manufacture of salt and the curing of skins, which they say cannot be done without it. I know that many gentlemen will laugh at this, but I assure them it is true. I may add that on all the roads they have shelters made of reeds or straw or grass so that they can retire when they wish to do so, and purge their bowels unseen by passers-by, and also in order that their excrement shall not be lost.

But why waste so many words on the goods in their great market? If I describe everything in detail I shall never be done. Paper, which in Mexico they call *amal*, and some reeds that smell of liquid amber, and are full of tobacco, and yellow ointments and other such things, are sold in a separate part. Much cochineal is for sale too, under the arcades of that market, and there are many sellers of herbs and other such things. They have a building there also in which three judges sit, and there are officials like constables who examine the merchandise. I am forgetting the sellers of salt and the makers of flint knives, and how they split them off the stone itself, and the fisherwomen and the men who sell small cakes made from a sort of weed which they get out of the great lake, which curdles and forms a kind of bread which tastes rather like cheese. They sell axes too, made of bronze and copper and tin, and gourds and brightly painted wooden jars.

Cue: Temple.

We went on to the great ***cue***, and as we approached its wide courts, before leaving the market-place itself, we saw many more merchants who, so I was told, brought gold to sell in grains, just as they extract it from the mines. This gold is placed in the thin quills of the large geese of that country, which are so white as to be transparent. They used to reckon their accounts with one another by the length and thickness of these little quills, how much so many cloaks or so many gourds of chocolate or so many slaves were worth, or anything else they were bartering.

» Working with Sources

1. How and why does Díaz use comparisons from other markets while describing the one in Tlatelolco?

2. What do the specific elements of this market suggest about the importance of trade and commerce in pre-Columbian Mexico?

SOURCE 15.4   Pedro Cieza de León on Incan roads

1541–1547

The Incas created an imperial communications and logistics infrastructure that was unparalleled in the Americas, with two highways extending to the north and south from Cuzco nearly the entire length of the empire. The roads, which were up to 12 feet wide, crossed the terrain as directly as possible, which clearly required a tremendous labor force to create. In many places, even today, the 25,000-mile road network still exists. Pedro Cieza de León was born in Spain in 1520 and undoubtedly traveled along the extensive, and still-functional, Roman road system of his native land as a child. When he arrived in the New World at the age of 13, he was captivated and impressed by the civilizations that the Spanish were supplanting. In 1541, he began writing his account of the Incas, tracing their heritage and government for the benefit of those who would never see the territory he did—or travel the roads that made his observations possible.

CHAPTER 42 (ii.xv)

Of how the buildings for the Lord-Incas were constructed, and the highways to travel through the kingdom [of Peru].

One of the things that most took my attention when I was observing and setting down the things of this kingdom was how and in what way the great, splendid highways we see throughout it could be built, and the number of men that must have been required, and what tools and instruments they used to level the mountains and cut through the rock to make them as broad and good as they are. For it seems to me that if the Emperor were to desire another highway built like the one from Quito to Cuzco, or that which goes from Cuzco to Chile, truly I do not believe he could do it, with all his power and the men at his disposal, unless he followed the method the Incas employed. For if it were a question of a road fifty leagues long, or a hundred, or two hundred, we can assume that, however rough the land, it would not be too difficult, working hard, to do it. But there were so long, one of them more than 1100 leagues, over mountains so rough and dismaying that in certain places one could not see bottom, and some of the sierras so sheer and barren that the road had to be cut through the living rock to keep it level and the right width. All this they did with fire and picks.

. . .

When a Lord-Inca had decided on the building of one of these famous highways, no great provisioning or levies or anything else was needed except for the Lord-Inca to say, let this be done. The inspectors then went through

Source: Pedro Cieza de León, *The Incas*, trans. Harriet de Onis, ed. Victor Wolfgang von Hagen (Norman: University of Oklahoma Press, 1959), 135–137.

the provinces, laying out the route and assigning Indians from one end to the other to the building of the road. In this way, from one boundary of the province to the other, at its expense and with its Indians, it was built as laid out, in a short time; and the others did the same, and, if necessary, a great stretch of the road was built at the same time, or all of it. When they came to the barren places, the Indians of the lands nearest by came with victuals and tools to do the work, and all was done with little effort and joyfully, because they were not oppressed in any way, nor did the Incas put overseers to watch them.

Aside from these, great fine highways were built, like that which runs through the valley of Xaquixahuana, and comes out of the city of Cuzco and goes by the town of Muhina. There were many of these highways all over the kingdom, both in the highlands and the plains. Of all, four are considered the main highways, and they are those which start from the city of Cuzco, at the square, like a crossroads, and go to the different provinces of the kingdom. As these monarchs held such a high opinion of themselves, when they set out on one of these roads, the royal person with the necessary guard took one [road], and the rest of the people another. So great was their pride that when one of them died, his heir, if he had to travel to a distant place, built his road larger and broader than that of his predecessor, but this was only if this Lord-Inca set out on some conquest, or [performed] some act so noteworthy that it could be said the road built for him was longer.

> ≫ **Working with Sources**

1. **How were the Incas' roads a manifestation of royal power, at least in Cieza de León's estimation?**

2. **What technical challenges faced the Incan road builders, and how did they overcome them?**

SOURCE 15.5 Garcilaso de la Vega, "The Walls and Gates of Cuzco"

1609–1616

The Incan city of Cuzco was an elongated triangle formed by the confluence of two rivers. At one end, enormous, zigzagging walls followed the contours of a steep hill. The walls were built with stone blocks weighing up to 100 tons and cut so precisely that no mortar was needed. The ruins of the walls were still visible after the Spanish siege of 1536 (as they are today), and they were a marvel to Garcilaso de la Vega, when he viewed them in the mid-sixteenth century. Garcilaso was born in 1539, the decade of the conquest of Peru, to a Spanish conqueror and a Native American princess,

Source: Garcilaso de la Vega, *Royal Commentaries of the Incas and General History of Peru*, trans. Harold V. Livermore, vol.1 (Austin: University of Texas Press, 1966), 463–468.

a second cousin of the last two Inca rulers. As a young man, Garcilaso left his native Peru, never to return. Toward the end of his life he retired to a secluded Spanish village, where he wrote his general history of the Incas. He was particularly proud of the monumental achievements of his Incan relatives and of the power that their construction projects represented.

CHAPTER XXVII

The fortress of Cuzco; the size of its stones.

The Inca kings of Peru made marvelous buildings, fortresses, temples, royal palaces, gardens, storehouses, roads, and other constructions of great excellence, as can be seen even today from their remaining ruins, though the whole building can scarcely be judged from the mere foundations.

The greatest and most splendid building erected to show the power and majesty of the Incas was the fortress of Cuzco, the grandeur of which would be incredible to anyone who had not seen it, and even those who have seen it and considered it with attention imagine, and even believe, that it was made by enchantment, the handiwork of demons, rather than of men. Indeed the multiplicity of stones, large and small, of which the three **circumvallations** are composed (and they are more like rocks than stones) makes one wonder how they could have been quarried, for the Indians had neither iron nor steel to work them with. And the question of how they were conveyed to the site is no less difficult a problem, since they had no oxen and could not make wagons: nor would oxen and wagons have sufficed to carry them. They were in fact heaved by main force with the aid of thick cables. The roads by which they were brought were not flat, but rough mountainsides with steep slopes, up and down which the rocks were dragged by human effort alone.

Circumvallations: Walls built around the city.

· · ·

CHAPTER XXVIII

The three circumvallations, the most remarkable part of the work.

On the other side, opposite this wall, there is a large level space. From this direction the ascent to the top of the hill is a gradual one up which an enemy could advance in order of battle. The Incas therefore made three concentric walls on the slopes, each of which would be more than two hundred fathoms long. They are in the shape of a half moon, for they close together at the ends to meet the other wall of smooth masonry on the side facing the city. The first of these three walls best exhibits the might of the Incas, for although all three are of the same workmanship, it is the most impressive and has the largest stones, making the whole construction seem incredible to anyone who has not seen it, and giving an impression of awe to the careful observer who ponders on the size and number of the stones and the limited resources of the natives for cutting and working them and setting them in their places.

· · ·

Almost in the middle of each wall there was a gate, and these gates were each shut with a stone as high and as thick as the wall itself which could be raised and lowered. The first of these was called Tiupuncu, "gate of sand," since the plain is rather sandy or gravelly at this point: *tiu* is "sand," or "a sandy place," and *puncu*, "gate, door." The second is called Acahuana Puncu, after the master mason, whose name was Acahuana, the syllable *ca* being pronounced deep down in the throat. The third is Viracocha Puncu, dedicated to the god Viracocha, the phantom we have referred to at length, who appeared to Prince Viracocha Inca and forewarned him of the rising of the Chancas, as a result of which he was regarded as the defender and second founder of Cuzco, and therefore given this gate with the request that he should guard it and defend the fortress as he had guarded the city and the whole empire in the past.

≫ Working with Sources

1. Why did the Incas feel the need to fortify Cuzco so heavily, and would these preparations have been successful in typical battle situations?

2. What aspect of the city's walls most arouses Garcilaso's admiration and wonder, and why?

PART FOUR

Interactions across the Globe

1450–1750

Starting around 1450, important changes can be detected in the patterns of world history. The religious civilizations that had emerged in the period after 600 CE continued to evolve, but the competing states that constituted these civilizations began to give way to new empires, such as those of the Mughals, the Ottomans, the Safavids, and the Habsburgs. China, historically an empire, had already reconstituted itself under the Ming after the collapse of the Mongol super-empire that had straddled Eurasia. Finally, on the Atlantic coast, smaller European countries, such as Portugal, Spain, the Netherlands, England, and France, were creating the first global seaborne empires. Large or small, land based or maritime, however, all of these empires employed the vitally important innovation of firearms. In addition, many reorganized themselves as centralized polities based on money economies, large bureaucracies, and professional armies. Locked into far-flung competition for resources, markets, and ideological influence, they interacted with each other with increasing intensity.

While this renewal of the drive for empire among these civilizations was a significant turning point in world history, two new phenomena appeared during the three centuries in question that would have further far-reaching implications. Indeed, they would ultimately provide the basis on which our modern society was to be built: the New Sciences (or Scientific Revolution) and the Enlightenment. Attempts to found an understanding of the universe on mathematics and experimentation would lead to science as the chief mode of interpreting the physical realm. Attempts to apply principles of science to understanding and improving human societies would lead to the concepts of individual rights, natural law, and popular sovereignty that would become the modern legacy of the Enlightenment. The combination of these two trends created the foundations of the *scientific–industrial society* that now dominates our modern global culture.

The process by which this formation of *scientific–industrial society* took place was, of course, extremely complex, and it is impossible for us to do more than suggest some of the larger patterns of it here. Moreover, because of the long-standing argument in Western historiography for European "exceptionalism"—that there was something unique in the European historical experience that preordained it to rise to

1440–1897 Benin kingdom, West Africa	**1492** Spanish conquest of Granada, expulsion of Jews, and discovery of the Americas	**ca. 1500** Beginning of Columbian Exchange	**1514** Nicolaus Copernicus formulates the heliocentric model
	1453 Ottoman capture of Constantinople	**1498** Vasco da Gama's circumnavigation of Africa and journey to India	**1511** First African slaves taken to Caribbean	**1517** Martin Luther publishes his 95 theses; beginning of Protestant Reformation

dominance—we must be careful to explore the various aspects of this process without sliding into easy assumptions about their inevitability. For example, one question that suggests itself is "To what extent did the societies of western Europe (what we have termed the 'religious civilization' of Western Christianity) part ways with the other religious civilizations of the world?" Here, aspects of the question are tantalizingly complex and, thus, have recently been the subject of considerable debate:

- On one hand, there appears to have been no movement comparable to that of the European Renaissance or Reformation arising during this time in the other parts of the world to create a new culture similar to that of Europe. The Middle East, India, and China for the most part continued ongoing cultural patterns, although often on considerably higher levels of refinement and sophistication. Recent scholarship on neglected cultural developments in these areas from 1450 to 1750 has provided ample proof for the continuing vitality of Islamic, Hindu, Buddhist, Confucian, and Daoist cultural traditions. Thus, former assumptions of stagnation or decline no longer seem supportable.
- On the other hand, Europe, like much of the rest of the world, remained rooted in agrarian–urban patterns until the effects of the Industrial Revolution began to be felt sometime after 1800. The centuries-old patterns in which the majority of the population was employed in agriculture and did not live in cities continued unchanged. Furthermore, through nearly this entire period, China and India were more populous and at least as wealthy and diversified in their economies and social structures as their European counterpart. The "great divergence," as scholars currently call it, happened only *after* the Western constitutional and industrial revolutions. Nonetheless, the overall wealth of European countries involved in the conquest and exploitation of the resources of the Americas and the development of global trading systems advanced immensely—as did knowledge of the globe as a whole. Thus, while India and China had long possessed immense and varied resources, Europeans were now acquiring and utilizing similar ones at an accelerating rate. This wealth and the patterns of its acquisition and distribution would eventually have far-reaching consequences.

It is important to emphasize that those developments we deem crucial today were not immediately apparent to the people living at the time. Indeed, for the great majority of people, even in 1750, much seemed to go on as before. Everywhere in the world empires continued to grow and decline, religious tensions continued to erupt into warfare, and rulers continued to ground their authority not in their peoples but in the divine. Thus, for a full understanding of world history during 1450–1750, one has to carefully balance cultural, political, social, and economic factors and constantly keep in mind that although change was certainly occurring, it was often too imperceptible for contemporaries to detect.

Thinking Like a World Historian

≫ What new and different patterns characterized the development of states and empires in the period 1450–1750?

≫ How did the emergence of centralizing states lead to more intensive and frequent interactions among empires in the period 1450–1750?

≫ How did the New Sciences and the Enlightenment lay the foundation for the scientific–industrial society that dominates our global culture today?

≫ To what extent did the societies of western Europe diverge from other civilizations in the period 1450–1750? Why is the notion of "exceptionalism" problematic in examining this question?

interactive timeline

1521, 1533
Spanish conquest of the Aztec and Inca Empires

1577
Matteo Ricci, first Jesuit missionary to arrive in China

1607
Founding of Jamestown, Virginia

1720
Edo, capital of Japan, world's largest city

1542–1605
Akbar, the most innovative of the Mughal rulers (India)

1604
Galileo Galilei formulates the mathematical law of falling bodies

1687
Isaac Newton unifies physics and astronomy

1736–1795
Reign of Qianlong emperor, China

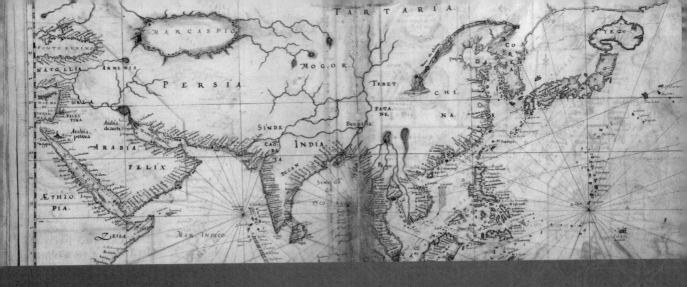

Western European Expansion and the Ottoman–Habsburg Struggle

Al-Hasan Ibn Muhammad al-Wazzan (ca. 1494–1550) was born into a family of bureaucrats in Muslim Granada soon after the Christian conquest of this kingdom in southern Iberia in 1492. Unwilling to convert to Christianity, Hasan's family emigrated to Muslim Morocco around 1499–1500 and settled in the city of Fez. Here, Hasan received a good education in religion, law, logic, and the sciences. After completing his studies, he entered the administration of the Moroccan sultan, traveling to sub-Saharan Africa and the Middle East on diplomatic missions.

In 1517, as he was returning home from a mission to Istanbul, Christian **corsairs** kidnapped him from his ship. Like their Muslim counterparts, these corsairs roamed the Mediterranean to capture unsuspecting travelers, whom they then held for ransom or sold into slavery. For a handsome sum of money, they turned the cultivated Hasan over to Pope Leo X (1513–1521), who ordered Hasan to convert to Christianity and baptized him with his own family name, Giovanni Leone di Medici. Hasan became known in Rome as Leo Africanus ("Leo the African"), in reference to his travels in sub-Saharan Africa. He stayed

ABOVE: This 1630 map by João Teixeira Albernaz the Elder (late 1500s–ca. 1662), member of a prominent family of Portuguese mapmakers, shows Arabia, India, and China.

for 10 years in Italy, initially at the papal court and later as an independent scholar in Rome. During this time, he taught Arabic to Roman clergymen, compiled an Arabic–Hebrew–Latin dictionary, and wrote an essay on famous Arabs. His most memorable and enduring work was a travelogue, first composed in Arabic and later translated into Italian, *Description of Africa*, which was for many years the sole source of information about sub-Saharan Africa in the Western Christian world.

After 1527, however, life became difficult in Rome. In this year, Charles V (r. 1516–1558), king of Spain and emperor of the Holy Roman Empire of Germany, invaded Italy and sacked the city. Hasan survived the sack of Rome but departed for Tunis sometime after 1531, seeking a better life in Muslim North Africa. Unfortunately, all traces of Hasan after his departure from Rome are lost. It is possible that he perished in 1535 when Charles V attacked and occupied Tunis (1535–1574), although it is generally assumed that he lived there until around 1550.

Seeing Patterns

》 What patterns characterized Christian and Muslim competition in the period 1300–1600? Which elements distinguished them from each other, and which elements were similar? How did the pattern change over time?

》 How did centralizing states in the Middle East and Europe function in the period 1450–1600? How did economics, military power, and imperial objectives interact to create the centralizing state?

》 Which patterns did cultural expressions follow in the Habsburg and Ottoman Empires? Why did the ruling classes of these empires sponsor these expressions?

The world in which Hasan lived and traveled was a Muslim–Christian world composed of the Middle East, North Africa, and Europe. Muslims on the Iberian Peninsula and in the Balkans bracketed this world, with the Western Christians in the center. Although Muslims and Christians traveled in much of this world more or less freely—as merchants, mapmakers, adventurers, mercenaries, or corsairs—the two religious civilizations were locked in a pattern of fierce competition. During 800–1050, the Muslims justified their conquests as holy wars (*jihads*), and during 1050–1300 the Christians retaliated with their Crusades and the *Reconquista* of Iberia.

By the fifteenth century, the Christians saw their liberation of Iberia and North Africa from Muslim rule and circumnavigation of the Muslims in the Mediterranean as steppingstones toward rebuilding the crusader kingdom of Jerusalem, which had been lost to the Muslims in 1291. Searching for a route that would take them around Africa, they hoped to defeat the Muslims in Jerusalem with an attack from the east. Driven at least in part by this search, the Christians discovered the continents of the Americas. For their part, the Muslims sought to conquer eastern and central Europe while simultaneously shoring up their defense of North Africa and driving the Portuguese out of the Indian Ocean. After a hiatus of several centuries—when commonwealths of states had characterized Western Christian and Islamic civilizations—imperial polities reemerged, in the form of the Ottoman and Habsburg Empires vying for world rule.

Corsairs: In the context of this chapter, Muslim or Christian pirates who boarded ships, confiscated the cargoes, and held the crews and travelers for ransom; they were nominally under the authority of the Ottoman sultan or the pope in Rome but operated independently.

The Muslim–Christian Competition in the East and West, 1450–1600

After a long period during which the Christian kings in Iberia found tributes by the Muslim emirs more profitable than war, in the second half of the fifteenth century the kings resumed the *Reconquista*. During the same time period, the small principality of the Ottomans took advantage of Mongol and Byzantine weakness to conquer lands in both Anatolia and the Balkans. After the Muslim conquest of Constantinople in 1453 and the Western Christian conquest of Granada in 1492, the path was open for the emergence of the Ottoman and Habsburg Empires.

Iberian Christian Expansion, 1415–1498

During a revival of anti-Muslim crusade passions in the fourteenth century, Portugal resumed its *Reconquista* policies by expanding to North Africa in 1415. Looking for a way to circumnavigate the Muslims, collect West African gold, and reach the Indian spice coast, Portuguese sailors and traders established fortified harbors along the African coastline. Castile and Aragon, not to be left behind, conquered Granada in 1492, occupied ports in North Africa, and sent Columbus to discover an alternate route to what the Portuguese were seeking. Although Columbus's discovery of America did not yield Indian spices, he delivered the prospects of a new continent to the rulers of Castile and Aragon (see Map 16.1).

Maritime Explorations   Portugal's resumption of the *Reconquista* had its roots in its mastery of Atlantic seafaring. In 1277–1281, mariners of the Italian city-state of Genoa pioneered commerce by sea between the Mediterranean and northwestern Europe. One port on the route was Lisbon, where Portuguese shipwrights and their Genoese teachers teamed up to develop new ships suited for the stormy Atlantic seas. In the early fifteenth century they developed the *caravel*, a small ship with high, upward-extending fore and aft sides, a stern rudder, and square as well as triangular lateen sails. With their new ships, the Portuguese became important traders between England and the Mediterranean countries.

The sea trade stimulated an exploration of the eastern Atlantic. By the early fifteenth century, the Portuguese had discovered the uninhabited islands of the Azores and Madeira, while the Castilians, building their own caravels, began a century-long conquest of the Canary Islands. Here, the indigenous, still Neolithic Berber inhabitants, the Guanches, put up a fierce resistance. But settlers, with the backing of Venetian investors, carved out colonies on conquered parcels of land, on which they enslaved the Guanches to work in sugarcane plantations. They thus adopted the sugarcane plantation system from the eastern Mediterranean, where it had Byzantine and crusader roots on the island of Cyprus, as discussed in greater detail in Chapter 18, and made it an Atlantic one.

Military orders: Ever since the early 1100s, the papacy encouraged the formation of monastic fighting orders, such as the Hospitalers and Templars, to combat the Muslims in the crusader kingdom of Jerusalem; similar *Reconquista* orders, such as the Order of Santiago and the Order of Christ, emerged in Iberia to eliminate Muslim rule.

Apocalyptic Expectations   Parallel with the Atlantic explorations, Iberian Christians began to rethink their relationship with the Muslims on the peninsula. The loss of the crusader kingdom in Palestine to the Muslim Mamluks in 1291 was an event that stirred deep feelings of guilt among the Western Christians. Efforts to dispatch military expeditions to reconquer Jerusalem failed, however, mostly because rulers in Europe—busy centralizing their realms—were now more interested in warring against each other for territorial gain. The failure did not dampen spiritual revivals, however, especially in the Franciscan and **military orders** of Iberia. These monks, often well connected with the Iberian royal courts as confessors, preachers, and educators, were believers in Revelation (Greek *Apokalypsis*)—that is, the imminent end of the world, the calamities of this end, and the Second Coming of Christ.

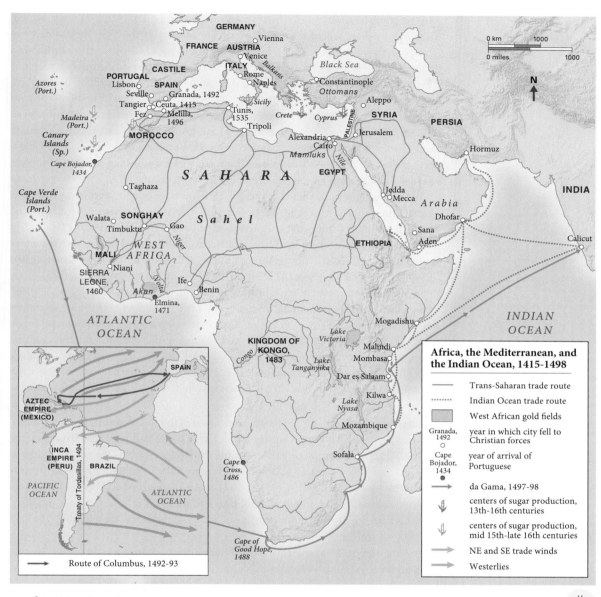

MAP **16.1 Africa, the Mediterranean, and the Indian Ocean, 1415–1498.**

interactive timeline

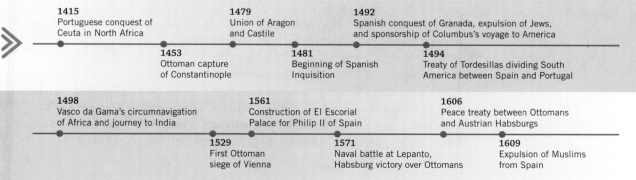

1415
Portuguese conquest of
Ceuta in North Africa

1453
Ottoman capture
of Constantinople

1479
Union of Aragon
and Castile

1481
Beginning of Spanish
Inquisition

1492
Spanish conquest of Granada, expulsion of Jews,
and sponsorship of Columbus's voyage to America

1494
Treaty of Tordesillas dividing South
America between Spain and Portugal

1498
Vasco da Gama's circumnavigation
of Africa and journey to India

1529
First Ottoman
siege of Vienna

1561
Construction of El Escorial
Palace for Philip II of Spain

1571
Naval battle at Lepanto,
Habsburg victory over Ottomans

1606
Peace treaty between Ottomans
and Austrian Habsburgs

1609
Expulsion of Muslims
from Spain

According to Revelation, Christ's return could happen only in Jerusalem, which, therefore, made it urgent for the Christians to reconquer the city. They widely believed that they would be aided by Prester John, an alleged Christian ruler at the head of an immense army from India or Ethiopia. In the context of the intense religious fervor of the period, Christians as well as Muslims saw no contradiction between religion and military conquest. A providential God, so they believed, justified the conquest of lands and the enslavement of the conquered. The religious justification of military action, therefore, was not a pretext for more base material interests (though these would be a likely effect of such conquests) but a proud declaration by believers that God was on their side to help them convert and conquer the non-Christian world—a declaration no longer acceptable today, of course.

In Portugal, political claims in the guise of end-time or apocalyptic expectations guided the military orders in "reconquering" Ceuta, a northern port city of the Moroccan sultans. The orders argued that prior to the Berber–Arab conquest of the early eighth century CE, Ceuta had been Christian and that it was therefore lawful to undertake its capture. Accordingly, a fleet under Henry the Navigator (1394–1460) took Ceuta in 1415, capturing a huge stock of West African gold ready to be minted as money. Henry, a brother of the ruling Portuguese king, saw himself as a precursor in the unfolding of apocalyptic events and invested huge resources into the search for the *Rio de Oro*, the West African "river of gold," thought to be the place where Muslims obtained their gold. By the middle of the fifteenth century, Portuguese mariners had reached the "gold coast" of West Africa (today's Ghana), where local rulers imported gold from the interior Akan fields, near a tributary of the Niger River—the "gold river" of the Muslim merchants.

map of the known world by Martellus, ca. 1489

Reforms in Castile The Portuguese renewal of the *Reconquista* stimulated a similar revival in Castile. For a century and a half, Castile had collected tributes from Granada instead of completing the reconquest of the peninsula. The revival occurred after the dynastic union of Castile and Aragon–Catalonia under their respective monarchs, Queen Isabella (r. 1474–1504) and King Ferdinand II (r. 1479–1516). The two monarchs embarked on a political and religious reform program designed to strengthen their central administrations and used the reconquest ideology to help speed up the reforms.

Among the political reforms was the recruitment of urban militias and judges, both under royal supervision, to check the military and judicial powers of the aristocracy. Religious reform focused on improved education for the clergy and stricter enforcement of Christian doctrine among the population at large. The new institution entrusted with the enforcement of doctrine was the Spanish Inquisition, a body of clergy first appointed by Isabella and Ferdinand in 1481 to ferret out any people whose beliefs and practices were deemed to violate Christian theology and church law. With their religious innovations, the monarchs regained the initiative from the popes and laid the foundations for increased state power.

The Conquest of Granada The *Reconquista* culminated in a 10-year campaign (1482–1492), now fought with cannons on both sides. In the end, Granada fell into Christian hands because the Ottomans, still consolidating their power in the Balkans, sent only a naval commander who stationed himself in North Africa and harassed Iberian ships. The Mamluks of Egypt, less powerful than the Ottomans, sent an embassy to Granada that made a feeble threat of retribution against Christians in Egypt and Syria. Abandoned by the Muslim powers, the last emir of Granada negotiated terms for an honorable surrender. According to these terms, Muslims who chose to stay as subjects of the Castilian crown were permitted to do so, practicing their faith in their own mosques.

The treaty did not apply to the Jews of Granada, however, who were forced either to convert to Christianity or emigrate. In the 1300s, anti-Jewish preaching by the Catholic clergy and riots by Christians against Jews in Seville had substantially reduced the Jewish population of some 300,000 at its peak (ca. 1050) to a mere 80,000 in 1492. Of this remainder, a majority emigrated in 1492 to Portugal and the Ottoman Empire, strengthening the urban population of the latter with their commercial and crafts skills. Portugal adopted its own expulsion decree in 1497. Thus, the nearly millennium-and-a-half-long Jewish presence in Sefarad, as Spain was called in Hebrew, ended, with an expulsion designed to strengthen the Christian unity of Iberia.

After the expulsion of the Jews, it did not take long for the Christians to violate the Muslim treaty of surrender. The church engaged in forced conversions, the burning of Arabic books, and transformations of mosques into churches, triggering an uprising of Muslims in Granada (1499–1500). Christian troops crushed the uprising, and Isabella and Ferdinand used it as an excuse to abrogate the treaty of surrender. In one province after another during the early sixteenth century, Muslims were forced to convert, disperse to other provinces, or emigrate.

Columbus's Journey to the Caribbean   At the peak of their royal power in early 1492, Isabella and Ferdinand seized a golden opportunity to catch up quickly with the Portuguese in the Atlantic. They authorized the seasoned mariner Christopher Columbus (1451–1506) to build two caravels and a larger carrack and sail westward across the Atlantic. Columbus promised to reach India ahead of the Portuguese, who were attempting to find a route to India by sailing around Africa. The two monarchs pledged money for the construction of ships from Castilian and Aragonese crusade levies collected from the Muslims.

In September, Columbus and his mariners departed from the Castilian Canary Islands, catching the favorable South Atlantic easterlies. After a voyage of a little over a month, Columbus landed on one of the Bahaman islands. From there he explored a number of Caribbean islands, mistakenly assuming that he was close to the Indian subcontinent. After a stay of 3 months, he left a small colony of settlers behind and returned to Iberia with seven captured Caribbean islanders and a small quantity of gold.

Columbus was a self-educated explorer. Through voracious but indiscriminate reading, he had accumulated substantial knowledge of such diverse subjects as geography, cartography, the Crusades, and the Apocalypse. On the basis of this reading (and his own faulty calculations), he insisted that the ocean stretching between western Europe and eastern Asia was relatively narrow. Furthermore, he fervently believed that God had made him the forerunner of an Iberian apocalyptic world ruler who would recapture Jerusalem from the Muslims just prior to the Second Coming of Christ (see Source 16.1).

For many years, Columbus had peddled his idea about reaching India (and subsequently Jerusalem) from the east at the Portuguese court. The Portuguese, however, while sharing Columbus's apocalyptic fervor, dismissed his Atlantic Ocean calculations as fantasies. Even in Castile, where Columbus went after his rejection in Portugal, it took several years and the victory over Granada before Queen Isabella finally listened to him. Significantly, it was at the height of their success at Granada in 1492 that Isabella and Ferdinand seized their chance to beat the Portuguese to Asia. Although disappointed by the meager returns of Columbus's first and subsequent voyages, Isabella and Ferdinand were delighted to have acquired new islands in the Caribbean, in addition to the Canaries. In one blow they had drawn even with Portugal.

Vasco da Gama's Journey to India   Portugal redoubled its efforts after 1492 to discover the way to India around Africa. In 1498, the king appointed an important court official and member of the crusading Order of Santiago, Vasco da Gama (ca. 1469–1524), to command four caravels for the journey to India. Da Gama, an experienced mariner, made good use of the accumulated Portuguese knowledge of seafaring in the Atlantic and guidance by Arab sailors in the Indian Ocean. After a journey of 6 months, the ships arrived in Calicut, the main spice trade center on the Indian west coast.

The first Portuguese mariner sent ashore by da Gama in Calicut encountered two North African Muslims, who addressed him in Castilian Spanish and Genoese Italian: "The Devil take you! What brought you here?" The mariner replied: "We came to seek Christians and spices." When da Gama went inland to see the ruler of Calicut, he was optimistic that he had indeed found what he had come for. Ignorant of Hinduism, he mistook the Indian religion for the Christianity of Prester John. Similarly ignorant of the conventions of the India trade, he offered woolen textiles and metal goods in exchange for pepper, cinnamon, and cloves. The Muslim and Hindu merchants were uninterested in these goods designed for the African market and demanded gold or silver, which the Portuguese had only in small amounts. Rumors spread about the Muslims plotting with the Hindus against the apparently penniless Christian intruders. Prudently, da Gama lifted anchor and returned home with small quantities of spices.

After these modest beginnings, however, within a short time Portugal had mastered the India trade. The Portuguese crown organized regular journeys around Africa, and when Portuguese mariners on one such journey—taking a far western route in the Atlantic—landed in northeast Brazil they claimed it for their expanding commercial network. During the early sixteenth century, the Portuguese India fleets brought considerable amounts of spices from India back to Portugal, threatening the profits of the Egyptian and Venetian merchants who had hitherto dominated the trade. Prester John, of course, was never found, and the project of retaking Jerusalem receded into the background.

Pedro Reinel's map of East Africa and the Indian Ocean, c. 1507

Rise of the Ottomans and Struggle with the Habsburgs for Dominance, 1300–1609

While Muslim rule disappeared in the late fifteenth century from the Iberian Peninsula, the opposite was happening in the Balkans. Here, the Ottoman Turks spearheaded the expansion of Islamic rule over Christians. By the late sixteenth century, when the East–West conflict between the Habsburgs and Ottomans reached its peak, entire generations of Croats, Germans, and Italians lived in mortal fear of the "terrible Turk" who might conquer all of Christian Europe.

Late Byzantium and Ottoman Origins   The rise of the Ottomans was closely related to the decline of Byzantium. The emperors of Byzantium had been able to reclaim their "empire" in 1261 from its Latin rulers and Venetian troops by allying themselves with the Genoese. This empire, which during the early fourteenth century included Greece and a few domains in western Anatolia, was no more than a midsize kingdom with modest agricultural resources. But it was still a valuable trading hub, thanks to Constantinople's strategic position as a market linking the Mediterranean with Slavic kingdoms in the Balkans and the Ukrainian–Russian principality of Kiev. Thanks to its commercial wealth, Byzantium experienced a cultural revival, which at its height featured the lively scholarly debate over Plato and Aristotle that exerted a profound influence on the western Renaissance in Italy (see Chapter 10).

Inevitably, however, both Balkan Slavs and Anatolian Turks appropriated Byzantine provinces in the late thirteenth century, further reducing the empire. One of the lost provinces was Bithynia, across the Bosporus in Anatolia. Here, in 1299, the Turkish warlord Osman (r. 1299–1326) gathered his clan and a motley assembly of Islamic holy warriors (Turkish *gazis*, including a local saint and his followers), as well as adventurers (including renegade Byzantines), and declared himself an independent ruler. Osman and a number of other Turkish lords in the region were nominally subject to the Seljuks, the Turkish dynasty which had conquered Anatolia from the Byzantines two centuries earlier but by the early 1300s was disintegrating.

During the first half of the fourteenth century, Osman and his successors emerged as the most powerful emirs by conquering further Anatolian provinces from Byzantium. The Moroccan Abu Abdallah Ibn Battuta (1304–1369), famous for his journeys through the Islamic world, Africa, and China, passed through western Anatolia and Constantinople during the 1330s, visiting several Turkish principalities. He was duly impressed by the rising power of the Ottomans, noting approvingly that they manned nearly 100 forts and castles and maintained pressure on the Eastern Christian infidels. In 1354, the Ottomans gained their first European foothold on a peninsula about 100 miles southwest of Constantinople. Thereafter, it seemed only a matter of time before the Ottomans would conquer Constantinople.

Through a skillful mixture of military defense, tribute payments, and dynastic marriages of princesses with Osman's descendants, however, the Byzantine emperors salvaged their rule for another century. They were also helped by Timur the Great (r. 1370–1405), a Turkish-descended ruler from central Asia who sought to rebuild the Mongol Empire. He surprised the Ottomans, who were distracted by their ongoing conquests in the Balkans, and defeated them decisively in 1402. Timur and his successors were unsuccessful with their dream of Neo-Mongol world rule, but the Ottomans needed nearly two decades (1402–1421) to recover from their collapse and reconstitute their empire in the Balkans and Anatolia. Under Mehmet II, "the Conqueror" (r. 1451–1481), they finally assembled all their resources to lay siege to the Byzantine capital.

Patterns Up Close | Shipbuilding

With the appearance of empires during the Iron Age, four regional but interconnected shipbuilding traditions—Mediterranean, North Sea, Indian Ocean, and China Sea—emerged.

In the Mediterranean, around 500 BCE, shipwrights began to use nailed planks for their war galleys as well as cargo transports, as evidenced by shipwrecks of the period. In the Roman Empire (ca. 200 BCE–500 CE), nailed planking allowed the development of the roundship (image *a*), a large transport 120 feet in length with a capacity of 400 tons of cargo transporting grain from Egypt to Italy. The roundship and its variations had double planking, multiple masts, and multiple square sails. After 100 BCE, the triangular (lateen) sail allowed for tacking (zigzagging) against the wind, greatly expanding shipping during a summer sailing season.

The Celtic North Sea tradition adapted to the Mediterranean patterns of the Romans. When the Roman Empire receded during the 300s CE, shipwrights in Celtic regions continued with their own innovations, shifting to frame-first construction for small boats in the 300s. At the same time, Norsemen, or Vikings, innovated by introducing overlapping (clinkered) plank joining for their eminently seagoing boats. The North Sea innovations, arriving as they did at the end of the western Roman Empire, remained local for nearly half a millennium.

The evolution of China into an empire resulted in major Chinese contributions to ship construction. In the Han period (206 BCE–220 CE) there is evidence from clay models of riverboats for the use of nailed planks. One model, dating to the first century CE, shows a central steering rudder at the end of the boat. At the same time, similar stern rudders appeared in the Roman Empire. Who adopted what from whom, if at all, is still an unanswered question.

Patterns of Shipbuilding. Left to right: Hellenistic-Roman roundship (*a*), Chinese junk (*b*) Indian Ocean dhow (*c*).

From Istanbul to the Adriatic Sea Similar to Isabella and Ferdinand's siege of Granada, Mehmet's siege and conquest of Constantinople (April 5–May 29, 1453) is one of the stirring events of world history. The Byzantines were severely undermanned and short of gunpowder, unable to defend the full length of the imposing land walls that protected the city. Although they had some help from Genoese, papal, and Aragonese forces, it was not nearly enough to make a difference. Using their superiority in troop strength of 11 to 1 for a tight siege, the Ottomans

Shipbuilding innovations continued after 600 CE. In Tang China, junks with multiple bulkheads (watertight compartments) and multiple layers of planks appeared. The average junk was 140 feet long, had a cargo capacity of 600 tons, and could carry on its three or four decks several hundred mariners and passengers (see image *b*). Junks had multiple masts and trapezoidal (lug) and square sails made of matted fibers and strengthened (battened) with poles sewed to the surface. The less innovative Middle Eastern, eastern African, and Indian dhow was built with sewed or nailed planks and sailed with lateen and square sails, traveling as far as southern China (see image *c*).

(d)

In western Europe, the patterns of Mediterranean and North Sea shipbuilding merged during the thirteenth century. At that time, northern shipwrights developed the cog as the main transport for Baltic grain to ports around the North Sea. The cog was a ship of some 60 feet in length and 30 tons in cargo capacity, with square sails and flush planking below and clinkered planking above the waterline. Northern European crusaders traveled during 1150–1300 on cogs via the Atlantic to the Mediterranean. Builders adapted the cog's clinker technique to the roundship tradition that Muslims as well as Eastern and Western Christians had modified in the previous centuries. Genoese clinkered roundships pioneered the Mediterranean–North Sea trade in the early fourteenth century (see image *d*).

Lisbon shipwrights in Portugal, learning from Genoese masters, borrowed from local shipbuilding traditions and Genoese roundship construction patterns for the development of the caravel around 1430. The caravel was a small and slender 60-foot-long ship with a 50-ton freight capacity, a stern rudder, square and lateen sails, and a magnetic compass (of Chinese origin).

(e)

The caravel and, after 1500, the similarly built but much larger galleon were the main vessels the Portuguese, Spanish, Dutch, and English used during their oceanic voyages from the mid-fifteenth to mid-eighteenth centuries (see image *e*).

Patterns of Shipbuilding (*Continued*). From top: Baltic cog (*d*), Iberian caravel (*e*). These ships illustrate the varieties of shipbuilding traditions that developed over thousands of years.

Questions

- How does the history of shipbuilding demonstrate the ways in which innovations spread from one place to another?

- Do the adaptations in shipbuilding that flowed between cultures that were nominally in conflict with each other provide a different perspective on the way these cultures interacted?

bombarded Constantinople's walls with heavy cannons. A weak section was on the northeastern side, along the harbor in the Golden Horn, where the walls were low. Here, the Byzantines had blocked off the entrance to the Golden Horn with a huge chain. In a brilliant tactical move, Mehmet circumvented the chain. He had troops drag ships on rollers over a hillside into the harbor. The soldiers massed on these ships were ready to disembark and assault the walls with the help of ladders. On the first sign of cracks in the northeastern walls, the Ottoman besiegers stormed the city.

Siege of Constantinople, 1453. Note the soldiers on the left pulling boats on rollers and wheels over the Galata hillside. With this maneuver, Sultan Mehmet II was able to circumvent the chain stretched across the entrance to the Golden Horn (in place of the anachronistic bridge in the image). This allowed him to speed up his conquest of Constantinople by forcing the defenders to spread their forces thinly over the entire length of the walls.

The last Byzantine emperor, Constantine XI, perished in the general massacre and pillage which followed the Ottoman occupation of the city (see Source 16.2).

Mehmet quickly repopulated Constantinople ("Istanbul" in Turkish, from Greek "to the city," *istin polin*) and appointed a new patriarch at the head of the Eastern Christians, to whom he promised full protection as his subjects. In quick succession, he ordered the construction of the Topkapı Palace (1459), the transfer of the administration from Edirne (which had been the capital since 1365) to Istanbul, and the resumption of expansion in the Balkans, where he succeeded in forcing the majority of rulers into submitting to vassal status. One of the Balkan lords resisting the sultan was Vlad III Dracul of Wallachia, who according to tradition in 1461–1462 impaled a contingent of Ottoman troops sent against him on sharpened tree trunks. Mehmet replaced Vlad with his more compliant brother, but the memory of the impalements lived on to inspire vampire folktales and, eventually, in 1897, the famous Gothic horror novel *Dracula*.

Mehmet's ongoing conquests eventually brought him to the Adriatic Sea, where one of his generals occupied Otranto on the heel of the Italian peninsula. The Ottomans were poised to launch a full-scale invasion of Italy from Otranto, when the sultan died unexpectedly. His successor evacuated Otranto, preferring to consolidate the Ottoman Empire in the Middle East, North Africa, and the Balkans before reconsidering an invasion of central and western Europe.

Imperial Apogee   Between 1500 and 1600 the Ottoman sultans succeeded magnificently in the consolidation of their empire. In 1514, with superior cavalry and infantry forces, cannons, and muskets, the Ottomans defeated the Persian Safavids in Iran, who had risen in 1501 to form a rival Shiite empire in opposition to the Sunni Ottomans. In the southern Middle East, intermittent tensions between the Ottomans and the Mamluk Turks in Egypt, Syria, and eastern Arabia gave way to open war in 1517. The Ottomans, again due to superior firepower, defeated the Mamluks and took control of western Arabia, including the holy pilgrimage city of Mecca. A year later, in 1518, Sultan Süleyman I, "the Magnificent" (r. 1520–1566), appointed a naval commander to drive the Spanish from a series of fortifications and cities in North Africa, which the latter had conquered in the name of the *Reconquista* in the 1490s and early 1500s.

In the Balkans, the Ottomans completed their conquests of Serbia and Hungary with the annexation of Belgrade and Buda (now part of Budapest) as well as a brief siege of Vienna in 1529, begun too late in the year and eventually stopped by the approaching winter. By the second half of the sixteenth century, when the submission of most of Hungary had been secured, the Ottoman Empire was a vast multiethnic and multireligious state of some 15 million inhabitants extending from Algeria in the Maghreb to Yemen in Arabia and from Upper Egypt to the Balkans and the northern shores of the Black Sea (see Map 16.2).

Morocco and Persia   In the period of 1450–1600, the two large empires of the Ottomans and Indian Mughals dominated Islamic civilization. Two smaller and more short-lived realms existed in Morocco and Persia, ruled by the Saadid

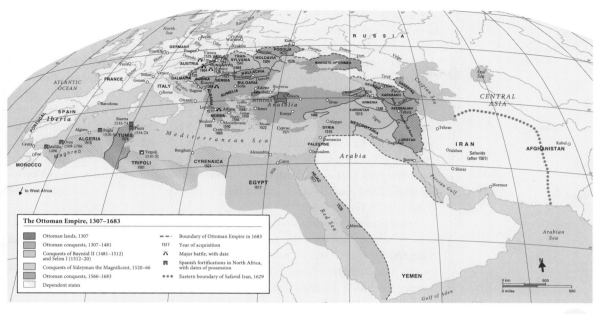

MAP **16.2 The Ottoman Empire, 1307–1683.**

map analysis

(1509–1659) and Safavid (1501–1722) dynasties, respectively. The Saadid sultans defended themselves successfully against the Ottoman expansion and liberated themselves from the Portuguese occupation of Morocco's Atlantic ports which had followed the conquest of Ceuta in 1415. In 1591, after their liberation, the Saadids sent a firearm-equipped army to West Africa in order to revive the gold trade, which had dwindled to a trickle after the Portuguese arrival in Ghana. The army succeeded in destroying the West African empire of Songhay but failed to revive the gold trade. Moroccan army officers assumed power in Timbuktu, and their descendants, the Ruma, became provincial lords independent of Morocco. The Saadids, unable to improve their finances, split into provincial realms. The still-reigning Alaouite dynasty of Moroccan kings replaced them in 1659.

The Safavids grew in the mid-1400s from a mixed Kurdish–Turkish mystical brotherhood in northwestern Iran into a Shiite warrior organization (similar to the Sunni one participating in the early Ottoman expansion) that carried out raids against Christians in the Caucasus. In 1501, the leadership of the brotherhood put forward the 14-year-old Ismail as the Hidden Twelfth Imam. According to Shiite doctrine, the Hidden Imam, or Messiah, was expected to arrive and establish a Muslim apocalyptic realm of justice at the end of time, before God's Last Judgment. This realm would replace the "unjust" Sunni Ottoman Empire. The Ottomans countered the Safavid challenge in 1514 with the Battle of Chaldiran, where they crushed the underprepared Safavids with their superior cannon and musket firepower. After his humiliating defeat, Ismail dropped his claim to messianic status, and his successors

Vlad Dracul next to Impaled Ottoman Soldiers. The woodcut depicts the alleged impalement of 1,000 Ottoman soldiers sent against Vlad Dracul, prior to Sultan Mehmet II leading a victorious campaign into Wallachia and removing Dracul from power. Dracul's cannibalism, suggested in the image, is not confirmed by historical sources.

assumed the more modest title of king (Persian *shah*) as the head of state, quite similar in many respects to that of the Ottomans.

a Safavid battle tunic

Learning from their defeat, the Safavids recruited a standing firearm-equipped army from among young Christians on lands conquered in the Caucasus. They held fast to Shiism, thereby continuing their opposition to the Sunni Ottomans, and supported the formation of a clerical hierarchy, which made this form of Islam dominant in Iran. As sponsors of construction projects, the Safavids greatly improved urbanism in the country. After moving the capital from Tabriz to the centrally located Isfahan in 1590, they built an imposing palace, administration, and mosque complex in the city. In a suburb they settled a large colony of Armenians, who held the monopoly in the production of Caspian Sea silk, a high-quality export product which the Dutch—successors of the Portuguese in the Indian Ocean trade—distributed in Europe.

As patrons of the arts, the shahs revived the ancient traditions of Persian culture to such heights that even the archrival Ottomans felt compelled to adopt Persian manners, literature, and architectural styles. Persian royal culture similarly radiated to the Mughals in India. Not everyone accepted Shiism, however. An attempt to force the Shiite doctrines on the Afghanis backfired badly when enraged Sunni tribes formed a coalition, defeated the Safavids, and ended their regime in 1722.

Rise of the Habsburgs   Parallel to the rise and development of the Ottomans and Safavids, Castile–Aragon on the Iberian Peninsula evolved into the center of a vast empire of its own. A daughter of Isabella and Ferdinand married a member of the Habsburg dynastic family, which ruled Flanders, Burgundy, Naples, Sicily, and Austria, as well as Germany (the "Holy Roman Empire of the German Nation," as this collection of principalities was called). Their son, Charles V (r. 1516–1558), not only inherited Castile–Aragon, now merged and called "Spain," and the Habsburg territories but also became the ruler of the Aztec and Inca Empires in the Americas, which Spanish adventurers had conquered in his name between 1521 and 1536 (see Chapter 18). In both Austria and the western Mediterranean the Habsburgs were direct neighbors of the Ottomans (see Map 16.3).

After a victorious battle against France in 1519, Charles V also won the title of emperor from the pope, which made him the overlord of all German principalities and supreme among the monarchs of Western Christianity. Although this title did not mean much in terms of power and financial gain in either the German principalities or Western Christianity as a whole, it made him the titular political head of Western Christianity and thereby the direct counterpart of Sultan Süleyman in the struggle for dominance in the Christian–Muslim world of Europe, the Middle East, and northern Africa. Both the Habsburgs and the Ottomans renewed the traditional Islamic–Christian imperialism which had characterized the period 600–950 and which had been replaced by the Muslim and Christian commonwealths of 950–1450.

Habsburg Distractions   Charles V faced a daunting task in his effort to prevent the Ottomans from advancing against the Christians in the Balkans and Mediterranean. Multiple problems in his European territories diverted his attention and forced him to spend far less time than he wanted on what Christians in most parts of Europe perceived as a pervasive Ottoman–Muslim threat. During the first three decades of

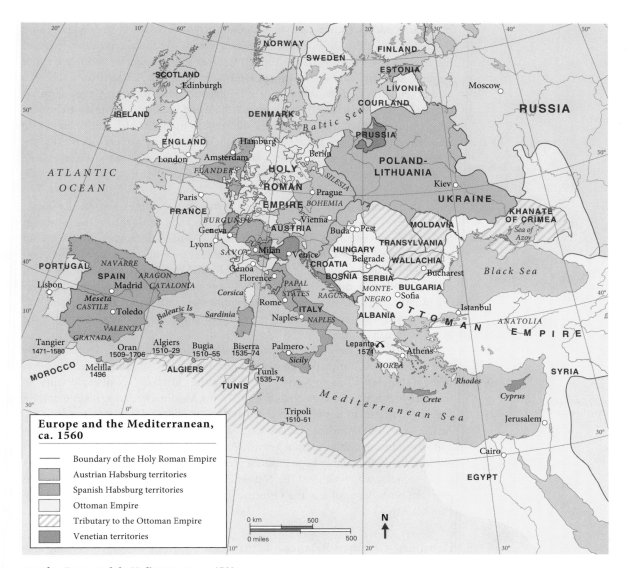

MAP 16.3 **Europe and the Mediterranean, ca. 1560.**

the sixteenth century, revolts in Iberia, the Protestant Reformation in the German states, and renewed war with France for control of Burgundy and Italy commanded Charles's attention.

The emperor's distractions increased further in 1534 when, in an attempt to drive the Habsburgs out of Italy, France forged an alliance with the Ottomans. This alliance horrified western Europe. It demonstrated, however, that the Ottomans, on account of their military advances against the Christians in eastern Europe and the western Mediterranean, had become crucial players in European politics. As fierce as the struggle between Muslims and Christians for dominance was, when the French king found himself squeezed on both sides of his kingdom by his archrival, Charles V, the Ottomans became his natural allies.

Habsburg and Ottoman Losses   All these diversions seriously strained Habsburg resources against the Ottomans, who pressed relentlessly ahead on the two fronts of the Balkans and North Africa. Although Charles V deputized his younger brother Ferdinand I to the duchy of Austria in 1521 to shore up the Balkan defenses, he was able to send him significant numbers of troops only once. After a series of dramatic defeats, Austria had to pay the Ottomans tribute and, eventually, even sign a humiliating truce (1562). On the western Mediterranean front, the Habsburgs did not do well either. Even though Charles V campaigned several times in person, most garrisons on the coast of Algeria, Tunisia, and Tripoli were too exposed to withstand the Ottoman onslaught by sea and by land. In 1556, at the end of Charles V's reign, only two of eight Habsburg garrisons had survived.

A third frontier of the Muslim–Christian struggle for dominance was the Indian Ocean. After Vasco da Gama had returned from India in 1498, the Portuguese kings invested major resources into breaking into the Muslim-dominated Indian Ocean trade. In response, the Ottomans made great efforts to protect existing Muslim commercial interests in the Indian Ocean. They blocked Portuguese military support for Ethiopia and strengthened their ally and main pepper supplier, the sultan of Aceh on the Indonesian island of Sumatra, by providing him with troops and weapons. War on land and on sea, directly and by proxy, raged in the Indian Ocean through most of the sixteenth century.

Portuguese trading posts in the Indian Ocean, 1630

In the long run, the Portuguese were successful in destroying the Ottoman fleets sent against them, but smaller convoys of Ottoman galleys continued to harass Portuguese shipping interests. As new research on the Ottoman "age of exploration" in the Indian Ocean has demonstrated, by 1570 the Muslims traded again as much via the Red Sea route to the Mediterranean as the Portuguese did by circumnavigating Africa. In addition, the Ottomans benefited from the trade of a new commodity—coffee, produced in Ethiopia and Yemen. Portugal (under Spanish rule 1580–1640) reduced its unsustainably large military presence in the Indian Ocean, followed by the Ottomans, which allowed the Netherlands in the early seventeenth century to overtake both Portugal and the Ottoman Empire in the Indian Ocean spice trade (see Map 16.4).

Habsburg–Ottoman Balance   In the 1550s, Charles V despaired of being able to ever master the many challenges posed by the Ottomans as well as by France and the Protestants. He decided that the only way to ensure the continuation of Habsburg power would be a division of his western and eastern territories. Accordingly, he bestowed Spain, Naples, the Netherlands, and the Americas on his son Philip II (r. 1556–1598). The Habsburg possessions of Austria, Bohemia, and the remnant of Hungary not lost to the Ottomans, as well as the Holy Roman Empire (Germany), went to his brother Ferdinand I (r. 1558–1564). Charles hoped that his son and brother would cooperate and help each other militarily against the Ottomans.

Moriscos: From Greek *maurus* ("dark"); Castilian term referring to North Africans and to Muslims under Spanish rule.

When Philip took over the Spanish throne, he realized, to his concern, that most of the Habsburg military was stationed outside Spain, leaving that country vulnerable to attack. As the Ottomans had recently conquered most Spanish strongholds in North Africa, a Muslim invasion of Spain was a distinct possibility. Fearful of **morisco** support for an Ottoman invasion of Spain, Philip's administration and the Inquisition renewed their decrees of conversion which had lain dormant for half a century.

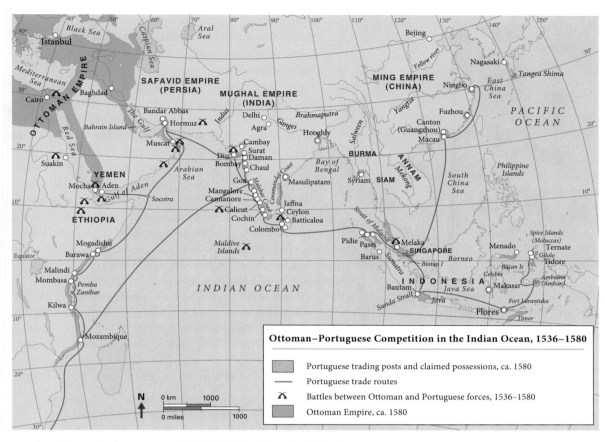

MAP **16.4** Ottoman–Portuguese Competition in the Indian Ocean, 1536–1580.

This sparked a massive revolt among the moriscos of Granada in 1568–1570, supported by Ottoman soldiers and Moroccan arms. Philip was able to suppress the revolt only after recourse to troops and firearms from Italy. To break up the dangerously large concentrations of Granadan moriscos in the south of Spain, Philip ordered them to be dispersed throughout the peninsula. At the same time, to alleviate the Ottoman naval threat, Philip, the pope, Venice, and Genoa formed a Holy Christian League. Its task was the construction of a fleet which was to destroy Ottoman sea power in the eastern Mediterranean. The fleet succeeded in 1571 in bottling up the entire Ottoman navy at Lepanto, in Ottoman Greece, destroying it in the ensuing firefight.

The Ottomans, however, had enough resources not only to rebuild their navy but also to capture the strategic port city of Tunis in 1574 from the Spaniards. With this evening of the scores, the two sides decided to phase out their unsustainable naval war in the Mediterranean. After this date, Venice was the only (but formidable) naval enemy of the Ottomans, at various times in control of Aegean islands and southern Greece. The Ottomans, for their part, turned their attention eastward, to the rival Safavid Empire, where they exploited a period of dynastic instability for the conquest of territories in the Caucasus (1578–1590). The staunch Catholic Philip II, for his part, was faced with the Protestant war of independence in the

Paolo Veronese, *Battle of Lepanto*, altar painting with four saints beseeching the Virgin Mary to grant victory to the Christians (ca. 1572). In the sixteenth century, the entire Mediterranean, from Gibraltar to Cyprus, was a naval battleground between Christians and Muslims. The Christians won the Battle of Lepanto thanks to superior naval tactics. At the end of the battle "the sea was entirely covered, not just with masts, spars, oars, and broken wood, but with an innumerable quantity of blood that turned the water as red as blood."

Netherlands. This war was so expensive that, in a desperate effort to straighten out his state finances, Philip II had to declare bankruptcy (1575) and sue for peace with the Ottomans (1580).

The Limits of Ottoman Power   After their victory over the Safavids, the Ottomans looked again to the west. While the peace with Spain was too recent to be broken, a long peace with Ferdinand I in Austria (since 1562) was ready to collapse. A series of raids and counter-raids at the Austrian and Transylvanian borders had inflamed tempers, and in 1593 the Ottomans went on the attack. Austria, however, was no longer the weak state it had been a generation earlier. Had it not been for a lack of support from the Transylvanian and Hungarian Protestants, who preferred the sultan to the Catholic emperor as overlord, the Austrians might have actually prevailed over the Ottomans.

Eventually, thanks to the Protestants' support, the Ottomans drew even on the battlefield with the Austrians. In 1606, the Ottomans and Austrian Habsburgs made peace again. With minor modifications in favor of the Austrians, the two sides returned to their earlier borders. The Austrians made one more tribute payment and then let their obligation lapse. Officially, the Ottomans conceded nothing, but in practical terms Austria was no longer a vassal state.

Expulsion of the Moriscos   In the western Mediterranean, the peace between the Ottomans and Spanish Habsburgs held. But Philip and his successors remained aware of the possibility of renewed Ottoman aid to the Iberian Muslims. Even though they had been scattered across the peninsula after 1570, the moriscos continued to resist conversion. Among Castilians, an intense debate began about the apparent impossibility of assimilating them to Catholicism in order to create a religiously unified state. The church advocated the expulsion of the moriscos, arguing that the allegedly high Muslim birthrate in a population of 7.5 million (mostly rural) Spaniards was a serious threat.

Fierce resistance against the proposed expulsion, however, rose among the Christian landowners in the southeastern province of Valencia. These landowners benefited greatly from the farming skills of the estimated 250,000 morisco tenant farmers who worked their irrigated rice and sugarcane estates. Weighing the potential Ottoman threat against the possibility of economic damage, the government decided in 1580 in favor of expulsion. Clearly, they valued Christian unity against the Ottomans more than the prosperity of a few hundred landowners in Valencia.

It took until 1609, however, before a compensation deal with the landowners in Valencia was worked out. In the following 5 years, some 300,000 moriscos were forcibly expelled from Spain, under often appalling circumstances: They had to leave all their possessions behind, including money and jewelry, taking only whatever clothes and household utensils they could carry. As in the case of the Jews a century earlier, Spain's loss was the Ottoman Empire's gain, this time mostly in the form of skilled irrigation farmers.

The Centralizing State: Origins and Interactions

The major technological change that occurred in the Middle East and Europe during 1250–1350 was the growing use of firearms. It took until the mid-1400s, however, before cannons and muskets were technically effective and reliable enough to make a difference in warfare. At this time, a pattern emerged whereby rulers created centralized states to finance their strategic shift to firearm-bearing infantries. They resumed the policy of conquest and imperialism, which had lain dormant during the preceding period, when the religious civilizations of Islam and Christianity had evolved into commonwealths of many competing realms. Both the Ottomans and the Habsburgs raised immense amounts of cash in silver and gold to spend on cannons, muskets, and ships for achieving world rule.

Expulsion of the Moriscos (secret Muslims) from Spain, 1609–1614. The moriscos had to leave all their valuables behind, carrying only their barest belongings. They were watched closely by Spanish soldiers, as seen in this etching.

State Transformation, Money, and Firearms

In the early stages of their realms, the kings of Iberia (1150–1400) and the Ottoman sultans (1300–1400), with little cash on hand, compensated military commanders for their service in battle with parcels of conquered land, or land grants. That land, farmed by villagers, generated rental income in kind for the officers. Once the Iberian and Ottoman rulers had conquered cities and gained control over long-distance trade, however, patterns changed. Rulers began collecting taxes in cash, with which they paid regiments of personal guards to supplement the army of land-grant officers and their retainers. They created the centralizing state, forerunner of the absolutist state of the early seventeenth century.

The Land-Grant System   When the Ottoman *beys*, or military lords, embarked on their conquests in the early 1300s, they created personal domains on the choice lands they had conquered. Here, they took rents in kind from the resident villagers to finance their small dynastic households. Their comrades in arms, such as members of their clan or adherents (many of whom were holy warriors and/or adventurers), received other conquered lands, from which they collected rents for themselves. As the Ottomans conquered Byzantine cities, first in Anatolia and then, in the second half of the 1300s, in the Balkans, they gained access to the **money economy**. They collected taxes in coins from the markets and tollbooths at city gates where foods and crafts goods were exchanged, as well as from the Christians and Jews subject to the head tax. The taxes helped in adding luxuries to the households of the Ottoman beys and enabling them to build palaces.

Money economy: Form of economic organization in which mutual obligations are settled through monetary exchanges; in contrast, a system of land grants, with its rents from peasants, obliges the landholders to provide military service, without payment, to the grantee (sultan or king).

Janissaries: Infantry soldiers recruited among the Christian population of the Ottoman Empire and paid from the central treasury.

Devşirme: The levy on boys in the Ottoman Empire; that is, the obligation of the Christian population to contribute adolescent males to the military and administrative classes.

As a consequence of the full conquest of the southern Balkans by the Ottoman Empire in the fifteenth and sixteenth centuries, both the land-grant system and the money economy expanded exponentially. An entire military ruling class of grant holders emerged, forming the backbone of the early Ottoman army and administration. The grant holders were cavalrymen who lived with their households of retainers in the villages and towns of the interior of Anatolia and the Balkans. Most of the time, they were away on campaign with the sultans, leaving managers in charge of the collection of rents from the villagers on their lands. At the conclusion of the period of rapid growth of the Ottoman Empire in the early years of the sixteenth century, the landed ruling class of cavalrymen numbered some 80,000, constituting a vast reserve of warriors for the mobilization of troops each summer.

The Janissaries   An early indicator of the significance of the money economy in the Ottoman Empire was the military institution of the **Janissaries**—troops which received salaries from the central treasury. This institution probably appeared during the second half of the fourteenth century and is first documented in 1395. It was based

on a practice (called **devşirme** [dev-SHIR-me]) of conscripting young boys, which palace officers carried out irregularly every few years among the empire's Christian population. For this purpose, the palace officers traveled to Christian villages, towns, and cities in the Balkans, Greece, and Anatolia. At each occasion, they selected boys between the ages of 6 and 16 and marched them off to Istanbul, where they were converted to Islam and trained as future soldiers and administrators. The boys and young men then entered the central system of palace slaves under the direct orders of the sultan and his viziers or ministers.

The *devşirme* contradicted Islamic law, which forbade the enslavement of "peoples of the Book" (Jews, Christians, and Zoroastrians). Its existence, therefore, documents the extent to which the sultans reasserted the Roman–Sasanid–Arab imperial traditions of the ruler making doctrine and law. Ruling by divine grace, the Ottomans were makers of their own law, called *kanun* (from Greek *kanon*). Muslim religious scholars, who had assumed the role of guardians of law and doctrine during the preceding commonwealth period of Islamic civilization (950–1300), had no choice but to accept sultanic imperialism and seek to adapt it to the Sharia as best they could.

Boy Levy (devşirme) in a Christian Village. This miniature graphically depicts the trauma of conscription, including the wailing of the village women and the assembly of boys waiting to be taken away by implacable representatives of the sultan.

Toward the first half of the fifteenth century, the sultans equipped their Janissaries with cannons and matchlock muskets. According to reports in Arabic chronicles, firearms first appeared around 1250 in the Middle East, probably coming from China. When the Janissaries received them, firearms had therefore undergone some 150 years of experimentation and development in the Middle East and North Africa. Even though the cannons and muskets were still far from being decisive in battle, they had become sophisticated enough to make a difference. By the mid-1400s, gigantic siege cannons and slow but reliable matchlock muskets were the standard equipment of Ottoman and other armies. The sultans relied on large numbers of indigenous, rather than European, gunsmiths, as new research in Ottoman archives has revealed (see Source 16.5).

Revenues and Money The maintenance of a salaried standing army of infantry soldiers and a central administration to provide the fiscal foundation would have been impossible without precious metals. Therefore, the Ottoman imperial expansion was driven by the need to acquire mineral deposits. During the fifteenth century the Ottomans captured the rich silver, lead, and iron mines of Serbia and Bosnia. Together with Anatolian copper, iron, and silver mines conquered earlier, the Balkan mines made the Ottomans the owners of the largest precious metal production centers prior to the Habsburg acquisition of the Mexican and Andean mines in the mid-1500s.

The sultans left the Balkan mining and smelting operations in the hands of preconquest Christian entrepreneurs from the autonomous Adriatic coastal city-state of Ragusa or Dubrovnik. These entrepreneurs were integrated into the Ottoman imperial money economy as tax farmers obliged to buy their right of operation from the government in return for reimbursing themselves from the mining and smelting profits. **Tax farming** was the preferred method of producing cash revenues for the central administration. The holders of tax farms delivered the profits from the production of metals, salt, saltpeter, and other minerals to the state, minus the commission they were entitled to subtract for themselves. They also collected the head tax—payable in money—from the Jews and Christians and the profits from the sale of the agricultural dues from state domains. Thus, tax farmers were crucial members of the ruling class, responsible for the cash flow in the state.

The right to mint silver into the basic coin of the empire was similarly part of the tax-farm regime, as were the market, city gate, and port duties. The tax-farm regime, of course, was crucially dependent on a strong sultan or chief minister, the grand vizier. Without close supervision, this regime could easily deteriorate into a state of decentralization, something which indeed eventually happened in the Ottoman Empire on a large scale, although not before the eighteenth century.

Süleyman's Central State The centralizing state of the Ottomans reached its apogee under Sultan Süleyman I, "the Magnificent." At the beginning of the sultan's reign, the amount of money available for expenditures was twice that of half a century earlier. By the end of his reign, this amount had again doubled. With this money, the sultan financed a massive expansion of the military and bureaucracy. Palace, military, and bureaucracy formed a centralized state, the purpose of which was to project power and cultural splendor toward its predominantly rural subjects in the interior as well as Christian enemies outside the empire.

Ottoman Siege of a Christian Fortress. By the middle of the fifteenth century, cannons had revolutionized warfare. Niccolò Machiavelli, ever attuned to new developments, noted in 1519 that "no wall exists, however thick, that artillery cannot destroy in a few days." Machiavelli could have been commenting on the Ottomans, who were masters of siege warfare. Sultan Mehmet II, the conqueror of Constantinople in 1453, founded the Imperial Cannon Foundry shortly thereafter; it would go on to make some of the biggest cannons of the period.

Tax farming: Governmental auction of the right to collect taxes in a district, market, or mine. The tax farmer advanced these taxes to the treasury and retained a commission.

The bureaucrats were recruited from two population groups. Most top ministers and officers in the fifteenth and sixteenth centuries came from the *devşirme* among the Christians. The conscripted boys learned Turkish, received an Islamic education, and underwent intensive firearm and (for some) horsemanship training, in preparation for salaried service in the Janissary army or administration.

The empire's other recruits came from colleges in Istanbul and provincial cities to which the Muslim population of the empire had access. Colleges were institutions through which ambitious villagers far from major urban centers could gain upward mobility. Graduates with law degrees found employment in the bureaucracy or as judges in the villages, towns, and cities. Muslims of Christian parentage made up the top layer of the elite, while Muslims of Islamic descent occupied the middle ranks.

Under Süleyman, the Janissaries comprised about 18,000 soldiers, divided into 11,000 musket-equipped troopers, a cavalry of 5,000, and 2,000 gunners who formed the artillery regiments. Most were stationed in barracks in and near the Topkapı Palace in Istanbul, ready to go on campaign at the sultan's command. Other Janissaries provided service in provincial cities and border fortresses. For his campaigns, the sultan added levies from among the cavalry troops in the towns and villages of the empire.

Typical campaigns involved 70,000 soldiers and required sophisticated logistics. All wages, gunpowder, and weapons and the majority of the foodstuffs were carried on wagons and barges, since soldiers were not permitted to provision themselves from the belongings of the villagers, whether friend or foe. Although the state collected heavy taxes, it had a strong interest in not destroying the productivity of the villagers (see Source 16.4).

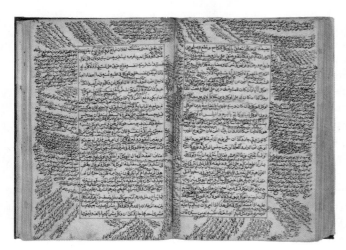

Ottoman Law Book. Covering the entire range of human activity—from spiritual matters, family relations, and inheritances to business transactions and crimes—the *Multaqa al-abhur* (*The Confluence of the Currents*) was completed in 1517 and remained for hundreds of years the authoritative source for many of the laws in the Ottoman Empire. It was written in Arabic by the legal scholar Ibrahim al-Halabi; later commentators added annotations in the margins and within the body of the text itself.

Charles V's Centralizing State   The centralizing state began in Iberia with the political and fiscal reforms of Isabella and Ferdinand and reached its mature phase under Charles V. From the late fifteenth century onward, Castile and Aragon shared many fiscal characteristics with those of the Ottomans. The Spanish monarchs derived cash advances from tax farmers, who organized the production and sale of minerals and salt. From other tax farmers, they received advances on the taxes collected in money from the movement of goods in and out of ports, cities, and markets, as well as on taxes collected in kind from independent farmers and converted through sale on urban markets. In addition, Muslims paid head taxes in cash. Most of the money taxes were also enforced in Flanders, Burgundy, Naples, Sicily, and Austria, after Iberia's incorporation into the Habsburg domain in 1516. Together, these taxes were more substantial than those of Spain, especially in highly urbanized Flanders, where the percentage of the urban population was about twice that of Spain.

From 1521 to 1536, the Spanish crown enlarged its money income by the one-fifth share to which it was entitled from looted Aztec and Inca gold and silver treasures. Charles V used these treasures to finance his expedition against Tunis. Thereafter, he collected a one-quarter share from the silver mines in the Americas that were brought into production beginning in 1545. Full production in the mines was not reached until the second half of the sixteenth century, but already under Charles V Habsburg imperial revenues doubled, reaching about the same level as those of the Ottomans. Thus, at the height of their struggle for dominance in the Muslim–Christian world, the Habsburgs and the Ottomans expended roughly the same amounts of resources to hurl against each other in the form of troops, cannons, muskets, and war galleys.

In one significant respect, however, the two empires differed. The cavalry ruling class of the Ottoman Empire was nonhereditary. Although land-grant holdings went in practice from father to son and then grandson, their holders had no recourse to the law if the sultans decided to replace them. By contrast, ever since the first half of the thirteenth century, when the Iberian kings were still lacking appreciable monetary resources, their landholders possessed a legal right to inheritance. The landholders met more or less regularly in parliaments (Spanish *cortes*), where they could enforce their property rights against the kings through majority decisions. When Isabella and Ferdinand embarked on state centralization, they had to wrestle with a powerful, landed aristocracy that had taken over royal jurisdiction and tax prerogatives (especially market taxes) on their often vast lands, including cities as well as towns and villages. The two monarchs took back much of the jurisdiction but were unable to do much about the taxes, thus failing in one crucial respect in their centralization effort. Although Habsburg Spain relied on precious metals as heavily as the Ottoman Empire did, it was in the end less centralized than that of the Ottomans.

The Habsburgs sought to overcome their lack of power over the aristocracy and the weakness of their Spanish tax base by squeezing as much as they could out of the Italian and Flemish cities and the American colonies. But in the long run their finances remained precarious, plentiful in some years but sparse in others. Relatively few Spanish aristocrats bothered to fulfill their traditional obligation to unpaid military service. Others who did serve forced the kings to pay them like mercenaries. As a result, in the administration and especially in the military, the kings hired as many Italians, Flemings, and Germans as possible. At times, they even had to deploy these mercenaries to Spain in order to maintain peace there. Most of these foreigners were foot soldiers, equipped with muskets.

The Ottoman and Habsburg patterns of centralized state formation bore similarities to patterns in the Roman and Arab Empires half a millennium earlier. At that time, however, the scale was more modest, given that the precious metals from West Africa and the Americas were not yet part of the trade network. In addition, earlier empires did not yet possess firearms, requiring an expensive infrastructure of charcoal and metal production, gunsmithing, saltpeter mining, and gunpowder manufacture. Thanks to firearms, the centralizing states of the period after 1450 were much more potent enterprises. They were established polities, evolving into absolutist and eventually national states.

Imperial Courts, Urban Festivities, and the Arts

Ottoman and Habsburg rulers set aside a portion of revenues to project the splendor and glory of their states to subjects at home as well as enemies abroad. They commissioned the building of palaces, mosques, and churches and sponsored public festivities. Since the administrators, nobility, tax farmers, and merchants had considerable funds, they also patronized writers, artists, and architects. Although Christian and Muslim artists and artisans belonged to different religious and cultural traditions and expressed themselves through different media, their artistic achievements were inspired by the same impulse: to glorify their states through religious expression.

The Ottoman Empire: Palaces, Festivities, and the Arts

The Ottomans built palaces and celebrated public feasts to demonstrate their imperial power and wealth. In Ottoman Islamic civilization, however, there were no traditions of official public art. The exception was architecture, where a veritable explosion of mosque construction occurred during the sixteenth century. Refined pictorial artistry, in the form of portraits, book illustrations, and miniatures, was found only inside the privacy of the Ottoman palace and wealthy administrative households. As in Habsburg Spain, theater and music enjoyed much support on the popular level, in defiance of official religious restrictions against these forms of entertainment.

The Topkapı Palace   When the Ottoman sultans conquered the Byzantine capital Constantinople in 1453, they acquired one of the great cities of the world. Although richly endowed with Roman monuments and churches, it was dilapidated and depopulated when the Ottomans took over. The sultans initiated large construction projects, such as covered markets, and populated the city with craftspeople and traders drawn from both the Asian and European sides of their empire. By 1600 Istanbul was again an imposing metropolis with close to half a million inhabitants, easily the largest city in Europe at that time.

One of the construction projects was a new palace for the sultans, the Topkapı Sarayı, or "Palace of the Gun Gate," begun in 1459. The Topkapı was a veritable minicity, with three courtyards, formal gardens, and forested hunting grounds. It also included the main administrative school for the training of imperial bureaucrats, barracks for the standing troops of the Janissaries, an armory, a hospital, and—most important—the living quarters, or harem, for the ruling family. Subjects were permitted access only through the first courtyard—reserved for imperial festivities—to submit their petitions to the sultan's council of ministers.

The institution of the harem rose to prominence toward the end of the reign of Süleyman. At that time, sultans no longer pursued marriage alliances with neighboring Islamic rulers. Instead, they chose slave concubines for the procreation of children, preferably boys. Concubines were usually from the Caucasus or other frontier regions, often Christian, and, since they were slaves, deprived of family attachments.

A concubine who bore a son to the reigning sultan acquired privileges, such as influence on decisions made by the central administration.

The head eunuch of the harem guard evolved into a powerful intermediary for all manner of small and large diplomatic and military decisions between the sultan's mother, who was confined to the harem, and the ministers or generals she sought to influence. In addition, the sultan's mother arranged marriages of her daughters to members of the council of ministers and other high-ranking officials. In the strong patriarchal order of the Ottoman Empire, it might come as a surprise to see women exercise such power, but this power evidently had its roots in the tutelage exercised by mothers over sons who were potential future sultans.

Imperial Hall, Topkapı Palace. The Ottomans never forgot their nomadic roots. Topkapı Palace, completed in 1479 and expanded and redecorated several times, resembles in many ways a vast encampment, with a series of enclosed courtyards. At the center of the palace complex were the harem and the private apartments of the sultan, which included the Imperial Hall, where the sultan would receive members of his family and closest advisors.

image analysis

Public Festivities   As in Habsburg Spain, feasts and celebrations were events that displayed the state's largesse and benevolence. Typical festivities were the Feast of Breaking the Fast, which came at the end of the fasting month of Ramadan, and the Feast of Sacrifice, which took place a month and a half later at the end of the Meccan pilgrimage. Festive processions and fairs welcomed the return of the Meccan pilgrimage caravan. Other feasts were connected with the birthday of the Prophet Muhammad and his journey to heaven and hell. Muslims believed that the Prophet's birth was accompanied by miracles and that the angel Gabriel accompanied him on his journey, showing him the joys of heaven and the horrors of hell. Processions with banners, music, and communal meals commemorated the birthdays of local Muslim saints in many cities and towns. As in Christian Spain, these feasts attracted large crowds.

Wrestlers, ram handlers, and horsemen performed in the Hippodrome, the stadium for public festivities. Elimination matches in wrestling determined the eventual champion. Ram handlers spurred their animals to gore one another with their horns. Horsemen stood upright on horses, galloping toward a mound, which they had to hit with a javelin. At the harbor of the Golden Horn, tightrope artists stood high above the water, balancing themselves on cables stretched between the masts of ships, as they performed juggling feats. Fireworks—featuring a variety of effects, noises, and colors—completed the circumcision festival in the evening. Court painters recorded the procession and performance scenes in picture albums. The sultans incorporated these albums into their libraries, together with history books recording in word and image their military victories against the Habsburgs (see Source 16.3).

Popular Theater   The evenings of the fasting month of Ramadan were filled with festive meals and a special form of entertainment, the Karagöz ("Black Eye") shadow theater. This form of theater came from Egypt, although it probably had Javanese–Chinese roots. The actors in the Karagöz theater used figures cut from thin, transparent leather, painted in primary colors, and fashioned with movable jaws and limbs. With brightly burning lamps behind them, actors manipulated

Ottoman Festivities, 1720. The sultan watches from a kiosk on the shore of the Golden Horn as artists perform high-wire acts, musicians and dancers perform from rowboats offshore, and high officials and foreign dignitaries view the festivities from a galleon.

the figures against a cloth screen. The audience was seated on the other side of the screen, following the plays with rapt attention (or not).

Among boys, a performance of the Karagöz theater accompanied the ritual of circumcision, a rite of passage from the ancient Near East adopted in Islamic civilization. The custom called for boys between the ages of 6 and 12 to be circumcised. Circumcision signified the passage from the nurturing care of the mother to the educational discipline of the father. Groups of newly circumcised boys were placed in beds from which they watched the Karagöz plays.

Mosque Architecture During the sixteenth century, the extraordinarily prolific architect Sinan (ca. 1492–1588) filled Istanbul and the earlier Ottoman capital Edirne with a number of imperial mosques, defined by their characteristic slender minarets. According to his autobiography, Sinan designed more than 300 religious and secular buildings, from mosques, colleges, and hospitals to aqueducts and bridges. Sultan Süleyman, wealthy officials, and private donors provided the funds. Sinan was able to hire as many as 25,000 laborers, enabling him to build each of his mosques in six years or less.

Sinan described the Shehzade and Süleymaniye mosques in Istanbul and the Selimiye mosque in Edirne as his apprentice, journeyman, and master achievements. All three followed the central dome-over-a-square concept of the Hagia Sophia, which in turn is built in the tradition

Selimiye and Hagia Sophia. The architect Sinan elegantly melded the eight, comparatively thin, columns inside the mosque (*a*) with the surrounding walls and allowed for a maximum of light to enter the building. In addition, light enters through the dome (*b*). Compare this mosque with the much more heavily built, late-Roman-founded Hagia Sophia (*c*).

of Persian and Roman dome architecture. His primary, and most original, contribution to the history of architecture was the replacement of the highly visible and massive four exterior buttresses, which marked the square ground plan of the Hagia Sophia, with up to eight slender pillars as hidden internal supports of the dome. His intention with each of these mosques was not massive monumentality but elegant spaciousness, giving the skylines of Istanbul and Edirne their unmistakable identity.

The Spanish Habsburg Empire: Popular Festivities and the Arts

The centrality of Catholicism gave the culture of the Habsburg Empire a strongly religious coloration. Both state-sponsored spectacles and popular festivities displayed devotion to the Catholic faith. More secular tendencies, however, began to appear as well, if only because new forms of literature and theater emerged outside the religious sphere as a result of the Renaissance. Originating in Italy and the Netherlands, Renaissance aesthetics emphasized pre-Christian Greek and Roman heritages, which had not been available to medieval Christian artists.

Capital and Palace   The Habsburgs focused relatively late on creating the typical symbols of state power and splendor—that is, a capital city and a palace. Most Spaniards lived in the northern third and along the southern and eastern rims of the Iberian Peninsula, leaving the inhospitable central high plateau, the Meseta, thinly inhabited. Catholicism was the majority religion by the sixteenth century and a powerful unifying force, but there were strong linguistic differences among the provinces of the Iberian Peninsula. Charles V resided for a while in a palace in Granada next door to the formerly Muslim Alhambra palace. Built in an Italian Renaissance–derived style and appearing overwhelming and bombastic in comparison to the outwardly unprepossessing Alhambra, Granada was too Moorish and, geographically, too far away in the south for more than a few Spanish subjects to be properly awed.

Only a few places in the river valleys traversing the Meseta were suited for the location of a central palace and administration. Philip II eventually found such a place near the city of Madrid (built on Roman–Visigothic foundations), which in the early sixteenth century had some 12,000 inhabitants. There, he had his royal architect in chief and sculptor Juan Bautista de Toledo (ca. 1515–1567), a student of Michelangelo, build the imposing Renaissance-style palace and monastery complex of El Escorial (1563–1584).

As a result, Madrid became the seat of the administration and later of the court. A large central square and broad avenue were cut across the narrow alleys of the old city, which had once been a Muslim provincial capital. People of all classes gathered in the square and avenue, to participate in public festivities and learn the latest news "about the intentions of the Grand Turk, revolutions in the Netherlands, the state of things in Italy, and the latest discoveries made in the Indies," as the writer Antonio de Liñán y Verdugo remarked in a work published in 1620.

Like its Italian paradigm, the architecture of the Spanish Renaissance emphasized the Roman imperial style—itself derived from the Greeks—with long friezes, round arches, freestanding columns, and rotunda-based domes. With this style, Spanish architects departed from the preceding Gothic, stressing horizontal extension rather than height and plain rather than relief or ornament-filled surfaces.

Passion play: Dramatic representation of the trial, suffering, and death of Jesus Christ; passion plays are still an integral part of Holy Week in many Catholic countries today.

Christian State Festivities   Given the close association between the state and the church, the Spanish crown expressed its glory through the observance of feast days of the Christian calendar. Christmas, Easter, Pentecost, Trinity Sunday, Corpus Christi, and the birthdays of numerous saints were the occasion for processions and/or **passion plays**, during which urban residents affirmed the purity of their Catholic faith. Throngs lined the streets or marched in procession, praying, singing, weeping, and exclaiming. During Holy Week, the week preceding Easter, Catholics—wearing white robes, tall white or black pointed hats, and veils over their faces—marched through the streets, carrying heavy crosses or shouldering wooden platforms with statues of Jesus and Mary. A variety of religious lay groups or confraternities competed to build the most elaborately decorated platforms. Members of flagellant confraternities whipped themselves. The physical rigors of the Holy Week processions were collective reenactments of Jesus' suffering on the Cross.

By contrast, the Corpus Christi (Latin, meaning "body of Christ") processions that took place on the Sunday after Trinity Sunday (several weeks after Easter) were joyous celebrations. Central to these processions was a platform with a canopy covering the consecrated host (bread believed to have been transfigured into the body of Jesus). Marchers dressed as giants, serpents, dragons, devils, angels, patriarchs, and saints participated in jostling and pushing contests. Others wore masks, played music, performed dances, and enacted scenes from the Bible. Being part of the crowd in the Corpus Christi processions meant partaking in a joyful anticipation of salvation.

The Auto-da-Fé   The investigation or proceeding of faith (Portuguese *auto-da-fé*, "act of faith") was a show trial in which the state, through the Spanish Inquisition, judged a person's commitment to Catholicism. Inquisitional trials were intended to display the all-important unity and purity of the Catholic Reformation. The Inquisition employed thousands of state-appointed church officials to investigate anonymous denunciations of individuals failing to conform to the prescribed doctrines and liturgy of the Catholic faith.

Suspected offenders, such as Jewish or Muslim converts to Catholicism or perceived deviants from Catholicism, had to appear before one of the 15 tribunals distributed throughout the country. In secret trials, officials determined the degree of the offense and the appropriate punishment. These trials often employed torture, such as stretching the accused on the rack, suspending them with weights, crushing hands and feet in an apparatus called "the boot," and burning them with firebrands. In contrast to the wide perception of the Inquisition as marked by pervasive cruelties, however, scholarship has emphasized that in the great majority of cases the punishments were minor, or the investigations did not lead to convictions.

Popular Festivities   *Jousts* (mock combats between contestants mounted on horseback) were secular, primarily aristocratic events, also frequently connected with dynastic occurrences. The contestants, colorfully costumed as Muslims, Turks, and Christians, rode their horses into the city square accompanied by trumpets and drums and led their horses through a precise and complex series of movements. At the height of the spectacle, contestants divided into groups of three or four at each end of the square. At a signal, they galloped at full speed past each other, hurling their javelins at one another while protecting themselves with their shields. The joust evolved eventually into exhibitions of dressage ("training"), cultivated by the Austrian Habsburgs, who in 1572 founded the Spanish Court Riding School in Vienna.

Bullfights, also fought on horseback, often followed the jousts. Fighting wild animals, including bulls, in spectacles was originally a Roman custom that had evolved from older bovine sacrifices in temples around the Mediterranean. During the Middle Ages, bullfights were aristocratic pastimes that drew spectators from local estates. Bullfighters, armed with detachable metal points on 3-foot-long spears, tackled several bulls in a town square, together with footmen who sought to distract the bulls by waving red capes at them. The bullfighter who stuck the largest number of points into the shoulders of the bull was the winner.

Theater and Literature   The dramatic enactments of biblical scenes in the passion plays and Corpus Christi processions were the origin of a new phenomenon in Italy and Spain, the secular theater. During earlier centuries, traveling troupes had often performed on wagons after processions. Stationary theaters with stages, main floors, balconies, and boxes appeared in the main cities of Spain during the sixteenth century. A performance typically began with a musical prelude and a prologue describing the piece, followed by the three acts of a drama or comedy. Brief sketches, humorous or earnest, filled the breaks. Plays dealt with betrayed or unrequited love, honor, justice, or peasant–nobility conflicts. Many were hugely successful, enjoying the attendance or even sponsorship of courtiers, magistrates, and merchants.

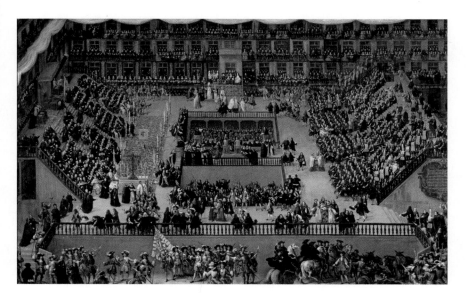

The Auto-da-Fé This detail from an 1683 painting by the Italian-born painter Francisco Rizi shows a huge assembly in the Plaza Mayor of Madrid. It captures the solemn spectacle of the trial: In the center, below a raised platform, the accused stand in the docket waiting for their convictions to be pronounced; ecclesisatical and civil authorities follow the proceedings from grandstands. On the left, an altar is visible: The celebration of mass was a common feature of the auto-da-fé.

El Greco, *View of Toledo*, ca. 1610–1614. The painting, now in the Metropolitan Museum of Art in New York City, illustrates El Greco's predilection for color contrasts and dramatic motion. Baroque and Mannerist painters rarely depicted landscapes, and this particular landscape is represented in eerie green, gray, and blue colors, giving the impression of a city enveloped in a mysterious natural or perhaps spiritual force.

interactive concept map

An important writer of the period was Miguel de Cervantes (1547–1616), who wrote his masterpiece, *Don Quixote*, in the new literary form of the novel. *Don Quixote* describes the adventures of a poverty-stricken knight and his attendant, the peasant Sancho Panza, as they wander around Spain searching for the life of bygone *Reconquista* chivalry. Their journey includes many hilarious escapades during which they run into the reality of the early modern centralizing state dominated by monetary concerns. Cervantes confronts the vanished virtues of knighthood with the novel values of the life with money.

Painters The outstanding painter of Spain during Philip II's reign was El Greco (Domenikos Theotokopoulos, ca. 1546–1614), a native of the island of Crete. After early training in Crete as a painter of Eastern Christian icons, El Greco went to Venice for further studies. In 1577, the Catholic hierarchy hired him to paint the altarpieces of a church in Toledo, the city in central Spain that was one of the residences of the kings prior to the construction of El Escorial in Madrid. El Greco's works reflect the spirit of Spanish Catholicism, with its emphasis on strict obedience to traditional faith and fervent personal piety. His characteristic style features elongated, pale figures surrounded by vibrant colors and represents a variation of the so-called mannerist style (with its perspective exaggerations), which succeeded the Renaissance style in Venice during the later sixteenth century.

>> Putting It All Together

The Ottoman–Habsburg struggle can be seen as another chapter in the long history of competition that began when the Achaemenid Persian Empire expanded into the Mediterranean and was resisted by the Greeks in the middle of the first millennium BCE. Although India and China were frequently subjected to incursions from central Asia, neither of the two had to compete for long with any of its neighbors. Sooner or later the central Asians either retreated or were absorbed by their victims. The Ottomans' brief experience with Timur was on the same order. But the Middle East and Europe were always connected, and this chapter, once more, draws attention to this connectedness.

There were obvious religious and cultural differences between the Islamic and Western Christian civilizations as they encountered each other during the Ottoman–Habsburg period. But their commonalities are equally, if not more, interesting. Most important, both Ottomans and Habsburgs were representatives of the return to imperialism, and in the pursuit of their imperial goals, both adopted the policy of the centralizing state with its firearm infantries and pervasive urban money economy. Both found it crucial to their existence to project their glory to the population at large and to sponsor artistic expression. In the long run, however, the imperial ambitions of the Ottomans and Habsburgs exceeded their ability to raise cash. Although firearms and a monetized urban economy made them different from previous empires, they were as unstable as all their imperial predecessors. Eventually, around 1600, they reached the limits of their conquests.

Review and Relate

Thinking Through Patterns

Examine the ways historians approach the big questions of this chapter.

In 1300, the Ottomans renewed the Arab-Islamic tradition of jihad against the Eastern Christian empire of Byzantium, conquering the Balkans and eventually defeating the empire with the conquest of Constantinople in 1453. They also carried the war into the western Mediterranean and Indian Ocean. In Western Christian Iberia, the rekindling of the reconquest after the lull of the thirteenth and fourteenth centuries was more successful. Invigorated by a merging of the concepts of the Crusade and the *Reconquista*, the Iberians expanded overseas to circumvent the Muslims and trade for Indian spices directly. The so-called Age of Exploration, during which Western Christians traveled to and settled in overseas lands, is deeply rooted in the Western traditions of war against Islamic civilization.

In the mid-1400s, the Middle East and Europe returned to the pattern of imperial state formation after a lull of several centuries, during which states had competed against each other within their respective commonwealths. The element which fueled this return was gunpowder weaponry. The use of cannons and handheld firearms became widespread during this time but required major financial outlays on the part of the states. The Ottomans and Habsburgs were the states with the most resources, and the Ottomans even assembled the first standing armies. To pay the musket-equipped soldiers, huge amounts of silver were necessary. The two empires became states based on a money economy: Bureaucracies maintained centralized departments that regulated the collection of taxes and the payroll of soldiers.

The rulers of these empires were concerned to portray themselves, their military, and their bureaucracies as highly successful and just. The state had to be as visible and benevolent as possible. Rulers, therefore, were builders of palaces, churches, or mosques. They celebrated religious and secular festivities with great pomp and

> ≫ **What patterns characterized the Christian and Muslim imperial competition in the period 1300–1600? Which elements distinguished them from each other, and which elements were similar? How did the pattern change over time?**

> ≫ **How did the centralizing state in the Middle East and Europe function in the period 1450–1600? How did economics, military power, and imperial objectives interact to create the centralizing state?**

> ≫ **Which patterns did cultural expressions follow in the**

Habsburg and Ottoman Empires? Why did the ruling classes of these empires sponsor these expressions?

encouraged ministers and the nobility to do likewise. In the imperial capitals, they patronized architects, artists, and writers, resulting in a veritable explosion of intellectual and artistic creativity. In this regard, the Ottomans and the Habsburgs followed similar patterns of cultural expression.

| Against the Grain

Consider this as a counterpoint to the main patterns examined in this chapter.

Tilting at Windmills

- What explains the lasting literary success of *Don Quixote*?

- Why has the phrase "tilting at windmills" undergone a change of meaning from the original "fighting imaginary foes" to "taking on a situation against all seeming evidence" in our own time?

Cervantes's *The Ingenious Gentleman Don Quixote of La Mancha* was an instant hit in the Spanish-speaking literary world of the early 1600s and contributed to the rise of the novel as a characteristic European form of literary expression. As stated in his preface, Cervantes composed his novel in opposition to the dominant literary conventions of his time, to "ridicule the absurdity of those books of chivalry, which have, as it were, fascinated the eyes and judgement of the world, and in particular of the vulgar."

Every episode in this novel, from the literary frame to its most famous story, Don Quixote's joust against windmills he believes to be fantastic giants, is cast in the forms of gentle, hilarious, or biting parodies of one or another absurdity in society. The frame is provided by the fictional figure of Cide Hamete Benengeli, a purportedly perfidious Muslim and historian who might or might not have been lying when he chronicled the lives of the knight Don Quixote and his squire Sancho Panza in the 74 episodes of the novel. Don Quixote's joust, or "tilting," against windmills has become a powerful metaphor for rebelling against the often overpowering conventions of society.

Don Quixote is today acclaimed as the second most printed text after the Bible. Over the past four centuries, each generation has interpreted the text anew. Revolutionary France saw Don Quixote as a doomed visionary; German Romantics, as a hero destined to fail; Communists, as an anti-capitalist rebel before his time; and secular progressives, as an unconventional hero at the dawn of modern free society. For Karl Marx, Don Quixote was the hidalgo who yearned for a return to the feudal aristocracy of the past which in his time was becoming a pleasure aristocracy, enjoying its useless life at the royal court and imitated later by the bourgeoisie. Sigmund Freud enjoyed reading and rereading *Don Quixote* throughout his life, looking at the knight-errant as "tragic in his helplessness while the plot is unraveled." In our own time, Don Quixote became the quintessential postmodern figure; in the words of Michel Foucault, his "truth is not in the relation of the words to the world but in that slender and constant relation woven between themselves as verbal signs. The hollow fiction of epic exploits has become the representative power of language. Words have swallowed up their own nature as signs." As a tragic or comic figure, Don Quixote continues to be the irresistible symbol of opposition.

Key Terms

audio flashcards

Corsairs 459	Military orders 460	Passion play 484
Devşirme 476	Money economy 475	Tax farming 477
Janissaries 476	Moriscos 472	

For additional resources, please go to
www.oup.com/us/vonsivers.
Please see the Further Resources section at the back of the book for additional readings and suggested websites.

Sources for Chapter 16

SOURCE 16.1

Christopher Columbus, *The Book of Prophecies*

1501–1502

Although he is more famous for his voyages—and for the richly detailed accounts he made of them—Columbus (1451–1506) also composed a book of prophetic revelations toward the end of his life, entitled *El Libro de las Profecias*. Written after his third voyage to the Americas, the book traces the development of God's plans for the end of the world, which could be hastened along, particularly by a swift and decisive move to reclaim Jerusalem from Muslim control. When Jerusalem was once more restored to Christian sovereignty, Columbus predicted, Jesus could return to earth, and all of the events foreseen in the Book of Revelation (and in various medieval revelations, as well) could unfold. It is helpful to place the plans for Columbus's original voyage in 1492 against the backdrop of his religious beliefs, as he encourages Ferdinand and Isabella to take their rightful place in God's mystical plan—as well as in Columbus's own cartographic charts.

Letter from the Admiral to the King and Queen [Ferdinand and Isabella]

. . .

Most exalted rulers: At a very early age I began sailing the sea and have continued until now. This profession creates a curiosity about the secrets of the world. I have been a sailor for forty years, and I have personally sailed to all the known regions. I have had commerce and conversation with knowledgeable people of the clergy and the laity. Latins and Greeks, Jews and Moors, and with many others of different religions. Our Lord has favored my occupation and has given me an intelligent mind. He has endowed me with a great talent for seamanship; sufficient ability in astrology, geometry, and arithmetic; and the mental and physical dexterity required to draw spherical maps of cities, rivers and mountains, islands and ports, with everything in its proper place.

During this time I have studied all kinds of texts: cosmography, histories, chronicles, philosophy, and other disciplines. Through these writings, the hand of Our Lord opened my mind to the possibility of sailing to the Indies and gave

Source: Christopher Columbus, *The Book of Prophecies*, ed. Roberto Rusconi, trans. Blair Sullivan, vol. 3 (Berkeley: University of California Press, 1997), 67–69, 75–77.

me the will to attempt the voyage. With this burning ambition I came to your Highnesses. Everyone who heard about my enterprise rejected it with laughter and ridicule. Neither all the sciences that I mentioned previously nor citations drawn from them were of any help to me. Only Your Highnesses had faith and perseverance. Who could doubt that this flash of understanding was the work of the Holy Spirit, as well as my own? The Holy Spirit illuminated his holy and sacred Scripture, encouraging me in a very strong and clear voice from the forty-four books of the Old Testament, the four evangelists, and twenty-three epistles from the blessed apostles, urging me to proceed. Continually, without ceasing a moment, they insisted that I go on. Our Lord wished to make something clearly miraculous of this voyage to the Indies in order to encourage me and others about the holy temple.

. . .

Most of the prophecies of holy Scripture have already been fulfilled. The Scriptures say this and the Holy Church loudly and unceasingly is saying it, and no other witness is necessary. I will, however, speak of one prophecy in particular because it bears on my argument and gives me support and happiness whenever I think about it.

I have greatly sinned. Yet, every time that I have asked, I have been covered by the mercy and compassion of Our Lord. I have found the sweetest consolation in throwing off all my cares in order to contemplate his marvelous presence.

I have already said that for the voyage to the Indies neither intelligence nor mathematics nor world maps were of any use to me; it was the fulfillment of Isaiah's prophecy. This is what I want to record here in order to remind Your Highnesses and so that you can take pleasure from the things I am going to tell you about Jerusalem on the basis of the same authority. If you have faith in this enterprise, you will certainly have the victory.

. . .

I said above that much that has been prophesied remains to be fulfilled, and I say that these are the world's great events, and I say that a sign of this is the acceleration of Our Lord's activities in this world. I know this from the recent preaching of the gospel in so many lands.

The Calabrian abbot Joachim said that whoever was to rebuild the temple on Mount Zion would come from Spain.

The cardinal Pierre d'Ailly wrote at length about the end of the religion of Mohammed and the coming of the Antichrist in his treatise *De concordia astronomicae veritatis et narrationis historicae* [*On the agreement between astronomical truth and historical narrative*]; he discusses, particularly in the last nine chapters, what many astronomers have said about the ten revolutions of Saturn.

>> Working with Sources

1. **How does Columbus appeal to the "crusading" goals of Ferdinand and Isabella, and why?**

2. **Would this appeal have found favor with the monarchs, given their other actions in Spain in 1492?**

SOURCE 16.2	Thomas the Eparch and Joshua Diplovatatzes, "The Fall of Constantinople"

1453

The siege and conquest of Constantinople by the Ottoman Turks under Mehmet II (r. 1451–1481) was one of the turning points of world history. Unfolding over two months between April 5 and May 29, 1453, the siege exposed the inability of the Byzantine emperor Constantine XI to withstand a sustained and massive attack. Outnumbering the defenders 11 to 1, the Ottomans battered Constantinople's walls with heavy cannons and took advantage of the natural weaknesses of the city's geography. This account, told by two survivors and (self-proclaimed) eyewitnesses to the siege and its aftermath, details some of the specific stages of the defeat—and the suffering for Christians that came as a result.

When the Turk then drew near to Pera in the fortified zone, he seized all the boats he could find and bound them to each other so as to form a bridge which permitted the combatants to fight on the water just as they did on land. The Turks had with them thousands of ladders which they placed against the walls, right at the place which they had fired [their cannon] and breached the wall, just as they did at the cemetery of St. Sebold. The Genoese handled this breach; they wanted to protect it with their ships because they had so many. In the army of the Turk the order had been given fifteen days before the attack that each soldier would carry a ladder, whether he was fighting on land or sea. There also arrived galleys full of armed men: it seemed that they were Genoese and that they had come to aid the besieged, but in fact they were Turks and they were slipping into the gates. Just as this was becoming less worrisome and the city seemed secure, there arrived under the flag of the Genoese several ships which repelled the Turks with great losses.

At dawn on Monday, 29 May, they began an attack that lasted all night until Tuesday evening and they conquered the city. The commander of the Genoese, who was leading the defense of the breach, pretended to be wounded and abandoned his battle station, taking with him all his people. When the Turks realized this, they slipped in through the breach. When the emperor of the Greeks saw this, he exclaimed in a loud voice: "My God, I have been betrayed!" and he suddenly appeared with his people, exhorting the others to stand firm and defend themselves. But then the gate was opened and the crush of people became such that the emperor himself and his [men] were killed by the Turks and the traitors.

Then the Turks ran to the Hagia Sophia, and all those whom they had imprisoned there, they killed in the first heat of rage. Those whom they found later, they bound with a cord around their neck and their hands tied behind

Source: trans. William L. North from the Italian version in A. Pertusi, ed., *La Caduta di Constantinopoli: Le testimonianze dei contemporanei* (Milan: Mondadori, 1976), 234–239, available online at https://apps.carleton.edu/curricular/mars/assets/Thomas_the_Eparch_and_Joshua_Diplovatatzes_for_MARS_website.pdf.

their backs and led them out of the city. When the Turk learned that the emperor had been killed in Constantinople, he captured the Grand Duke who was governing in the emperor's stead and had the Grand Duke's son beheaded and then the Grand Duke himself. Then he seized one of the Grand Duke's daughters who was quite beautiful and made her lie on the great altar of Hagia Sophia with a crucifix under her head and then raped her. Then the most brutish of the Turks seized the finest noble women, virgins, and nuns of the city and violated them in the presence of the Greeks and in sacrilege of Christianity. Then they destroyed all the sacred objects and the bodies of the saints and burned everything they found, save for the cross, the nail, and the clothing of Christ: no one knows where these relics ended up, no one has found them. They also wanted to desecrate the image of the Virgin of St. Luke by stabbing six hundred people in front of it, one after another, like madmen. Then they took prisoner those who fell into their hands, tied them with a rope around the neck and calculated the value of each one. Women had to redeem themselves with their own bodies, men by fornicating with their hands or some other means. Whoever was able to pay the assessed amount could remain in his faith and whoever refused had to die. The Turk who had become governor of Constantinople, named Suleiman in German, occupied the temple of Hagia Sophia to practice his faith there. For three days the Turks sacked and pillaged the city, and each kept whatever he found—people and goods—and did with them whatever he wished.

. . .

All this was made known by Thomas the Eparch, a count of Constantinople, and Joshua Diplovatatzes. Thutros of Constantinople translated their Greek into "welisch" and Dumita Exswinnilwacz and Matheus Hack of Utrecht translated their welisch into German.

» **Working with Sources**

1. **What does this account suggest about the preparedness of the Turks for the sack of Constantinople—and the lack of preparation on the part of the Byzantine defenders?**

2. **What details indicate that the taking of Constantinople was seen as a "religious" war on the Ottoman side?**

| SOURCE 16.3 | Evliya Çelebi, "A Procession of Artisans at Istanbul" |

ca. 1638

Born on the Golden Horn and raised in the sultan's palace in Istanbul, Çelebi traveled throughout Ottoman domains between 1640 and 1680. He published an account of his travels and experiences as the *Seyahatname*, or *Book of Travels*. In the first of his 10 books in the document, Çelebi

Source: Robert Dankoff, *An Ottoman Mentality: The World of Evliya Çelebi*, 2nd ed. (Leiden, the Netherlands: Brill, 2006), 86–89.

provides a lengthy description of Istanbul around the year 1638, including a panoramic view of 1,100 artisan and craft guilds. The numbers and diversity of trades represented underscore the extent of Ottoman commerce—as well as the pride of place each of the city's working people claimed as their due.

The numbers in brackets refer to the order of listing in this chapter.

I: Ship-captains [7] vs. Saddlers [30]

Following the bakers [6], the saddlers wished to pass, but the ship-captains and sea-merchants raised a great fuss. When Sultan Murad got wind of the matter, he consulted with the ulema and the guild shaikhs. They all agreed that it made sense for the ship-captains to proceed after the bakers, because it was they who transported the wheat, and the bakers were dependent on them, and also because Noah was their patron saint.

Comment: the saddlers do not reappear until much later, between the tanners [29] and the shoemakers [31].

. . .

III: Egyptian Merchants [9] vs. Butchers [10]

Following the procession of these Mediterranean Sea captains, the butchers were supposed to pass, according to imperial decree. But all the great Egyptian merchants, including the dealers in rice, hemp, Egyptian reed mats, coffee and sugar gathered together and began quarreling with the butchers. Finally they went before the sultan and said: "My padishah, our galleons are charged with transporting rice, lentils, coffee and hemp. They cannot do without us, nor we without them. Why should these bloody and tricky butchers come between us? Plagues have arisen from cities where they shed their blood, and for fear of this their stalls and shambles in other countries are outside of the city walls. They are a bloody and filthy band of ill-omen. We, on the other hand, always make Istanbul plentiful and cheap with grains of all sorts."

Now the butchers' eyes went bloodshot. "My padishah," they said, "Our patron saint is Butcher Cömerd and our occupation is with sheep, an animal which the Creator has made the object of mercy, and whose flesh He has made lawful food for the strengthening of His servants' bodies. Bread and meat are mentioned as the foremost of God's gifts to mankind: with a small portion of meat, a poor man can subsist for five or six days. We make our living with such a lawful trade, and are known for our generosity (*cömerdlik*). It is we who make Istanbul plentiful and cheap. As for these merchants and dealers and profiteers: concerning them the Koran says (2:275), 'God has made selling lawful and profiteering unlawful'. They are such a despised group that after bringing their goods from Egypt they store it in magazines in order to create a shortage, thus causing public harm through their hoarding.

. . .

"Egyptian sugar? But in the Koran the rivers of paradise are praised as being made 'of pure honey' (47:15). Now we have honey from Turkey, Athens,

Wallachia, Moldavia, each with seventy distinct qualities. Furthermore, if my padishah wished, thousands of quintals of sugar could be produced in Alanya, Antalya, Silifke, Tarsus, Adana, Payas, Antakya, Aleppo, Damascus, Sidon, Beyrut, Tripoli and other such provinces—enough to make it plentiful and cheap throughout the world—so why do we need your sugar?

"As for coffee: it is an innovation; it prevents sleep; it dulls the generative powers; and coffee houses are dens of sedition. When roasted it is burnt; and in the legal compilations known as *Bezzaziye* and *Tatarhaniye* we have the dictum that 'Whatever is carbonized is absolutely forbidden'—this holds even for burnt bread. Spiced sherbet, pure milk, tea, fennel, salep, and almond-cream—all these are more wholesome than coffee."

. . .

To these objections of the butchers, the Egyptian merchants replied:

. . . "It is true that Turkey has no need of sugar and hemp, and that European sugar is also very fine. But tell us this, O band of butchers: what benefit and return do you offer to the public treasury?"

The butchers had nothing to say to this, and the Egyptian merchants continued: "My padishah, the goods arriving in our galleons provide the public treasury an annual revenue of 11,000 purses from customs dues. As a matter of justice ('*adalet ederseñiz*) we ought to have precedence in the Muhammadan procession, and the butchers ought to come after us." The *şeyhülislam* Yahya Efendi and Mu'id Ahmed Efendi cited the hadith, "The best of men is he who is useful to mankind," and the sultan gave the Egyptian merchants a noble rescript authorizing them to go first, and the butchers to go second.

> » **Working with Sources**

1. **Why did the order in which they appeared in the procession matter so much to these particular groups?**

2. **How did appeals to the Quran accentuate or diminish their case to be placed ahead in the procession?**

SOURCE 16.4

Ogier Ghiselin de Busbecq, "The Court of Suleiman the Magnificent"

1581

Ghiselin (1522–1592) was a Flemish ambassador who represented the Austrian Habsburgs at the court of Suleiman the Magnificent (1520–1566) in Istanbul. In 1581, he published an account of his time among the Ottomans as *Itinera Constantinopolitanum et Amasianum* (*Travels in*

Source: Wayne S. Vucinich, *The Ottoman Empire: Its Record and Legacy* (Princeton, NJ: Van Nostrand, 1965), 127–129.

Constantinople and Asia Minor). In this segment of his travel narrative, he draws attention to the personal habits and behaviors of a contemporary emperor—one who saw himself as the heir to the Romans as well as to the other monarchs who had held Constantinople/Istanbul.

The Sultan was seated on a very low ottoman, not more than a foot from the ground, which was covered with a quantity of costly rugs and cushions of exquisite workmanship; near him lay his bow and arrows. His air, as I said, was by no means gracious, and his face wore a stern, though dignified, expression. On entering we were separately conducted into the royal presence by the chamberlains, who grasped our arms.... After having gone through a pretense of kissing his hand, we were conducted backwards to the wall opposite his seat, care being taken that we should never turn our backs on him. The Sultan then listened to what I had to say; but the language I held was not at all to his taste, for the demands of his Majesty breathed a spirit of independence and dignity . . . and so he made no answer beyond saying in a tetchy way, "Giusel, giusel," i.e. well, well . . .

. . .

I was greatly struck with the silence and order that prevailed in this great crowd. There were no cries, no hum of voices, the usual accompaniments of a motley gathering, neither was there any jostling; without the slightest disturbance each man took his proper place according to his rank. The Agas, as they call their chiefs, were seated, to wit, generals, colonels (*bimbashi*), and captains (*soubashi*). Men of a lower position stood. The most interesting sight in this assembly was a body of several thousand Janissaries, who were drawn up in a long line apart from the rest; their array was so steady and motionless that, being at a little distance, it was some time before I could make up my mind as to whether they were human beings or statues; at last I received a hint to salute them, and saw all their heads bending at the same moment to return my bow.

. . .

When the cavalry had ridden past, they were followed by a long procession of Janissaries, but few of whom carried any arms except their regular weapon, the musket. They were dressed in uniforms of almost the same shape and colour, so that you might recognize them to be the slaves.... There is only one thing in which they are extravagant, viz., plumes, head-dresses, etc., and veterans who formed the rear guard were specially distinguished by ornaments of this kind. The plumes which they insert in their frontlets might well be mistaken for a walking forest.

≫ Working with Sources

1. Why were order and discipline apparently so important at Suleiman's court?

2. Why might Ghiselin have found the Janissaries so particularly impressive?

SOURCE 16.5   Janissary Musket

ca. 1750–1800

The Janissaries constitute the most famous and centralized of the Ottomans' military institutions. A feared and respected military force, the Janissaries were Christian-born males who had been seized from their homes as boys, converted to Islam, and then trained as future soldiers and administrators for the Turks. Under the direct orders of the sultan and his viziers, the Janissaries were equipped with the latest military innovations. These units received cannons and matchlock (later flintlock, below) muskets. The muskets continued their evolution in the Janissaries' hands, becoming standard equipment for Ottoman and other armies.

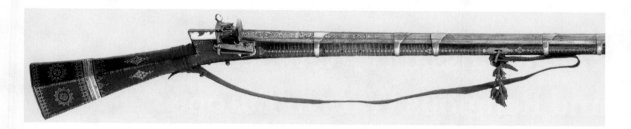

» Working with Sources

1. What does the elaborate decoration of this musket suggest about its psychological as well as its practical effects?

2. Was this firearm likely to have been produced by indigenous, rather than European, gunsmiths? Why or why not?

AXIOMATA
SIVE
LEGES MOTUS

Lex. I.

Corpus omne perseverare in statu suo quiescendi vel movendi uniformiter in directum, nisi quatenus a viribus impressis cogitur statum illum mutare.

Rojectilia perseverant in motibus suis nisi quatenus a resistentia aeris retardantur & vi gravitatis impelluntur deorsum. Trochus, cujus partes cohærendo perpetuo retrahunt sese a motibus rectilineis, non cessat rotari nisi quatenus ab aere re-

Lex. III.

Actioni contrariam semper & æqualem esse reactionem : sive corporum duorum actiones in se mutuo semper esse æquales & in partes contrarias dirigi.

Quicquid premit vel trahit alterum, tantundem ab eo premitur vel trahitur. Siquis lapidem digito premit, premitur & hujus digitus a lapide. Si equus lapidem funi alligatum trahit, retrahetur etiam & equus æqualiter in lapidem: nam funis utrinq; distentus eodem relaxandi se conatu urgebit Equum versus lapidem, ac lapidem versus equum, tantumq; impediet progressum unius quantum promovet progressum alterius. Si corpus aliquod in corpus aliud impingens, motum ejus vi sua quomodocunq; mutaverit, idem quoque vicissim in motu proprio eandem mutationem in partem contrariam vi alterius (ob æqualitatem pressionis mutuæ) subibit. His actionibus æquales fiunt mutationes non velocitatum sed motuum, (scilicet in corporibus non aliunde impeditis :) Mutationes enim velocitatum, in contrarias itidem partes factæ, quia motus æqualiter mutantur, sunt corporibus reciproce proportionales.

>> Chapter 17   1450–1750

The Renaissance, New Sciences, and Religious Wars in Europe

Though less celebrated than many of her male contemporaries, one of the most remarkable scientific minds of the seventeenth century was Maria Cunitz (ca. 1607–1664). Under the tutorship of her father, a physician, she became accomplished in six languages (Hebrew, Greek, Latin, Italian, French, and Polish), the humanities, and the sciences. For a number of years, while the Thirty Years' War (1618–1648) raged in Germany and her home province of Silesia, Cunitz and her Protestant family sought refuge in a Cistercian monastery in neighboring Catholic Poland. There, under difficult living conditions, she wrote *Urania propitia* (*Companion to Urania*), in praise of the Greek muse and patron of astronomy. When the family returned to Silesia after the war, Cunitz lost her scientific papers and instruments in a fire, but she continued to devote her life to science through her careful astronomical observations.

Cunitz's book is a popularization of the astronomical tables of Johannes Kepler (1571–1630), the major scientific innovator remembered today for his discovery of the elliptical trajectories of the planets. Cunitz's book makes corrections in Kepler's tables and offers simplified calculations of star positions. Writing in both Latin and German, she published it privately

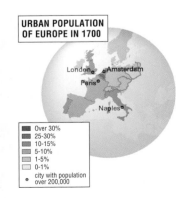

URBAN POPULATION OF EUROPE IN 1700

London Amsterdam
Paris
Naples

- Over 30%
- 25-30%
- 10-15%
- 5-10%
- 1-5%
- 0-1%
- • city with population over 200,000

ABOVE: In his *Principia Mathematica*, first published in 1687, Isaac Newton (1643–1727) unified physics and astronomy into a single mathematic system.

in 1650. It was generally well received, although there were a few detractors who found it hard to believe that a woman could succeed in the sciences. Whatever injustice was done to her during her lifetime, today the scientific community has made amends. A crater on Venus has been named after her, and a statue of her stands in the town where she grew up.

Cunitz lived in a time when Western Christianity had entered the age of early global interaction, from 1450 until 1750. During most of this time, Europe remained institutionally similar to the other parts of the world, especially the Middle East, India, China, and Japan. Rulers throughout Eurasia governed by divine grace. All large states followed patterns of political centralization. Their urban populations were nowhere more than 20 percent, and their economies depended on the productivity of agriculture. As research on China, the Middle East, and India during 1450–1750 has shown, there was no "great divergence" in the patterns of political organization, social formation, and economic production between Western Christianity and the other religious civilizations until around 1750.

Culturally, however, northwestern Europe began to move in a different direction from Islamic, Hindu, Neo-Confucian, and Buddhist civilizations after 1500. New developments in the sciences and philosophy in England, France, the Netherlands, and parts of Germany initiated new cultural patterns for which there was no equivalent in the other parts of Eurasia, including southern Europe. As significant as these patterns were, for almost the entire span of time between 1500 and 1750 the new mathematized sciences remained limited to a few hundred and later to a few thousand educated persons, largely outside the ruling classes. Their ideas and outlooks diverged substantially from those represented by the Catholic and Protestant ruling classes and resulted frequently in tensions or, in a few cases, even repression of scientists by the authorities. The new scientific and intellectual culture broadened into a mass movement only after 1750. The subsequent Industrial Revolution of modernity was rooted in this movement.

Thee European Renaissance, Baroque, and New Sciences formed a cultural sequence that broke with much that had been inherited from medieval times. It began with the appropriation of the Greek and Roman cultural heritage, allegedly absent from the Middle Ages, by a small educated elite. In their enthusiasm for all things Greek and Roman, however, the members of this elite overestimated the extent of their break from the Middle Ages. In today's view from a greater distance, we think of this break as far less radical, with much in culture remaining unchanged. Many centuries were needed before the new cultural pattern initiated by Renaissance, Baroque, and the New Sciences became a general phenomenon.

Seeing Patterns

≫ What were the reasons for the cultural change that began in Europe with the Renaissance around 1400? In which ways were the subsequent patterns of cultural change different from those in the other religious civilizations of Eurasia?

≫ When and how did the mathematization of the sciences begin, and how did it gain popularity in northwestern Europe? Why is the popularization of the sciences important for understanding the period 1500–1750?

≫ What were the patterns of centralized state formation and transformation in the period 1400–1750? How did the Protestant Reformation and religious wars modify these patterns?

Similarly, the political and social changes of the period 1400–1750 have to be balanced against the inherited continuities. The rise of firearm-equipped armies of foot soldiers was a new phenomenon, but the use of these infantries by rulers to further increase their centralizing powers was an inheritance from the Middle Ages. The idea of a religious return to the roots of Christianity, pursued by the leaders of the Protestant Reformation, can also be traced back to the Middle Ages. When rulers used the Reformation for their centralizing ambitions, however, the ensuing religious wars became a new phenomenon. Overall, the seeds of an eventual departure of Western Christianity from the general patterns of agrarian–urban society were planted around 1500. But for a long time thereafter these seeds remained largely underground, and the "great divergence" from the agrarian–urban patterns of Islamic, Hindu, and Chinese civilizations began only after 1750.

Cultural Transformations: Renaissance, Baroque, and New Sciences

The **Renaissance** was a period of cultural transformation which in the fifteenth century followed the scholastic Middle Ages in Western Christianity. In many ways, the Renaissance was an outgrowth of scholasticism, but its thinkers and artists saw themselves as having broken away from scholastic precepts. They considered their period a time of "rebirth" (which is the literal meaning of "renaissance" in French). During this period they were powerfully influenced by the writings of Greek and Hellenistic-Roman authors who had been unknown during the scholastic age. In the sixteenth century, the Renaissance gave way to the Baroque in the arts and the **New Sciences**. Thus, the Renaissance was just the first of a sequence of periods of cultural transformation following each other in rapid succession.

Renaissance: "Rebirth" of culture based on new publications and translations of Greek, Hellenistic, and Roman authors whose writings were previously unknown in Western Christianity.

New Sciences: Mathematized sciences, such as physics, introduced in the 1500s.

The Renaissance and Baroque Arts

Beginning around 1400 in Italy and spreading later through northwestern Europe, an outpouring of learning, scholarship, and art came from theologians, philosophers, writers, painters, architects, and musical composers. These thinkers and artists benefited from Greek and Hellenistic-Roman texts which scholars had discovered recently in mostly Eastern Christian archives in Byzantium. In addition, in the early fifteenth century Byzantine scholars from Constantinople arrived in Italy with further newly rediscovered texts, which had a profound impact. The emerging cultures of the Renaissance and Baroque were creative adaptations of those Greek and Hellenistic-Roman writings to the cultural heritage of Western Christianity. Out of this vibrant mixture arose the overarching movement of **humanism**.

Humanism: Intellectual movement focusing on human culture, in such fields as philosophy, philology, and literature, and based on the corpus of Greek and Roman texts.

New Manuscripts and Printing   Eastern Christian Byzantium experienced a cultural revival between its recovery in 1261 from the Latin interlude and its collapse in 1453 when the Muslim Ottomans conquered Constantinople. During this revival, scholars engaged in a vigorous debate about the compatibility of Plato and Aristotle with each other. The debate made Italian scholars fully aware of how much of Greek literature was still absent from Western Christianity. For example, at the time they possessed just two of Plato's 44 dialogues. Italians invited about a dozen Eastern Christian scholars, who brought manuscripts to Florence, Rome, and Venice to translate and teach. Their students became fluent in Greek and translated Hesiod and Homer, some Greek tragedies and comedies, Plato and the Neo-Platonists, the remaining works of Aristotle, Hellenistic scientific texts, and the Greek church fathers. Western Christianity had finally absorbed the ancient heritage.

The work of translation was helped by the development of a more rounded, simplified Latin script, which replaced the angled, dense Gothic script used since the 1150s. In addition, the costly vellum (scraped leather) writing material on which many manuscripts had been laboriously written was replaced by cheaper paper, which had been introduced from Islamic Spain in the early twelfth century and had become common in the rest of Europe by 1400. Experimentation in the 1430s with movable metal typeface resulted in the innovation of the printing press. A half-century later, with more than 1,000 printers all over Europe and more than 8 million books in the hands of readers, a veritable printing revolution had taken place in Europe.

Philology and Political Theory   The flood of new manuscripts and the renewed examination of existing manuscripts in libraries encouraged the study of Greek, Latin, and Hebrew philology. Scholars trained in these languages edited critical texts based on multiple manuscripts. The best known among these philologists was the Dutchman Desiderius Erasmus (1466–1536), who published an edition of the Greek and Latin New Testaments in 1516. Critical textual research, which became central to subsequent scholarship, can trace its foundations to the Renaissance.

Another type of critical stance emerged as a central element in political thought. In *The Prince*, Niccolò Machiavelli (1469–1527) reflected on the ruthless political competition among the princes of Europe for dominance over his hopelessly disunited native Italy. What Italy needed in his own generation, Machiavelli argued, was a unifier who possessed what Aristotle discussed in Book 5 of his *Politics*, namely a person of intuitive strength, valor, or indomitable spirit (Italian, *virtù*) to take the proper steps—subtle or brutal—when political success was to be achieved. Many Renaissance scholars preferred Plato, but Machiavelli remained faithful to Aristotle, the superior political realist—an Aristotle held in high esteem centuries later by the American founding fathers.

Bookseller. By 1600, the increase in literacy levels combined with widespread printing of books, pamphlets, and tracts had made people like this itinerant bookseller in Italy a commonplace sight throughout much of Europe.

interactive timeline

| 1506–1558 Reign of King Charles V of Spain | 1517 Martin Luther posts his 95 theses; beginning of Protestant Reformation | 1545 Beginning of Catholic Reformation | 1565–1620 Dutch Protestant war of liberation from Spain | 1589–1610 Reign of King Henry IV of France |

| 1514 First formulation of the heliocentric solar system by Nicolaus Copernicus | 1524–1525 German Peasants' War | 1562–1598 French war of religion | 1571–1630 Johannes Kepler, discoverer of the elliptical paths of the planets |

| 1556–1598 Reign of King Philip II of Spain, the Netherlands, and the Americas | 1618–1648 Thirty Years' War in Germany | 1643–1715 King Louis XIV of France | 1688 "Glorious Revolution" in England | 1740–1786 Frederick II, builder of the centralizing state of Prussia |

| 1604 Galileo Galilei's first formulation of the mathematical law of falling bodies | 1639–1660 Religious wars and aftermath in England, Scotland, and Ireland | 1687 Isaac Newton unifies physics and astronomy | 1690 Denis Papin's first steam engine |

Albrecht Dürer, *The Fall of Man (Adam and Eve)*, 1504

The Renaissance Arts   In Italy, the reception of the new texts of the fifteenth century was paralleled by a new artistic way of looking at the Roman past and the natural world. The first artists to adopt this perspective were the sculptor Donatello (ca. 1386–1466) and the architect Filippo Brunelleschi (1377–1446), who received their inspiration from Roman imperial statues and ruins. The artistic triumvirate of the high Italian Renaissance was composed of Leonardo da Vinci (1452–1519), Michelangelo (1475–1564), and Raphael (1483–1520). Inspired by the Italian creative outburst, the Renaissance flourished also in Germany, the Netherlands, and France, making it a Europe-wide phenomenon (see Source 17.4).

The earliest musical composers of the Renaissance in the first half of the fifteenth century were Platonists, who considered music a part of a well-rounded education. The difficulty, however, was that the music of the Greeks or Romans was completely unknown. A partial solution for this difficulty was found through emphasizing the relationship between the word—that is, rhetoric—and music. In the sixteenth century this emphasis coincided with the Protestant and Catholic demand for liturgical music, such as hymns, masses, and *madrigals* (verses sung by unaccompanied voices). A pioneer of this music was the Italian composer Giovanni Pierluigi da Palestrina (ca. 1525–1594), who represented Renaissance music at its most exquisite.

The theater was a relatively late expression of the Renaissance. The popular mystery, passion, and morality plays from the centuries prior to 1400 continued in Catholic countries. In Italy, in the course of the fifteenth century, the *commedia dell'arte* (a secular popular theater) emerged, often using masked actors in plays of forbidden love, jealousy, and adultery. In England during the sixteenth century the popular traveling theater troupes became stationary and professional, attracting playwrights who composed more elaborate plays. Sponsored by the aristocracy and the Elizabethan court, playwrights wrote hundreds of scripts—some 600 are still extant—beginning in the 1580s. The best known among these playwrights was William Shakespeare (1564–1616), who also acted in his tragedies and comedies.

The Baroque Arts   The Renaissance gave way around 1600 to the Baroque, which dominated the arts until about 1750. Two factors influenced its emergence. First, the Protestant Reformation, Catholic Reformation, and religious wars changed the nature of patronage, on which architects, painters, and musicians depended. Many Protestant churches, opposed to imagery as incompatible with their view of early Christianity, did not sponsor artists for the adornment of their buildings with religious art. Wealthy urban merchants, often Protestant, stepped into the breach but avoided paintings with religious themes, preferring instead secular portraits, still lifes, village scenes, and landscapes.

Second, the predilection for Renaissance measurement, balance, and restraint gave way in both Catholic and Protestant regions to greater spontaneity and dramatic effect. Even more pronounced was the parallel shift in church and palace architecture to a "baroque" voluptuousness of forms and decorations, exemplified by Bavarian and Austrian Catholic churches, the Versailles Palace, and St. Paul's Cathedral in London, all completed between 1670 and 1750. Baroque music, benefitting from ample church and palace patronage and exemplified by the Italian Antonio Vivaldi (1678–1741) and the German Johann Sebastian Bach (1685–1750), experienced a veritable explosion of unrestrained exploration.

Renaissance Art. Brunelleschi's cupola for the cathedral of Florence, completed in 1436, was one of the greatest achievements of the early Renaissance (*a*). Raphael's *School of Athens* (1509–1510) depicts some 50 philosophers and scientists, with Plato (in red tunic) and Aristotle (blue) in the center of the painting (*b*). Peter Brueghel's *The Harvesters* (1565) shows peasants taking a lunch break (*c*).

image analysis

The New Sciences

Eastern Christian scholars invited from Byzantium to Florence in Italy during the first half of the fifteenth century brought with them Hellenistic scientific treatises, which aroused great interest among Italian Renaissance scholars. Battle lines were drawn between those scholars who continued to adhere to the Aristotelian-scholastic scientific method, even though this method had undergone significant changes during the 1300s, and scholars (such as Copernicus) who were more interested in newly translated mathematical, astronomical, and geographical texts. Eventually, in the 1600s, two scientific pioneers—Galileo and Newton—abandoned much of the *qualitative* scientific method of Aristotelian scholasticism in favor of the quantitative, *mathematized* science of physics. In the eighteenth century, Newton's unified astronomical-physical-based science of a mechanical, deterministic universe became the foundation for the development of modern scientific–industrial society.

Copernicus's Incipient New Science   According to Aristotle, nature was composed of the four elements of (in ascending order of lightness) earth, water, air, and fire. In astronomical terms, he thought that these elements formed distinct layers, together shaping the world. In geographical terms, however, it was obvious to Aristotle that not all earth was submerged by water. He knew that Europe, Asia, and Africa formed a contiguous land mass of continents above water. Aristotle did not resolve the contradiction in his writings, but subsequent medieval scholars sought to find a resolution. They developed the theory of the "floating apple," whereby they assumed that most of earth was submerged, and a minimal protruding amount—the three continents—was surrounded everywhere by water.

During the Renaissance, the *Geography*, written by the Hellenistic cosmographer Ptolemy (see Chapter 5), became available from Constantinople. This important work proposed the geographical concept of a globe composed of a single sphere of intermingled earth and water. When Nicolaus Copernicus (1473–1543) appeared on the scene, scholars were still grappling with these competing theories of the floating apple and the intermingled earth–water spheres.

Copernicus was born in Torun, a German-founded city which had come under Polish rule a few years before his birth. He began his studies at the University of Kraków, the only eastern European school to offer courses in astronomy. During the years 1495–1504, he continued his studies—of canon law, medicine, geography, cosmography, and astrology—at Italian universities. In 1500 he briefly taught mathematics in Rome and perhaps read Greek astronomical texts translated from Arabic in the library of the Vatican. Eventually, Copernicus graduated with a degree in canon law and took up an administrative position at the cathedral of Torun, which allowed him time to pursue astronomical research.

Sometime between 1507 and 1514 Copernicus realized that the discovery of the Americas in 1492 provided a decisive empirical proof for the theory of the world as a single earth–water sphere. During this time, it is likely that he saw the new world map by the German cartographer Martin Waldseemüller (ca. 1470–1520), which made him aware of the existence of the Americas as hitherto unknown inhabited lands on the other side of the world. Much more land protruded from the water and was not limited to the interconnected land mass of Eurasia–Africa, than had been previously assumed in the floating-apple theory.

Copernicus's heliocentric universe

As a result, this theory became questionable. Copernicus firmly espoused the Ptolemaic theory of the single intermingled water–earth sphere with mountainous protrusions. A globe with well-distributed water and land masses is a perfect body that moves in perfect circular paths, so he argued further, and formulated his hypothesis, according to which the earth is a body that has the same appearance and performs the same motions as the other bodies in the planetary system. The discovery of the Americas, therefore, can be considered as the empirical trigger that convinced Copernicus of the correctness of his trigonometric calculations, which removed the earth from the center of the planetary system and made it revolve around the sun.

Galileo's Mathematical Physics   During the near century between the births of Copernicus and Galileo Galilei (1564–1642), mathematics—with its two branches of Greek geometry and Arabic algebra—improved considerably. Euclid's *Elements*, badly translated from Arabic in the late twelfth century, with a garbled definition of proportions, was retranslated correctly from the original Greek in 1543. Shortly thereafter, the new translation in 1544 of a text on floating and descending bodies by the Hellenistic scholar Archimedes (287–212 BCE) attracted intense scholarly attention. The text, unknown to the Muslims, had been translated from the Greek in the thirteenth century but subsequently remained unappreciated, on account of its incompatibility with the then-prevailing Aristotelian scholasticism.

What was required for a scholar critical of scholastic traditions was to combine geometry, algebra, and Archimedean physics. In 1604, that scholar appeared in the person of Galileo, when he formulated his famous mathematical "law of falling bodies." It is true that this law had been foreshadowed by the reflections of scholastic scholars at the University of Oxford's Merton College and the University of Paris in

Waldseemüller's 1507 World Map. The German mapmaker Martin Waldseemüller was the first western Christian to draw a world map which included the newly discovered Americas. He gave them the name "America" after the Italian explorer Amerigo Vespucci (1454–1512), who was the first to state that the Americas were a separate land mass, unconnected to Asia. The single copy of Waldseemüller's map still extant is among the holdings of the US Library of Congress.

image analysis

the 1300s. But these earlier scholars reflected on the logical and/or geometric properties of motion only "according to imagination." Galileo was the scholar who systematically combined imagination with empirical research and experimentation and thereby became the founder of what we now call the (mathematized) New Sciences.

Running Afoul of the Church   Galileo was not only a physicist but also a first-rate astronomer, one of the first to use a telescope, which had been recently invented in Flanders. On the basis of his astronomical work, in 1610 he received a richly endowed appointment as chief mathematician and philosopher at the court of the Medici, the ruling family of Florence. But his increasing fame also attracted the enmity of the Catholic Church.

As a proponent of Copernican heliocentrism, Galileo seemed to contradict the passage in the Hebrew Bible where God recognized the motion of the sun around the earth. (In Joshua 10:12–13, God stopped the sun's revolution for a day, in order to allow the Israelites to win a critical battle against the Amorites.) In contrast to the more tolerant pope at the time of Copernicus, the Roman Inquisition favored a strictly literal interpretation of this passage, which implied that God had halted the sun's motion around the earth. In 1632 Galileo found himself condemned to house arrest and forced to make a public repudiation of heliocentrism (see Source 17.5).

The condemnation of Galileo had a chilling effect on scientists in the southern European countries where the Catholic Reformation was dominant (see p. 499). Prudent patrons reduced their stipends to scientists, and scientific research subsequently declined. During the seventeenth century, interest in the New Sciences

Galileo's views of the moon

shifted increasingly to France, Germany, the Netherlands, and England. In these countries, no single church authority, of either the Catholic or the Protestant variety, was sufficiently dominant until the end of the seventeenth century to enforce the literal understanding of scripture. As a result, these countries produced numerous mathematicians, astronomers, physicists, and inventors, Catholic as well as Protestant. The New Scientists in northern Europe had a certain liberty that their southern colleagues lacked. It was this relative intellectual freedom, not any great sympathy on the part of religious authorities for the New Sciences, which allowed the latter to flourish, especially in the Netherlands and England.

Iberian Natural Sciences   The shift of New Sciences research to northwestern Europe notwithstanding, southern European countries such as Spain were well situated to make substantial scientific contributions, even if not in the New Sciences. Hundreds of botanists, geographers, ethnographers, physicians, and metallurgists fanned out across the new colonies to take advantage of what their northern colleagues in the New Sciences could not do: They researched the new plants, diseases, peoples, and mineral resources of the New World, Africa, and Asia with the traditional descriptive and qualitative methods of the natural sciences and accumulated a voluminous amount of knowledge. For long periods, the Habsburg monarch kept the manuscripts with this knowledge under wraps, fearful that his colonial competitors would benefit from them—hence it was only through recent research efforts that the Iberian contributions to the sciences in the 1500s and 1600s have become more widely known.

Isaac Newton's Mechanics   In the middle of the English struggles between the Protestants and the Catholic/Catholicizing Stuart monarchs, Isaac Newton (1643–1727) brought the New Sciences of Copernicus and Galileo to their culmination. As a professor at the University of Cambridge, he worked in the fields of mathematics, optics, astronomy, physics, alchemy, and theology. His primary early contribution was calculus, a new field in mathematics, which he developed at the same time as the German philosopher Gottfried Wilhelm Leibniz (1646–1716). Later in his career, Newton unified the fields of physics and astronomy, establishing the so-called Newtonian synthesis. His *Mathematical Principles of Natural Philosophy*, published in 1687, was the towering achievement of the New Sciences. It established a deterministic universe following mathematical rules and formed the basis of science until the early twentieth century, when Albert Einstein's relativity theory superseded Newtonianism.

The New Sciences and Their Social Impact

Scientists in the seventeenth century were in close communication with each other. They met in scientific societies or residential salons. Popularizers introduced an increasingly large public to the New Sciences. Scientists carried out experiments with constantly improved scientific instruments, such as telescopes, microscopes, thermometers, and barometers. Experience with barometers led technically versatile scientists and engineers to experiment with vacuum chambers and cylinders operating with condensing steam. Experimentation culminated with the invention of the steam engine in England in 1712.

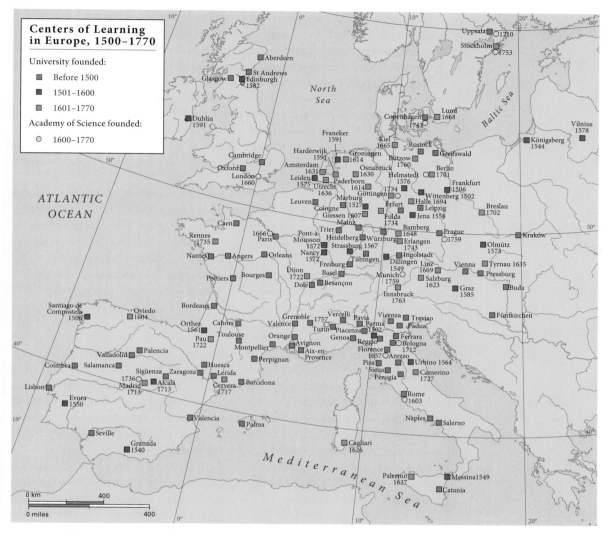

Centers of Learning in Europe, 1500–1770

University founded:
- Before 1500
- 1501–1600
- 1601–1770

Academy of Science founded:
- 1600–1770

MAP **17.1** **Centers of Learning in Europe, 1500–1770.**

map analysis

New Science Societies   When the Catholic Reformation drove the New Sciences to northwestern Europe, the Italian-style academies gave way to chartered scientific societies, such as the Royal Society of London (1660) and the Paris Academy of Sciences (1666). Other countries, like Prussia, Russia, and Sweden, soon followed suit. These societies employed staffs of administrators, co-opted scientists as fellows, held regular discussion meetings, challenged their fellows to answer scientific questions, awarded prizes, and organized field trips and expeditions. They also published transactions, correspondences, and monographs. Many societies attracted thousands of members—famous pioneers, obscure amateurs, technically proficient tinkerers, theoretical mathematicians, daring experimenters, and flighty dreamers—representing an important cross section of seventeenth-century urban society in northwest Europe (see Map 17.1).

Other popularizers were textbook authors and itinerant lecturers who addressed audiences of middle-class amateurs, instrument makers, and specialized craftspeople, especially in England and the Netherlands. Many lecturers toured coffeehouses, urban residences, country estates, and provincial schools. Coffeehouses allowed the literate urban public to meet, read the daily newspapers (first appearing in the early seventeenth century), and exchange ideas. Coffee, introduced from Ethiopia and Yemen via the Ottoman Empire in the sixteenth century, was the preferred nonalcoholic social drink before the arrival of tea in the later eighteenth century. Male urban literacy is estimated to have exceeded 50 percent in England and the Netherlands during this period, although it remained considerably lower in France, Germany, and Italy.

Some lecturers were veritable entrepreneurs of the speaking circuit, teaching a kind of "Newtonianism lite" for ladies and gentlemen with little time or patience for serious study. Other lecturers set up subscriptions for month-long courses. Wealthy businessmen endowed public lectures and supported increasingly elaborate experiments and expensive laboratory equipment. In the first half of the eighteenth century, the New Science triumphed in northwestern Europe in a scientifically and technically interested public of experimenters, engineers, instrument makers, artisans, business people, and lay folk.

Women, Social Salons, and the New Science   Women formed a significant part of this public. In the fields of mathematics and astronomy, Sophie Brahe (1556–1643), sister of the Danish astronomer Tycho Brahe (1546–1601), and Maria Cunitz (see chapter-opening vignette) were the first to make contributions to the new astronomy of Copernicus and Kepler. According to estimates, in the second half of the seventeenth century some 14 percent of German astronomers were women. A dozen particularly prominent female astronomers practiced their science privately in Germany, Poland, the Netherlands, France, and England.

Another institution which helped in the popularization of the New Sciences was the salon. As the well-furnished, elegant living room of an urban residence, the salon was both a domestic chamber and a semipublic meeting place for the urban social elite to engage in conversations, presentations, and experiments. The culture of the salon emerged first in Paris sometime after the closure of the court-centered Palace Academy in the 1580s. Since the Catholic French universities remained committed to Aristotelian scholasticism, the emerging stratum of educated urban aristocrats and middle-class professionals turned to the salons as places to inform themselves about new scientific developments. Furthermore, French universities as well as scientific academies refused to admit women, in contrast to Italian and German institutions. The French salon, therefore, became a bastion of well-placed and respected female scholars.

One outstanding example of French salon science was Gabrielle-Emilie du Châtelet (1706–1749). In her youth, Châtelet fulfilled her marital duties to her husband, the Marquis of Châtelet. She had three children before turning to the sciences. In one of the Paris salons she met François Marie Arouet, known as Voltaire (1694–1778), the eighteenth-century Enlightenment writer, skeptic, satirist, and amateur Newtonian. Châtelet and Voltaire became intimate companions under the benevolent eyes of the marquis at the family estate in Lorraine in northeastern France. Although Voltaire published prolifically, Châtelet eventually outstripped him both in research and scientific understanding. Her lasting achievement was the translation of Newton's *Mathematical Principles* into French, published in 1759.

Discovery of the Vacuum Among the important scientific instruments of the day were telescopes, microscopes, and thermometers. It was the barometer, however, that was the crucial instrument for the exploration of the properties of the vacuum and condensing steam, eventually leading to the invention of the steam engine. The scientist laying the groundwork for the construction of the barometer was Evangelista Torricelli (1608–1647), a mathematician and assistant of Galileo. In collaboration with Florentine engineers, he experimented with mercury-filled glass tubes, demonstrating the existence of atmospheric pressure by the air and of vacuums in the tubes.

A few years later, the French mathematician and philosopher Blaise Pascal (1623–1662) had his brother-in-law haul a mercury barometer up a mountain to demonstrate lower air pressures at higher altitudes. Soon thereafter, scientists discovered the connection between changing atmospheric pressures and the weather, laying the foundations for weather forecasting. The discovery of the vacuum, the existence of which Aristotle had held to be impossible, made a deep impression on the scientific community in the seventeenth century and was an important step toward the practical application of the New Sciences to mechanical engineering in the eighteenth century.

New Scientist. Maria Cunitz is honored today with a sculpture in Świdnica, Poland, where she grew up.

The Steam Engine The French Huguenot scientist and engineer Denis Papin (ca. 1647–1712) took the first crucial step from the vacuum chamber to the steam engine. In 1690, when he was a court engineer and professor in Germany, Papin constructed a cylinder with a piston. Weights, via a cord and two pulleys, held the piston at the top of the cylinder. When heated, water in the bottom of the cylinder turned into steam. When subsequently cooled through the injection of water, the steam condensed, forcing the piston down and lifting the weights up. Papin spent his last years (1707–1712) in London, where the Royal Society of London held discussions of his papers, thereby alerting engineers, craftspeople, and entrepreneurs in England to the steam engine as a labor-saving machine. In 1712, the mechanic Thomas Newcomen built the first steam engine to pump water from coal mine shafts.

Altogether, it took a little over a century, from 1604 (Galileo) to 1712 (Newcomen), for Europeans to apply the New Sciences to engineering—that is, the construction of the steam engine. Had it not been for the New Sciences, this engine—based on contracting steam—would not have been invented. (Hero of Alexandria, who invented steam-driven machines in the first century CE, made use of the expanding force of steam.) Prior to 1600, mechanical inventions—such as the

Vacuum Power. In 1672, the mayor of Magdeburg, the New Scientist Otto von Guericke, demonstrated the experiment that made him a pioneer in the understanding of the physical properties of the vacuum. In the presence of German Emperor Ferdinand III, two teams of horses were unable to pull the two sealed hemispheres apart. Guericke had created a vacuum by pumping out the air from the two sealed copper spheres.

wheel, the compass, the stern rudder, and the firearm—were constructed by anonymous tinkerers with a good commonsense understanding of nature. In 1700, engineers had to have at least a basic understanding of mathematics and such abstract physical phenomena as inertia, gravity, vacuums, and condensing steam if they wanted to build a steam engine or other complex machinery.

The New Sciences: Philosophical Interpretations

The New Sciences engendered a pattern of radically new intellectual, religious, and political thinking, which evolved in the course of the seventeenth and early eighteenth centuries. This thought was largely incompatible with the inherited medieval scholasticism. It eventually evolved into a powerful instrument of critique of Christian doctrine and the constitutional order of the absolutist states. Initially, the new philosophical interpretations were confined to a few thinkers, but through the new concept of the social contract in the course of the 1700s they became a potent political force.

Descartes's New Philosophy   After the replacement of qualitative with mathematical physics, brought about by Galileo with his law of descending bodies, the question arose whether Aristotelian philosophy and Catholic theology were still adequate for the understanding of reality. New Scientists perceived the need to start philosophizing and theologizing from scratch. The first major New Scientist who, in his own judgment, started a radical reconsideration of philosophy from the ground up was the Frenchman René Descartes (1596–1650). He earned a degree in law, traveling widely after graduation. In the service of the Dutch and Bavarian courts, he bore witness to the beginning of the Thirty Years' War and its atrocities committed in the name of religious doctrines. During the war, he spent two decades in the Netherlands, studying and teaching the New Sciences. His principal innovation in mathematics was the discovery that geometry could be converted through algebra into analytic geometry.

Descartes was shocked by the condemnation of Galileo and decided to abandon all traditional propositions and doctrines of the church as well as Aristotelianism.

Realizing that his common sense (that is, the five senses of seeing, hearing, touching, smelling, and tasting) was unreliable, he determined that the only reliable body of knowledge was thought, especially mathematical thought. As a person capable of thought, he concluded—bypassing his unreliable senses—that he existed: "I think, therefore I am" (*cogito ergo sum*). A further conclusion from this argument was that he was composed of two radically different substances, a material substance consisting of his body (that is, his senses) and another, immaterial substance consisting of his thinking mind. According to Descartes, body and mind, although joined through consciousness, belonged to two profoundly different realms of reality.

Descartes, selections from *A Discourse on Method* (1637)

Variations on Descartes's New Philosophy Descartes's radical distinction between body and mind stimulated a lively debate among a growing circle of philosophers of the New Sciences. Was this distinction only conceptual while reality was experienced as a unified whole? If the dualism was real as well as conceptual, which substance was more fundamental, sensual bodily experience or mental activity, as the creator of the concepts of experience? The answers of three philosophers— Baruch Spinoza, Thomas Hobbes, and John Locke—stood out in the 1600s. They set the course for two major directions of philosophy during the so-called Enlightenment of the 1700s (see Chapter 23), one Continental European and the other Anglo-American.

For Baruch Spinoza (1632–1677), Descartes's distinction between body and mind was to be understood only in a conceptual sense. In our daily experience we do not encounter either bodies or minds but persons endowed with both together. He therefore abandoned Descartes's distinction and developed a complicated philosophical system that sought to integrate Galilean nature with the ideas of God, the Good in ethics, and the Just in politics into a unified whole. The Jewish community of Amsterdam, into which he had been born, excommunicated him for heresy, since he seemed to make God immanent to the world. But he enjoyed a high esteem among fellow philosophers on the continent who appreciated his effort to moderate Descartes's radical mind–body distinction.

Both Thomas Hobbes (1588–1679) and John Locke (1632–1704) not only accepted Descartes's radical distinction; they furthermore made the body the fundamental reality and the mind a dependent function. Consequently, they focused on the bodily passions, not reason, as the principal human character trait. For Hobbes, the violent passions of aggression and fear were constitutive of human nature. He speculated that individuals in the primordial state of nature were engaged in a "war of all against all." To survive, they forged a social contract in which they transferred all power to a sovereign. Hobbes's famous book *Leviathan* (1651) can be read as a political theory of absolute rule, but his ideas of a social contract and transfer of power nevertheless imply a sprinkling of constitutionalism.

frontispiece to *Leviathan*

Locke, who lived through the less violent phases of the English religious wars, focused on the more benign bodily passion of acquisitiveness. Primordial individuals, so he argued, engaged as equals in a social contract for the purpose of erecting a government that protected their properties and, more generally, established a civil society governed by law. With Hobbes and Locke a line of new thought came to its conclusion, leading from Galileo's mathematized physics and Descartes's two substances to the ideas of absolutism as well as democratic constitutionalism.

Locke, *An Essay Concerning Human Understanding* (1690)

Mapping the World

The world—its shape, its size, its orientation—has been rendered so thoroughly knowable by modern technology that we fail to appreciate how long it took to map the planet scientifically.

In 1400, no accurate map of the world existed anywhere on the planet. Prior to the first Portuguese sailing expeditions down the west coast of Africa in the 1420s and 1430s, mariners all over the world relied on local knowledge of winds, waves, and stars to navigate. The Portuguese were the first to use science to sail, adapting highly sophisticated scholarship in trigonometry, astronomy, and solar timekeeping developed in previous centuries by Jewish and Muslim scientists in Iberia.

Crucial to this novel approach was latitude. Mathematically challenging, fixing exact latitude required precise calculations of the daily changes in the path of the sun relative to the earth and determination of the exact height of the sun. The invention of the nautical astrolabe in 1497 by the Jewish scientist Abraham Zacuto aided this process tremendously. Determining longitude was also important, and Jewish scientists in Portugal adapted a method based on the pioneering work of the Islamic astronomer al-Biruni (973–1048).

Although primarily resting on achievements in astronomical observation and measurement in the Jewish and Islamic scientific traditions, the new maps of the fifteenth century also drew on an innovation from another part of the world: the compass. Originating in China, the compass was first widely used as a navigational

Centralizing States and Religious Upheavals

The pattern of the centralizing state transforming the institutional structures of society was characteristic not only of the Ottoman and Habsburg Empires during 1450–1750, as we have seen in Chapter 16, but also of other countries of Europe, the Middle East, and India. The financial requirements for sustaining such a state required everywhere a reorganization of the relationship among rulers, ruling classes, and regional as well as local forces. The Protestant Reformation and religious wars slowed the pattern of central state formation, but once the religious fervor died down, two types of states emerged: the French, Russian, and Prussian landed centralizing state and the Dutch and English naval centralizing state.

The Rise of Centralized Kingdoms

The shift from feudal mounted and armored knights to firearm-equipped professional infantries led to the emergence of states whose rulers sought to strengthen the power of their administrations. Rulers sought to centralize state power, collect higher taxes to subsidize their infantries, and curb the decentralizing forces of the nobility, cities, and other local institutions. Not all autonomous units (such as city-states, city-leagues, and religious orders dating to the previous period, 600–1450) were able to survive the race to centralization. A winnowing process occurred during 1450–1550, which left only a few territorially coherent kingdoms in control of European politics.

instrument by Muslim sailors during the twelfth century. In the thirteenth century, mapmakers in the Mediterranean began to include compasses on portolans, or nautical charts, enabling sailors to follow their direction on a map.

With an accurate science for fixing latitude and improved knowledge for longitude (determining precise longitude would not be achieved until 1774 with the invention of the marine chronometer), the science of cartography was transformed in the fifteenth and sixteenth centuries. Any place on earth could be mapped mathematically in relation to any other place, and the direction in which one place lay in relation to another could be plotted using compass lines. By 1500 mapmakers could locate any newly discovered place in the world on a map, no matter how remote.

Portolan by Pedro Reinel. Drawn in 1504 by the great Portuguese cartographer Pedro Reinel (ca. 1462–ca. 1542), this nautical chart (portolan) shows compass lines and is the earliest known map to include lines of latitude.

Questions

- How were adaptations from various cultural traditions essential to the transformation of cartography in the fifteenth and sixteenth centuries?

- How are developments in cartography in this time period an example of the shift from descriptive science to mathematical science?

The Demographic Curve   Following the demographic disaster of the Black Death in 1348 and its many subsequent cycles, the population of the European states expanded again after 1470. It reached its pre-1348 levels around 1550, with some 85 million inhabitants (not counting the Spanish Habsburg and Ottoman Empires). The population continued to grow until about 1600 (90 million), when it entered a half-century of stagnation during the coldest and wettest period in recorded history, the Little Ice Age (1550–1750).

During 1650–1750, the population rose slowly at a moderate rate from 105 to 140 million. In 1750, France (28 million) and Russia (21 million) were the most populous countries, followed by Germany (18 million), Italy (15 million), Poland (13 million), England (7 million), and the Netherlands and Sweden (2 million each). While the population figures of the individual countries for the most part bore little resemblance to their political importance during 1450–1750, as we shall see, the overall figures for Europe demonstrate that Western Christianity had risen by 1750 to the status of demographic equivalence to the two leading religious civilizations of India (155 million) and China (225 million).

A Heritage of Decentralization   Bracketed between the two empires of the Ottomans and Habsburgs at either geographical end, Western Christian Europe during the second half of the fifteenth century was a quilt of numerous independent or autonomous units, including the nascent centralizing kingdoms of France and England, the Hanseatic League of trading cities, the territory ruled by the Catholic crusading order of Teutonic Knights, and the small kingdoms of Denmark, Sweden,

Norway, Poland–Lithuania, Bohemia, and Hungary. It furthermore comprised the principalities and cities of Germany, the duchy of Burgundy, the Alpine republic of Switzerland, and the city-states of Italy. At the northeastern periphery was the Grand Duchy of Moscow, representing Eastern Christianity after the fall of Byzantium to the Ottomans in 1453. In this quilt, the majority of units competed vigorously with each other, seeking either to exploit the new possibilities which armies of mercenaries with firearms gave them or to survive as best as possible with just a handful of mercenaries.

TABLE 17.1 Victims of State Centralization in Europe, 1450–1600.

- Duchy of Burgundy, absorbed by France, 1477
- City-states Milan, Naples, taken by France 1499–1501
- Rest of Italy, except Venice, taken by Spain, 1550s
- Kingdoms of Bohemia and rump Hungary taken by Austrian Habsburgs, 1526; majority of Hungary to the Ottoman Empire
- Calais, last toehold of England on continent, to France, 1558
- Hanseatic League of ports in northern Europe, centered on the Free Cities of Lübeck and Hamburg, de facto dissolved 1669
- Duchy of Prussia lost by Teutonic Order to the kingdom of Poland, 1525; Prussia as fief of the kingdom of Poland, under its own dynasty of the Hohenzollern
- Prussia united with Brandenburg, 1618; Hohenzollerns as Polish vassals in Prussia and Habsburg vassals in Brandenburg
- Sweden independent from Denmark, 1523

Military and Administrative Capacities   In the course of the sixteenth century, some kingdoms turned their mercenary troops into standing armies and stationed them in star-shaped forts. These forts were a fifteenth-century Italian innovation that made walls more resistant to artillery fire and trapped attackers in cross fires. Habsburg imperial as well as Dutch troops introduced the line infantry in the course of the sixteenth century. In this formation, three- to six-deep lines of musketeers advanced on a broad front toward the enemy, with the front line firing, stepping back to reload, and making room for the next line to step forward and repeat the actions. Since the line formation required extensive peacetime drills and maneuvers, the regimental system came into use. Soldiers formed permanent regiments and wore standardized, multicolored uniforms.

The French-invented flintlock gradually replaced the matchlock musket during 1620–1630, the advantage being that the flint produced a spark more quickly than the wick fuse. Similarly, during 1660–1700 the French introduced and gradually improved the bayonet—a sharp knife fixed to the end of the muzzle. With the appearance of the bayonet, pikemen, equipped with thrusting spears-cum-battle-axes for the protection of musketeers in hand-to-hand combat, were phased out. By 1750, armies in the larger European countries were both more uniform in their armaments and larger, increasing from a few thousand to tens of thousands of soldiers (see Map 17.2).

The military forces devoured copious amounts of tax money. Accordingly, taxes expanded substantially during the period 1450–1550. But rulers could not raise land, head, and commerce taxes without the formal (in assemblies) or informal (based on customs and traditions) assent of the ruling classes and cities. Similarly, villagers voted with their feet when taxes became too oppressive. The taxation limits were reached in most European countries in the mid-sixteenth century, and for the next two centuries rulers could raise additional finances only to the detriment of

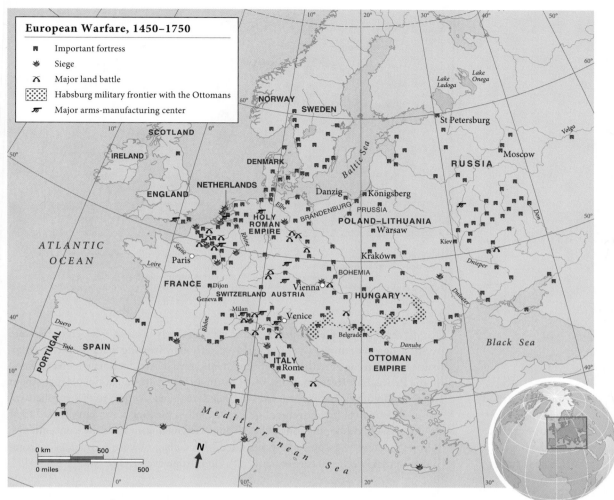

MAP **17.2 European Warfare, 1450–1750.**

their previously acquired central powers, such as by borrowing from merchants and selling offices. The Netherlands was an exception. Only there did the urban population rise from 10 to 40 percent, willing to pay higher taxes on expanded urban manufactures and commercial suburban farming. The Dutch government also derived substantial revenues from charters granted to armed overseas trading companies. Given the severe limits on revenue-raising measures in most of Europe, the eighteenth century saw a general deterioration of state finances, which eventually became major contributing factors to the American and French Revolutions.

The Protestant Reformation, State Churches, and Independent Congregations

Parallel to the growing centralism of the kings, the popes restored the central role of the Vatican in the church hierarchy, after the devastating Great Schism of competing papal lines (1305–1415). Outwardly, the popes displayed this restoration through expensive Vatican construction projects that aroused considerable criticism outside

Musketeers. These pictures from an English illustrated drill manual demonstrate the steps by which a seventeenth-century musketeer "makes ready" his weapon, typically in less than 30 seconds. In battle, a sergeant would stand alongside each company of musketeers, organizing its movements and volley fire. Once a rank of musketeers had discharged its weapons, it would move out of the way for another rank to fire. If combat was joined at close quarters, the musketeers would use their rifle butts as clubs.

Protestant Reformation: Broad movement to reform the Roman Catholic Church, the beginnings of which are usually associated with Martin Luther.

Rome, especially in Germany, where the leading clergy under a weak emperor were more strongly identified with Rome than elsewhere. Growing literacy and lay religiosity helped in the growth of a profound theological dissatisfaction, which exploded in the **Protestant Reformation**. The Reformation began as an antipapal movement of reform in the early sixteenth century that demanded a return to the simplicity of early Christianity. The movement quickly engulfed the kingdoms and divided their ruling classes and populations alike. Vicious religious wars were the consequence. Although these wars eventually subsided, the divisions were never healed completely and mark the culture of many areas in Europe even today.

Background to the Reformation   Several religious and political changes in the fifteenth century led to the Protestant Reformation. One important religious shift was the growth of popular theology, a consequence of the introduction of the printing press (1454–1455) and the distribution of printed materials. A flood of devotional tracts, often read aloud to congregations of illiterate believers, catered to the spiritual interests of ordinary people. Many Christians attended Mass daily, confessed, and did penance for their sins. Wealthy Christians endowed saint cults, charitable institutions, or confraternities devoted to the organization of processions and passion plays. Poor people formed lay groups or studied scripture on their own and devoted themselves to the simple life of the early Christians. More Europeans than in previous centuries had a basic, though mostly literal, understanding of Christianity.

An important political change in the fifteenth century was an increasing inability for the popes, powerful in Rome, to appoint archbishops and bishops outside Italy. The kings of France, Spain, England, and Sweden were busy transforming their kingdoms into centralized states, in which they reduced the influence of the popes. Only in Germany, where the powers of the emperor and the rulers in the various principalities canceled each other out, was the influence of the popes still strong. What remained to the popes was the right to collect a variety of dues in the kingdoms of Europe. They used these dues to finance their expensive and, in the eyes of many,

Erasmus, *Julius Excluded from Heaven* (1514)

luxuriously worldly administration and court in Rome, from which they engaged in European politics. One of the dues was the sale of **indulgences**, which, in popular understanding, were tickets to heaven. Many contemporary observers found the discrepancy between declining papal power and the remaining financial privileges disturbing and demanded reforms.

Luther's Reformation   One such observer was Martin Luther (1483–1546), an Augustinian monk, ordained priest, and New Testament professor in northeastern Germany. Luther was imbued with deep personal piety and confessed his sins daily, doing extensive penance. After a particularly egregious sale of indulgences in his area, in 1517 he wrote his archbishop a letter with 95 theses in which he condemned the indulgences and other matters as contrary to scripture. Friends translated the theses from Latin into German and made them public. What was to become the Protestant Reformation had begun.

News of Luther's public protest traveled quickly across Europe. Sales of indulgences fell off sharply. In a series of writings, Luther spelled out the details of the church reform he envisaged. One reform proposal was the elevation of original New Testament scripture over tradition—that is, over canon law and papal decisions. Salvation was to be by faith alone; good works were irrelevant. Another reform was the declaration of the priesthood of all Christians, doing away with the privileged position of the clergy as mediators between God and believers who could forgive sins. A third reform was a call to German princes to begin church reform in their own lands through their power over clerical appointments, even if the Habsburg emperor was opposed. Finally, by translating the Bible into German, Luther made the full sacred text available to all who, by reading or listening, wanted to rely solely on scripture as the source of their faith. Luther's Bible was a monument of the emerging literary German language. A forceful and clear writer in his translation and own publications, Luther fully explicated the basics of Protestantism.

Reaction to Luther's Demands   Both emperor and pope failed in their efforts to arrest Luther and suppress his call for church reform. The duke of Saxony was successful in protecting the reformer from seizure. Emperor Charles V, a devout Catholic, considered Castile's successful church reform of half a century earlier to be fully sufficient. In his mind, Luther's demands for church reform were to be resisted. Two other pressing concerns, however, diverted the emperor's attention. First, the Ottoman-led Islamic threat, in eastern Europe and the western Mediterranean, had to be met with decisive action. Second, his rivalry with the French king precluded the formation of a common Catholic front against Luther. Enthusiastic villagers and townspeople in Germany exploited Charles's divided attention and abandoned both Catholicism and secular obedience. A savage civil war, called the Peasants' War, engulfed Germany from 1524 to 1525, killing perhaps as many as 100,000 people.

Luther and other prominent reformers were horrified by the carnage. They drew up church ordinances that regulated preaching, church services, administrative councils, education, charity, and consistories for handling disciplinary matters. In Saxony, the duke endorsed this order in 1528. He thereby created the model of Lutheran Protestantism as a state religion, in which the rulers were protectors and supervisors of the churches in their territories. A decade later, Saxony was fully Lutheran.

A minority of about half a dozen German princes and the kings of Denmark and Sweden followed suit. In England, Protestants gained strength in the wake of

Indulgence: Partial remission of sins after payment of a fine or presentation of a donation. Remission would mean the forgiveness of sins by the Church, but the sinner still remained responsible for his or her sins before God.

Anti-Catholic Propaganda.
This anonymous woodcut of
1520 by a German satirist
depicts the devil (complete with
wings and clawed feet) sitting
on a letter of indulgence and
holding a money collection box.
The devil's mouth is filled with
sinners who presumably bought
letters of indulgence in good
faith, thinking they had been
absolved of their sins.

the break with Rome by Henry VIII (r. 1509–1547) and his assumption of church leadership in his kingdom. Although remaining Catholic, he surrounded himself with religious reformers and proclaimed an Anglican state church whose creed and rites combined elements of Catholicism and Protestantism. In Switzerland, several cantons adopted the religious reforms of Huldrych Zwingli (1484–1531). In Scotland, the reforms of John Knox (1514–1572) became the foundation for the state church. Thus, most of northern Europe followed a pattern of alliances between Protestant reformers and the state (see Map 17.3).

Calvinism in Geneva and France In France, as in England, the king controlled all church appointments. King Francis I, however, did not take the final step toward the creation of an independent state church. Since he competed with Charles V of the Habsburg Empire for dominance over the papacy in Italy, he had to appear especially loyal and devout. When a few Protestants in France went public with their demands for church reform, Francis I gave them the stark choice of exile or burning at the stake.

One reformer who chose exile was the French lawyer John Calvin (Jean Cauvin, 1509–1564). During his exile, he passed at one point through Geneva, where a French friend of his beseeched him to help him in preaching the faith. Calvin relented and began a stormy and at one point interrupted career as the city's religious reformer. Geneva—not yet part of Switzerland and under the nominal rule of the duke of Savoy (himself under the nominal rule of the Habsburgs)—was unsure about which path of reform to embrace. It took Calvin well into the 1550s before his form of Protestantism prevailed in the city.

As expressed in Calvin's central work, *Institutes of the Christian Religion* (1536), and numerous other writings, a crucial doctrine of Calvin's was *predestination*. According to this doctrine, God has "predestined" each human prior to birth for heaven or hell. Believers could only hope, through faith alone, that sometime during a life of moral living they would receive a glimpse of their fate. In contrast to Luther, however, Calvin made the enforcement of morality through a formal code, administered by local authorities, part of his version of Protestantism.

Interestingly, this code did not prohibit the taking of interest on loans. While Luther as well as the Catholic Church, in accordance with scripture, condemned all interest as usury, Calvin considered a few percentage points to be entirely justifiable. The strong condemnation of interest on loans in the Hebrew Bible was rooted in the precariousness of Mediterranean rain-fed agriculture: Several years of drought could drive farmers into total dependence on landlords if the latter demanded interest on loans. By placing moneylending into the increasingly urban context of the 1500s, Calvin displayed a greater sense of economic reality than Luther. Acquiring wealth with the help of money and thereby perhaps gaining a glimpse of one's fate became one of the hallmarks of Calvinism. Wealth began to become respectable in Christian society.

Calvin died in his Genevan exile, but Geneva-trained Calvinist preachers went to France and the Netherlands in the mid-1500s. Under the protection of local

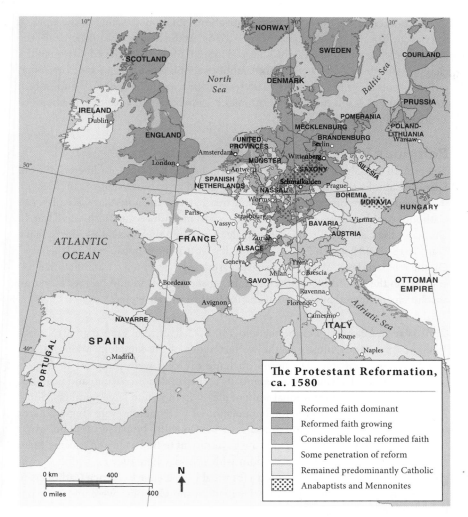

MAP **17.3** **The Protestant Reformation, ca. 1580.**

magistrates, they organized the first clandestine independent Calvinist congregations. Calvinist religious self-organization by independent congregations thus became a viable alternative to Lutheran state religion (see Source 17.2).

The Catholic Reformation   The rivalry between Spain and France made it initially difficult for the popes to tackle the problem of Catholic reforms in order to meet the Protestant challenge. When they finally called together the Council of Trent (1545–1563), they abolished payment for indulgences and phased out other church practices considered to be corrupt. These actions launched the **Catholic Reformation**, an effort to gain back dissenting Catholics. Supported by the kings of Spain and France, however, the popes made no changes to the traditional doctrines of faith together with good works, priestly mediation between believer and God, and monasticism. They even tightened church control through the revival of the papal Inquisition and a new Index of Prohibited Books.

Catholic Reformation: Also Counter-Reformation. Reaffirmation of Catholic papal supremacy and the doctrine of faith together with works as preparatory to salvation; such practices as absenteeism (bishops in Rome instead of in their bishoprics) and pluralism (bishops and abbots holding multiple appointments) were abolished.

To counterbalance these punitive institutions, the popes furthered the work of the Basque priest Ignatius Loyola (1491–1556). At the head of the new order of the Society of Jesus, or Jesuits, Loyola devoted himself tirelessly to the education of the clergy, establishment of a network of Catholic schools and colleges, and conversion of Protestants as well as non-Christians by missionaries to the Americas and eastern Asia. Thanks to Jesuit discipline, Catholics regained a semblance of self-assurance against the Protestants.

Religious Wars and Political Restoration

The growth of Calvinism led to a civil war in France and a war of liberation from Spanish Catholic rule in the Netherlands in the later sixteenth century. In England, the slow pace of reform in the Anglican Church, with which neither Calvinists nor Catholics could identify, erupted in the early seventeenth century into a civil war. In Germany, the Catholic–Protestant struggle turned into the devastating Thirty Years' War (1618–1648), which France and Sweden won at the expense of the Habsburgs. On the religious level, Western Christians grudgingly accepted denominational toleration; on the political level, the centralizing states evolved into polities based on absolutism, tempered by provincial and local administrative practices.

Civil War in France   During the mid-1500s, Calvinism in France grew to about 1,200 congregations, mostly in the western cities of the kingdom, where literate merchants and craftspeople catering to trade overseas were receptive to Protestant publications. Calvinism was essentially an urban denomination; and peasants, rooted more deeply in traditional ways of life, did not join in large numbers. Some 2 million, or 10 percent of the total population of 18.5 million, were Huguenots, as the Protestants were called in France. They continued to be persecuted, but given their numbers, it was impossible for the government to imprison and execute them all. In 1571, they even met in a kingdom-wide synod, where they ratified their congregational church order. They posed a formidable challenge to French Catholicism.

In many cities, relations between Huguenots and Catholics were uneasy. From time to time, groups of agitators crashed each other's church services. Hostilities escalated after 1560 when the government weakened under a child king and was unable to deal with the increasingly powerful Huguenots. In four western cities the Huguenots achieved self-government and full freedom of religious practice from the crown. Concerned to find a compromise, in 1572 the now reigning king married his sister to the leader of the Huguenots, King Henry III of Navarre (later King Henry IV of France, 1589–1610), a Protestant of the Bourbon family in southwestern France. Henry detested the fanaticism that surrounded him.

Only 6 days after the wedding, on St. Bartholomew's Day (August 24, 1572), outraged members of the Catholic aristocracy perpetrated a wholesale slaughter of thousands of Huguenots. This massacre, in response to the assassination of a French admiral, occurred with the apparent connivance of the court. For over a decade and a half, civil war raged, in which Spain aided the Catholics and Henry enrolled German and Swiss Protestant mercenaries. A turning point came only in 1589 when Henry of Navarre became King Henry IV of France. Surviving nearly three-dozen plots against his life, the new king needed 9 years and two conversions to Catholicism—"Paris is well worth a Mass," he is supposed to have quipped—before he was able to calm the religious fanaticism among the majority of French people.

With the Edict of Nantes in 1598, he decreed freedom of religion for Protestants. A number of staunch Catholic adherents were deeply offended by the edict as well as the alleged antipapal policies of Henry IV. The king fell victim to an assassin in 1610. Catholic resentment continued until 1685, when King Louis XIV revoked the edict and triggered a large-scale emigration of Huguenots to the Netherlands, Germany, England, and North America. At last, France was Catholic again.

The Dutch War of Independence   In the Netherlands, the Spanish overlords were even more determined to keep the country Catholic than the French monarchs. When Charles V resigned in 1556 (effective 1558), his son Philip II (r. 1556–1598) became king of Spain and the Netherlands, consisting of the French-speaking regions of Wallonia in the south and the Dutch-speaking regions of Flanders and Holland in the north. Like his father, Philip was a staunch supporter of the Catholic Reformation. He asked the Jesuits and the Inquisition to aggressively persecute the Calvinists. For better effect, Philip subdivided the bishoprics into smaller units and recruited clergymen in place of members of the nobility.

In response, in 1565 the nobility and Calvinist congregations rose in revolt. They dismantled the bishoprics and cleansed the churches of images and sculptures, thereby triggering what was to become a Protestant war of Dutch liberation from Catholic Spanish overlordship (1565–1621). Philip retaliated by sending in an army that succeeded in suppressing the liberation movement. He reimposed Catholicism, and executed thousands of rebels, many of them members of the Dutch aristocracy.

Remnants of the rebellion struggled on and, in 1579, renewed the war of liberation in three of the 17 northern provinces making up the Netherlands. Later joined by four more provinces, the people in these breakaway regions called themselves members of the "United Provinces of the Dutch Republic." Spain refused to recognize the republic and kept fighting until acute Spanish financial difficulties prompted the truce of 1609–1621. Although drawn into fighting again during the Thirty Years' War, the Netherlands gained its full independence eventually in 1648.

first Dutch national atlas, 1622

Civil War in England   As in the Netherlands, the prevalent form of Protestantism in England was Calvinism. During the sixteenth century, the Calvinists numbered about 10 percent in a kingdom of some 7 million in which the Anglican Church encompassed the vast majority of subjects. English Catholics numbered 3 percent, but contrary to the Calvinists they refused to recognize the king as the head of the Anglican church. The percentage of Calvinists was the same as in France before 1685, but the partially reformed Anglican Church under the tolerant queen Elizabeth I (1533–1603) was able to hold them in check.

The Calvinists were, furthermore, a fractious group, encompassing moderate and radical tendencies that neutralized each other. Among the radicals were the Puritans, who demanded the abolition of the Anglican clerical hierarchy and a new church order of independent congregations. When Anglican Church reform slowed with the arrival of the Stuart monarchs on the throne of England (1603–1685), unfortunately the balance among the religious tendencies unraveled. As rulers of England, the Stuarts were officially heads of the Anglican state church, but except for the first king, the three successors were either Catholics or Catholic sympathizers. Since they were furthermore rulers of what was called the England of the Three Kingdoms they found it impossible to maneuver among the demands of the English

Puritans, Scottish Presbyterians (self-governing regional Calvinists), and Catholic Irish. The issue of how little or how far the Anglican Church had been reformed away from Catholicism and how dominant it should be in the three realms became more and more divisive (see Source 17.1).

In addition, the Stuarts were intent on building their version of the centralized state. They collected taxes without the approval of Parliament. Many members resented being bypassed since Parliament was the constitutional co-sovereign of the kingdom. A slight majority in the House of Commons was Puritan, and what they considered the stalled church reform added to their resentment. Eventually, when all tax resources were exhausted, the king had to call Parliament back together. The two sides were unable, however, to come to an agreement and civil war broke out. Since this war was also a conflict among the Three Kingdoms, it had both religious and regional aspects (1639–1651).

The war was generally less vicious than that in France. Nevertheless, because of widespread pillage and destruction of crops and houses, the indirect effects of the war for the population of thousands of villages were severe. The New Model Army, a professional body of 22,000 troops raised by the Puritan-dominated English Parliament against the royal forces, caused further upheavals by cleansing villages of their "frivolous" seasonal festivals, deeply rooted in local traditions. In the end, the monarchy was replaced with a republican theocracy, the "Commonwealth of England."

Republic, Restoration, and Revolution   The ruler of this theocracy, Oliver Cromwell (r. 1649–1658), was a Puritan member of the lower nobility (the gentry) and a commander in the New Model Army. After dissolving Parliament, Cromwell handpicked a new Parliament but ruled for the most part without its consent. Since both Scotland and Ireland were opposed to the English Puritans, Cromwell waged a savage war of submission against the two. The Dutch and Spanish, also opponents of the Puritans, were defeated in naval wars that substantially increased English shipping power in the Atlantic. But fear among the gentry in Parliament of a permanent centralized state led to a refusal of further financial subsidies for the military. After Cromwell's death in 1658, it took just 3 years to restore the Stuart monarchy and the Anglican state church to their previous places.

The recalled Stuart kings, however, resumed the policies of centralization. As before, the kings called Parliament together only sparingly and raised funds without its authorization. But their standing army of 30,000, partially stationed near London, was intended more to intimidate the parliamentarians than to subjugate them. In 1687, the king, James II (r. 1685–1688), even espoused a major plan of reform, as new research has shown. In the "Glorious Revolution" of 1688, a defiant Parliament deposed the king and made his daughter Mary and her Dutch husband William the new co-regents.

The Thirty Years' War in Germany   As religious tensions were mounting in England during the early seventeenth century, similar tensions erupted into a full-blown war in Germany, bringing about the second such conflagration in a century, the Thirty Years' War. As we saw earlier, even though the rulers of the German principalities had made either Catholicism or Protestantism their state religion, minorities were tolerated or even admitted to offices. The Jesuit-educated Ferdinand II (r. 1619–1637), ruler of the Holy Roman Empire, however, refused to appoint Protestants in majority-Protestant Bohemia, of which the Habsburgs were kings since 1526. In response, Protestant leaders in 1618 renounced Ferdinand's authority and made the Calvinist prince of the Palatinate in the Rhineland their new king. With these events in Protestant Bohemia, open hostilities between the religious denominations began in Germany.

In a first round of war (1619–1630), Ferdinand and the Catholic princes suppressed the Bohemian rebellion and slowly advanced toward northern Germany, capturing Lutheran territories for reconversion to Catholicism and defeating Denmark. In 1630, however, the Lutheran king Gustavus II Adolphus (r. 1611–1632) of Sweden intervened. The king's main goal was the creation of a Swedish-Lutheran centralized state around the Baltic Sea, a project already begun before the Thirty Years' War.

Centralizing States at War. German imperial troops besiege Swedish troops in the northern German city of Stralsund in 1628. The etching shows typical features of the centralizing state, from top to bottom: galleon-style warships (successors of the caravel); a star-shaped fort (an Italian innovation) designed to withstand artillery barrages; the medieval walls of the city; musket-equipped infantry troops; field cannons; and the colorful Baroque uniforms worn by the musketeers of the period.

By aiding the German Lutherans, he hoped to consolidate or even increase his predominance in the region. Louis XIII (r. 1610–1643) of France granted Sweden financial subsidies, since he was concerned that Ferdinand's victories would further strengthen the Habsburg Spanish–Flemish–Austrian–German–Italian grip around France. With the politically motivated alliance between Sweden and France, the German Catholic–Protestant war turned into a war for state dominance in Europe.

The Swedes were initially successful but withdrew when Gustavus II Adolphus fell unexpectedly in battle. Ferdinand decided to compromise with the Protestant princes of Germany, by reestablishing the prewar divisions, in order to keep the French out of the war. But Louis XIII entered anyway, and during the next 13 years, French armies sought to cut the Habsburg supply lines from Italy to the Netherlands by occupying Habsburg Alsace. Swedish armies, exploiting the French successes against the Habsburgs, fought their way back into Germany. In the end, the Austrian–German Habsburgs, pressured on two sides and exhausted from the war, agreed in October 1648 to the Peace of Westphalia.

The agreement provided for religious freedom in Germany and ceded Habsburg territories in Alsace to France and the southern side of the Baltic Sea to Sweden. It granted territorial integrity to all European powers. The Spanish Habsburgs continued their war against France until 1659, when they also bowed to superior French strength, giving up parts of Flanders and northeastern Spain. In the Caribbean, Spain lost territories to France, the Netherlands, and England, accelerating the decline of Spain's overseas power. France emerged as the strongest country in Europe, and the Spanish-dominated Caribbean became an area of open power rivalry (see Map 17.4).

Absolutism in France?   During its period of greatest political dominance, France came under the rule of its longest-reigning monarch, King Louis XIV (1643–1715). He was of small stature—for which he compensated with high-heeled shoes—but his hardy constitution and strong self-discipline helped him to dominate even the most grueling meetings with his advisors. He enjoyed pomp and circumstance and built Versailles—his gigantic palace and gardens near Paris, populated with 10,000 courtiers, attendants, and servants—into a site of almost continuous feasting, entertainment, and intrigue. It was here that Louis, the "Sun King," beamed benevolently with his "absolute" divine mandate upon his aristocracy and commoners alike (see Source 17.3).

Versailles played an important role in Louis' efforts to undercut the power of the nobility. Anyone with any aspirations of attracting the king's attention had to come to the palace to attend him. He kept both friends and potential enemies close by, forcing them to spend themselves lavishly into ruin to keep up with the fashions inspired by the king. Like the Tokugawa shoguns in Edo, Japan, he bypassed them administratively and ruled through central bureaucratic institutions (see Chapter 21).

Absolutism: Theory of the state in which the unlimited power of the king, ruling under God's divine mandate, was emphasized. In practice, it was neutralized by the nobility and provincial and local communities.

In practice, the French **absolutism** of Louis XIV and his eighteenth-century successors, as well as absolutism in other European countries, was a complex mixture of centralized and decentralized forces. On one hand, after the end of the religious wars in 1648, mercenary armies under autonomous dukes and counts disappeared from the European scene, replaced by permanent armies or navies under the central command of royal relatives or favorites. The kings also no longer called their assemblies of nobles and notables together to have new taxes approved (in France from 1614 to 1789), and thus many of the nobility's tax privileges disappeared.

On the other hand, the kings of the seventeenth century were acutely aware that true absolutism was possible only if the taxes were collected by centrally salaried

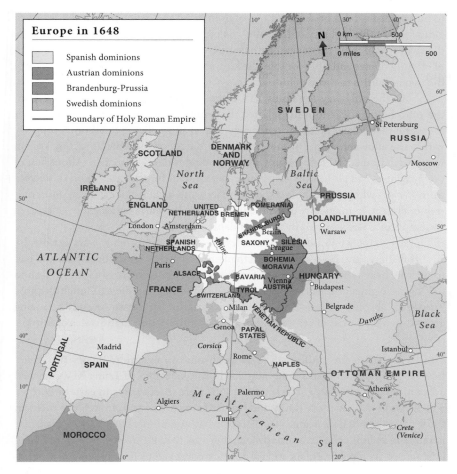

MAP **17.4 Europe in 1648.**

employees. It was physically impossible, however, to transport tax revenues, in the form of silver money and grain, from the provinces to the capital, pay the central bureaucrats, and then cart the remaining money back to the provinces to pay salaried tax collectors there. A centrally paid bureaucracy would have required a central bank with provincial branches, using a credit and debit system. The failed experiment with such a bank in Paris from 1714 to 1720 demonstrates one such effort to find a solution to the central salarization problem. The bank's short life demonstrates that absolute central control was beyond the powers of the kings.

Instead, the kings had to rely on subcontracting out most offices and the collection of most taxes to the highest bidders, who then helped themselves to the collection of their incomes. Under Louis XIV, a total of 46,000 administrative jobs were available for purchase in Paris and the provinces. Anyone who had money or borrowed it from financiers was encouraged to buy an office—from the old aristocracy receiving rents from the farmers on their rural estates to ordinary merchants' sons with law degrees borrowing money from their fathers.

Once in office, these officers were often forced by the government to grant additional loans to the crown. To retain their loyalty, the government rewarded them with first picks for retaining their offices within the family. They were also privileged to buy landed estates or acquire titles of nobility to the secondary (and less presti-gious) tier of the "nobility of the robe" (as opposed to the old first-tier "nobility of the sword," which by the seventeenth century was demilitarized). With this system of offering offices and titles for sale, the king sought to bind the financial interests of the two nobilities to those of his own.

About the only way for Louis XIV to keep a semblance of a watchful eye on the officeholders was to send salaried, itinerant *intendants* around the provinces to ensure that collecting taxes, rendering justice, and policing functioned properly within the allowable limits of the "venality of office," as the subcontracting system was called. Louis XIV had roughly one intendant for each province. About half of the provinces had *parlements*—appointed assemblies for the ratification of decrees from Paris—whose officeholders, drawn from the local noble, clerical, and com-moner classes, frequently resisted the intendants. The Paris *parlement* even refused to accept royal writs carried by the intendants.

In later years, when Louis XIV was less successful in his many wars against the rival Habsburgs and Protestant Dutch than previously, the crown overspent and had to borrow heavily with little regard for the future. Louis' successors in the second half of the eighteenth century were saddled with crippling debts. French-inspired European "absolutism" was thus in practice a careful (or not so careful) balancing act between the forces of centralization and decentralization in the states of Europe.

The Rise of Russia   Although France's absolutism was more theory than prac-tice, its glorious ideological embodiment in the Versailles of Louis XIV spawned adaptations across Europe. These adaptations were most visible in eastern Europe, which was populated more thinly and had far fewer towns and cities. Since rulers in those areas did not have a large reservoir of urban commoners to aid them as admin-istrators in building the centralized state, they had to make do with the landowning aristocracy. As a result, rulers and aristocracy connived to finance state centraliza-tion through an increased exploitation of the farmers in the villages: In the 1600s, their legal status deteriorated, their tax liabilities increased, and they became serfs.

Tsar (or Czar): Derived from "Caesar," title used by the Russian rulers to emphasize their imperial ambitions.

In Russia, **Tsar** Peter I, "the Great" (r. 1682–1725), of the Eastern Christian Romanov dynasty, was a towering figure who singlehandedly sought to establish the French-type centralized state during his lifetime. At nearly 7 feet tall, Peter was an imposing, energetic ruler, controllable only by his second wife (and former mis-tress) Catherine, a warmhearted woman and beloved tsarina. Peter invited western European soldiers, mariners, administrators, craftspeople, scholars, and artists into his service and succeeded within just a few years in building a disciplined army and imposing navy. He built ports on the Baltic Sea and established the new capital of St. Petersburg, distinguished by many very beautiful palaces and official buildings.

Peter the Great, "Decree on the Invitation to Foreigners" (1702)

A typical example among the thousands invited to Russia by the tsar was Peter von Sivers, a Danish mariner (and ancestor of one of the coauthors of this book) who rose to the position of admiral in the Baltic fleet that broke Swedish dominance in northern Europe. Since the tsar was not able to pay these advisors salaries (any more than Louis XIV could pay salaries to advisors to the French court), he gave many western officers estates with serfs in the Baltic provinces and Finland, con-quered from Sweden, and made them aristocrats in his retinue.

The Russian military was completely reorganized by the tsar. After an early rebel-lion, Peter savagely decimated the inherited firearm regiments and made them part

A World Turned Upside Down. In this popular satirical woodcut of 1766, based on a similar woodcut from the early 1700s, the mice are capturing and burying the cat: In other words, Peter the Great has turned the world upside down with his reforms.

of a new army recruited from the traditional Russian landed nobility. Both classes of soldiers received education at military schools and academies and were required to provide lifelong service. In order to make his soldiers look more urban, Peter decreed that they shave their traditional beards and wear European uniforms or clothes. Every twentieth peasant household had to deliver one foot soldier to conscription. A census was taken to facilitate the shift from the inherited household tax on the villagers to a new capitation tax collected by military officers. In the process, the remaining free farmers outside the estate system of the aristocracy found themselves classified and taxed as serfs, unfree to leave their villages. The result of Peter's reforms was a powerful, expansionary centralizing state that played an increasingly important role among European kingdoms during the eighteenth century (see Map 17.5).

The Rise of Prussia   Similar to Russia, the principality of Prussia-Brandenburg was underurbanized. It had furthermore suffered destruction and depopulation during the Thirty Years' War. When the Lutheran Hohenzollern rulers embarked on the construction of a centralized state in the later seventeenth century, they first broke the tax privileges of the landowning aristocracy in the Estates General and raised taxes themselves through agents. As in Russia, farmers who worked on estates held by landlords were serfs. Since there were few urban middle-class merchants and professionals, the kings enrolled members of the landlord aristocracy in the army and civilian administration.

Elevated by the Habsburg Holy Roman emperor from the status of dukes to that of kings in 1701, the Hohenzollern monarchs systematically enlarged the army, employing it during peacetime for drainage and canal projects as well as palace construction in Berlin, the capital. Under Frederick II, "the Great" (1740–1786), Prussia pursued an aggressive foreign policy, capturing Silesia from the Habsburgs in a military campaign. Frederick also expended major efforts to attracting immigrants, intensifying agriculture, and establishing manufacturing enterprises. Prussia emerged as a serious competitor of the Habsburgs in the Holy Roman Empire of Germany.

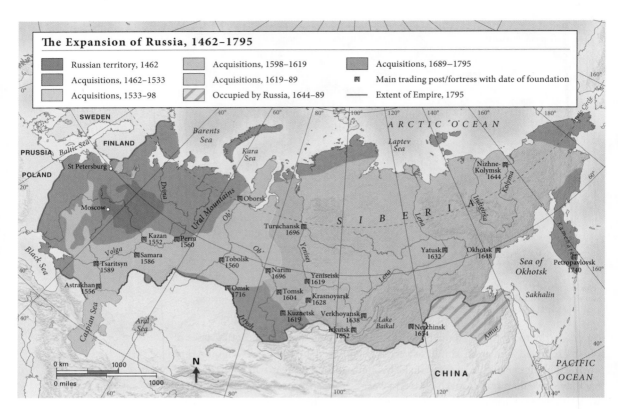

MAP **17.5** **The Expansion of Russia, 1462–1795.**

English Constitutionalism In contrast to Prussia, France, Spain, Austria, and other European states, England had since 1450 a political system ruled by a king or a queen, with a Parliament composed of the aristocracy as well as representatives of towns and cities. Only in England did the interests of the nobility and the urban merchants gradually converge: Younger sons, unable to inherit the family estate, sought their fortunes in London. Rulers on the European continent financed their early centralizing states through raising indirect taxes on sales, commerce, imports, and exports, affecting cities more than noble estates. In England, the cities allied with the aristocracy in resisting indirect tax increases and forcing the throne to use the less ample revenues of its royal estates to pay soldiers. Efforts of the Stuart kings to create a centralized land-based state based on firearm infantries failed. Instead, the ruling class preferred to build a centralized naval state. After the Glorious Revolution of 1688, England became the dominant power on the world's oceans.

After its victory over the Stuart kings, Parliament consolidated its financial powers through the creation of the Bank of England in 1694, two decades before a similar but ill-fated attempt in France. When Mary and William died without children, England continued in 1714 with a king from the principality of Hannover in Germany distantly related to the previous royals. Around the same time, England and Scotland united, creating the United Kingdom. Parliament collected higher taxes than France and, through its bank, was able to keep its debt service low during the early 1700s. The navy grew twice as large as that of France and was staffed by a well-salaried, disciplined military, while the few land troops, deemed superfluous, were mostly low-paid Hessian-German mercenaries. A rudimentary two-party system of

Prussian Military Discipline. The Prussian line infantry made full use in the mid-1700s of flintlock muskets, bayonets, and drilling.

two aristocracy–merchant alliances came into being. The two parties were known as the Tories and the Whigs, the former more royalist and the latter more parliamentarian, with the Whigs in power for most of the first half of the eighteenth century.

❯ Putting It All Together

interactive concept map

Prior to 1500, all religious civilizations possessed sophisticated mathematics and practiced variations of qualitative sciences, such as astrology, geography, alchemy, and medicine. The one exception was trigonometry-based astronomy in Islamic, Hindu, and Christian religious civilizations, pioneered by the Hellenistic scholar Ptolemy (Chapter 5). Physics became the second mathematical science in the early 1500s, but only in Western Christianity. This transformation of the sciences, however, had no practical (that is, engineering) consequences prior to the invention of the steam engine in the 1700s and the subsequent industrialization of England in the 1800s. Furthermore, the mathematization of physics did little to influence the continued prevalence of qualitative description as the methodology of the other sciences. Astrology, alchemy, and medicine continued with what we regard today as outmoded qualitative theories well into the nineteenth century.

Most important, the rise of the New Sciences should not be confused with the vast political, social, economic, and cultural changes, called "modernity" after 1800, which propelled the West on its trajectory of world dominance. Although the West began to acquire its specific scientific and philosophical identity with the introduction of the mathematical sciences in the century between Copernicus and Galileo (1514-1604), the impact of these sciences on the world was felt only after 1800 when they were applied to industry. Once this application gathered momentum, in the nineteenth century, Asia and Africa had no choice but to adapt to modern science and industrialization.

Review and Relate

| Thinking Through Patterns

Examine the ways historians approach the big questions of this chapter.

> What were the reasons for the cultural changes that began in Europe around 1450? In which ways were the patterns of cultural changes during 1450–1750 different from those in the other religious civilizations of Eurasia?

Located far from the traditional agrarian–urban centers of Eurasia, Western Christianity repeatedly adapted its culture (particularly theological, philosophical, scientific, and artistic forms of expression) in response to outside stimuli coming from Islamic and Eastern Christian civilizations. Without these stimuli, the Renaissance, Baroque, New Science, and Enlightenment would not have developed. In contrast, the Middle East, Byzantium, India, and China, originating firmly within the traditional agrarian–urban centers, received far fewer outside stimuli prior to the scientific–industrial age. Scholars and thinkers in these religious civilizations did not feel the same pressure to change their cultural heritage and adapt as their colleagues in Western Christianity did.

> When and how did the New Sciences begin, and how did they gain popularity in northwestern European society? Why is the popularization of the New Sciences important for understanding the period 1450–1750?

The discovery of the two new continents of the Americas prompted Nicolaus Copernicus to reject Aristotle's astronomical theory of spheres and to posit a sun-centered planetary system. Copernicus's new approach to science continued with Galileo Galilei's discovery of the mathematical law of falling bodies in physics and was completed when Isaac Newton unified physics and astronomy. The New Sciences became popular in educated urban circles in northwestern Europe, where Catholic and Protestant Church authorities were largely divided. In southern Europe, where the Catholic Reformation was powerful and rejected Galileo, the adoption of the New Sciences occurred more slowly. As scientists in northwestern Europe discovered, the New Sciences possessed practical applicability: After studying the properties of condensing steam and the vacuum, scientists and mechanics began experimenting with steam engines, which served as the principal catalysts for the launching of the scientific–industrial age.

> What were the patterns of centralized state formation and transformation in the period 1450–1750? How did the Protestant Reformation and religious wars modify these patterns?

European kingdoms, such as France, Sweden, and Prussia, expanded their powers of taxation to the detriment of the nobility. With the accumulated funds, they hired and salaried mercenary infantries equipped with firearms, using them to conquer land from their neighbors. The religious wars of the 1500s and 1600s strengthened centralization efforts and hastened the demise of the nobility as an obstacle to the centralized state. In England, Parliament blocked the Stuart kings from building a landed central state and instead pursued the construction of a naval state, which succeeded a similar one built by the Netherlands in 1688.

Against the Grain

Consider this as a counterpoint to the main patterns examined in this chapter.

The Digger Movement

I n April 1649, toward the end of the English Civil War and just 3 months after the execution of King Charles I, a group of 70, mostly landless, farmers and day laborers occupied "common" (public) land near Walton, Surrey (about 25 miles south of London), to establish a colony. As the farmers and laborers dug up the soil and sowed the ground with parsnips, carrots, and beans, they came to be called the "Diggers."

Driven off by enraged small landowners who benefited greatly from the use of common land for grazing sheep and cutting timber, a much-reduced group of colonists moved on to common land in nearby Cobham in August 1649. After some delay, this time it was the gentry with their manor rights to the common land who destroyed the Diggers' cottages and fields in the winter of 1650. The Diggers, although ultimately unsuccessful, made a much-publicized statement that public land was "the treasure of all people" and should not be reserved for the benefit of anyone, be they gentry or even small property owners—a bold demand which ran counter to the rapidly increasing privatization of land and commercialization of agriculture.

The leader of the group was Gerrard Winstanley (1609–1670), an embittered former cloth merchant in London who had to abandon his trade in 1643 after he became insolvent. He struggled to regain his solvency in the countryside of Surrey, at one point working as a grazier of cattle. Parts of Surrey had suffered substantial hardship during the Civil War, having been forced to provision and quarter troops. In a flurry of pamphlets between 1648 and 1650 Winstanley explained the motives and goals of the Diggers most eloquently, displaying a remarkable familiarity with local affairs. In addition, he had a superb ability to make these affairs relevant, in the religious idiom of Protestantism, for England as a whole. He was the first to clearly identify the problem of the rising numbers of rural landless laborers victimized by the increasing commercialization of agriculture in England—a labor force that continued to increase until the industrializing cities of the later 1700s eventually absorbed them.

- Was Winstanley hopelessly utopian in his efforts to establish farmer communities on common land in England?

- How have other figures in world history sympathized with the lot of poor and landless farmers and attempted reform (or revolution) on their behalf?

Key Terms

🔊
audio flashcards

Absolutism 516	Indulgence 509	Renaissance 492
Catholic Reformation 511	New Sciences 492	Tsar (or Czar) 518
Humanism 492	Protestant Reformation 508	

For additional resources, please go to
www.oup.com/us/vonsivers.
Please see the Further Resources section at the back of the book for additional readings and suggested websites.

Sources for Chapter 17

| SOURCE 17.1 | Examination of Lady Jane Grey, London |

1554

Jane Grey, the granddaughter of Henry VIII's sister Mary, was born in 1537, the same year as Edward VI, the only surviving son of the king who had sought a male heir so desperately. Jane, who like Edward was raised in the Protestant religion Henry had introduced to England, proved a diligent and intellectually gifted teenager. In spite of her youth and gender, Jane corresponded with Protestant authorities on the Continent, but fast-moving events in England precluded further study. When Edward died without an heir in 1553, the throne passed, by prearranged agreement, to his fiercely Catholic half-sister Mary.

However, in order to forestall a Catholic successor—and the dramatic rollback of the Protestant reforms instituted by Henry's and Edward's Church of England—Jane's relatives proclaimed her queen. Her rule lasted a mere nine days. She was imprisoned in the Tower of London by Mary, who was then forced to consider whether Jane's execution was warranted. Shortly before Jane's death, at age 16, Queen Mary sent her own chaplain, Master Feckenham (sometimes rendered as "Fecknam") to try to reconcile Jane to the Catholic faith. The results of this attempt were triumphantly recorded in John Foxe's *Acts and Monuments*, published after the Protestant Queen Elizabeth had triumphed over Mary and the Catholics. Although the conversation recorded here is not a trial transcript—and is a highly partisan account—it does distill some of the central issues that divided Catholics and Protestants in an extremely chaotic and violent period.

> **FECKNAM:** "I am here come to you at this present, sent from the queen [Mary] and her council, to instruct you in the true doctrine of the right faith: although I have so great confidence in you, that I shall have, I trust, little need to travail with you much therein."
>
> **JANE:** "Forsooth, I heartily thank the queen's highness, which is not unmindful of her humble subject: and I hope, likewise, that you no less will do your duty therein both truly and faithfully, according to that you were sent for."

· · ·

Source: "The Examination of Lady Jane Grey (1554)," from Denis R. Janz, ed., *A Reformation Reader: Primary Texts with Introductions*, 2nd ed. (Minneapolis, MN: Fortress, 2008), 360–362, taken from *The Acts and Monuments of John Foxe* (London: Seeleys, 1859), 415–417.

FECKNAM: "How many sacraments are there?"

JANE: "Two: the one the sacrament of baptism, and the other the sacrament of the Lord's Supper."

FECKNAM: "No, there are seven."

JANE: "By what Scripture find you that?"

FECKNAM: "Well, we will talk of that hereafter. But what is signified by your two sacraments?"

JANE: "By the sacrament of baptism I am washed with water and regenerated by the Spirit, and that washing is a token to me that I am the child of God. The sacrament of the Lord's Supper, offered unto me, is a sure seal and testimony that I am, by the blood of Christ, which he shed for me on the cross, made partaker of the everlasting kingdom."

FECKNAM: "Why? What do you receive in that sacrament? Do you not receive the very body and blood of Christ?"

JANE: "No, surely, I do not so believe. I think that at the supper I neither receive flesh nor blood, but bread and wine: which bread when it is broken, and the wine when it is drunken, put me in remembrance how that for my sins the body of Christ was broken, and his blood shed on the cross; and with that bread and wine I receive the benefits that come by the breaking of his body, and shedding of his blood, for our sins on the cross."

FECKNAM: "Why, doth not Christ speak these words, 'Take, eat, this is my body?' Require you any plainer words? Doth he not say, it is his body?"

JANE: "I grant, he saith so; and so he saith, 'I am the vine, I am the door'; but he is never the more for that, the door or the vine. Doth not St. Paul say, 'He calleth things that are not, as though they were?' God forbid that I should say, that I eat the very natural body and blood of Christ: for then either I should pluck away my redemption, or else there were two bodies, or two Christs. One body was tormented on the cross, and if they did eat another body, then had he two bodies: or if his body were eaten, then was it not broken upon the cross; or if it were broken upon the cross, it was not eaten of his disciples."

. . .

With these and like such persuasions he would have had her lean to the [Catholic] church, but it would not be. There were many more things whereof they reasoned, but these were the chiefest.

After this, Fecknam took his leave, saying, that he was sorry for her: "For I am sure," quoth he, "that we two shall never meet."

JANE: "True it is," said she, "that we shall never meet, except God turn your heart; for I am assured, unless you repent and turn to God, you are in an evil case. And I pray God, in the bowels of his mercy, to send you his Holy Spirit; for he hath given you his great gift of utterance, if it please him also to open the eyes of your heart."

≫ Working
with Sources

1. **What does this source reveal about the religious education of young people in the extended royal household during the final years of Henry VIII and the reign of Edward VI?**

2. **How does the literal interpretation of the Bible enter into this discussion, and why?**

| SOURCE 17.2 | Sebastian Castellio, *Concerning Whether Heretics Should Be Persecuted* |

1554

In October 1553, the extraordinarily gifted Spanish scientist Michael Servetus was executed with the approval and the strong support of John Calvin and his followers in Geneva. The charge was heresy, specifically for denying the existence of the Trinity and the divinity of Christ, and the method of execution—burning at the stake—elicited commentary and protest from across Europe. One of the fullest and most sophisticated protests against this execution was issued by Sebastian Castellio, a professor of Greek language and New Testament theology in the Swiss city of Basel. His book *De Haereticis* is a collection of opinions, drawn from Christian writers, from both before and after the Protestant Reformation and across 15 centuries. It is more than an academic exercise, however, as this dedication of the Latin work to a German noble demonstrates.

Turks: Muslims.

From the Dedication of the book to Duke Christoph of Württemberg:
    . . . And just as the **Turks** disagree with the Christians as to the person of Christ, and the Jews with both the Turks and the Christians, and the one condemns the other and holds him for a heretic, so Christians disagree with Christians on many points with regard to the teaching of Christ, and condemn one another and hold each other for heretics. Great controversies and debates occur as to baptism, the Lord's Supper, the invocation of the saints, justification, free will, and other obscure questions, so that Catholics, Lutherans, Zwinglians, Anabaptists, monks, and others condemn and persecute one another more cruelly than the Turks do the Christians. These dissensions arise solely from ignorance of the truth, for if these matters were so obvious and evident as that there is but one God, all Christians would agree among themselves on these points as readily as all nations confess that God is one.

Source: Sebastian Castellio, *Concerning Heretics, Whether They Are to Be Persecuted and How They Are to Be Treated, A Collection of the Opinions of Learned Men Both Ancient and Modern*, trans. Roland H. Bainton, (New York: Octagon, 1965), 132–134.

What, then is to be done in such great contentions? We should follow the counsel of Paul, "Let not him that eateth despise him that eateth not . . . To his own master he standeth or falleth" [Romans 14:3–4]. Let not the Jews or Turks condemn the Christians, nor let the Christians condemn the Jews or Turks, but rather teach and win them by true religion and justice, and let us, who are Christians, not condemn one another, but, if we are wiser than they, let us also be better and more merciful. This is certain that the better a man knows the truth, the less is he inclined to condemn, as appears in the case of Christ and the apostles. But he who lightly condemns others shows thereby that he knows nothing precisely, because he cannot bear others, for to know is to know how to put into practice. He who does not know how to act mercifully and kindly does not know the nature of mercy and kindness, just as he who cannot blush does not know the nature of shame.

If we were to conduct ourselves in this fashion we should be able to dwell together in concord. Even though in some matters we disagreed, yet should we consent together and forbear one another in love, which is the bond of peace, until we arrive at the unity of the faith [Ephesians 4:2–3]. But now, when we strive with hate and persecutions we go from bad to worse. Nor are we mindful of our office, since we are wholly taken up with condemnation, and the Gospel because of us is made a reproach unto the heathen [Ezekiel 22:4], for when they see us attacking one another with the fury of beasts, and the weak oppressed by the strong, these heathen feel horror and detestation for the Gospel, as if it made men such, and they abominate even Christ himself, as if he commanded men to do such things. We rather degenerate into Turks and Jews than convert them into Christians. Who would wish to be a Christian, when he saw that those who confessed the name of Christ were destroyed by Christians themselves with fire, water, and the sword without mercy and more cruelly treated than brigands and murderers? Who would not think Christ a **Moloch**, or some such god, if he wished that men should be immolated to him and burned alive? Who would wish to serve Christ on condition that a difference of opinion on a controversial point with those in authority would be punished by burning alive at the command of Christ himself more cruelly than in the bull of **Phalaris**, even though from the midst of the flames he should call with a loud voice upon Christ, and should cry out that he believed in Him? Imagine Christ, the judge of all, present. Imagine Him pronouncing the sentence and applying the torch. Who would not hold Christ for a Satan? What more could Satan do than burn those who call upon the name of Christ?

Moloch: A Phoenician deity who, according to the Bible, demanded the sacrifice of human children.

Phalaris: Tyrant in pre-Christian Sicily who burned victims alive in a giant bronze bull.

≫ **Working with Sources**

1. Was Castellio minimizing the significant theological disputes that had arisen as a result of the Reformation? Were his objections directly applicable to the Servetus case?

2. What did Castellio see as the practical, as well as the theological, consequences of burning those perceived to be "heretics"? Is he convincing on this point?

SOURCE 17.3 Duc de Saint-Simon, "The Daily Habits of Louis XIV at Versailles"

ca. 1715

Anoble at Louis XIV's court at Versailles, Louis de Rouvroy, the duc de Saint-Simon (1675–1755), would achieve lasting fame after his death with the publication of his copious, frank, and witty observations of the court. While resident at Versailles for brief periods after 1702 until the king's death in 1715, Saint-Simon paid particular attention to the maneuverings of his fellow aristocrats. He managed to garner the resentment of many of them, especially the king's illegitimate children, "the Bastards," who held a prominent place at court. His accounts of the daily routine of life at Versailles, and the central position of the king who had famously declared, "L'état, c'est moi!," are often applied today to spectacles that can also be described as at once grand and a little absurd.

At eight o'clock the chief valet de chambre on duty, who alone had slept in the royal chamber, and who had dressed himself, awoke the King. The chief physician, the chief surgeon, and the nurse (as long as she lived), entered at the same time. The latter kissed the King; the others rubbed and often changed his shirt, because he was in the habit of sweating a great deal. At the quarter [hour], the grand chamberlain was called (or, in his absence, the first gentleman of the chamber), and those who had, what was called the *grandes entrées*. The chamberlain (or chief gentleman) drew back the curtains which had been closed again, and presented the holy water from the vase, at the head of the bed. These gentlemen stayed but a moment, and that was the time to speak to the King, if any one had anything to ask of him; in which case the rest stood aside. When, contrary to custom, nobody had aught to say, they were there but for a few moments. He who had opened the curtains and presented the holy water, presented also a prayer-book. Then all passed into the cabinet of the council. A very short religious service being over, the King called, they re-entered. The same officer gave him his dressing-gown; immediately after, other privileged courtiers entered, and then everybody, in time to find the King putting on his shoes and stockings, for he did almost everything himself and with address and grace. Every other day we saw him shave himself; and he had a little short wig in which he always appeared, even in bed, and on medicine days. He often spoke of the chase, and sometimes said a word to somebody. No toilette table was near him; he had simply a mirror held before him.

As soon as he was dressed, he prayed to God, at the side of his bed, where all the clergy present knelt, the cardinals without cushions, all the laity remaining standing; and the captain of the guards came to the balustrade during the prayer, after which the King passed into his cabinet.

Source: *Memoirs of the Duc de Saint-Simon*, trans. Bayle St. John, ed. W. H. Lewis (New York: Macmillan, 1964), 140–141, 144–145.

He found there, or was followed by all who had the entrée, a very numerous company, for it included everybody in any office. He gave orders to each for the day; thus within half a quarter of an hour it was known what he meant to do; and then all this crowd left directly. The bastards, a few favourites, and the valets alone were left. It was then a good opportunity for talking with the King; for example, about plans of gardens and buildings; and conversation lasted more or less according to the person engaged in it.

. . .

At ten o'clock his supper was served. The captain of the guard announced this to him. A quarter of an hour after the King came to supper, and from the antechamber of Madame de Maintenon [his principal mistress] to the table again, any one spoke to him who wished. This supper was always on a grand scale, the royal household (that is, the sons and daughters of France), at table, and a large number of courtiers and ladies present, sitting or standing, and on the evening before the journey to Marly all those ladies who wished to take part in it. That was called presenting yourself for Marly. Men asked in the morning, simply saying to the King, "Sire, Marly." In later years, the King grew tired of this, and a valet wrote up in the gallery the names of those who asked. The ladies continued to present themselves.

. . .

Ruelle: The "little path" between a bed and the wall.

The King, wishing to retire, went and fed his dogs; then said good night, passed into his chamber to the ***ruelle*** of his bed, where he said his prayers, as in the morning, then undressed. He said good night with an inclination of the head, and whilst everybody was leaving the room stood at the corner of the mantelpiece, where he gave the order to the colonel of the guards alone. Then commenced what was called the *petit coucher*, at which only the specially privileged remained. That was short. They did not leave until he got into bed. It was a moment to speak to him.

» Working with Sources

1. **Why does Saint-Simon pay particular attention to moments of the day during which a courtier could speak directly with the king?**

2. **What does the combination of religious and secular pursuits in the king's daily habits suggest about life at his court?**

SOURCE 17.4

Giorgio Vasari, *The Life of Michelangelo Buonarroti*

1550

Trained as a painter, architect, and goldsmith, Giorgio Vasari (1511–1574) practiced various artistic trades, but is most renowned today as the first art historian. His *Lives of the Most Eminent Painters, Sculptors,*

Source: Giorgio Vasari, *The Lives of the Artists*, trans. Julia Conaway Bondanella and Peter Bondanella (New York: Oxford University Press, 1998), 418–420; 427–428.

and Architects, first published in 1550, is the principal source of information about the most prominent artists of the European Renaissance. Having studied under the great artist Michelangelo Buonarroti (1475–1564), Vasari was particularly keen to tell this story. In these scenes from his biography of Michelangelo, Vasari draws attention to his master's early training, as well as the prominent roles Lorenzo il Magnifico de' Medici and ancient sculpture played in his artistic development.

In those days Lorenzo de' Medici the Magnificent kept Bertoldo the sculptor in his garden near Piazza San Marco, not so much as the custodian or guardian of the many beautiful antiquities he had collected and assembled there at great expense, but rather because he wished above all else to create a school for excellent painters and sculptors . . . Thus, Domenico [Ghirlandaio] gave him some of his best young men, including among others Michelangelo and Francesco Granacci; and when they went to the garden, they found that Torrigiani, a young man of the Torrigiani family, was there working on some clay figures in the round that Bertoldo had given him to do.

After Michelangelo saw these figures, he made some himself to rival those of Torrigiani, so that Lorenzo, seeing his high spirit, always had great expectations for him, and, encouraged after only a few days, Michelangelo began copying with a piece of marble the antique head of an old and wrinkled faun with a damaged nose and a laughing mouth, which he found there. Although Michelangelo had never before touched marble or chisels, the imitation turned out so well that Lorenzo was astonished, and when Lorenzo saw that Michelangelo, following his own fantasy rather than the antique head, had carved its mouth open to give it a tongue and to make all its teeth visible, this lord, laughing with pleasure as was his custom, said to him: "But you should have known that old men never have all their teeth and that some of them are always missing." In that simplicity of his, it seemed to Michelangelo, who loved and feared this lord, that Lorenzo was correct; and as soon as Lorenzo left, he immediately broke a tooth on the head and dug out the gum in such a way that it seemed the tooth had fallen out, and anxiously awaited Lorenzo's return, who, after coming back and seeing Michelangelo's simplicity and excellence, laughed about it on more than one occasion, recounting it to his friends as if it were miraculous. . . .

. . .

Around this time it happened that Piero Soderini saw the statue [the David, finished in 1504], and it pleased him greatly, but while Michelangelo was giving it the finishing touches, he told Michelangelo that he thought the nose of the figure was too large. Michelangelo, realizing that the Gonfaloniere [a civic official in Florence] was standing under the giant and that his viewpoint did not allow him to see it properly, climbed up the scaffolding to satisfy Soderini (who was behind him nearby), and having quickly grabbed the chisel in his left hand along with a little marble dust that he found on the planks in the scaffolding, Michelangelo began to tap lightly with the chisel, allowing the dust to fall little by little without retouching the nose from the way it was. Then, looking down at the Gonfaloniere who stood there watching, he ordered:

"Look at it now."

"I like it better," replied the Gonfaloniere: "you've made it come alive."

Thus Michelangelo climbed down, and, having contented this lord, he laughed to himself, feeling compassion for those who, in order to make it appear that they understand, do not realize what they are saying; and when the statue was finished and set in its foundation, he uncovered it, and to tell the truth, this work eclipsed all other statues, both modern and ancient, whether Greek or Roman; and it can be said that neither the Marforio in Rome, nor the Tiber and the Nile of the Belvedere, nor the colossal statues of Monte Cavallo can be compared to this David, which Michelangelo completed with so much measure and beauty, and so much skill.

≫ Working with Sources

1. **How do these anecdotes illustrate the relationship between artists and their patrons (and funders) during the Renaissance?**

2. **How did Michelangelo deal with the legacy of artists from Greco-Roman antiquity?**

SOURCE 17.5

Galileo Galilei, Letter to the Grand Duchess Christina de' Medici

1615

This famous letter is often cited as an early sign of Galileo's inevitable conflict with church authorities over the Copernican system of planetary motion—and the theory's theological, as well as its scientific, ramifications. Galileo (1564–1642) would be condemned to house arrest in 1632 and forced to make a public repudiation of the heliocentric theory first advanced by Copernicus in the sixteenth century. However, Galileo's connection to the renowned Medici family of Florence was also cause for comment—and caution—from 1610, when he received an appointment and their implicit endorsement.

Constructing a telescope in 1609 (which he proudly claimed could "magnify objects more than 60 times"), Galileo trained it on the moons of Jupiter, which he tracked over several days in 1610. Having named these objects for the Medici family, he rushed these and many other astronomical observations into print in the *Sidereus Nuncius* (*The Starry Messenger*). Inviting other scientists to "apply themselves to examine and determine" these planetary motions, Galileo demonstrated a preference

---

Source: Galileo Galilei, *The Essential Galileo*, ed. and trans. Maurice A. Finocchiaro (Indianapolis: Hackett, 2008), §4.2.5—4.2.6, 140–144.

for the Copernican theory and elicited sharp responses, particularly from church officials. In 1615, the dowager Grand Duchess Christina, mother of his patron, Cosimo II, expressed her own reservations about the implications of the Copernican theory for a passage in the Old Testament. Galileo's response attempts, or seems to attempt, to reconcile experimental science and received religion.

Thus let these people apply themselves to refuting the arguments of Copernicus and of the others, and let them leave its condemnation as erroneous and heretical to the proper authorities; but let them not hope that the very cautious and very wise Fathers and the Infallible One with his absolute wisdom are about to make rash decisions like those into which they would be rushed by their special interests and feelings. For in regard to these and other similar propositions which do not directly involve the faith, no one can doubt that the Supreme Pontiff always has the absolute power of permitting or condemning them; however, no creature has the power of making them be true or false, contrary to what they happen to be by nature and de facto. So it seems more advisable to first become sure about the necessary and immutable truth of the matter, over which no one has control, than to condemn one side when such certainty is lacking; this would imply a loss of freedom of decision and of choice insofar as it would give necessity to things which are presently indifferent, free, and dependent on the will of the supreme authority. In short, if it is inconceivable that a proposition should be declared heretical when one thinks that it may be true, it should be futile for someone to try to bring about the condemnation of the earth's motion and sun's rest unless he first shows it to be impossible and false.

There remains one last thing for us to examine: to what extent it is true that the Joshua passage [Joshua 10:12–13] can be taken without altering the literal meaning of the words, and how it can be that, when the sun obeyed Joshua's order to stop, from this it followed that the day was prolonged by a large amount.

. . .

I think therefore, if I am not mistaken, that one can clearly see that, given the Ptolemaic system, it is necessary to interpret the words in a way different from their literal meaning. Guided by St. Augustine's very useful prescriptions, I should say that the best nonliteral interpretation is not necessarily this, if anyone can find another which is perhaps better and more suitable. So now I want to examine whether the same miracle could be understood in a way more in accordance with what we read in Joshua, if to the Copernican system we add another discovery which I recently made about the solar body. However, I continue to speak with the same reservations—to the effect that I am not so enamored with my own opinions as to want to place them ahead of those of others; nor do I believe it is impossible to put forth interpretations which are better and more in accordance with the Holy Writ.

Let us first assume in accordance with the opinion of the above-mentioned authors, that in the Joshua miracle the whole system of heavenly motions was stopped, so that the stopping of only one would not introduce unnecessarily universal confusion and great turmoil in the whole order of nature.

. . .

Furthermore, what deserves special appreciation, if I am not mistaken, is that with the Copernican system one can very clearly and very easily give a literal meaning to another detail which one reads about the same miracle; that is, that the sun stopped in the middle of heaven. Serious theologians have raised a difficulty about this passage: it seems very probable that, when Joshua asked for the prolongation of the day, the sun was close to setting and not at the meridian; for it was then about the time of the summer solstice, and consequently the days were very long, so that if the sun had been at the meridian then it does not seem likely that it would have been necessary to pray for a lengthening of the day in order to win a battle, since the still remaining time of seven hours or more could very well have been sufficient.

. . .

We can remove this and every other implausibility, if I am not mistaken, by placing the sun, as the Copernican system does and as it is most necessary to do, in the middle, namely, at the center of the heavenly orbs and of the planetary revolutions; for at any hour of the day, whether at noon or in the afternoon, the day would not have been lengthened and all heavenly turnings stopped by the sun stopping in the middle of the heavens, namely, at the center of the heavens, where it is located. Furthermore, this interpretation agrees all the more with the literal meaning inasmuch as, if one wanted to claim that the sun's stopping occurred at the noon hour, then the proper expression to use would have been to say that it "stood still at the meridian point," or "at the meridian circle," and not "in the middle of the heaven"; in fact, for a spherical body such as heaven, the middle is really and only the center.

> **» Working with Sources**

1. How does Galileo deal with the apparently irreconcilable conclusions of science and the Bible?

2. How would you characterize Galileo's tone in his analysis of the verses from the Book of Joshua?

New Patterns in New Worlds

COLONIALISM AND INDIGENOUS RESPONSES IN THE AMERICAS

Alonso Ortíz was a deadbeat. He fled from his creditors in Zafra, Estremadura, in southwestern Spain, in the early 1770s to find a new life in the Americas. In Mexico City, with the help of borrowed money, he set up shop as a tanner. His business flourished, and, with a partner, Ortíz expanded into two rented buildings. Eight Native American employees, whom he had trained, did the actual labor of stomping the hides in the vats filled with tanning acids. A black slave, belonging to his partner, was the supervisor. Happy that he no longer had to take his shoes off to work, Ortíz concentrated on giving instructions and hustling up business.

Ortíz's situation in Mexico City was not entirely legal, however. He had left his wife, Eleanor González, and children alone in Zafra, though the law required that families should be united. The authorities rarely enforced this law, but that was no guarantee for Ortíz. Furthermore, he had not yet sent his family any remittances, leaving Eleanor to rely on the largesse of her two brothers back home in Estremadura for survival. And then there was still the debt. Ortíz had reasons to be afraid of the law.

To avoid prosecution, Ortíz wrote a letter to Eleanor. In this letter, he proudly described the comfortable position he had achieved. He announced that his kind business partner was sending her a sum of money sufficient

THE AMERICAS
IN 1750

- Spanish
- Portuguese
- British
- French
- Dutch

ABOVE: **In his monumental *Historia de la conquista de México*, written more than 150 years after the events described, Antonio de Solís (1610–1686) depicted the meeting of Moctezuma and Cortés .**

to begin preparations for her departure from Spain. To his creditors, Ortíz promised to send 100 tanned hides within a year. "Your arrival would bring me great joy," he wrote to Eleanor, reneging on an original promise to have already returned home to Spain. Evidently aware of her reluctance to join him in Mexico, Ortíz closed his letter with a request to grant him 4 more years abroad and to do so with a notarized document from her hand. Unfortunately, we do not know her answer.

The Ortíz family drama gives a human face to European colonialism and emigration to the "New World" of the Americas. Like Alonso Ortíz, some 300,000 other Spaniards left the "Old World" (Europe, contiguous with Asia and Africa) between 1500 and 1800. They came alone or with family, temporarily or for good, and either failed or succeeded in their new lives. A few hundred letters by emigrants exist, giving us glimpses of their lives in Mexico, Peru, and other parts of the Americas conquered by the Spanish and Portuguese in the sixteenth century. As these relatively privileged immigrants settled, they hoped to build successful enterprises using the labor of Native Americans as well as that of black slaves imported from Africa. The example of Ortíz shows that even in the socially not very prestigious craft of tanning a man could achieve a measure of comfort by having people of even lower status working for him.

Seeing Patterns

> What is the significance of western Europeans acquiring the Americas as a warm-weather extension of their northern continent?

> What was the main pattern of social development in colonial America during the period 1500–1800?

> Why and how did European settlers in South and North America strive for self-government, and how successful were they in achieving their goals?

Beginning in the sixteenth century, the Americas became an extension of Europe. European settlers extracted mineral and agricultural resources from these new lands. In Europe these resources had become increasingly expensive and impractical to produce (if they could be produced at all). A pattern emerged in which gold and silver, as well as agricultural products that could not be grown in Europe's cooler climate, were intensively exploited. In their role as supplementary subtropical and tropical extensions of Europe, the Americas became a crucial factor in Europe's changing position in the world. First, Europe acquired large quantities of precious metals, which its two largest competitors, India and China, lacked. Second, with its new access to warm-weather agricultural products, Europe rose to a position of agrarian autonomy similar to that of India and China. In terms of resources, compared with the principal religious civilizations of India and China, Europe grew between 1550 and 1800 from a position of inferiority to one of near parity.

The Colonial Americas: Europe's Warm-Weather Extension

The European extension into the subtropical and tropical Americas followed Columbus's pursuit of a sea route to India and its spices that would circumvent the Mediterranean and its dominance by Muslim traders. The Spaniards justified the conquest of these new continents and their Native American inhabitants with

Land-labor grant (*encomienda*): Land grant by the government to an entrepreneur entitling him to use forced indigenous or imported slave labor on that land for the exploitation of agricultural and mineral resources.

Bartolomé de las Casas, from *A Short Account of the Destruction of the Indies* (1542)

Christ's command to convert the heathen in the Spanish Habsburg World Empire, the glorious final empire before Christ's return. They financed their imperial expansion as well as their wars against Ottoman and European rivals with American gold and silver, leaving little for domestic investment in productive enterprises. A pattern evolved in which Iberian settlers transformed the Americas into mineral-extracting and agrarian colonies based on either cheap or forced labor.

The Conquest of Mexico and Peru

The Spanish conquerors of the Aztec and Inca Empires, although few in number, succeeded by exploiting internal weaknesses in the empires. They swiftly eliminated the top of the power structures, paralyzing the decision-making apparatuses long enough for their conquests to succeed. Soon after the conquests, the Old World disease of smallpox—to which New World inhabitants had never been exposed and therefore had never developed immunity—ravaged the Native American population and dramatically reduced the indigenous labor force. To make up for this reduction, colonial authorities imported black slaves from Africa for employment in mines and in agriculture. Black Africans, who had long been in contact with Eurasia, were, like Europeans, less susceptible to smallpox. A three-tiered society of European immigrants, Native Americans, and black slaves emerged in the Spanish and Portuguese Americas.

From Trading Posts to Conquest   Columbus had discovered the Caribbean islands under a royal commission, which entitled him to build fortified posts and to trade with the indigenous Taínos. Friendly trade relations with the Taínos, however, quickly deteriorated into outright exploitation, with the Spaniards usurping the traditional entitlements of the Taíno chiefs to the labor of their fellow men, who panned gold in rivers or mined it in shallow shafts. With the help of **land-labor grants** (Spanish *encomiendas*), the Spanish took over from the Taíno chiefs and, through forced labor, amassed sizable quantities of gold. What had begun as trade-post settlement turned into full-blown conquest of land.

The Spaniards conquered the Caribbean islands not only through force. Much more severe in its consequences was the indirect conquest through disease. The Old World disease of smallpox quickly wiped out an estimated 250,000 to 1 million Taínos on the larger northern islands as well as the less numerous Caribs on the smaller southern islands. Isolated since the Ice Age from the rest of humankind, Native Americans possessed no immunity against smallpox and were similarly ravaged by other introduced diseases.

Protests, mostly among members of the clergy, arose against both the brutal labor exploitation by the conquerors and the helplessness of the Taínos against disease. Unfortunately, the protesters remained a small minority, even within the clergy. One notable protestor was Bartolomé de las Casas (1474–1566), from a family of merchants in Seville. Las Casas had practiced law before emigrating to Hispaniola, where he received an *encomienda*. After becoming a priest in 1510 and later a Dominican monk, however, he became a bitter opponent of the land-labor grant system, which finally came to an end after 1542 with the introduction of the *repartimiento* system (see p. 534).

First Mainland Conquests   Another early settler on Hispaniola was Hernán Cortés (1485–1547). His father was a lower-level nobleman in Estremadura, a rough, formerly Islamic frontier region in southwestern Iberia. Chosen by his parents for a career in law, Cortés learned Latin but left the university before graduation. After his arrival in the New World in 1504, he advanced quickly from governmental scribe in Hispaniola to mayor of Santiago in Cuba. Thanks to several labor grants, he became rich. When the Cuban governor asked him in the fall of 1518 to equip and lead a small preparatory expedition for trade and exploration to the Yucatán Peninsula in southeastern Mexico, Cortés enthusiastically agreed. Within a month he assembled 300 men, considerably exceeding his contract. The governor tried to stop him, but Cortés departed quickly for the American mainland.

Cultural Intermediary. The Tabascans gave Malinche, or Doña Marina, to Hernán Cortés as a form of tribute after they were defeated by the Spanish. Malinche served Cortés as a translator and mistress, playing a central role in Cortés's eventual victory over the Aztecs. She was in many respects the principal face of the Spanish and is always depicted center stage in Native American visual accounts of the conquest.

As the Cuban governor had feared, Cortés did not bother with trading posts in Yucatán. The Spanish had previously learned of the existence of the Aztec Empire, with its immense silver and gold treasures. In a first encounter, Cortés's motley force—numbering by now about 530 Spanish men—defeated a much larger indigenous force at Tabasco. The Spaniards' steel weapons and armor proved superior in hand-to-hand combat to the obsidian-spiked lances and wooden swords, as well as quilted cotton vests of the defenders.

Among the gifts of submission presented by the defeated Native Americans in Tabasco was Malinche, a Nahuatl [NA-hua]-speaking woman. Her widowed Aztec mother had sold her into slavery to the Tabascans after her remarriage. Malinche quickly learned Spanish and became the consort of Cortés, teaching him about the subtleties of Aztec culture. In her role as translator, Malinche was nearly as decisive as Cortés in shaping events. Indeed, Aztecs often used the name of Malinche when addressing Cortés, forgetting that her voice was not that of Cortés. With Tabasco conquered, Cortés quickly moved on; he was afraid that the Cuban governor, who was in pursuit, would otherwise force him to return to Cuba.

Conquest of the Aztec Empire On the southeast coast of Mexico, Cortés founded the city of Veracruz as a base from which to move inland. In the city, he had his followers elect a town council, which made Cortés their head and chief justice, allowing Cortés to claim legitimacy for his march inland. To prevent opponents in his camp from notifying the Cuban governor of his usurpation of authority, Cortés

interactive timeline

1492	1516–1556	1521
Christopher Columbus lands in the Caribbean	Reign of Charles V, Habsburg king of Spain and the Americas	Spanish conquest of the Aztec Empire in Mexico

1500	1519–1521	1532–1533
Pedro Álvares Cabral claims Brazil for Portugal	Reign of Cuauhtémoc, last ruler of the Aztec Empire	Reign of Atahualpa, last ruler of the Inca Empire

1533	1607	1690
Spanish conquest of the Inca Empire in Peru	Jamestown, Virginia, first permanent English settlement	Gold discovered in Brazil

1545	1608
Founding of silver mine of Potosí	Quebec City, first permanent French settlement

Cortés and the conquest
of the Aztec Empire

had all ships stripped of their gear and the hulls sunk. Marching inland, the Spaniards ran into resistance from indigenous people, suffering their first losses of horses and men. Although bloodied, they continued their march with thousands of Native American allies, most notably the Tlaxcalans, traditional enemies of the Aztecs. The support from these indigenous peoples made a crucial difference when Cortés and his army reached the court of the Aztecs.

When Cortés arrived at the city of Tenochtitlán on November 2, 1519, the emperor Moctezuma II (r. 1502–1519) was in a quandary over how to react to these invaders whose depredations neither his tributaries nor his enemies had been able to stop. To gain time, Moctezuma greeted the Spaniard in person on one of the causeways leading to the city and invited him to his palace. Cortés and his company, now numbering some 600 Spaniards, took up quarters in the palace precincts. After a week of gradually deteriorating discussions, Cortés suddenly put the incredulous emperor under house arrest and made him swear allegiance to Charles V.

Before being able to contemplate his next move, however, Cortés was diverted by the need to march back east, where troops from Cuba had arrived to arrest him. After defeating those troops, he pressed the remnants into his own service and returned to Tenochtitlán. During his absence, the Spaniards who had remained in Moctezuma's palace had massacred a number of unarmed Aztec nobles participating in a religious ceremony. An infuriated crowd of Tenochtitlán's inhabitants invaded the palace. In the melee, Moctezuma and some 200 Spaniards died. The rest of the Spanish fled for their lives, retreating east to their Tlaxcalan allies, who, fortunately, remained loyal. Here, after his return, Cortés devised a new plan for capturing Tenochtitlán.

"The Capture of
Tenochtitlán"

After 10 months of preparations, the Spaniards returned to the Aztec capital. In command now of about 2,000 Spanish soldiers and assisted by some 50,000 Native American troops, Cortés laid siege to the city, bombarding it from ships he had built in the lake and razing buildings during forays onto land. After nearly 3 months, much of the city was in ruins, fresh water and food became scarce, and smallpox began to decimate the population of some 3–4 million inhabitants in the Mexican Basin and 25 million throughout the Aztec Empire. On August 21, 1521, the Spaniards and their allies stormed the city and looted its gold treasury. They captured the fiercely resisting last emperor, Cuauhtémoc [cu-aw-TAY-moc], a few days later and executed him in 1525, thus ending the Aztec Empire (see Map 18.1 and Source 18.1).

Conquest of the Inca Empire At about the same time, a relative of Cortés, Francisco Pizarro (ca. 1475–1541), conceived a plan to conquer the Andean empire of the Incas (which, in 1492, comprised some 9–12 million inhabitants). Pizarro, like Cortés born in Estremadura, was an illegitimate and uneducated son of an infantry captain from the lower nobility. Arriving in Hispaniola as part of an expedition in 1513 that went on to discover Panama and the Pacific, he became mayor of Panama City, acquired some wealth, and began to hear rumors about an empire of gold and silver to the south. After a failed initial expedition, he and 13 followers captured some precious metal from an oceangoing Inca sailing raft. Receiving a permit to establish a trading post from Charles V, Pizarro departed with a host of 183 men in late December 1530.

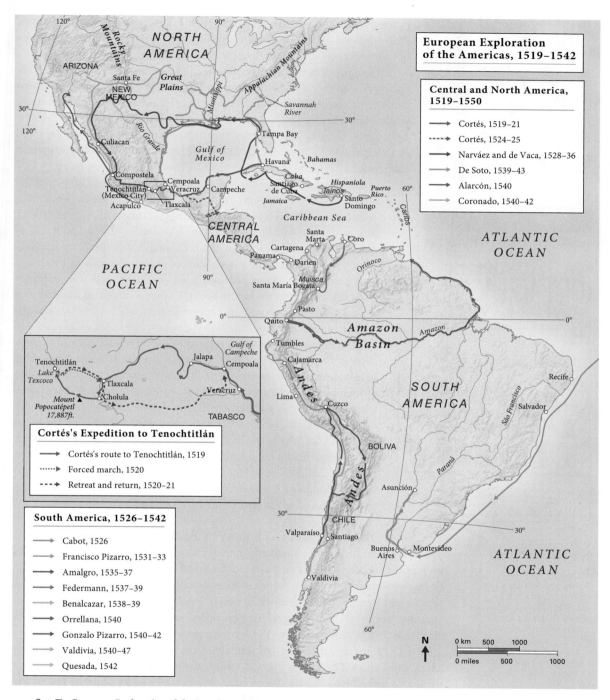

European Exploration of the Americas, 1519–1542

Central and North America, 1519–1550

→ Cortés, 1519–21
┄┄→ Cortés, 1524–25
→ Narváez and de Vaca, 1528–36
→ De Soto, 1539–43
→ Alarcón, 1540
→ Coronado, 1540–42

Cortés's Expedition to Tenochtitlán

→ Cortés's route to Tenochtitlán, 1519
┈┈→ Forced march, 1520
┄┄→ Retreat and return, 1520–21

South America, 1526–1542

→ Cabot, 1526
→ Francisco Pizarro, 1531–33
→ Amalgro, 1535–37
→ Federmann, 1537–39
→ Benalcazar, 1538–39
→ Orrellana, 1540
→ Gonzalo Pizarro, 1540–42
→ Valdivia, 1540–47
→ Quesada, 1542

MAP **18.1** **The European Exploration of the Americas, 1519–1542.**

In a grimly fortuitous bit of luck for Pizarro, smallpox had preceded him in his expedition. In the later 1520s, the disease had ravaged the Inca Empire, killing the emperor and his heir apparent and leading to a protracted war of succession between two surviving sons. Atahualpa, in the north, sent his army south to the capital, Cuzco, where

ATAHUALLPA. INCA XIIII.

Conquest by Surprise. The Spanish conqueror Francisco Pizarro captured Emperor Atahualpa (*top*) in an ambush. Atahualpa promised a roomful of gold in return for his release, but the Spaniards collected the gold and murdered Atahualpa (*bottom*) before generals of the Inca army could organize an armed resistance.

it defeated his half-brother, Huáscar. When Pizarro entered the Inca Empire, Atahualpa was encamped with an army of 40,000 men near the northern town of Cajamarca, on his way south to Cuzco to install himself as emperor.

Arriving at Cajamarca, Pizarro succeeded in arranging an unarmed audience with Atahualpa in the town square. On November 16, 1532, Atahualpa came to this audience, surrounded by several thousand unarmed retainers, while Pizarro hid his soldiers in and behind the buildings around the square. At a signal, these soldiers rushed into the square. Some soldiers captured Atahualpa to hold him hostage. In the ensuing bloodbath, not one Spanish soldier was killed. The whole massacre was over in less than an hour.

With his ambush, Pizarro succeeded in paralyzing the Inca Empire at the very top. Without their emperor, Atahualpa, none of the generals in Cuzco dared to seize the initiative. Instead of ordering his generals to liberate him, Atahualpa sought to satisfy the greed of his captors with a room full of gold and silver as ransom. In the following 2 months, Inca administrators delivered immense quantities of precious metals to Pizarro in Cajamarca. During the same time, however, the Spanish were in fear of being attacked from the north. Spanish officers subjected Atahualpa to a mock trial and executed the hapless king on July 26, 1533, hoping to keep the Incas disorganized.

And indeed, the northern forces broke off their march and thereby allowed the Spaniards to take the capital. The Spaniards did so against minimal resistance, massacring the inhabitants and stripping Cuzco of its immense gold and silver treasures. Pizarro did not stay long in the now worthless, isolated city in the Andes. In 1535 he founded a new capital, Lima, which was more conveniently located on the coast and about halfway between Cajamarca and Cuzco. At this time, Incas in the south finally overcame their paralysis. Learning from past mistakes, they avoided mass battles, focused on deadly guerilla strikes, and rebuilt a kingdom that held out until 1572. It was only then that the Spanish gained full control of the Inca Empire.

The Portuguese Conquest of Brazil The Portuguese were not far behind the Spaniards in their pursuit of conquest. Navigators from both Spain and Portugal had first sighted the Brazilian coast in 1499–1500, and the Portuguese quickly claimed it for themselves. Brazil's indigenous population at that time is estimated to have amounted to nearly 5 million. The great majority lived in temporary or permanent villages based on agriculture, fishing, and hunting. Only a small minority in remote areas of the Amazon were pure foragers.

The Portuguese were interested initially in trade with the villagers, mostly for a type of hardwood called brazilwood, which was used as a red dye. When French traders appeared, ignoring the Portuguese commercial treaties with the tribes, the Portuguese crown shifted from simple trade agreements to trading-post settlements. This involved giving land grants to commoners and lower noblemen with the obligation to build fortified coastal villages for settlers and to engage in agriculture and friendly trade. By the mid-sixteenth century, a handful of these villages became successful, their inhabitants intermarrying with the surrounding indigenous chieftain families and establishing sugarcane plantations.

Explanations for the Spanish Success   The slow progression of the Portuguese in Brazil is readily understood. But the stupendous victories of handfuls of Spaniards over huge empires with millions of inhabitants and large cities defy easy explanation. Five factors invite consideration.

First, and most important, the conquistadors went straight to the top of the imperial pyramid. The emperors and their courts expected diplomatic deference from inferiors, among whom they included the minuscule band of Spaniards. Confronted, instead, with a calculated combination of arrogance and brutality, the emperors and courts were thrown off balance by the Spaniards, who ruthlessly exploited their opportunity. As the emperors were removed from the top level, the administration immediately below them fell into paralysis, unable to seize the initiative and respond in a timely fashion.

Second, both the Aztec and Inca Empires were relatively recent creations in which there were individuals and groups who contested the hierarchical power structure. The conquistadors either found allies among the subject populations or encountered a divided leadership. In either case, they were able to exploit divisions in the empires.

Third, European-introduced diseases, traveling with or ahead of the conquerors, took a devastating toll. In both empires, smallpox hit at critical moments during or right before the Spanish invasions, causing major disruptions.

Fourth, thanks to horses and superior European steel weapons and armor, primarily pikes, swords, and breastplates, small numbers of Spaniards were able to hold large numbers of attacking Aztecs and Incas at bay in hand-to-hand combat. Contrary to widespread belief, cannons and matchlock muskets were less important, since they were useless in close encounters. Firearms were still too slow and inaccurate to be decisive.

A fifth factor, indigenous religion, was probably of least significance. According to some now-outdated interpretations, Moctezuma was immobilized by his belief in a prophecy that he would have to relinquish his power to the savior Quetzalcoatl returning from his mythical city of Tlapallan on the east coast (see Chapter 15). Modern scholarship provides convincing reasons, however, to declare this prophecy a postconquest legend, circulated by Cortés both to flatter Charles V and to aggrandize himself as the predicted savior figure bringing Christianity.

The Establishment of Colonial Institutions

The Spanish crown established administrative hierarchies in the Americas, similar to those of the Aztecs and Incas, with governors at the top of the hierarchy and descending through lower ranks of functionaries. A small degree of settler autonomy

Brazil in 1519. This early map is fairly accurate for the northern coast but increasingly less accurate as one moves south. First explorations of the south by both Portuguese and Spanish mariners date to 1513–1516. Ferdinand Magellan passed through several places along the southern coast on his journey around the world in 1520–1521. The scenes on the map depict Native Americans cutting and collecting brazilwood, the source of a red dye much in demand by the Portuguese during the early period of colonization.

Spanish Steel. The *Lienzo de Tlaxcala*, from the middle part of the sixteenth century, is our best visual source for the conquest of Mexico. In this scene, Malinche, protected by a shield, directs the battle on the causeway leading to Tenochtitlán. The two Spanish soldiers behind her, one fully armored, brandish steel swords, which were more effective than the obsidian blades carried by the Aztec defenders (one of whom is dressed in leopard skins), shown on the left.

Creoles: American-born descendants of European, primarily Spanish, immigrants.

was permitted through town and city councils, but the crown was determined to make the Americas a territorial extension of the European pattern of centralized state formation. Several hundred thousand settlers (including Alonso Ortíz) found a new life in the Americas, mostly as urban craftspeople, administrators, and professionals. By the early seventeenth century, a powerful elite of Spanish who had been born in America, called **Creoles** (Spanish *criollos*) was in place, first to assist and later to replace most of the administrators sent from Spain in the governance of the Americas (see Map 18.2).

From Conquest to Colonialism   The unimaginable riches of Cortés and Pizarro inspired numerous further expeditions. Adventurers struck out with small bands of followers into Central and North America, Chile, and the Amazon. Their expeditions, however, yielded only modest amounts of gold and earned more from selling captured Native Americans into slavery. In the north, expeditions penetrated as far as Arizona, New Mexico, Texas, Oklahoma, Kansas, and Florida but encountered only villagers and the relatively poor Pueblo towns. No new golden kingdoms (the mythical El Dorado, or "golden city") beyond the Aztec and Inca Empires were discovered in the Americas.

In the mid-sixteenth century, easy looting was replaced by a search for the mines from where the precious metals came. In northern Mexico, Native Americans led a group of soldiers and missionaries in 1547 to a number of rich silver mines. In addition, explorers discovered silver in Bolivia (1545) and northern Mexico (1556), gold in Chile (1552), and mercury in Peru (1563). The conquistadors shifted from looting to the exploitation of Native American labor in mines and in agriculture.

In a small number of areas, indigenous peoples resisted incorporation into the Spanish colonies. Notably, in southern Chile the Mapuche repulsed all attempts by the Spanish to subdue them. They had already prevented the Incas from expanding their empire to the southern tip of the continent. Initially, in 1550–1553 the Spanish succeeded in establishing a number of forts and opening a gold mine. But in campaign after campaign they failed to gain more than a border strip with an adjacent no-man's-land. In 1612 they agreed to a temporary peace which left the majority of the Mapuche independent.

Another Native American people who successfully resisted the Spanish conquest were the Asháninka in the Peruvian rain forest. Located along the Eno River, one of the headwater tributaries of the Amazon, they were the first standing in the way of the Spanish attempts to extend their dominance from Peru eastward. The Asháninka exploited hillside salt veins in their region and were traders of goods between the Andes and the rain forest. Although Jesuits and later Franciscans established missions among the Asháninka in the 1600s, they failed to make many converts. It was only in 1737 that the Spanish finally built a fort in the region—a first step toward projecting colonial power into the rain forest.

Bureaucratic Efficiency   During the first two generations after the conquest, Spain maintained an efficient colonial administration, which delivered between 50

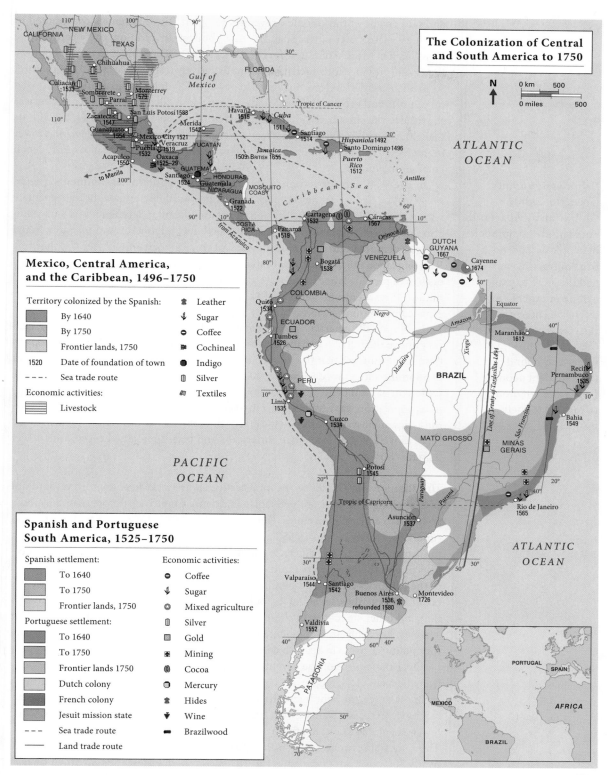

The Colonization of Central and South America to 1750

N

0 km 500
0 miles 500

Mexico, Central America, and the Caribbean, 1496–1750

Territory colonized by the Spanish:

▨	By 1640
▨	By 1750
▨	Frontier lands, 1750
1520	Date of foundation of town
- - -	Sea trade route

Economic activities:

▤	Livestock

✿	Leather		
↓	Sugar		
⊖	Coffee		
✽	Cochineal		
●	Indigo		
⃞	Silver		
▨	Textiles		

Spanish and Portuguese South America, 1525–1750

Spanish settlement:

▨	To 1640
▨	To 1750
▨	Frontier lands, 1750

Portuguese settlement:

▨	To 1640
▨	To 1750
▨	Frontier lands 1750
▨	Dutch colony
▨	French colony
▨	Jesuit mission state
- - -	Sea trade route
——	Land trade route

Economic activities:

⊖	Coffee
↓	Sugar
◉	Mixed agriculture
⃞	Silver
▢	Gold
✚	Mining
◉	Cocoa
◐	Mercury
✿	Hides
♥	Wine
▬	Brazilwood

MAP 18.2 **The Colonization of Central and South America to 1750.**

map analysis

and 60 percent of the colonies' revenues to Spain. These revenues contributed as much as one-quarter of the Spanish crown budget. In addition, the viceroyalty of New Spain in Mexico remitted another 25 percent of its revenues to the Philippines, the Pacific province for which it was administratively responsible from 1571 onward. As in Spain, settlers in New Spain had to pay up to 40 different taxes and dues, levied on imports and exports, internal trade, mining, and sales. The only income tax was the tithe to the church, which the administration collected and, at times, used for its own budgetary purposes. Altogether, however, for the settlers the tax level was lower in the New World than in Spain, and the same was true for the English and French colonies in North America.

Labor assignment (*repartimiento*): Obligation by villagers to send stipulated numbers of people as laborers to a contractor, who had the right to exploit a mine or other labor-intensive enterprise; the contractors paid the laborers minimal wages and bound them through debt peonage (repayment of money advances) to their businesses.

In the 1540s the government introduced rotating **labor assignments** (*repartimientos*) to phase out the *encomiendas* that powerful owners sought to perpetuate within their families. This institution of rotating labor assignments was a continuation of the *mit'a* system, which the Incas had devised as a form of taxation, in the absence of money and easy transportation of crops in their empire (see Chapter 15). Rotating labor assignments meant that for fixed times a certain percentage of villagers had to provide labor to the state for road building, drainage, transportation, and mining. Private entrepreneurs could also contract for indigenous labor assignments, especially in mining regions.

In Mexico the *repartimiento* fell out of use in the first half of the seventeenth century due to the toll of recurring smallpox epidemics on the Native American population. It is estimated that the indigenous population in the Americas, from a height of 54 million in 1550, declined to 10 million by 1700 before recovering again. The replacement for the lost workers was wage labor. In highland Peru, where the indigenous population was less densely settled and the effects of smallpox were less severe, the assignment system lasted to the end of the colonial period. Wage labor expanded there as well. Wages for Native Americans and blacks remained everywhere lower than for those for Creoles.

The Rise of the Creoles Administrative and fiscal efficiency, however, did not last very long. The wars of the Spanish Habsburg Empire cost more than the crown was able to collect in revenues. King Philip II (r. 1556–1598) had to declare bankruptcy four times between 1557 and 1596. In order to make up the financial deficit, the crown began to sell offices in the Americas to the highest bidders. The first offices put on the block were elective positions in the municipal councils. By the end of the century, Creoles had purchased life appointments in city councils as well as positions as scribes, local judges, police chiefs, directors of processions and festivities, and other sinecures. In these positions, they collected fees and rents for their services. Local oligarchies emerged, effectively ending whatever elective, participatory politics existed in Spanish colonial America.

Over the course of the seventeenth century a majority of administrative positions became available for purchase. The effects of the change from recruitment by merit to recruitment by wealth on the functioning of the bureaucracy were far-reaching. Creoles advanced on a broad front in the administrative positions, while fewer Spaniards found it attractive to buy their American positions from overseas. The only opportunities which European Spaniards still found enticing were the nearly 300 positions of governors and inspectors, since these jobs gave their owners the right to subject the Native Americans to forced purchases of goods, yielding huge profits. For the most part, wealthy Spanish merchants delegated junior partners to these highly lucrative activities. By 1700, the consequences of the Spanish crown selling most of its American administrative offices were a decline in the competence of office holders, the emergence of a Creole elite able to bend the Spanish administration increasingly to its will, and a decentralization of the decision-making processes.

Northwest European Interference   As Spain's administrative grip on the Americas weakened during the seventeenth century, the need to defend the continents militarily against European interlopers arose. At the beginning, there were European privateers, holding royal charters, who harassed Spanish silver shipments and ports in the Caribbean. In the early seventeenth century, the French, English, and Dutch governments sent ships to occupy the smaller Caribbean islands not claimed by Spain. Privateer and contraband traders stationed on these islands engaged in further raiding and pillaging, severely damaging Spain's monopoly of shipping between Europe and the Caribbean.

engraving showing English attack on the Spanish settlement of St. Augustine, Florida, 1589

Conquests of Spanish islands followed in the second half of the century. England captured Jamaica in 1655, and France colonized western Hispaniola (Saint-Domingue) in 1665, making it one of their most profitable sugar-producing colonies. Along the Pacific coast, depredations continued into the middle of the eighteenth century. Here, the galleons of the annual Acapulco–Manila fleet carrying silver from Mexico to China and returning with Chinese silks, porcelain, and lacquerware were the targets of English privateers. Over the course of the seventeenth century, Spain allocated one-half to two-thirds of its American revenues to the increasingly difficult defense of its annual treasure fleets and Caribbean possessions.

Bourbon Reforms   After the death of the last, childless Habsburg king of Spain in 1700, the new French-descended dynasty of the Bourbons made major efforts to regain control over their American possessions. They had to begin from a discouragingly weak position as nearly 90 percent of all goods traded from Europe to the Americas were of non-Spanish origin. Fortunately, population increases among the settlers as well as the Native Americans (after having overcome their horrific losses to disease) offered opportunities to Spanish manufacturers and merchants. After several false starts, in the middle of the eighteenth century the Bourbon reform program began to show results.

The reforms aimed at improved naval connections and administrative control between the mother country and the colonies. The monopolistic annual armed silver fleet was greatly reduced. Instead, the government authorized more frequent single sailings at different times of the year. Newly formed Spanish companies, receiving exclusive rights at specific ports, succeeded in reducing contraband trade. Elections took place again for municipal councils. Spanish-born salaried officials replaced scores of Creole tax and office farmers. The original two viceroyalties were subdivided into four, to improve administrative control. The sale of tobacco and brandy became state monopolies. Silver mining and cotton textile manufacturing were expanded. By the second half of the eighteenth century, Spain had regained a measure of control over its colonies.

As a result, government revenues rose substantially. Tax receipts increased more than twofold, even taking into account the inflation of the late eighteenth century.

In the end, however, the reforms remained incomplete. Since the Spanish economy was not also reformed, in terms of expanding crafts production and urbanization, the changes did not diminish the English and French dominance of the import market by much. Spain failed to produce textiles, metalwares, and household goods at competitive prices for the colonies; thus the level of English and French exports to the Americas remained high.

Early Portuguese Colonialism   In contrast to the Spanish Americas, the Portuguese overseas province of Brazil remained initially confined to a broad coastal strip, which developed only slowly during the sixteenth century. The first governor-general arrived in 1549. He and his successors (after 1640 called "viceroys," as in the Spanish colonies) were members of the high aristocracy, but their positions were salaried and subject to term limits. As the colony grew, the crown created a council in the capital of Lisbon for all Brazilian appointments and established a high court for all judicial affairs in Bahia in northern Brazil. Commoners with law degrees filled the nonmilitary colonial positions. In the early seventeenth century, however, offices became as open to purchase as in the Spanish colonies, although not on the city council level, where a complex indirect electoral process survived.

Jesuits converted the Native Americans, whom they transported to Jesuit-administered villages. Colonial cities and Jesuits repeatedly clashed over the slave raids of the "pioneers" (*bandeirantes*) in village territories. The bandeirantes came mostly from São Paulo in the south and roamed the interior in search of human prey. Native American slaves were in demand on the wheat farms and cattle ranches of São Paulo as well as on the sugar plantations of the northeast. Although the Portuguese crown and church had, like the Spanish, forbidden the enslavement of Native Americans, the bandeirantes exploited a loophole. The law was interpreted as allowing the enslavement of Native Americans who resisted conversion to Christianity. For a long time, Lisbon and the Jesuits were powerless against this flagrantly self-interested interpretation.

Expansion into the Interior   In the middle of the seventeenth century, the Jesuits and Native Americans finally succeeded in pushing many bandeirantes west and north, where they switched from slave raiding to prospecting for gold. In the far north, however, the raids continued until 1680, when the Portuguese administration finally prevailed and ended Native American slavery, almost a century and a half after Spain. Ironically, it was mostly thanks to the "pioneer" raids for slaves that Brazil expanded westward, to assume the borders it has today.

As a result of gold discoveries in Minas Gerais in 1690 by bandeirantes, the European immigrant population increased rapidly, from 1 to 2 million during the 1700s. Minas Gerais, located north of Rio de Janeiro, was the first inland region of the colony to attract settlers. By contrast, as a result of smallpox epidemics beginning in the 1650s in the Brazilian interior, the Native American population declined massively, not to expand again until the end of the eighteenth century. To replace the lost labor, Brazilians imported slaves from Africa, at first to work in the sugar plantations and, after 1690, in the mines, where their numbers increased to two-thirds of the labor force. In contrast to Spanish mines, Brazilian mines were surface operations requiring only minimal equipment outlays. Most blacks worked with pickaxes and shovels. The peak of the gold boom came in the 1750s, when the importance of gold was second only to that of sugar among Brazilian exports to Europe.

Early in the gold boom, the crown created the new Ministry of the Navy and Overseas Territories, which greatly expanded the administrative structure in Brazil. It established 14 regions and a second high court in Rio de Janeiro, which replaced Bahia as the capital in 1736. The ministry in Lisbon ended the sale of offices, increased the efficiency of tax collection, and encouraged Brazilian textile manufacturing to render the province more independent from English imports. By the mid-1700s, Brazil was a flourishing overseas colony of Portugal, producing brazilwood, sugar, gold, tobacco, cacao, and vanilla for export.

North American Settlements Efforts at settlement in the less hospitable North America in the sixteenth century were unsuccessful. Only in the early part of the seventeenth century did French, English, and Dutch merchant investors succeed in establishing small communities of settlers on the coast, who grew their own food on land purchased from the local Native American villagers. These settlements were Jamestown (founded in 1607 in today's Virginia), Quebec (1608, Canada), Plymouth and Boston (1620 and 1630, respectively, in today's Massachusetts), and New Amsterdam (1625, today's New York). Subsistence agriculture and fur, however, were meager ingredients if the settlements were to prosper. The settlements struggled through the seventeenth century, sustained either by Catholic missionary efforts or by the Protestant enthusiasm of the Puritans who had escaped persecution in England. Southern places like Jamestown survived because they adopted tobacco, a warm-weather plant, as a cash crop for export to Europe. In contrast to Mexico and Peru, the North American settlements were not followed—at least not at first—by territorial conquests (see Map 18.3).

Native Americans European arrivals in North America soon began supplementing agriculture with trade. They exchanged metal and glass wares, beads, and seashells for furs, especially beaver pelts, with the Native American groups of the interior. The more these groups came into contact with the European traders, however, the more dramatic the demographic impact of the trade on them was: Smallpox, already a menace during the 1500s in North America, became devastating as contacts intensified. In New England, for example, of the approximately 144,000 estimated Native Americans in 1600, fewer than 15,000 remained in 1620.

The introduction of guns contributed an additional lethal factor to trading arrangements, as English, French, and Dutch traders provided their favorite Native

Mine Workers. The discovery of gold and diamonds in Minas Gerais led to a boom, but did little to contribute to the long-term health of the Brazilian economy. With the Native American population decimated by disease, African slaves performed the backbreaking work.

Samuel de Champlain's map of the northeast coast of North America, ca. 1607

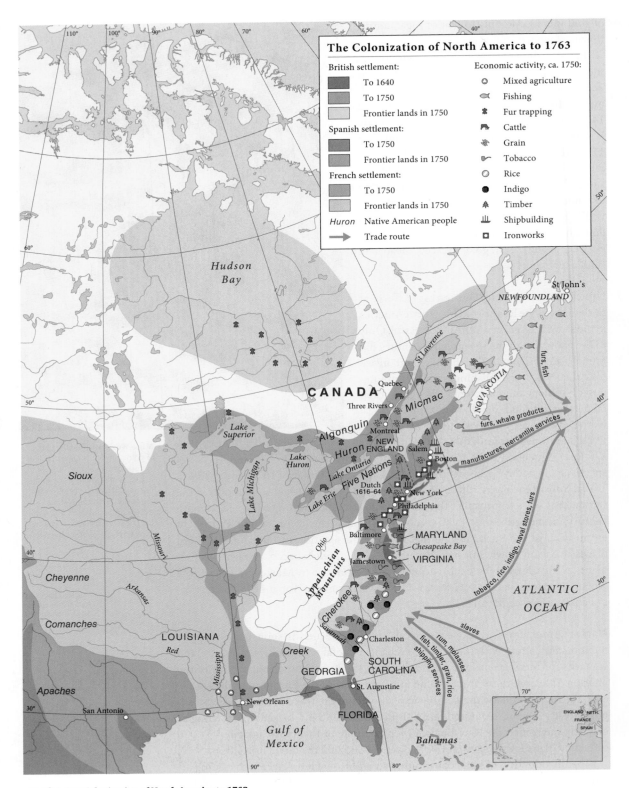

The Colonization of North America to 1763

British settlement:
- To 1640
- To 1750
- Frontier lands in 1750

Spanish settlement:
- To 1750
- Frontier lands in 1750

French settlement:
- To 1750
- Frontier lands in 1750

Huron Native American people
→ Trade route

Economic activity, ca. 1750:
- Mixed agriculture
- Fishing
- Fur trapping
- Cattle
- Grain
- Tobacco
- Rice
- Indigo
- Timber
- Shipbuilding
- Ironworks

MAP 18.3 **The Colonization of North America to 1763.**

American trading partners with flintlocks in order to increase the yield of furs. As a result, in the course of the 1600s the Iroquois in the northeast were able to organize themselves into a heavily armed and independent-minded federation, capable of inflicting heavy losses on rival groups as well as on European traders and settlers.

Farther south, in Virginia, the Jamestown settlers encountered the Powhatan confederacy. These Native Americans, living in some 200 well-fortified, palisaded villages, dominated the region between the Chesapeake Bay and the Appalachian Mountains. Initially, the Powhatan supplied Jamestown with foodstuffs and sought to integrate the settlement into their confederation. When this attempt at integration failed, however, benevolence turned to hostility, and the confederacy raided Jamestown twice in an attempt to rid their region of foreign settlers. But the latter were able to turn the tables and defeat the Powhatan in 1646, thereafter occupying their lands and reducing them to small scattered remnants. Pocahontas, the daughter of the Powhatan chief at the time of the foundation of Jamestown, was captured during one of the raids, converted to Christianity, and lived in England for a number of years as the wife of a returning settler. The decline of the Powhatan in the later 1600s allowed English settlers to move westward, in contrast to New England in the north, where the Iroquois, although allied with the English against the French, blocked any western expansion.

John Smith, excerpt from *The Generall Historie of Virginia* (1624)

The Iroquois were fiercely determined to maintain their dominance of the fur trade and wrought havoc among the Native American groups living between New England and the Great Lakes. In the course of the second half of the 1600s they drove many smaller groups westward into the Great Lakes region and Mississippi plains, where these groups settled as refugees. French officials and Jesuit missionaries sought to create some sort of alliance with the refugee peoples, to counterbalance the powerful Iroquois to the east. Many Native Americans converted to Christianity, creating a Creole Christianity similar to that of the Africans of Kongo and the Mexicans after the Spanish conquest of the Aztecs.

Major population movements also occurred farther west on the Great Plains, where the Apaches arrived from the Great Basin in the Rockies. They had captured horses which had escaped during the Pueblo uprising of 1680–1695 against Spain. The Comanches, who arrived at the same time also from the west and on horses, had, in addition, acquired firearms and around 1725 began their expansion at the expense of the Apaches. The Sioux from the northern forests and the Cheyenne from the Great Basin added to the mix of federations on the Great Plains in the early 1700s. At this time, the great transformation of the Native Americans in the center of North America into horse breeders and horsemen warriors began. Smallpox epidemics did not reach the Plains until the mid-1700s while in the east the ravages of this epidemic had weakened the Iroquois so much that they concluded a peace with the French in 1701.

Land Sale. Signatures of the leaders of the Iroquois federation on a treaty with Thomas and Richard Penn in 1736. By the terms of this treaty the Iroquois sold lands west of the Susquehanna River to the sons of the founders of the English colony of Pennsylvania. The leaders of the six nations that made up the Iroquois federation (Mohawk, Oneida, Onondaga, Cayuga, Seneca, and Tuscarora) signed with their pictograms. Their names were added later.

French Canada The involvement of the French in the Great Lakes region with refugees fleeing from the Iroquois was part of a program of expansion into the center of North America, begun in 1663 (see Source 18.4). The governor of Quebec had dispatched explorers, fur traders, and missionaries not only into the Great Lakes region but also into the Mississippi valley. The French government then sent farmers, craftspeople, and young single women from France with government-issued agricultural implements and livestock to establish settlements. The most successful settlement was in the subtropical district at the mouth of the Mississippi, called "La Louisiane," where some 300 settlers with 4,000 African slaves founded sugar plantations. Immigration was restricted to French subjects and excluded Protestants. Given these restrictions, Louisiana received only some 30,000 settlers by 1750, in contrast to English North America, with nearly 1.2 million settlers by the same time.

Colonial Assemblies As immigration to New England picked up, the merchant companies in Europe, which had financed the journeys of the settlers, were initially responsible for the administration of about a dozen settlement colonies. The first settlers to demand participation in the colonial administration were Virginian tobacco growers with interests in the European trade. In 1619 they deputized delegates from their villages to meet as the House of Burgesses. They thereby created an early popular assembly in North America, assisting their governor in running the colony. The other English colonies soon followed suit, creating their own assemblies. In contrast to Spain and Portugal, England—racked by its internal Anglican–Puritan conflict—was initially uninvolved in the governance of the overseas territories.

When England eventually stepped in and took the governance of the colonies away from the charter merchants and companies in the second half of the seventeenth century, it faced entrenched settler assemblies, especially in New England. Only in New Amsterdam, conquered from the Dutch in 1664–1674 and renamed "New York," did the governor initially rule without an assembly. Many governors were deputies of wealthy aristocrats who never traveled to America but stayed in London. These governors were powerless to prevent the assemblies from appropriating rights to levy taxes and making appointments. The assemblies thus modeled themselves after Parliament in London. As in England, these assemblies were highly select bodies that excluded poorer settlers, who did not meet the property requirements to vote or stand for elections.

Territorial Expansion Steady immigration, also from the European mainland, encouraged land speculators in the British colonies to cast their sights beyond the Appalachian Mountains. (According to historical convention, the English are called "British" after the English–Scottish union in 1707.) In 1749, the Ohio Company of Virginia received a royal permit to develop land, together with a protective fort, south of the Ohio River. The French, however, also claimed the Ohio valley, considering it a part of their Canada–Mississippi–Louisiana territory. A few years later, tensions over the valley erupted into open hostility. Initially, the local encounters went badly for the Virginian militia and British army. In 1755, however, the British and French broadened their clash into a worldwide war for dominance in the colonies and Europe, the Seven Years' War of 1756–1763.

powder horn, ca. 1757

The Seven Years' War   Both France and Great Britain borrowed heavily to pour resources into the war. England had the superior navy and France the superior army. Since the British navy succeeded in choking off French supplies to its increasingly isolated land troops, Britain won the war overseas. In Europe, Britain's failure to supply the troops of its ally Prussia against the Austrian–French alliance caused the war on that front to end in a draw. Overseas, the British gained most of the French holdings in India, several islands in the Caribbean, all of Canada, and all the land east of the Mississippi. The war costs and land swaps, however, proved to be unmanageable for both the vanquished and the victor. The unpaid debts became the root cause of the American, French, and Haitian constitutional revolutions that began 13 years later. Those revolutions, along with the emerging industrialization of Great Britain, signaled the beginning of the modern scientific–industrial age in world history.

The Making of American Societies: Origins and Transformations

The patterns which made the Americas an extension of Europe emerged gradually and displayed characteristics specific to each region. On one hand, there was the slow transfer of the plants and animals native to each continent, called the **Columbian Exchange** (see "Patterns Up Close"). On the other hand, Spain and Portugal adopted different strategies of mineral and agricultural exploitation. In spite of these different strategies, however, the settler societies of the two countries in the end displayed similar characteristics.

Columbian Exchange: Exchange of plants, animals, and diseases between the Americas and the rest of the world.

Exploitation of Mineral and Tropical Resources

The pattern of European expansion into subtropical and tropical lands began with the Spanish colonization of the Caribbean islands. When the Spanish crown ran out of gold in the Caribbean, it exported silver from Mexico and Peru in great quantities to finance a centralizing state that could compete with the Ottomans and European kings. By contrast, Portugal's colony of Brazil did not at first mine for precious metals, and consequently the Portuguese crown pioneered the growing of sugar on plantations. Mining would be developed later. The North American colonies of England and France had, in comparison, little native industry at first. By moving farther south, however, they adopted the plantation system for indigo and rice and thus joined their Spanish and Portuguese predecessors in exploiting the subtropical–tropical agricultural potential of the Americas.

Silver Mines   When the interest of the Spaniards turned from looting to the exploitation of mineral resources, two main mining centers emerged: Potosí in southeastern Peru (today Bolivia) and Zacatecas and Guanajuato in northern Mexico. For the first 200 years after its founding in 1545, Potosí produced over half of the silver of Spanish America. In the eighteenth century, Zacatecas and Guanajuato jumped ahead of Potosí, churning out almost three times as much of the precious metal. During the same century, gold mining in Colombia and Chile rose to importance as well, making the mining of precious metals the most important economic activity in the Americas.

The Columbian Exchange

Few of us can imagine an Italian kitchen without tomatoes or an Irish meal without potatoes or Chinese or Indian cuisine without the piquant presence of chilies, but until fairly recently each of these foods was unknown to the Old World. Likewise, the expression "As American as apple pie" obscures the fact that for millennia apples, as well as many other frequently consumed fruits, such as peaches, pears, plums, cherries, bananas, oranges, and lemons, were absent from the New World. It was not until the sixteenth century, when plants, animals, and microbes began to flow from one end of the planet to another, that new patterns of ecology and biology changed the course of millions of years of divergent evolution.

When historians catalog the long list of life forms that moved across the oceans in the Columbian Exchange, pride of place is usually reserved for the bigger, better-known migrants like cattle, sheep, pigs, and horses. However, the impact of European weeds and grasses on American grasslands, which made it possible for the North American prairie and the South American pampas to support livestock, should not be overlooked. By binding the soil together with their long, tough roots, these "empires of the dandelion" provided the conditions for the grazing of sheep, cattle, and horses, as well as the planting of crops like wheat.

The other silent invader that accompanied the conquistadors was, of course, disease. Thousands of years of mutual isolation between the Americas and Afro-Eurasia rendered the immune systems of Native Americans vulnerable to the scourges that European colonists unwittingly brought with them. Smallpox, influenza, diphtheria, whooping cough, typhoid, chickenpox, measles, and meningitis wiped out millions of Native Americans—by some estimates, the native populations of Mesoamerica and the Andes plummeted by 90 percent in the period 1500–1700. In comparison, the contagions the New World was able to reciprocate upon the Old World—syphilis and tuberculosis—did not unleash nearly the same devastation, and the New World origin of these diseases is still debated.

It is therefore obvious that the big winner in the Columbian Exchange was western Europe, though the effects of the New World bounty took centuries to be fully discerned. While Asia and Africa also benefited from the Columbian Exchange in the forms of new foods that enriched diets, the Europeans got a continent endowed with a warm climate in which they could create new and improved versions of their homelands. The Native Americans were nearly wiped out by disease, their lands

Innovations, such as the "patio" method, which facilitated the extraction process through the use of mercury, and the unrestrained exploitation of indigenous labor made American silver highly competitive in the world market. Conditions among the Native Americans and blacks employed as labor were truly abominable. Few laborers lasted through more than two forced recruitment (*repartimiento*) cycles before they were incapacitated or dead.

Given gaps in bookkeeping and high levels of smuggling, scholars have found it extremely difficult to estimate the total production of the American mines from 1550 to 1750. The best current estimate is that Spanish America produced 150,000

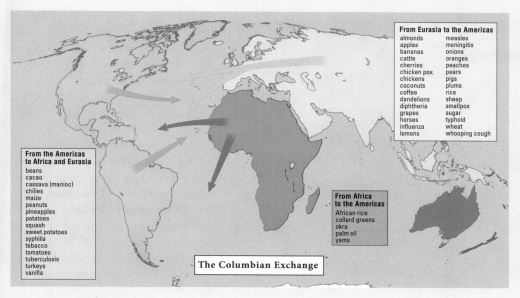

MAP **18.4 The Columbian Exchange.**

appropriated, and the survivors either enslaved or marginalized. The precipitous drop in the population of Native Americans, combined with the tropical and semi-tropical climate of much of the Americas, created the necessary conditions for the Atlantic slave trade. The population losses from this trade were monumental, although the Columbian Exchange, which brought manioc and corn to Africa, balanced these losses to a degree.

Questions

- Can the Columbian Exchange be considered one of the origins of the modern world? How? Why? How does the Columbian Exchange demonstrate the origins, interactions, and adaptations model that is used throughout this book?

- Weigh the positive and negative outcomes of the Columbian Exchange. Is it possible to determine whether the overall effects of the Columbian Exchange on human society and the natural environment were for the better or for the worse?

tons of silver (including gold converted into silver weight). This quantity corresponded to roughly 85 percent of world production. The figures underline the extraordinary role of American silver for the money economies of Europe, the Middle East, and Asia, especially China.

Since the exploitation of the mines was of such central importance, for the first century and a half of New World colonization the Spanish crown organized its other provinces around the needs of the mining centers. Hispaniola and Cuba in the Caribbean were islands which had produced foodstuffs, sugar, and tobacco from the time of Columbus but only in small quantities. Their main function was to

The Silver Mountain of Potosí. Note the patios in the left foreground and the water-driven crushing mill in the center, which ground the silver-bearing ore into a fine sand that then was moistened, caked, amalgamated with mercury, and dried on the patio. The mine workers' insect-like shapes reinforce the dehumanizing effects of their labor.

map of Mexican town drawn by indigenous artists, 1579

feed and protect Havana, the collection point for Mexican and Peruvian silver and the port from where the annual Spanish fleet shipped the American silver across the Atlantic.

A second region, Argentina and Paraguay, was colonized as a bulwark to prevent the Portuguese and Dutch from cutting across the southern end of the continent and accessing Peruvian silver. Once established, the two colonies produced wheat, cattle, mules, horses, cotton, textiles, and tallow to feed and supply the miners in Potosí. The subtropical crop of cotton, produced by small farmers, played a role in Europe's extension into warm-weather agriculture only toward the end of the colonial period.

A third colonial region, Venezuela, began as a grain and cattle supply base for Cartagena, the port for the shipment of Colombian gold, and Panama and Portobelo, ports for the transshipment of Peruvian silver from the Pacific to Havana. Its cocoa and tobacco exports flourished only after the Dutch established themselves in 1624 in the southern Caribbean and provided the shipping. Thus, three major regions of the Spanish overseas empire in the Americas were mostly peripheral as agricultural producers during the sixteenth century. Only after the middle of the century did they begin to specialize in tropical agricultural goods, and they were exporters only in the eighteenth century. By that time, the Dutch and English provided more and more shipping in the place of the Spanish.

Wheat Farming and Cattle Ranching   To support the mining centers and administrative cities, the Spanish colonial government encouraged the development of agricultural estates (*haciendas*). These estates first emerged when conquistadors used their *encomienda* rights to round up Native American labor to produce subsistence crops. Native American tenant farmers were forced to grow wheat and raise cattle, pigs, sheep, and goats for the conquerors, who were now agricultural entrepreneurs. In the latter part of the sixteenth century, the land grants gave way to rotating forced labor as well as wage labor. Owners established their residences and built dwellings for tenant farmers on their estates. A landowner class emerged.

Like the conquistadors before, a majority of landowners produced wheat and animals for sale to urban and mining centers. Cities purchased wheat and maintained granaries in order to provide for urban dwellers in times of harvest failure. Entrepreneurs received commissions to provide slaughterhouses with regular supplies of animals. As the Native American population declined in the seventeenth century and the church helped in consolidating the remaining population in large villages, additional land became available for the establishment of estates. From 1631 onward, authorities granted Spanish settler families the right to maintain their estates undivided from generation to generation. Through donations, the church also acquired considerable agricultural lands. Secular and clerical landowning interests supported a powerful upper social stratum of Creoles from the eighteenth century onward.

Plantations and Gold Mining in Brazil   Brazil's economic activities began with brazilwood, followed by sugar plantations, before gold mining rose to prominence in the eighteenth century. A crisis hit sugar production in 1680–1700, mostly as a result of the Dutch beginning production of sugar in the Antilles. It was at that time that the gold of Minas Gerais, in the interior of Brazil, was discovered.

Gold-mining operations in Brazil during the eighteenth century were considerably less capital-intensive than the silver mines in Spanish America. Most miners were relatively small operators with sieves, pickaxes, and a few black slaves as unskilled laborers. Many entrepreneurs were indebted for their slaves to absentee capitalists, with whom they shared the profits. Since prospecting took place on the land of Native Americans, bloody encounters were frequent. Most entrepreneurs were ruthless frontiersmen who exploited their slaves and took no chances with the indigenous people. Brazil produced a total of 1,000 tons of gold in the eighteenth century, a welcome bonanza for Portugal at a time of low agricultural prices. Overall, minerals were just as valuable for the Portuguese as they were for the Spanish.

Plantations in Spanish and English America   The expansion of plantation farming in the Spanish colonies was a result of the Bourbon reforms. Although sugar, tobacco, and rice had been introduced early into the Caribbean and southern Mexico, it was only in the expanded plantation system of the eighteenth century that these crops (plus indigo, cacao, and cactuses as host plants for cochineal) were produced on a large scale for export to Europe. The owners of plantations did not need expensive machinery and invested instead in African slave labor, with the result that the slave trade hit full stride, beginning around 1750.

English Northeast American settlements in Virginia and Carolina exported tobacco and rice beginning in the 1660s. Georgia was the thirteenth British colony, founded in 1733 as a bulwark against Spanish Florida and a haven for poor Europeans. In 1750 it joined southern Carolina as a major plantation colony and rice and indigo producer. In the eighteenth century, even New England finally had its own export crop, in the form of timber for shipbuilding and charcoal production in Great Britain, at the amazing rate of 250 million board-feet per year by the start of the nineteenth century. These timber exports illustrate an important new factor appearing in the Americas in the eighteenth century. Apart from the cheap production of precious metals and warm-weather crops, the American extension of Europe became increasingly important as a replacement for dwindling fuel resources across much of northern Europe. Altogether, it was thanks to the Americas that mostly cold and rainy Europe rose successfully into the ranks of the wealthy, climatically balanced, and populated Indian and Chinese empires.

Social Strata, Castes, and Ethnic Groups

The population of settlers in the New World consisted primarily of Europeans who came from a continent that had barely emerged from its population losses to the Black Death. Although population numbers were rising again in the sixteenth century, Europe did not have masses of emigrants to the Americas to spare. Given the small settler population of the Americas, the temptation to develop a system of forced labor in agriculture and mining was irresistible. Since the Native Americans and African slaves pressed into labor were ethnically so completely different from the Europeans, however, a social system evolved in which the latter two not only were economically underprivileged but also made up the ethnically nonintegrated lowest rungs of the social ladder. A pattern of legal and customary discrimination evolved which, even though partially vitiated by the rise of ethnically mixed groups, prevented the integration of American ethnicities into settler society.

The Social Elite   The heirs of the Spanish conquistadors and estate owners—farmers, ranchers, and planters—maintained city residences and employed managers on their agricultural properties. In Brazil, cities emerged more slowly, and for a long time estate owners maintained their manor houses as small urban islands. Estate owners mixed with the Madrid- and Lisbon-appointed administrators and, during the seventeenth century, intermarried with them, creating the top tier of settler society known as Creoles, some 4 percent of the population. In a wider sense, the tier included also merchants, professionals, clerks, militia officers, and the clergy. They formed a relatively closed society in which descent, intermarriage, landed property, and a government position counted more than money and education.

In the seventeenth and eighteenth centuries, the estate owners farmed predominantly with Native American forced labor. They produced grain and/or cattle, legumes, sheep, and pigs for local urban markets or mining towns. In contrast to the black slave plantation estates of the Caribbean and coastal regions of Spanish and Portuguese America, these farming estates did not export their goods to Europe. From the beginning of colonialism, furthermore, Madrid and Lisbon discouraged estate owners, as well as farmers in general, from producing cash crops, such as olive oil, wine, or silk, to protect their home production.

As local producers with little competition, farming and ranching estate owners did not feel market pressures. Since they lived for the most part in the cities, they exploited their estates with minimal investments and usually drew profits of less than 5 percent of annual revenues. They were often heavily indebted, and as a result there was often more glitter than substance among the landowning Creoles.

Lower Creoles   The second tier of Creole society consisted of people like Alonzo Ortíz, the tanner introduced at the beginning of this chapter. Even though of second rank, they were privileged European settlers who, as craftspeople and traders, theoretically worked with their hands. In practice, many of them were owner-operators who employed Native Americans and/or black slaves as apprentices and journeymen. Many invested in small plots of land in the vicinity of their cities, striving to rise into the ranks of the landowning Creoles.

Wealthy weavers ran textile manufactures mostly concentrated in the cities of Mexico, Peru, Paraguay, and Argentina. In some of these manufactures, up to 300 Native American and black workers produced cheap, coarse woolens and a variety of cottons on dozens of looms. Men were the weavers and women the spinners—in contrast to the pre-Columbian period, when textile manufacture was entirely a woman's job. On a smaller scale, manufactures also existed for pottery and leather goods. On the whole, the urban manufacturing activities of the popular people, serving the

Textile Production. Immigrants from Spain (like Alonso Ortíz, discussed at the beginning of the chapter), maintained workshops (*obrajes*) as tanners, weavers, carpenters, or wheelwrights. As craftspeople producing simple but affordable goods for the poor, they remained competitive throughout the colonial period, in spite of increasingly large textile, utensil, and furniture imports from Europe. At the same time, indigenous textile production by native women continued as in the preconquest period, albeit under the constraints of labor services imposed by officials or clergy, as shown in these examples.

poor in local markets, remained vibrant until well into the nineteenth century, in spite of massive European imports. Prior to the arrival of railroads, the transportation of imports into the interior of the Americas was prohibitively expensive.

Mestizos and Mulattoes   The mixed European–Native American and European–African populations had the collective name of "caste" (*casta*), or ethnic group. The term originated in the desire of the Iberian and Creole settlers to draw distinctions among degrees of mixture in order to counterbalance as much as possible the masses of Native Americans and Africans, especially from the eighteenth century onward. The two most important castes were the *mestizos* (Spanish) or *mestiços* (Portuguese) who had Iberian fathers and Native American mothers, and *mulatos*, who had Iberian fathers and black mothers. By 1800 the castas as a whole formed the third largest population category in Latin America (20 percent), after Native Americans (40 percent) and Creoles (30 percent). In Brazil, black freedmen and mulattoes were numerically even with Creoles (28 percent each), after black slaves (38 percent) and before Native Americans (6 percent in the settled provinces outside Amazonia). In both Spanish and Portuguese America, there were also a small percentage of people descended from Native American and black unions. Thus, most of the intermediate population groups were sizable, playing important neutralizing roles in colonial society, as they had one foot in both the Creole and subordinate social strata (see Figure 18.1).

As such neutralizing elements, mestizos and mulattoes filled lower levels of the bureaucracy and the lay hierarchy in the church. They held skilled and supervisory positions in mines and on estates. In addition, in the armed forces mulattoes dominated

Race, Class, and Gender in Colonial Mexico. An outraged black woman defends herself against an aggressive Creole man, with a fearful mulatta child clinging to the woman's skirt.

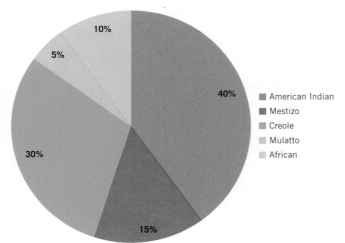

Figure 18.1 Ethnic Composition of Latin America, ca. 1800.

the ranks of enlisted men; in the defense militias, they even held officer ranks. In Brazil, many mulattoes and black freedmen were farmers. Much of the craft production was in their hands. A wide array of laws existed to keep mestizos and mulattoes in their peculiarly intermediate social and political positions.

Women   The roles played by women depended strongly on their social position. Well-appointed elite Creole households followed the Mediterranean tradition of secluding women from men. Within the confines of the household, elite women were persons of means and influence. They were the owners of substantial dowries and legally stipulated grooms' gifts. Often, they actively managed the investment of their assets. Outside their confines, however, even elite women lost all protection. Crimes of passion, committed by honor-obsessed fathers or husbands, went unpunished. Husbands and fathers who did not resort to violence nevertheless did not need witnesses to obtain court judgments to banish daughters or wives to convents for alleged lapses in chastity. Thus, even elite women were bound by definite limits set by a patriarchal society.

On the lower rungs of society, be it popular Creole, mestizo, mulatto, or Native American, gender separation was much less prevalent. After all, everyone in the family had to work in order to make ends meet. Men, women, and children shared labor in the fields and workshops. Girls or wives took in clothes to wash or went out to work as domestics in wealthy households. Older women dominated retail in market stalls. As in elite society, wives tended to outlive husbands. In addition, working families with few assets suffered abandonment by males. Women headed one-third of all households in Mexico City, according to an 1811 census. Among black slaves in the region of São Paulo, 70 percent of women were without formal ties to the men who fathered their children. Thus, the most pronounced division in colonial society was that of a patriarchy among the Creoles and a slave society dominated by women, with frequently absent men—an unbridgeable division that persists still today.

Native Americans   In the immediate aftermath of the conquest, Native Americans could be found at all levels of the social scale. Some were completely marginalized in remote corners of the American continents. Others acculturated into the ranks of the working poor in the silver mines or textile manufactures. A few even formed an educated Aztec or Inca propertied upper class, exercising administrative functions

Illustration from an Indian Land Record. The Spaniards almost completely wiped out the Aztec archives after the conquest of Mexico; surviving examples of Indian manuscripts are thus extremely rare. Although the example shown here, made from the bark of a fig tree, claims to date from the early 1500s, it is part of the so-called Techialoyan land records created in the seventeenth century to substantiate native land claims. These "títulos primordiales," as they were called, were essentially municipal histories that documented in text and pictures local accounts of important events and territorial boundaries.

in Spanish civil service. Social distinctions, however, disappeared rapidly during the first 150 years of Spanish colonialism. Smallpox reduced the Native American population by nearly 80 percent. Diseases were more virulent in humid, tropical parts of the continent than in deserts, and the epidemics took a far greater toll on dense, settled populations than they did on dispersed forager bands in dry regions. In the Caribbean and on the Brazilian coast, Native Americans disappeared almost completely; in central and southern Mexico, their population shrank by two-thirds. It was only in the twentieth century that population figures reached the preconquest level again in most parts of Latin America.

Apart from European diseases, the native forager and agrarian Native Americans in the Amazon, Orinoco, and Maracaibo rain forests were the least affected by European colonials during the period 1500–1800. Not only were their lands economically the least promising, but they also defended those lands successfully with blowguns, poison darts, and bow and arrow. In many cold and hot arid or semiarid regions, such as Patagonia, southern Chile, the Argentine grasslands (*pampas*), the Paraguayan salt marshes and deserts, and northern Mexican mountains and steppes, the situation was similar. In these lands, the seminomadic Native Americans quickly adopted the European horse and became highly mobile warrior peoples in defense of their mostly independent territories.

The villagers of Mexico, Yucatán, Guatemala, Colombia, Ecuador, and Peru had fewer choices. When smallpox reduced their numbers in the second half of the sixteenth century, state and church authorities razed many villages and concentrated the survivors in *pueblos de indios*. Initially, the Native Americans put up strong resistance against these resettlements by repeatedly returning to their destroyed old settlements. From the middle of the seventeenth century, however, the pueblos were fully functional, self-administering units, with councils (*cabildos*), churches, schools, communal lands, and family parcels.

The councils were important institutions of legal training and social mobility for ordinary Native Americans. Initially, the traditional "noble" chiefly families descending from the preconquest Aztec and Inca ruling classes were in control as administrators. The many village functions, however, for which the *cabildos* were responsible allowed commoners to move up into auxiliary roles. In some of these roles, they had opportunities to learn the system and acquire modest wealth. Settlers constantly complained about insubordinate Native Americans pursuing lawsuits in the courts. Native American villages were closed to settlers, and the only outsiders admitted were Catholic priests. Contact with the Spanish world remained minimal, and acculturation went little beyond official conversion to Catholicism. Village notaries and scribes were instrumental in preserving Nahuatl in Mexico and Quechua in Peru, making them into functional, written languages. Thus, even in the heartlands of Spanish America, Native American adaptation to the rulers remained limited.

Unfortunately, however, tremendous demographic losses made the Native Americans in the pueblos vulnerable to the loss of their land. Estate owners expanded their holdings, legally and illegally, in spite of the heroic litigation efforts of the villages opposed to this expansion (see Source 18.3). When the population rebounded, many estates had grown to immense sizes. Villages began to run out of land for their inhabitants. Increasing numbers of Native Americans had to rent land from estate owners or find work on estates as farmhands. They became estranged from their villages, fell into debt peonage, and entered the ranks of the working poor in the countryside or city, bearing the full brunt of colonial inequities.

New England Society   For a long time in the early modern period, the small family farm, where everyone had to work to eke out a precarious living, remained the norm for the majority of New England's population. Family members specializing in construction, carpentry, spinning, weaving, or ironworks continued to be restricted to small perimeters around their villages and towns. An acute lack of money and cheap means of transportation hampered the development of market networks in the interior well into the 1770s. The situation was better in the agriculturally more favored colonies in the Mid-Atlantic, especially in Pennsylvania. Here, farmers were able to produce marketable quantities of wheat and legumes for urban markets. The number of plantations in the south rose steadily, demanding a substantial increase in numbers of slaves (from 28,000 in 1700 to 575,000 in 1776), although world market fluctuations left planters vulnerable. Except for boom periods in the plantation sector, the rural areas remained largely poor.

Real changes occurred during the early eighteenth century in the urban regions. Large port cities emerged which shipped in textiles and ironwares from Europe in return for timber at relatively cheap rates. The most important were Philadelphia (28,000 inhabitants), New York (25,000), Boston (16,000), and Newport, Rhode Island (11,000). A wealthy merchant class formed, spawning urban strata of professionals (such as lawyers, teachers, and newspaper journalists). Primary school education was provided by municipal public schools as well as some churches, and evening schools for craftspeople existed in some measure. By the middle of the eighteenth century a majority of men could read and write, although female literacy was minimal. Finally, in contrast to Latin America, social ranks in New England were less elaborate.

The Adaptation of the Americas to European Culture

European settlers brought two distinct cultures to the Americas. In the Mid-Atlantic, Caribbean, and Central and South America, they brought with them the Catholic Reformation, a culture and perspective that resisted the New Science of Galileo and the Enlightenment thought of Locke until the late eighteenth century. In the northeast, colonists implanted dissident Protestantism as well as the Anglicanism of Great Britain and the Presbyterianism of Scotland. The rising number of adherents of the New Science and Enlightenment in northwestern Europe had also a parallel in North America. In general, settlers and their locally born offspring were proud of their respective cultures, which, even though provincial, were dominant in what they prejudicially viewed as a less civilized, if not barbaric, Native American environment.

Catholic Missionary Work From the beginning, Spanish and Portuguese monarchs relied heavily on the Catholic Church for their rule in the new American provinces. The pope granted them patronage over the organization and all appointments on the new continents. A strong motive driving many in the church as well as society at large was the belief in the imminent Second Coming of Jesus. This belief was one inspiration for the original Atlantic expansion (see Chapter 16). When the Aztec and Inca Empires fell, members of the Franciscan order, the main proponents of the belief in the imminence of the Second Coming, interpreted it as a sign of the urgent duty to convert the Native Americans to Christianity. If Jesus's kingdom was soon to come, according to this interpretation, all humans in the Americas should be Christians.

Jesuit missionaries, from the Church of San Pedro in Lima, Peru, ca. 1700

Thousands of Franciscan, Dominican, and other preaching monks, later followed by the Jesuits, fanned out among the Native Americans. They baptized them, introduced the sacraments (Eucharist, baptism, confession, confirmation, marriage, last rites, and priesthood), and taught them basic theological concepts of Christianity. The missionaries learned native languages, translated the catechism and New Testament into those languages, and taught the children of the ruling native families how to read and write. Thanks to their genuine efforts to understand the Native Americans on their own terms, a good deal of preconquest Native American culture was recorded without too much distortion.

The role and function of saints as mediators between humans and God formed one element of Catholic Christianity to which Native Americans acculturated early. Good works as God-pleasing human efforts to gain salvation in the afterlife formed another. The veneration of images of the Virgin Mary and pilgrimages to the chapels and churches where they were kept constituted a third element. The best-known example of the last element is Our Lady of Guadalupe, near Mexico City, who in 1531 appeared in a vision to a Native American in the place where the native goddess Tonantzin used to be venerated. On the other hand, the Spanish Inquisition also operated in the Spanish and Portuguese colonies, seeking to limit the degree to which Catholicism and traditional religion mingled (see Source 18.2). The church treaded a fine line between enforcement of doctrine and leniency toward what it determined were lax or heretical believers.

Earliest representation of the Madonna and Child created by Indians in the New World (1531)

Education and the Arts The Catholic Reformation expressed itself also in the organization of education. The Franciscans and Dominicans had offered general education to the children of settlers early on and, in colleges, trained graduates for

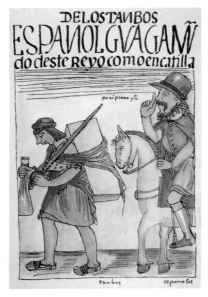

Spanish Cruelty to Incas.
Felipe Guamán Poma de Ayala, a Peruvian claiming noble Inca descent, was a colonial administrator, well educated and an ardent Christian. He is remembered today as a biting critic of the colonial administration and the clergy, whom he accused of mistreating and exploiting the Andean population, as in this colored wood print.

illustration from
Willem Piso's *Natural History of Brazil* (1637)

missionary work. The first New World universities, such as Santo Domingo (1538), Mexico City, and Lima (both 1553), taught theology, church law, and Native American languages. Under the impact of the Jesuits, universities broadened the curriculum, offering degrees also in secular law, Aristotelian philosophy, the natural sciences, and medicine. Although the universities did not admit the New Sciences and Enlightenment of northwestern Europe into their curriculum, there was nevertheless considerable scientific research on tropical diseases, plants, and animals as a counterbalance. The vast extent of this research, long kept secret by the Spanish and Portuguese monarchs from their European competitors, is becoming gradually known only now.

Furthermore, missionary monks collected and recorded Native American manuscripts and oral traditions, such as the Aztec *Anales de Tula* and the Maya *Popol Vuh*. Others wrote histories and ethnographies of the Taíno, Aztec, Maya, Inca, and Tupí peoples. Bartolomé de las Casas, Toribio Motolonía de Benavente, Bernardino de Sahagún, Diego de Landa, Bernabé Cobo, and Manuel da Nóbrega are merely a handful of noteworthy authors who wrote about the Native Americans. Many labored for years, worked with legions of informers, and produced monumental tomes.

A number of Native American and mestizo chroniclers, historians, and commentators on the early modern state and society are similarly noteworthy. Muñoz Camargo was a Tlaxcaltecan; Fernando de Alva Ixtlixóchitl and Fernando Alvarado Tezózomoc were Mexican mestizos; and Juan de Santa Cruz Pachacuti Yamqui and Felipe Inca Garcilaso de la Vega were Peruvian mestizos, all writing on their native regions. Felipe Guamán Poma de Ayala (ca. 1535–1616), a native Peruvian, is of particular interest. He accompanied his 800-page manuscript, entitled (in English translation) *The First New Chronicle and Good Government*, with some 400 drawings of daily-life activities in the Peruvian villages. These drawings provide us with invaluable cultural details, which would be difficult to render in writing. Unfortunately, King Philip II of Spain, a relentless proponent of the Catholic Reformation, took a dim view of authors writing on Native American society and history. In 1577 he forbade the publication of all manuscripts dealing with what he called idolatry and superstition. Many manuscripts lay hidden in archives and did not see the light of day until modern times.

Protestantism in New England

From the start, religious diversity was a defining cultural trait of English settlements in North America. The spectrum of Christian denominations ranged from a host of English and continental European versions of Protestantism to Anglicanism and a minority of Catholics. As if this spectrum had not been sufficiently broad, dissenters frequently split from the existing denominations, moved into new territory, and founded new settlements. Religiosity was a major characteristic of the early settlers.

An early example of religious splintering was the rise of an antinomian ("anti-law") group within Puritan-dominated Massachusetts. The Puritans dominant in this colony generally recognized the authority of the Anglican Church but strove to move it toward Protestantism from within. The preachers and settlers represented in the General Court, as their assembly was called, were committed to the Calvinist balance between "inner" personal grace obtained from God and "outer" works according to the law. The antinomian group, however, digging deep into early traditions in Christianity, advocated an exclusive commitment to inner grace through spiritual perfection.

Their leader was Anne Hutchinson, an early and tireless proponent of women's rights and an inspiring preacher. She was accused of arguing that she could recognize those believers in Calvinist Protestantism who were predestined for salvation and that these believers would be saved even if they had sinned. After a power struggle with the deeply misogynistic magistrates opposed to influential women, the General Court prevailed and forced the antinomians to move to Rhode Island in 1638.

The New Sciences in the New World. This painting by Samuel Collings, *The Magnetic Dispensary* (1790), shows how men and women, of lay background, participated in scientific experiments in the English colonies of North America, similar to educated middle-class people in western Europe at the same time.

The example of Hutchinson is noteworthy because it led to the founding of Harvard College in 1636 by the General Court. Harvard was the first institution of higher learning in North America, devoted to teaching the "correct" balanced Calvinist Protestantism. Later, the college functioned as the main center for training the colony's ministers in Puritan theology and morality, although it was not affiliated with any specific denomination.

New Sciences Research   As discussed in Chapter 17, the New Sciences had found their most hospitable home in northwestern Europe by default. The rivalry between Protestantism and Catholicism had left enough of an authority-free space for the New Sciences to flourish. Under similar circumstances—intense rivalry among denominations—English North America also proved hospitable to the New Sciences. An early practitioner was Benjamin Franklin (1706–1790), who began his career as a printer, journalist, and newspaper editor. Franklin founded the University of Pennsylvania (1740), the first secular university in North America, and the American Philosophical Society (1743), the first scientific society. This hospitality for the New Sciences in North America was quite in contrast to Latin America, where a uniform Catholic Reformation prevented its rise.

Witch Hunts   In the last decade of the seventeenth century, a high level of religious intensity and rivalry was at the root of a witchcraft frenzy which seized New England. The belief in witchcraft was the survival on the popular level of the ancient concept of a shared mind or spirit that allows people to influence each other, either positively or negatively. Witches, male and female, were persons exerting a negative influence, or black magic, on their victims. In medieval Europe, the church had kept witchcraft out of sight, but in the wake of Protestantism and the many challenges to church authority it had become more visible. In the North American colonies, with no overarching religious authority, the visibility of witchcraft was particularly high.

The one case where this sensitivity erupted into hysteria was that of Salem, Massachusetts. Here, the excitement erupted in 1692 with Tituba, a Native American

Witch Trial. In the course of the 1600s, in the relatively autonomous English colonies of Northeast America, more persons were accused, tried, and convicted of witchcraft than anywhere else. Of the 140 persons coming to trial between 1620 and 1725, 86 percent were women. Three witch panics are recorded: Bermuda, 1651; Hartford, Connecticut, 1652–1665; and Salem, Massachusetts, 1692–1693. This anonymous American woodcut of the early 1600s shows one method to try someone for witchcraft: swim or float if guilty, or sink if innocent.

interactive concept map

slave from Barbados who worked in the household of a pastor. Tituba practiced voodoo, the West African–originated, part-African and part-Christian religious practice of influencing others. When a young daughter and niece in the pastor's household suffered from convulsions, mass hysteria broke out, in which 20 women accused of being witches were executed, although Tituba, ironically, survived. A new governor finally calmed the passions and restored order (see Source 18.5).

Revivalism   Religious fervor expressed itself also in periodic Protestant renewal movements, among which the "Great Awakening" of the 1730s and 1740s was the most important. The main impulse for this revivalist movement came from the brothers John and Charles Wesley, two Methodist preachers in England who toured Georgia in 1735. Preachers from other denominations joined, all exhorting Protestants to literally "start anew" in their relationship with God. Fire-and-brimstone sermons rained down on the pews, reminding the faithful of the absolute sovereignty of God, the depravity of humans, predestination to hell and heaven, the inner experience of election, and salvation by God's grace alone. Thus, revivalism, recurring with great regularity to the present, became a potent force in Protestant America, at opposing purposes with secular founding-father constitutionalism.

Putting It All Together

During the period 1500–1800 the contours of a new pattern in which the Americas formed a resource-rich and warm-weather extension of Europe took shape. During this time, China and India continued to be the most populous and wealthiest agrarian–urban regions of the world. Scholars have estimated China's share of the world economy during this period as comprising 40 percent. India probably did not lag far behind. In 1500, Europe was barely an upstart, forced to defend itself against the push of the Ottoman Empire into eastern Europe and the western Mediterranean. But its successful conquest of Iberia from the Muslims led to the discovery of the Americas. Possession of the Americas made Europe similar to China and India in that it now encompassed, in addition to its northerly cold climates, subtropical and tropical regions which produced rich cash crops as well as precious metals. Over the course of 300 years, with the help of its American extension, Europe narrowed the gap between itself and China and India, although it was only after the beginning of industrialization, around 1800, that it eventually was able to close this gap.

Narrowing the gap, of course, was not a conscious policy in Europe. Quite the contrary, because of fierce competition both with the Ottoman Empire and internally, much of the wealth Europe gained in the Americas, especially silver, was wasted on warfare. The centralizing state, created in part to support war, ran into insurmountable budgetary barriers, which forced Spain into several state bankruptcies. Even mercantilism, a logical extension of the centralizing state, had limited effects. Its centerpiece, state support for the export of manufactures to the American colonies, functioned unevenly. The Spanish and Portuguese governments, with weak urban infrastructures and low manufacturing capabilities, especially in textiles, were unable to enforce this state-supported trade until the eighteenth century and even then only in very limited ways. France and especially England practiced mercantilism more successfully but were able to do so in the Americas only from the late seventeenth century onward, when their plantation systems began to take shape. Although the American extension of Europe had the potential of making Europe self-sufficient, this potential was realized only partially during the colonial period.

A fierce debate has raged over the question of the degree of wealth the Americas added to Europe. On one hand, considerable quantitative research has established that the British slave trade for sugar plantations added at best 1 percent to the British gross domestic product (GDP). The profits from the production of sugar on the English island of Jamaica may have added another 4 percent to the British GDP. Without doubt, private slave-trading and sugar-producing enterprises were at times immensely profitable to individuals and groups, not to mention the mining of silver through forced labor. In the larger picture, however, these profits were considerably smaller if one takes into account the immense waste of revenues on military ventures—hence the doubts raised by scholars today about large gains made by Europe through its American colonial acquisitions.

On the other hand, the European extension to the Americas was clearly a momentous event in world history. It might have produced dubious overall profits for Europe, but it definitely encouraged the parting of ways between Europe on one hand and Asia and Africa on the other, once a new scientific–industrial society began to emerge around 1800.

Review and Relate

| Thinking Through Patterns

Examine the ways historians approach the big questions of this chapter.

In their role as supplementary subtropical and tropical extensions of Europe, the Americas had a considerable impact on Europe's changing position in the world. First, Europe acquired large quantities of precious metals, which its two largest competitors, India and China, lacked. Second, with its new access to warm-weather agricultural products, Europe rose to a position of agrarian autonomy similar to that of India and China. In terms of resources, compared with the principal religious civilizations of India and China, Europe grew between 1550 and 1800 from a position of inferiority to one of near parity.

≫ **What is the significance of western Europeans acquiring the Americas as a warm-weather extension of their northern continent?**

>> **What was the main pattern of social development in colonial America during the period 1500–1800?**

Because the numbers of Europeans who emigrated to the Americas was low for most of the colonial period—just 300,000 Spaniards left for the New World between 1500 and 1800—they never exceeded the numbers of Native Americans or African slaves. The result was a highly privileged settler society that held superior positions on the top rung of the social hierarchy. In principle, given an initially large indigenous population, labor was cheap and should have become more expensive as diseases reduced the Native Americans. In fact, labor always remained cheap, in part because of the politically supported institution of forced labor and in part because of racial prejudice.

>> **Why and how did European settlers in South and North America strive for self-government, and how successful were they in achieving their goals?**

Two contrasting patterns characterized the way in which European colonies were governed. The Spanish and Portuguese crowns, primarily interested in extracting minerals and warm-weather products from the colonies, had a strong interest in exercising as much centralized control over their possessions in the Americas as they could. In contrast, the British crown granted self-government to the northeast American colonies from the start, in part because the colonies were initially far less important economically and in part because of a long tradition of self-rule at home. Nevertheless, even though Latin American settlers achieved only partial self-rule in their towns and cities, they destroyed central rule indirectly through the purchase of offices. After financial reforms, Spain and Portugal reestablished a degree of central rule through the appointment of officers from the home countries.

| Against the Grain

Consider this as a counterpoint to the main patterns examined in this chapter.

Juana Inés de la Cruz

In the wake of the Protestant and Catholic Reformations of the 1500s, it was no longer unusual for European women to pursue higher education. In the considerably more conservative Latin American colonies of Spain, Juana Inés de la Cruz (1651–1695) was less fortunate, even though her fame as the intellectually most brilliant figure of the seventeenth century in the colonies endured.

De la Cruz was the illegitimate child of a Spanish immigrant father and a Creole mother. She grew up on the hacienda of her maternal grandfather, in whose library she secretly studied Latin, Greek, and Nahuatl, and also composed her first poems. Unable as a woman to be admitted to the university in Mexico City, de la Cruz nevertheless was fortunate to receive further education from the wife of the vice regent of New Spain. In order to continue her studies and eschewing married life in the ruling class, in 1668 she entered a convent. Here, she continued to study and write hundreds of poems, comedies, religious dramas, and theological texts. Her seminars with courtiers and scholarly visitors were a major attraction in Mexico City.

In 1688, however, she lost her protection at court with the departure of her vice-regal supporters for Spain. Her superior, the archbishop of Mexico, was an open misogynist, and even though her confessor and the bishop of Puebla were admirers, their admiration had limits. A crisis came in 1690 when the bishop of Puebla published de la Cruz's critique of a famous sermon of 1650 by the Portuguese Jesuit António Vieira on Jesus's act of washing his disciples' feet, together with his own critique of de la Cruz. The complex theological arguments addressed the question of whether the foot washing was an inversion of the master–slave (Vieira) or master–servant (de la Cruz) relationship—a theological question unresolved in the Gospels, as well as among the Christian churches in the subsequent centuries. De la Cruz viewed Vieira's interpretation as more hierarchical–male and her own interpretation as more humble–female.

A year later, in 1691, de la Cruz wrote a highly spirited, lengthy riposte to the bishop's apparently well-meaning advice to her in his critique to be more conscious of her status as a woman. Her message was clear: Even though women had to be silent in church, as St. Paul had taught, neither study nor writing were prohibited for women. Before the church could censor her, in 1693 Juana Inés de la Cruz stopped writing. She died two years later.

- Why were the Latin American colonies more socially conservative than Europe?

- Was de la Cruz right to stop her correspondence with the Mexican clergy in 1693?

Key Terms

audio flashcards

Columbian Exchange 541
Creoles 532

Labor assignment
(*repartimiento*) 534

Land-labor grant
(*encomienda*) 526

For additional resources, please go to
www.oup.com/us/vonsivers.
Please see the Further Resources section at the back of the book for additional readings and suggested websites.

Sources for Chapter 18

SOURCE 18.1 ## Hernán Cortés, *Second Letter from Mexico to Emperor Charles V*

1522

With a handful of untrained and poorly equipped soldiers, Hernán Cortés overthrew the powerful Aztec civilization between 1519 and 1521. Born in Spain around 1485, Cortés decided to inform the king of Spain (and Holy Roman emperor) Charles V of his achievements, in a series of written updates. Despite their ostensible purpose, these "letters" were designed for more than the edification and delight of the emperor. Like Julius Caesar's dispatches from the Gallic Wars of the 50s BCE—in which at least one million Gauls were purportedly killed and another million enslaved—these accounts were designed for broad public consumption. Each letter was sent to Spain as soon as it was ready, and it seems likely that Cortés's father, Martín, arranged for their immediate publication. Over the course of these five published letters, although Cortés developed a persona for himself as a conquering hero and agent of imperial power, he also exposed the ruthlessness and brutality of his "conquest" of Mexico.

From henceforth they offered themselves as vassals of Your Sacred Majesty and swore to remain so always and to serve and assist in all things that Your Highness commanded them. A notary set all this down through the interpreters which I had. Still I determined to go with them; on the one hand, so as not to show weakness and, on the other, because I hoped to conduct my business with Mutezuma from that city because it bordered on his territory, as I have said, and on the road between the two there is free travel and no frontier restrictions.

When the people of Tascalteca saw my determination it distressed them considerably, and they told me many times that I was mistaken, but since they were vassals of Your Sacred Majesty and my friends they would go with me to assist me in whatever might happen. Although I opposed this and asked them not to come, as it was unnecessary, they followed me with some 100,000 men, all well armed for war, and came within two leagues of the city. After much

Source: Hernán Cortés, *Letters from Mexico*, ed. and trans. Anthony Pagden (New Haven, CT: Yale University Press, 1986), 72–74.

persuasion on my part they returned, though there remained in my company some five or six thousand of them. That night I slept in a ditch, hoping to divest myself of these people in case they caused trouble in the city, and because it was already late enough and I did not want to enter too late. The following morning, they came out of the city to greet me with many trumpets and drums, including many persons whom they regard as priests in their temples, dressed in traditional vestments and singing after their fashion, as they do in the temples. With such ceremony they led us into the city and gave us very good quarters, where all those in my company were most comfortable. There they brought us food, though not sufficient.

. . .

During the three days I remained in that city they fed us worse each day, and the lords and principal persons of the city came only rarely to see and speak with me. And being somewhat disturbed by this, my interpreter, who is an Indian woman from Putunchan, which is the great river of which I spoke to Your Majesty in the first letter, was told by another Indian woman and a native of this city that very close by many of Mutezuma's men were gathered, and that the people of the city had sent away their women and children and all their belongings, and were about to fall on us and kill us all; and that if she wished to escape she should go with her and she would shelter her. All this she told to Gerónimo de Aguilar, an interpreter whom I acquired in Yucatán, of whom I have also written to Your Highness; and he informed me. I then seized one of the natives of this city who was passing by and took him aside secretly and questioned him; and he confirmed what the woman and the natives of Tascalteca had told me. Because of this and because of the signs I had observed, I decided to forestall an attack, and I sent for some of the chiefs of the city, saying that I wished to speak with them. I put them in a room and meanwhile warned our men to be prepared, when a harquebus was fired, to fall on the many Indians who were outside our quarters and on those who were inside. And so it was done, that after I had put the chiefs in the room, I left them bound up and rode away and had the harquebus fired, and we fought so hard that in two hours more than three thousand men were killed.

. . .

After fifteen or twenty days which I remained there the city and the land were so pacified and full of people that it seemed as if no one were missing from it, and their markets and trade were carried on as before. I then restored the friendly relations between this city of Curultecal and Tascalteca, which had existed in the recent past, before Mutezuma had attracted them to his friendship with gifts and made them enemies of the others.

≫ **Working with Sources**

1. **Does Cortés offer a justification for his treatment of the people of Tascalteca? Why or why not?**

2. **What were the risks associated with Cortés's reliance on translators as he conquered the natives of Mexico?**

SOURCE 18.2 Marina de San Miguel's Confessions before the Inquisition, Mexico City

1598–1599

The Inquisition was well established in Spain at the time of Cortés's conquest in the 1520s. A tribunal of the Holy Office of the Inquisition came in the conquistadors' wake, ultimately established at Mexico City in 1571 with authority to regulate Catholic morality throughout "New Spain." Most of the Inquisition trials concerned petty breaches of religious conduct, but others dealt with the much more serious crime of heresy. In November 1598, the Inquisition became alarmed about the rise of a group who believed that the Day of Judgment was at hand. Among the group denounced to the Holy Office was Marina de San Miguel, a Spanish-born woman who held a high status due to her mystical visions. Her confessions reveal the degree to which admissions of "deviance" could be extorted from a victim. In March 1601, Marina was stripped naked to the waist and paraded upon a mule. Forced to confess her errors, she was sentenced to 100 lashes with a whip. Confined to a plague hospital, she died some time later.

First Confession

In the city of Mexico, Friday, November 20, 1598. The Lord Inquisitor *licenciado* don Alonso de Peralta in his morning audience ordered that a woman be brought before him from one of the secret prisons of this Holy Office. Being present, she swore an oath *en forma devida de derecho* under which she promised to tell the truth here in this audience and in all the others that might be held until the determination of her case, and to keep secret everything that she might see or believe or that might be talked about with her or that might happen concerning this her case.

. . .

She was asked if she knows, presumes, or suspects the cause for her arrest and imprisonment in the prisons of the Holy Office. . . . The inquisitor said that with her illness she must have imagined it. And she says that she wants to go over her memory so that she can tell the truth about everything that she might remember.

With this the audience ceased, because it was past eleven. The above was read and she approved it and signed it. And she was ordered to return to her cell, very admonished to examine her memory as she was offered to do.

. . .

Source: Jacqueline Holler, "The Spiritual and Physical Ecstasies of a Sixteenth-Century Beata: Marina de San Miguel Confesses Before the Mexican Inquisition," in Richard Boyer and Geoffrey Spurling, eds., *Colonial Lives: Documents on Latin American History, 1550–1850* (New York: Oxford University Press, 2000), 79–98.

Third Confession

In the city of Mexico, Tuesday, November 24, 1598. . . .

She said that what she has remembered is that in the course of her life some spiritual things have happened to her, which she has talked about to some people. And she believes that they have been the cause of her imprisonment, because they were scandalized by what she told them.

· · ·

And then she opened her eyes and began to shake and get up from the bench on which she was seated, saying, "My love, help me God, how strongly you have given me this." And among these words she said to the Lord Inquisitor that when she is given these trances, she should be shaken vigorously to awaken her from her deep dream. Then she returned to being as though sleeping. The inquisitor called her by her name and she did not respond, nor the second time. And the third time she opened her eyes and made faces, and made signs with her hands to her mouth.

· · ·

Sixth Confession

In the city of Mexico, Monday, January 25, 1599. . . .

She said that it's like this. . . . She has been condemned to hell, because for fifteen years she has had a sensual temptation of the flesh, which makes her perform dishonest acts with her own hands on her shameful parts. She came to pollution [orgasm] saying dishonest words that provoke lust, calling by their dishonest names many dirty and lascivious things. She was tempted to this by the devil, who appeared to her internally in the form of an Angel of Light, who told her that she should do these things, because they were no sin. This was to make her abandon her scruples. And the devil appeared to her in the form of Christ our Redeemer, in such a way that she might uncover her breasts and have carnal union with him. And thus, for fifteen years, she has had carnal union occasionally from month to month, or every two months. And if it had been more she would accuse herself of that too, because she is only trying to save her soul, with no regard to honor or the world. And the carnal act that the devil as Angel of Light and in the form of Christ had with her was the same as if she had had it with a man. And he kissed her, and she enjoyed it, and she felt a great ardor in her whole body, with particular delight and pleasure.

· · ·

Eighth Confession

In the city of Mexico, Wednesday, January 27, 1599. . . .

But all the times she had the copulation with the devil in the form of Christ she doubted whether it was the devil or not, from which doubts one can infer that she did not believe as firmly as she ought to have that such things could not possibly be from Christ. In this she should urgently discharge her conscience. . . .

· · ·

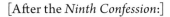

[After the *Ninth Confession*:]

In the city of Mexico, Tuesday, Day of the Purification of our Lady, February 2, 1599, the Lord Inquisitor in his afternoon audience ordered Marina de San Miguel brought before him. And once present she was told that if she has remembered anything in her case she should say it, and the truth, under the oath that she has made.

She said no. . . .

> ≫ Working
> with Sources

1. **What does this document indicate about the working methods of the Inquisition (and their "successes") in Mexico in the 1590s?**

2. **Does the Inquisition seem to have been more concerned about Marina's sexuality than her mystical experiences?**

SOURCE 18.3   Nahuatl Land Sale Documents, Mexico

ca. 1610

After the conquest of the Aztec imperial capital of Tenochtitlán, Spaniards turned their attention to the productive farmland in the surrounding countryside, which was inhabited by Nahuatl-speaking native people. By the late sixteenth century, Spaniards began to expand rapidly into this territory. They acquired estates in a variety of ways, from royal grants to open seizure of property. Nevertheless, the purchase of plots of land from individual Nahuas was also common—although sometimes the sellers came to regret the transaction and petitioned higher authorities for redress of their grievances.

Altepetl: City-state.

Teopixqui: Priest, in Nahuatl.

Tlaxilacalli: Subunit of an *altepetl*.

Here in the *altepetl* Santo Domingo Mixcoac, Marquesado del Valle, on the first day of July of the year 1612, I, Joaquín de San Francisco, and my wife, Juana Feliciana, citizens here in the *altepetl* of Santa María Purificación Tlilhuacan, sell to Dr. Diego de León Plaza, *teopixqui*, one field and house that we have in the *tlaxilacalli* Tlilhuacan next to the house of Juan Bautista, Spaniard. Where we are is right in the middle of [in between] their houses. And now we receive [the money] in person. The reason we sell it is that we have no children to whom it might belong. For there is another land and house, but [the land] here we can no longer [work] because it is really in the middle of [land belonging to] Spaniards. [The land] is not *tributario*, for my father, named Juan Altamirano, and my mother, María Catalina, really left it to me. And now I give it to [the doctor] very voluntarily. And now he is personally giving me 130 pesos. Both my wife and I receive it in person before the witnesses. And the

Source: Rebecca Horn, "Spaniards in the Nahua Countryside: Dr. Diego de León Plaza and Nahuatl Land Sale Documents (Mexico, Early Seventeenth Century)," in Richard Boyer and Geoffrey Spurling, eds., *Colonial Lives: Documents on Latin American History, 1550–1850* (New York: Oxford University Press, 2000), 102–103, 108–109.

tribute will be remedied with [the price]; it will pay it. The land [upon which tribute is owed] is at Colonanco. It is adjacent to the land of Miguel de Santiago and Lucas Pérez. And the witnesses [are] Antonio de Fuentes and señora Inés de Vera and Juana de Vera, Spanish women (and the Nahuas) Juan Josef, Gabriel Francisco, María, Mariana, and Sebastián Juan. And because we do not know how to write, I, Joaquín [de San] Francisco, and my wife asked a witness to set down [a signature] on our behalf [along with the notary?] Juan Vázquez, Spaniard. Witnesses, Antonio de Fuentes, [etc.] Before me, Matías Valeriano, notary. And both of them, he and his wife [Joaquín de San Francisco and Juana Feliciana], received the 140 pesos each three months, [presumably paid in installments?] before the witnesses who were mentioned. Before me, Matías Valeriano, notary.

. . .

[Letter of complaint to the authorities of Santo Domino Mixcoac, on the behalf of a group of Nahuas, undated:]

We are citizens here in Santo Domingo Mixcoac. We state that we found out that Paula and Juana and María and Catalina and Inés and Anastacia complain about the **teniente** before you [the *corregidor, gobernador, regidores*, etc.]. It is Antonio de Fuentes whom they are accusing because they say he mistreats them. [They say] he robs [people's land].

Teniente: Lieutenant.

. . .

And now [the] Spaniard Napolles disputes with the *teniente*. And Napolles goes around to each house exerting pressure on, forcing many people [to say "get rid of the *teniente*"]. [He says:] "Let there be no officer of the justice. I will help you expel the *teniente* because we will be happy if there is no officer of the law on your land." Napolles, Spaniard, keeps a woman at his house and he is forcing her. For this reason [the authorities] arrested him for concubinage. They gave him a fine about which he became very angry and they arrested him. He stole four pigs, the property of a person named Francisco Hernández, Spaniard, and because of that they arrested him. He was scorched [burned] for their relatives accuse them.

. . .

And so now with great concern and with bowing down we implore you [the *corregidor, gobernador,* and *regidores*, etc.] and we ask for justice. Everyone knows how [the blacks and *mestizos*] mistreat us. They don't go to confession. They are already a little afraid and are already living a little better. And we ask for justice. Let them be punished. We who ask it are Juan Joseph, Francisco de San Juan, and Francisco Juan.

≫ **Working with Sources**

1. **Why do the documents incorporate Nahuatl terms at some times but not at others?**

2. **How do the documents illustrate the various levels of justice available to native people and to "Spaniards"?**

SOURCE 18.4 *The Jesuit Relations,*
French North America

1649

*T*he Jesuit Relations are the most important documents attesting to the encounter between Europeans and native North Americans in the seventeenth century. These annual reports of French missionaries from the Society of Jesus document the conversions—or attempted conversions—of the various indigenous peoples in what is today the St. Lawrence River basin and the Great Lakes region. When they arrived on the banks of the St. Lawrence in 1625, French Jesuits were entering a continent still very much under control of First Nations peoples, who were divided by their own ethnic and linguistic differences. Even the catchall terms "Huron" and "Iroquois" masked their nature as confederacies, composed of several distinct nations, who had joined together prior to the arrival of Europeans.

When the Jesuits made headway with one group, they usually lost initiative with the group's rivals—and sometimes found themselves in the midst of a conflict that they could barely understand or appreciate. This section of the *Relations* concerns the torture and murder of Jean Brébeuf, who had lived among the Hurons at various points from the 1620s through the 1640s, observing their culture and systematically attempting to convert them to Catholicism. However, when an Iroquois raiding party invaded his settlement, the depth of the Hurons' Christian commitment—and his own—would be tested.

The sixteenth day of March in the present year, 1649, marked the beginning of our misfortunes—if an event, which no doubt has been the salvation of many of God's elect, can be called a misfortune.

The Iroquois, enemies of the Hurons, arrived by night at the frontier of this country. They numbered about a thousand men, well furnished with weapons, most of them carrying firearms obtained from their allies, the Dutch. We had no knowledge of their approach, although they had started from their country in the autumn, hunting in the forests throughout the winter, and had made a difficult journey of nearly two hundred leagues over the snow in order to take us by surprise. By night, they reconnoitered the condition of the first place upon which they had designs. It was surrounded by a pine stockade fifteen or sixteen feet in height, and a deep ditch with which nature had strongly fortified this place on three sides. There remained only a small space that was weaker than the others.

It was at this weak point that the enemy made a breach at daybreak, but so secretly and promptly that he was master of the place before anyone could mount a defense. All were then sleeping deeply, and they had no time to recognize the danger. Thus this village was taken, almost without striking a blow and with only ten Iroquois killed. Part of the Hurons—men, women, and

Source: Paul Ragueneau, "Relation of 1648–49," in Allan Greer, ed., *The Jesuit Relations: Natives and Missionaries in Seventeenth-Century North America* (Boston: Bedford/St. Martin's, 2000), 112–115.

children—were massacred then and there, while the others were made captives and were reserved for cruelties more terrible than death.

. . .

The enemy did not stop there, but followed up his victory, and before sunrise he appeared in arms to attack the town of St. Louis, which was fortified with a fairly good stockade. Most of the women and the children had just gone from it upon hearing the news which had arrived regarding the approach of the Iroquois. The people of greatest courage, about eighty persons, being resolved to defend themselves well, courageously repulsed the first and the second assaults, killing about thirty of the enemy's boldest men, in addition to many wounded. But finally, the larger number prevailed, as the Iroquois used their hatchets to undermine the palisade of stakes and opened a passage for themselves through some considerable breaches.

About nine o'clock in the morning, we perceived from our house at St. Marie the fire which was consuming the cabins of that town, where the enemy, after entering victoriously, had reduced everything to desolation. They cast into the flames the old, the sick, the children who had not been able to escape, and all those who, being too severely wounded, could not have followed them into captivity. At the sight of those flames, and by the color of the smoke which issued from them, we understood sufficiently what was happening, for this town of St. Louis was no more than a league distant from us. Two Christians who escaped the fire arrived about this time and confirmed this.

In this town of St. Louis were at that time two of our fathers, Father Jean de Brébeuf and Father Gabriel Lalemant, who had charge of a cluster of five towns. These formed but one of the eleven missions of which we have spoken above, and we call it the mission of St. Ignace.

Some Christians had begged the fathers to preserve their lives for the glory of God, which would have been as easy for them as for the more than five hundred persons who went away at the first alarm, for there was more than enough time to reach a place of safety. But their zeal could not permit such a thing, and the salvation of their flock was dearer to them than the love of their own lives. They employed the moments left to them as the most previous which they had ever had in the world, and through the heat of the battle their hearts were on fire for the salvation of souls.

Catechumens: Native converts who had not yet been baptized.

Neophytes: Recently baptized Christians.

One was at the breach, baptizing the **catechumens**, and the other was giving absolution to the **neophytes**. Both of them urged the Christians to die in the sentiments of piety with which they consoled them in their miseries. Never was their faith more alive, nor their love for their good fathers and pastors more keenly felt.

An infidel, seeing the desperate situation, spoke of taking flight, but a Christian named Etienne Annaotaha, the most esteemed in the country for his courage and his exploits against the enemy, would never allow it. "What!" he said. "Could we ever abandon these two good fathers, who have exposed their lives for us? Their love for our salvation will be the cause of their death, for there is no longer time for them to flee across the snows. Let us then die with them, and we shall go together to heaven." This man had made a general confession a few days previously, having had a presentiment of the danger awaiting him and saying that he wished that death should find him disposed for Heaven. And indeed he, as well as many other Christians, had abandoned themselves to fervor in a manner so extraordinary that we shall never be sufficiently able to bless the guidance of God over so many predestined souls. His divine providence continues lovingly to guide them in death as in life.

> **Working with Sources**

1. How well do the Jesuits seem to have understood the conflicts among native peoples in this region?

2. How was Ragueneau's reporting of the battle designed to highlight the "success" of the mission, despite an apparent setback?

SOURCE 18.5

The Salem Witch Trials, British North America

1692

The witch hunt that took place in Salem, Massachusetts, in 1692 has been frequently (if sensationally) depicted in modern films and plays. But a reading of the extant documents used in the trial of the supposed witches provides a more nuanced insight into the process of denunciation, conviction, and execution that unfolded in this persecution, which was among the last in the Western world. Although the Salem witch hunt resulted in the conviction of 30 and the execution of 19, the total number of persons who had been formally accused reached 164. Doubts about the guilt of those executed eventually led to a reconsideration of the procedures used in the trial, and the governor of the colony abruptly suspended the trials in the autumn of 1692. In spite of the admission by some of the Salem jurors that they had been mistaken, the judgments passed on seven of the convicted were not reversed until 2001.

Samuel Gray of Salem, aged about 42 years, testifieth and saith that about fourteen years ago, he going to bed well one [a.m.] one Lord's Day at night, and after he had been asleep some time, he awakened and looking up, saw the house light as if a candle or candles were lighted in it and the door locked, and that little fire there was raked up. He did then see a woman standing between the cradle in the room and the bedside and seemed to look upon him. So he did rise up in his bed and it vanished or disappeared. Then he went to the door and found it locked, and unlocking and opening the door, he went to the entry door and looked out and then again did see the same woman he had a little before seen in the room and in the same garb she was in before. Then he said to her, "What in the name of God do you come for?" Then she vanished away, so he locked the door again and went to bed, and between sleeping and waking he felt something come to his mouth or lips cold, and thereupon started and looked up again and did see the same woman with some thing between both her hands holding before his mouth upon which she moved. And the child in the cradle gave a great screech out as if it was greatly hurt and she disappeared, and taking the child up could not quiet it in some hours from which time the

Source: Brian P. Levack, ed., *The Witchcraft Sourcebook* (New York: Routledge, 2004), 225–226, 228–229.

child that was before a very lively, thriving child did pine away and was never well, although it lived some months after, yet in a sad condition and so died. Some time after within a week or less he did see the same woman in the same garb and clothes that appeared to him as aforesaid, and although he knew not her nor her name before, yet both by the countenance and garb doth testify that it was the same woman that they now call Bridget Bishop, alias Oliver, of Salem. Sworn Salem, May 30th 1692.

. . .

The deposition of Joseph Ring at Salisbury, aged 27 years, being sworn, saith that about the latter end of September last, being in the wood with his brother Jarvis Ring hewing of timber, his brother went home with his team and left this deponent alone to finish the hewing of the piece for him for his brother to carry when he came again. But as soon as his brother was gone there came to this deponent the appearance of Thomas Hardy of the great island of Puscataway, and by some impulse he was forced to follow him to the house of Benovy Tucker, which was deserted and about a half a mile from the place he was at work in, and in that house did appear Susannah Martin of Amesbury and the aforesaid Hardy and another female person which the deponent did not know. There they had a good fire and drink—it seemed to be cider. There continued most part of the night, [the] said Martin being then in her natural shape and talking as if she used to. But towards the morning the said Martin went from the fire, made a noise, and turned into the shape of a black hog and went away, and so did the other. Two persons go away, and this deponent was strangely carried away also, and the first place he knew was by Samuel Woods' house in Amesbury.

. . .

The deposition of Thomas Putnam, aged 40 years and [Edward Putnam] aged 38 years, who testify and say that we have been conversant with the afflicted persons or the most of them, as namely Mary Walcott, Mercy Lewes, Elizabeth Hubbard, Abigail Williams, Sarah Bibber and Ann Putnam junior and have often heard the aforementioned persons complain of Susannah Martin of Amesbery [sic] torturing them, and we have seen the marks of several bites and pinches which they say Susannah Martin did hurt them with, and also on the second day of May 1692, being the day of the examination of Susannah Martin, the aforenamed persons were most grievously tortured during the time of her examination, for upon a glance of her eyes they were struck down or almost choked and upon the motion of her finger we took notes they were afflicted, and if she did but clench her hands or hold her head aside the afflicted persons aforementioned were most grievously tortured, complaining of Susannah Martin for hurting them.

» Working with Sources

1. **What do these documents suggest about the (supposed) powers of witches, especially in terms of acting at a distance upon their victims?**

2. **Although all of the witnesses in this set of documents were men, do they reveal something about the connection between witchcraft accusations and gender?**

> Chapter 19   1450–1800

African Kingdoms, the Atlantic Slave Trade, and the Origins of Black America

THE ATLANTIC WORLD, 1500–1800

I t was a claim the Catholic Capuchin monks of the kingdom of Kongo vigorously denounced as a heretical abomination. Dona Beatriz Kimpa Vita (1684–1706), people claimed, had been reborn as St. Anthony of Padua. For many subjects of the kingdom, this claim was perfectly reasonable as part of an African Christian spirituality in which a gifted person could enter other people's minds and assume their identity. But the monks prevailed. The king of Kongo had Dona Beatriz condemned after a trial and burned at the stake.

Dona Beatriz had been intellectually precocious. In her childhood, her family had her initiated in a *kimpasi* enclosure as a *nganga marinda* (a Kikongo word derived from "knowledge" or "skill"). Such enclosures at the edges of towns and cities were common and contained altars with crosses and censers (for burning incense). The enclosures also included statues believed to be capable of recognizing evildoers, animal claws to grab them, horns to mark the line between the worlds of nature and the spirit, and animal tails as symbols of power. In her initiation ceremony, the head

ABOVE: **In this watercolor by Capuchin monk Antonio Cavazzi (1621–1678), a European monk and Kongo natives participate in a religious procession.**

woman of the enclosure put the young Dona Beatriz into a trance that enabled her to recognize and repel all the troubling forces that might disturb a person or the community.

The people in Kongo were very much aware, however, that not all *ngangas* were benevolent. Some *ngangas* were thought to misuse their spiritual powers and engage in witchcraft. For the missionary Capuchin monks, preaching the Catholic Reformation in the 1500s and 1600s, all *ngangas* were seen as witches. Whether the young Dona Beatriz was intimidated by the monks' denunciations or not, she followed the church ruling on witches, renounced her initiation, married, and pursued the domestic life of any other young woman in Kongo society.

But Dona Beatriz's spiritual path did not end here. In 1704, she again underwent a series of deep religious transformations in which she "died," only to be reborn as St. Anthony of Padua (1195–1231), a Portuguese Franciscan monk and one of the patron saints of Portugal. Devotees of the saint believe he blesses marriages and helps people find lost items. With her new saintly and male identity, more powerful than her earlier one as a *nganga*, Dona Beatriz preached a novel and inspiring vision: She was God's providential figure, arrived to restore the Catholic faith and reunify the kingdom of Kongo, both of which she saw as having been torn asunder during nearly half a century of dynastic disunity and civil war (1665–1709).

After her spiritual rebirth, Dona Beatriz immediately went to Pedro IV, king of Kongo (r. 1695–1718), and his Capuchin ally, the chief missionary Bernardo da Gallo, and accused them of being laggards in their efforts to restore the faith and unity of the kingdom. Pedro, perhaps impressed with her claims and the potential power at her command, temporized in his response. Bernardo, however, subjected Dona Beatriz to an angry interrogation about her faith and alleged saintly possession. In a startling and, for Bernardo, alarming parallel to Martin Luther's arguments during the Protestant Reformation nearly two centuries before, Beatriz countered with a remarkable attack on the Catholic cornerstone of sacraments. Intention or faith alone, she argued, not the sacraments of the church, would bring salvation. Unlike Luther, however, Dona Beatriz did not derive her convictions from the letters of St. Paul in the New Testament but from her *nganga* initiation: It was her good intentions that distinguished her from the malevolent witch.

Unable to arrive at a plan of action, the king and Bernardo let Beatriz go. In a journey reminiscent of that of Joan of Arc, she led a growing crowd of followers to the ruined capital of Kongo, M'banza (called São Salvador by the Portuguese). There, she trained "little Anthonies" as missionaries to convert the Kongolese to her new Antonian–African Christianity. Under the

Seeing Patterns

》 **What was the pattern of kingdom and empire formation in Africa during the period 1500–1800?**

》 **How did patterns of plantation slavery evolve in the Atlantic and the Americas?**

》 **What are the historic roots from which modern racism evolved?**

protection of a rival of the king, Beatriz was at the pinnacle of her spiritual power when everything unraveled. Though already married, she gave birth to a child conceived with one of her followers. She did so secretly at her ancestral home in King Pedro's territory, evidently in a deep crisis over her spiritual mission. Allies of the king discovered the lovers by accident and arrested them. They brought them before Pedro, who, in the meantime, had decided to reject Beatriz's challenge and silence her. After a state trial—the church stayed out of the proceedings—Beatriz, her companion, and the baby were executed by the favored means of punishing heretics—burning at the stake.

The story of Dona Beatriz illustrates a major pattern discussed in this chapter: the process by which many Africans adapted their religious heritage to the challenge of European Christianity. Europeans arrived on the western coast of Africa in the late fifteenth century as both missionaries and merchants—at times also as slave traders and slave raiders. Africans responded with gold, goods, and their own adaptive forms of Christianity, as well as efforts—as in Kongo, Angola, and Benin—to limit the slave trade in accordance with their own political interests. Elsewhere, however, Africans also exploited and adapted indigenous systems of household, agricultural, administrative, and military slavery to reap voluminous profits from the developing Atlantic human traffic. The unprecedented massive transfer of African slaves to the plantations and mines of the Americas brought to those continents a vast and complex array of peoples from foragers and herders to villagers and city dwellers, representing a wide variety of religious experiences—including those of both Islam and Christianity. In many cases, their cultures would not only survive in the Americas under extraordinarily difficult circumstances but become foundational in the new societies being created there.

African States and the Slave Trade

In the north of sub-Saharan Africa the pattern of Islamic and Christian dynastic state formation that had been ongoing for centuries continued to dominate herder and village societies in the period 1500–1800. An invasion by Muslim forces from Morocco during the sixteenth century, however, ended the trend toward empire building in West Africa and strengthened the forces of decentralization. By contrast, in the savanna and Great Lakes regions of central Africa, improved agricultural wealth and intensified regional trade helped perpetuate the kingdom formation already under way. An important set of institutions in the chiefdoms and states of Africa was slavery, though its form and character were far different from the chattel slavery that would characterize the Americas. When the Europeans inserted themselves into these systems, they profoundly altered them to benefit their own interests in the production of warm-weather cash crops on American plantations. The implications of the new trade provided both enormous opportunities and horrific challenges for African traders and local leaders. As the Mediterranean slave trade had for Venetian, Genoese, and North African traffickers, the growing Atlantic slave trade appealed to some West African rulers as a path to enhanced wealth and power, and they enriched themselves through warfare, raids, and trading. More often, however, rulers tried by various means to resist what ultimately became the greatest forced migration in human history.

The End of Empires in the North and the Rise of States in the Center

The Eurasian empires with universal ambitions of the premodern world united peoples of many different religions, languages, and ethnic affiliations. Mali (1240–1460) was the first African empire that was similar to the empires of Eurasia in this respect. Mali's successor state, the focus of this section, was the even larger Songhay Empire (1460–1591). Though vast, it lasted only a short time.

Origins of the Songhay Songhay was initially a tributary state of Mali. It was centered on the city of Gao downstream on the Niger River from the agricultural center of Jenné-jeno and the commercial and scholarly center of Timbuktu (see Source 19.1). Gao's origins dated to 850, when it emerged as the end point of the eastern trans-Saharan route from Tunisia and Algeria, parallel to the more heavily traveled western route from Morocco. Gao was located at the northern end of the Songhay Empire, near the Niger Bend, and was inhabited by the Songhay, an ethnic grouping composed of herders, villagers, and fishermen.

The Songhay were ethnically distinct from the Soninke of the kingdom of ancient Ghana and the Malinke of the Mali Empire farther west. Their homeland was located to the east and southeast of the Niger Bend. At the end of the eleventh century, the leading clans of the Songhay, profiting from the trans-Saharan trade, converted to Islam. Two centuries later the warriors among them assumed positions of leadership as vassals of the *mansa*, or emperor, of Mali.

The Songhay Empire The Songhay began their imperial expansion in the mid-1400s, toward the end of the dry period in West Africa (1100–1500), during which control of the steppe region was sometimes difficult to maintain. Mali, which had its center in the much wetter savanna, lost its northern outpost, Timbuktu, to the Songhay in 1469. In the following decades, Mali slowly retreated southwestward. Eventually, it became a minor vassal of the Songhay. At its height, the Songhay Empire stretched from Hausaland in the savanna southeast of Gao all the way westward to the Atlantic coast (see Map 19.1).

As in the previous centuries in ancient Ghana and Mali, the decisive difference that elevated the Songhay emperors (*askiyas*) above their vassals was their

interactive timeline

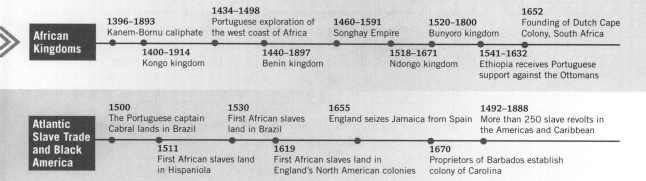

African Kingdoms					
	1396–1893 Kanem-Bornu caliphate	**1434–1498** Portuguese exploration of the west coast of Africa	**1460–1591** Songhay Empire	**1520–1800** Bunyoro kingdom	**1652** Founding of Dutch Cape Colony, South Africa
	1400–1914 Kongo kingdom	**1440–1897** Benin kingdom	**1518–1671** Ndongo kingdom	**1541–1632** Ethiopia receives Portuguese support against the Ottomans	

Atlantic Slave Trade and Black America				
	1500 The Portuguese captain Cabral lands in Brazil	**1530** First African slaves land in Brazil	**1655** England seizes Jamaica from Spain	**1492–1888** More than 250 slave revolts in the Americas and Caribbean
	1511 First African slaves land in Hispaniola	**1619** First African slaves land in England's North American colonies	**1670** Proprietors of Barbados establish colony of Carolina	

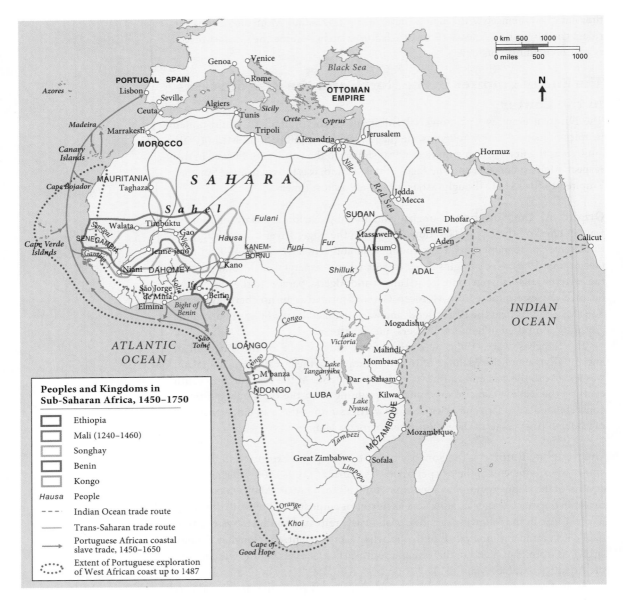

MAP **19.1 Peoples and Kingdoms in Sub-Saharan Africa, 1450–1750.**

taxation of the gold trade. The gold fields of the Upper Niger, Senegal, and Black Volta Rivers in the southern rain forest were outside the empire, but merchant clans, often accompanied by troop detachments, transported the gold to Timbuktu and Gao. Here, North African merchants exchanged their Mediterranean manufactures and salt for gold, slaves, and kola nuts. Agents of the *askiyas* in these cities collected market taxes in the form of gold. Agricultural taxes and tributes supported kingdoms; long-distance trade was needed in addition for an empire to come into being.

Songhay's Sudden End   After the initial conquests, the Songhay Empire had little time to consolidate its territory on a more peaceful footing. After just over a century of dominance, the Songhay Empire came to a sudden end in 1591 when a Moroccan force invaded from the north. The invasion was prompted by Moroccan sultans who had successfully driven the Portuguese from their Atlantic coast but were concerned about the flourishing Portuguese trade for gold on the West African coast. They therefore decided to find and occupy the West African gold fields in the rain forest themselves, thus depriving the Portuguese of their supply.

However, after defeating Songhay, they were unable to march any farther, lacking necessary logistical support from Morocco through the Sahara. Although the officers initially turned the Niger delta and Bend into a Moroccan province, within a generation they assimilated into the West African royal clans. As a result, imperial politics in West Africa disintegrated, together with much of the trans-Saharan gold trade, which was siphoned off by the Portuguese on what became known as the Gold Coast (modern Ghana).

The Eastern Sahel and Savanna   The steppes between Songhay in the west and Ethiopia in the northeastern highlands near the Red Sea also were home to Islamic regimes governing moderate to large territories. Kanem-Bornu (1396–1893) was a long-lived Islamic realm, calling itself a caliphate, but with a majority of subjects following local African religious traditions. Located in both the steppe and savanna, it was based on a slave and ivory trade with the Mediterranean and on agriculture and fishing for its internal organization on the south side of Lake Chad. Kanem-Bornu's imperial frontier was in the southwest, where it waged long intermittent wars with the savanna kingdoms of Hausaland.

The Hausa kingdoms, numbering about half a dozen, had formed during the height of the Mali-dominated trans-Saharan trade as southeastern extensions of this trade into rain-forest Africa. Although they were under frequent attack by Songhay and Kanem-Bornu during the period 1500–1800, the Hausa kingdoms enjoyed periods of independence during which many of the ruling clans converted to Islam. Like their northern neighbors, they maintained cavalry forces, which—apart from military purposes—served to protect the caravans of the traders. In addition to taxing these traders, the Hausa kings collected dues from the villagers. Craftspeople produced pottery, iron implements and utensils, cotton cloth, basketry, leather goods, and iron weapons. Miners and smiths smelted and forged copper, iron, and steel. Although more agricultural in orientation, the Hausa kingdoms closely resembled their northern neighbors in the steppe.

Farther east, in the steppe between Lake Chad and the Nile, the Fur and the Funj, cattle-breeding clan-lineage federations, converted fully to Islam, from the royal clans down to the commoners. In contrast, in West Africa only the dynasties and merchants became Muslim. Their leaders adopted the title "sultan" and became increasingly Arabized in the period 1500–1800, while Christianity along the Upper Nile disappeared completely.

South Central Africa   On the southern side of the rain forest, the eastern part of the southern savanna and the Great Lakes area in central Africa remained outside the reach of the slave trade. As a result, their populations continued to grow. Large numbers of farmer and cattle herder groups, organized in chiefdoms, inhabited these regions. In the eastern savanna, the kingdom of Luba emerged before 1500, while others followed at various intervals thereafter.

A steady increase in regional trade for copper, iron, salt, dried fish, beads, cloth, and palm oil enabled chieftain clans to consolidate their rule and enlarge their holdings into kingdoms. Living in enclosures and surrounded by "courts," or ruling-class settlements, kings maintained agricultural domains worked by slaves. Villages nearby delivered tribute in the form of foodstuffs. From the mid-seventeenth century onward, the American-origin staples corn and cassava (manioc) broadened the food supply. Tributaries at some distance delivered prestige goods, especially copper and ironware, as well as beads. At times, the kings mobilized thousands of workers to build moats and earthworks around their courts, which became centers of incipient urbanization processes.

The Great Lakes region, to the north, south, and west of Lake Victoria, was a highly fertile eastward extension of the southern savanna supporting two annual crops of sorghum and sesame, as well as banana groves and herds of cattle. Traders distributed salt, iron, and dried fish. Agriculture, cattle breeding, and trade supported intense political competition in the region. Small agricultural–mercantile kingdoms shared the region, but sometime in the sixteenth century cattle breeders—the Luo, relatives of the Shilluk—arrived from southern Sudan and shook up the existing political and social structures. Pronounced disparities in cattle ownership emerged on the rich pasture lands. Cattle lords, bolstered by their new wealth and status, rose as competitors of the kings.

North of Lake Victoria, the Bunyoro kingdom, based on agriculture and regional trade, held the cattle lords at bay, while on the south side of the lake the cattle lords created new small kingdoms. After a while dominant cattle breeders and inferior farmers settled into more or less unequal relations of mutual dependence. Under the colonial system in the nineteenth century, these unequal relations froze into a caste system in which the dominant but minority Tutsi cattle breeders were continually at odds with the majority Hutu farmers. (The tensions in this social situation were part of a combination of factors that ultimately—under the conditions of modernity—led to the mass killings and genocide committed by the Hutus against the Tutsis in the modern state of Rwanda in 1993–1994.) Farther south the pre-1500 tradition of gold-mining kingdoms, such as Great Zimbabwe, continued. But here the interaction of Africa with Portugal set the kingdoms on a different historical trajectory.

Portugal's Explorations along the African Coast and Contacts with Ethiopia

The Portuguese expansion into North Africa and the exploration of the African coast were outgrowths of both the *Reconquista* and religious crusading impulses. Mixed in with these religious motives was the practical necessity of financing the journeys of exploration through profits from trade. The combination of the two guided Portugal within a single century around the African continent to India. Along the coast, the Portuguese established forts as points of protection for their merchants. In Ethiopia they supported the Christian kingdom there with military aid, providing protection against the Ottomans in Yemen, just across the Red Sea.

Chartered Explorations in West Africa   Henry the Navigator (1394–1460), brother of the ruling king, a principal figure of the Portuguese *Reconquista* and chief embodiment of the crusading zeal, occupied the Moroccan port of Ceuta in 1415. He claimed that Ceuta had been Christian prior to the Berber–Arab conquest and subsequent Islamization of Iberia. He also wished to renew crusading for the reconquest of Jerusalem, lost to the Muslims in 1291. But the merchant wing of the Lisbon court was wary of the military expenditures. During the fifteenth century, campaigns for the military occupation of other cities of Morocco, mostly along the Atlantic coast, alternated with voyages financed by Portuguese groups of merchants and aristocrats for commerce along the West African coast.

In 1434, mariners discovered that ships could overcome adverse currents and winds and return from the West African coast by sailing out into the Atlantic, setting course for the newly discovered islands of the Canaries, Madeira, and Azores, before turning east toward Lisbon. It was the impossibility of returning along the coast from the southern part of West Africa that had doomed all previous efforts. Sailors either had to return by land, via the Sahara to the Mediterranean, or they disappeared without a trace. Thus, sailing south in the Atlantic and developing a route by which to return was a decisive step toward circumnavigating the continent.

Between 1434 and 1472, through a combination of royally chartered, merchant-financed voyages, as well as public state-organized expeditions, Portuguese mariners explored the coast as far east as the Bight of Benin. Trade items included European woolens and linens, which were exchanged for gold, cottons, and Guinea pepper. Small numbers of African slaves were included early on as trade items, mostly through purchases from chieftains and kings. Several uninhabited tropical islands off the coast were discovered during this time, and the Portuguese used slaves for the establishment of sugar plantations on them. They shipped other slaves to Europe for domestic employment, adding to the long-standing Mediterranean and trans-Saharan practice of household slavery.

excerpt from Gomes Eannes de Azurara, *The Chronicle of the Discovery and Conquest of Guinea* (1453)

Portugal and Ethiopia   By the second half of the fifteenth century, private merchant interests focused on developing trade in West Africa provided few incentives for further explorations. It required the military wing of the Portuguese court to revive crusading. From 1483 through 1486 the king organized state expeditions for further expansion from the Bight of Benin south to the Congo River. Here, mariners sailed upstream in hopes of linking up with Prester John (see Chapter 16), a mythical Christian king believed to live in India or Ethiopia who could help Portugal in the reconquest of Jerusalem. Instead of Prester John, the Portuguese mariners encountered the ruler of the powerful kingdom of Kongo, who converted to Christianity and established close relations with Portugal.

A few years later, after Christopher Columbus had sailed to the Americas for Castile–Aragon in 1492, the Portuguese crown continued the search for a way to India or Ethiopia, a route presumed to lie around the southern tip of Africa. Eventually, Vasco da Gama circumnavigated the southern tip, established trade outposts in Swahili city-states of East Africa, and reached India in 1498. From this point Portuguese development of the Indian spice trade grew in importance.

The Portuguese discovered in the early sixteenth century that the Ethiopian kingdom was extremely weak in the face of the aggressive Muslim sultanate of Adal, on the Red Sea to the east. Until the end of the fifteenth century, Ethiopia had been a powerful Coptic Christian kingdom in the highlands of northeastern Africa. Its people practiced a productive plow-based agriculture for wheat and teff (a local grain), and its kings controlled a rich trade of gold, ivory, animal skins, and slaves from the southern Sudan through the Rift Valley to the Red Sea (see Chapter 14).

excerpt from *The Fetha Nagast* (ca. 1450)

Prester John. The legend of Prester John, a Christian ruler whose lost kingdom in northeast Africa, surrounded by Muslims and pagans, captivated the European imagination from the twelfth through the seventeenth centuries. Purportedly a descendant of one of the Three Magi, Prester John (or Presbyter John) presided over a realm full of riches and fabulous creatures, originally assumed to be in India.

Possession of a Red Sea port for this trade, however, was a bone of contention between Ethiopia and Adal during the first half of the sixteenth century.

A Christian incursion into Muslim territory in 1529 triggered a response by Adal in the form of a furiously destructive Muslim holy war. Ethiopia would have been destroyed in this war had it not been for the timely arrival in 1541 of a Portuguese fleet with artillery and musketeers. For its part, Adal received Ottoman Muslim artillery and musketeer support from Yemen, but 2 years later, after several fierce battles, the Christians prevailed.

Ethiopia paid a high price for its victory, however. Adal Muslim power was destroyed, but in its place, the Ottomans took over the entire west coast of the Red Sea, mostly in order to keep out Portugal. Non-Christian cattle breeders from the southwest occupied the Rift Valley, which separated the northern and southern Ethiopian highlands and had been depopulated during the Christian–Muslim wars. Cut off by the newcomers, Christians in the southern highlands were left to their own devices, surviving in small states. Small numbers of Portuguese stayed in Ethiopia, with Jesuit missionaries threatening to dominate the Ethiopian church, which had long followed its own traditions, as well as the kings. In 1632 the Ethiopian king expelled the Jesuits and consolidated the kingdom as a shrunken power within much smaller borders.

Initially, Ethiopian culture continued to be active under the initative of the court, expressed mostly through theological writings and iconic paintings. But from about 1700 Ethiopia decentralized into provincial lordships with little interest in their cultural heritage. Only in the mid-nineteenth century, in response to the Western challenge, did the kings take back their power from the provincial lords.

Coastal Africa and the Atlantic Slave Trade

After Portuguese mariners had circumnavigated Africa, they initially focused on developing their spice trade with India. Gradually, however, they also built their

(a) **Elmina as it appeared in a European etching from 1562.**   *(b)* **Outer defensive walls.**

Elmina. This town in present-day Ghana was, along with the village of São Jorge da Mina, the first Portuguese fortified trading post on the African coast, from 1482 until it passed to the Dutch in 1637. Merchants used it for storing the goods they traded and for protection in case of conflicts with Africans. It was staffed by a governor and 20–60 soldiers along with a priest, surgeon, apothecary, and a variety of craftspeople. Throughout the first half of the sixteenth century Elmina was also the center of Portuguese slaving activities.

Atlantic slave trade, which took off in the early seventeenth century, to be followed by mariner-merchants from other European countries. To understand the pattern underlying the slave trade from 1500 to 1800 it is crucial to be aware of the importance of slavery within the African historical context. Different kinds of slavery existed in a number of regions in Africa. In many places, a form of slavery existed in the place of land ownership. The more slaves a household, clan leader, chief, or king owned, to work at home or in the fields, the wealthier he was. This form of **household slavery** was the most common variety.

Trade Forts   Early on, in the 1440s, Portuguese mariners raided the West African coast in the region defined by the Senegal and Gambia Rivers—Senegambia—for slaves. But they suffered losses since the performance and reliability of their muskets was not yet superior to the precisely aimed poisoned arrows of the Africans. Furthermore, dwelling in a rain forest with its many rivers opening to the coast, West Africans possessed a well-developed tradition of boatbuilding and coastal navigation. Boats hollowed out from tree trunks could hold as many as 50 warriors. These warriors paddled swiftly through the estuaries and mangrove swamps along the coast and picked off the mariners from their caravels with their archery if they approached the coast in a hostile manner. The Portuguese thus learned to set foot on the beach in a less threatening way and began what developed into a lucrative coastal fort trade in a variety of items, including slaves.

Through treaties with local African leaders, Portugal acquired the right to build posts or forts from which to trade. Africans involved in trade in these regions produced a variety of items that were soon in demand in Europe. They wove colorful cotton cloth and wore it by the yard. A particular kind of bark or leaf cloth from central West Africa was at times highly sought in Portugal and the Caribbean. For a long time, Senegambian mats were preferred as bedcovers in Europe. In many places, Africans smelted iron and forged steel that was of higher quality than that of iron-poor Portugal.

Trade, as in most other parts in the world during the period 1500–1800, was for expensive luxury goods, not ordinary articles of daily life. Merchants had to be able to achieve high profits while carrying comparatively little to weigh them down. African rulers purchased luxuries in order to engage in conspicuous consumption, fashion display, and lavish gift giving—all ways to enhance their status and cement

Household slavery: African chiefs and kings maintained large households of retainers, such as administrators, soldiers, domestics, craftspeople, and farmers; many among these were slaves, acquired through raids and wars but also as a form of punishment for infractions of royal, chiefly, or clan law.

Portuguese Traders. This brass plaque, from about the middle of the sixteenth century, decorated the palace of the Benin *obo* and shows two Portuguese traders. The fact they are holding hands suggests that they could be father and son.

power relations. They sold slaves to the Europeans in a similar fashion, as luxuries in return for luxuries. Thus, scarcity raised demand on both sides in their respective quest for luxury items.

African Slavery Sub-Saharan Africa—with few long rivers and immense equatorial rain forests—was a vast region with enormous hurdles to a shift in patterns from local self-sufficiency to exchange agriculture and urbanization. Inland exchanges of food for manufactured goods over distances greater than 20 miles were for the most part prohibitively expensive. Because of the tsetse fly (see Chapter 6), human portage or animal transport, the only available forms of moving goods, was limited to highly valuable merchandise, such as salt, copper, and iron. Everything else was manufactured within self-sufficient households, such as pottery, textiles, mats, basketry, utensils, implements, leather goods, and weapons, alongside a full range of agricultural goods.

Such self-sufficiency required large households. In villages with limited outside trade, the polygamous household with the largest number of males and females employed at home and in the fields was the wealthiest. To increase his wealth further, a household master often raided neighboring villages and acquired captives, to be enslaved and put to work inside and outside the household. Not surprisingly, therefore, slave raiding and household slavery were general features in sub-Saharan African societies, though some peoples like the San of southern Africa lacked the institution altogether. The more stratified slaveholding societies were—with chiefly or royal institutions such as central administrations, armies, and juridical and fiscal offices—the more slaves rose into positions of responsibility and, frequently, autonomy. This was especially the case in the large empires like Mali and Songhay, where a variety of institutions of servitude existed outside of the category of household slavery. Thus, as in a number of societies outside of Africa, the varieties of slavery in sub-Saharan Africa tended to be highly complex and flexible in structure and function.

Limited Slave Trade from Benin When Portugal began the slave trade to supply labor for its sugar plantations on West African offshore islands, African chiefs and kings had to evaluate the comparative value of slaves for their households or for sale. The kingdom of Benin in the rain-forest region west of the Niger delta was an early example of this calculation. The ruler Ewuare (r. 1440–1473) was the first to rise to dominance over chiefs (*azuma*) and assume the title of king (*obo*). Through conquests in all directions, Ewuare acquired large numbers of slaves who were employed in his army and for the construction of extensive earthworks protecting the capital, Benin City.

Early trade contacts between Portuguese mariners and Benin intensified when the successor of Ewuare granted permission to build a fort on the coast in 1487. But the king kept the exchange of palm oil, ivory, woolens, beads, pepper, and slaves for guns, powder, metalware, salt, and cottons under close control. A generation later, when the kings prohibited the sale of male slaves, the Portuguese promptly abandoned their fort. Later, a compromise was reached whereby a limited number of slaves were traded, perhaps some 30 percent of the total trade volume between Portugal and Benin, in return for firearms. The kingdom admitted missionaries and members of the dynasty acculturated to the Portuguese, making Benin increasingly economically diversified and culturally complex.

Slave exports remained restricted during the following two centuries, while Benin was a strong, centralized state. Under subsequent weak kings, decentralization set in. Provincial chiefs began to compete with each other, requiring increased numbers of firearms. To buy more weapons, toward the end of the seventeenth century a weak Benin palace lifted the restrictions on the slave trade. Even more weapons were purchased, and slaves were sold during a civil war in the first half of the eighteenth century. But the kingdom reunified, and the palace never lost complete control over Benin's trade with the Portuguese and, from the mid-seventeenth century onward, Dutch and British merchants. Compared to the slave trade farther west on the West African coast, the large centralized kingdom of Benin with its high internal demand for slave labor remained a modest exporter of slaves and thus retained a considerable degree of autonomy and agency.

The Kingdom of Kongo   Farther south, on the central West African coast, the Portuguese established trade relations with several coastal kingdoms, among which Kongo and Ndongo were the most important. These kingdoms were located south of the Congo River, with rain forest to the north and savanna to the south. Kongo, the oldest and most centralized kingdom in the region, emerged about 1400, or a century before the arrival of the Portuguese. Its capital, M'banza (São Salvador), was 20 miles inland in the fertile highlands. With 60,000 inhabitants in the sixteenth century, its size was comparable to such European cities as London, Amsterdam, Moscow, and Rome at the time. M'banza also contained a large palace population and a royal domain, where slaves farmed sorghum, millet, and corn.

Within a radius of some 20 miles, the kings governed a region of about 300,000 independent villagers directly. To defend their rule, they relied on a standing army of 5,000 troops, including 500 musketeers, in the sixteenth century. They appointed members of the royal family as governors, who were entitled to rents but were also obliged to deliver taxes in kind to the palace. In addition, the kings collected a head tax in the form of cowrie shells, an indication that farmers engaged in a limited form of trading their agricultural surplus on markets in the capital to obtain the shells for the tax. This region of direct rule was marked by a unified law and administration. Royal appointees traveled around to represent the royal writ. Farther away, vassal kings, called dukes (Portuguese *duque*), governed and sent tribute or gifts to the capital. They sometimes rebelled and broke away; thus, the territory of Kongo, similar to that of Songhay, shifted constantly in size.

The kings of Kongo converted to Christianity early and sent members of the ruling family to Portugal for their education. Portuguese missionaries converted the court and a number of provincial chiefs. Among the ruling class, many read and wrote Portuguese and Latin fluently, impressing European aristocrats with their comportment whenever they went on missions. Muslim ethnic stereotypes against "reddish" Christians and Christian stereotypes and patronizing attitudes against dark Muslims, called *moros*, and, by extension, black people from sub-Saharan Africa had existed for a long time in Iberia and expressed themselves in Portugal's dealings with Kongo (see Source 19.2).

Kongolese royalty wore Portuguese dress, listened to church music and hymns, and drank wine imported from Madeira. Lay assistants converted many urban and villager commoners to Catholicism, and schoolmasters instructed children at churches and chapels. The result was an African Creole culture, in which the veneration of territorial and ancestral spirits was combined with Catholicism. As the story of Dona Beatriz Kimpa Vita demonstrates, this Creole culture should not be viewed as a simple copy of European culture. Instead, as with the Creole cultures of the Americas, it was a creative adaptation of traditions: in this case, of Portuguese Catholicism to the indigenous African spiritual and cultural heritage, in the same way that East and West Africa adapted to Coptic Christianity or Islam and represented genuine variations of African culture.

Kongo began to sell slaves to Portuguese traders as early as 1502 for labor on the sugar plantations of the island of São Tomé. By the mid-1500s, the kings permitted the export of a few thousand slaves a year. But Portugal wanted more slaves, and in 1571 the crusader king Sebastião I (r. 1557–1578), who renewed Henry the Navigator's devotion to territorial conquest, chartered a member of the aristocracy with creating a colony in the adjacent kingdom of Ndongo for the mining of salt and silver by slaves. At first, this holder of the charter assisted the king of Ndongo in defeating rebels; but when his colonial aims became clear, the king turned against him, and a full-scale Portuguese war of conquest and for slaves erupted.

In this war, which lasted with short interruptions from 1579 to 1657, the Portuguese allied themselves with Ibangala bands. The Ibangala were a large group of loosely organized, fierce warriors from the eastern outreaches of Kongo and Ndongo into central Africa who raided in both kingdoms for slaves. Their propaganda as well as their swift campaigns threw the population into fear and turmoil. Tales of cannibalism and the forcible recruitment of child soldiers spread by word of mouth. The Ibangala reputation for fierceness was enhanced by their consumption of large quantities of palm wine and imported Portuguese wine from the Canaries, the latter received from traders in payment for slaves. Together, a few hundred Portuguese musketeers and tens of thousands of Ibangalas raided the kingdoms of Ndongo and Kongo for slaves, often capturing as many as 15,000 a year.

The war reduced the resourceful Queen Nzinga (r. 1624–1663) of Ndongo to a guerilla fighter. In the end, thanks to an alliance with some Ibangalas, she re-created a kingdom, greatly reduced in size, that also engaged in the slave trade. The widening conflict also spilled over into Kongo, where Portuguese and allied Ibangala troops exploited a long civil war (1665–1709) and enslaved even Catholic and Antonian (followers of Dona Beatrice) Christians. The war expanded further when new entrants onto the scene, the Dutch West India Company, mistakenly assumed that the small numbers of Portuguese troops would be no match in a quick conquest for the coastal forts. Thanks to Brazilian help, however, Portugal was able to drive out the Dutch. The latter decided to return to a more peaceful trade for slaves from other fortified strongholds on the African west coast.

The Dutch in South Africa

In 1652, the Dutch built a fort on the South African coast to supply fresh water and food to ships traveling around the Cape of Good Hope. Employees of the company, working on time contracts, grew wheat on small

Kongolese Cross of St. Anthony. Considered an emblem of spiritual authority and power, the Christian cross was integrated into Kongo ancestral cults and burial rituals and was believed to contain magical protective properties. In Antonianism, the religious reform movement launched by Dona Beatriz, or Kimpa Vita, in 1704, St. Anthony of Padua, a thirteenth-century Portuguese-born saint, became known as Toni Malau, or "Anthony of Good Fortune," and was the patron of the movement. His image was widely incorporated into religious objects and personal items, such as this cross.

Queen Nzinga. In this contemporary engraving, Queen Nzinga is shown conducting negotiations with the Portuguese in 1622. She sits on a slave's back to avoid having to stand in the presence of a person beneath her rank.

lots and bought cattle from the Khoi, local cattle breeders. A few wealthy landowners imported the first black slaves in 1658, from Dahomey, on the West African coast, to convert the original Dutch smallholdings into larger wheat and grape plantations. Gradually, a culturally Dutch settler society emerged, which included Protestants fleeing religious persecution in France and Germany.

The majority of these settlers were urban craftspeople and traders, while most of the actual farmers employed slaves from Mozambique, Madagascar, and even as far away as Indonesia, the center of Dutch colonial ambitions in the East Indies. Around 1750, there were about 10,000 *Boers* (Dutch for "farmer") in the Cape Colony, easily outnumbered by slaves. Through relentless land expansion into the interior, ranchers destroyed the Khoi, forcing their absorption into other local groups. The Boers governed themselves, following the model of Dutch representative institutions. Their descendants, who called themselves "Afrikaners," would one day fight the Zulu for land and the British for independence and create the system of apartheid in South Africa. Today, they share political power and a troubled political legacy with their black African countrymen.

American Plantation Slavery and Atlantic Mercantilism

The patterns of African slavery were quite different from the patterns of American plantation slavery. While European slave traders exploited existing African slave systems, the American plantation slave system had its roots in the Eastern Christian religious civilization of Byzantium. There, the Roman institution of agricultural

map analysis: the spread of sugar cultivation

estate slavery had survived, in both law and practice. Imperial estates on the Mediterranean islands of Cyprus and Crete employed Muslim prisoners as well as captives from the Russian steppes as slaves for the cultivation of such labor-intensive crops as wine and olive oil. After 1191, when crusaders conquered Cyprus from Byzantium, crusader landlords and Venetian and Genoese merchants expanded into sugar production, which had been introduced from Iran to the eastern Mediterranean by the Muslims. (Sugarcane was domesticated in New Guinea ca. 8000 BCE, and sugar refining was developed in India during the 300s CE.) From the early 1400s onward, Venetians, Spaniards, and Portuguese established slave-based sugarcane plantations on the islands of Madeira, the Canaries, and São Tomé off the West African coast.

The Special Case of Plantation Slavery in the Americas

In examining the rise and perpetuation for more than three centuries of the patterns of American **plantation slavery**, a number of questions arise: How many Africans were forcibly taken from Africa to the Americas? Who were they, and who were the people who exploited their labor? What institutions were created to capture, transport, supply, and work slaves? What did the labor of the African slaves help to build? And, perhaps most of all, why did this system develop the way it did—and last so long?

Plantation slavery: Economic system in which slave labor was used to grow cash crops such as sugarcane, tobacco, and cotton on large estates.

Numbers   The enslavement of Africans for labor in the Western Hemisphere constituted the largest human migration—voluntary or involuntary—in world history before the later nineteenth century. Though it is estimated that millions of Africans had earlier been taken into servitude in the Muslim world from the eighth to the fourteenth century, their numbers are dwarfed by those shipped across the Atlantic from the fifteenth through the early nineteenth century.

While the figures have been hotly debated by scholars and activists over recent decades, the latest estimates put the numbers of Africans shipped out of Africa at around 12.5 million—more than twice the number taken in the so-called Oriental slave trade to the Middle East and Indian Ocean basin during the period 700–1500. Nearly half of these slaves, 5.8 million, went to Brazil. While historical demographers and other scholars try to determine how many slaves died in the process of being transferred to the African coast after their initial capture and how many more perished at sea, their conclusions are at present only tentative. However, most estimates place the numbers of slaves lost during these transfers at 1.4 million, or 12 percent, with a total of 11 million reaching the American shores. These figures, it should be noted, exclude the numbers killed in the African slave raids and wars themselves, which will probably never be precisely known (see Map 19.2).

Chattel: Literally, an item of movable personal property; chattel slavery is the reduction of the status of the slave to an item of personal property of the owner, to dispose of as he or she sees fit.

Chattel Slavery   By the mid-eighteenth century African slaves everywhere in the New World had been reduced to the status of **chattel**. The perfect expression of this condition may be found in the famous Dred Scott decision, handed down by the US Supreme Court a century later, in 1857. In the court's opinion, the chief justice, Roger B. Taney, forcefully stated that black African slaves "had no rights which a white man was bound to respect."

Within this statement we see another qualitatively different element from earlier kinds of slavery: what came to be known as the "color line." While color was sometimes not the determining factor in the early years of American slavery, it had very

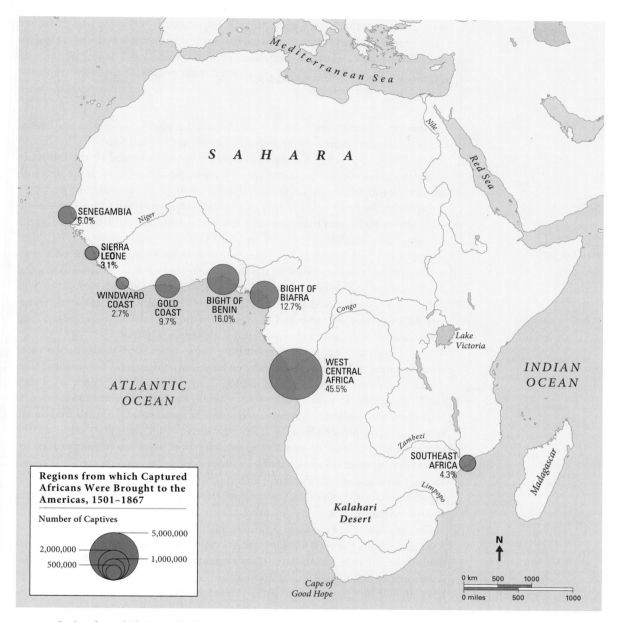

MAP **19.2** **Regions from which Captured Africans Were Brought to the Americas, 1501–1867.**

much come to be so by the eighteenth century. The equation of blackness with slavery prompted assumptions over time of African inferiority and created the basis for the modern expression of the phenomenon of racism, a problem that has plagued all societies touched by the institution of African slavery to this day (see Source 19.5).

Historians have long debated the role of present-day sensibilities and issues in the study of the past. The practice of looking at the past through the lens of the present is called **presentism**. Of course, everyone brings his or her own views and biases along when studying history. Historians, however, consciously try to distance

Presentism: A bias toward present-day attitudes, especially in the interpretation of history.

themselves from these while attempting to empathetically enter the past. Nowhere is this problem more evident than in looking for the origins of the plantation system and African slavery. Here, the origins are certainly modest and distant in time and present many alternatives. But, above all, what those origins led to remains repellent to our present sensibilities.

Caribbean Plantations   Soon after the first European voyages to the Americas and the establishment of Spanish settlements in the Caribbean, the indigenous population of Taínos and Caribs all but disappeared, decimated by the European smallpox against which the native peoples were helpless. Beginning in the sixteenth century, Native Americans on the mainland were similarly decimated by smallpox. To replenish the labor force, as early as 1511, the Spanish crown authorized the importation of 50 African slaves for gold mining on the island of Hispaniola. In the following decades thousands more followed for work on newly established sugar plantations. The Africans, at this point primarily from Senegambia, shared a similar set of disease immunities with the Europeans. They were acclimated to tropical conditions and had no home base in the American islands to which to flee. For their European overlords, this made them ideal workers. Indeed, by the late sixteenth century African slaves outnumbered Europeans on the Spanish-controlled islands and in Mexico and Peru, where they were primarily involved in mining.

Apart from mining, plantation work for sugar production is among the most arduous forms of labor. Sugarcane leaves have sharp edges, and the mature stalks must be cut down forcefully with *machetes*—long, heavy knives. The stalks are then bundled, loaded into a cart, and carried to a mill. The early mills utilized horizontal rotating millstones (later versions used stone or metal rollers) turned by human, animal, or water power. Once the stalks were crushed and their juice extracted, the waste was used as food for animals and, occasionally, slaves. The refining process involved boiling successive batches of juice, itself a hot and taxing process. The charred animal bones added to the refining, for whitening the crystallizing sugar, were often supplemented by those of deceased slaves, thus contributing a particularly sinister element to the process.

The average slave field hand on a sugar plantation was estimated to live just 5 or 6 years. Early on, the workforce was largely male, which meant that there were relatively few children to replenish the slave population. With the price of slaves low and the mortality rate high, it was economically more desirable to literally work slaves to death and buy more than to make the extra investments necessary to cultivate families. Not surprisingly, revolts, work slowdowns, and sabotage of equipment and cargoes were frequent, with punishments being severe and public. Slaves were flogged and branded for minor infractions and maimed, castrated, hanged, burned, and sometimes dismembered for more severe crimes.

Mercantilism in Action in the Caribbean   With the decline of Spanish power and the rise of the North Atlantic maritime states during the seventeenth century, a profound shift of the political balance in the Caribbean took place. Portugal, Spain, the Netherlands, Great Britain, and France all followed a similar path to enrichment that came to be known as **mercantilism**—that is, the assumption that the wealth of the state depends on having the maximum amount of gold and silver in its treasury. Thus, states should keep their economies blocked off from competitors and import

engraving showing African slaves working in the mines of Hispaniola (1595)

Mercantilism: Political theory according to which the wealth derived from the mining of silver and gold and the production of agricultural commodities should be restricted to each country's market, with as little as possible expended on imports from another country.

Grinding Sugarcane. The steps in the making of refined sugar were elaborate and backbreaking. In the center, a wagon brings the harvested cane in from the fields, while slaves in the foreground sort the stalks under the watchful eyes of an overseer. The wind-powered mill uses rollers to crush the cane and extract its juice for boiling.

as little and export as much as possible. Colonies were seen as vital to this economic system, because they supplied raw materials to the European homeland and provided safe markets for goods manufactured in the home country.

It followed that one way to enhance your riches was to capture those of your rivals. Thus, from the late sixteenth through the early eighteenth centuries, the navies of the Dutch, English, French, Spanish, and Portuguese all attacked each other's shipping interests and maritime colonies. The Spanish, with their lucrative treasure fleets from Acapulco and through the Caribbean along the Spanish Main, were the favorite targets of all. Moreover, all of these governments issued "letters of marque" allowing warships owned by individuals or companies called **privateers** to prey on the shipping of rival powers for a share in the prize money they obtained. Not surprisingly, a number of individuals also went into this business for themselves as pirates.

The growing trade in plantation commodities from the Caribbean compelled Spain's European competitors to oust the Spanish from their valuable sugar islands. Thus, the rising naval power of England seized Jamaica from Spain in 1655. France, by the mid-seventeenth century the premier continental European power, followed a decade later in seizing the western part of Hispaniola, which came to be called Saint-Domingue.

This process was accompanied by two developments that enhanced the mercantilist economies of both powers. First, English and French as well as Dutch merchants became involved in the African slave trade, usurping the Portuguese near-monopoly on the traffic. The second was that the growing demand for molasses (a syrup that is a by-product of sugar refining) and the even greater popularity of its fermented and distilled end product, rum, pushed both sugar planting and slavery to heights

Privateers: Individuals or ships granted permission to attack enemy shipping and to keep a percentage of the prize money the captured ships brought at auction; in practice, privateers were often indistinguishable from pirates.

that would not reach their peak until after 1750. As we will see in more detail, sugar, slaves, molasses, and rum form the vital legs of the famous triangular trade that sustained the Atlantic economic system.

The human toll, however, was appalling. Barbados, for example, was settled initially in 1627 by English planters, who grew tobacco, cotton, indigo, and ginger, employing English and Irish **indentured laborers**. In 1640, however, planters switched to the more profitable sugarcane. English and Irish indentured laborers now proved so unwilling to leave their home countries for Barbados that law courts in the home ports resorted to convicting them on trumped-up charges and sentencing them to "transportation." Many others were tricked or seized by press-gangs and sent there. So great was the mortality of their African counterparts that they had to be shipped to the sugar islands at a rate of two to one in order to keep the population from declining.

Indentured laborers: Poor workers enrolled in European states with an obligation to work in the Americas for 3–7 years in return for their prepaid passage across the Atlantic.

The Sugar Empire: Brazil   The Portuguese first planted sugarcane as a crop in Brazil in the 1530s, well before Caribbean planters began to grow it and a generation after the original trade in brazilwood (a red dye) was established. Portuguese colonists turned to the production of sugar because, unlike their counterparts in the Caribbean, Mexico, and Peru, they did not find any gold or silver. Like the Spanish, the Portuguese crown repeatedly issued edicts to the colonists to refrain from enslaving indigenous people for work on the sugar plantations; these edicts, however, were widely ignored. In addition, in the 1530s, the Portuguese trading network on the central African coast began to supply the colony with African slaves. By the end of the century, a dramatic rise in demand for sugar in Europe increased the importation of African slaves, of which the Portuguese carefully cultivated their carrying monopoly.

The insatiable demand of the sugar industry for slaves received a further boost in 1680 when enslavement of Indians was finally abolished, and in 1690 the discovery of gold in Minas Gerais, in the interior, led to a gold boom and increased demand for labor even more. Brazil ultimately became the final destination of nearly half of all the slaves transported to the Americas. Indeed, Brazil went on to be the largest slave state in the world, with about two-fifths of its entire population consisting of people of African descent, and was the last country in the Americas to give up the institution, in 1888 (see Map 19.3).

slaves working in a sugar mill in Brazil, ca. 1658

Slavery in British North America

Modern historians have identified a plantation zone which, in 1750, extended unbroken from the Chesapeake Bay in England's North American colonies to Brazil, embracing the entire Caribbean. This zone represented a pattern unprecedented in world history. No system of cash cropping had ever extended over so much territory or brought so much profit to its owners and investors. It created the largest demand for human labor yet seen, which after 1700 was satisfied almost exclusively through the African slave trade. As we noted in the beginning of this section, this in turn created a nearly immutable color line that defined a permanent underclass and identified blackness with slavery and inferiority. Though it was eventually destined to die out in the northernmost British and French possessions as well as the northern United States, legal slavery at one time extended far beyond the plantation zone into what is now Canada.

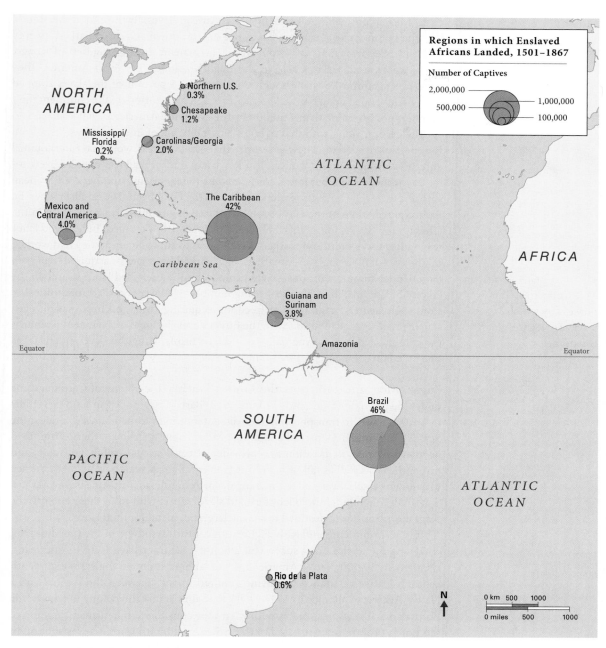

MAP **19.3 Regions in which Enslaved Africans Landed, 1501–1867.**

The "Sot Weed" Enterprise   As we saw in preceding chapters, the first permanent English settlements in the Americas were the for-profit enterprise at Jamestown in 1607 and the religious "errand in the wilderness" of the initial settlements in
Massachusetts from 1620 on. Both would soon count Africans among them, though
their descendants in Jamestown would be by far the more economically important.
In August of 1619 a Dutch privateer surprised a Portuguese slaver en route to Vera

Cruz, Mexico, and relieved her of 60 of her African slaves. By the end of the month, the ship put in at the struggling enterprise of Jamestown and disembarked "twenty and odd Negroes," some of whom were Christians from the kingdom of Kongo. These were the first slaves sold in the English colonies of North America. They would be far from the last. Though only about 3–5 percent of the slaves shipped from Africa ended up in North America, through procreation on the continent their numbers grew to more than 4 million by the eve of the American Civil War.

Their labor, along with that of increasing numbers of indentured workers from Europe, was needed for a new enterprise that, it was hoped, would save the colonial enterprise from failure: tobacco. The Powhatan and other local peoples grew tobacco for themselves, but it was considered by the increasing numbers of European smokers to be inferior to the varieties grown in the Caribbean. The English, however, had acquired some of the Caribbean plants and begun intensive cultivation in the Chesapeake Bay region of this "sot weed," as it came to be called. Indentured labor was widely used, but those workers were bound to stay only until they had worked off the cost of their passage. After that, they worked for wages or acquired their own land. Under these conditions, slaves came to be the preferred labor source in the colony of Virginia. Though a surprising number of Africans earned **manumission** from their owners, gaining their freedom, acquiring land, and on occasion even starting their own plantations with their own slaves during the seventeenth century, the colonial authorities eventually passed laws firmly fixing the slave underclass as one based on color.

Manumission: The process by which slaves are legally given freedom.

Sugar, Rice, and Indigo in the Lower South   The colony of Carolina came under the purview of the Lords Proprietors in Barbados, who began sending settlers in 1670 as a way to transport religious dissenters and to form a bulwark against the Spanish in Florida. As part of a vast pine forest running from southern Virginia to northern Florida, its position as a provider of naval stores—pitch, tar, rosin, and turpentine—as well as tall, straight tree trunks for ships' masts, was vital in the age of wooden vessels. Even today, the state of North Carolina's nickname is "the Tarheel State." Although indentured laborers and slaves were involved in these enterprises, plantation crops were destined to see the largest demand for their labor.

In the seventeenth and early eighteenth centuries, settlers in the Carolinas ran what was by far the most successful attempt ever to enslave Native Americans. As many as 50,000 Native American slaves labored there by the early eighteenth century. Native resistance to slaving resulted in war between the settlers and a Native American alliance in 1715–1717 that almost lost the colony for the Lords Proprietors. The settlers, angry with what they considered the mismanagement of the Lords Proprietors, appealed to the crown, and South Carolina was split off in 1719 and set up as a royal colony shortly thereafter. Deprived of Native Americans for slaves, the colonies began to import large numbers of West African slaves as the Dutch dominance of the trade gave way to the British. This initial wave of slave immigration ultimately grew to a point that made South Carolina the only North American colony, and later state, in which African Americans outnumbered those of European descent.

In addition, South Carolina produced many of the same plantation commodities as Brazil and the Caribbean (such as sugarcane, molasses, and rice), along with one vitally important new addition: indigo, which was destined to become the colony's most important cash crop until the cotton boom of the nineteenth century.

The dark blue dye produced from the tropical plant *Indigofera tinctoria* had been grown extensively throughout Asia, the ancient Mediterranean, and North and West Africa. A similar American species, *Indigofera suffruticosa*, had long been in use in Mexico and Central America. Maritime countries with Indian and East Asian connections imported vast quantities of it into Europe, while the Spanish began to cultivate the American variety. Sales in northern Europe were initially hampered because there indigo competed with the local production of dyes made from the woad plant. Restrictions on imports were gradually lifted, and South Carolina entered an indigo boom starting in the 1740s. The burgeoning need for labor in planting, stripping the leaves, fermenting, cleaning, draining, scraping, and molding the residue into balls or blocks—all accompanied by a considerable stench—drove the slave trade even further.

TO BE SOLD, on board the Ship *Bance-Island*, on tuesday the 6th of *May* next, at *Ashley-Ferry*; a choice cargo of about 250 fine healthy NEGROES, just arrived from the Windward & Rice Coast. —The utmost care has already been taken, and shall be continued, to keep them free from the least danger of being infected with the SMALL-POX, no boat having been on board, and all other communication with people from *Charles-Town* prevented.

Austin, Laurens, & Appleby.

N. B. Full one Half of the above Negroes have had the SMALL-POX in their own Country.

Advertisement for a Slave Auction. In this notice from 1766, potential slave buyers in Charleston, South Carolina, are informed of the time and place for the sale of a "choice cargo" of recently arrived Africans. As Charleston was undergoing a smallpox epidemic at the time, potential customers are reassured that the captives are healthy and likely to be immune to the disease.

The last new English possession in southern North America prior to 1750 was Georgia. The southern regions of what was to become the colony of Georgia had been claimed by the Spanish as early as 1526 as part of their exploration of Florida and the Gulf Coast. Attempts by the French to found a colony near Port Royal, South Carolina, and Fort Caroline (near present-day Jacksonville) in the 1560s were ultimately undone. With the expansion of the English presence in the seventeenth century and the French concentrating on their vast claims in Canada and the Mississippi valley, the territory between Carolina and the Spanish fort at St. Augustine became increasingly disputed.

Into this situation stepped James Oglethorpe (1696–1785), the only founder of an English colony in North America who lived to see it become part of the United States. Oglethorpe's vision was to set up a colony for England's poor, debtors (who would otherwise be imprisoned), and dispossessed. He obtained a royal charter for his idea and in 1733 landed with his first band of settlers at the site of the modern city of Savannah. After buying land from the local Native Americans, he began to develop the colony as a free area in which slavery was banned. The Spanish attempted to claim Georgia in 1742 but were repulsed. Pressed by settlers bringing their slaves in from South Carolina, Georgia's ban on slave labor was soon rescinded. By the end of Oglethorpe's life, which he spent in retirement in England, Georgia had developed its own slave-based plantation economy, producing rice, sugar, indigo, and, on the Sea Islands along the coast, a fine, long-fiber variety of cotton, which proved to be a harbinger of the commodity that would ensure slavery's survival in the United States until 1865.

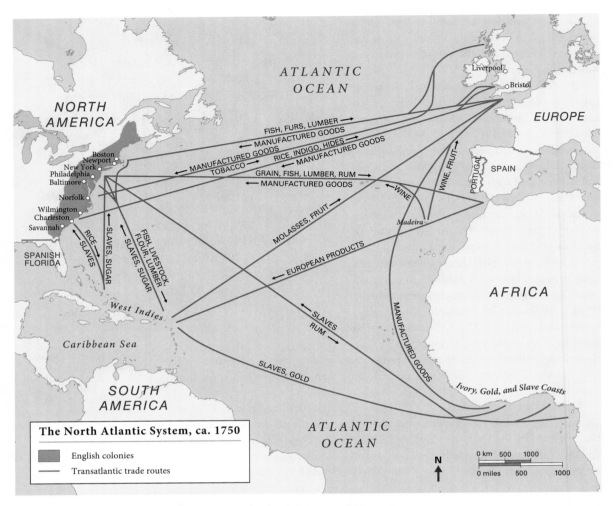

MAP **19.4** **The North Atlantic System, ca. 1750.**

The Fatal Triangle: The Economic Patterns of the Atlantic Slave Trade

As mentioned, the European countries that successively dominated the transportation of slaves from the West African coast moved steadily northward in a pattern that paralleled their naval and merchant marine power. That is, during the fifteenth and sixteenth centuries, Portugal had an effective monopoly on the trade from outposts in Senegambia, Elmina, and Ndongo. The success of Dutch and English privateers encouraged more concerted economic warfare and, with it, the seizure by the Dutch of Elmina in 1637. Now it was the Dutch who became the principal slave carriers, part of a pattern of aggressive colonizing that made the Netherlands the world's richest country in per capita terms through much of the seventeenth century. The rise of England's naval power at the expense of the Dutch and the fading of the Spanish and Portuguese naval presence allowed the English—and, to a lesser extent, the

French—to dominate the slave trade. By the mid-eighteenth century, as the trade approached its height, it had become the base upon which the world's most lucrative economic triangle was constructed (see Map 19.4).

Rum, Guns, and Slaves   As we have seen, England's colonies in the Americas, especially those in the Caribbean, were by the eighteenth century producing valuable crops, including sugar, tobacco, cotton, and indigo, for export to the Old World. Tobacco was raised mainly in England's North American colonies, along with some cotton for export to England, though at this point England still imported most of its cotton from India. So profitable were these exports that, in keeping with the policy of mercantilism, the crown passed a series of acts in 1651 and 1660 that produced even greater profits for merchants in the motherland. The Navigation Acts required that all goods imported to England from American colonies had to be transported only on English ships, thereby guaranteeing a virtual monopoly on transatlantic trade.

British merchants acquired enormous profits through their colonial trading practices, particularly with the Atlantic colonies. We are afforded a good example of how this worked through an analysis of the **Atlantic system**, or the "triangular trade." In general terms, British ships would leave home ports in either their North American colonies or Britain with goods of various kinds, then travel to ports along the western coast of Africa, where these goods would be exchanged for African slaves; these ships would then sail across the Atlantic, where slaves would be exchanged for goods produced in western Atlantic colonies; and finally, these goods would be carried back to the home port.

One common pattern consisted of the following stages: An English ship loaded with New England rum would sail from Europe to the western coast of Africa, where the rum would be exchanged for a cargo of slaves; laden with slaves, the ship would then sail westward across the Atlantic to sugar colonies in the Caribbean, where the slaves would be exchanged for a cargo of molasses; the ship would sail to New England, where the molasses would be processed into rum. A variant pattern consisted of British ships leaving their home ports—increasingly Liverpool and Bristol, the ports that benefited most dramatically from the slave trade—loaded with manufactured goods, such as guns, knives, textiles, and assorted household wares. They would sail to the western coast of Africa, where these goods would be exchanged for a cargo of slaves, then sail westward across the Atlantic to the British colony of Virginia, where their human cargo would be exchanged for tobacco; they would then sail eastward across the Atlantic to their home ports in Britain, where the tobacco would be unloaded and then sold to British and European merchants.

The Middle Passage   Following capture in Africa, prisoners were usually marched to slave markets and embarkation ports roped, chained, or ganged together by forked tree limbs. Slave lots were then wholesaled to middlemen or auctioned directly to foreign factors. From this point they would be imprisoned in fortified slave pens called "barracoons" until the next ship bound for their sale destination arrived. But it was on the voyage from Africa to the Americas, the infamous "Middle Passage," that the full horror of the slave's condition was most vividly demonstrated (see Source 19.3).

Atlantic system: Economic system in which European ships would exchange goods for slaves in West Africa and slaves would then be brought to America and exchanged for goods that would be carried back to the home port.

portrait of Ayuba Suleiman Diallo (1733)

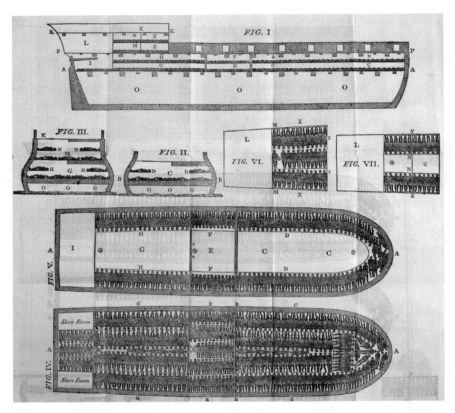

Plan of a Slave Ship, 1789. This image, based on the *Brooks*, a Liverpool slave ship, was one of the first to document the horrors of the slave trade. It shows the captives laid like sardines below deck. In such conditions slaves perished at the rate of 10–30 percent during the Middle Passage. The engraving was widely distributed by British abolitionists, who eventually succeeded in banning the trade in 1807.

Because the profits involved in transportation were so high for captains, officers, and even crewmen, they constantly experimented with ways to pack the maximum number of human beings into the holds of their ships. Because a certain percentage of mortality was expected during a voyage that lasted from a few weeks to nearly 2 months, some ship captains favored "tight packing"—deliberate overcrowding on the assumption that a few more captives might survive than on a ship with fewer captives but a higher rate of survival. On the other hand, some captains favored the "loose pack" method, with the assumption that a higher number would survive if given marginally more room. In either case, conditions were abominable.

Due to well-founded fears of slave mutiny, the holds of slave ships were locked and barred and the hatchways and vents covered with iron gratings. The slaves were chained to tiny bunks arranged in tiers configured to maximize the space of the hold. Food was minimal, usually corn mush, and sanitation nonexistent. Small groups of captives would be brought up on deck on a rotating basis to be haphazardly washed of their vomit and feces with buckets of frigid ocean water thrown at them by the crew. They would then be "danced" for minimal exercise and sent back down, and the next group would be brought up. The dead, sick, and resistant would simply be thrown overboard. The ship and crew were also well armed to fight off mutineers and attacks by competitors or pirates. On landing at their destination, the slaves were again barracooned, cleaned up, and given better meals pending their auction to individual buyers. In the process somewhere between 10 and 30 percent of them died en route.

Culture and Identity in the African Diaspora

The original meaning of the term "diaspora" referred to the dispersal of the Jews around the Roman Empire after their revolt of the first century CE was put down. Scholars now use the term more generally for the wide dispersal by forced or voluntary migration of any large group. In the case of the **African diaspora**, in which Africans moved to nearly all parts of the Americas primarily through the slave trade, the story is far too varied and complex for us to do more than note some general patterns related to culture and identity.

African diaspora: Dispersal of African peoples throughout the world, particularly the Americas, as part of the trans-Atlantic slave trade.

A New Society: Creolization of the Early Atlantic World

As discussed earlier in this chapter, one of the effects of the Portuguese implantation on African coasts through trade forts and colonies was the adaptation of coastal African societies to Western Christianity and Portuguese culture. These societies were highly diverse. Some were clan or lineage based and welcomed trade with outsiders; others were militarily oriented and saw the new arrivals as unwelcome competitors; still others were kingdoms, some of which cooperated intermittently or permanently with the Portuguese and later with the Dutch, English, and French. Depending on the type or intensity of interaction, African Creole cultures emerged—that is, cultures in which some adaptation to Catholicism occurred and in which Africans appropriated certain outside cultural elements into their own heritage.

In earlier scholarship this creolization was often described as resulting in certain elements of an alien, colonizing culture uneasily grafted onto "genuine" Africanness. As in the case of Dona Beatriz and the rise of a Kongolese Catholicism, however, Creole culture has to be seen as an "authentic" phenomenon in its own right. This is similarly true for black Creole cultures in the Americas. Africans arrived with either their own local spiritual traditions or as Christians and Muslims, since foreign and indigenous slave raiders penetrating inland Africa made no religious distinctions among their victims. Either way, African slaves adapted to their plantation life through creolization or, as African Christian or Muslim Creoles, through further creolization, a process that expressed itself in distinct languages or dialects as well as synthetic (or hybrid) religious customs. Adaptation was thus not simple imitation but a creative transformation of cultural elements to fit the new conditions of a life of forced labor abroad.

Recent scholarship suggests that a key formative element in the development of culture and identity of Africans in the Americas lay in the influence of the central African Creoles from Kongo and Ndongo (today's Congo and Angola) up to the middle of the seventeenth century. The Christianity of some believers and its later variants helped to nurture this religion among Africans in the new lands, especially when it was reinforced by the religious practices of the slave owners. The mix of language and terms for a multitude of objects similarly gave the early arrivals a certain

Voodoo and Other New World Slave Religions

Altar and Shrine from the Interior of the Historic Voodoo Museum in New Orleans.

One prominent pattern of world history that we have seen a number of times already is the way indigenous elements work to shape the identity of imported religions as they are taken up by their new believers. Buddhism in China and Japan, for example, adopted elements from Daoism and Chinese folk beliefs as well as spirits and demons from Shinto. Christianity added Roman and Germanic elements to its calendar of holidays, architecture, and cult of saints. Islam in Iran and India and Christianity in Africa underwent similar processes. In Kongo, for example, the African Christian cult of St. Anthony merged Portuguese Catholic and Kongolese spiritual traditions into a new church. This trend of interaction continues today, where we find the African Christian churches among the fastest growing in the world and increasingly sending clergy and missionaries to Europe and the United States.

In the Americas three main strains of this kind of interaction and adaptation of imported and indigenous traditions developed over time and are still widely practiced today: Santeria is found primarily in Cuba and among the Spanish-speaking Africans of the Caribbean but is now also in the larger cities of North America with communities of Caribbean immigrants; vodoun, usually written as "voodoo,"

degree of agency and skill in navigating the institutions of slavery as they were being established.

An example of a Creole language that has survived for centuries is Gullah, used by the isolated slave communities along the coastal islands of South Carolina and Georgia and still spoken by their descendants today. In Haiti, Creole (*Kreyòl*) is not only the daily spoken language but one also used in the media and in literary works. (French is recognized as the other national language, especially in law and official pronouncements.) Creole cultures thus typically involve not only the phenomenon of adaptation but also multiple identities—in language, religion, and culture.

Music and Food   It can justifiably be said that the roots of most popular music in the Americas may be found in Africa. Regardless of where they came from in Africa, slaves brought with them a wide variety of musical instruments, songs, and chants, all of which contributed to shaping the musical tastes of their owners and society at large. The widespread use of rhythmic drumming and dance in African celebrations, funerals, and even coded communications has come down to us today as the basis for music as diverse as Brazilian samba, Cuban and Dominican rumba and merengue, New Orleans jazz, and American blues, rock and roll, soul, and hip-hop. It is difficult to imagine American country and western music, or bluegrass, without the

developed in Haiti and old Saint-Domingue and is widely practiced among African-descended French speakers around the Caribbean and in areas of Louisiana; and the adherents of Candomblé are mostly confined to Brazil.

All three are syncretic religions composed of elements that appear disconnected to outsiders but which practitioners see as part of an integrated whole. They intermingle Roman Catholic saints with West African natural and ancestral spirits and gods, see spiritual power as resident in natural things, and incorporate images of objects to represent a person or thing whose power the believer wants to tap or disperse (as in the use of so-called voodoo dolls). They also hold that proper ritual and sacrifices by priests and priestesses can tune into the spirits of the natural world. In some cases, they see these practices as curing sicknesses and raising the dead—the source of the famous "zombie" legends. Such innovations allowed the slaves to create a religious and cultural space in which they carved out autonomy from their masters—indeed, in which they *were* the masters. They also provided a kind of alternate set of beliefs which could be invoked alongside more mainstream Christian practices. In a real sense, they provided a precious degree of freedom for people who had almost no other form of it.

Mami Wata. Both a protector and a seducer, Mami Wata is an important spirit figure throughout much of Africa and the African Atlantic. She is usually portrayed as a mermaid, a snake charmer, or a combination of both.

Questions

- How do black Christianity and voodoo religion show the new patterns of origins, interaction, and adoption that emerged after 1500?

- Can you think of more recent examples of syncretic religions? If so, which ones? Why are they syncretic?

modern descendant of a West African stringed instrument we know today as the banjo. The chants of field hands, rhyming contests, and gospel music contributed mightily to many of these genres.

Like music, cuisine passed easily across institutional barriers. Here, the dishes that most Americans consider "southern" have in many cases deep African roots. The first rice brought to the Carolinas was a variety native to the Niger inland delta in West Africa. Africans brought with them the knowledge of setting up and running an entire rice-based food system, which was established in the Carolina lowlands and Gulf Coast. The yam, the staple of West African diets, also made its way to the Americas. The heart of Louisiana Creole cooking, including rich and spicy gumbos, "dirty rice," jambalaya, and other dishes, comes from the use of the African vegetable okra and a heady mixture of African, American, and Asian spices along with rice.

Plantation Life and Resistance   Although nineteenth-century apologists for slavery frequently portrayed life under it as tranquil, the system was in fact one of constant real and implied violence.

Most slaves reconciled themselves to their condition and navigated it as best they could, but the reminders of their status were constantly around them. Obviously, those who endured the Middle Passage had violence thrust upon them immediately

Slave Culture. This ca. 1790 painting from Beaufort, South Carolina, shows the vibrancy of African American culture in the face of great hardship. Note the banjo, whose origins lie in West Africa and which would have a great impact on the development of American music.

upon capture. Even those born into slavery, however, lived in squalid shacks or cabins; ate inadequate rations, perhaps supplemented with vegetables they were allowed to grow themselves; and spent most of their waking hours at labor.

Those working as house servants had a somewhat easier life than field hands. In some cases, they were the primary guardians, midwives, wet nurses, and even confidants of their masters' families. Often, there was considerable expressed affection between the household slaves and the master's family. But more often, this was tempered by the knowledge that they or their family members could be sold at any time, that infractions would be severely punished, and that they would be treated as unruly, temperamental children at best.

As we saw earlier, field hands led a far harder and shorter life. The price of slavery for the master was eternal vigilance; his nightmare was slave revolt. Over the years a variety of methods were developed to keep slaves in line and at their work. Overseers ran the work schedules and supervised punishments; drivers kept slaves at their work with a long bullwhip in hand to beat the slow or hesitant. Slaves leaving plantations on errands had to carry passes, and elaborate precautions were taken to discourage escape or even unauthorized visits to neighboring plantations. In the Carolinas, for example, owners spread tar on fence rails so that slaves attempting to climb or vault them would be marked for easy detection. Runaways were pursued with relentless determination by trackers with bloodhounds and flogged, branded, maimed, or castrated when returned.

Given these conditions, slave behaviors designed to try to manage their work on their own terms or to get back at their owners were frequent. Slaves staged work slowdowns, feigned illnesses, sabotaged tools and equipment, or pretended not to understand how to perform certain tasks. Kitchen slaves would sometimes spit or urinate into soups or gravies. Despite the risks involved, runaways were quite

Punishing Slave Revolts. John Gabriel Stedman (1744–1797) was a British–Dutch soldier and writer whose years in Surinam, on the northern coast of South America, were recorded in *The Narrative of a Five Year Expedition against the Revolted Negroes of Surinam* (1796). With its graphic depictions of slavery it became an important tract in the abolitionist cause. In this illustration, *A Negro Hung Alive by the Ribs to a Gallows*, engraved by the famous artist and Romantic poet William Blake (1757–1827), Stedman shows a rebel who was hung by his ribs for two days as punishment for his crimes. Masters routinely cut off the noses of their slaves, burnt them alive, and whipped them to death with impunity.

common. Later, in the United States in the 1850s, enforcement of the Fugitive Slave Act would be a prime factor driving the country toward civil war.

Despite all their precautions, slave owners throughout the Americas constantly faced the prospect of slave insurrection. By some estimates, there were more than 250 slave uprisings involving 10 or more slaves during the four centuries of Atlantic slavery. The most famous of these revolts in the United States was that of Nat Turner in Virginia in 1831. In 2016 a feature-length drama titled *Birth of a Nation* about Turner's rebellion was released—its title meant to counter the racist sentiments of the famous film of that name released a century before. In some cases, these rebellions were successful enough for the slaves to create their own isolated settlements where they could, for a time, live in freedom. These escapees were called *Maroons*. Three of the more successful Maroon settlements existed in Jamaica, Colombia, and Surinam. In Brazil, slaves developed their own system of weaponless martial arts called *capoeira*, in which fighters walk on their hands and use their legs to strike. Map 19.5 lists some of the larger slave insurrections from 1500 to 1850.

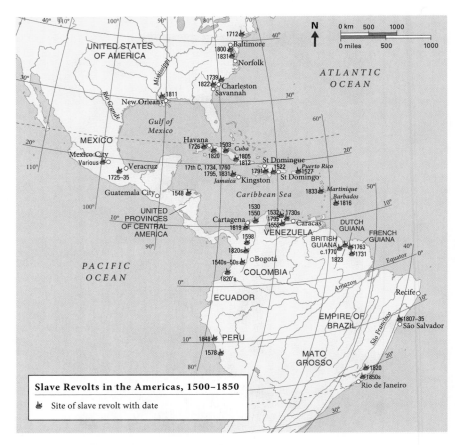

MAP **19.5** **Slave Revolts in the Americas, 1500–1850.**

interactive concept map

≫ Putting It All Together

Portugal, the Netherlands, England, France, and Spain built up a fully evolved pattern of trading for plantation slaves on the Atlantic coast of Africa in the course of the sixteenth and seventeenth centuries. The trade took off toward the end of the sixteenth century, with 28,000 slaves annually, and by 1700 it had reached 80,000 annually, where it stayed until the early nineteenth century, when the slave trade was abolished. As for the patterns of state formation in Africa, on the whole, the more powerful a kingdom was, the fewer slaves it sold, given its own labor requirements. Conversely, the more conducive the circumstances were to the collapse of chiefly or royal rule and the emergence of raider societies such as the Imbangala, Ashante, or Dahomey, the more damaging the impact was on a given population. Thus, no global judgment is possible. Undoubtedly, in some regions of western and central Africa the effects were grave, while in others, often directly adjacent, the impact was less decisive. Nonetheless, the period marked a profound transformation, with many areas depopulated by the slave trade, some enhanced through the trade and the introduction of new food crops like maize and cassava, and others undergoing creolization to some degree.

The interaction and adaptation patterns of Europeans and Africans in Africa and Europeans, Africans, and Native Americans in the Caribbean and Americas over the course of three centuries (1500–1800) created not just a new, two-hemisphere world system of trade but a new kind of society as well. The Atlantic slave trade was the foundation on which the mass production of cash crops and commodities, the first world pattern of its kind, was brought into being. This economic sphere was by far the richest of its kind in the world, but with it came the creation of an enduring social underclass and the foundation of modern racism.

Yet even as early as the 1750s, one finds the origins of the abolition movement—the international movement to end first the slave trade and ultimately slavery itself. Among the leaders of Europe's Enlightenment, thinkers were already calling for the end of the trade and institution. Within a few decades, works like the memoirs of the former slave and abolitionist Olaudah Equiano (ca. 1745–1797, see Source 19.4) would push the movement forward, as would the work of England's William Wilberforce (1759–1833), who actually lived to see the outlawing of the trade and of English slavery itself. Elsewhere, it would take a revolution, as in Haiti, or a civil war, as in the United States, for abolition to occur. In the Atlantic world, slavery finally ended in Brazil in 1888. But it persists informally in India, Africa, and the Middle East even today.

Review and Relate

Thinking Through Patterns

Examine the ways historians approach the big questions of this chapter.

What is remarkable about Africa during these 300 years is that it continued its pattern of kingdom and empire formation and actually did so on an accelerated pace, on the basis of increased intra-African trade. The half dozen examples analyzed in this chapter could be applied to another dozen states. In the interior of Africa the pattern continued in spite of the demographic effects (in whatever form they had in specific regions) of the Atlantic slave trade.

» **On what was the pattern of kingdom and empire formation in Africa based during the period 1500–1800?**

The pattern of plantation production evolved over several centuries before it was transplanted to the islands of the Atlantic and the Caribbean as well as the Americas. It was above all a system for growing labor-intensive cash crops—indigo, sugar, tobacco—that relied increasingly on African slave labor. By 1800, the demand for plantation commodities by Europeans and the guns, textiles, rum, and other manufactured goods that Africans took in trade for slaves swelled the system to huge proportions. In turn, the mercantilist economics of western Europe regulated the trade within an efficient, tightly controlled, triangular system.

The gradual domination of African slavery in the Americas and Caribbean over other kinds of servitude created a pattern of racism, in which blackness was permanently associated with slavery. As the economics of slavery became entrenched, the participants in the system answered the criticism of slavery on moral grounds by

» **How did the patterns of slave trade and plantation slavery evolve**

**in the Atlantic and
the Americas?**

claiming that black Africans were inherently inferior and thus deserved to be enslaved. The argument was essentially circular: They were enslaved because they were inferior, and they were inferior because they were slaves.

≫ **What are the
historic roots from
which modern racism
evolved?**

In North America, long after slavery was abolished, these attitudes were preserved in law and custom in many places and reinforced during the colonization of Africa in the nineteenth century and in the practice of segregation in the United States. In Latin America—although racism is no less pervasive—racial views are more subtle. People describing themselves as *mulato*, *sambo*, or *pardo* have had a better chance to be recognized as members of their own distinct ethnic groups than in the United States, where until recently the census classified people simply as either black or Caucasian. The 2010 census form, however, expanded its choices to 14 racial categories and allowed people to check multiple boxes. Clearly, the complexities of race and ethnicity in the Americas are continuing to evolve.

| **Against the Grain**

Consider this as a counterpoint to the main patterns examined in this chapter.

Oglethorpe's Free Colony

- Why were institutions of slavery so prevalent in so many places in the world?

- Even though many people found slavery to be immoral on humanitarian and even economic grounds, the institution persisted for centuries in the Atlantic world. Why do you think it proved so difficult to dismantle?

Set against the backdrop of both expanding colonial slavery and the hardening of the so-called color line, James Oglethorpe's dream of a colony of Georgia in which both slavery and rum were to be banned, and where the colonists were to consist of the "worthy poor" freed from the threat of debtor's prison, would appear to defy the patterns of the times. Oglethorpe, as a young member of the House of Commons, was appalled at the conditions of London prisons and perhaps even more by the practice of imprisoning debtors and forcing them to pay for their own upkeep while incarcerated. Appointed to a parliamentary committee investigating the situation, he developed a scheme that he hoped would solve several problems plaguing English society: growing indebtedness on the part of the working poor and the jobless; rampant alcoholism fueled by cheap rum and gin; and migration to cities by the landless.

His solution was to found a colony as a haven for those most afflicted by these ills. He bought land at fair prices from the Creek people, ensured that skilled craftsmen and laborers were among the initial settlers, and laid out what became the city of Savannah in a design that called for houses with ample lots, a 45-acre farm outside the city for self-sufficiency, and numerous common areas and squares to create close-knit neighborhoods. To ensure that the labor of the immigrants would be valued, slavery was strictly forbidden, as was the slave-produced product of rum. While scholars differ on whether he was a true abolitionist, he did declare slavery to be "immoral" and felt that it violated English law.

As we saw in this chapter, however, his visionary aims ultimately ran aground on the shoals of the colony's position on the border with Spanish Florida. With Oglethorpe's retirement to England in 1750, his fellow trustees returned control of the colony to the British crown, and the ban on slavery was rescinded. The invention of the cotton gin in the 1790s began a process by which that commodity would become the most valuable export in the world and the bulwark of the US economy. And as cotton became king, the slave state of Georgia would be at the epicenter of its expansion.

Key Terms

audio flashcards

African diaspora   583
Atlantic system   581
Chattel   572
Household slavery   567

Indentured laborers   576
Manumission   578
Mercantilism   574
Plantation slavery   572

Presentism   573
Privateers   575

For additional resources, please go to
www.oup.com/us/vonsivers.
Please see the Further Resources section at the back of the book
for additional readings and suggested websites.

📄 **Sources for Chapter 19**

SOURCE 19.1	**Abd al-Rahman al-Saadi** **on the scholars of Timbuktu**

ca. 1655

Born in Timbuktu in 1596, Abd al-Rahman al-Saadi wrote, in Arabic, a chronicle titled *Tarikh al-Sudan* (*History of the Sudan*). The document addresses the political, cultural, and religious history of the Songhay state in the fifteenth and sixteenth centuries, and it also offers detailed accounts of various states in the Niger River valley into al-Saadi's own day. Al-Saadi was particularly interested in the impact of Islamic thought and culture on the African kingdoms, as the following excerpt demonstrates. The document was discovered by a German explorer in the 1850s during his visit to Timbuktu.

This is an account of some of the scholars and holymen who dwelt in Timbuktu generation after generation—may God Most High have mercy on them, and be pleased with them, and bring us the benefit of their *baraka* in both abodes—and of some of their virtues and noteworthy accomplishments. In this regard, it is sufficient to repeat what the trustworthy shaykhs have said, on the authority of the righteous and virtuous Friend of God, locus of manifestations of divine grace and wondrous acts, the jurist *Qāḍī* Muhammad al-Kābarī—may God Most High have mercy on him. He said: "I was the contemporary of righteous folk of Sankore, who were equaled in their righteousness only by the Companions of the Messenger of God—may God bless him and grant him peace and be pleased with all of them."

Hizb: Segment.

Among them were (1) the jurist al-Hājj, grandfather of *Qāḍī* 'Abd al-Rahmān b. Abī Bakr b. al-Hājj. He held the post of *qāḍī* during the last days of Malian rule, and was the first person to institute recitation of half a ***hizb*** of the Qur'ān for teaching purposes in the Sankore mosque after both the mid-afternoon and the evening worship. He and his brother Sayyid Ibrāhīm the jurist left Bīru to settle in Bangu. His tomb there is a well-known shrine, and it is said he is a **badal**. The following account is related on the authority of our virtuous and ascetic shaykh, the jurist al-Amīn b. Ahmad, who said, "In his day the Sultan of Mossi came campaigning as far as Bangu, and people went out to fight him. It so happened that a group of people were sitting with al-Hājj at that moment, and he uttered something over [a dish of] millet and told them

Badal: Elevated rank of saints in the Sufi hierarchy.

Source: Abd al-Rahman al-Saadi, *Timbuktu and the Songhay Empire*, trans. John Hunwick (Leiden, the Netherlands: Brill, 2003), 38–40.

to eat it. They all did so except for one man, who was his son-in-law, and he declined to do so because of their relationship by marriage. Then the holyman said to them, "Go off and fight. Their arrows will do you no harm." All of them escaped harm except for the man who did not eat, and he was killed in that battle. The Sultan of Mossi and his army were defeated and driven off, having gained nothing from the people of Bangu, thanks to the *baraka* of that sayyid.

From him is descended the Friend of God the Most High the jurist Ibrāhīm, son of the Friend of God Most High, the jurist *Qādī* 'Umar who lived in Yindubu'u, both of whom were righteous servants of God. It was Askiya *al-hājj* Muhammad who appointed 'Umar *qādī* of that place. From time to time one of his sister's sons used to visit Timbuktu, and the jurist *Qādī* Mahmūd complained to Askiya *al-hājj* Muhammad that this man was slandering them to the people of Yindubu'u. When the Askiya visited Tila the jurist *Qādī* 'Umar came with a group of men from Yindubu'u to pay him a courtesy call. The Askiya inquired after his sister's son, so 'Umar presented him to him. The Askiya said, "You are the one who was been sowing discord between the jurist Mahmūd and your maternal uncle." The *qādī* was annoyed, and retorted, "You, who appointed one *qādī* in Timbuktu and another in Yindubu'u, are the one sowing discord." Then he got up angrily and went off to the waterfront, saying to his companions, "Let us go off and cross the river and be on our way." When they got there, he wanted to cross it, but they said, "It is not yet time for the ferry. Be patient until it comes." He replied, "What if it does not come?" They realised that he was prepared to cross the river without a boat. So they restrained him and sat him down until the ferry came, and they all crossed over together— may God have mercy on them and bring us benefit through them. Amen!

> ≫ **Working with Sources**

1. Why did the scholars and holy men of Timbuktu draw a visitor's attention?

2. Are there indications in this document of a culture that was still fusing Islamic and non-Islamic traditions together?

SOURCE 19.2

Letter of Nzinga Mbemba (Afonso I) of Kongo to the King of Portugal

1526

A Portuguese sailor came into contact with the Kingdom of Kongo, which occupied a vast territory along the Congo River in central Africa, in 1483. When he returned in 1491, he was accompanied by Portuguese priests and Portuguese products, and in the same year the Kongolese king

Source: https://www2.stetson.edu/secure/history/hy10430/afonso.html

and his son were baptized as Catholics. When the son succeeded his father in 1506, he took the Christian name Afonso and promoted the introduction of European culture and religion within his kingdom. His son Henrique was educated in Portugal and became a Catholic bishop. However, Afonso's kingdom began to deteriorate in subsequent decades, as the Portuguese made further inroads into his territory, pursuing ruthless commercial practices and trading in slaves captured in his dominions. In 1526, the king sent desperate letters to King João III of Portugal, urging him to control his own subjects and to respect the alliance—and the common Catholic faith—that bound the Europeans and the Africans.

Sir, Your Highness should know how our Kingdom is being lost in so many ways that it is convenient to provide for the necessary remedy, since this is caused by the excessive freedom given by your agents and officials to the men and merchants who are allowed to come to this Kingdom to set up shops with goods and many things which have been prohibited by us, and which they spread throughout our Kingdoms and Domains in such an abundance that many of our vassals, whom we had in obedience, do not comply because they have the things in greater abundance than we ourselves; and it was with these things that we had them content and subjected under our vassalage and jurisdiction, so it is doing a great harm not only to the service of God, but the security and peace of our Kingdoms and State as well.

And we cannot reckon how great the damage is, since the mentioned merchants are taking every day our natives, sons of the land and the sons of our noblemen and vassals and our relatives, because the thieves and men of bad conscience grab them wishing to have the things and wares of this Kingdom which they are ambitious of; they grab them and get them to be sold; and so great, Sir, is the corruption and licentiousness that our country is being completely depopulated, and Your Highness should not agree with this nor accept it as in your service. And to avoid it we need from those (your) Kingdoms no more than some priests and a few people to teach in schools, and no other goods except wine and flour for the holy sacrament. That is why we beg of Your Highness to help and assist us in this matter, commanding your factors that they should not send here either merchants or wares, because it is our will that in these Kingdoms there should not be any trade of slaves nor outlet for them. Concerning what is referred [to] above, again we beg of Your Highness to agree with it, since otherwise we cannot remedy such an obvious damage. Pray Our Lord in His mercy to have Your Highness under His guard and let you do forever the things of His service. I kiss your hands many times. . . .

(At our town of Kongo, written on the sixth day of July in 1526.)

Moreover, Sir, in our Kingdoms there is another great inconvenience which is of little service to God, and this is that many of our people, keenly desirous as they are of the wares and things of your Kingdoms, which are brought here by your people, and in order to satisfy their voracious appetite, seize many of our people, freed and exempt men, and very often it happens that they kidnap even noblemen and the sons of noblemen, and our relatives, and take them to be sold to the white men who are in our Kingdoms; and for this purpose they have concealed them; and others are brought during the night so that they might not be recognized.

And as soon as they are taken by the white men they are immediately ironed and branded with fire, and when they are carried to be embarked, if they are caught by our guards' men the whites allege that they have bought them but they cannot say from whom, so that it is our duty to do justice and to restore to the freemen their freedom, but it cannot be done if your subjects feel offended, as they claim to be.

And to avoid such a great evil we passed a law so that any white man living in our Kingdoms and wanting to purchase goods in any way should first inform three of our noblemen and officials of our court whom we rely upon in this matter, and these are Dom Pedro Manipanza and Dom Manuel Manissaba, our chief usher, and Goncalo Pires our chief freighter, who should investigate if the mentioned goods are captives or free men, and if cleared by them there will be no further doubt nor embargo for them to be taken and embarked. But if the white men do not comply with it they will lose the aforementioned goods. And if we do them this favor and concession it is for the part Your Highness has in it, since we know that it is in your service too that these goods are taken from our Kingdom, otherwise we should not consent to this. . . .

(date of letter, October 18, 1526)

> **Working with Sources**

1. **What do these documents indicate about the intersections of international commerce and the slave trade?**

2. **In what terms does King Afonso issue his protest to the Portuguese king, and why?**

SOURCE 19.3

Documents concerning the slave ship *Sally*, Rhode Island

1765

Rhode Islanders were the principal American slave traders during the eighteenth century, during which a total of approximately 1,000 slave-trading voyages set out from the colony to Africa. The "triangular trade" among the Atlantic seaboard, the Caribbean, and West Africa was the main source of great wealth for many families in this small British settlement. Among these families was that of John Brown, whose donation to a struggling college in Providence would lead to the renaming of the institution in his honor. Aware of their university's explicit connection to the profitable and lethal slave trade, archivists at Brown University have attempted to tell the

Source: John Carter Brown Library. http://cds.library.brown.edu/projects/sally/documents.html

full story of voyages like that of the *Sally*. In the excerpts that follow, lines from the ship's log are annotated with details of the events they describe; italicized text is transcribed directly from the log.

Log Book From the Slave Ship *Sally*.

December 11, 1764: At James Fort, on the River Gambia

By early December, the Sally had arrived at James Fort, the primary British slave "factory" on Africa's Windward Coast. Located fifteen miles from the mouth of the Gambia River, James Fort was the collection point for slaves coming down from the interior, and British and North American ships routinely stopped there to acquire provisions and slaves. On December 11, Hopkins purchased thirteen Africans from Governor Debatt, the British official who ran the fort, in exchange for 1,200 gallons of rum and sundry stores.

June 8, 1765: "Woman Slave hanged her Self between Decks"

While most slave ships worked their way along the coast, the Sally appears to have remained largely in one place, apparently at a small British slave "factory" near the mouth of the River Grande, in what is today Guinea-Bissau. Hopkins traded rum with passing slave ships, acquiring manufactured goods like cloth, iron bars, and guns, which he then used to acquire slaves. On June 8, 1765, he purchased his 108th captive. That same day, an enslaved woman committed suicide. She was the second captive to die on the ship.

Newport July 17, 1765
Sir

Having heard by Capt Morris that you had Lost all your Hands in the River Basa I came down here, last Evening on purpose to Take Some method to suply the

misfortune as much as Possable, by the Two Vessels Just about sailing from this place Capt Briggs & Capt Moor but Receiving your Letter of ye 15th May this morning which giving us Such favourable accounts of your Circumstance from what we had heard Quite aleviates our Misfortune and prevents dewing any thing further than Writing you by these opertunitys principaly to Inform you that (Notwithstanding our first orders to you & our Letter to Barbadoes of ye 4th Ultimo advising you to go to South Carolina,) that the market there is Surpriseingly Glutted with Slaves So that it will not by any means do to go there Therefore Recomend if you Can get £20 Sterling for your Well Slaves Land at Barbadoes to sell there . . . and Lay out ye Neet proceed in 30 hogshead Rum 8 or 10 hogshead Sugar & 3 or 4 Baggs of Cotton the remainder in full Weight money or Good Bills but money full Weight is 5 percent better for us than bills and proceed home, without giving yourself any further trouble about Loading with Salt But if your Slaves Should be in good order and you Cannot get that proceed to Jamaica and there Dispose of them for ye same of pay & proceed home, but Notwithstanding what we here advise if you think any other port in the Westindes will Do better Considering all ye Risque, you are At full Liberty to go and Inshort do by Vessel & Cargo in that Respect as if She wass your own all friends and particularly your family is Well
M

2
Burroughs is this morning gone to Providence in order to Carry your Letter to Mrs Hopkins. you may depend. . . . Friends nor money shall not be Wanting to make the Insurance you Wish for to your Wife whose Letter Mr Burrows opend in order to Relieve the aprehentions of his father & family from ye Maloncholy Tale Brought by Capt Morris
I am for Self & Co. your Assured Frend
MB
Copy Letter
to Capt Esek
Hopkins July
1765

July 17, 1765: The Browns receive word from Hopkins

In June, 1765, after months with no news from the Sally, the Browns received reports that the ship and crew had been lost. Those rumors were contradicted on July 17, when a letter belatedly arrived from Hopkins, safe on the River Grande. Though Hopkins reported the loss of one crewman and substantial loss of his cargo through leakage, the Browns were elated. Your letter "Quite Aleviates our Misfortune," they wrote.

August 20, 1765: The Sally embarks for the Americas

On August 20, 1765, more than nine months after his arrival on the African coast, Hopkins acquired his 196th and final captive. Nineteen Africans had already died on the ship. A twentieth captive, a "woman all Most dead," was left behind as a present for Anthony, the ship's "Linguister," or translator. At least twenty-one Africans had been sold to other slave traders on the coast, bringing the Sally's "cargo" to about 155 people.

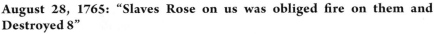

August 28, 1765: "Slaves Rose on us was obliged fire on them and Destroyed 8"

Four more Africans died in the first week of the Sally's return voyage. On August 28, desperate captives staged an insurrection, which Hopkins and the crew violently suppressed. Eight Africans died immediately, and two others later succumbed to their wounds. According to Hopkins, the captives were "so Desperited" after the failed insurrection that "Some Drowned them Selves Some Starved and Others Sickened & Dyed."

October, 1765: The Sally arrives in the West Indies

The Sally reached the West Indies in early October, 1765, after a transatlantic passage of about seven weeks. After a brief layover in Barbados, the ship proceeded to Antigua, where Hopkins wrote to the Browns, alerting them to the scope of the disaster. Sixty-eight Africans had perished during the passage, and twenty more died in the days immediately following the ship's arrival, bringing the death toll to 108. A 109th captive would later die en route to Providence.

November 16, 1765: "Sales of Negroes at Public Vendue"

When they dispatched the Sally, the Brown brothers instructed Hopkins to return to Providence with four or five "likely lads" for the family's use. The rest of the Sally survivors were auctioned in Antigua. Sickly and emaciated, they commanded extremely low prices at auction. The last two dozen survivors were auctioned in Antigua on November 16, selling, in one case, for less than £5, scarcely a tenth of the value of a "prime slave."

» Working with Sources

1. **How do these documents illuminate the economic and market forces that were bound up in the transatlantic slave trade?**

2. **What were the practical consequences of viewing human slaves as a commercial product?**

SOURCE 19.4

The Interesting Narrative of the Life of Olaudah Equiano

1789

This autobiography of a slave who would emerge as a leading voice in the abolitionist cause has been enormously significant for understanding Atlantic slavery. Equiano claimed to have been born a prince among the Igbo people of modern Nigeria around 1745, kidnapped as a child, and transported across the ocean to the West Indies and Virginia. Named by his first (of several) masters after the sixteenth-century king Gustav I of Sweden,

---

Source: Henry Louis Gates, Jr., ed., *The Classic Slave Narratives* (New York: Mentor, 1987), 99–100, 102–103.

"Gustavus Vas[s]a" would travel throughout the southern American colonies and the Caribbean, always longing to achieve his freedom. Shaming his Quaker master into honoring a promise, Equiano was freed in 1765, but he continued to suffer the indignities and risks attending a free black man living in a slave society. His published memoir was designed to galvanize antislavery forces, and his work elicited sufficient sympathy and respect to contribute to the abolition of the British slave trade (though not slavery itself) in 1807.

We set sail once more for Montserrat, and arrived there safe; but much out of humour with our friend, the silversmith. When we had unladen the vessel, and I had sold my venture, finding myself master of about forty-seven pounds, I consulted my true friend, the Captain, how I should proceed in offering my master the money for my freedom. He told me to come on a certain morning, when he and my master would be at breakfast together. Accordingly, on that morning I went, and met the Captain there, as he had appointed. When I went in I made my obeisance to my master, and with my money in my hand, and many fears in my heart, I prayed him to be as good as his offer to me, when he was pleased to promise me my freedom as soon as I could purchase it. This speech seemed to confound him; he began to recoil; and my heart that instant sunk within me. "What," said he, "give you your freedom? Why, where did you get the money? Have you got forty pounds sterling?" "Yes, sir," I answered. "How did you get it?" replied he. I told him, "very honestly." The Captain then said he knew I got the money very honestly and with much industry, and that I was particularly careful. On which my master replied, I got money much faster than he did; and said he would not have made me the promise which he did, had he thought I should have got the money so soon. "Come, come," said my worthy Captain, clapping my master on the back. "Come, Robert, (which was his name) I think you must let him have his freedom. You have laid your money out very well; you have received good interest for it all this time, and here is now the principal at last. I know Gustavus has earned you more than a hundred a year, and he will still save you money, as he will not leave you. Come, Robert, take the money." My master then said, he would not be worse than his promise; and, taking the money, told me to go to the Secretary at the Register Office, and get my manumission drawn up.

These words of my master were like a voice from heaven to me: in an instant all my trepidation was turned into unutterable bliss, and I most reverently bowed myself with gratitude, unable to express my feelings, but by the overflowing of my eyes, and a heart replete with thanks to God; while my true and worthy friend, the Captain, congratulated us both with a peculiar degree of heartfelt pleasure.

. . .

During our stay at this place [Savannah, Georgia], one evening a slave belonging to Mr. Read, a merchant of Savannah, came near our vessel, and began to use me very ill. I entreated him, with all the patience of which I was master, to desist, as I knew there was little or no law for a free negro here. But the fellow, instead of taking my advice, persevered in his insults, and even struck me. At this I lost all temper, and fell on him, and beat him soundly. The next morning his master came to our vessel, as we lay alongside the wharf, and desired me to come ashore that he might have me flogged all round the town, for beating his negro slave! I told him he had insulted me, and had given the provocation by first striking me. I had also told my Captain the whole affair that morning, and desired him to go along with me to Mr. Read, to prevent bad consequences; but he said that it did not signify, and if Mr. Read said any thing he would make matters up, and desired me to go to work, which I accordingly did.

The Captain being on board when Mr. Read came and applied to him to deliver me up, he said he knew nothing of the matter, I was a free man. I was astonished and frightened at this, and thought I had better keep where I was, than go ashore and be flogged round the town, without judge or jury. I therefore refused to stir; and Mr. Read went away, swearing he would bring all the constables in the town, for he would have me out of the vessel. When he was gone, I thought his threat might prove too true to my sorrow; and I was confirmed in this belief, as well by the many instances I had seen of the treatment of free negroes, as from a fact that had happened within my own knowledge here a short time before.

There was a free black man, a carpenter, that I knew, who for asking a gentleman that he had worked for, for the money he had earned, was put into gaol; and afterwards this oppressed man was sent from Georgia, with false accusations, of an intention to set the gentleman's house on fire, and run away with his slaves. I was therefore much embarrassed, and very apprehensive of a flogging at least. I dreaded, of all things, the thoughts of being stripped, as I never in my life had the marks of any violence of that kind. At that instant a rage seized my soul, and for a little I determined to resist the first man that should attempt to lay violent hands on me, or basely use me without a trial; for I would sooner die like a free man, than suffer myself to be scourged, by the hands of ruffians, and my blood drawn like a slave.

>> **Working with Sources**

1. **What did being free mean to Equiano? Was he disappointed in his change of status?**

2. **What role does the captain play in the narrative at this point?**

SOURCE 19.5

Casta paintings, Mexico

Eighteenth century

Some of the most remarkable visual records of colonial Mexico are the series of paintings called "casta" paintings, illustrating every racial combination of Spanish, mestizo, black, Native American, and other types thought possible in the New Spain of the eighteenth and early nineteenth

Source: De Espanol y Negra, Mulato (From Spaniard and Black, Mulatto), attributed to Jose de Alcibar, c. 1760. Denver Art Museum: Collection of Frederick and Jan Mayer. Photo © James O. Milmoe

centuries. Casta paintings were always created in a series, and each picture usually contains a male–female couple and at least one child. Occasionally more than one child and even other animal or human figures are depicted. At the top or bottom of the painting is an inscription that explains the racial mix shown in the image. At least 50 groups of these paintings have been identified, although very few survive today in complete series.

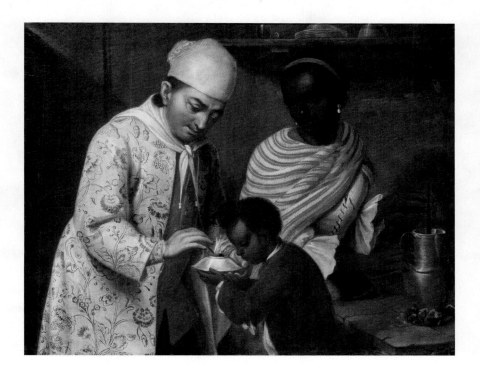

≫ Working with Sources

1. How do the inscription and the image work together, and what was the entire painting meant to convey?

2. Analyze the clothing styles depicted in the painting; do these clothes provide any indication of a "reality" that may appear in the work?

>> Chapter 20   1400–1750

The Mughal Empire

MUSLIM RULERS AND HINDU SUBJECTS

Central
Asia

Southeast
Asia

**MUGHAL
INDIA,
ca. 1700**

INDIAN
OCEAN

J une 17, 1631, could hardly have been a less auspicious day for the family of the Mughal emperor Shah Jahan. Though he ruled over the most powerful empire in India's history and commanded unprecedented wealth, the emperor's beloved wife, Mumtaz Mahal, had just died in giving birth to their fourteenth child. The royal family was naturally plunged into mourning, a grief conveyed by the following lines read at the announcement of her death:

The world is a paradise full of delights,

Yet also a rose bush filled with thorns;

He who picks the rose of happiness

Has his heart pierced by a thorn.

Shah Jahan himself, however, plumbed far greater depths of depression. His beard turned gray, and it was said that he wept for nearly 2 years afterward. Indeed, his eyes grew so weak from his tears that he needed to wear glasses to read his daily correspondence. Inconsolable for months on end, he finally resolved to build a magnificent tomb complex for Mumtaz Mahal over her burial site along the Jumna (or Yamuna) River near the giant fortress at Agra. At a time when monumental building projects were

ABOVE: **The Taj Mahal (1631–1653), a magnificent architectural synthesis of Hindu and Muslim influences and Persian classicism.**

the order of the day for Mughal rulers, this tomb, with its balance of deceptively simple lines, harmony of proportion, and technical skill, would become the most recognized symbol of India throughout the world: the Taj Mahal.

Beyond its architectural elegance, however, the Taj Mahal also conveys a great deal of information about the circumstances of Mughal rule in India, particularly about the attempted syncretism of Muslim rulers and Hindu subjects we first saw in Chapter 12. Like their predecessors, the Mughals discovered the difficulties of being an ethnic and religious minority ruling a huge and diverse population. By Shah Jahan's time, moreover, religious revival was sweeping Islamic India and earlier Mughal rulers were subject to criticism about their laxity in ruling according to Islamic law and the accommodations they had made with India's other religious communities. Shah Jahan therefore devoted himself anew to a study of the Quran and re-solved to rule insofar as it was possible according to Islamic precepts. Over the coming decades, such policy changes would raise tensions between Hindus and Muslims.

Seeing Patterns

≫ What were the strengths and weaknesses of Mughal rule?

≫ What was the Mughal policy toward religious accommodation? How did it change over time?

≫ What factors account for the Mughal decline during the eighteenth century?

The gleaming white stone dome and minarets of Shah Jahan's architectural masterpiece are the centerpiece of a much larger complex that is, in fact, a vision of the entrance to paradise recreated on earth. The complex is, as one scholar put it, a vast **allegory** of Allah's judgment in paradise on the day of the resurrection. In the end, Mughal ambition to create an empire as the earthly expression of this vision lent itself to that empire's ultimate decline. The constant drive to bring the remaining independent Indian states under Mughal control continually strained imperial resources. Dynastic succession almost always resulted in internal wars fought by rival claimants to the Mughal mantle. By the eighteenth century, prolonged rebellion and the growing power of the East India Companies of the European powers would conspire to send the dynasty into a downward spiral from which it never recovered. But its most visible symbol, the Taj Mahal—literally the "Crown Palace"—remains the emblem of India's peak as an ambitious attempt at creating a syncretic religious civilization in the modern period.

Allegory: A literary, poetic, dramatic, pictorial, or architectural device in which the parts have symbolic value in depicting the meaning of the whole.

History and Political Life of the Mughals

Though we have noted previously that relations between Muslims and India's other religions were *syncretic*—that despite attempts to integrate them more thoroughly into India's larger religious mosaic, they coexisted, sometimes on difficult or hostile terms, but remained largely separate from the other traditions. Yet the political and social systems created by the Mughals were in many respects a successful *synthesis*. That is, the Mughals brought with them a tradition that blended the practices of what social scientists call an "extraction state"—one that supplies itself by conquest and plunder—with several centuries of ruling more settled areas. This legacy would guide them as they struggled with a set of problems similar to those faced by rulers in other areas in creating an empire centered on one religion. Aided in their conquests by the new military technologies of cannon and small firearms, the Mughals created a flexible bureaucracy with a strict hierarchy of ranks and sophisticated separation of powers but with ultimate power concentrated in the hands of the emperors. Like those of the Chinese and Ottomans, the system was easily expanded into newly conquered areas, gave considerable free rein to the ambitious, and weathered all the major political storms it encountered until its decline during the eighteenth century.

From Samarkand to Hindustan

As we have seen in earlier chapters, the rise to prominence of speakers of Turkic languages of the Altaic group had taken place over the course of many centuries. From at least the time of the Huns, these groups regularly coalesced into potent raiding and fighting forces, often putting together short-lived states such as those of the Toba in fifth- and sixth-century China, the Uighurs in the eighth and ninth centuries, and, most important, the Mongols in the twelfth and thirteenth centuries. But the Mongol Empire, the largest in world history, as we have seen soon fell apart, and in its wake the central Asian heartland of the Turkic peoples—roughly speaking, from the Sea of Azov to the western reaches of present-day Mongolia—evolved into a patchwork of smaller states, many of whose rulers claimed descent from Genghis Khan. With the ousting of the Mongol Yuan dynasty from China in 1368, the eastern regions of this vast territory were thrown into further disarray, which set the stage for another movement toward consolidation.

The Empire of Timur   Aided by the ease of travel within the Mongol Empire, Islam had by the fourteenth century become the dominant religion among the central Asian Turkic peoples. By this time some of the Turkic groups, like the Seljuks and the Ottomans, had long since moved into the eastern Mediterranean region and Anatolia. In the interior of central Asia, however, the memory of the accomplishments of the Mongol Empire among the inhabitants of Chagatai—the area given to Genghis Khan's son of that name—was still fresh. Their desire for a new Mongol Empire, now coupled with Islam, created opportunities for military action to unite the settled and nomadic tribes of Chagatai. The result by the end of the fourteenth century was the stunning rise of Temur Gurgan (r. 1370–1405), more widely known by a variation of the Persian rendering of his name, Timur-i Lang, as Timur the Lame, or Tamerlane.

What little is known about Timur's early years has been clouded by the mystique he cultivated as a ruler, which continued to grow long after his death. Though he came close to matching the conquests of Genghis Khan, his forebearers were not direct descendants of the conqueror. He therefore devised genealogies connecting him to the dominant Mongol lines to give him legitimacy as a ruler, and he even found a direct descendant of Genghis Khan to use as a figurehead for his regime. He also portrayed himself as a man whose destiny was guided by God from humble beginnings to world domination.

From 1382, when he secured the region of his homeland around the capital, the Silk Road trading center of Samarkand, until his death in 1405, Timur ranged widely through western central Asia, Afghanistan, northern India, Iran, Anatolia, and the eastern Mediterranean lands (see Map 20.1). Like his model, Genghis

Khan, he proved surprisingly liberal in his treatment of certain cities that surrendered peacefully. Many more times, however, he reduced besieged cities to rubble, slaughtered the inhabitants, and erected pyramids of skulls as a warning to others to submit.

At the time of his death in 1405, Timur was contemplating the invasion of Ming China. This, however, never came to pass, and Timur's empire, like that of Genghis Khan, did not long outlast him. As it fell apart, the various Chagatai peoples largely resumed their local feuds, once again leaving the way open for a strong military force to impose order.

Babur and the Timurid Line in India   By the beginning of the sixteenth century, the region from Samarkand south into the Punjab in northern India had largely become the province of feuding Turkic tribes and clans of Afghan fighters, many of whom had migrated south to serve with the Lodi sultans of India. Into this volatile environment was born Zahir ud-Din Muhammad Babur (1483–1530, r. 1526–1530). (Zahir's nickname, "Babur," rooted in the Indo-European word for "beaver," was no longer understood by Turkish or Persian speakers, who assumed that it was connected with the Turkish word *baber* for "tiger.") Babur's claims to legitimate rule were considerable: His father was a direct descendant of Timur, while his mother claimed the lineage of Genghis Khan.

At 14, Babur conquered Samarkand, though he was soon forced out by a competing tribe. Like Timur and Genghis Khan, his accomplishments as a youthful prodigy led him to believe that God had provided him with a special destiny to fulfill. This belief sustained him during the next several years when, out of favor with certain powerful relatives, he roamed the border regions seeking an opportunity to return to power.

In 1504, accompanied on a campaign by his strong-willed mother, Babur moved into Afghanistan, captured Kabul, and went on to raid points farther south over the following decade. By 1519, he stepped up his raids into northern India with a view to subjugating and ruling it. After 7 more years of campaigning, this goal was achieved. In 1526, Babur's army of approximately 12,000 met the forces of Sultan Ibrahim Lodi, whose army boasted perhaps 100,000 men and 1,000 elephants, at Panipat, near Delhi. Though the sultan enjoyed such vast numerical superiority, Babur's forces employed the new technologies of matchlock muskets

MAP **20.1 Area Subjugated by Timur-i Lang, 1360–1405.**

interactive timeline

1336–1405
Timur (Tamerlane), founder
of Timurid line of rulers

1483–1530
Babur, founder of Timurid
line in India—the Mughals

1542–1605
Akbar, most innovative
of Mughal rulers

1627–1657
Shah Jahan, builder
of the Taj Mahal

1618–1707
Aurangzeb, last powerful
Mughal ruler

1707–1858
Ebbing of Mughal power in
India; rise of British influence

1739
Invasion by Persians; looting of
Delhi; taking of Peacock Throne

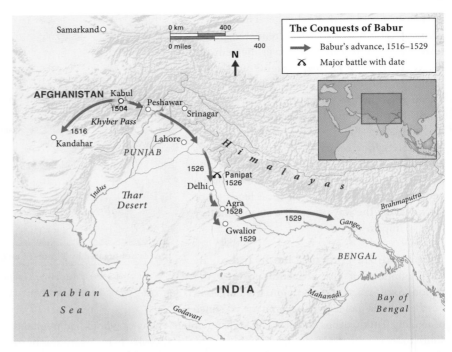

MAP 20.2 **The Conquests of Babur.**

Portrait of Babur. This imagined portrait of Babur was done about 60 years after his death. He is shown receiving representatives of the Uzbeks of Central Asia and the Rajputs of India in an audience dated December 18, 1528.

and field cannon to devastating effect. In the end, the Lodi sultan was killed, along with many of the Afghan tribal chiefs whose forces made up the bulk of his army, and Babur's way was now clear to consolidate his new Indian territories.

Victory at Panipat was swiftly followed by conquest of the Lodi capital of Agra and further success over the Hindu Rajputs in 1528. On the eve of his death in December 1530, Babur controlled an enormous swath of territory extending from Samarkand in the north to Gwalior in India in the south (see Map 20.2). For Babur and his successors, their ruling family would always be the "House of Timur," prompting historians to sometimes refer to the line as the Timurids. Because of their claims to the legacy of Genghis Khan, however, they would be better known to the world as the Mughals (from "Mongols").

Loss and Recovery of Empire   As had been the case so many times in the past with other newly conquered empires, the House of Timur's new rulers were now faced with the problem of consolidating, organizing, and administering Babur's vast domain. Like Timur before him, Babur had given comparatively little thought to the arts of peace. Now it fell on his son Humayun (r. 1530–1556) to create a state. Unfortunately, Humayun's interests were aimed more toward Islamic Sufi mysticism, poetry, astrology, and at times wine and opium than they were toward responsible leadership. Though chroniclers have generally been critical of him for losing much of Babur's legacy, he tapped a considerable reservoir of courage and determination to ultimately win it back.

A chronic problem for the long-term health of the dynasty was the **institution-alization** of traditional nomadic succession practices among the Mughal rulers. Though only one son was designated as the ruler's successor, the others were given substantial territories to govern within the empire, a situation that frequently led to conflict. In addition to such ongoing family difficulties, Humayun faced various hostile military forces still active in unconquered areas of northern India and Afghanistan. An Afghan leader named Sher Khan Sur managed to unite many of these forces and invaded the extreme eastern region of Bengal. Twice routed, Humayun fled to Persia in 1540, where, utterly humiliated, he was forced to convert to Shia Islam in a desperate bid to court the favor of the Safavid ruler, Shah Tahmasp. As distasteful as this was for him as a Sunni Muslim, he now at least had Persian backing and proceeded to move into Afghanistan and, ultimately, to Delhi. By 1555, after 15 years of exile and fighting, the dynasty was restored. For Humayun, however, the peace brought only a brief respite. In a final irony for this scholarly man, he tripped on his robe while descending the staircase from the roof terrace of his palace library, his arms laden with books, while attempting to kneel at the sound of the muezzin's call to prayer. After several days he died of his injuries in January 1556.

Institutionalization: The creation of a regular system for previously improvised or ad hoc activities or things, such as law codes to replace local customs.

Consolidation and Expansion   Because of the difficulties involved in Humayun's own accession to the throne, his death was kept secret for several weeks, while the court worked out plans for a regency for the emperor's son, 14-year-old Jalal ud-Din Akbar (r. 1556–1605). His military education began quickly as Humayun's old enemy, Sher Khan Sur, sent an army to attack Delhi in 1557. In a close fight, Mughal forces finally carried the day. Over the next year and a half, they secured the eastern, southern, and western flanks of their lands, bringing them conclusively into the Mughal fold and again anchoring Islam in the former areas of its influence—"Hindustan."

Upon finally seizing power in a palace coup, Akbar plunged into renewed campaigning in quest of more territory. Along the way, he seemed at once determined to master all India by any military means necessary yet also intolerant of cruelties practiced by his subordinates in his name. Akbar abhorred religious violence of any kind and spent much of his rule attempting to reconcile the different religious traditions of his empire. In the end his attempts, though remarkably far-sighted, would prove futile and earn him the enmity of many of his fellow Muslims, who felt he had become an unbeliever.

As a warrior Akbar was far more successful. Through the 1560s, aided by capable military advisors, Mughal armies continued to push the boundaries of the empire west, south, and east. In 1562 they subdued Malwa and in 1564 Gondwana; in 1568, the great Rajput fortress of Chitor fell. This string of victories continued into the next decade, with the long-sought conquest of Gujarat taking place in 1573. Turning eastward, Akbar set his sights on Bengal, which, along with the neighboring regions of Bihar and Orissa, fell to the Mughals by the mid-1570s. They remained, however, volatile and hostile to Mughal occupation. Both Muslim and Hindu princes in the region continued their campaigns of resistance into the following decades (see Map 20.3).

Humayun Being Received by the Persian Shah Tahmasp. This gouache rendering of a pivotal moment in Mughal dynastic history is by the late sixteenth-century Indian painter Sanwalah. Although all seems cordial between the two men and Humayun was treated well by the Shah, a number of accounts claim that he was threatened with execution if he did not convert to Shia Islam.

Visions of Akbar. A depiction of Akbar from ca. 1630 shows him in all of his religious glory: surrounded by a luminous halo, surmounted by angels glorifying him and holding his crown, and graced with the holiness to make the lion lie down with the heifer.

In the meantime, resistance and rebellion periodically plagued other areas of the empire. In central Asia, as early as 1564, a rebellion of Uzbek Mughal allies required a skilled combination of violence and diplomacy to defuse. At the same time, revolts in Malwa and Gujarat required reconquest of those territories. In order to keep the old Islamic heartland of northern India—Hindustan—under firm Mughal control, the Mughals built fortresses at strategic points throughout their inner domains as well as along the frontier. Among the most important of these were Allahabad, Lahore (in modern Pakistan), Ajmer (the Amber Fort in Jaipur), and the largest—the famous Red Fort in Delhi.

The New City   In addition to fielding large armies—one European observer estimated that the army he accompanied on one of Akbar's campaigns surpassed 100,000—and huge, expensive forts, the immense revenues of the Mughal lands allowed other monumental projects to be undertaken. In an effort to show solidarity with his non-Muslim subjects, Akbar had married a Hindu Rajput princess named Manmati. Manmati had twins, who tragically died, and a distraught Akbar sought advice from a famous Sufi holy man named Salim Chishti (sometimes spelled as Chisti). Salim told Akbar that he would ultimately have a son. When that son—named Salim in

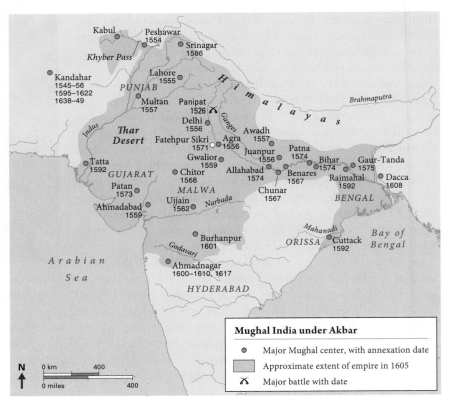

MAP 20.3 **Mughal India under Akbar.**

honor of the holy man—was born, Akbar began to build a city on the site of Salim Chishti's village of Sikri. Fatehpur Sikri, as the new city was known when it was completed in 1571, was built from the same red sandstone as the great fort at Agra, 26 miles away. Akbar's instincts for design and dynastic propaganda were everywhere evident within the city. At its center was the mosque, which housed the tomb of Salim Chishti and became an object of veneration and pilgrimage for Indian Sufis. Despite its amenities, however, the city was untenable in the long run and ultimately abandoned because there was simply not enough available water to sustain the population.

The Summer and Autumn of Empire

In a way, the saga of Fatehpur Sikri runs parallel to Mughal fortunes over the next century. The military accomplishments of the dynasty are in many ways spectacular, but they were eventually worn down by internal rebellion and succession struggles; the immense fortunes of the rulers were ultimately squeezed by the needs of defense and of ostentation to demonstrate power; and new economic and, ultimately, military competitors arrived on the scene with the coming of the Europeans.

The Revolt of the Sons In 1585, Akbar left Fatehpur Sikri with his army for Lahore, which he would make his temporary capital for most of the rest of his life. Once again, the Afghan princes were chafing under Mughal domination and intriguing with the Uzbeks and Safavid Persians to wrest local control for themselves. For Akbar, as for his predecessors, it was vital to maintain a hold over these areas because of their historical connection to the peoples of Chagatai and the need to keep control of the essential Silk Road trade. Now the key city of Kandahar, in modern Afghanistan, was in Safavid Persian hands, disrupting Mughal control of the trade. For the next 13 years, Akbar and his generals fought a long, stubborn war to subdue the Afghans and roll back the Safavids. Though his forces were defeated on several occasions, in the end the Mughals acquired Sind and Kashmir, subdued for a time the region of Swat, and, with the defection of a Safavid commander, occupied Kandahar. By 1598, the regions in question were secure enough for Akbar to move back to Agra.

Salim Chishti's Tomb at Fatehpur Sikri. The tomb of the Sufi mystic Salim Chishti shows the sense of restrained flamboyance that marks the mature Mughal architectural style. The Chishtis had long been revered by India's Sufis, and Salim's simple, elegant tomb, with its domed sarcophagus, multihued marble, and Quranic inscriptions, quickly became a favorite pilgrimage site. Surrounding it is one of the red sandstone courtyards of Akbar's Fatehpur Sikri.

In 1600, Akbar embarked on his last great campaign against the remaining free Muslim sultanates of central India. These were reduced within a year, but Akbar was now faced with a domestic crisis. His son Salim launched a coup and occupied the fort at Agra. Salim declared himself emperor, raised his own army, and even had coins struck with his name on them. In the end, one of Akbar's wives and a group of court women were able to reconcile Akbar and Salim. Salim was confined within the palace amid intrigues that threatened to bypass him as heir in favor of his own son, Khusrau. In the end, however, he retained his position, and upon Akbar's death on October 25, 1605, Salim acceded to the throne as Jahangir (r. 1605–1627).

A Jesuit describes Akbar (1582)

Renewed Expansion of the "War State"   As if to underscore the dynasty's continual problems with orderly succession, Jahangir's son Khusrau left the palace, quickly put a small army together, and marched on Lahore. When negotiations with his son went nowhere, Jahangir's forces swiftly defeated the insurgents. To impart to his son a special horror at what he had done, Khusrau was made to watch his comrades put to death by impalement—a punishment also used in the Ottoman Empire by the vassal Vlad "the Impaler" Dracula (Chapter 16). Sharpened posts were driven through their midsections and planted in the ground so that they would die slow, agonizing deaths suspended in the air. The doomed soldiers were made to salute Khusrau, who was forced to ride among them in a macabre military review. Undeterred, Khusrau rebelled again, and on failing this time, was blinded and imprisoned for his efforts.

As one scholar writes, "Under Jahangir the empire continued to be a war state attuned to aggressive conquest and territorial expansion." This now meant pushing south into the Deccan and periodically resecuring Afghanistan and its adjacent regions. A move into Bengal, however, foreshadowed a major clash with a very different kind of enemy: the Shan people of Southeast Asia called the Ahoms. Southeast Asia was where the expanding cultural and political influence of China met that of Hindu and Buddhist India. In the case of the Ahoms, the territory in question was in the vicinity of Assam, along the Brahmaputra River to the north of Burma and Thailand. Though they had recently converted to Hinduism, the Ahoms had no caste system and drew upon a legacy of self-confident expansion that the Mughals had not encountered before in their opponents. With little fixed territory to defend because of their mobility, the Ahoms proved the most stubborn enemies the empire had yet encountered. Year after year, Jahangir's armies labored to secure the northeastern territories only to have the Ahoms bounce back and mount fresh offensives against them. Though both sides employed troops armed with matchlocks and cannon, neither side could obtain a clear tactical edge, and their wars dragged on for decades.

More culturally and psychologically threatening to the Mughals was their relationship with the empire to their west, Safavid Persia. Both sides constantly jockeyed for position against each other and periodically went to war. There was also intense religious rivalry, with the predominantly Sunni Mughals and Shiite Safavid Persians each denouncing the other as heretical unbelievers. For the Mughals, moreover, it was particularly galling that they owed the survival of their dynasty in part to the Persian shah Tahmasp, who had given aid to Humayun—forcing him to convert to Shiism in return.

In addition, among the sizable number of Persians and Shiites within the Mughal elites there was a pronounced feeling that Persian culture, language, and literature were superior to those of the Turks and Muslim India as a whole. In some respects, both Persians and "Persianized" Indians saw Muslim India as a kind of cultural colonial outpost, in much the same way that Chinese sophisticates viewed the high cultures of Japan, Korea, and Vietnam. This made for a complex set of relations between the two empires, with both vying for power in religious and cultural terms as much as in the political and military realm.

New Directions in Religious Politics   After Jahangir died of a fever in October 1627, his oldest son, Khurram, outmaneuvered his younger brother for the throne and reigned as Shah Jahan (r. 1627–1657). His rule coincided with perhaps the high point of Mughal cultural power and prestige, as reflected in its iconic building, the Taj Mahal. However, his record is less spectacular in political and military terms. In this case, the Mughal obsession with controlling the northern trade routes coincided with the need to take back the long-contested great fort at Kandahar, once again in Persian hands. Thus, Shah Jahan spent much of his reign on the ultimately fruitless drive to finally subdue the northwest.

As we noted earlier, the reign of Akbar and, to a considerable extent, that of Jahangir had marked a time of extraordinary religious tolerance. The attraction of both men to the Sufi school of Salim Chishti, with its mystical leanings and parallels with similar Hindu movements, created a favorable emotional environment for religious pluralism. It also made Muslims, for whom strict adherence to Sunni doctrine was necessary to guard against undue Persian Shia influence, apprehensive. Others, noting the ability of Hindus to incorporate the gods and beliefs of other faiths into their own, feared that the ruling Muslim minority might ultimately be assimilated into the Hindu majority.

With Shah Jahan, however, we see a definite turn toward a more legalistic tradition. Under the influence of this trend among leading Sunni theologians, Shah Jahan began to block construction and repair of non-Muslim religious buildings, instituted more direct state support for Islamic festivals, and furnished lavish subsidies for Muslim pilgrims to Mecca. The old ideal of a unified Muslim world governed by Quranic law steadily gained ground at the Mughal court and would see its greatest champion in Shah Jahan's son Aurangzeb. In the meantime, the trend lent itself to the creation of a new capital, Shajahanabad Delhi, today one of the "seven cities" that make up the modern metropolis of Delhi–New Delhi complete with the largest mosque—Jama Masjid—a college (*madrasa*), and hospital complex in India—and, of course, the Taj Mahal at Agra.

The Pinnacle of Power   The ascendancy of Aurangzeb (r. 1658–1707) was marked yet again by the now all-too-familiar pattern of princely infighting. In this case it was brought on by the extended illness of Shah Jahan in 1657. A four-way struggle broke out among the sons of Shah Jahan and his beloved Mumtaz Mahal. Although Shah Jahan soon recovered, he returned to Agra broken and depressed, while his sons fought bitterly for control. By 1661 three had been defeated and killed, leaving Aurangzeb in control of the empire. Shah Jahan lived on in captivity until 1666.

Aurangzeb's long rule, despite its violent birth, seemed to begin auspiciously enough. Renewing the Mughal bid to expand into the northeastern areas controlled

Akbar's Attempt at Religious Synthesis

Like their predecessors, the Mughals as Muslim rulers in India were faced with an immense array of diverse, and sometimes antagonistic, religious and cultural traditions. Amid this "religious syncretism," as we have termed it, Akbar's innovation within the world-historical pattern of religious civilizations was to create a new religion that would encompass these traditions and bind his followers directly to him as emperor and religious leader: to create an Indian "religious synthesis."

Already graced with a larger-than-life reputation for charisma and openness, he was also resistant to the strictures of Sunni Islam or any other organized religion. As a boy, he was condemned by his tutors as uneducable because he remained unable to read or write. Some scholars have suggested that he was dyslexic. Perhaps because of this, he developed an extraordinary memory for literature and poetry. Some have also suggested that his illiteracy was in emulation of the stories of the early holy men, who found illumination directly from God. In any case, his tastes within Islam centered on Sufi mysticism, which had a long tradition of tolerance and eclecticism. This openness encouraged him to study the mystical traditions of the Hindus, Parsis (Zoroastrian immigrants from Persia), and Christians. After establishing himself at Fatehpur Sikri, he sponsored regular Thursday-night theological debates, mostly among Muslim scholars but gradually including Hindus, Parsis, and in 1578 Catholic missionaries. He honored many of the cultural traditions of India's various religions as well: He wore his hair long under his turban like the Sikhs and some Hindus, coined emblems of the sun to honor the Parsis, and kept paintings of the Virgin Mary as a nod to the Christians.

Akbar Presiding Over a Religious Debate. Akbar's distaste for religious orthodoxy manifested itself most dramatically in his conducting regularly held debates among theologians from many of India's faiths. Here, a discussion is taking place with two Jesuit missionaries, Fathers Rudolph Aquaviva and Francis Henriquez (dressed in black) in 1578. Interestingly, the priests had unfettered access to Akbar, were free to preach, and even gave instruction to members of Akbar's family at his request.

by the Ahoms, his armies fought them to a standstill in the early 1660s and made them Mughal clients. When Mughal control of the area around Kabul and the Khyber Pass was threatened by a revolt of local tribesmen, Aurangzeb fought several stubborn campaigns to retain control of the region and bought off other potentially troublesome groups with lavish gifts.

With these campaigns, the political power of the Mughals reached perhaps its greatest extent. But the period also marked a watershed in at least two respects. First, it saw the opening of decades-long wars with the Hindu Marathas, in which the empire's cohesion was steadily eroded. In addition, the various trading companies of the English, French, and Dutch expanded their own fortified outposts in Indian ports outside Mughal domains. As Mughal power was sapped by the revolts of the eighteenth century, the companies' armed forces became important players in regional politics.

During one particularly lavish and bloody hunting party in 1578, he had a sudden, intense mystical experience. Like Ashoka so long before him—of whom Akbar was completely unaware—he was now appalled by the destruction and waste in which he had participated. Out of this experience and his religious consultations, he gradually developed a personal philosophy he called *sulh-i kull*—"at peace with all." While this did not end his military campaigns, which he saw as ordained by God, it did push him to develop a new religion he called *din-i ilahi* (divine faith). Akbar shrewdly directed the movement at key courtiers, nobles, and those aspiring to gain favor from the regime. He devised elaborate rituals in which adherents swore loyalty to him not only as emperor but as the enlightened religious master of the new sect. Borrowing heavily from Sufi mysticism, Persian court protocols, Zoroastrian sun and fire veneration, and even Muslim- and Christian-influenced spiritualism, he sought to at once limit the power of Sunni Islamic clerics and draw followers of other religions to what he taught was a "higher" realm, one that embraced all religions and provided the elect with secret insights into their ultimate truths.

In the end, however, despite its creative merging of the needs of state and religion to overcome what had been considered deep religious and cultural divisions, Akbar's attempt must be counted as a failure. While some Hindu and Muslim courtiers embraced *din-i ilahi* enthusiastically for its perceived religious truths, many did so for opportunistic reasons, and it was roundly condemned by most Sunni theologians. And while Akbar's personal magnetism was able to hold the sect together during his lifetime, his successors not only repudiated it but swung increasingly in the direction of stricter Sunni Islam.

Questions

- How does Akbar's attempt at religious syncretism demonstrate the pattern of origins–innovations–adaptations that informs the approach of this book?

- Why was Akbar's attempt to create a new divine faith doomed to failure?

The other watershed was Aurangzeb's bid for a more effective "Islamification" of Mughal India. Aurangzeb's vision for the empire was rule by Islamic Sharia law. As an Islamic state, connected to the larger commonwealth of Islamic states, he believed that Mughal rule should be primarily for the benefit of Muslims. This was an almost complete repudiation of his great-grandfather Akbar's vision of religious transcendence. While Aurangzeb stopped short of forcible conversion, he did offer multiple inducements to bring unbelievers into the faith. Elites who converted to Islam were given lavish gifts and preferential assignments, while those who did not convert found themselves isolated from the seat of power. Discriminatory taxes were also levied on unbelievers, including a new tax on Hindu pilgrims. Zealous Muslim judges in various cities prompted protests from Hindus regarding their rulings. Moving a step beyond the actions of Shah Jahan, Aurangzeb ordered the demolition of dozens of Hindu temples that had not been constructed or repaired according to state-approved provisions. The most unpopular measure, however, was the reimposition of the hated *jizya* tax on unbelievers, which had been abolished by Akbar.

The new religious policies also created problems in dealing with self-governing, non-Muslim groups within the empire. The legacy of distrust of the Mughals among the Sikhs, who blended Hindu and Muslim traditions, was enhanced by Aurangzeb's heavy-handed attempts to intervene in the selection of a new Sikh guru, or religious leader, and by the destruction of some Sikh temples. When the Sikhs did not choose the candidate Aurangzeb favored, the emperor arrested the other candidate for allegedly converting Muslims and had him executed. His son and successor, Gobind Singh, would later lead a full-blown Sikh revolt.

The Maratha Revolt   Notwithstanding these internal problems, Aurangzeb's military prowess netted him key areas that had long eluded Mughal efforts: Bijapur, Golconda, and much of the Maratha lands of the Deccan region of south-central India. Yet even here, the preconditions were already in place for a rebellion that would sap the strength of the empire for generations.

The Hindu Marathas, like the inhabitants of many regions bordering Mughal India, had evolved working relationships with the old Muslim sultanates that, over time, were annexed by the Timurids. For the earlier Mughal rulers, it was often enough for these small states to remit tribute and, on occasion, supply troops in order to retain their autonomy. For Aurangzeb, however, commitment to a more robust and legalistic Islam also meant political expansion of the Mughal state. This was justified on the religious grounds that the sultanates to the south had drifted from correct observance of Quranic law; that it was permissible to confiscate the lands of unbelievers; and that unbelievers would more likely convert if guided by proper Muslim rulers. Hence, Aurangzeb spent much of the last two decades of his life campaigning to bring central India under his sway.

Despite the tenacity of Maratha resistance, Aurangzeb's carrot-and-stick strategy—supporting pro-Mughal factions among the Maratha leaders, lavishing money and gifts on Maratha converts and deserters, and fielding large armies to attack Maratha fortifications—was successful. In the early 1690s 11 Maratha strongholds fell to his forces. Yet prolonged fighting, with the emperor staying in the field year after year, also led to problems at court and in the interior of the empire.

The demands of constant campaigning reduced the flow of money and goods from south to north and east to west across central India. Moreover, by the early eighteenth century, the Maratha frontier, far from being steadily worn down, was actually expanding into Mughal areas. The Marathas had set up their own administrative system with its own forts and tax base and encouraged raids on Mughal caravans and pack trains. By the time of Aurangzeb's death in 1707, the Marathas were noticeably expanding their sway at Mughal expense. With the weakening of the Mughal interior, Persia took the opportunity to settle scores. The Persians sent an expeditionary force that sacked Delhi in 1739 and carried off Shah Jahan's fabled Peacock Throne—from this time forward associated with the monarchs of Persia and Iran, rather than with India and the Mughals.

The East India Companies   Within a dozen years of Vasco da Gama's first voyage to India in 1498, armed Portuguese merchant ships seized the port of Goa in 1510. Portugal's pioneering efforts in capturing the spice trade and setting up fortified bases from which to conduct business were swiftly imitated by other European maritime countries. For the English, Dutch, and French, these enterprises were conducted by royally chartered companies, which were given a monopoly over their country's trade within a certain region. Because these companies were operating thousands of miles from home in areas that were often politically chaotic, they acted much like independent states. They maintained fortified warehouses, their armed merchant ships functioned as naval forces, and they assembled their own mercenary armies.

The Dutch Trading Post at Hugli, 1665. The mid-seventeenth century was the high point of Dutch influence and trade in Asia, and the Dutch East India Company was one of the most powerful entities in the region. This fortified outpost on the Hugli River was typical of European trading establishments in the region during the late sixteenth and most of the seventeenth centuries. By the end of the century, however, the Dutch would be supplanted on the Hugli by their archrivals, the English, who would establish their own base, which would swiftly grow into the great trading center of Calcutta.

Throughout the seventeenth century English, French, and Dutch enterprises largely supplanted Portuguese influence in the region, while the location of their trading ports outside Mughal lands allowed them considerable freedom. European naval prowess had by this time also surpassed that of any of the Indian states, and European ships controlled the sea-lanes to Indian ports. Thus the companies grew richer and more powerful and increasingly found themselves involved in local politics. For the English, the acquisition of Bombay (Mumbai) from Portugal in the 1660s gave the company a superb harbor. In 1690, after unwisely becoming involved in a struggle with Aurangzeb, English traders were pushed down the Hugli (also Hoogli or Hooghly) River in Bengal and began building a new trading station called Calcutta (not to be confused with the port of Calicut, on the west coast of India). By 1750, the power of the Dutch in India had been eclipsed by that of the British and French East India Companies. With the victory of the British East India Company commander, Robert Clive, at Plassey over the French forces in 1757 came British domination of Bengal and, by century's end, much of northern India.

Administration, Society, and Economy

One of the large patterns characteristic of the period under consideration in this section is a pronounced trend toward centralization. In a way, this phenomenon is not surprising, since the creation of states and empires requires power at the center to hold the state together, ensure consistent governance, provide for revenues, and maintain defense. What is noteworthy, however, is that in widely separate regions throughout Eurasia a variety of states concurrently reached a point where their governments, with armies now aided by firearms, made concerted efforts to focus more power than ever at the center. As part of this trend toward the development of centralizing states, some form of enforcement of approved religion or belief system legitimating the rulers was also present. As we saw in the Ottoman and Habsburg Empires in Chapter 16 and in seventeenth-century France and other European countries in Chapter 17, the trend was toward what came to be called "absolutism," with vast powers concentrated in the person of the monarch. In China and Japan, as we will see in Chapter 21, it meant additional

The ideal of a Muslim ruler: excerpt from *Rulings on Temporal Government* by Barni (ca. 1358)

powers concentrated in the hands of the emperor (China) and shogun (Japan). For Mughal India, the system that attempted to coordinate and balance so many disparate and often hostile elements of society is sometimes called "autocratic centralism." While never as effective as the Chinese bureaucratic system or as tightly regulated as absolutist France, its policies and demands stretched into the lives of its inhabitants in often unexpected ways.

Mansabdars and Bureaucracy

As we saw earlier, Babur and his successors found themselves forced to govern a largely settled, farming and city-dwelling society, whose traditions, habits, and (for the majority) religious affiliations were different from their own. While not unfamiliar with settled societies, the nomadic Timurids initially felt more comfortable in adapting their own institutions to their new situation and then grafting them onto the existing political and social structures. The result was a series of hybrid institutions that, given the tensions within Indian society, worked remarkably well when the empire was guided by relatively tolerant rulers but became increasingly problematic under more dogmatic ones.

Political Structure   The main early challenge faced by the Timurids was how to create a uniform administrative structure that did not rely on the unusual gifts of a particular ruler. It was the problem of moving from what social scientists call "charismatic leadership" (in which loyalty is invested in a leader because of his personal qualities) to "rational–legal" leadership (in which the institution itself commands primary respect and loyalty). Thus, Akbar created four principal ministries: one for army and military matters; one for taxation and revenue; one for legal and religious affairs; and one for the royal household.

Under the broad central powers of these ministries, things functioned much the same on the provincial and local levels. The provincial governors held political and military power and were responsible directly to the emperor. In order to prevent their having too much power, however, the fiscal responsibility for both the civil and military affairs of the provinces was in the hands of officers who reported to the finance minister. Thus, arbitrary or rebellious behavior could, in theory at least, be checked by the separation of financial control.

Administrative Personnel   One key problem faced by the Mughals was similar to that confronting the French king Louis XIV and the Tokugawa shoguns in Japan during the following century—that is, how to impose a centralized administrative system on a state whose nobles were used to wielding power themselves. In all three cases, the solutions were remarkably similar. For the Mughals, India's vast diversity of peoples and patchwork of small states offered a large pool of potential noble recruits, and the competition among the ambitious for imperial favor was intense. The Timurid rulers were careful to avoid overt favoritism toward particular ethnic, or even religious, groups; and though most of their recruited nobility were Sunni Muslims, Hindus and even Shiite Muslims were also represented.

The primary criteria—as one would expect in a centralizing state—were military and administrative skills. An elaborate, graded system of official ranks was created in which the recipients, called *mansabdars*, were awarded grants of land and the revenues those working the land generated. In turn the mansabdars were responsible for remitting the correct taxes and, above a certain rank, for furnishing men and materiel for the army. Standards for horses, weapons, and physical qualities for soldiers, to which recruiters were expected to adhere, were established by the central government. The positions in the provincial governments and state ministries were filled by candidates from this new mansabdar elite chosen by the court. Thus, although the nobles retained considerable power in their own regions, they owed their positions to the court and had no hope of political advancement if they did not get court preferment.

The Mughal Early Modern Economy

Mughal India had a vigorous trade and manufacturing economy, though, as with all agrarian-based societies, land issues and agriculture occupied the greatest part of the population. Unlike the societies of China, Japan, Korea, and Vietnam, which were influenced to a greater or lesser degree by Neo-Confucian ideas that regarded commerce as vaguely disreputable, Hindu, Muslim, Buddhist, and Jain traditions reserved an honored place for commerce and those who conducted it. Thus, Mughal economic interests routinely revolved around keeping the flow of goods moving around the empire, maintaining a vigorous import and export trade, and, as we have seen, safeguarding access to the Silk Road routes.

Agriculture and Rural Life   The basic administrative unit of rural India at the time of the Mughals was the *pargana*, a unit comprising an area usually containing a town and from a dozen to about 100 villages. It was in the pargana that the lowest levels of officialdom had met the network of clan and caste leaders of the villages under both the Hindu rajas and the Muslim sultans before the Timurids, and this pattern continued over the coming centuries. But because the earliest years of the Mughals were marked by conquest and plunder, and later by an administrative apparatus that contented itself with taxation and defense at the local level, life in the villages tended to go on much as it had before the conquest. Thus, the chief duties of the *zamindars*, as the local chiefs and headmen were called, were to channel the expansive and competitive energies among local clans, castes, and ethnic and religious groups into activities the Mughals considered productive. In border areas especially, this frequently involved clearing forests for farmland, harvesting tropical woods and products for market, and often driving off bands of foragers from the forests and hills.

Agricultural expansion went hand in hand with systematic integration of the rural and urban economies. One enormous obstacle facing the Mughals, which had faced previous regimes, was efficiency and equity in rural taxation. Grain and other agricultural commodities provided the bulk of Indian tax revenues, but vast differences in regional soil conditions, climate, and productivity made uniform tax rates extremely difficult to enforce. During Akbar's reign, therefore, massive surveys of local conditions were conducted to monitor harvests and grain prices over 10-year periods. These were then compiled into data tables used by local officials to calculate expected harvests and tax obligations. Imperial and local officials would sign agreements as to grain amounts to meet tax obligations over a set period. These obligations, like the Chinese "single-whip" system (see Chapter 21), would then be paid in silver or copper coin in four installments.

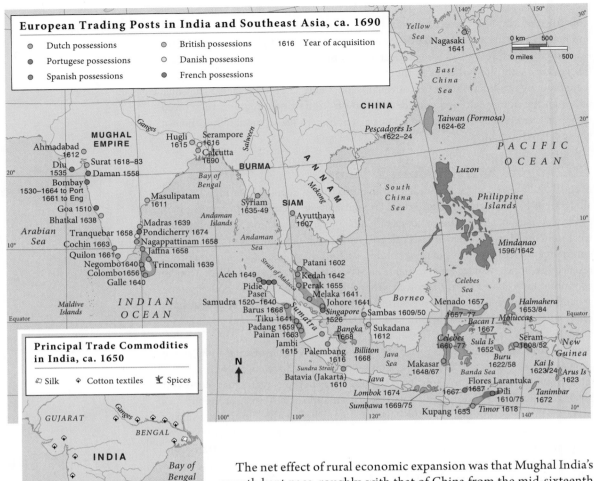

MAP 20.4 **European Trading Ports in India and Southeast Asia, ca. 1690.**

map analysis

The net effect of rural economic expansion was that Mughal India's growth kept pace, roughly, with that of China from the mid-sixteenth century to the beginning of the nineteenth. Expansion in Bengal and northeast India of wet rice cultivation and the introduction of American crops such as maize and potatoes in dryer areas allowed for a population increase from about 150 million in 1600 to 200 million in 1800. Moreover, acreage under cultivation increased by perhaps as much as one-third over this same period. Preferential tax rates on tobacco, indigo, sugarcane, cotton, pepper, ginger, and opium ensured that supplies of these coveted trade items would be secure. India began a burgeoning silk industry during this time as well. Thus, revenues more than doubled between Akbar's and Aurangzeb's reigns, to about 333.5 million rupees a year, while the increase in population meant that the per capita tax burden actually went down.

International Trade India had been the center of Indian Ocean trade for nearly two millennia before the rise of the Mughals, but the advent of the world trading systems being created by the Atlantic maritime states added a vastly expanded dimension to this commerce. The intense and growing competition among the English, Dutch, and French East India Companies meant that Indian commodities were now being shipped globally, while imports of American silver and food and cash crops were growing annually. By the mid-seventeenth century, the Dutch and English dominated maritime trade in Indian spices. Between 1621 and 1670, for example, Indian exports of pepper to Europe doubled to 13.5 million pounds. An often added bonus was Indian saltpeter, a vital component of gunpowder, used as ships' ballast (see Map 20.4).

Perhaps of even more long-term importance, however, was the growth of India's textile trade. Here, French access to Bengali silk contributed immensely to French leadership in European silk products, while Indian indigo supplied European needs for this dye until slave production of it in the Americas lowered its cost still further. Most momentous of all, though, was the rapid rise of Indian cotton exports. Lighter and more comfortable than wool or linen, Indian cotton *calicoes* (named for Indian port of Calicut) proved immensely popular for underwear and summer clothing. Indeed, the familiar term "pajamas" comes from the Hindi word *pajama*, the lightweight summer garments worn in India and popularized as sleepwear in Europe.

Society, Family, and Gender

Though the majority of the material in this chapter describes the activities of the Muslim Timurids in Indian history and society, it must be kept in mind that the vast majority of people in all areas of India were Hindus rather than Muslims. Thus, although the laws and customs of the areas controlled by the Mughals had a considerable effect on all members of Indian society, most of the everyday lives of Indians at the pargana, village, clan, and family levels went on much as it had before the arrival of the Mughals—or, for that matter, before the arrival of Islam.

Caste, Clan, and Village

As we saw in earlier chapters, the ties of family, clan, and caste were the most important for the majority of Indians (most of whom were Hindu), particularly in rural society, which comprised perhaps 90 percent of the subcontinent's population. Even after the reimposition of the tax on unbelievers by Aurangzeb and the restrictions on the building and rehabilitating of Hindu temples, Hindu life at the local level went on much as it had before. Indeed, many new converts to Islam retained their caste and clan affiliations, especially in areas in which caste affiliation was determined by language, village designation, or profession.

For rural Indian society, however, even in areas under Muslim control for centuries, religious and cultural tensions as well as local friction with central authority were present. Thus, during the reign of Akbar, whose tolerant rule eased tensions somewhat, clan archives are relatively quiet; in contrast, during Aurangzeb's long rule and periods of internal conflict, these same archives bristle with militia drives and petitions for redress of assorted grievances. In areas only marginally under Mughal control, clan councils offered resources for potential rebels.

Family and Gender

For the Indian elites outside the areas of Mughal control, family life of the higher castes went on largely as it had from the time of the Guptas. The "twice-born" Hindus of the brahman varna went through lengthy training and apprenticeship in the household of a trusted guru in preparation for their roles as religious and societal leaders through their various stages of life.

1630 Portuguese map of Asia

Jahangir's Influential Wife, the Former Persian Princess Nur Jahan, in Her Silk Gauze Inner-Court Dress.

image analysis

Women, who in the pursuit of dharma it was said are "worthy of worship," nevertheless spent most of their lives in seclusion. Whether among the highest castes or the lowest, their primary duties still included the running of the household and childrearing. Among the elites, where education in literature, poetry, and basic mathematics was also available to certain women, maintaining the household accounts, supervising servants, as well as education in the arts of living and loving as depicted in the *Kama Sutra* were also considered part of a wife's proper knowledge. In all cases, however, as in China, the "inner" world of the household and the "outer" world of business, politics, warfare, and so on were clearly defined by gender. In rural areas, the lives and work of peasant families, though generally guided by traditional gender roles, were more flexible in that large collective tasks such as planting and harvesting required the participation of both men and women.

The conquests of the Mughals brought with them a somewhat different temperament among their elites. The nomadic Turkic peoples of the Asian steppes, with their reliance on mobility and herding and organization around small groups of fiercely independent families and clans, had not developed the elaborate class, caste, and gender hierarchies of their settled neighbors. Women could, and often did, exercise a far greater degree of power and influence than even among the Hindu, Sikh, or Muslim elites in India.

Even after the conversion of these nomadic peoples to Islam, this tradition of female independence continued among the Timurids. As we saw earlier, for example, Babur's mother played a vital role in his rise to power, and emperors' wives, like Mumtaz Mahal, exercised a considerable degree of control in the imperial household. Moreover, since marriages played a vital role in cementing diplomatic and internal relations, women exercised a good deal of influence in terms of the extension of imperial power. Nur Jahan (d. 1645), the striking Persian princess married to Jahangir, played a leading role in court politics and in mediation during the succession wars at the end of Jahangir's reign. Indeed, Jahangir turned the running of the empire over to her on several occasions, stating that he felt quite secure with it in her capable hands.

As the Mughals assimilated local Muslim elites, the court quickly set up the harem as an institution of seclusion and protection for court women. Yet within the harem, women enjoyed considerable freedom, constructed their own hierarchies among the imperial wives and their attendants, and celebrated their own holidays and ceremonies largely insulated from the influence of men. It was in many respects a kind of alternative women's society, in which a distinct system of values was instilled in daughters and, crucially, women newly married into the household. For these women, navigating the harem's social relationships was of supreme importance, since the inner harmony of the court—and sometimes human lives—depended on it.

Science, Religion, and the Arts

While the advancement of science and technology in Mughal India did not match the pace set during the scientific revolution in western Europe, there were nonetheless several noteworthy developments in weaponry, mathematics, and astronomy. In terms of religion, as we have seen, the great theological differences between Hindus and Muslims persisted—and with the reign of Aurangzeb increased. Again, however, the tendency of Hinduism to assimilate other traditions and the relative compatibility of Islamic Sufi practices with other mystical traditions did sometimes decrease tensions. This, of course, was most dramatically seen with Akbar's efforts at bridging the religious gaps of his empire. Finally, one could say that where attempts at reconciling religions failed, language, literature, art, and architecture often succeeded and left a brilliant legacy of cultural synthesis.

Lahore fort, a masterpiece of Mughal architecture

Science and Technology

As they had done for centuries already, Muslim scholars in India drew on the rich scientific history of the subcontinent and merged it with their efforts at preserving, commenting on, and transmitting the ancient Greco-Roman and Persian achievements. Among the most important developments in this regard, as we have seen in other chapters, was the spreading of the Indian decimal number system and the use of zero as a placeholder in mathematical computations. This had already had a profound effect on the development of European science, which forever after referred to that system as "Arabic numerals." Among the developments that directly fostered the rise of Muslim empires, none was more important than the rapid development of gunpowder weapons.

New Directions in Firearms in the Gunpowder Empires   The spread of firearms from China and the shift in emphasis among weapons developers from rockets to tubular weapons firing projectiles is an extraordinarily complex subject and one littered with claims and counterclaims for the ultimate sources of particular innovations. We can say, however, that by the beginning of the sixteenth century, the armies of the major European kingdoms, Ming China, Ottoman Turkey, and Persia had all become accustomed to employing cannons and explosive charges for besieging fortresses, were developing more convenient and effective small arms for their infantries, and were beginning to employ lighter, more portable cannons as field guns for pitched battles. The use of these weapons became so pervasive and the changes that accompanied them so important that scholars often refer to the states of the Mughals, Persians, and Ottomans as the **gunpowder empires**.

Given the desire on the part of all armies to expand their firepower, it is not surprising that a gifted engineer, astronomer, and philosopher named Fathullah Shirazi (ca. 1580) came up with a design for a multibarreled gun—similar to one designed by Leonardo da Vinci—for Akbar's armies. In this case, 12–16 light cannons were mounted side by side on a gun carriage and fired by the operator in quick succession.

Gunpowder empires: Muslim-ruled empires of the Ottomans, Safavids, and Mughals that used cannons and small arms in their military campaigns, 1450–1750.

Mathematics and Astronomy   India's long history of mathematical innovation merged with Muslim work on astronomical observation to make impressive advances

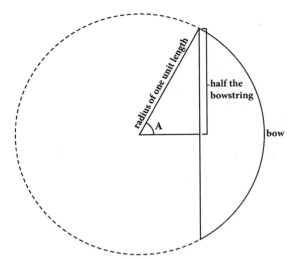

Origins of the Trigonometric Sine of an Angle as Described by Indian Mathematicians. Indian mathematicians did pioneering work in all of the areas of mathematics, particularly arithmetic and geometry. Hindu geometers knew of the trigonometric sine of an angle from at least the eighth century CE, if not earlier. In the early ninth century, the great Arabic mathematician al-Khwarizmi described the sine of an angle in his treatise on "Hindu" numbers, which was subsequently translated into Latin in the twelfth century. Through a series of mistranslations from one language to another, the original Sanskrit word for sine, *jya-ardha* ("half the bowstring"), ended up being rendered as "sinus" in Latin and other European languages—the modern sine.

in celestial calculation. A century before Akbar, Indian mathematicians had pushed their calculations of the value of pi to nine decimal places and expanded their facility with trigonometry to the point where some of the fundamental concepts of infinite series and calculus had been worked out.

Like other agrarian peoples reliant on an accurate calendar for the yearly agricultural and ceremonial cycle, Mughal rulers had a vital interest in knowing when unusual celestial phenomena such as comets, eclipses, and meteor showers were due and in having explanations for them ready at hand. Using extremely fine calculations and careful observation, the astronomers of the Kerala school, active from the fourteenth to the sixteenth centuries, had calculated elliptical orbits for the visible planets a century in advance of Johannes Kepler and suggested systems of planetary orbits similar to those of both Tycho Brahe and Copernicus (Chapter 17).

Religion: In Search of Balance

As scholars have often noted, Indian Islam went through relatively open, inclusive, and Sufi-oriented cycles—most notably in this chapter during the reigns of Babur, Humayun, and Akbar—and phases in which a more rigorous attention to orthodox Sunni practices and the desire to connect with Muslim communities beyond India prevailed, such as during the reigns of Jahangir, Shah Jahan, and especially Aurangzeb. These periods, as we have already seen, had a profound effect on the relations of minority Muslim rulers with non-Muslim subjects. But they also played an important role in mandating which forms of Islam would be most influential in Mughal India and the relations of the Mughals with the Muslims of other regions.

The Position of Non-Muslims in Mughal India   As we have seen in earlier chapters, despite profound theological differences between the monotheism of Islam and the profuse polytheism of popular Hindu religious traditions, there was a degree of attraction between the adherents of the two religions. As was the case with mystical and devotional sects of both, they saw a commonality in their ways of encountering the profound mysteries of faith. Thus, Akbar's grounding in Islamic Sufi mysticism made him interested in, and receptive to, Hindu mystical traditions. For their part, in addition to the mystical elements of Islam—in any case accessible only to a relative few—far more Hindus of the lower castes were attracted to the equality before God of all Islamic believers. Thus, like Buddhism before it, Islam promised emancipation from the restrictions of the caste system and a shared brotherhood of believers without regard for ethnicity, race, job, or social position.

More generally, however, the religious divisions remained difficult to reconcile. From the time of the first occupation of territories by Muslim armies in the seventh century, nonbelievers had been granted the legal status of protected peoples (Chapter 10). That is, they were allowed to worship as they pleased and govern according to their own religious laws. There were also inducements and penalties aimed at conversion to Islam. Unbelievers were subject to the *jizya* and pilgrimage taxes, and they suffered job discrimination in official circles, all of which disappeared once they converted. For their part, Hindus considered Muslims to be ritually un-clean (*mlecchha*), and upper-caste members underwent elaborate purification rites after coming into contact with them.

Yet the presence of a vastly larger Hindu population also meant that considerable accommodation had to be made by the rulers in order to run the empire effectively and even more to maintain order at the local level. Akbar, as we noted earlier, banned the discriminatory taxes on unbelievers. In addition, the financial skills of Hindus and Jains were increasingly sought by the court, and their status rose further when Akbar made a Hindu his finance minister and employed Hindu court astrologers. Perhaps of even more symbolic and political importance was the habit of Mughal rulers of occasionally marrying Hindu women.

The position of Christians was similar. They, along with Jews, were considered "people of the Book" and therefore protected but still subject to the same taxes and impediments before the reign of Akbar. While the position of Christian mis-sionaries in Mughal lands was often precarious, the reverence with which Mus-lims regarded the biblical prophets and Jesus also helped to smooth diplomatic relations at court. Akbar invited Jesuits to his debates, and paintings of Christian religious figures, especially the Virgin Mary, can be found in Mughal depictions of court life.

Mughal painting showing the crucifixion and the Virgin Mary (1600)

Yet this period of relative religious openness peaked with Akbar, and the pen-dulum soon began to swing back with increasing speed. Mughal receptiveness of Islamic mysticism and other religions, as most dramatically displayed by Akbar's new *din-i ilahi* religion, offended more orthodox Sunni Muslims. Their influence was felt at court during the reign of Jahangir and especially during that of Shah Jahan, who merged love and piety in the form of the Taj Mahal. It reached its zenith during Aurangzeb's reign. As Mughal lands stretched to their greatest extent, the austere Aurangzeb reimposed the taxes on unbelievers and purged many Hindus from his court.

Islamic Developments   While the vast majority of India's Muslims remained adherents of the Sunni branch of Islam and Hanafi school of interpretation of Islamic law, there were also several noteworthy developments in other areas. First, as we have noted several times already, there was an influential Shiite presence in India. For centuries, Shiites had migrated into Hindu areas of southern India, where, despite being a notable minority, they generally escaped the discrimination at the hands of Sunnis characteristic of the north. In addition, Mughal relations with Safavid Persia, where Shia Islam was the official state religion, meant a certain influ-ence on the Mughal court was unavoidable. Hence, Akbar studied mystical elements of Shiism, while Jahangir married the Safavid princess Nur Jahan, probably the most powerful woman of the Mughal period.

Literature and Art

The Mughal period was one of India's most prolific in terms of its profusion of literary genres. Moreover, literature, art, and architecture were the areas in which India's rich multicultural environment produced its most arrestingly synthetic works. In translation projects, classical Persian works, poetry in nearly all of India's languages, and even treatises on law and theology, Indian writers borrowed freely and frequently from each other. In painting, realistic portraits of personages and dramatic contemporary and historical scenes were recorded; and of course the great buildings of the era remain for many the "authentic" symbols of India.

New Literary Directions   As they had been for centuries in Islamic India, Arabic and Persian remained the principal literary languages. The use of both, however, was considerably enlivened by the introduction of the latest wave of Turkic terms by the Chagatai–Turkic Mughals. Chagatai itself remained in use among the elites until the nineteenth century, while many of its loan words, along with a considerable Persian and Arabic vocabulary, were grafted onto the base of Sanskrit to form the modern languages of Hindi and Urdu. Regional languages, such as Kashmiri and Bengali, also rose to prominence for both literary and general use.

Ironically, one of the catalysts for the explosion of literary work from the mid-sixteenth to the mid-seventeenth centuries came from the Mughals's most humiliating period. The exile of Humayun to Persia in the 1540s coincided with the Persian Shah Tahmasp embarking on a program of self-denial and abstinence in response to criticism about the worldliness of his court. Writers, painters, and poets who suddenly found themselves out of favor at the Persian court attached themselves to Humayun. They followed him to India, where their talents enlivened the arts already developing there. Their classical Arab and Persian verse forms were ultimately adopted into Urdu. By the following century, these forms had matured with the verses of Qudsi and Abu Talib Kalim (d. 1602), whose verses were considered models of adept compression of emotion.

Though Sunni scholarship languished somewhat under Akbar, Sufi works proliferated, many borrowing concepts and terminology from non-Islamic sources. The most famous of these was Muhammad Ghauth Gwaliori's *The Five Jewels*, which tapped sources from Hindu and Muslim astrology and Jewish Kabbala traditions, as well as Sufi mysticism. By Aurangzeb's reign, the pendulum had swung back to the more Mecca-centered, prophetic, and exclusive strain in Indian Islam. Thus, the works tended to be more often treatises on Islamic law, interpretation of *hadith*—the traditions of the Prophet—and Sunni works on theology.

Art and Painting   One of the more interesting aspects of Islam as practiced by the Mughals—as well as the Safavid Persians and Ottomans—is that the injunctions against depicting human beings in art were often widely ignored in the inner chambers and private rooms of the court. Of course, during Aurangzeb's long reign, there was a marked drop in artistic output because of his much stricter interpretation of proper Islamic behavior.

Not surprisingly, Akbar had a direct hand in the creation of what is considered to be the first painting in the "Mughal style"—a combination of the extreme delicacy of Persian miniature work with the vibrant colors and taste for bold themes of Hindu painters. Akbar inherited two of the master painters who accompanied Humayun from Persia, and the contact they acquired with Hindu works under Akbar's patronage resulted in hundreds of Mughal **gouache** works,

Gouache: Watercolors with a gum base.

including the colossal illustrated *Hamzanama* of 1570. The Persian tradition of miniature painting flourished under the Mughals. Illustrations of Muslim and Hindu religious themes and epics were perennial favorites, as were numerous depictions of imperial *durbars*—receptions requiring noble attendance at court. These usually included authentic portraits of key individuals and provide scholars with important clues as to the identities of courtiers and dignitaries. Mughal artists often passed their skills on within their families over generations and represented an important subset of members at the imperial court and among the entourages of regional elites.

By the end of the sixteenth century, a new influence was beginning to affect Mughal art: Europeans. The realistic approach of European artists and their use of perspective began to be felt at the courts of Akbar and Jahangir. One prominent female artist, Nadira Banu, specialized in producing Flemish-style works. Some took European paintings and added Mughal touches—flatter backgrounds, gold leaf, and mosques in the distance. The period of Akbar's religious experiments also prompted an unparalleled interest among Mughal painters in Christian religious figures. Depictions of Christ from the gospels and from Muslim tales were popular fare, as were angels; even more so was the figure of the Virgin, a picture of whom even appears in a portrait of Jahangir. It was perhaps the most dramatic meeting of cultural influences since the era of the Gandharan Buddhas that were fashioned in the style of the Greek god Apollo.

The *Hamzanama* (Book of Hamza). Akbar so enjoyed the *Hamzanama*, a heroic romance about the legendary adventures of the Prophet Mohammad's uncle Amir Hamza, that he commissioned an illustrated version in 1562. This painting from Akbar's version shows the prophet Elijah rescuing Hamza's nephew Prince Nur ad-Dahr.

Architecture   Nowhere was the Mughal style more in evidence than in the construction of tombs and mausoleums. The most prominent of these, the Taj Mahal, was introduced in the opening to this chapter and needs little additional discussion. The ethereal lightness of so colossal a construction and the perfection of its layout make it the most distinctive construction of its kind. Europeans sometimes assumed that its architects were influenced by French or Italian artistic trends, though this remains a subject of debate. The chief architect, Ustad Ahmad Lahori (d. 1649), also designed the famous Red Fort of Shah Jahan's city, Shahjahanabad. During the high point of Mughal wealth and power, several Mughal emperors built entire cities. By far the most famous of these, as we have previously seen, was Akbar's Fatehpur Sikri. Not to be outdone, of course, Shah Jahan created his own city complex at Delhi, Shahjahanabad.

As one would expect, just as they were integral to the tomb complexes of the Mughals, mosques would be among the empire's most important constructions. Many were built as shrines at holy sites or to mark significant events in the lives of holy men or martyrs. Once again, a distinctive style emerged in which the basic form of the dome symbolically covering the world and the slender arrow of the minaret pointing heavenward interacted with central Asian, Persian, and even Hindu architectural influences. The largest Mughal mosques, like the Friday Delhi Mosque (Jama Masjid) in Shahjahanabad and Aurangzeb's huge Badshahi Mosque in Lahore, contain immense courtyards, surrounded by cloisters leading to small rooms for intimate gatherings, domed areas for men and women, and distinctive minarets with fluted columns and bell-shaped roofs. One mosque in Burhanpur built by Shah Jahan even has Sanskrit translations of Quranic verses in it. As scholars have noted, the location of many of the largest mosques, like those of some European cathedrals, is adjacent to government buildings and forts in order to demonstrate the seamless connections of these religious civilizations.

interactive concept
map

❯ Putting It All Together

The rise of the Turkic central Asian peoples to prominence and power, from the borders of successive Chinese dynasties to Anatolia and the domains of the Ottomans, and with the Timurids or Mughals in India, is one of the most dramatic sagas of world history. In India, this latest group of outside conquerors faced what might be called the "great question" of the subcontinent: how to create a viable state out of so many long-standing religious traditions, many of which are in direct opposition to each other. Even before the coming of Islam, rulers such as Ashoka felt the need to use transcendent concepts, such as dharma, to try to bridge cultural and religious gaps. The Guptas, for their part, tried to use state-supported Hinduism. With the arrival of Islam, a new religion that stood in opposition to the older Hindu pattern of assimilation of gods and favored instead the conquest and conversion of opponents, a divide was created, which persists to this day. It should be remembered that, as recent scholarship has shown, even within these dramatically opposed religious traditions, much more accommodation than previously supposed took place. The later development of Sikhism, as another attempt at a syncretic bridge across India's religious divide, both added to attempts at greater tolerance and at times contributed to religious tensions.

Against this backdrop the accomplishments of the Mughals must be weighed as significant in terms of statecraft and artistic and cultural achievement, and perhaps less so in religious areas. At its height, Mughal India was the most populous, wealthy, politically powerful, and economically vibrant empire in the world next to China. It thus allowed the Mughal rulers unprecedented wealth and financed the proliferation of monumental architecture that became forever identified with India: the Red Fort, Fatehpur Sikri, and, above all, the Taj Mahal.

Yet, for all its wealth and power, the Mughal dynasty was plagued by problems that ultimately proved insoluble. The old nomadic succession practices of the Timurids repeatedly led to palace revolts by potential heirs. These wars in turn encouraged conflict with internal and external enemies who sensed weakness at the core of the regime. Protracted conflicts in Afghanistan, with Safavid Persia, and in Bengal also bled this centralized state of resources. Finally, the Maratha wars slowly wore down even the semblance of unity among the rulers following Aurangzeb.

But perhaps an equally important factor in the ultimate dissolution of the empire was that of Hindu–Muslim syncretism. Here, we have two of the world's great religions interacting with each other in prolonged and profound ways, with the added complication of Muslim rulers and Muslims in general being a minority among the subcontinent's people. Despite the flexibility of the early rulers in trying to deemphasize the more oppressive elements of Islamic rule in Hindu India—most dramatically, Akbar through his effort to create an entirely new religion—the attempt at a stricter orthodoxy under Aurangzeb hardened Hindu–Muslim and Sikh divisions for centuries to come.

Throughout the period, one other factor loomed larger day by day as the dynasty went into decline. The well-financed and well-armed trading companies of the Europeans, increasingly adept at reading Indian politics, gradually moved into positions of regional power. By 1750, they were on the cusp of changing the political situation completely. Indeed, the seeds that had been planted by 1750 would soon be reaped as the first great clash of mature religious civilizations with the new industrially based societies. By 1920, all of these religious civilizations would be gone.

Review and Relate

Thinking Through Patterns

Examine the ways historians approach the big questions of this chapter.

The weaknesses are probably more obvious than the strengths at first glance. Two things are immediately apparent: first, the position of the Mughals as an ethnic and religious minority ruling a vastly larger majority population and, second, the conflict-prone succession practices of the older central Asian Turkic leaders. The minority position of the Mughals aggravated long-existing tensions between Hindu subjects and Muslim rulers in India, of which the Mughals were to be the last line. In an age of religious civilizations, where some kind of unity of religion was the ideal, this put considerable strains on the Mughals as rulers—as it did the Ottomans in predominantly Christian lands and Catholics and Protestants in Europe. Central Asian Turkic succession practices almost always guaranteed conflict when it was time for a new ruler to accede the throne. Nearly every Mughal successor during this period ended up having to fight factions and family to gain the empire.

> **What were the strengths and weaknesses of Mughal rule?**

In some respects the strengths of Mughal rule developed in reaction to these problems. Babur and Akbar, in particular, were extraordinarily tolerant rulers in terms of religion. When later rulers like Aurangzeb returned to strict Sunni Islamic policies, it prompted resistance, especially among Hindus. Also, while Mughal rulers were never able to completely free themselves from succession struggles, they succeeded in setting up a well-run fiscal–military state with the mansabdar system, largely undercutting old local and regional loyalties and tying the new loyalty to the state. Like France, the Ottomans, and the Confucian states of eastern Asia, the development of bureaucratic forms was an important earmark of the early modern era.

> **What was the Mughal policy toward religious accommodation? How did it change over time?**

As we noted, Mughal rulers faced the problem confronted by nearly all "religious civilizations": Religious orthodoxy was seen, in theory, as a vital element of loyalty to the state. But for the Mughals, as for previous Muslim rulers in India, the desire for strict adherence to Muslim law was always tempered by the problem of Islam being a minority religion in India. Here, as we saw, the early Mughal rulers—Babur, Humayun, Akbar—were far less tied to strict Sunni Islam than their successors. Thus, their way of ruling was to uphold Sunni Islam as the approved state religion but to scrupulously refrain from forcing Muslim practices on other religious groups. Akbar went so far as to create a new religion and held Thursday-night discussions with leaders of other religions to find ways to satisfy the desires of all. With Shah Jahan, however, the reaction building among reform-minded Sunni Muslims to this liberalization turned into enforcing more strict practices, which peaked during the long reign of Aurangzeb. By the end of Aurangzeb's reign the Sikhs were near revolt and the long Hindu Maratha revolt was in full swing. But even during this period, local religious customs remained largely intact and, indeed, often thrived.

> **What factors account for the Mughal decline during the eighteenth century?**

At the beginning and for much of the eighteenth century, Mughal India was the second richest and most prosperous empire in the world, after China. But by 1750 it was already in pronounced decline. A large part of this was due to rebellions by the Sikhs, Rajputs, and especially the Marathas that raged off and on through the century. By the 1750s as well, the European trading companies with their small but well-trained armies were becoming locally powerful. Here, the great milestone would take place during the Seven Years' War (1756–1763), when the British East India Company eliminated its French competitors and in essence took over the rule of Bengal from its headquarters in Calcutta. Within 100 years it would take over all of India.

Against the Grain

Consider this as a counterpoint to the main patterns examined in this chapter.

Sikhism in Transition

• Why would both Hindus and Muslims express hostility toward a religion that claims to want to transcend the differences between them? Did the Sikhs appear to have any alternatives to becoming a fighting faith in order to ensure their survival?

As we saw in Chapter 13, the example of Zen Buddhism affords an example of a pacifistic religious tradition that was taken up by warrior classes. In some respects, Sikhism underwent a similar transformation, though not as thoroughgoing as that of Zen, and one that took place for very different reasons. As we remember from Chapter 12, the Sikhs had started from an avowedly peaceful premise: that the tension, and even all-out warfare, between Hindus and Muslims must somehow be transcended. Influenced by poets and mystics like Kabir and Guru Nanak, and drawing upon the emotional connections experienced by Muslim Sufis and Hindu Bhakti devotees who proclaimed that "there is no Hindu; there is no Musselman [Muslim]," the Sikhs had emerged during the sixteenth century as an entirely new religious movement.

Yet, far from providing a model for the two contending religions to emulate, Sikhs were viewed with suspicion by both. Although they attracted enough of a following to remain vital to the present day, their attempts at transcendence were viewed in much the same light as Akbar's attempts at a new religious synthesis were. Though they were awarded the city of Amritsar, the Golden Temple of which became their religious center, Mughal repression of the Sikhs under Aurangzeb in the seventeenth century provoked a prolonged rebellion, which turned them into a fierce fighting faith in self-defense. The Sikhs established control of most of the Punjab region during the eighteenth-century decline of the Mughals. During the days of British rule, the reputation of the Sikhs as fierce fighters prompted the British to employ them as colonial troops and policemen throughout their empire. Even after independence, smoldering disputes between the government and Sikhs urging local autonomy for Punjab led to the assassination of Indian Prime Minister Indira Gandhi in retaliation for a government operation to forcibly remove a Sikh splinter group from the Golden Temple in 1984.

- Why does it seem that, on the whole, what we have termed "religious civilizations" have difficulty tolerating different religious traditions within their domains? Does loyalty to a state require loyalty to its approved religion(s) as well? Why?

Key Terms

Allegory   593
Gouache   614
Gunpowder empires   611
Institutionalization   597

audio flashcards

For additional resources, please go to
www.oup.com/us/vonsivers.
Please see the Further Resources section at the back of the book for additional readings and suggested websites.

📄 Sources for Chapter 20

SOURCE 20.1	Babur, *The Baburnama*

ca. 1528

Zahiruddin Muhammad Babur (1483–1530) was born a prince of Fergana in Transoxiana (modern Uzbekistan and Tajikistan), a region that had been conquered (briefly) by the army of Alexander the Great in the 320s BCE and more recently by Babur's ancestor Timur-i Lang, or Tamerlane (r. 1370–1405). Driven from his homeland, Babur conquered neighboring kingdoms and moved south into Afghanistan, capturing Kabul in 1504. By 1519, he stepped up his raids into northern India, and his highly mobile, if vastly outnumbered, army defeated Sultan Ibrahim Lodi at Panipat in 1526. Victory at Panipat was followed by the conquest of the Lodi capital of Agra and further defeats of Hindu leaders in northern India. Babur's dynasty would become known as the Mughals (from "Mongols"), but his legacy can also be gauged from the success of his memoirs, the *Baburnama*. Composed and reworked throughout his life, the *Baburnama* is the first true autobiography in Islamic literature, and it can be read for insights into his own character as well as the military tactics he employed on the battlefield.

On Wednesday afternoon the twenty-eighth of Rajab [May 10], I entered Agra and camped in Sultan Ibrahim's quarters.

From the year 910 [1504–05], when Kabul was conquered, until this date I had craved Hindustan. Sometimes because my **begs** had poor opinions, and sometimes because my brothers lacked cooperation, the Hindustan campaign had not been possible and the realm had not been conquered. Finally all such impediments had been removed. None of my little begs and officers were able any longer to speak out in opposition to my purpose. In 925 [1519] we led the army and took Bajaur by force in two or three **gharis**, massacred the people, and came to Bhera. The people of Bhera paid ransom to keep their property from being plundered and pillaged, and we took four hundred thousand shahrukhis worth of cash and goods, distributed it to the army according to the number of liege men, and returned to Kabul.

Begs: Subordinate rulers.

Ghari: Measure of time, about 24 minutes.

Source: *The Baburnama: Memoirs of Babur, Prince and Emperor*, trans. and ed. Wheeler M. Thackston (New York: Oxford University Press, 1996), 328–329, 330, 331.

From that date until 932 [1525–26], we led the army to Hindustan five times within seven or eight years. The fifth time, God through his great grace vanquished and reduced a foe like Sultan Ibrahim and made possible for us a realm like Hindustan. From the time of the Apostle until this date only three padishahs gained dominion over and ruled the realm of Hindustan. The first was Sultan Mahmud Ghazi, who, with his sons, occupied the throne of Hindustan for a long time. The second was Sultan Shihabuddin Ghuri and his slaves and followers, who ruled this kingdom for many years. I am the third. My accomplishment, however, is beyond comparison with theirs, for when Sultan Mahmud subdued Hindustan, the throne of Khurasan was under his control, the rulers of Khwarazm and the marches were obedient to him, and the padishah of Samarkand was his underling. If his army was not two hundred thousand strong, it must have been at least one hundred thousand. Moreover, his opponents were rajahs. There was not a single padishah in all of Hindustan. Every rajah ruled independently in a different region.

. . .

Hindustan is a vast and populous kingdom and a productive realm. To the east and south, in fact to the west too, it ends at the ocean. To the north is a mountain range that connects the mountains of the Hindu Kush, Kafiristan, and Kashmir. To the northwest are Kabul, Ghazni, and Kandahar. The capital of all Hindustan is Delhi. After Sultan Shihabuddin Ghuri's reign until the end of Sultan Firozshah's, most of Hindustan was under the control of the Delhi sultans. Up to the time that I conquered Hindustan, five Muslim padishahs and two infidels had ruled there. Although the mountains and jungles are held by many petty rays and rajahs, the important and independent rulers were the following five.

. . .

Of the infidels, the greater in domain and army is the rajah of Vijayanagar. The other is Rana Sanga, who had recently grown so great by his audacity and sword. His original province was Chitor. When the sultans of Mandu grew weak, he seized many provinces belonging to Mandu, such as Ranthambhor, Sarangpur, Bhilsan, and Chanderi. Chanderi had been in the ***daru'l-harb*** for some years and held by Sanga's highest-ranking officer, Medini Rao, with four or five thousand infidels, but in 934 [1528], through the grace of God, I took it by force within a ghari or two, massacred the infidels, and brought it into the bosom of Islam, as will be mentioned.

All around Hindustan are many rays and rajahs. Some are obedient to Islam, while others, because they are so far away and their places impregnable, do not render obedience to Muslim rulers.

Daru'l-harb: "Abode of war," Islamic term for non-Islamicized countries.

> » Working with Sources

1. **Why was it important for Babur to display his knowledge of the history and geography of Hindustan?**

2. **Was he driven by a "crusading" goal to liberate Hindustan from control by the "infidels" and convert its inhabitants to Islam?**

| SOURCE 20.2 | # Muhammad Dara Shikuh, *The Mingling of Two Oceans* |

ca. 1650s

The eldest son of Shah Jahan, the fifth Mughal emperor, Dara Shikuh was defeated by his younger brother in a struggle for power in 1658. The victorious brother, Muhiuddin, ruled as the Emperor Aurangzeb, and he had Dara declared, by a court of nobles and clergy, an apostate from Islam and assassinated in 1659. Dara left behind a remarkable series of writings, advocating an enlightened program of harmonizing the various, bitterly opposed religions of the subcontinent. He had developed friendships with Sikhs, followed a Persian mystic, and completed a translation of 50 Upanishads from their original Sanskrit into Persian in 1657. His most famous work, the *Majma-ul-Bahrain* (*The Mingling of Two Oceans*), addressed the overlapping ideas of Hindu and Muslim mysticism. His attempt to combine the traditions into a coherent whole may have been rejected by his fervently Muslim brother, but he also represents a strain of ecumenical thought within the Mughal Empire.

X. Discourse on the Vision of God (*Rūyat*).

The Indian monotheists call the Vision of God, *Sāchātkār*, that is, to see God with the (ordinary) eyes of the forehead. Know that the Vision of God, either by the Prophets, may peace be on them, or by the perfect divines, may their souls be sanctified, whether in this or the next world and whether with the outer or the inner eyes, cannot be doubted or disputed; and the "men of the Book" (*ahl-i-kitāb*), the perfect divines and the seers of all religions—whether they are believers in the Kur'ān, the Vedas, the Book of David or the Old and the New Testaments—have a (common) faith in this respect. Now, one who disbelieves the beholding of God is a thoughtless and sightless member of his community, the reason being: if the Holy Self is Omnipotent, how can He not have the potency to manifest himself? This matter has been explained very clearly by the 'Ulamā of the Sunnī Sect. But, if it is said, that (even) the Pure Self (*dhāt-i-baht*) can be beheld, it is an impossibility; for the Pure Self is elegant and undetermined, and, as He cannot be determined, He is manifest in the veil of elegance only, and as such cannot be beheld, and such beholding is an impossibility. And the suggestion that He can be beheld in the next and not in this world, is groundless, for if He is Omnipotent, He is potent to manifest Himself in any manner, anywhere and at any time He likes. (I hold) that one who cannot behold Him here (i.e., in this world) will hardly behold Him there (i.e. in the next world); as He has said in the Holy verse: "And whoever is blind in this, he shall (also) be blind in the hereafter" [Qur'an 17:72].

The *Mu'tazila* and the *Shī'a* doctors, who are opposed to *rūyat* (Beholding), have committed a great blunder in this matter, for had they only denied the capability of beholding the Pure Self, there would have been some justification, but their denial of all forms of *rūyat* is a great mistake; the reason being

Source: Muhammad Dara Shikuh, *The Mingling of Two Oceans*, trans. and ed. M. Mafuz ul-Haq (Calcutta: Asiatic Society of Bengal, 1929), 50–53.

that most of the Prophets and perfect divines have beheld God with their ordinary eyes and have heard His Holy words without any intermediary and,
now, when they are, by all means, capable of hearing the words of God, why
should they not be capable of beholding Him? Verily, they must be so; and, just
as it is obligatory to have faith in God, the Angels, the (revealed) Books, the
Prophets, the Destiny, the Good and the Evil, and the Holy Places, etc., so it is
obligatory and incumbent to have faith in *rūyat*.

. . .

Now, the beholding of God is of five kinds: first, in dream with the eyes
of heart; secondly, beholding Him with the ordinary eyes; thirdly, beholding
Him in an intermediate state of sleep and wakefulness, which is a special kind
of Selflessness; fourthly, (beholding Him) in (a stage of) special determination; fifthly, beholding the One Self in the multitudinous determinations of
the internal and external worlds. In such a way beheld our Prophet, may peace
be on him, whose "self" had disappeared from the midst and the beholder
and the beheld had merged in one and his sleep, wakefulness and selflessness
looked as one and his internal and the external eyes had become one unified
whole—such is the state of perfect *rūyat*, which is not confined either to this or
the next world and is possible everywhere and at every period.

XI. Discourse on the Names of God, the Most High (*Asmāi Allāh Taʿālā*).

Know that the names of God, the Most High, are numberless and beyond comprehension. In the language of the Indian divines, the Absolute, the Pure, the
Hidden of the hidden and the Necessary Self is known as *asan, tirgun, nirankār,
niranjan, sat* and *chit*. If knowledge is attributed to Him, the Indian divines des-
ignate Him as *chitan*, while the Muslims call Him *ʿAlīm* (Knowing).

≫ **Working with Sources**

1. **To what extent, and in what specific ways, did Dara Shikuh represent an ecumenical spirit with respect to Islam and other religions?**

2. **How does Dara Shikuh anticipate and address the objections of others within the Muslim community?**

SOURCE 20.3 # Edicts of Aurangzeb

1666–1679

When he became emperor in 1658, Aurangzeb attempted a radical
"Islamification" of Mughal India, imposing a strict interpretation of
Sharia law and implementing reforms that he thought would benefit Muslims
more than adherents of other religions. Repudiating his great-grandfather
Akbar's vision of religious transcendence and harmony but stopping short of
forcible conversion, Aurangzeb offered incentives to non-Muslims to convert,

Source: http://www.aurangzeb.info/2008/06/exhibit-no_7171.html.

destroyed many of their temples, and reimposed the hated *jizya* tax. This tax on Hindus had been abolished by Akbar in 1564, and its reinstatement by Aurangzeb in 1679 triggered mass protests and violent reactions from authorities in many cities. Revolts among Sikhs and among Hindus left the Mughal Empire weakened and in decline by the time of Aurangzeb's death in 1707. An excerpt from his proscriptions is offered below.

Exhibit No. 6: Keshava Rai Temple. "Even to look at a temple is a sin for a Musalman," Aurangzeb. Umurat-i-Hazur Kishwar-Kashai Julus (R.Yr.) 9, Rabi II 24 / 13 October 1666.

'It was reported to the Emperor (Aurangzeb) that in the temple of Keshava Rai at Mathura, there is a stone railing presented by Bishukoh (one without dignity i.e. Prince Dara, Aurangzeb's elder brother). On hearing of it, the Emperor observed, "In the religion of the Musalmans it is improper even to look at a temple and this Bishukoh has installed this kathra (barrier railing). Such an act is totally unbecoming of a Musalman. This railing should be removed (forthwith)." His Majesty ordered Abdun Nabi Khan to go and remove the kathra, which is in the middle of the temple. The Khan went and removed it. After doing it he had audience. He informed that the idol of Keshava Rai is in the inner chamber. The railing presented by Dara was in front of the chamber and, formerly, it was of wood. Inside the kathra used to stand the sevakas of the shrine (pujaris etc.) and outside it stood the people (khalq)'.

Exhibit No. 7: Demolition of Kalka's Temple - I. Siyah Waqa'i- Darbar Regnal Year 10, Rabi I, 23 / 3 September 1667.

'The asylum of Shariat (Shariat Panah) Qazi Abdul Muqaram has sent this arzi to the sublime Court: a man known to him told him that the Hindus gather in large numbers at Kalka's temple near Barahapule (near Delhi); a large crowd of the Hindus is seen here. Likewise, large crowds are seen at (the mazars) of Khwaja Muinuddin, Shah Madar and Salar Masud Ghazi. This amounts to bid'at (heresy) and deserves consideration. Whatever orders are required should be issued.

Saiyid Faulad Khan was thereupon ordered (by the Emperor) to send one hundred beldars to demolish the Kalka temple and other temples in its neighbourhood which were in the Faujdari of the Khan himself; these men were to reach there post haste, and finish the work without a halt'.

Exhibit No. 8: Demolition of Kalka Temple II. Siyah Akhbarat-i-Darbar-i-Mu'alla Julus 10, Rabi II 3 / 12 September 1667.

'Saiyad Faulad Khan reported that in compliance with the orders, beldars were sent to demolish the Kalka temple which task they have done. During the course of the demolition, a Brahmin drew out a sword, killed a bystander and then turned back and attacked the Saiyad also. The Brahmin was arrested'.

Exhibit No. 16: Reimposition of Jizyah by Aurangzeb. (2nd April 1679)

'As all the aims of the religious Emperor were directed to the spreading of the law of Islam and the overthrow of the practices of the infidels, he issued orders to the high diwani officers that from Wednesday, the 2nd April 1679 / 1st Rabi I, in obedience to the Quranic injunction, "till they pay commutation money (Jizyah) with the hand in humility," and in agreement with the canonical tradition, Jizyah should be collected from the infidels (zimmis) of the capital and the provinces. Many of the honest scholars of the time were appointed to discharge the work (of collecting Jizyah). May God actuate him (Emperor Aurangzeb) to do that which He loves and is pleased with, and make his future life better than the present'.

» **Working with Sources**

1. **How did the legacy of Akbar's and Dara's ecumenism influence Aurangzeb's policies?**

2. **What was the stated purpose of the reimposition of financial penalties on non-Muslims? Was this policy likely to have the effect he intended?**

SOURCE 20.4

Muhammad Ghawth Gwaliori, *The Five Jewels*

ca. 1526

In sixteenth-century Hindustan, the Sufi mystic Muhammad Ghawth Gwaliori claimed to have experienced an astounding ascension through multiple heavenly spheres up to the throne of God. This intensely personal experience, which he underwent in his 20s, occurred within a volatile political and social context. Born around 1501, Ghawth left home at age 12 to further his religious education and to undertake a series of mystic initiations that prepared him for his ascension in 1526. Ghawth lived during the rule of Humayun, when Mughal control was still tentative, and Akbar was still a young man. After his mystical experiences made him famous, Ghawth was seen as a spiritual support for the Mughal regime. When Humayun fell from power in 1540, Ghawth was persecuted by a group of Afghan warlords who followed a more orthodox form of Islam and attacked the reality—as well as the political implications—of his mystical experiences.

We reached the limit of the fourth heavenly sphere; the sphere split open; the stars waned like glowing crescents. I passed up into the heaven. The spirits of all the prophets came forward to greet me. They all shook my hand joyfully, along with the angels of that sphere. They praised me and their faces lit up, saying, "We have been waiting for so long, asking the Lord when you would

Source: Excerpts from Scott A. Kugle, "Heaven's Witness: The Uses and Abuses of Muhammad Ghawth's Mystical Ascension," *Journal of Islamic Studies*, 14 (2003): 17–20.

be passing by this way. On the day that the Prophet ascended along this route, there were with him some saints, and you were one of them. However, at that time, you were in the form of pure spirit. In contrast, this time you are fully attached to your body! This is a completely new and different spectacle." They stood around amazed at my appearance. I ascended with 'Alī and Abū Bakr, until we neared the limit of the fifth heavenly sphere.

. . .

The fourth heaven split open; the stars flared up, blazing brightly. I ascended into the fifth heavenly sphere. Such wondrous and strange things came into sight while all the angels of that sphere came forward into my presence. They carried in their hands pages, like those of a book. I asked, "What are these pages?" They answered, "These are the registers of Might which will consume the people consigned to the flames. They haven't been displayed yet or made public, but they record all the people's deeds." I asked, "Where are the people of the flames?" They invited me to come this way in order to see. When I came forward, I saw a chamber formed from the purest substance of Divine wrath. In it, there were many beings sitting, all in the shape of women. One woman among them was explaining clearly the meaning of Divine unity [*tawhīd*]. I asked, "Who is that woman who is teaching so eloquently?" They answered, "That is the mother of all humankind, Eve!"

I rushed forward to greet her and pay my respects, and asked her, "Why have you, a true Muslim, appeared in the midst of all the people who are overcome by Divine wrath?" Eve replied, "We are the most comprehensive, most perfect and most beautiful of all the manifestations of the Divine. We are called 'the People of Divine Might' who are the manifestation of Allah's attribute of utter singularity." I requested Eve to explain this to me further; she said, "The authority of Allah's beauty is delegated to the prophets, and that authority has already come to its full completion long ago and its delegation is now over. Then the saints were raised up and were given authority. To the saints was delegated the authority of Allah's beauty mixed with Allah's might. Now listen, these women whom you see here are the messengers who will be sent to the people punished in hell fire. They are called 'the People of Divine Might.' They each wish to raise people up from the fires of hell into the realm of pure Divine might. The Prophet himself revealed this from the inner world when he said, 'Women are the emissaries of Satan.'"

. . .

The heaven split open and we ascended into it. The essences both lofty and lowly appeared before me. I hesitated there, thinking that, if I don't understand the appearance of these essences, I will have no way to advance religious knowledge and intuitive knowledge [*'ilm-i dīnī o 'ilm-i ladūnī*]. My thoughts inclined to find out what religious knowledge really looked like. At that moment, Jesus spoke to me, saying, "Have you ever seen the four Imams [who fashioned the structure of Islamic law]?" I answered, "No." Jesus directed me to look at a certain place in the vastness; there I saw the four Imams standing together, each disputing with the others, saying, "No, no, the certain truth is this, not that." I thought to myself, if this is the outer knowledge of religion, then what is the inner knowledge of intuition? The thought simply flashed in my mind, but I didn't say anything to that effect. Just then, all the Divine names of Allah emerged, each in the particular dimension of its knowability, from the realm of the primal archetypes. Each took a distinct shape, giving rise to the whole multitude of perceptible and existent forms. I could see the continuity between the Divine names and all the created forms that arose from their various natures. I could see the universe contained within the relation between the Divine names that prepared the universe for its worldly existence.

> **Working with Sources**

1. What do the inclusion of Ali, Eve, and Jesus in Ghawth's mystical vision suggest about religious culture in sixteenth-century Hindustan?

2. What might one learn from Ghawth's vision about the Sufi view of gender and the roles of women?

SOURCE 20.5 ## Calico textile

ca. 1806

Calico was a fine printed cotton cloth first imported to England from Calicut, on the western shore of the subcontinent, by the British East India Company. A domestic manufacture of calico-inspired textiles followed, as English artisans attempted to mimic the bright colors, careful weaving, and intricate designs of Indian cloth. This example commemorates Vice Admiral Lord Nelson, a British naval hero of the Napoleonic Wars and the American War of Independence. Nelson, who died in the Battle of Trafalgar in 1805, was buried in St. Paul's Cathedral after an elaborate funeral service.

> **Working with Sources**

1. What specific elements are incorporated into this commemorative calico, and how are they symbolic of Nelson's military career?

2. How were the interests of the British East Indies Company furthered by internal conflict on the subcontinent in the seventeenth and eighteenth centuries?

Source: National Maritime Museum, London.

> Chapter 21   1500–1800

Regulating the "Inner" and "Outer" Domains

CHINA AND JAPAN

The time seemed right for a letter home. In only 2 weeks the Japanese invasion force had captured the Korean capital of Seoul, and the skill and firepower of the Japanese warriors seemed to let them brush their opponents aside at will. The Japanese commander, Toyotomi Hideyoshi, was a battle-hardened commoner who had risen through the ranks of his patron, Oda Nobunaga, as Oda fought to unite Japan before his assassination in 1582. Now, a decade later, Hideyoshi, as he was still known (as a commoner he had no surname and had only been given the family name Toyotomi by the imperial court in 1586) had embarked on an audacious campaign to extend his power to the Asian mainland. Six years before, he had written his mother that he contemplated nothing less than the conquest of China. Now seemed like a good time to inform her that his goal might actually be within his grasp.

As if in an eerie foreshadowing of another Korean conflict to come centuries later, however, the Japanese soon faced a massive Chinese and Korean counterattack and became mired in a bloody stalemate, their guns and

ABOVE: This scene, 1 of 15 from the handscroll painting *A Visit to the Yoshiwara* by Hishikawa Mononobu (ca. 1625–1694), depicts the "floating world" of Tokugawa Japan.

tactics barely enough to compensate for the determination and numbers of their enemies. After 4 more years of negotiation punctuated by bitter fighting, Hideyoshi finally withdrew to Japan. One final invasion attempt of Korea in 1597 collapsed when his death the following year set off a bloody struggle for succession, which ultimately placed in power the Tokugawa family, who would go on to rule Japan for more than 250 years.

Hideyoshi's dream of conquering China was, in a sense, a quest to claim the wellsprings of Japanese civilization as well. The episode brought together the politics, cultures, and fortunes of three of the four fiercely independent realms that together wove the primary strands of an East Asian pattern of history. The fourth, Vietnam, while not involved in this particular struggle, had been subject to similar pressures of Chinese cultural and political diffusion for eighteen centuries. The rise of Japanese power represents a vitally important pattern of world history, which we have seen in other areas, such as the Mediterranean and the expanding kingdoms of Europe: A state on the periphery absorbs innovation from a cultural center, in this case China, and then becomes a vital center itself. And like the other states in the region, Japan had absorbed the structures of "religious civilizations," as we have termed them—in this case, the philosophical system of Neo-Confucianism.

Of equal importance, Hideyoshi's invasion was made possible in part by the arrival of a new factor: the appearance of the first Europeans in the region. While their arrival in the sixteenth century provided only the smallest inkling of the reversals of fortune to come, by the middle of the nineteenth century their presence would create a crisis of power and acculturation for all of East Asia. For Japan, the industrializing West would then become a new center from which to draw innovation. For the present, however, European intrusions provided powerful incentives for both China and Japan to turn inward to safeguard their own security and stability.

Late Ming and Qing China to 1750

Proclaimed as a new dynasty in 1368, the Ming in its early years appears to have followed the familiar pattern of the "dynastic cycle" of previous dynasties. Having driven out the Mongol remnant, the Hongwu emperor and his immediate successors consolidated their rule, elevated the Confucian bureaucracy to its former place, and set up an administrative structure more focused on the person of the emperor than in previous dynasties. In 1382, the Grand Secretariat was created as the top governmental board below the emperor. Under the Grand Secretariat were the six boards, the governors and governors-general of the provinces, and lower-level officials of various degrees down to the district magistrate.

In this section we will also take up the question of China's retreat from its greatest period of maritime expansion in the early 1400s—and sudden withdrawal to concentrate on domestic matters. Why such an abrupt change in policy? What factors led to the ultimate decline of the Ming dynasty and the rise to power of the Manchus, a bordering nomadic people who drove out the Ming and created China's last imperial dynasty, the Qing [ching]? By what means did the Manchus create a

Seeing Patterns

≫ Why did late Ming and early Qing China look inward after such a successful period of overseas exploration?

≫ How do the goals of social stability drive the policies of agrarian states? How does the history of China and Japan in this period show these policies in action?

≫ In what ways did contact with the maritime states of Europe alter the patterns of trade and politics in eastern Asia?

≫ How did Neo-Confucianism in China differ from that of Tokugawa Japan?

state in which, despite being a tiny ruling minority, they held their grip on power into the twentieth century? Finally, what faint hints of the dynasty's problems appeared during its time of greatest power in the mid-eighteenth century?

From Expansion to Exclusion

During the late fourteenth and early fifteenth centuries, while China was rebuilding from the war to drive out the Mongols, the more pressing problems of land distribution and tenancy had abated somewhat. As in Europe, the depopulation of some areas from fighting and banditry and the lingering effects of the Black Death (which had reduced China's population from perhaps 100 million to about 60 million) had raised the value of labor, depressed the price of land, and increased the proportional amount of money in circulation. While the problems of land tenure would recur, another period of relief from their full effects soon came, albeit indirectly, from the creation of overseas empires by the Portuguese and the Spanish in the sixteenth century. The resulting Columbian Exchange saw the circulation of a number of new food crops on a global scale that had a substantial impact on the world's agricultural productivity (see Chapter 18).

New Food Crops   In addition to new, higher-yielding rice strains from Southeast Asia, the Chinese began to cultivate sugarcane, indigo, potatoes, sweet potatoes, maize (corn), peanuts, and tobacco that came from Africa and the Americas by way of the Spanish in the Philippines and the Portuguese at Macau. Corn and potatoes, versatile crops suitable for cultivation in a variety of marginal environments, accounted for a considerable increase in the arable land within China. Peanuts, sugarcane, indigo, and tobacco quickly established themselves as important cash crops.

Aided by the productivity of these new crops, China's population grew from its low of perhaps 60 million at the beginning of the Ming period to an estimated 150 million by 1600. There was also a marked growth in urbanism as market towns and regional transshipment points multiplied. The efficiency of Chinese agriculture, the continued incorporation of marginal and border lands into production, and the refinement of the empire's immense internal trade all contributed to another doubling of the population to perhaps 300 million by 1800. This accelerating growth began China's movement toward what some historical demographers have argued was a *high-level equilibrium trap*—a condition in which the land was approaching its maximum potential for feeding an increasing population but the economy had not reached a point of disequilibrium that could only be corrected by a technological and/or institutional change. In this schema, for example, the unbalanced nature of England's economy in the mid-eighteenth century created an environment favorable to the capital investment and technological innovations in the textile industry that began the Industrial Revolution. China, which continued to have abundant labor, no large pool of capital in search of investment, and no obvious need for more efficient agriculture or labor-saving machinery would go through the nineteenth century in a "balanced" state but one in which the growing population was slowly squeezed into impoverishment (see Map 21.1). Though the outlines of this theory were drawn in the early 1970s, its viability and fine points are still under debate today.

China and the World Commercial Revolution   China's rapid recovery, particularly as the sixteenth century brought new crops from the Americas, placed the late Ming and Qing Empires in the center of an increasingly extensive and complex

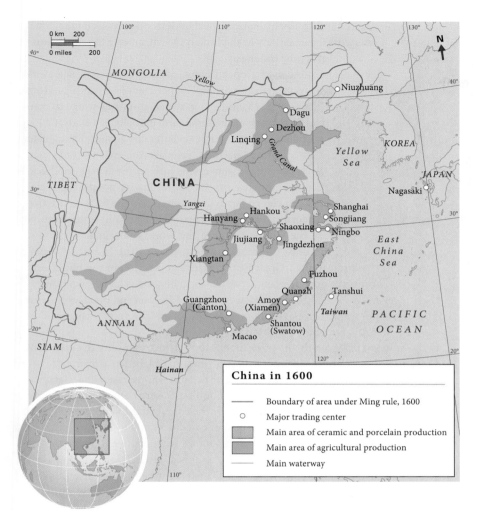

MAP 21.1 **China in 1600.**

worldwide commercial revolution (see "Patterns Up Close"). The competition for markets among the emerging maritime Atlantic states of Europe pushed them to develop ever-widening trade networks in the Indian and Pacific Oceans, along the African coast, and in the Americas. In all of these regions (except the Americas)

interactive timeline

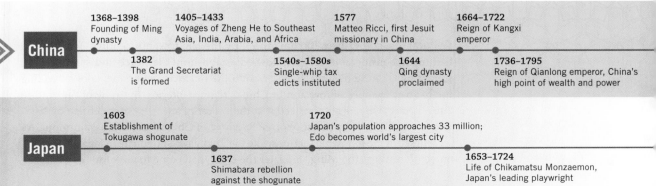

China				
1368–1398 Founding of Ming dynasty	**1405–1433** Voyages of Zheng He to Southeast Asia, India, Arabia, and Africa	**1577** Matteo Ricci, first Jesuit missionary in China	**1664–1722** Reign of Kangxi emperor	
	1382 The Grand Secretariat is formed	**1540s–1580s** Single-whip tax edicts instituted	**1644** Qing dynasty proclaimed	**1736–1795** Reign of Qianlong emperor, China's high point of wealth and power

Japan		
1603 Establishment of Tokugawa shogunate	**1720** Japan's population approaches 33 million; Edo becomes world's largest city	
	1637 Shimabara rebellion against the shogunate	**1653–1724** Life of Chikamatsu Monzaemon, Japan's leading playwright

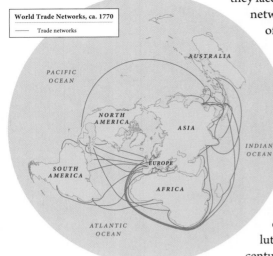

World Trade Networks, ca. 1770

——— Trade networks

PACIFIC OCEAN

AUSTRALIA

NORTH AMERICA

ASIA

INDIAN OCEAN

EUROPE

SOUTH AMERICA

AFRICA

ATLANTIC OCEAN

MAP 21.2 **World Trade Networks, ca. 1770.**

they faced stiff competition from local traders long involved in regional networks, particularly in the Indian Ocean, among the many ports of what is now Indonesia.

Among the European states, commercial, political, and religious competition resulted in policies of mercantilism (see Chapters 17, 18, and 19) in which countries strove to control sources of raw materials and markets. Similarly, China and Japan (by the early seventeenth century) sought to tightly control imports, regulate the export trade, and keep potentially subversive foreign influences in check. China's immense production of luxury goods, the seclusion policies of Japan and Korea, and the huge and growing demand for porcelain, tea, silk, paper, and cotton textiles made the Chinese empire the world's dominant economic engine until the productive capacity of the Industrial Revolution vaulted Great Britain into that position in the nineteenth century. Indeed, recent work by world historians has shown how extensively China's economy powered that of Eurasia and much of the rest of the world before what Kenneth Pomeranz has called "the great divergence" of Western economic ascendancy (see Map 21.2).

In the midst of this growth, the government took steps to simplify the system of land taxation. *Corvée* labor—the required contribution of labor as a form of tax—was effectively abolished. As in previous regimes, land was assessed and classified according to its use and relative productivity. Land taxes were then combined into a single bill, payable in silver by installments over the course of the year: the so-called single-whip tax system. The installment plan allowed peasants to remain relatively solvent during planting season when their resources were depleted, thus reducing the need to borrow at high rates from moneylenders at crucial times of the yearly cycle. Significantly, the requirement that the tax payment be in silver also played a crucial role in the increasing monetization of the economy. This was aided considerably by the increasing amounts of silver entering the Chinese economy by means of the Manila trade. Merchants from south China exchanged spices and Chinese luxury goods such as porcelain (see "Patterns Up Close") in Manila in the Spanish-controlled Philippines for Spanish silver from the Americas. Manila thus became a vital axis around which the trade economies of three continents revolved. Though ultimately eclipsed in trade share and economic importance with the rise of the Canton system in the eighteenth century, Spanish (and later Mexican) silver continued to be the preferred medium of exchange for Chinese merchants for more than three centuries.

Regulating the Outer Barbarians   By the late fifteenth century, Ming China had made considerable progress toward establishing the peace and stability long sought by Chinese regimes. In addition to the practical requirements of defending the historic avenues of invasion in China's remote interior, the view of the empire cultivated by China's elites placed it at the center of a world order defined by Neo-Confucian philosophy and supported by a host of Chinese cultural assumptions. As we will see in the following sections, like the Tokugawa shogunate in Japan in the seventeenth century, the Ming, and later the Qing, had come to view foreign influence as less "civilized" and far too often injurious to established social order. Hence, successive rulers placed severe restrictions on maritime trade and conceived of diplomatic relations primarily in commercial terms. "All the world is one family," imperial proclamations routinely claimed, and the emperor was conceived as the father, in Confucian terms, of this world-family system. "Tribute missions," a term sometimes (though somewhat misleadingly) applied to this diplomatic–commercial relationship, were sent from Korea, Vietnam, the Ryukyu Islands, and occasionally Japan to pay periodic ceremonial visits to the emperor, who then bestowed presents on the envoys and granted them permission to trade in China. This arrangement worked reasonably well within the long-standing hierarchy of the Confucian cultural sphere. By the late eighteenth century, however, it came into direct conflict with the more egalitarian system of international trade and diplomacy that had evolved in the West.

The Ming in Decline   Despite the increased attention directed at the Mongol resurgence of the 1440s, periodic rebellions in the north and northwest punctuated the late fifteenth and sixteenth centuries. The huge commitment of Chinese troops in Korea against the forces of the Japanese leader Hideyoshi during his attempted invasion of Korea and China from 1592 to 1598 weakened the dynasty further during a crucial period that saw the rise of another regional power: the Manchus. By the turn of the seventeenth century, under the leadership of Nurhachi (r. 1616–1626) and Abahai (r. 1636–1643), the Manchus, an Altaic-speaking farming, hunting, and fishing people related to the Jurchens inhabiting the northeastern section of the Ming domain, had become the prime military force of the area, and dissident Chinese sought them as allies. In 1642, in the midst of factional warfare among the Ming, the Chinese general Wu Sangui invited the Manchu leader Dorgon to cross the Great Wall where it approaches the sea at Shanhaiguan. For the Chinese, this event would come to carry the same sense of finality as Caesar's crossing of the Rubicon: The Manchus occupied Beijing in 1644 and declared the founding of a new regime, the Qing, or "pure," dynasty. Like the defeated remnant of the Nationalist regime in 1949, some Ming loyalists fled to the island of Taiwan, where they expelled the Dutch (who had established a trading base there) and held on until succumbing to Qing forces in 1683.

The Spring and Summer of Power: The Qing to 1750

Like the Toba and Mongols before them, the Manchus now found themselves in the position of having to "dismount and rule." A good deal of preparation for this had already taken place within the borderland state they had created for themselves—for a time, successfully isolated by the Ming—on the Liaodong Peninsula of south Manchuria. Long exposure to Chinese culture and Confucian administrative practices provided models that soon proved adaptable by Manchu leaders within the larger environment of China proper.

The Banner System   The **banner system**, under which the Manchus were organized for military and tax purposes, was also expanded under the Qing to provide for segregated Manchu elites and garrisons in major cities and towns. Under the banner system, the Manchu state had been divided into eight major military and ethnic (among them Manchu, Han Chinese, and Mongolian) divisions, each represented by a distinctive banner. Within each division, companies were formed of

East Asia and Southeast Asia as shown in a 1625 Chinese map

Banner system: The organizational system of the Manchus for military and taxation purposes; there were eight banners under which all military houses were arranged, and each was further divided into blocks of families required to furnish units of 300 soldiers to the Manchu government.

Patterns Up Close

The "China" Trade

Ming and Qing China may be said to be at the heart of two innovations of enormous importance to the patterns of world history. The first is one that we have tracked through all of the chapters in this book pertaining to China: the technical and aesthetic development of ceramics, culminating in the creation of true porcelain during the Song period (960–1279). The early Ming period saw the elaboration of the use of kaolin white clays with what are called "flux" materials—minerals, metals, and compounds—that can fuse with the clay under extremely high temperatures to form durable glazes and striking artistic features. Thus, the Song and Yuan periods were characterized by pure white and celadon green wares, some with a purposely created "crackle" glaze on them, while by the Ming period, highly distinctive blue and white ware—the result of employing pigments with cobalt oxide imported from the areas around modern Iran and Iraq—set the world standard for elegance.

Porcelain Vase, Ming Period. Porcelain ware of the Song and Ming periods is among the most coveted Chinese art objects even today. Here we have a Ming vase showing characteristically vibrant colors and a degree of technical perfection indicative of the best Chinese pottery works, such as Jingdezhen. The motif of the grass carp on the vase is symbolic of endurance and perseverance, and thus associated with the god of literature and scholarship.

The artistic excellence of Chinese porcelain, like earlier styles of Chinese ceramics, spawned imitations throughout the Chinese periphery. By 1500, porcelain works in Korea, Japan, and Vietnam supplied a burgeoning market both at home and throughout East and Southeast Asia. While these regional manufacturers for the most part followed the designs of the Chinese imperial works at Jingdezhen, some, especially the Japanese ceramicist Chojiro, preferred highly rustic, rough-hewn earthenware designs with glazes that formed spontaneous designs as the pieces were fired—the famous raku ware. Thus there was already a highly developed regional market for what was, at the time, arguably the world's most highly developed technology.

The period from 1500 to the mid-nineteenth century brings us to the second great innovation in which China was the driving force: the world market for porcelain.

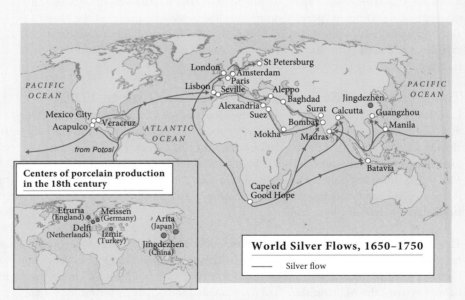

Centers of porcelain production in the 18th century

Etruria (England) Meissen (Germany) Arita (Japan)
Delft (Netherlands) Izmir (Turkey)
Jingdezhen (China)

World Silver Flows, 1650–1750

—— Silver flow

MAP 21.3 **Silver Flows and Centers of Porcelain Production.**

China's wares had found customers for centuries in nearly every corner of Eurasia and North and East Africa. Shipwrecks have been found in the Straits of Malacca laden with Ming porcelain; traders in the Swahili cities along the East African coast were avid collectors, while Africans farther inland decorated their graves with Chinese bowls. All stops on the Silk Road had their precious supplies of porcelain, while the Ottoman Turks did their best to copy the blue and white Ming wares in their own factories at Izmir.

Before the sixteenth century, a trickle of Ming porcelain also made its way to Europe. With the establishment of the first European trade empires, however, the demand for porcelain skyrocketed. Portuguese, Spanish, and later Dutch, French, English, and (after 1784) American merchants all sought porcelain in ever-increasing amounts. From 1500 to 1800 it was arguably the single most important commodity in the unfolding world commercial revolution. While estimates vary, economic historians have suggested that between one-third and one-half of all the silver produced in the Americas during this time went to pay for porcelain. Incoming ships often used the bulk cargoes of porcelain as ballast, and foreign merchants sent custom orders to their Chinese counterparts for Chinese-style wares designed for use at Western tables. Such was the prominence of this "export porcelain" in the furnishings of period homes that scarcely any family of means was without it (see Map 21.3).

With the prominence of mercantilist theory and protectionism toward home markets during the seventeenth and eighteenth centuries, it is not surprising that foreign manufacturers sought to break the Chinese monopoly. During Tokugawa times, the Japanese, for example, forced a group of Korean potters to labor at the famous Arita works to turn out Sino–Korean designs; the Dutch marketed delftware as an attempt to copy Chinese "blue willow" porcelain. It was not until German experimenters in Saxony happened upon a workable formula for hard-paste porcelain—after years of trial and error, even melting down Chinese wares for analysis—that their facility at Meissen began to produce true porcelain in 1710. Josiah Wedgwood set up his own porcelain factory in 1759 in England. But Chinese manufacturers would still drive the market until the end of the nineteenth century. And fine porcelain would forever carry the generic name of "china" regardless of its origins.

Porcelain Candlestick for the Export Market, Qing Period. By the early 1700s, luxury exports from China such as porcelain, lacquerware, and, of course, tea had become important staples of European maritime trade. Export porcelain—either items made to order by Chinese porcelain works for overseas buyers or generic ones made to suit European and colonial tastes—had become such a big business that cheaper pieces were sometimes actually used as ship's ballast on the homeward voyages. Shown here is a candlestick for use in a European home with Chinese motifs of vessels at the top. The cobalt blue color is characteristic of the Ming and Qing designs.

Questions

- How does the development of porcelain serve as an example of Chinese leadership in technical innovation during the premodern and early modern periods?

- How did the emergence of a global trading network after 1500 affect both the demand for porcelain and its impact on consumer tastes?

300 fighters recruited from families represented by that banner. Originally devised for a mobile warrior people, the system eventually became the chief administrative tool of the Manchu leadership. It was now introduced into China in such a way as to establish the Manchus as a hereditary warrior class occupying its own sections of major Chinese cities. The Han, or ethnic Chinese, forces were organized into their own "Armies of the Green Standard," so named for the color of the flags they carried.

Minority Rule   Always conscious of their position as a ruling minority in China, with their numbers comprising only about 2 percent of the population, the Manchus, like the Mongols before them, sought to walk a fine line between administrative and cultural adaptation and the kind of complete assimilation that had characterized previous invaders. Chinese and Manchus were scrupulously recruited in equal numbers for high administrative posts; Manchu quotas in the examination system were instituted; edicts and memorials were issued in both Chinese and Manchu; Qing emperors sought to control the empire's high culture; and, of course, Manchu "bannermen" of the various garrisons were kept in their own special quarters in the towns and cities. In addition, the Manchu conqueror Dorgon instituted the infamous "queue edict" in 1645: All males, regardless of ethnicity, were required on pain of death to adopt the Manchu hairstyle of a shaved forehead and long pigtail in the back—the queue—as the outward sign of loyalty to the new order. This hairstyle can be seen in early photographs taken of Chinese men until the Qing dynasty fell in 1912. As a darkly whimsical saying put it, "Keep the hair, lose the head; keep the head, lose the hair."

The results, however, were bloody and long lasting. The queue edict provoked revolts in several cities, and the casualties caused by their suppression may have numbered in the hundreds of thousands. For the remainder of the Qing era, rebels and protesters routinely cut their queues as the first order of business; during China's Taiping Rebellion (1851–1864), perhaps the bloodiest civil war in human history, insurgents were known as "the long-haired rebels" for their immediate abandonment of the Qing hairstyle.

As the Manchus consolidated their rule, however, their conception of their empire grew far more expansive. That is, while the Han Chinese were by far the largest ethnic group, the Manchus conceived of their state as one embodying in a more or less egalitarian sense all of the peoples within it. By the time of the Kangxi, Yongzheng, and Qianlong emperors, Qing concepts of the state had become remarkably inclusive, embracing nearly all of the minorities recognized by the People's Republic today. While rebellions were put down ruthlessly, and conquest of western lands proceeded apace, the incorporated peoples were seen as partners in a world empire.

excerpts from the Kangxi emperor on ruling (1717)

Creating the New Order   Though the Qing kept the centralized imperial system of the Ming largely intact, while importing the banner system as a kind of Manchu parallel administrative apparatus, they also made one significant addition to the uppermost level of the bureaucracy. While retaining the Ming Grand Secretariat, the emperor Kangxi's successor, Yongzheng, set up an ad hoc inner advisory body called the Grand Council in 1733. Over the succeeding decades the Grand Council became the supreme inner advisory group to the emperor, while the Grand Secretariat was relegated to handling less crucial "outer" matters of policy making and implementation.

For much of the seventeenth century, however, the pacification of the empire remained the primary task. Under the able leadership of Nurhachi's great-grandson, the Kangxi emperor (r. 1661–1722), the difficult subjugation of the south was concluded, the Revolt of the Three Feudatories (1673–1681) ultimately crushed, and the naval stronghold of the Ming pretender called Koxinga by the Dutch captured on Taiwan in 1683.

As had been the case in past dynasties, the Qing sought to safeguard the borders of the empire by bringing peoples on the periphery into the imperial system through a judicious application of the carrot and the stick, or, as it was known to generations of Chinese strategists, the "loose rein" and "using barbarians to check barbarians." In practical terms, this meant a final reckoning with the Mongols in the 1720s by means of improved cannon and small arms, along with bribes and presents to friendly chieftains, and the intervention of the Qing in religious disputes regarding Tibetan Buddhism, which had also been adopted by a number of the Mongol groups. Toward this end, the Qing established a protectorate over Tibet in 1727, with the Dalai Lama ruling as the approved temporal and religious leader. To cement the relationship further, the emperor built a replica of a Tibetan stupa just outside the Manchu quarter in Beijing and a model of the Dalai Lama's Potala Palace at the emperor's summer retreat in Jehol [yeh-HOLE].

Tibetan Stupa and Temple, Beijing. This marble chorten, the Tibetan version of the Buddhist stupa, or reliquary, was built by the Qianlong emperor for the visit of the Panchen Lama in 1779, in part to cement the new Sino–Tibetan relationship growing from the establishment of a Qing protectorate over Tibet.

The Qianlong Emperor With the traditional threats from the borders now quashed, the reign of the Qianlong [chien-LUNG] emperor, from 1736 to 1795, marked both the high point and the beginning of the decline of the Qing dynasty— and of imperial China itself. The period witnessed China's expansion to its greatest size during the imperial era. This was accompanied by a doubling of its population to perhaps 300 million by 1800. By almost any measure, its internal economy dwarfed that of any other country and equaled or surpassed that of Europe as a whole until the Industrial Revolution was well under way.

The Qing army, though perhaps already eclipsed in terms of discipline and training by the leading nations of Europe, was still many times larger than that of any potential competitor. Moreover, Qianlong wielded this power successfully a number of times during his reign, with expeditions against pirates and rebels on Taiwan and in punitive campaigns against Vietnam, Nepal, and Burma between 1766 and 1792 (see Map 21.4). During his long life, he also tried, with limited success, to take up the writing brush of a scholar and connoisseur, creating the collection of art that is today the core of the National Palace Museum's holdings on Taiwan. Under his direction, the state sponsored monumental literary enterprises on a scale still awesome to contemplate today. Based on the small but steady stream of information on the Qing Empire circulating around Europe, it seemed to some that the Chinese had solved a number of the problems of good government and might provide practical models of statecraft for Europeans to emulate.

Early European Contacts Ironically, it was precisely at the time that China abandoned its oceanic expeditions that tiny Portugal on the Atlantic coast began eyeing its expansion to Ceuta in North Africa (see Chapters 16, 18, 19). By the 1440s,

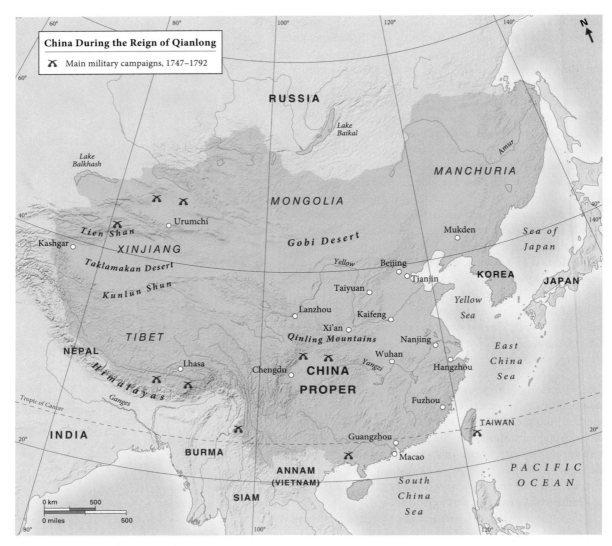

MAP **21.4** **China during the Reign of Qianlong.**

map analysis

Portuguese navigators had rounded the bulge of West Africa and opened commercial relations with the coastal kingdoms there. Scarcely a decade after Vasco da Gama arrived in Calicut in 1498, the first Portuguese ships appeared in Chinese waters. By 1557, these *Folangqi*—the Chinese transliteration of "Franks," a generic term for Europeans transmitted by the Arabs to Malacca, where it was transformed into *Ferenghi* [fa-REN-gee]—had wrested the first European colony from the Chinese at Macau. It was destined to be the longest-lived European colony as well, remaining under Portuguese control until 1999. From this point on, through merchants and missionaries, the contacts would frequently be profitable—and, sometimes, disastrous. Ultimately, they provided some of the most far-reaching interactions of world history.

Missionaries   The arrival of the first European merchants in East Asia was followed shortly by that of the first Catholic missionaries. Although the crusading impulse was still very much alive in Christian dealings with Muslim merchants in the Indies, Christian missionaries (at first from the Franciscan and Dominican orders and later from the Jesuits) were quick to realize the vast potential for religious conversions in China and Japan. The various missionary orders set up headquarters in Malacca, and in 1549 the Franciscan Francis Xavier landed in Japan. The endemic conflict among the *daimyo* (regional warlords) of Japan helped create a demand for Western goods, especially firearms, and the association of these with Christianity allowed considerable progress to be made in gaining conversions. China, however, required a vastly different strategy.

Wary of potentially disruptive foreign influences, the Ming at first refused entry to missionaries. Once admitted, the Franciscans and Dominicans, with their limited training in Chinese language and culture, made little headway. Additionally, their efforts were largely aimed at seeking conversions among the poor, which won them scant respect or influence among China's elite. The Jesuits, however, tried a different tack. Led by Matteo Ricci (1552–1610) and his successors Adam Schall von Bell (1591–1666) and Ferdinand Verbiest (1623–1688), they immersed themselves in the classical language and high culture of the empire and gained recognition through their expertise in mathematics, astronomy, military science, and other European learning sought by the imperial court. Jesuit advisors served the last Ming emperors as court astronomers and military engineers and successfully made the transition to the new dynasty. The high point of their influence was reached during the reign of the Qing Kangxi emperor (1661–1722). With Schall as the official court astronomer and mathematician and an entire European-style observatory set up in Beijing, Kangxi actively considered conversion to Catholicism.

The papacy, however, had long considered Jesuit liturgical and doctrinal adaptations to local sensibilities problematic. In the case of China, competition among the three orders for converts and disturbing reports from the Franciscans and Dominicans regarding the Jesuits' alleged tolerance of their converts' continued veneration of Confucius and maintenance of ancestral shrines set off the "rites controversy." This was worsened in the eyes of the papacy by the Jesuits' acquiescence to the use of tea and rice for the Eucharist instead of bread and wine. After several decades of intermittent discussion, Kangxi's successor, Yongzheng, banned the order's activities in China in 1724. Christianity and missionary activity were thus driven underground, though the Qing would retain a Jesuit court astronomer into the nineteenth century.

Matteo Ricci and Li Paul. The cross-cultural possibilities of sixteenth- and seventeenth-century Sino–Western contact were perhaps best exemplified by the activities of the Jesuit Matteo Ricci (1552–1610). Ricci predicated his mission in China on a respectful study of the language and classical canon of the empire coupled with a thorough knowledge of the new mathematics and astronomy of the West. Here, he is pictured with one of his most prominent converts, a literatus and veteran of the war against the Japanese in Korea, Li Yingshi. Upon his conversion in 1602, Li took the Christian name of Paul.

The Canton Trade While China's commerce with the maritime Atlantic states grew rapidly in the eighteenth century, the Europeans had not yet been fully

Canton Factories, ca. 1800. Under the "Canton system" begun in 1699, all maritime trade with the Europeans was tightly controlled and conducted through the single port of Canton, or Guangzhou. Foreign merchants were not allowed to reside within the walled city, so they constructed their own facilities along the Pearl River waterfront. Though it kept profits high for the concerned parties, the restrictiveness of the system caused nineteenth-century merchants and diplomats to push the Chinese to open more ports to trade, which proved to be a major sticking point in Sino–Western relations.

incorporated into the Qing diplomatic system. A century before, the expansion of Russia into Siberia and the region around the Amur River had prompted the Qing to negotiate the Treaty of Nerchinsk in 1689. Under its terms, negotiated with Kangxi's Jesuit advisors acting as interpreters and go-betweens, the Russians agreed to abandon their last forts along the Amur and were given rights to continue their lucrative caravan trade in the interior. Formal borders were established in Manchuria, and the first attempts at settling claims to the central Asian regions of Ili and Kuldja were made. Significantly, Russian envoys were also permitted to reside in Beijing but in a residence like those used by the temporary envoys of tribute missions.

The situation among the European traders attempting to enter Chinese seaports, however, was quite different. The British East India Company, having established its base at Calcutta in 1690, soon sought to expand its operations to China. At the same time, the Qing, fresh from capturing the last Ming bastion on Taiwan and worried about Ming loyalists in other areas, sought to control contact with foreign and overseas Chinese traders as much as possible, while keeping their lucrative export trade at a sustainable level. Their solution, implemented in 1699, was to permit overseas trade only at the southern port of Guangzhou [GWAHNG-joe], more widely known as Canton. The local merchants' guild, or *cohong* (in pinyin, *gonghang*), was granted a monopoly on the trade and was supervised by a special official from the imperial Board of Revenue. Much like the Tokugawa in seventeenth-century Japan, the Qing permitted only a small number of foreigners, mostly traders from the English, French, and Dutch East India Companies, to reside at the port. They were confined to a small compound of foreign "**factories**," were not permitted inside the city walls, and could not bring their wives or families along. Even small violations of the regulations could result in a suspension of trading privileges, and all infractions and disputes were judged according to Chinese law. Finally, since foreign affairs under these circumstances were considered a dimension of trade, all diplomatic issues were settled by local officials in Canton.

Factory: Here, the place where various "factors" (merchants, agents, etc.) gathered to conduct business.

The eighteenth century proved to be a boom time for all involved in the Canton trade, and the British in particular increasingly viewed it as a valuable part of their growing commercial power. While the spread of tea drinking through Europe and its colonies meant that tea rapidly grew to challenge porcelain for trade supremacy, silk also grew in importance, as well as lacquerware, wicker and rattan furniture, and dozens of other local specialties increasingly targeted at the export market. After 1784, the United States joined the trade; but despite the growing American presence, it was the British East India Company that dominated the Canton factories. Both the cohong and foreign chartered companies carefully guarded their respective monopolies, and the system worked reasonably well in keeping competition low and profits high on all sides.

Village and Family Life

Just as the effort toward greater control and centralization was visible in the government and economy of China during the Ming and Qing, it also reverberated within the structures of Chinese village life. While much of local custom and social relations among the peasants still revolved around family, clan, and lineage—with the scholar-gentry setting the pace—new institutions perfected under the Ming and Qing had a lasting impact into the twentieth century.

Organizing the Countryside   During the sixteenth century, the administrative restructuring related to the consolidation of the tax system into the single-whip arrangement led to the creation of the *lijia* system. All households were placed into officially designated villages for tax purposes; 10 households made up a *jia*, and 100 households comprised a *li*, whose headmen, appointed by the magistrate, were responsible for keeping tax records and labor dues.

While the lijia system was geared primarily toward more efficient tax collection and record keeping, the *baojia* (see Chapter 12) system functioned as a more far-reaching means of government surveillance and control. The baojia system required families to register all members and be organized into units of 10 families, with one family in each unit assuming responsibility for the other nine. Each of these responsible families was arranged in groups of 10, and a member of each was selected to be responsible for that group of 100 households, and so on up to the *bao*, or 1,000-household level. Baojia representatives at each level were to be chosen by the families in the group. These representatives were to report to the magistrate on the doings of their respective groups and held accountable for the group's behavior.

Glimpses of Rural Life   As with other agrarian–urban empires, much of what little we know about Chinese peasant life comes to us through literary sources. Most of these were compiled by the scholar-gentry, though starting in the seventeenth century a small but influential number of chronicles were also produced by Westerners traveling in China. Based on these accounts, some generalizations can be made about rural and family life in Ming and Qing times.

Chinese Commercial Enterprises. The growing volume and profits of the export trade encouraged further development and specialization of long-standing Chinese domestic industries during the eighteenth and nineteenth centuries. Moneychangers known as shroffs (a) were involved in testing the quality of silver taken from foreign concerns in exchange for Chinese goods. A worker and overseer demonstrate the operation of a silk reeling machine (b). Women worked to sort tea; in this photograph (c), packing chests for tea are stacked behind the sorters. The hairstyle of the men in these photos—shaved forehead with long braid called a queue—was mandatory for all Chinese males as a sign of submission to the Qing.

First, while the introduction of new crops during the period had brought more marginal land under cultivation, allowed for a huge increase in the population, and helped lend momentum to the trend toward more commercialization of agriculture, the work, technology, and overall rhythms of peasant life had changed little over the centuries.

Second, as with gathering political tensions, some early signs of economic stress were already present toward the end of Qianlong's reign. Chief among these was the problem of absentee landlordism. This would grow increasingly acute as the vitality of the commercial networks and market towns of central and southern China increased and the gentry were drawn away from the countryside by urban opportunities and amenities. In addition, successful tea, cotton, silk, and luxury goods traders frequently retained their compounds in the cities while buying land and degrees and becoming scholar-gentry, further increasing the incidence of absenteeism in the countryside. During the next century, with the dislocations of the Opium Wars, the Taiping Rebellion, and the foreign treaty ports, the problem of absentee landlordism greatly accelerated.

Third, as we have seen before, pressures on patterns of village life tended to be magnified in the lives of women and girls. Elite women were routinely educated to be as marriageable as possible. Study of proper Confucian decorum, writing model essays, chanting poetry, and developing a firm grasp of the *Xiaojing* (*Classic of Filial Piety*) were central to their lessons. As noted earlier, women were expected to be modest and obedient and were usually separated from and subordinate to men. Marriage and property laws were set up to reinforce these qualities. In addition to the emphasis placed on mourning by both sexes, widows were expected to remain single and be subordinate to their oldest sons. As also noted previously, the custom of foot binding had long since become institutionalized, though in some areas— among southern China's Hakka minority, for example—it never caught on. The sale of infant girls and, in extreme cases, female infanticide rose markedly in rural areas during times of war, famine, or other social stresses. It should be remembered, however, that, as in previous Chinese dynasties, the dominance of women over the "inner realm" of the family remained largely complete, though this realm was never considered equal in importance to the outer sphere of men's activities.

Science, Culture, and Intellectual Life

As we saw in Chapter 12, the Ming dynasty in many ways marked the high point as well as the beginning of the decline of China's preeminent place as a world technological innovator. One area in which this became painfully evident by the eighteenth and nineteenth centuries was in military matters.

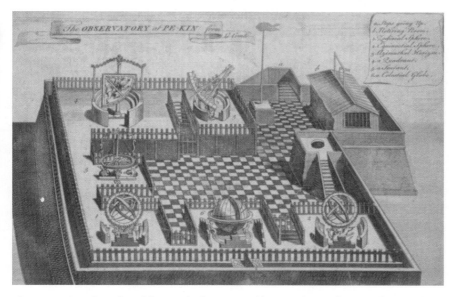

Observatory in Beijing. One of the ways the Jesuits were able to gain favor at the imperial courts of two successive dynasties was through the New Sciences of the West. Jesuit mathematicians, technical advisors, mapmakers, and astronomers found an eager reception among their Chinese counterparts, the fruits of which included armillary spheres (pictured on the left and right foreground) and the celestial globe (center). The instruments were cast by Chinese artisans to the specifications of the Jesuit court mathematician Ferdinand Verbiest in the 1680s.

Superpower   The Ming at their height have been described by some Chinese scholars as a military superpower. Perhaps most important in this regard was that the ascendancy of the Ming in 1368 marked the beginning of what one historian has called a "military revolution" in the use of firearms. The first use of metal gun barrels in the late thirteenth century spurred the rapid development of both cannon and small arms—so much so that by the mid-fifteenth century the Ming arsenal at Junqiju [JWUN-chee-joo] was producing thousands of cannon, handguns, and "fire lances" every year. By one estimate, in 1450 over half of the Ming frontier military units had cannon and one-third of all troops carried firearms. As early as the 1390s large shipborne cannon were already being installed in naval vessels. Indeed, court historians of the late Ming credited nearly all the military successes of the dynasty to the superiority of their firearms.

By the Qing period, however, following the pacification of the realm, the need for constant improvement of arms was seen as increasingly costly and unnecessary. While marginal improvements were made in the **matchlock** firing mechanisms of Chinese small arms, such improvements as were made in larger guns were largely directed by European missionary advisors to the throne.

Matchlock: An early type of gun in which the gunpowder charge is ignited by a burning taper (the "match") attached to the trigger mechanism.

Science and Literature   In geography, mathematics, and astronomy a fruitful exchange was inaugurated between European Jesuit missionaries and a small but influential group of Chinese officials in the seventeenth and eighteenth centuries. The most lasting legacy of this meeting was the European-style observatory in Beijing and a number of new maps of the world based on sixteenth- and seventeenth-century explorations. Unfortunately, by the nineteenth century these were all but forgotten, and the inadequacy of the geographical knowledge of Chinese officials in policy-making positions was soon all too apparent.

As in seventeenth-century France, the centralizing tendency of the government of China led to the exercise of considerable control in the cultural realm through patronage, monopoly, and licensing. As Manchus, the Kangxi, Yongzheng, and Qianlong emperors strove to validate their reigns by being patrons of the arts and aspiring to high levels of connoisseurship and cultivation of the best of the literati. As in other centralizing realms, they not only set the tone in matters of aesthetics but also used mammoth cultural projects to direct the energies of scholars and officials into approved areas. At the same time, they sought to quash unorthodox views through lack of support and, more directly, through literary inquisitions. Kangxi, for example, sponsored the compilation of a huge dictionary of approved definitions of Chinese characters—still considered a primary reference work today. Under his direction, the commentaries and interpretations of Neo-Confucianism championed by the Song philosopher Zhu Xi became the approved versions. Kangxi's 13 sacred edicts, embodying maxims distilled in part from Zhu Xi's thought, became the official Qing creed from 1670 on. Anxious to legitimize themselves as culturally "Chinese," Kangxi and Qianlong sponsored huge encyclopedia projects. Qianlong's effort, at 36,000 volumes, was perhaps the most ambitious undertaking of its kind ever attempted.

Neo-Confucian Philosophy   While the urge to orthodoxy pervaded both dynasties, considerable intellectual ferment was also brewing beneath the surface of the official world. As we saw in Chapter 12, in the sixteenth century the first major new directions in Neo-Confucianism were being explored by Wang Yangming

(1472–1529). While Wang's school remained a popular one, his emphasis on intuition, on a kind of enlightenment open to all, and, more and more, on a unity of opposites embracing different religious and philosophical traditions placed his more radical followers increasingly on the fringes of intellectual life. In addition, the Qing victory ushered in an era of soul-searching among Chinese literati and a wholesale questioning of the systems that had failed in the face of foreign conquest.

Two of the most important later figures in Qing philosophy were Huang Zongxi [hwang zung-SHEE] (1610–1695) and Gu Yanwu [goo yen-WOO] (1613–1682). Both men's lives spanned the Qing conquest, and like many of their fellow officials, both men concluded that the collapse of the old order was in part due to a retreat from practical politics and too much indulgence in the excesses of the radicals of the Wang Yangming school. With a group of like-minded scholars, they based themselves at the Donglin Academy, founded in 1604. There, they devoted themselves to reconstituting an activist Confucianism based on rigorous self-cultivation and on remonstrating with officials and even the court. One outgrowth of this development, which shares interesting parallels with the critical textual scholarship of the European Renaissance, was the so-called Han learning movement. Convinced that centuries of Buddhism, religious Daoism, and Confucian commentaries of questionable value had diverted Confucianism from the intent of the sages, Han learning sought to recover the original meaning of classic Confucian works through exacting textual scholarship and systematic philology, or historical linguistics. The movement, though always on the fringe of approved official activities, peaked in the eighteenth century and successfully uncovered a number of fraudulent texts, while setting the tone for critical textual analysis during the remainder of the imperial era.

The Arts and Popular Culture Although China's artists and writers clung to an amateur ideal of the "three excellences" of poetry, painting, and calligraphy, increasing official patronage ensured that approved schools and genres of art would be maintained at a consistent, if not inspired, level of quality. Here, the Qianlong emperor was perhaps the most influential force. Motivated in part by a lifelong quest to master the fine arts, he collected thousands of paintings—to which he added, in the tradition of Chinese connoisseurs, his own colophons—rare manuscripts, jade, porcelain, lacquerware, and other objets d'art. Because the force of imperial patronage was directed at conserving past models rather than creating new ones, the period is not noteworthy for stylistic innovation. One interesting exception to this, however, was the work of the Jesuit painter Giuseppe Castiglione (1688–1766). Castiglione's access to Qianlong resulted in a number of portraits of the emperor and court in a style that merged traditional Chinese subjects and media with Western perspective and technique. Evidence of this synthesis can also be seen in the Italianate and Versailles-inspired architecture at the emperor's Summer Palace just outside of Beijing.

Local Custom and Religion Chinese cities and villages were populated by storytellers, corner poets, spirit mediums, diviners, and a variety of other sorts of entertainers. While village social life revolved principally around clan and family

Qianlong Emperor (1736–1795). One of the more interesting cross-cultural interactions during the early Qing period was that inspired by the Jesuit missionary Giuseppe Castiglione (1688–1766). Trained as an architect and painter, Castiglione (Chinese name Lang Shining) arrived in Beijing in 1715 and served as court painter to emperors Kangxi, Yongzheng, and Qianlong. He influenced Chinese painters in the use of Western perspective and also absorbed Chinese techniques of portraiture and landscape painting. Here, the young Qianlong emperor is shown in his imperial regalia—including his robes of imperial yellow with dragon motifs—but with an authentically detailed face gazing confidently at the viewer.

functions, popular culture was also dominated by Daoism, Buddhism, and older traditions of local worship, all with their own temples, shrines, and festivals. The oldest beliefs of the countryside involving ancestral spirits, "hungry ghosts" (roaming spirits of those not properly cared for in death), fairies, and demons were enhanced over the centuries by a rich infusion of tales of Daoist adepts and "immortals," *yijing* diviners, Buddhist bodhisattvas, and underworld demons. Popular stories incorporating all of these, like *A Journey to the West*, continued to be popular fare for the literate as well as for storytellers and street performers.

excerpts from Pu Songling, *Strange Tales from a Chinese Studio* (1740)

One of the richest glimpses into local society comes from Pu Songling's (1640–1715) *Strange Tales from the "Make-Do" Studio*, sometimes rendered in English as *Strange Tales from a Chinese Studio*. Though considered a master stylist among his circle of friends, Pu never progressed beyond the provincial-level examinations and spent most of his life in genteel poverty. He traveled extensively, collecting folktales, accounts of local curiosities, and especially stories of the supernatural. His stories are available to us today thanks to the foresight of his grandson, who published them in 1740. In Pu's world, "fox-fairies" appear as beautiful women, men are transformed into tigers, the young are duped into degenerate behavior—with predictable consequences—and crooked mediums and storytellers take advantage of the unwary.

The Long War and Longer Peace: Japan, 1450–1750

As we recall from Chapter 13, the struggles by court factions in Japan's capital of Heian-Kyo (Kyoto) had ultimately resulted in the creation of the office of the *shogun*, the chief military officer of the realm, in 1185. Actual executive power gradually receded from the emperor's hands, however, into the shogun's, and by the fourteenth century the emperor had become in reality the puppet of his first officer. As we also saw, a fundamental shift occurred with the attempt by Emperor Go-Daigo to reassert his prerogatives in 1333. When his one-time supporter Ashikaga Takauji expelled him and set up his headquarters in the capital, power and prestige were pressed together once again, with profound political and cultural consequences for Japan. Courtly elegance insinuated itself into the brutal world of the warrior, while power, intrigue, and ultimately a prolonged and debilitating civil war would ravage the capital until it ended with Japan's unification.

The price of unification, however, was high. As we saw in the opening vignette of this chapter, the first of Japan's unifiers, Oda Nobunaga, was assassinated for his efforts; the invasions of Korea undertaken by his successor Hideyoshi resulted in the loss of hundreds of thousands of lives. The final custodians of Japanese unification, the Tokugawa family, created a system over several generations that they hoped would preserve Japan forever in a state of unity and seclusion. Yet over the two and a half centuries of the Tokugawa peace, forces were building that would allow Japan to vault into the modern world with unprecedented speed in the late nineteenth century.

The Struggle for Unification

As we have seen, the fundamental instability of the Ashikaga regime lent itself to the continual contesting for the shogun's office among the more powerful *daimyo*, or regional warlords. In 1467, these factional battles finally erupted into a devastating civil war that would last off and on for more than a century. The opening phase of this struggle, the Onin War, lasted 10 years and devastated the city of Kyoto, while leaving the imperial court barely functional and the shogunate in tatters. With no real center of power, a bitter struggle of all against all among the daimyos continued into the 1570s.

Oda Nobunaga and Toyotomi Hideyoshi For the Japanese, the period was called *Gekokujo*, or "those below toppling those above." By the mid-sixteenth century, a handful of daimyos began the painful process of consolidating their power and securing allies. One important factor in deciding the outcome of these wars was the result of intrusion from the outside. By the 1540s, the first Portuguese and Spanish merchants and missionaries had arrived in southern Japan. One daimyo who was quick to use the newcomers and their improved small arms to his advantage was Oda Nobunaga, the son of a small landholder who had risen through the ranks to command. Oda employed newly converted Christian musketeers to secure the area around Kyoto and had largely succeeded in unifying the country when he was assassinated in 1582. His second in command, Hideyoshi, whom we met in the opening of this chapter, was another commoner who had risen through the ranks. Now he assumed Oda's mantle and systematically brought the remaining daimyos under his sway over the next nine years.

Hideyoshi viewed a foreign adventure at this point as an excellent way to cement the loyalties of the newly subdued daimyos. In addition, the army he had put together—battle hardened, well trained, with perhaps the largest number of guns of any force in the world at the time—might prove dangerous to disband. Hence, as early as 1586 he announced his grandiose plans to conquer China itself. Thus, in 1592 he set out with a massive expeditionary force, which at its peak numbered over 200,000 men. Though his supply lines were harassed unmercifully by the Korean naval forces in their well-armored "turtle ships," the Japanese made good progress up the peninsula until massive Chinese counterattacks slowly eroded their gains and decimated large stretches of Korea.

Hideyoshi's adventure ended when he turned homeward to Japan with the remnants of his army in 1596. His stature as a commander and force of personality kept his coalition of daimyos together until his death during his troubled second Korean campaign in 1598.

The coalition then broke in two, and a civil war began between Tokugawa Ieyasu, the charismatic leader of the eastern coalition of daimyos, and their western counterparts. In the fall of 1600, the back of the western coalition was broken by the Tokugawa victory at the Battle of Sekigahara, near Kyoto. Ieyasu, who claimed to be a descendant of the Minamoto clan, the original shoguns, laid claim to the office and was officially invested with it in 1603. His accession marked the beginning of

Toyotomi Hideyoshi (1536–1598). Portraits of Japanese daimyo and shoguns tend to position them in similar ways, looking to the front left, with stiff, heavily starched official robes that reflect their austerity and dignity. In this 1601 portrait, done several years after his death, Hideyoshi is shown in a typical pose, with the signs of his adopted family and imperial crests around the canopy to denote his role of imperial guardian.

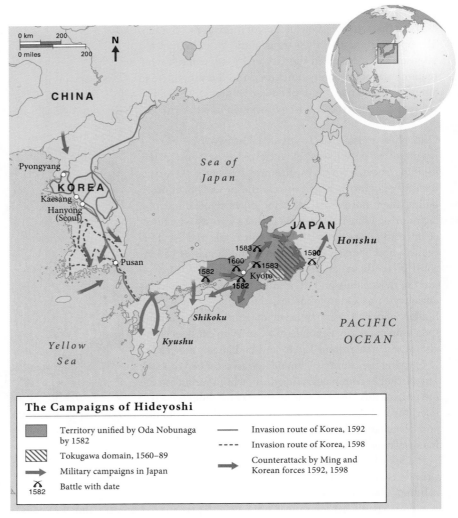

MAP **21.5** **The Campaigns of Hideyoshi.**

Japan's most peaceful, most secluded, and perhaps most thoroughly regulated and policed interval in its long history. Breaking precedent, the Tokugawas would create a hereditary shogunate, organized along Chinese Neo-Confucian models of morality and government, that would last until 1867 (see Map 21.5).

The Tokugawa *Bakufu* to 1750

The realm that Tokugawa Ieyasu (1542–1616) had won at the Battle of Sekigahara was one that had been scarred by seemingly endless warfare and social disruption. The daimyos and samurai, their armies as large as hundreds of thousands of soldiers in some cases, employed some of the most advanced military technology in the world, but their depredations had broken old loyalties and alliances. The intrusion of European missionaries and merchants, along with their converts and agents, contributed to the social ferment. The brief interlude of unity behind Hideyoshi's continental adventures had thoroughly unraveled and, indeed, had been a contributing cause of the civil war that had brought Ieyasu to power.

Ieyasu's assumption of the shogunate in 1603 thus began a process of unparalleled centralization and stabilization in Japan that would last until 1867. Initially, however, seclusion did not figure among its principles. In fact, under the direction of European advisors, Ieyasu and his son Hidetada (1579–1632) laid plans to build a powerful naval and merchant fleet during their first decade of rule. Seclusion did not emerge as the shogunate's policy until the 1630s. The most pressing order of business was to erect a system within which to place all the daimyos that would at once reward the loyal and keep a watchful eye on the defeated.

"Tent Government"   The system devised under the Tokugawa *bakufu* ("tent government," referring to the shogun's official status as the emperor's mobile deputy) was called *sankin kotai*, the "rule of alternate attendance." An inner ring of daimyo holdings was annexed by the Tokugawa family and administered by their retainers. All daimyos were then given either *fudai*, or "inner" domains, if they had been allies of the Tokugawa, or *tozama*, "outer" domains, if they had ultimately surrendered to Ieyasu's eastern coalition. The shogunate placed its new headquarters in the Tokugawa castle in Edo, the future city of Tokyo. In order to ensure their loyalty, all outer daimyos were required to reside in the capital in alternate years and return to their domains during the off years. Members of their families were required to stay as permanent hostages in Edo. Daimyos were also required to bring their most important retainers and their households with them during their stays. Almost from the beginning, therefore, the main roads to Edo, most famously the Tokaido, were the scene of constant daimyo processions. Like the great pilgrimage routes of Islam, Buddhism, and Christianity, these roads spurred enormous commerce and the creation of an array of services to meet the needs of the constant traffic. And like the French nobility a few decades later at Versailles, the daimyos found both their power and their purses increasingly depleted.

Freezing Society   In turning the office of shogun over to his son Hidetada in 1605, Ieyasu made it legally hereditary for the first time. With the possibility of revolt always just under the surface, Ieyasu stayed on as regent and pursued further measures to enhance the stability of the regime. Under his grandson Iemitsu (1604–1651), most of the characteristic Tokugawa policies in this regard became institutionalized. The shogunate declared that, like in the *jati* system in India, the members of the officially recognized classes in Japan—daimyos, samurai, peasants, artisans, merchants—and their descendants would be required to stay in those classes forever. The Tokugawa adopted Neo-Confucianism as the governing ideology, thus joining the commonwealth of Confucian "religious civilizations" in the region, and its long-established precepts of filial piety, models of ethical behavior, and unswerving loyalty to the government were incorporated into the new law codes.

Significant differences, however, separated the practice of this system in Japan from similar, concurrent systems in China, Korea, and Vietnam. In China and Vietnam, a civil service had long been in place, complete with a graded system of examinations from which the best candidates would be drawn for duty. The situation in Japan was closer to that of Korea, in which the *Yangban* were already a hereditary aristocracy in the countryside and so monopolized the official classes. Japan, though, differed even further because the samurai and daimyos were now not just a hereditary class of officials but a military aristocracy as well. Not only was the low position traditionally given to the military in Chinese Confucianism totally reversed, but the daimyo and samurai had absolute, unquestioned power of life and death over all commoners. Like their counterparts in China, they were expected to have mastered the classics and the refined arts of painting, poetry, and calligraphy. But official reports and popular literature are full of accounts of samurai cutting down hapless peasants who failed to bow quickly enough to daimyo processions or who committed other infractions, no matter how trivial.

Giving Up the Gun   In order to ensure that the samurai class would be free from any serious challenge, the government required them to practice the time-honored skills of swordsmanship, archery, and other forms of individual martial arts. But the rapid development of firearms and their pervasive presence in the realm remained a threat to any class whose skills were built entirely around hand-to-hand combat. Thus, in a way perhaps unique among the world's nations, the Tokugawa literally "gave up the gun." Tokugawa police conducted searches for forbidden weapons among commoners and destroyed almost the entire stock of the nation's firearms. A few museum pieces were kept as curiosities, as were the bronze cannon in some of the Tokugawa seaside forts. Thus, weapons that had been among the most advanced in the world when they were cast in the 1600s were the ones that confronted the first foreign ships nearly 250 years later in 1853.

As the shogunate strove to impose peace on the daimyo and bring stability to the populace, it became increasingly anxious to weed out disruptive influences. In addition to the unsettling potential of the country's guns, therefore, the Tokugawa began to restrict the movements of foreigners, particularly missionaries. From the earliest days of European arrivals in Japan, subjects of competing countries and religions had brought their quarrels with them, often involving Japanese as allies or objects of intrigue. The influence of the missionaries on the growing numbers of Japanese Christians—perhaps 200,000 by the 1630s—was especially worrisome to those intent on firmly establishing Neo-Confucian beliefs and rituals among the commoners. Moreover, the bitter duel between Catholic and Protestant missionaries and merchants carried its own set of problems for social stability, especially in the ports, where the majority of such activities tended to take place.

Christian Martyrs. Beginning in 1617 and culminating in the suppression of a rebellion by impoverished Christian peasants in 1637–1638, missionaries and their converts to the foreign faith were brutally persecuted by the Tokugawa. Wholesale massacres and even crucifixions along the main roads were not uncommon, or, as in this engraving, hanging clergy—in this case Jesuits—upside down and setting them on fire.

Tokugawa Seclusion   Ultimately, therefore, missionaries were ordered to leave the country, followed by the merchants. The English and Spanish withdrew in the 1620s, while the Portuguese stayed until 1639. Ultimately, only the Dutch, Koreans, and Chinese were allowed to remain, in small, limited numbers and subject to the pleasure of the shogunate. Further, in 1635 it was ruled that Japanese subjects would be forbidden to leave the islands and that no oceangoing ships were to be built. Any Japanese who left would be considered traitors and executed upon return. Like the Canton system later in Qing China, foreign merchants would be permitted only in designated areas in port cities and could not bring their families with them. The only Europeans permitted to stay, the Dutch, were chosen because they appeared to be the least affected by the religious bickering that characterized their European counterparts. They were, however, restricted to a tiny island called Dejima (also known as Deshima) built on a landfill in Nagasaki harbor. In return for the privilege, they were required to make yearly reports in person to the shogun's ministers on world events. Over time, the collections of these reports found a small but willing readership among educated and cultured Japanese. This "Dutch learning" and the accounts of Chinese and Korean observers formed the basis of the Japanese view of the outside world for over two centuries. Like European learning in Korea and Vietnam, it also provided useful examples for reformers to use in critiquing Neo-Confucian society.

Trampling the Crucifix   Much less tolerance was shown to Japan's Christian community. Dissatisfaction with the new Tokugawa strictures provoked a rebellion at Shimabara just outside Nagasaki in 1637 by Christian converts and disaffected samurai. As the revolt was suppressed, many of those facing the prospect of capture and execution by the Tokugawa flung themselves into the volcanic hot springs nearby. Those who were captured were subjected to what their captors understood to be appropriate European-style punishment: Instead of being burned at the stake, they were clustered together and roasted to death inside a wide ring of fire. Subsequently, remaining missionaries were sometimes crucified upside down, while suspected converts were given an opportunity to "trample the crucifix" to show they had discarded the new faith. Those who refused to convert back to approved faiths were imprisoned or executed. In the end, perhaps 37,000 people were killed.

For all their attempts at suppressing the religion, however, tens of thousands continued to practice in secret until Christianity was declared legal again during the reign of Emperor Meiji (r. 1867–1912). Though foreign ships would occasionally attempt to call at Japanese ports, by the eighteenth century Europeans generally

Dutch Ships in Nagasaki Harbor. This detail from a 1764 map shows Dutch and Japanese ships in Nagasaki harbor. The Japanese ships are dwarfed by the much larger Dutch sailing vessels. The small fan-shaped area connected to the town of Nagasaki was the only place where the Dutch were allowed to disembark and trade. They were forbidden to cross the causeway into the city itself.

steered clear of the islands. As we will see in Chapter 24, however, by the middle decade of the nineteenth century the opening of more ports in China for trade, the growth of the whaling industry, and the quest for gold in California would all conspire to change this situation forever.

Growth and Stagnation: Economy and Society

While a number of the processes begun under earlier shogunates continued during the seventeenth and eighteenth centuries, their pace quickened immensely. Perhaps most dramatically, by 1750, Japan had become one of the most urbanized societies on earth, next to the Netherlands. Edo itself reached a million people, making it arguably the world's largest city. Osaka and Kyoto were both approaching 400,000, and perhaps as much as 10 percent of Japan's population lived in cities with populations above 10,000 (see Map 21.6). In a way, such explosive growth is even more remarkable given that the Tokugawa placed strict curbs on travel within their realms. Commoners, for example, were not to leave their home districts without permission from the local authorities. On the other hand, as we have seen, the law of alternate attendance ensured an immense and growing traffic in and out of the major cities along the major routes

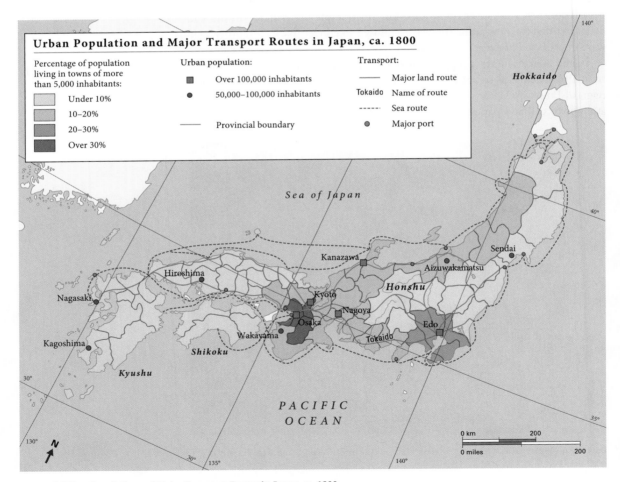

MAP **21.6** **Urban Population and Major Transport Routes in Japan, ca. 1800.**

into Edo. The vast array of services required to support that traffic aided urban and suburban growth and had the effect of spreading the wealth down to the urban merchants, artisans, entertainers, bathhouse proprietors, and even refuse collectors.

Population, Food, and Commerce   Perhaps a more direct cause of this urbanization may be found in the growth of the population as a whole. By various estimates, Japan may have had as many as 33 million people in 1720. The efficiency of small-scale, intensive rice and vegetable farming, aided by easy-to-operate, simple machines such as the Chinese-style "climbing stair" or "dragon wheel" pump made Japanese agriculture the most efficient in the preindustrial world. Such efficiencies would create one of the most densely populated rural landscapes in the world even into the twentieth century.

As we have noted, various Tokugawa policies aimed at stabilizing the country politically and socially had the unanticipated effect of spurring the economy. A number of factors contributed to this in addition to the forced movement of the daimyos and their retinues in alternate years. The Tokugawa tax structure set quotas of rice for each village, rather than for individuals, and left the individual daimyos responsible for remitting these to the capital. Thus, an immense traffic in bulk rice further spurred the carrying trade along the roads and in the coastal waters. In addition to guaranteeing provisions for the cities, the need to convert rice to cash for the treasury contributed greatly to building a banking and credit infrastructure. Indeed, the practice of merchant bankers advancing credit to wholesalers against anticipated rice crops created what some scholars have called an early kind of futures market. The progress of the famous Mitsui *zaibatsu*, or cartel, of the nineteenth and twentieth centuries followed such a route, its members starting in 1670 as dry goods merchants and gradually moving into the position of bankers for the shogunate.

The tastes of the three largest cities—Edo, with its high concentration of the wealthy and well connected; Kyoto, with its large retinue of the imperial household; and Osaka, the chief port—created a huge demand for evermore sophisticated consumer goods and services. Such enterprises as sake brewing, wholesaling dried and prepared foods, running bathhouses, and managing large studios of artisans all became booming businesses. Even the import and export trades, slowed to a relative trickle by government regulations, proved quite lucrative for the few engaged in them. Books, porcelains, lacquerware, and objets d'art were exchanged for Japanese hard currency. Indeed, the vibrancy of Japanese urban life and a burgeoning middle class created what scholars have sometimes called the "democratization of taste." That is, what was once the strict province of the court, daimyo, and samurai was now widely available to anyone who had the money and interest to afford it. Moreover, the new moneyed classes were also creating new directions in the arts and entertainment. Hence without pushing the parallels too far, the economic forces in Tokugawa Japan were creating within their secluded environment conditions not unlike those developing in England—though conspicuously minus the overseas colonies.

Rural Transformations   Life in rural areas underwent certain changes as well. As they had with the military houses, the Tokugawa promulgated Neo-Confucian rules for the comportment of families and their individual members. Like parish churches in Europe, each local Buddhist temple was to keep registers of the villagers in its district. Weddings, funerals, travel, rents, taxes, and so forth were subject to

Woodblock Print of the Fish Market at the East Side of Nihonbashi (The Bridge of Japan). The Tokugawa period, with its long interlude of peace and prosperity, was Japan's first great age of urban life. The constant traffic of daimyo progressions along the main roads and the large coasting trade along the Inland Sea ensured a growing middle class of artisans, tradespeople, and merchants. The capital, Edo, had ballooned to over a million people on the eve of the American intrusion; and the bustle of the capital is illustrated in this panel depicting a famous fish market.

official permission through either the village headman or the samurai holding a position equivalent to a magistrate. Within these strictures, however, and subject to the hereditary occupation laws, families, clans, and villages were relatively autonomous.

This was especially true of rural families, in which men, women, and children commonly worked together on their plots. While the "inner domain," so central to Neo-Confucian thought as the strict province of women, retained a good deal of that character, there were also many areas that mitigated it. Men, for example, routinely helped in the everyday tasks of childrearing. As late as the 1860s, foreign observers reported watching rural groups of men minding infants while their wives were engaged in some collective task. Women in cities and larger villages routinely ran businesses, especially those involved in entertainment. Indeed, the women of the famous geisha houses, owned and run by women, were renowned for their skills, education, wit, and refinement. Even on a more humble level, women ran bathhouses, taverns, restaurants, and retail establishments of all sorts. Interestingly, by the eighteenth century, merchants increasingly utilized the spinning and weaving talents of rural and semirural women in parceling out the various steps in textile manufacturing to them—a Japanese version of the English "putting out system."

The Samurai in Peacetime   As time went by, the position of the samurai in rural society changed as well. Though he was expected to hone his military skills, his role as an official and Neo-Confucian role model gradually became paramount. Samurai existed on stipends, either directly from the Tokugawa or from their local daimyo. These, however, were no guarantee of prosperity, and by the later eighteenth century the samurai living in genteel poverty had become something of a popular stereotype. In many areas, they functioned as schoolmasters and founded village academies in the local temples for the teaching of practical literacy and correct moral behavior. By the mid-nineteenth century Japan may have had the world's highest level of functional literacy. As in Korea, this proved important in popularizing new crops or agricultural techniques.

By the middle of the eighteenth century there were signs of tension among the aims of the government in ensuring peace and stability, the dynamism of the internal economy, and the boom in population. Like China a century later, some scholars contend that Japan had approached the limit of the ability of the land to support its people. In fact, Japan's population remained remarkably steady from the middle of the eighteenth century to the latter nineteenth. Repeated signs of creeping rural impoverishment and social unrest manifested themselves, however, and were often noted by commentators. Inflation in commodity prices ran ahead of efforts to increase domain revenues, squeezing those on fixed incomes and stipends. Efforts to keep rural families small enough to subsist on their plots led to an increasing frequency of infanticide. Compounding such problems were large-scale famines in 1782 and 1830. By the early nineteenth century, there was an increasing perception that the government was gradually losing its ability to care for the populace.

Hothousing "Japaneseness": Culture, Science, and Intellectual Life

As with so many elements of Japanese cultural history, existing genres of art—major styles of painting, poetry, and calligraphy—continued to flourish among the daimyos and samurai, while exerting an increasing pull on the tastes of the new middle classes. Indeed, Zen-influenced **monochrome** painting, the ideals of the tea ceremony championed by Sen Rikyu, the austere Noh theater, and the abstract principles of interior design and landscape gardening were carefully preserved and popularized until they became universally recognized as "Japanese."

New Theater Traditions   Traditional cultural elements coexisted with new forms, with some adapting aspects of these earlier arts and others conceived as mass entertainment. Among the former was the development of *bunraku*, the elaborate puppet theater still popular in Japan today. Bunraku puppets, perhaps one-third life size, generally took three puppeteers to manipulate. Their highly facile movements and facial expressions staged against a black backdrop to conceal their handlers readily allowed the audience to suspend disbelief and proved a highly effective way to popularize the older Noh plays. But renowned playwrights soon wrote special works for these theaters as well.

The most revered was Chikamatsu Monzaemon [chick-ah-MAT-soo mon-ZAE-mon] (1653–1724), who skillfully transferred the tragically noble sentiments of the best Noh works into contemporary themes. The fatal tension between love and social obligation, for example, made his *Love Suicide at Sonezaki* wildly popular with Edo audiences. His most famous work, *The Forty-Seven Ronin*, written in 1706, is based on a 1703 incident in which the daimyo of 47 samurai was killed by a political opponent, leaving them as *ronin*—masterless. Out of loyalty to their dead daimyo the ronin kill his assassin in full knowledge that their lives will then be forfeit to the authorities, a price they stoically go on to pay.

Originally written for bunraku, *The Forty-Seven Ronin* was adapted a few decades later as a work for *kabuki*, the other great mass entertainment art of Tokugawa Japan. Because kabuki was originally a satirical and explicitly bawdy form of theater, the government banned women from appearing in it, hoping to sever its association with

Monochrome: Single-color; in East Asian painting, a very austere style popular in the fourteenth and fifteenth centuries, particularly among Zen-influenced artists.

Two Courtesans. During the late seventeenth century, the new genre of ukiyo-e, "pictures of the floating world," developed and remained popular through the nineteenth century. Finely wrought woodblock prints in both monochrome and color, they take their name from the pleasure districts whose people and scenes were favorite subjects. This work is from a series by the noted artist Kitagawa Utamaro (ca. 1753–1806) on famous courtesans of the "Southern District," part of the Shinagawa section of Edo.

image analysis

prostitution. Female impersonators as actors continued its risqué reputation, however, while more serious works also drew immense crowds to the pleasure districts, to which the theaters were by law segregated. Kabuki remained by far the most popular Japanese mass entertainment, and interestingly, given the medium's off-color reputation, *The Forty-Seven Ronin* remained the most frequently performed play throughout the Tokugawa period.

The era also marked the golden age of the powerfully brief poetic form of *haiku*, the most famous practitioner of which was the renowned Matsuo Basho (1644–1694). As a poet he used a dozen pen names; he took "Basho" from the banana plant he especially liked in his yard. In poems like "Old Battlefield" the 17-syllable couplets compressed unbearable emotion and release in a way that has made them a treasured form in Japan and, more recently, in much of the world.

The visual arts found new forms of expression through the widespread use of fine woodblock printing, which allowed popular works to be widely duplicated. The new genre was called *ukiyo-e*, "pictures of the floating world," a reference to the pleasure quarters on the edge of the cities that furnished many of its subjects. Though largely scorned by the upper classes, it remained the most popular form of advertising, portraiture, and news distribution until the end of the nineteenth century, when it began to be supplanted by photography. During Tokugawa times, one of the most famous practitioners of the art was Kitagawa Utamaro (1753–1806), whose studies of women became forever associated with Japanese perceptions of female beauty. In the works of Katsushika Hokusai (1760–1849) and Ando Hiroshige (1797–1858) scenes like Hokusai's *Thirty-Six Views of Mt. Fuji*, or, like Utamaro's work, gentle snowfalls on temples, formed many of the first popular images that nineteenth-century Westerners had of Japan.

≫ Putting It All Together

During the late Ming and early Qing periods, imperial China achieved social and political stability and developed the world's largest economy. Yet, by the second part of the eighteenth century, internal problems were already germinating that would come to the surface in succeeding decades. In the following century, these initial cracks in the empire's structure would continue to grow and have a profound impact on China's fortunes.

The arrival of large numbers of foreign traders who brought with them the new technologies of the first scientific–industrial societies, combined with China's profound self-confidence in its own culture and institutions, added more pressure to an already volatile internal situation and ultimately created an unprecedented challenge

interactive concept map

for China. Over the coming decades, Chinese expectations of being able to civilize and assimilate all comers would dissolve, along with the hope that a renewed faithfulness to Confucian fundamentals would produce the leaders necessary to navigate such perilous times. But at the halfway mark of the eighteenth century, the Chinese still expected that they would successfully regulate the "inner" and "outer" domains of their empire and keep pernicious foreign influences at arm's length.

Ravaged by a century of warfare and foreign intrusion, Japan also sought to regulate its inner and outer domains and minimize outside influences. As with China, however, the stability perfected by the Tokugawa shogunate in the seventeenth and eighteenth centuries would be increasingly threatened in the nineteenth by the growing commercial power of the Europeans and Americans. Before the nineteenth century was finished, China would be rent by the bloodiest civil war in human history, while Japan would experience its own civil war and, in its aftermath, install a unified government under an emperor for the first time since the twelfth century. In the final years of the nineteenth century, Japan would once again invade Korea to attack China—this time with very different results. In the process, the historical relationship of more than two millennia between the two countries would be altered forever.

Review and Relate

Thinking Through Patterns

Examine the ways historians approach the big questions of this chapter.

In some respects the problem is similar to that faced by planners for defense spending in nations today: Why maintain huge, expensive systems when there are no enemies against which to use them? While the commercial prospects for China's fleets grew in prominence, maritime trade was simply not essential to the Chinese economy at that point. Moreover, urgent defense preparations were needed in the overland north against the resurgent Mongols. It is important to remember that the discontinuation of the fleets seems like a mistake in hindsight because of what happened to China hundreds of years later due to a lack of adequate naval defenses. At the time, however, these measures seemed both rational and appropriate to the Chinese and outside observers.

» **Why did late Ming and early Qing China look inward after such a successful period of overseas exploration?**

One almost universal pattern of world history among agrarian states is that their governments adopt policies aimed at promoting social stability. The reason for this is that, in short, nearly everything depends on having reliable harvests. Given the agricultural techniques and technologies of preindustrial societies, the majority of the population must be engaged in food production to ensure sufficient surpluses to feed the nonproducing classes. If such a society places a premium on change and social mobility, it risks chronic manpower shortages and insufficient harvests. Thus, social classes—whether in feudal Europe, India, China, or Japan—are carefully delineated, and the state directs its policies toward eliminating social upheaval.

» **How do the goals of social stability drive the policies of agrarian states? How does the history of China and Japan in this period show these policies in action?**

> **In what ways did contact with the maritime states of Europe alter the patterns of trade and politics in eastern Asia?**

> **How did Neo-Confucianism in China differ from that of Tokugawa Japan?**

In both China and Japan, these connections resulted in severe restrictions on maritime trade: the Canton system in China and the seclusion policies of the Tokugawa in Japan. Earlier, the Chinese emperor had welcomed Jesuit missionaries for their expertise in mathematics and science and even considered conversion to Catholicism. But the backlash against "subversive" influence induced the Qing to drive Christianity underground. In Japan such contact had earlier injected European influences into Japan's civil wars, and the reaction against this was Tokugawa seclusion.

The fundamental difference was that Japan was a military society, which adopted the forms and structures of Neo-Confucianism to make the daimyo and samurai into officials. They therefore were expected to maintain this civil role as bureaucrats but also to stand ready to fight if need be. The low esteem in which the military was held in China was just the inverse of that of the martial elites of Japan. Another key difference was that officials in China were selected on the basis of competitive examinations, thus creating some social mobility. In Japan, the social classes were frozen and no exams were offered for potential officials.

| Against the Grain

Consider this as a counterpoint to the main patterns examined in this chapter.

Seclusion's Exceptions

- While the attempts by China, Korea, and Japan to keep out foreign influences may strike us as impractical, many nations today still seek to limit foreign influences, particularly in the realm of culture. What are the advantages and disadvantages of such policies? Are they inevitably self-defeating?

- Were the policies of turning inward among these agrarian–urban societies part of larger historical patterns at work during this time? Why or why not?

Despite Japan's *sakoku* (closed country) policies of seclusion during the Tokugawa era, scholars have long understood that the country was more porous than popularly supposed. This was of course most true for Chinese and Korean merchants doing business in Japan. Formal relations of a sort with Korea on a more or less equal footing were maintained by the Tokugawa through the lord of the Tsushima *han*, or feudal domain, who also maintained a trading post in the Korean port of Pusan. Korean vessels, like those of the Chinese, were permitted to put in at Nagasaki, and Korean goods were in high enough demand that the shogunate's attempts to curtail silver exports were generally waived for Korean trade. Moreover, more than a dozen Korean trade missions traveled to the shogun's court during the Tokugawa period.

No official exchanges with Chinese representatives took place either in Edo or Beijing, since neither side wanted to be seen as the junior partner in the Neo-Confucian hierarchy of diplomacy by the so-called tribute mission system. In addition to the predominance of Chinese ships at Nagasaki, however, both Chinese and Japanese merchants took advantage of a loophole in the sovereignty of the Ryukyu Islands to trade there. China and Japan both insisted that the islands were their protectorate, though the Japanese domain of Satsuma had captured Okinawa in 1609. The leaders in

Okinawa, however, sent trade and tribute missions to both China and Japan in order to safeguard their freedom of action, thus keeping the conduit for trade semiofficially open for both sides.

The Dutch remained the European exceptions. In part, this was a condition they had helped engineer themselves: They had continually warned the Tokugawa about the sinister religious intentions of their Iberian competitors, suggesting that the Dutch alone should handle Japan's European trade. Indeed, though the volume of China's trade in Japan was many times larger, it was the Dutch who retained yearly access to the shogunate. Though their power and influence in European markets ebbed considerably during the eighteenth and early nineteenth centuries, their influence among the small but intellectually vital circle of Japanese scholars and leaders engaged in *rangaku*—"Dutch learning"—remained strong right up to the time of the coming of Perry's "Black Ships" in 1853. Thus, as one scholar of Japan has put it, "The Nagasaki door was always ajar and sometimes wide open."

Key Terms

audio flashcards

Banner system 625	Factory 633	Monochrome 647

For additional resources, please go to
www.oup.com/us/vonsivers.
Please see the Further Resources section at the back of the book for additional readings and suggested websites.

Sources for Chapter 21

SOURCE 21.1   Treaty between Koxinga and the Dutch government, Formosa

1662

In the seventeenth century, the Manchus crossed the Great Wall, captured Beijing, and founded a new regime, the Qing, or "pure," dynasty. Some Ming loyalists fled to the island of Formosa (Taiwan), off the Chinese coast, where they expelled the Dutch. The Europeans had established a trading base on the island, and the document below demonstrates the negotiated surrender of this fort to Koxinga.

Treaty made and agreed upon; from the one side, by His Highness the LORD TEIBINGH TSIANTE TEYSIANCON KOXIN, who has besieged Castle Zeelandia on Formosa since 1st May 1661 up till this 1st day of February 1662; and from the other side, as representing the Dutch Government, by the Governor of the said Castle, FREDERIK COYETT, and his Council, consisting of the undernoted eighteen Articles:

Article 1

All hostilities committed on either side to be forgotten.

Article 2

Castle Zeelandia, with its outworks, artillery, remaining war materiel, merchandise, money, and other properties belonging to the Honourable Company, to be surrendered to LORD KOXINGA.

Article 3

Rice, bread, wine, arack, meat, pork, oil, vinegar, ropes, canvas, pitch, tar, anchors, gunpowder, bullets, and linen, with such other articles as may be required by the besieged during their voyage to Batavia, to be taken aboard the Company's ships in keeping with instructions from the before-mentioned Governor and Council.

Article 4

All private movable property inside the Castle or elsewhere belonging to officers of the Dutch Government, shall first be inspected by LORD KOXINGA's delegates, and then placed on board the said ships.

. . .

Source: William Campbell, *Formosa under the Dutch* (London: Kegan Paul, Trench, Trubner, 1903), 455–456.

Article 9

Every servant of the Company, now imprisoned by the Chinese in Formosa, shall be liberated within eight or ten days, and those who are in China, as soon as possible. Servants of the Company who are not imprisoned in Formosa shall be granted a free pass to reach the Company's ships in safety.

Article 10

The said LORD KOXINGA shall now return to the Company the four captured boats, with all their accessories.

Article 11

He shall also provide a sufficient number of vessels to take the Honourable Company's people and goods to their ships.

Article 12

Vegetables, flesh-meat, and whatever else may be necessary to sustain the Company's people during their stay, shall daily be provided by His Highness's subjects at a reasonable price.

Article 13

So long as the Honourable Company's people remain on land before embarkation, no soldier or other subject of LORD KOXINGA shall be permitted to enter the Castle (unless on service for the Company), to approach the outworks nearer than the **gabions**, or to proceed further than the palisades erected by order of His Highness.

Gabion: A cage or box filled with rocks or sand; used in military fortifications.

Article 14

No other than a white flag shall float from the Castle until the Honourable Company's people have marched out.

. . .

Article 18

All misunderstandings, and every important matter overlooked in this Agreement, shall immediately be dealt with to the satisfaction of both parties, upon notice having been given on either side.

LORD CHEN CH'ENG-KUNG, [L. S.]
FREDERIK COYETT, [L. S.]

≫ Working with Sources

1. How and why did the forces of Lord Koxinga attempt to negotiate a less humiliating surrender for the Dutch? What were the long-term goals of both sides to the treaty?

2. Is Koxinga negotiating with the Dutch government, or more with a private corporation in the area?

SOURCE 21.2   Matteo Ricci, *China in the Sixteenth Century*

ca. 1600

When European Christian missionaries first came to Ming China, they made very little progress in converting the Chinese, in large part due to their limited training in Chinese language and culture. When he arrived in China in 1583, the Jesuit Matteo Ricci (1552–1610) encouraged his followers to immerse themselves in the language and to become conversant with the rich traditions of Chinese literature. He also came to be respected by, and especially helpful to, the emperor, as he offered his expertise in the sciences and mathematics to the imperial court. With a European Jesuit (Adam Schall von Bell) as the official court astronomer to Kangxi, there were reports that the Emperor himself considered converting to Catholicism. Nevertheless, not every encounter between Chinese and Europeans went so smoothly, as the following anecdote from Ricci's diary reveals.

Of late they [the Chinese] had become quite disturbed by the coming of the Portuguese, and particularly so because they can do nothing about it, due to the great profit reaped from Portuguese traders by the public treasury and by certain influential merchants. Without referring to the public treasury or to the merchants who come from every other province, they complain that the foreign commerce raises the price of all commodities and that outsiders are the only ones to profit from it. As an expression of their contempt for Europeans, when the Portuguese first arrived they were called foreign devils, and this name is still in common use among the Cantonese.

The citizens of Sciauquin have their own particular reasons for hating the strangers. They are afraid that the Portuguese merchants will get into the interior of the realm with the missionaries, and their fears are not without some foundation. The frequent visits of the Fathers to the town of Macao and their growing intimacy with the Governor have already aroused their antipathy. There is nothing that stirs them up like a wide-spreading slander, and they had a good one in the story that the tower which had been built at such great expense, and with so much labor, was erected at the request of the foreign priests. This probably had its origin in the fact that the tower was completed while the Fathers were building their mission houses. This false rumor had such an effect that the people called it the Tower of the Foreigners instead of The Flowery Tower, as it was named. As a result of the animosity which grew out of this incident, when they realized that they could not drive out the Mission, as

Source: Matthew Ricci, *China in the Sixteenth Century*, trans. Louis Gallagher (New York: Random House, 1953), 161–165.

they wanted to, they took to insulting the missionaries whenever an occasion occurred or they could trump up a reason for doing so. It was quite annoying and dangerous to be made a continual target for stones hurled from the tower, when people came there every day to play games, the purpose for which these towers are built. Not a stone was thrown at the Mission House from the high tower nearby that missed its roof as a target. These showers of stones were heaviest when they knew that there were only one or two of the servants at home. Another silly reason for their taking offense was that the doors of our house, which were kept open for inspection while it was being built, were now kept closed according to the rule of our Society. What they wanted to do was to use the house as they did their temples of idols, which are always left wide open and are often the scenes of uncouth frivolity.

It happened one day, when their insolence became really unbearable, that one of our servants ran out and seized a boy, who had been throwing stones at the house, and dragging him inside threatened to bring him to court. Attracted by the shrieking of the boy, several men, who were known in the neighborhood, ran into the house to intercede for the culprit, and Father Ricci ordered that he be allowed to depart without further ado. Here was a good pretext for a major calumny, and two of the neighbors who disliked the Fathers went into conference with a bogus relative of the boy, who knew something about court procedure. Then they trumped up a story that the boy had been seized by the Fathers and hidden in their house for three days, that he had been given a certain drug, well known to the Chinese, which prevented him from crying out, and that the purpose of it all was to smuggle him back to Macao, where they could sell him into slavery. The two men were to be called in as witnesses.

. . .

[A trial takes place before the Governor, and he hears the "witnesses" to the crime.]

. . .

Finally, in order to save the Father present from any embarrassment, he [the Governor] declared him [Ricci] wholly innocent and. . . his next move was to summon the three members of the building commission, who were at the tower on the day the incident occurred. The plaintiff requested that he call in the neighbors also, the real authors of the charge, who had a full knowledge of all its details. The Governor dismissed the multitude and, as he was leaving, he forbade the Father to leave the court. In the meantime, and in deep humiliation, the Father betook himself to prayer, commending his cause and its solution to God, to the Blessed Mother and to the Saints.

. . .

Then he [the Governor] told the missionary and his interpreter and the three Commissioners that he had heard enough of this affair, and that they might return to their homes and their business.

. . .

On the following day the Governor sent a solemn document to be posted at the main entrance of the Mission House. This notice, after explaining that the foreigners were living here with permission of the Viceroy, stated that certain unprincipled persons, contrary to right and reason, were known to have molested the strangers living herein, wherefore: he, the Governor, strictly forbade under severest penalty that anyone from now on should dare to cause them further molestation.

> **» Working with Sources**

1. What seems to have been Ricci's attitude toward Chinese customs and religious practices?
2. To what extent did trade rights and religious goals intersect in this setting? What was in the immediate and long-term interests of the Chinese "hosts" of the mission?

SOURCE 21.3   # Emperor Qianlong's Imperial Edict to King George III

1793

The reign of Qianlong (r. 1736–1795) marked both the high point and the beginning of the decline of the Qing dynasty. Several European nations, driven by their desire to corner the market on the lucrative Chinese trade, sent representatives to Qianlong's court. In 1793, Great Britain dispatched Lord Macartney, its first envoy to China, to obtain safe and favorable trade relations for his country. In response, Qianlong composed a letter to King George III (r. 1760–1820) detailing his objections and conditions, which Macartney conveyed back to Britain. The terms of this letter underscore Qianlong's subtle understanding of global economic conditions and the maintenance of a balance between the interests of various nations.

You, O King, live beyond the confines of many seas, nevertheless, impelled by your humble desire to partake of the benefits of our civilisation, you have dispatched a mission respectfully bearing your memorial. Your Envoy has crossed the seas and paid his respects at my Court on the anniversary of my birthday. To show your devotion, you have also sent offerings of your country's produce.

I have perused your memorial: the earnest terms in which it is couched reveal a respectful humility on your part, which is highly praiseworthy. In consideration of the fact that your Ambassador and his deputy have come a long

---

Source: E. Backhouse and J. O. Bland, *Annals and Memoirs of the Court of Peking* (Boston: Houghton Mifflin, 1914), 322–331.

way with your memorial and tribute, I have shown them high favour and have allowed them to be introduced into my presence. To manifest my indulgence, I have entertained them at a banquet and made them numerous gifts. I have also caused presents to be forwarded to the Naval Commander and six hundred of his officers and men, although they did not come to Peking, so that they too may share in my all-embracing kindness.

As to your entreaty to send one of your nationals to be accredited to my Celestial Court and to be in control of your country's trade with China, this request is contrary to all usage of my dynasty and cannot possibly be entertained. It is true that Europeans, in the service of the dynasty, have been permitted to live at Peking, but they are compelled to adopt Chinese dress, they are strictly confined to their own precincts and are never permitted to return home. You are presumably familiar with our dynastic regulations. Your proposed Envoy to my Court could not be placed in a position similar to that of European officials in Peking who are forbidden to leave China, nor could he, on the other hand, be allowed liberty of movement and the privilege of corresponding with his own country; so that you would gain nothing by his residence in our midst.

Moreover, our Celestial dynasty possesses vast territories, and tribute missions from the dependencies are provided for by the Department for Tributary States, which ministers to their wants and exercises strict control over their movements. It would be quite impossible to leave them to their own devices. Supposing that your Envoy should come to our Court, his language and national dress differ from that of our people, and there would be no place in which to bestow him. It may be suggested that he might imitate the Europeans permanently resident in Peking and adopt the dress and customs of China, but, it has never been our dynasty's wish to force people to do things unseemly and inconvenient. Besides, supposing I sent an Ambassador to reside in your country, how could you possibly make for him the requisite arrangements? Europe consists of many other nations besides your own: if each and all demanded to be represented at our Court, how could we possibly consent? The thing is utterly impracticable. How can our dynasty alter its whole procedure and system of etiquette, established for more than a century, in order to meet your individual views? If it be said that your object is to exercise control over your country's trade, your nationals have had full liberty to trade at Canton for many a year, and have received the greatest consideration at our hands. Missions have been sent by Portugal and Italy, preferring similar requests. The Throne appreciated their sincerity and loaded them with favours, besides authorising measures to facilitate their trade with China. You are no doubt aware that, when my Canton merchant, Wu Chao-ping, who was in debt to foreign ships, I made the Viceroy advance the monies due, out of the provincial treasury, and ordered him to punish the culprit severely. Why then should foreign nations advance this utterly unreasonable request to be represented at my Court? Peking is nearly two thousand miles from Canton, and at such a distance what possible control could any British representative exercise?

· · ·

Yesterday your Ambassador petitioned my Ministers to memorialise me regarding your trade with China, but his proposal is not consistent with our dynastic usage and cannot be entertained. Hitherto, all European nations, including your own country's barbarian merchants, have carried on their trade with our Celestial Empire at Canton. Such has been the procedure for many years, although our Celestial Empire possesses all things in prolific abundance and lacks no product within its own borders. There was therefore no need to import the manufactures of outside barbarians in exchange for our own produce. But as the tea, silk and porcelain which the Celestial Empire produces, are absolute necessities to European nations and to yourselves, we have permitted, as a signal mark of favour, that foreign hongs [merchant firms] should be established at Canton, so that your wants might be supplied and your country thus participate in our beneficence. But your Ambassador has now put forward new requests which completely fail to recognise the Throne's principle to "treat strangers from afar with indulgence," and to exercise a pacifying control over barbarian tribes, the world over. Moreover, our dynasty, swaying the myriad races of the globe, extends the same benevolence towards all. Your England is not the only nation trading at Canton. If other nations, following your bad example, wrongfully importune my ear with further impossible requests, how will it be possible for me to treat them with easy indulgence? Nevertheless, I do not forget the lonely remoteness of your island, cut off from the world by intervening wastes of sea, nor do I overlook your excusable ignorance of the usages of our Celestial Empire. I have consequently commanded my Ministers to enlighten your Ambassador on the subject, and have ordered the departure of the mission. But I have doubts that, after your Envoy's return he may fail to acquaint you with my view in detail or that he may be lacking in lucidity, so that I shall now proceed . . . to issue my mandate on each question separately. In this way you will, I trust, comprehend my meaning. . . .

. . .

(7) Regarding your nation's worship of the Lord of Heaven, it is the same religion as that of other European nations. Ever since the beginning of history, sage Emperors and wise rulers have bestowed on China a moral system and inculcated a code, which from time immemorial has been religiously observed by the myriads of my subjects. There has been no hankering after heterodox doctrines. Even the European (missionary) officials in my capital are forbidden to hold intercourse with Chinese subjects; they are restricted within the limits of their appointed residences, and may not go about propagating their religion. The distinction between Chinese and barbarian is most strict, and your Ambassador's request that barbarians shall be given full liberty to disseminate their religion is utterly unreasonable.

It may be, O King, that the above proposals have been wantonly made by your Ambassador on his own responsibility, or peradventure you yourself are ignorant of our dynastic regulations and had no intention of transgressing them when you expressed these wild ideas and hopes. . . . If, after the receipt of this explicit decree, you lightly give ear to the representations of your subordinates and allow your barbarian merchants to proceed to Chêkiang and

Tientsin, with the object of landing and trading there, the ordinances of my Celestial Empire are strict in the extreme, and the local officials, both civil and military, are bound reverently to obey the law of the land. Should your vessels touch the shore, your merchants will assuredly never be permitted to land or to reside there, but will be subject to instant expulsion. In that event your barbarian merchants will have had a long journey for nothing.

> **» Working with Sources**

1. How did Qianlong attempt to keep China and Great Britain on an equal footing, and in what specific regards?

2. How effectively does the emperor balance courtesy and warning in his letter?

SOURCE 21.4 Chikamatsu Monzaemon, *Goban Taiheiki*

1710

This one-act puppet play is one of the first fictionalized (though only thinly disguised) treatments of a famous event that occurred in Tokugawa Japan in 1701–1703. The historical incident began with a knife attack by the daimyo (feudal lord) Asano Naganori on an imperial official named Kira Yoshinaka. Whatever the justice of the provocation, Asano had committed a serious breach in conduct and was forced to pay the most severe penalty. Even though Kira had suffered only a minor wound to his face, Asano was commanded to commit *seppuku*, ritual suicide. When he did so, his 47 samurai vassals were left leaderless (*rōnin*), but they swore to avenge Asano's memory by killing Kira.

In January 1703, the 47 rōnin entered Kira's home, chasing him and killing several of his retainers and wounding others, including Kira's grandson. When they finally trapped and overcame Kira, the rōnin cut off his head and brought it to their master's grave. However, they then decided to turn themselves in to the authorities and commit *seppuku* themselves, true to their code until the bitter end. In order to elude the censors, Chikamatsu altered the names, condensed some of the main details, and offered a judge that was more sympathetic to the rōnin cause. The essential story would reemerge repeatedly in popular culture (both Japanese and non-Japanese) down to the present day.

Source: Jacqueline Miller, "A Chronicle of Great Peace Played Out on a Chessboard: Chikamatsu Monzaemon's Goban Taiheiki," *Harvard Journal of Asiatic Studies*, 46 (1986), 221–267, 263–267.

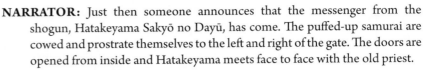

NARRATOR: Just then someone announces that the messenger from the shogun, Hatakeyama Sakyō no Dayū, has come. The puffed-up samurai are cowed and prostrate themselves to the left and right of the gate. The doors are opened from inside and Hatakeyama meets face to face with the old priest.

HATAKEYAMA: "Last night the retainers of En'ya Hangan forced their way into the mansion of Kō no Moronao in order to take revenge on the enemy of their lord, and killed him. As samurai, this has earned them both merit and praise. But they showed no respect for the fact that the shogun's palace was in the vicinity and disturbed the peace of Kamakura. It is the shogun's decision that these men be placed in the charge of Niki and Ishidō, and he orders that today they all cut open their bellies in front of the grave of En'ya. He also grants the head of Moronao to his only son, Moroyasu, and orders you to deliver it to him."

NARRATOR: The head priest accepts the written decree. He prepares a container for the head and sees to it that the arrangements are properly carried out.

HATAKEYAMA: "Let a member of Lord Moroyasu's household who has some semblance of respectability receive the head."

NARRATOR: At this, a chief retainer, Misumi no Gunji, announces his name in an imposing fashion, but there seems to be little honor for him when he returns with heavy heart, bearing the head of his useless master. Told that they ought to begin their preparations right away, the priests place En'ya's shrine in the center. They then place tatami mats to the right and left and spread white sand in front to soak up the blood that will be spilled. Behind they draw a white curtain and set out cushions covered in white silk. And on footed trays they place the knives for the suicides of the more than forty men.

Samurai throughout Kamakura pay solemn visits to the shrines, praying to the tutelary gods of warriors that they themselves, as military men, will be favored with the same good fortune. Poets write sheaves of verse about grief, and litterateurs search for rhymes to express their sorrow. Everyone, regardless of rank, age or sex, regrets this parting and they jostle each other in their haste to gather at the Kōmyōji. There, the scene in front of the gates resembles a fair.

Now the time has come—it is noon. As the moment of death approaches, the official observer, the Lord of Nagoya in Bizen, arrives at the Kōmyōji. Then, beginning with those who will act as seconds, all the officials, including the recording clerks and supervisors, accept their respective commissions and take their places on this formal occasion.

· · ·

LORD OF NAGOYA: "The shogun declares that the forty and more retainers of En'ya Hangan, in avenging their late lord by killing Kō no Moronao, committed an act of unprecedented loyalty, with each man worth a thousand. He is deeply impressed and would like to save their lives, but they erred in taking up arms in this age of great peace and by troubling the shogun's direct vassal. The government has no choice but to order them to commit seppuku. Under strong officers there are no weak soldiers. Your loyalty has reminded him of the benevolence of En'ya Hangan while he was alive. There is no doubt about the claim to succession of En'ya's only son, Takeōmaro, and the shogun decrees that he shall govern the two provinces of Izumo and Hōki. Go to the underworld and report this to your lord with gratitude. Now quickly cut your bellies!"

NARRATOR: He announces this in a loud voice, and the men lower their heads, weeping or laughing in their joy. One by one they remove their sleeveless over-robes. Yuranosuke takes the knife and stabs himself in the left side. As he does so, Rikiya, too, stabs himself. One by one they all stab themselves and, having done so, pull the blade across. At the same time and in the same place, sitting to the right and left of their master's grave, they have all cut their bellies, for the bond over three lives is strong. Finally all have been beheaded by their seconds, and the temple quickly becomes a graveyard. The *rōnin* leave their names on stones that will stand for ages to come. The foundation of the success of their lord's descendants and house, their prosperity and unbounded good fortune, lies in those honest hearts filled with loyalty and filial spirit. They conformed to the laws of both heaven and earth, and the gods and buddhas graciously watched over them.

≫ Working with Sources

1. **Why does the court official express sympathy for the rōnin and still persist in enforcing the sentence against them?**

2. **Is Chikamatsu's admiration for the actions of the rōnin justified by the historical reality of the period and original circumstances?**

SOURCE 21.5

Honda Toshiaki, "Secret Plan for Managing the Country"

1798

Drawing on the conclusions of his "Western" education, Japanese economist Honda Toshiaki (1749–1821) advocated a three-pronged plan of action to level the playing field between the Tokugawa shogunate and European powers. Having studied mathematics as a young man, Honda learned the Dutch language and studied Dutch medicine, astronomy, and military science. The choice of Dutch was fortuitous, since these were the only Europeans permitted to remain in Japan after 1639. Nevertheless, it was the prowess of these particular Europeans in shipping and trade, dependent on a scientific and mathematical knowledge of navigation, that most interested

Source: Ryusaku Tsunoda, William Theodore de Bary, and Donald Keene eds., *Sources of Japanese Tradition* (New York: Columbia University Press, 1964), vol. 2, 51–53.

Honda. This section of his "Secret Plan" addresses the need for the emperor to control ships and shipping in order to ensure Japanese prosperity.

As long as there are no government-owned ships and the merchants have complete control over transport and trade, the economic conditions of the samurai and farmers grow steadily worse. In years when the harvest is bad and people die of starvation, the farmers perish in greater numbers than any other class. Fields are abandoned and food production is still further reduced. There is then insufficient food for the nation and much suffering. Then the people will grow restive and numerous criminals will have to be punished. In this way citizens will be lost to the state. Since its citizens are a country's most important possession, it cannot afford to lose even one, and it is therefore most unfortunate that any should be sentenced to death. It is entirely the fault of the ruler if the life of even a single subject is thereby lost.

. . .

Some daimyo have now ceased to pay their retainers their basic stipends. These men have had half their property confiscated by the daimyo as well, and hate them so much that they find it impossible to contain their ever accumulating resentment. They finally leave their clan and become bandits. They wander lawlessly over the entire country, plotting with the natives who live on the shore, and thus entering a career of piracy. As they become ever more entrenched in their banditry one sees growing a tendency to revert to olden times.

It is because of the danger of such occurrences that in Europe a king governs his subjects with solicitude. It is considered to be the appointed duty of a king to save his people from hunger and cold by shipping and trading. This is the reason why there are no bandits in Europe. Such measures are especially applicable to Japan, which is a maritime nation, and it is obvious that transport and trade are essential functions of the government.

Ships which are at present engaged in transport do not leave coastal waters and put out to sea. They always have to skirt along the shore, and can navigate only by using as landmarks mountains or islands within visible range. Sometimes, as it inevitably happens, they are blown out to sea by a storm and lose their way. Then, when they are so far away from their familiar landmarks that they can no longer discern them, they drift about with no knowledge of their location. This is because they are ignorant of astronomy and mathematics, and because they do not possess the rules of navigation. Countless ships are thereby lost every year. Not only does this represent an enormous annual waste of produce, but valuable subjects also perish. If the methods of navigation were developed, the loss at sea of rice and other food products would be reduced, thus effecting a great saving. This would not only increase the wealth of the nation, but would help stabilize the prices of rice and other produce throughout Japan. The people, finding that they are treated equally irrespective of occupation and that the methods of government are fair, would no longer harbor any resentment, but would raise their voices in unison to pray for the prosperity of the rulers. By saving the lives of those subjects who would otherwise be lost at sea every year, we shall also be able to make up for our past shame, and will keep foreign nations from learning about weak spots in the institutions of Japan from Japanese sailors shipwrecked on their shores. Because of these and numerous other benefits to be derived from shipping, I have termed it the third imperative need.

» **Working with Sources**	**1.** How does Toshiaki use comparisons to European practices to solidify his case regarding imperial control of shipping?
	2. How does he envision the ideal relationship between the emperor and his people? What should be the emperor's central principle in ruling?

PART FIVE

The Origins of Modernity

1750–1900

What we have termed "modernity" in this section may be said to have begun roughly around 1800 in western Europe and may be characterized as the product of what historian Eric Hobsbawm (1917–2012) called the "twin revolutions" of the late eighteenth century. One of these was the new political landscape brought into being by the trio of constitutional revolutions in North America, France, and Haiti, which dealt a telling blow to the concept of traditional monarchical rule by divine right and introduced popular sovereignty as the new justification for political power. The other was the Industrial Revolution, which began in England with the introduction of steam-driven-machine–produced textiles and other goods. Scientific–industrial modernity, with its developing constellation of values marked by experimentation; political, social, and technological progress; social mobility; and secularism, was thus set on a path to displacing the older agrarian–urban order of religious civilizations that had been characterized by hierarchy, natural order, patriarchy, and divinely ordained morality and law. This transition is, in fact, still ongoing. Although the old agrarian–urban political order has been almost universally superseded, its values still contend with those of modernity in many parts of the world today.

The Origins of Modernity

The political and industrial revolutions that define modernity have intellectual roots reaching back to the 1500s. As scholars increasingly recognize, the discovery of the Americas, as well as the Copernican revolution in astronomy, provided powerful incentives for the introduction of new patterns of science and political philosophy. For more than two centuries, however, these ideas remained the province of only a small intellectual elite.

Political and Industrial Revolutions

By the 1700s, however, adherents of the new science and philosophy among urban, educated administrators and professionals in northwestern Europe had grown in numbers and began to become influential in society. In Britain, the *theory* of the social contract

1765
James Watt perfects the steam engine

1798–1801
Napoleon's occupation of Egypt

1832
Greece wins independence from the Ottomans

1848
Karl Marx and Friedrich Engels publish *The Communist Manifesto*

1776–1804
American, French, and Haitian Revolutions

1815
Congress of Vienna

1839–1876
Tanzimat reforms in the Ottoman Empire

1853–1854
Commodore Perry opens trade and diplomatic relations with Japan

entered into the *practice* of constitutionalism following the Glorious Revolution of 1688. Both were vastly expanded by thinkers during the eighteenth-century Enlightenment and helped to inspire the American, French, and Haitian Revolutions. These were narrow revolutions in the sense of ending monarchical–aristocratic rule—courageous revolts during still deeply religious times. Nonetheless, this era set the emancipation of humanity from the confining traditions of the past as a goal to be achieved. And in the case of Haiti, the idea that "all men are created equal," emblazoned earlier in the American Declaration of Independence and echoed in the French Declaration of the Rights of Man, formed the basis of a successful slave rebellion against revolutionary France itself.

The Industrial Revolution, beginning around 1800 in Great Britain, was a socially transformative and self-sustaining sequence of technical inventions and their commercial applications. Britain industrialized during the first half of the 1800s through steam-driven iron foundries, textile factories, overland transportation, and ocean travel. In a second wave, Germany and the United States industrialized, with the introduction of chemicals, electricity, and motorcars into the factory system. The two waves of industrialization created an unequal class system, with a citizenry composed of both landed aristocrats—fading in power as the old agrarian–urban order decayed—and a new, dynamic urban middle class amassing political and economic power. But the equally new phenomenon of the industrial working class, bidding for political, social, and economic equality, added a volatile social factor to the mix as its members sought to make good on the promises of the constitutional revolutions.

Resistance and Adaptation to the Western Challenge

The twin political–industrial revolutions in Europe were a major factor in the mid-nineteenth-century expansion of the existing seaborne European empires in Asia and Africa. Postrevolutionary France renewed its competition with Britain, and both later used "gunboat diplomacy" to establish favorable commercial conditions and trade outposts. From here, these two European nations, and others, proceeded to compete in imperial conquests for what they now considered to be strategically important territories across the globe.

The traditional agrarian and religious empires and states of Asia and Africa responded to the increasingly superior military power of the European maritime empires and the United States during the 1800s with both resistance and adaptation. Resisting with traditional armies and weapons, however, became more difficult as the 1800s unfolded and the industrial development of the West spawned new and sophisticated weaponry. "Adaptation," as it occurred under the duress of imperialism, was a creative process in which the states under challenge selected generic elements from the constitutional and industrial revolutions that had made the West powerful and attempted to harmonize them with their inherited traditions.

Thinking Like a World Historian

≫ What were the origins of the "twin revolutions" of the late eighteenth century? How did they combine to create what we call "modernity"?

≫ Why were the values of scientific–industrial society opposed to the older agrarian–urban order? Why does this conflict still persist in many parts of the world today?

≫ What patterns of resistance and adaptation characterized the responses of traditional agrarian and religious empires to European military power and expansion?

interactive timeline

1857
Sepoy Rebellion, India

1868–1912
Reign of Emperor Meiji, Japan

1878–1885
Independence of Serbia, Montenegro, Romania, and Bulgaria

1888
End of slavery, Brazil

1894–1895
Sino-Japanese War

1904–1905
Russo-Japanese War

1861
Emancipation of serfs in Russian Empire

1869
Opening of Suez Canal

1884
Hiram Maxim invents the first fully automatic machine gun

1900
Boxer Rebellion

1905
Albert Einstein publishes theory of relativity

1908
"Young Turks" rise to power in Ottoman Empire

> Chapter 22   1750–1871

Patterns of Nation-States and Culture in the Atlantic World

THE NORTH ATLANTIC, 1750-1880

When the French Revolution broke out in 1789, a young Caribbean mulatto named Vincent Ogé (ca. 1755–1791) was in France on business. His extended family of free light-skinned blacks owned a coffee plantation and a commercial business with black slaves on Saint-Domingue [SAN-dow-MANG] (modern Haiti). Caught up in the excitement of 1789, Ogé embraced the French revolutionary principles of liberty, equality, and fraternity with great enthusiasm and quickly became an adherent of French constitutionalism: The former absolute monarchy in France was swiftly reorganized to incorporate a written constitution and an elected National Assembly. As part of the general atmosphere of emancipation so prevalent during the early part of the Revolution, he joined the antislavery Society of the Friends of Blacks in Paris and demanded that French constitutionalism be extended to Saint-Domingue.

In a short time the society's efforts appeared to bear fruit. In March 1790, the National Assembly granted self-administration to the colonies, and Ogé returned to Saint-Domingue full of hope that he would be able to participate as a free citizen in the island's governance. But the French governor stubbornly refused to admit mulattoes as citizens of the new order.

ABOVE: Thousands of Polish soldiers joined Napoleon's forces sent to Haiti in 1802, depicted here in Battle on Santo Domingo *by Polish painter January Sucholdoski (1797–1875).*

Ogé and a group of friends therefore joined a band of 250–300 freedmen and took up arms to carve out a stronghold for themselves in the north of the island by arresting plantation owners and occupying their properties. One plantation owner later testified that the rebels looted and killed during their uprising but that Ogé himself was a man of honor who treated his prisoners fairly and even left this owner in the possession of his arms.

After only a few weeks of fighting, however, government troops pushed the rebels into the Spanish eastern part of the island. Ogé and his followers surrendered after being guaranteed their safety. But the Spanish governor betrayed his prisoners, turning them over to the French. After a trial for insurrection in February 1791, Ogé and 19 followers were condemned to death. Ogé suffered particularly barbaric tortures before expiring: Executioners strapped him spread-eagle on a wagon wheel and systematically broke his bones with an iron bar until he was dead.

Seeing Patterns

≫ How did the pattern of constitutionalism, emerging from the American and French Revolutions, affect the course of events in the Western world during the first half of the nineteenth century?

≫ In what ways did ethnic nationalism differ from constitutionalism, and what was its influence on the formation of nation-states in the second half of the nineteenth century?

≫ What were the reactions among thinkers and artists to the developing pattern of nation-state formation? How did they define the intellectual–artistic movements of romanticism and realism?

The Ogé insurrection was a prelude of the Haitian Revolution, which began in August 1791 as a rebellion against discrimination and culminated with the achievement of independence under a black government in 1804. It was the third of the great constitutional-nationalist revolutions—after the American and French Revolutions—that inaugurated, with the Industrial Revolution, the modern period of world history. The new pattern of constitutional nation formation encouraged other peoples who possessed a cultural but not political unity to strive for their own ethnic nation-states. Italians and Germans united in their own states, and Irish, Scots, and Welsh strove for autonomy within the United Kingdom.

The political ferment which led to the three constitutional revolutions was part of a larger cultural ferment called the Enlightenment. The rising urban middle classes of professionals, officials, and entrepreneurs embraced the New Sciences and their philosophical interpretations, which not only provided the intellectual ammunition for the revolutions but also stimulated entirely new forms of cultural creativity in the movements of romanticism and realism.

Origins of the Nation-State, 1750–1815

The Glorious Revolution of 1688 in England (Great Britain after 1707) bestowed rights and duties on English subjects who had never enjoyed them before. In this revolution, for the first time in Europe, the traditional divine rights of a monarch were curbed. A century later, the innovative ideas of *subjects* becoming *citizens* with constitutionally guaranteed rights and duties and of Parliament representing the citizens spread from Great Britain to North America, France, and Haiti. Beyond the Glorious Revolution, however, the American, French, and Haitian Revolutions were more radical in the sense that they rejected the British compromise of royal and parliamentary power and led to republican, middle-class, or liberated slave nation-states without traditional divine-right monarchies.

The American, French, and Haitian Revolutions

The American and French Revolutions were, in part, consequences of the Seven Years' War, in which Great Britain and France fought for the dominance of their respective seaborne empires in the world. The governments of both kingdoms went deeply into debt to wage the war. They owed this debt to their wealthy subjects, many of whom were landowners and administrators forming the ruling class. To pay back the debt, the kings had to go to all of their subjects and raise their taxes. The incongruence of monarchs holding the mass of their subjects responsible for their debts to a few wealthy subjects was apparent to a large number of people, who therefore formulated political principles of reform and, ultimately, revolution. Once the revolutions were under way, the American and French revolutionary principles of freedom and equality had repercussions in the wider Atlantic world, first in Haiti and ultimately in the Latin American colonies of Spain and Portugal (Chapter 27).

Conditions for Revolution in North America   When Britain won the Seven Years' War, it acquired France's trade forts in India as well as French possessions in Canada and the Ohio–Mississippi River valleys. France turned what remained of Louisiana over to its ally Spain (which had lost Florida to Britain) and retreated entirely from the continent of North America. But the British victory and territorial gains came at the price of a huge debt: The payment of the interest alone devoured most of the country's regular annual budget. Taxes had to be raised domestically as well as overseas, and in order to do so the government had to strengthen its administrative hand in an empire that had grown haphazardly and, in North America, without much oversight.

By 1763, the 13 North American colonies had experienced both rapid demographic and powerful economic growth. Opening lands beyond the Appalachian Mountains into the Ohio valley would relieve a growing population pressure on the strip of land along the Atlantic coast that the colonies occupied. Environmental degradation, through overplanting and deforestation, had increased the landless population and contributed to the presence of growing numbers of poor people in the burgeoning cities of Philadelphia, Boston, and New York.

The occupation of new land across the Appalachians, on the other hand, increased the administrative challenges for the British. They had to employ large numbers of standing troops to protect not only the settlers from the hostility of the Native Americans but also the Native Americans from aggression by settlers. Grain, timber, and tobacco exports had made the colonies rich prior to 1763, but the war boom inevitably gave way to a postwar bust. While new land created new opportunities, the economic slump created hardships (see Map 22.1).

In view of the complicated political and economic situation in the North American colonies, the British government failed to devise a clear plan for strengthening its administrative as well as taxing powers. It was particularly inept with the imposition of new taxes intended to help in the reduction of the national debt. In 1765, it introduced the Stamp Act, forcing everyone to pay a tax on the use of paper, whether for legal documents, newspapers, or even playing cards. The tax was to be used for the upkeep of the standing troops, many of which were withdrawn from the Ohio valley and ordered to be quartered in the colonies for the enforcement of the increased taxes.

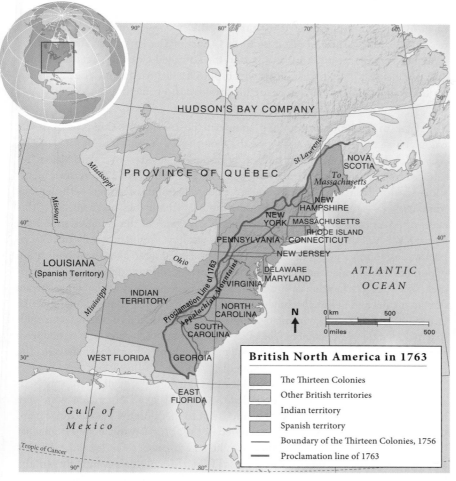

MAP **22.1 British North America in 1763.**

Countdown to War   A firestorm of protest against the Stamp Act broke out among the urban lower-middle ranks of shopkeepers, small merchants, mechanics, and printers, who organized themselves in groups such as the Daughters of Liberty and Sons of Liberty. The Daughters declared a highly successful boycott of British goods and promoted the production of homespun textiles. In Boston, one of the flashpoints of unrest, the British administration offended colonists of the upper urban class when it dissolved the Massachusetts Assembly for opposing the tax. The British Parliament withdrew the Stamp Act in 1766 when exports fell, but replaced it with indirect taxes on a variety of commodities. Although these taxes were less visible, there were still levied without the colonies' consent.

The one indirect tax which aroused particular anger among the American colonists was the tea tax. This tax was actually a subsidy to keep the near-bankrupt East India Company afloat and had nothing to do either with America or Britain's debt.

interactive timeline

1700–1800 Enlightenment	1775–1783 American Revolution	1799–1815 Napoleonic era	1815 Congress of Vienna	1870 Unification of Italy
1756–1763 Seven Years' War	1789–1799 French Revolution	1804 Beethoven's *Eroica*	1848 Political and economic revolts in Europe	1871 Unification of Germany

In 1773 the colonists protested the tax with the symbolic dumping of a cargo of tea into Boston Harbor. In response to this "Boston Tea Party," Britain closed the harbor, demanded restitution, and passed the so-called Coercive Acts (called the "Intolerable Acts" in the colonies), which put Massachusetts into effective bankruptcy. Both sides now moved inexorably toward a showdown.

The War of Independence   To countermand the British Coercive Acts, the colonial assemblies came together in the Continental Association of 1774–1776, which decided on an economic boycott of Britain. In an effort to isolate Massachusetts from the Association, British troops ventured out in April 1775 to seize an assumed cache of arms and ammunition in Concord. A militia of farmers—the famous "minutemen"—stopped the British, inflicting heavy casualties on them. After this clash of forces, war broke out in earnest, and delegates of the colonies appointed George Washington, a former officer from a wealthy Virginian family of tobacco planters, as commander of the colonists' troops. A year later, after the mobilization of popular forces and in the hope of garnering foreign support, delegates of the colonies issued the Declaration of Independence. This declaration was a highly literate document steeped in Enlightenment thought. Its author was Thomas Jefferson, like Washington the son of a Virginian planter, with an advanced university education that included the New Sciences. The great majority of the delegates who signed were also educated men of means—planters, landowners, merchants, and lawyers. The urban middle class was clearly in command.

Central to the declaration was the idea that the equality of all "men" was "self-evident." The declaration tacitly excluded the one-fifth of all Americans who were black slaves and the half who were women, not to mention the Native Americans. On the other hand, the signers also excluded Locke's property ownership from what they considered to be the most valuable rights of citizens and rendered these rights as "life, liberty, and the pursuit of happiness." When the colonists eventually won the War of Independence in 1783, the founders created a revolutionary federal republic with a Congress that was more representative of its citizens than the Parliament in Great Britain but still excluded a substantial proportion of inhabitants.

The Early United States   The new republic's initial years were fraught with organizational difficulties. The governing document, the Articles of Confederation, granted so much power to the individual states that they operated like separate countries. In 1787, a constitutional convention came together in Philadelphia to create a far more effective federal constitution. Careful to add checks and balances in the form of a bicameral legislature and separation of powers into legislative, executive, and judicial branches, the new constitution seemed to embody many of the ideals of the Enlightenment—including a set of 10 initial amendments: the Bill of Rights. Though still imperfect—particularly in sidestepping the contentious issue of slavery—it provided a model for nearly all the world's constitutions that followed. A later commentator praised it as "a machine that would go of itself"; another, more critical one called its checks and balances "a harmonious system of mutual frustration." In 1789, under the new system, George Washington was elected the first president of the United States.

Though the new republic fell far short of what we would consider today to be "representative"—until 1820 voting rights were restricted to white males with

Thomas Paine, *Common Sense* (1776)

property—its abolition of the divine right of monarchical rule and its replacement by the sovereignty of the people was for most people a previously unimaginable reversal of the natural order of things. In this respect, the American and French Revolutions signaled the inauguration of a new pattern of state formation and the advent of modernity.

Conditions for the French Revolution   King Louis XVI (r. 1774–1792) and the French government had watched the American War of Independence with great sympathy, hoping for an opportunity to avenge the kingdom's defeat in the Seven Years' War. France supplied the Americans with money, arms, and officers, and in 1778–1779, in alliance with Spain, waged war on Great Britain. The French–Spanish entry into the war forced Britain into an impossible defense of its entire colonial empire. Although mounting a creditable military effort, Britain conceded defeat in 1783 in the hope of escaping with minimal territorial losses, apart from the North American colonies. Indeed, in the peace negotiations France and Spain made few territorial gains. The French government furthermore had to begin exorbitant payments—much higher than what Britain faced after the Seven Years' War—on the interest for the loans to carry out the war. Crippling debt, which the French government was ultimately unable to pay, played a large role in establishing the preconditions underlying the outbreak of the French Revolution.

As in America, the French population had increased sharply during the 1700s. Food production could barely keep up, and inflation increased. As new scholarship has shown, the rural economy responded to the rising demand, though with difficulty, and in the region of Paris, production for the market was highly profitable. Furthermore, colonial trade with the Caribbean colonies boomed. Had it not been for the debt, the government would have been well financed: It collected direct taxes as well as monies from compulsory loans and the sale of titles and offices to a large upper stratum of ordinary people of means—merchants, lawyers, and administrators. These people were deeply invested in the regime, buying themselves into the ranks of the aristocracy and benefiting from administrative offices handling the kingdom's tax revenue. Although claiming to be the absolute authority, the king in reality shared power and wealth with a large ruling class of old and new aristocrats as well as aspiring ordinary urban people of wealth.

In 1781, suspicions arose about the solvency of the regime when the finance minister quit. He had kept the extent of the subsidies for the American revolutionaries a government secret. But the government continued to borrow, especially when bad weather leading to two poor harvests in 1786–1787 diminished tax revenues. The hardship caused by these two years became crucial for the eventual revolution in 1789: Without reserves in grain and animals, the peasants suffered severe famine and grew increasingly angry when government imports intended to help ended up in the hands of profiteers and hoarders.

By 1788, the government was unable to make payments on short-term loans and had to hand out promissory notes, with bankruptcy looming in the background. As in Britain in the 1760s, a reform of the tax system became unavoidable. At first, the king sought to initiate this reform with the help of a council of appointed notables. When this failed, he held elections for a general assembly to meet in Versailles (called the Estates-General, last convened in 1614). Voters, defined as males over 25 who were French and paid taxes, met in constituent meetings in their districts across

France, according to their "estate" as clergy, aristocrats, or commoners. Peasants met in large numbers in the "third estate," or commoner meetings; but the deputies they elected to meet in Paris were overwhelmingly administrators, lawyers, doctors, academics, businessmen, and debt holders. At the request of the king, the deputies composed petitions in which they listed their grievances about taxes, waste, luxury at court, and ministerial "despotism" to form the basis for the reform legislation.

The most famous among the petitions was the pamphlet of the priest Emmanuel-Joseph Sieyès [see-YES], entitled *What Is the Third Estate?* Although he was a member of the clergy and therefore part of the first estate, Sieyès was elected as a commoner from Paris and became one of the leading intellectual figures in the Revolution. In his pamphlet he put forward the revolutionary idea that the French nation of 25 million *was* the third estate, while the other two estates, totaling 200,000 members, were no more than a tiny fraction. The third estate, embodying Rousseau's idea of the "general will" of the nation, should alone form a "national assembly" and translate this general will into a constitution, fiscal reform, and the abolition of aristocratic privileges.

Amid widespread unrest and rioting among peasants in many places in France and workers in Paris, the third estate now outmaneuvered the other estates and the king. In June 1789 it seceded from the Estates-General and declared itself the National Assembly. Pressured by the pro-aristocracy faction at court, the king issued a veiled threat: If the Assembly would not accept his reform proposals, he said, "I alone should consider myself their [the people's] representative." The king then reinforced his troops in and around Paris and Versailles and dismissed his popular finance minister, who had brought some famine relief in spring. Parisians, afraid of an imminent military occupation of the city, swarmed through the streets on July 14, 1789. They provisioned themselves with arms and gunpowder from arsenals, gunsmith shops, and the Bastille, the royal fortress and prison inside Paris, which they stormed.

Three Phases of the Revolution   The French Revolution, unfolding from 1789 to 1799, went through the three phases of constitutional monarchy (1789–1792), radical republicanism (1792–1795), and military consolidation (1795–1799). The first phase began with the "great fear" of near anarchy, which reigned during July and August 1789. People in the provinces, mostly peasants, chased many of their aristocratic and commoner landlords from their estates. Paris, too, remained in an uproar, since food supplies, in spite of a good harvest, remained spotty. Agitation climaxed in October when thousands of working women, many with arms, marched from Paris to Versailles, forcing the king to move to Paris and concern himself directly with their plight. No longer threatened by the king, the National Assembly issued the Declaration of the Rights of Man and of the Citizen (1789), subjected the Catholic Church to French civil law (1790), established a constitutional monarchy (1791), and issued laws ending the unequal taxes of the Old Regime (1792)—four major reforms carried out in the spirit of constitutionalism.

The second phase of the Revolution (1792–1795), the period of radical republicanism, began when the revolutionaries found themselves unable to establish a stable constitutional regime. After the king tried unsuccessfully to flee Paris with his unpopular Austrian-born, Habsburg wife, Marie-Antoinette, to a monarchist

stronghold in eastern France in the summer of 1791, Austria and Prussia threatened to intervene if the king and queen were harmed. Patriotic feelings were aroused, and the idea of preventive war gained adherents. In April 1792 the government declared war on its eastern neighbors, to which many aristocratic families had fled.

Events quickly escalated, with republicans deposing the king and holding elections for a new assembly, the National Convention, to draw up a constitution. In the following year, the republicans executed the royal couple and created a conscript army, to regain control of the borders. Fears of plots from outside France as well as among the revolutionaries led to the formation of the Committee of Public Safety. This committee, the executive organ of the National Convention, ruthlessly eliminated some 30,000 real and suspected "reactionaries" during its "Reign of Terror," making mockery of the Revolution's Declaration of the Rights of Man and universal male suffrage.

The Revolution entered its third phase (1795–1799) after the army had succeeded in securing the borders at the end of 1793. A growing revulsion at the Reign of Terror led to the emasculation of the Committee of Public Safety and its eventual replacement by the Directory in November 1795. A new constitution and bicameral legislature were created, but political and financial stability remained elusive. The Directory depended increasingly on the army to survive. What was originally an untrained conscript army of able-bodied male civilians had become highly professionalized during two years of constant warfare and was the only stable institution in France.

Within the army, a brash young brigadier general named Napoleon Bonaparte (1769–1821), of minor aristocratic Corsican descent, was the most promising commander. From 1796 to 1798 Napoleon scored major victories against the Austrians in northern Italy and invaded Egypt, which he occupied in preparation for an invasion of British India. But, thwarted by a pursuing British fleet, he returned to France and overthrew the ineffective Directory in November 1799, thus ending the Revolution.

The French Revolution. After the storming of the Bastille (top left), the French Revolution gained momentum when Parisian women marched to Versailles, demanding that the king reside in Paris and end the famine there (top right). The inevitability of a republic became clear when the king and queen were captured after they attempted to flee (bottom right).

Maximilien de Robespierre, "Report of the Principles of Public Morality " (1794)

The Guillotine

It is estimated that during the period of the Terror (June 1793–July 1794) the guillotine was responsible for around 2,600 executions in Paris alone and for perhaps as many as 16,600 throughout France. This iconic symbol of grisly public executions is attended by many myths. Among these is the idea that the guillotine was invented by—and took its name from—one Dr. Guillotin solely for the purpose of speeding up executions of perceived enemies of the republic during the infamous Reign of Terror. Neither of these notions is true, however. Indeed, the actual train of events is far more compelling—and ironic.

The Execution of Marie-Antoinette. During the radical republican period of the French Revolution, the Committee of Public Safety had Queen Marie-Antoinette condemned to death for treason after a show trial. She was executed on October 16, 1793, 9 months after the execution of her husband, Louis XVI.

Far from appearing for the first time during the French Revolution, the first known model of a "decapitation machine" is probably the Halifax Gibbet, in use in England from around 1300 until 1650. Another model, the Scottish Maiden, was derived from the Halifax Gibbet and used in 150 executions from 1565 until 1708. It was subsequently turned over to a museum in Edinburgh in 1797 and may have earlier served as a model for the French machine.

When and how did the instrument first appear in France? Ironically, it came as an indirect result of efforts to end the death penalty. During the early days of the Revolution the National Assembly pondered the abolition of the death penalty in France altogether. On October 10, 1789, the Assembly was addressed by Dr. Joseph Ignace Guillotin (1738–1814),

Revival of Empire   Once in power, Napoleon embarked on sweeping domestic reforms that, taken together, curtailed much of the revolutionary fervor and restored order and stability in France. His crowning achievement was the reform of the French legal system, promulgated in the Civil Code of 1804, which in theory established the equality of all male citizens before the law but in reality imposed restrictions on many revolutionary freedoms. In 1804 Napoleon sealed his power by crowning himself emperor of the French. Secure in his authority at home, he now struck out on a lengthy campaign of conquest in Europe. Victory followed on victory from 1805 to 1810, resulting in the French domination of most of Continental Europe.

The goal was the construction of an Enlightenment-influenced but newly aristocratic European empire, land-based and in the tradition of the Habsburgs, Ottomans, and Russians (see Map 22.3). With this empire, he planned to form a Continental counterweight to the maritime British Empire that was unchallengeable in the Atlantic and Indian Oceans. The failure of Napoleon's Russian campaign in 1812, however, marked the beginning of the end of Napoleon's grand scheme. An alliance of Great Britain, Austria, Prussia, and Russia ended Napoleon's empire

founder of the French Academy of Medicine and a staunch opponent of capital punishment, who urged the assembly to at the very least find "a machine that beheads painlessly," if they could not ultimately agree to stop executions altogether. Toward this end Guillotin presented sketches of the kind of machine he had in mind, but his initial design was rejected, followed by a second rejection on December 1 of the same year. In 1791 the Assembly finally agreed to retain the death penalty, noting that "every person condemned to the death penalty shall have his head severed." But instead of adopting Dr. Guillotin's design, the Assembly accepted a model designed by Dr. Antoine Louis, secretary of the Academy of Surgery; Dr. Louis then turned to a German engineer, Tobias Schmidt, who constructed the first version of the "painless" decapitation machine. It was not until April 25, 1792, that the guillotine, nicknamed "Louisette" after Dr. Louis, claimed its first victim. It is not clear when the name was changed to "guillotine" (the final "e" was added later), but historians speculate that Dr. Guillotin's early advocacy of quick and painless executions was a major factor. As for Dr. Guillotin himself, the crowning irony was that, after fighting a losing battle with the government to change the name of the machine because of embarrassment to his family, he changed his own name and retreated to the obscurity he had come to crave.

Questions

- Can the guillotine be viewed as a practical adaptation of Enlightenment ideas? If so, how?

- Why do societies like France in the late eighteenth century debate the means they use to execute prisoners? What are the criteria by which one form of execution is considered more humane than others?

in 1815 and inaugurated the restoration of the pre–French Revolution regimes in Europe.

Conditions for the Haitian Revolution   French Saint-Domingue was one of the richest European colonies, based on plantations that produced vast amounts of sugar, indigo, coffee, and cotton for export to the Old World. At the time of the French Revolution, the colony produced nearly half of the world's sugar and coffee. Originally, it had been a Spanish possession. But as Spain's power slipped during the seventeenth and eighteenth centuries, France took advantage of the situation and established its colony on the western part of the island. In the following century, settlers enjoyed French mercantilist protectionism for splendid profits from their slave plantations.

In the second half of the 1700s, some 30,000 white settlers, 28,000 mulattoes (holding about one-third of the slaves), and about 500,000 black plantation and household slaves formed an extremely unequal colonial society. Similarly extreme inequalities existed only in Brazil and Jamaica. When France, like Britain and Spain

Punishment of a slave on the estate of Charles Balthazar Julien Févret de Saint-Mémin.
This watercolor vividly depicts the vast differences between the slave strapped to a frame and the
completely unconcerned estate owner on horseback. During the uprising of 1791 slaves occupied the
great majority of estates, ended slavery, and drove their owners into exile. Saint-Mémin, whose mother
was Creole, waited for a decade in the United States for the return of his estate before giving up and
returning to France.

after the Seven Years' War, tightened colonial controls, the French administrators
in Haiti were afraid that the white and mulatto plantation owners would form a
united resistance. In order to split the two, they introduced increasingly racist measures to deprive the mulattoes of their privileges. It was this increasing split which
created the conditions for Vincent Ogé's uprising discussed in the vignette of this
chapter and eventually for the slave rebellion once the French Revolution itself
was under way.

Revolt of the Slaves   After the failure of Ogé's uprising, resentment continued to
simmer among the mulattoes in the south as well as the black slaves in the north of
Haiti. Resentment turned into fury when the white settler Provincial Assembly refused any concessions even though the French revolutionary National Constituent
Assembly in May 1791 granted citizen rights to mulattoes whose parents were free.
Aware of the by now open hostility between the mulattoes and whites, slaves seized
the opportunity for their own rebellion in August 1791. The leaders of the slaves
were overseers, coachmen, or managers on plantations who called the slaves under
their authority to arms. Almost simultaneously, but with little coordination, the mulattoes of the south rose in rebellion as well. Within weeks, the slave and mulatto
rebellion had 100,000 followers and encompassed the entire northern and southern
provinces of the colony. The settlers were well armed but suffered heavy losses under
the onslaught of overwhelming numbers.

  With the rebellion taking an increasingly severe toll on the economy, the Assembly in Paris sent commissioners and troops in November 1791 and April 1792

The Haitian Revolution

to reestablish order. Neither commission made much headway, largely because of the unrelenting hostility of the whites, especially lower-class whites in urban centers. In their desperation to gain support, even from the blacks, the second commission made the momentous decision in August 1793 to abolish slavery. This decision, however, failed to rally the black military leaders who had allied themselves with the Spanish rulers of the eastern half of the island, Santo Domingo. Revolutionary France had been embroiled in war against Spain and Britain since early 1793, and the latter had invaded the French held part in the summer of 1793. Spain and Britain looked like inevitable victors, and the commissioners' emancipation declaration appeared to have been too little too late.

MAP **22.2** **The Haitian Revolution.**

Both invasions stalled, however, largely because of the impact of tropical diseases catching up with the British occupation forces (1793–1797). A by now sympathetic Assembly in Paris confirmed the emancipation declaration in February 1794, and the French position on the island began to improve. In May 1794, a shrewd black rebel leader from the north, François-Dominique Toussaint Louverture (ca. 1743–1803), decided that the tide was turning. He left the Spanish with his 4,000 troops and joined the French, whose numbers had dwindled to a few thousand (see Map 22.2). Toussaint, grandson of a vassal king (*onto*) in Benin, West Africa, had obtained his freedom in the 1770s. For a short period he had leased a coffee farm with a number of slaves, but after financial difficulties he went back to the plantations of his former owner as a coachman. Upon his return to the French in 1794, he accommodated himself with the mulatto faction of the rebellion in the south. In the following years, the northern blacks and southern mulattoes transformed the rebellion into a full-fledged revolution.

Nation-State Building   During the violent events of 1791–1794, many plantation owners had fled the colony. The former slaves carved out plots for themselves on deserted plantations and grew subsistence crops for their families. Toussaint remained committed to the plantation system, however, in order to supply revenues for his state-building ambitions. He dispatched his officers to the countryside to force former slaves to resume production, with moderate success. In 1801, Toussaint was sufficiently powerful to assume the governorship of Saint-Domingue from the French officials in a soft coup and proclaim a constitution that incorporated the basic principles of French constitutionalism. By this time, the civil administration was reasonably functional again, and efforts were under way to build local courts and schools to broaden the revolution.

But Toussaint still had to reckon with Atlantic politics. Napoleon Bonaparte, in control of France since 1799, was at that time determined to rebuild the French overseas empire. In Egypt (perhaps with plans to continue to India) he was thwarted by the British, but in the Americas he was successful in purchasing Louisiana from Spain in 1800 (ceded after the Seven Years' War of 1758–1763). With the defeat of Austria in 1802, Napoleon was able to get its ally Britain to

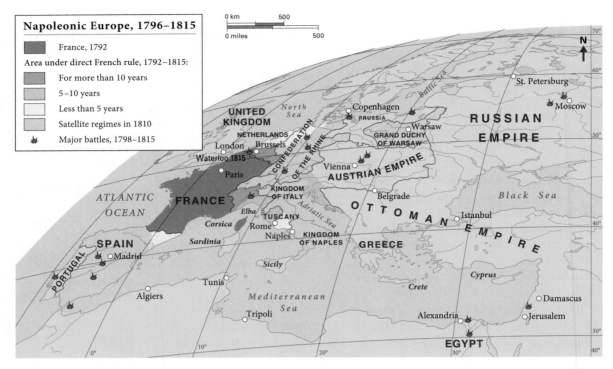

MAP **22.3** **Napoleonic Europe, 1796–1815.**

speeches and
letters of Toussaint
L'Ouverture on the
Haitian Revolution
(1793–1800)

recognize the French Republic and make peace. Immediately, Napoleon dispatched troops to Saint-Domingue to add the colony to Louisiana and revive the French Atlantic empire. Toussaint was well prepared for the invasion, but when the French landed in February 1802 several of his officers surrendered without a fight. As the French advanced into the island against declining resistance, one general, Jean-Jacques Dessalines, betrayed Toussaint to the French in June 1802. After his arrest, Toussaint was sent to France, where he died in April 1803. The revolution seemed to be finished.

Jean-Jacques Dessalines (r. 1802–1806) was a former slave from northern Haiti who, as a roofer, was of higher rank than the plantation slaves. Toussaint had made him the point man for the repair of the plantation system but without giving him the preferential role that he thought he deserved. Seemingly obedient to the French, Dessalines waited for the dreaded yellow fever to take its toll among the invaders. When more than two-thirds of the French forces were dead by the summer of 1802, Napoleon realized that his Atlantic dream was unrealizable. He sold Louisiana to the United States in April 1803 and withdrew the remnants of his troops from Saint-Domingue in November 1803. On January 1, 1804, Dessalines assumed power and declared the colony's independence.

Subsequently, he made himself emperor, to counter Napoleon, and renamed the country Haiti, its supposed original Taíno name. When he changed the constitution in favor of autocratic rule, he provoked a conspiracy against himself, which culminated in his assassination in 1806. In the aftermath, the state split into an autocratically ruled black north with a state-run plantation economy and a more democratic mulatto south with privatized economy of small farms (1806–1821).

Of the three revolutions resulting in the new form of the republican nation-state based on a constitution, that of Haiti is clearly the one that realized the Enlightenment principles of liberty, equality, and fraternity most fully. By demonstrating the power of the new ideology of constitutionalism, it inaugurated a new pattern of state formation in world history not only among the new white and mixed-race urban middle classes but also among the uprooted black African underclass of slaves.

Enlightenment Culture: Radicalism and Moderation

The American, French, and Haitian Revolutions were embedded in the culture of the **Enlightenment** (ca. 1700–1800). The origins of this culture lay in the new math-ematized sciences, which inspired a number of thinkers, such as Descartes, Spinoza, Hobbes, and Locke, to create new philosophical interpretations (see Chapter 17). The radical interpretation was materialism, according to which all of reality con-sisted of matter and Descartes's separate substance of mind or reason could either be dispensed with or be explained as a by-product of matter. Moderates held on to Descartes's mind or reason as a separate substance, struggling to explain its presence in reality. The radical Enlightenment tradition evolved primarily in France, most prominently among the so-called Encyclopedists, who were materialists and agnos-tics or even atheists. The moderate tradition found adherents in Germany, where the Enlightenment mingled with national awareness.

Enlightenment: European intellectual movement (1700–1800) growing out of the New Sciences and based largely on Descartes's concept of reality consisting of the two separate substances of matter and mind.

The Enlightenment and Its Many Expressions

Energetic writers popularized the new, science-derived philosophy in eighteenth-century France, Holland, England, and Germany. Thousands subscribed to Enlightenment-themed books, pamphlets, and newspapers and attended acad-emies, salons, and lectures. The audiences were still a minority, however, even among the growing middle class of urban administrators, professionals, mer-chants, and landowners, not to mention the 80 percent or more of the population engaged in the crafts and in farming. But their voices as radical or moderate "pro-gressives" opposing tradition-bound ministers, aristocrats, and clergy became measurably louder.

It was the late eighteenth-century generation of this vociferous minority that was central to the revolutions in America and France and—a minority within the minority—in the French slave colony Haiti. They translated their New Sciences–derived conception of reality into such "self-evident" ideals as life, liberty, equality, social contract, property, representation, nation, popular sovereignty, and constitu-tion. In the wider, more broadly conceived culture of the Enlightenment, they fash-ioned new forms of expression in the arts and thereby made the Enlightenment a broad movement.

Denis Diderot and the *Encyclopédie* The idea to bring together all the new knowledge accumulated since the Renaissance and the advent of the New Sciences in an alphabetically organized encyclopedia appeared first in England in 1728. A French publisher decided in 1751 to have it translated. But under the editorship of, for the most part, Denis Diderot (1713–1784) it became a massively expanded work in its own right. He poured all his energy into writing entries and soliciting contributions from the "republic of letters," as the French Enlightenment thinkers were called.

Many entries dealt with delicate subjects, such as science, industry, commerce, freedom of thought, slavery, and religious tolerance, sometimes edited by the cautious publisher without Diderot's knowledge. Publication itself was not easy, since the Catholic Church and the French crown banned the project as subversive for several years and forced it during this time to continue in secret. But the roughly 4,000 subscribers received their twenty-eighth and last volume in 1772, ready and able to assimilate everything modern and urbane gentlemen and gentlewomen should know.

Philosophy and Morality

Jean-Jacques Rousseau (1712–1778), in contrast to his atheist Enlightenment colleagues of the *Encyclopédie*, was a firm believer in the religious morality of the masses. The son of a cultivated and music-loving Geneva watchmaker, Rousseau was philosophically moderate, even if emotionally fragile and at times given to paranoia. To the consternation of the radicals in France, he espoused in his *Social Contract* (1762) the notion that humans had suffered a steady decline from their "natural" state ever since civilization began and imposed its own arbitrary authority on them. The radicals held that even though humans had lost their natural state of freedom and equality and had come under arbitrary authority, they were experiencing a steady progress of civilization toward ever-improving degrees of freedom and equality. Rousseau did share with his former friends a low opinion of the absolutist French regime, of which he ran afoul just as much as they did. But he had little faith in such concepts as popular sovereignty, elections, and electoral reforms that they propagated. Instead, he believed that people, rallying in a nation, should express their unity directly through a "general will," a sort of direct democracy—more applicable to his native city of Geneva than to a large nation like France.

Jean-Jacques, Rousseau, excerpts from *A Discourse on the Origin of Inequality* (1755)

Philosophy and the Categorical Imperative

Immanuel Kant (1724–1804), a much more disciplined philosopher than Rousseau, was a firm believer in the progress of civilization and history, as expressed in his *Perpetual Peace* (1795). In fact, he quite immodestly thought of himself as having performed a second "Copernican turn" in modernity with his two main books, *Critique of Pure Reason* and *Critique of Practical Reason* (1781–1787). Like all Enlightenment thinkers, Kant took Descartes as his point of departure. But he rejected both the two-substance theory of Descartes and the materialist turn of Locke and the radical French Enlightenment. Even though he admitted that sensory or bodily experience was primary, he insisted that this experience could be understood only through the categories of the mind or reason which were not found in experience. Reason conditioned experience; it was not its own susbtance.

In contrast to Rousseau with his traditional Christian ethics, Kant sought to build morality on reason. He came to the conclusion, therefore, that this morality had to be erected on the basis of the *categorical imperative*: to act in such a way that the principle of your action can be a principle for anyone's action. This highly abstract principle later entered modern thought as the basis for concrete human rights, with their claim to universality, as in the Charter of the United Nations (1945).

Economic Liberalism The Enlightenment also saw the birth of the academic discipline of economics. French and British thinkers who were appalled by the inefficient administration of finances, taxes, and trade by the regimes in their countries found the official pursuit of mercantilism wanting. As discussed in previous chapters, mercantilism was the effort to import as little as possible, except from the warm-weather colonies, and develop domestic crafts so as to export manufactured goods in exchange for the commodities of the colonies. Opposed to mercantilist state control in France, the so-called physiocrats argued that individual freedom and equality should be the principles of the economy. The state should reduce taxes and other means of control to a minimum so that entrepreneurism in the general population could flourish. It should adopt a policy of *laissez-faire* [les-say-FAIR]— that is, "hands-off."

The Scottish economist Adam Smith (1723–1790), who spent some time in Paris and was familiar with many of the physiocrats, developed a British version of laissez-faire economics. In his *Inquiry into the Nature and Causes of the Wealth of Nations* (1776) Smith argued that if the market were largely left to its own devices, without many state regulations and restrictions, it would regulate itself through the forces of supply and demand, appropriate prices, and so forth. It would then move in the direction of increasing efficiency as if guided by "an unseen hand." Smith became the founding father of modern economics, whose ideas are still regularly invoked today.

Literature and Music As in the other fields of modern cultural expression, the Enlightenment also inspired writers and composers. Noteworthy among them were Johann Wolfgang von Goethe (1749–1832) and Wolfgang Amadeus Mozart (1756–1791), sons of a lawyer and a court musician, respectively. Among Goethe's numerous poems, novels, plays, and even scientific works (on color) was his drama *Faust,* about an ambitious scientific experimenter who sells his soul to the devil to acquire mastery of nature. Faust became a metaphor for modernity—for the technicians and engineers whose dominance of natural forces runs roughshod over environmental concerns, as we would say today. Mozart was a child prodigy who composed an astounding number of symphonies, operas, and chamber music pieces. One of his best-known operas is *The Magic Flute*, a work displaying the influence of the Freemasons, a fraternal association popular in Enlightenment Europe devoted to "liberty, fraternity, and equality"—principles which the French Revolution borrowed as its motto.

The imperial turn of the French Revolution under Napoleon may be said to have effectively ended the Enlightenment. A few years later, with the fall of Napoleon and the restoration of monarchies, the European kings actively worked to rescind its effects, and in the face of overwhelming power, the Enlightenment constitutionalists went either silent or underground.

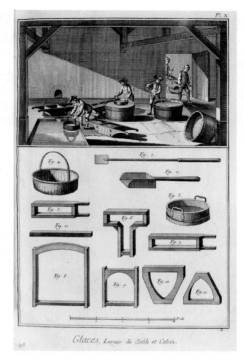

Glaces, Lavage du Sable et Calcin.

The *Encyclopédie*. Denis Diderot's massive work promoted practical, applied science, such as this illustration showing glassmaking.

Adam Smith, excerpts from *The Wealth of Nations* (1776)

Grimm's Fairy Tales. Perhaps the most famous collection of folktales in the Western tradition, *Children's and Household Stories* (1812), was assembled by Wilhelm and Jakob Grimm as a way to preserve their country's cultural commonality and to rekindle in their countrymen an appreciation for their Germanic roots. The stories they collected, such as "Rapunzel," shown in this illustration, were brought together through fieldwork and by peasant women who would visit the Brothers Grimm and recite stories that awoke "thoughts of the heart."

The Other Enlightenment: The Ideology of Ethnic Nationalism

The constitutionalists who led the revolutions of 1776–1804 in America, France, and Haiti proclaimed universal human rights in centuries-old monarchical states that had evolved into overseas empires. Ethnic descent or linguistic affiliations did not play a part in their revolutionary actions. After 1815, however, these affiliations began to play increasingly important roles.

Constitutionalism versus Ethnic Nationalism   In Great Britain's North American colonies, prior to the Revolution the great majority of the constitutionalists were "British," which meant that they were Englishmen, with minorities from among the Irish, Welsh, and Scots. Neither the English nor the minorities expressed their ethnic identities in the British colonies and in Britain not until the later 1800s. In France, the Parisians, who expressed the constitionalism of the French Revolution in their grammatically complex "high" French, assumed that constitutionalism was nevertheless easily understood and accepted by the provincials. Nearly half of the population in the provinces spoke dialects that were often incomprehensible to the Parisians. The other half spoke no French at all and were ethnically either Celtic or German. But no provincials or ethnic Celts and Germans drew support for expressing their separate ethnic identities in the 1700s, and—in contrast to Britain—not even in the 1800s. It was the Parisian Frenchness which eventually became the identity of what we call the French nation and it did so on the basis of the constitutional program of the French Revolution.

Overseas Haiti presents the remarkable case of a rebellion in favor of French metropolitan constitutionalism. After the Haitians achieved their independence, they elevated their West/Central African ethnic heritage and spoken language, Kreyòl, into their national identity, deemphasizing their French constitutional heritage.

German Cultural Nationalism   In contrast to Great Britain and France, Germany was politically fragmented during the 1700s. Even though it had always possessed a central ruling institution, its imperial, rather than royal, constitution made for a much higher degree of political decentralization than in the English and French kingdoms. In addition, many Germans in eastern Europe were widely dispersed among people with different linguistic, cultural, and even religious heritages, such as Czechs, Slovaks, Hungarians, Poles, and Russians. Educated Germans, such as urban professionals, administrators, and educators, clearly shared a common culture wherever they lived, but in the absence of a strong central state, this culture was largely nonpolitical.

A central figure in articulating the commonly shared culture into a linguistic ideology was Johann Gottfried Herder (1744–1803). Herder's father was an elementary schoolteacher and Lutheran church warden in eastern Germany. At college, Herder studied with Kant but also with others under whose influence he became familiar with Pietism, a Lutheran version of the medieval Catholic mystical tradition. Employed first as a preacher and then as an administrator at assorted courts in central Germany, he published widely as a literary critic and was on close terms with

Goethe and other German Enlightenment figures. In his writings, such as *On the Origin of Language* (1772), Herder sought to meld the diffuse cultural heritage into a more or less coherent ideology of Germanness combined with the Enlightenment. This ideology, so he hoped, would be preached not only to the educated but to the people in general through school curricula, history, and the arts.

The Herder-inspired ethnic version of the Enlightenment received a major boost during the French Revolution. Many Germans began to realize that any adoption of French constitutionalism made sense only in a politically united Germany. Before any unification plan could mature, however, Napoleon ended the French Revolution, declared himself emperor, and proceeded to defeat Prussia and Austria. With this, he aroused patriotic passions for liberation from French rule and hopes for a unified Germany under a constitutional government. The figure who decisively advanced in his writings from Herder's cultural Germanness to a fully developed political Germanness was Johann Gottlieb Fichte (1762–1814), a philosophy professor appalled by Napoleon's imperial conquests in Europe. Time seemed ripe for the realization of German political unification on the basis of a marriage of constitutionalism and ethnic nationalism. Instead, the eventual failure of Napoleon's conquests opened the door for a restoration of the pre-1789 monarchies.

Johann Gotlieb Fichte, excerpts from "Addresses to the German Nation" (1807–1808)

The Growth of the Nation-State, 1815–1871

Napoleon's defeat in Russia in 1812 and the Congress of Vienna of 1815 were the principal occasions for rulers to turn back the clock in Europe. Monarchies and aristocracies reappeared throughout the continent, and the restored kings allowed only for the barest minimum of popular representation in parliaments. By contrast, in Anglo-America, the supremacy of constitutionalism was unchallenged during the 1800s. Here, a pattern of increasing citizen participation in the constitutional process manifested itself, although not without challenges, which culminated in the American Civil War.

Restoration Monarchies, 1815–1848

For a full generation, monarchists in Europe sought to return to the politics of absolutism. This return required repression and elaborate political manipulation to keep the now-identifiable middle class of public employees, professionals, schoolteachers, and factory entrepreneurs away from meaningful political participation. A "Concert of Europe" emerged in which rulers avoided intervention in the domestic politics of fellow monarchs, except in cases of internal unrest.

The Congress of Vienna   European leaders met in 1815 at Vienna after the fall of Napoleon in an effort to restore order to a war-torn continent. The driving principle at the session was monarchical conservatism, articulated mainly by Prince Klemens von Metternich (1773–1859), Austria's prime minister. An opponent of constitutionalism, Metternich was determined to resist the aspirations of the still-struggling middle classes outside France, which he regarded with contempt.

To accomplish his objective of reinstituting kings and emperors ruling by divine grace, Metternich had the Congress hammer out two principles: legitimacy and

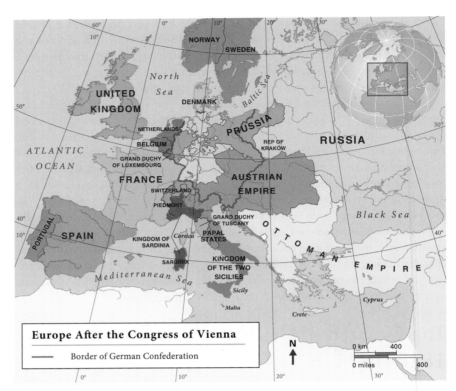

MAP 22.4 **Europe after the Congress of Vienna.**

balance of power. The principle of legitimacy was conceived as a way to both recognize exclusive monarchical rule in Europe and to reestablish the borders of France as they were in 1789. The principle of the balance of power involved a basic policy of preventing any one state from rising to dominance over any other. Members agreed to convene at regular intervals in the future in what they called the "Concert," so as to ensure peace and tranquility in Europe. What is remarkable about this is that, with only minor exceptions, this policy of the balance of power remained intact for more than half a century (see Map 22.4).

As successful as the implementation of these two principles was, the solution devised for the German territories—now no longer with an overall ruler since the Holy Roman Empire was dissolved in 1806—was less satisfactory. The Congress of Vienna created an unwieldy and weak confederation of 39 German states, including the empire of Austria and the kingdoms of Prussia, Denmark, and the Netherlands. Prussia and Austria promptly embarked on a collision course over dominance in the confederation, with Prussia keeping the initiative and creating a customs union in 1834. Prussia's main purpose with this union was to find outlets for its rising industrial and commercial interests in the northern German Ruhr region. Constitutionalist and republican Germans disliked the confederation as well, since they had no meaningful voice in it. Thus, by resolving the overall issue of coexistence among the German states, but not of their fragmentation, the Congress was only partially successful.

Further Revolutions in France   In keeping with the principle of legitimacy, the Congress restored the French Bourbon monarchy with the coronation of King Louis XVIII (r. 1814–1824), a brother of Louis XVI. Louis, even though determined to restore full absolutist powers, was indecisive as to which republican institutions to abolish first. Playing for time, he tolerated the "White Terror," during which the returning aristocracy and other royalists pursued revenge for their sufferings during the Revolution. When Louis died in 1824 the conservatives succeeded in putting Charles X (1824–1830), a second brother of Louis XVI, on the throne. Charles took the extreme course of restoring the property of the aristocracy lost during the Revolution and reestablishing the crown's ties to the Catholic Church.

Republican reaction to Charles's restoration policy was swift. In two elections, the republicans won a majority and overthrew the king. But they stopped short of abolishing the monarchy and elevated Louis-Philippe (1830–1848), son of a pro-republican duke who had been guillotined and had fought in the republican guards during 1789–1792, to the throne. Under this "bourgeois king," as he was sometimes caricatured, however, rising income gaps in the middle class as well as difficult living conditions among the nascent industrial working class led to new tensions. In the ensuing revolution of 1848, in which thousands of workers perished, the adherents of restoration and republicanism attempted another compromise: Louis-Philippe went into exile, and the parliament elected Louis-Napoleon Bonaparte (r. 1848–1852; self-declared emperor 1852–1870), a nephew of the former emperor, as president.

Rebellion. Following the successful revolution of 1848 that ended the monarchy of Louis-Philippe in France, similar uprisings broke out across Europe. This image shows the Berlin Alexander Square barricades of March 1848.

Uprisings across Europe   After the revolution in Paris, uprisings occurred in the spring of 1848 in cities such as Berlin, Vienna, Prague, Budapest, Palermo, and Milan, as well as in three Irish counties. In Prussia the king seemingly bowed to pressure from revolutionaries and promised constitutional reforms. In Austria, hit by uprisings in multiple cities and by multiple nationalities, both the emperor and Metternich, the driving forces of 1815, resigned. The successors, with Russian help, slowly regained military control over the Italians, Czechs, and Hungarians, as well as Austrians.

In the German Confederation, also hit by uprisings, moderate and republican delegates convened a constitutional assembly in Frankfurt in May 1848. This assembly elaborated the basic law for a new, unified state for German speakers and elected a provisional government. The new hard-line Austrian emperor, however, refused to let go of his non-German subjects. Therefore, the constitution joined only the German Federation and Prussia (also with non-German minorities) into a unitary state, with the provision for a future addition of German-speaking Austria. Against strong resistance by republicans, the delegates offered the Prussian king a new hereditary imperial crown in the name of the German people. But the king, unwilling to accept the principle of popular sovereignty, refused the crown "of clay." This refusal turned the tide against the Frankfurt Assembly. Moderate delegates departed, and radical ones instigated revolts. Prussian troops stepped in and relieved a group of grateful regional monarchs of their insurrectionists. By July 1849, the provisional Frankfurt government had come to an end and Germany's constitutional experiment was over.

Ethnic Nationalism in Italy   Italy was as fragmented politically as Germany, but unlike Germany it was also largely under foreign domination. Austria controlled the north directly and the center indirectly through relatives from the Habsburg dynasty. The monarchy of Piedmont in the northwest, the Papal States in the center, and the kingdom of Naples and Sicily (the "Two Sicilies") were independent but administratively and financially weak. After the Metternich restoration, the Italian dynasties had made concessions to constitutionalists, but Austria repressed uprisings in 1820–1821 and 1831–1832 without granting liberties. The republican Carbonari inspired both uprisings; they were members of the crafts guild of charcoal burners who had formed Enlightenment fraternities similar to the Freemasons during the eighteenth century. After their decisive defeat in 1831, the remnants formed the Young Italy movement.

Realistic second-generation politicians of the Restoration recognized that the middle-class ethnic nationalism coming to the fore in 1848 was a potent force that could be harnessed. By remobilizing this force in the 1860s, they would be able to end state fragmentation and make Italy and Germany serious players in the European Concert. These politicians were more sympathetic to French-style constitutionalism than the Restoration politicians but still opposed to republicanism. Their pursuit of realpolitik—exploitation of political opportunities—resulted in 1870–1871 in the transformations of the Italian kingdom of Piedmont and the German Empire of Prussia into the ethnic nation-states of Italy and Germany.

The Italian politician who did the most to realize Italy's unification was the prime minister of Piedmont-Sardinia, Count Camillo di Cavour (1810–1861). Cavour was the scion of an old aristocratic family in northwestern Italy with training as a military officer. While in the army, he read widely among French and British political philosophers and became a constitutionalist. A supporter of Adam Smith's liberal trade economics, he imported South American guano fertilizer and grew cash crops, like sugar beets, on his estate. As prime minister he was the driving force behind the development of railroads and thereby laid the foundations for the industrialization of northwest Italy.

With the backing of his similarly liberal-minded king, Victor Emanuel II (r. 1849–1878), he began the Italian unification process under decidedly trying circumstances. With the help of an alliance with France, he was able to provoke Austria, ruler of much of northern Italy, into a war in spring 1859. The allied forces defeated Austria, although not decisively, and in a compromise settlement, Piedmont gained adjoining Lombardy and five regions in north-central Italy. A year later Cavour occupied the Papal States and accepted the offer of Giuseppe Garibaldi (1807–1882) to add adjoining Naples and Sicily to a now largely unified Italy.

Garibaldi, a mariner from Nice in the northwest (present-day France), was a Carbonaro and Young Italy republican nationalist with a colorful career as a freedom fighter not only in Italy but also in Brazil and Uruguay. Dressed in his trademark red gaucho shirt with poncho and sombrero, the inspiring Garibaldi attracted large numbers of volunteers wherever he went to fight. Cavour died shortly afterward and did not live to see Piedmont transform itself into Italy. In the years from 1866 to 1870, the expanded Piedmont exploited the Prussian–Austrian war of 1866 to annex Venetia and then took advantage of the Franco-Prussian war of 1870 for the occupation of Rome. (Because of the Prussian threat Napoleon III recalled his French garrison in Rome which he had sent there against the threat of a campaign by the republican Garibaldi.) Thus Italy was unified by a king and his aristocratic prime minister, both moderate constitutionalists (though not republicans). As realistic politicians they dipped into a rising Italian ethnic nationalism to bring about unification.

Bismarck and Germany   In contrast to Italy, neither King Wilhelm I (r. 1861–1888) nor his chancellor (prime minister) Otto von Bismarck (in office 1862–1890) in Prussia had deep sympathies for constitutionalism. By combining their antipathies and forming a coalition of convenience, they succeeded in keeping the constitutionalists in the Prussian parliament in check. But they realized they could dip into the ethnic nationalism that had poured forth in 1848, using it for their version of realpolitik.

Bismarck was a Prussian aristocrat with a legal education rather than a military career. He was multilingual, widely read, and experienced in the diplomacy of the European Concert. He realized that Prussia, a weak player in the Concert, had a chance for greater influence only if the kingdom could absorb the German Federation. For Prussia to do so, Bismarck argued, it had to progress from talk about unification, as in Frankfurt, to military action, using "blood and iron." From the time of his appointment to 1871, he systematically maneuvered Prussia into an internationally favorable position for the coup that would eventually bring unification: war with France.

First, he exploited a succession crisis in Denmark for a combined Prussian–Austrian campaign to annex Denmark's southern province of Schleswig-Holstein in 1865. Then, when Austria objected to the terms of annexation, he declared war on Austria (1866). After Prussia won, Bismarck dissolved the German Confederation and annexed several German principalities. In France, Louis-Napoleon Bonaparte was

Bismarck. Bismarck, a Prussian from the aristocratic Junker [YOON-ker] landowner class, was known for his stern, formidable, shrewd, and calculating character and personality; thus, he was nicknamed the "Iron Chancellor." As a consummate practitioner of *Realpolitik*, Bismarck skillfully combined diplomacy with war in order to achieve the unification of Germany in 1871.

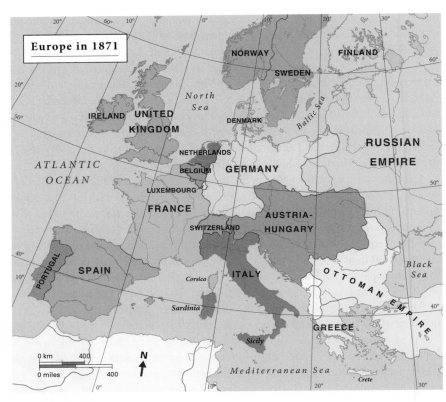

MAP **22.5 Europe in 1871.**

greatly concerned about the rising power of Prussia. He had carried out a coup d'état in 1852, ending the Second Republic and declaring himself emperor in imitation of his uncle—an act that prompted the readily quotable Karl Marx to claim that "history always repeats itself, the first time as tragedy, the second time as farce." A distraction on his eastern flank was not at all what Emperor Napoleon III desired.

But he carelessly undermined his own position. First, he prevented a relative of King Wilhelm from succeeding to the throne of Spain after it fell vacant. But when he demanded additional assurances that Prussia would not put forward candidates for any other thrones in the future, the canny Bismarck outmaneuvered him. He advised King Wilhelm to refuse the demand and edited the refusal in such a way as to make it insulting to the French. France then declared war on Prussia but was defeated (1870).

Now Bismarck had the upper hand that he had been diligently working to gain. He used it to annex Alsace-Lorraine from the French, carried out the final unification of Germany, and elevated the new state to the status of empire in April 1871 (see Map 22.5). In the meantime, French republicans had proclaimed the Third Republic (September 1870) and deposed Napoleon III (March 1871). While the so-called Second German Empire was consolidated from the start, the French Republic struggled until 1875 to find its republican constitutional order (on this struggle, see "Against the Grain").

Nation-State Building in Anglo-America, 1783–1900

After the independence of the United States in 1783, both the United States and Great Britain were free to pursue their versions of constitutional state development.

The old and new monarchies and ethnic movements which complicated state formation in central Europe did not affect the United States, giving rise instead to a long tradition among American historians of claiming American "exceptionalism." While it is indeed true that the growth of the United States in the 1800s followed its own trajectory, there is also no question that the underlying pattern of modern state formation was not unlike that of the other two constitutionally governed countries, France and Great Britain: Neither was much affected by ethnic nationalism.

The United States   During the first half of the nineteenth century the newly independent North American states not only prospered but also began a rapid westward expansion. As this process unfolded, toward 1850 it became increasingly apparent that sectional differences were developing in the process. Whereas the North developed an industrial and market-driven agricultural economy, the South remained primarily agrarian, relying heavily upon the production of cotton for its economic vitality. Even more, the South relied upon vast numbers of slaves to work the fields of the cotton plantations. Cotton was the main fiber for the industrial production of textiles, and it not only defined the wealth of the plantation owners but led them to see chattel slavery as the only viable means to keep the "cotton kingdom" prosperous. In defense of its stance, the South increasingly relied upon the notion of states' rights in opposition to federal control. With the acquisition of new territory extending to the Pacific coast after the war with Mexico from 1846 to 1848 and the push of settlement beyond the Mississippi, the vital question of which of the new territories would become "free states" and "slave states" resulted in increasing tensions between North and South.

The result was an attempt by a number of southern states to secede and form a new union, the Confederate States of America. When the new administration of President Abraham Lincoln attempted to suppress this movement, the disastrous American Civil War (1861–1865) ensued. Resulting in an enormous loss of life—more than 600,000 combatants on both sides were killed—the Civil War finally ended with a northern victory in 1865. There were several major results of the conflict, not least of which was an enhanced unification of the country during the occupation of the southern states, where federal troops enforced the policies of Reconstruction (1865–1877). First, Lincoln's concept of the primacy of national government over individual assertions of states' rights was now guaranteed. Second, slavery was abolished and slaves were granted full citizenship. Third, the rebuilding of the country and opening of the West resulted in a period of remarkable growth, facilitated especially by the expansion of a national network of railroads. By 1900, about 200,000 miles of uniform-gauge track crisscrossed the country, and the United States was on its way to becoming the world's predominant industrial power (see Map 22.6).

Carl Schurz," Report on the Condition of the South" (1865)

The price of reintegrating the old South into the new order was the end of Reconstruction and the reversion over the course of two generations to an imposition of de facto peonage on its black citizens. Indeed, between 1877 and 1914 state legislatures in the South systematically stripped African Americans of voting rights by means of poll taxes and literacy tests and imposed formal and informal segregation in social and public accommodations. These were enforced by law and all too often by lynchings and other forms of violence. In order to accommodate the sensibilities of white

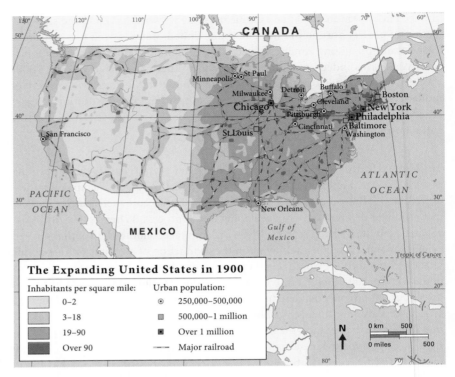

MAP 22.6 **The Expanding United States in 1900.**

southerners regarding race, most northern policy and opinion makers gradually backed away from the views espoused by the champions of racial equality during Reconstruction and gave tacit acquiescence to southern efforts to maintain white hegemony. The drive for full civil rights would thus occupy a sizable share of American domestic policy debates throughout the twentieth century.

Native Americans While blacks made uneven advances during the 1800s, Native Americans suffered unmitigated disasters. When the Louisiana Purchase in 1803 (see p. 665) nearly doubled the size of the United States, politicians quickly conceived of the idea of moving Native Americans from their eastern homelands to the new territories. For their part, Native Americans realized that only a large-scale unification would help them to stay put, especially in the South (Georgia, Alabama, and Florida) and the Midwest (Ohio, Indiana) where white settler encroachment was strong after independence.

In the Midwest, Tecumseh (1768–1812) and his brother Tenskwatawa (1775–1836) renewed the prophecies of unification that had been in circulation since the mid-1700s. Tecumseh traveled widely between the Midwest and South, seeking to forge a Native American resistance federation. Tenskwatawa, claiming his authority from visions of the Master of Life, the spirit of spirits in the world, preached that Native Americans needed to reject white culture and return to traditional life. In Tippecanoe, a newly founded town in Indiana, thousands of followers from a variety of nations came together, but suffered a severe defeat at the hands of US troops in 1811. The defeat ended the dream of Native American unity.

A Sauk Indian leader describes relations with Americans (1832)

In the South, discriminatory legislation and brutal assaults by the states made it more and more difficult for Native American nations to survive on their lands. With the declared intention of helping these nations against the states, in 1830 the federal government issued the Indian Removal Act. In fact, however, this act only deepened the sufferings of the Native Americans: A quarter never made it on the "Trail of Tears" to their designated new homeland, Oklahoma, dying on the way from disease and deprivation. The survivors settled and reconstructed their agriculture, schools, and councils as best as they could, having to accommodate the regular arrival of newly displaced Native Americans from the East in the subsequent decades.

Destruction of the Buffalo Herds   By mid-century, white ranchers and miners began to encroach on the lands farther west of the Mississippi, and beyond Missouri, already a state in 1821. Again, the federal government passed a law supposedly protecting the Native Americans of the Plains from increasingly bloody clashes with advancing whites by creating "reservations" (1851). The obligation, especially for such free-roaming groups as the Sioux and Apache, to stay on reservations rather than to hunt freely was a first aggravation. Further affronts came through the Homestead Act (1862), the construction of the transcontinental railroad (1863–1869), and the rapid appearance of towns and cities along the railroad corridors. The worst injury was the destruction of the gigantic herds of buffalo (bison), the hunting of which formed the principal livelihood of the Native Americans on the Plains.

Within a mere two decades (1865–1884), some 10–15 million animals were slaughtered until fewer than 1,000 remained. Research in the early 2000s has demonstrated that new chemical methods developed in 1871 in Britain and Germany made the tanning of the thick buffalo skin feasible for high-quality shoe leather and industrial belting, greatly stimulating the hunt for hides. In the American Indian Wars (1862–1890), the Native Americans defended their homelands tenaciously but ultimately in vain. Once more, visionaries sought to unify the various groups through the Ghost Dance, enacting a prophecy of the return of the buffalo herds and the disappearance of the whites. The Native Americans' last stand was at Wounded Knee Creek, South Dakota, in December 1890. Defeated and demoralized by 1900, the remaining quarter-million indigenous people (down from 600,000 in 1800) found themselves on 310 reservations on 2.3 percent of American soil.

Reform Measures   As in other Western nation-states, rapid industrialization produced social and labor unrest in the United States, resulting in the reforming initiatives of the Progressive era, which extended from 1890 to 1914. Although the later nineteenth century is referred to as the Gilded Age, epitomized by the staggering wealth of industrial tycoons like Andrew Carnegie (1835–1919) and John D. Rockefeller (1839–1937), all was not well beneath the surface. Big business had grown to such an extent that in the early 1900s a few hundred firms controlled two-fifths of all American manufacturing. The "trust buster" president, Theodore Roosevelt (in office 1901–1909), and Congress ended the

Two Girls of the Hopi Nation with Their Characteristic Hairstyles and Blankets. The Hopi live in the American Southwest, today's Arizona. They are best known as sophisticated farmers in adobe pueblos, some of which were built into the rock walls of canyons. In 1680, the Hopi rebelled for a dozen years against Spanish missionaries and colonists in their midst, achieving a degree of autonomy as a result. The United States organized the nation in 1882 into the Hopi Reservation.

monopolies of many firms, Rockefeller's Standard Oil among them, which had to divide itself into 30 smaller companies. A new Department of Commerce and Labor (1903) and the Pure Food and Drug and Meat Inspection Acts (1906) helped the hard-pressed workers and consumers. With the Federal Reserve Act (1913) and the Federal Trade Commission Act (1914) Congress created an overall framework for the supervision of the financial and business sectors. As many people at the time realized, a free market prospered only with at least a minimum of regulations.

Great Britain   The pattern of constitutional nation-state construction that Britain followed in the eighteenth and nineteenth centuries was gradual and uninterrupted by wars. Challenges did not come from a civil war but from the rise of linguistic nationalisms outside the English core. The first signs of Irish nationalism, based not only in ethnic and linguistic but also religious traditions, appeared after the Great Famine of 1845–1849. Rural production and land issues were the main points of contention, leading to demands for home rule or even independence. A Protestant landlord class still controlled most of the land, which was farmed by Catholic tenant farmers. During the worldwide Long Depression of 1873–1896 Irish farmers received low prices for their crops but no reductions in rent. A "land war" (mass protests against tenant evictions) ensued which the British Army sought to quell. This eventually led in 1898 to local government for the Irish and in 1903–1909 to land reform.

Scotland, traditionally divided between the Highlands and Lowlands, developed an ethnolinguistic sense of its identity only slowly. The development began on the level of folklore, with the revival of Scottish dress and music (clan tartans, kilts, and bagpipes). More serious issues came to the fore in 1853 when the Scots, upset by their perception that the British government paid more attention to Ireland, founded an association for the vindication of Scottish rights. But they had to wait until 1885, when the British government appointed the first secretary for Scotland.

Welsh nationalism arose in the context of industrialization and the development of a Welsh working class, which organized uprisings in the 1830s. Religious issues, mostly related to opposition to the Church of England among nonconformists (e.g., Methodists, Quakers, and Presbyterians), and education issues surrounding the so-called Treachery of the Blue Books added to the unrest. A governmental report of 1847, bound in blue covers, found that education in Wales was substandard: Sunday schools were the only schools offering education in Welsh, while regular schools used English as the language of instruction for children who spoke only Welsh. Both issues were the focus of most Welsh nationalist agitation in the second half of the 1800s, but it was not until 1925, with the foundation of the Party of Wales, that Welsh nationalism became a force of its own.

While ethnic nationalisms arose around the English core, Parliament, the guardian of British constitutionalism, undertook major legal reforms of its constitutional order in the course of the 1800s. As industrialization progressed, both Liberals and Conservatives took cognizance of the growing middle and working classes. The Great Reform Bill of 1832 shifted seats from southern districts to the more populated and industrialized center and north. The repeal of the Corn Laws in 1846 liberated imports and made grain cheaper, and the Second Reform Act of 1867 extended

excerpt from "The Treachery of the Blue Books" (1847)

the franchise to larger numbers of working-class voters. The end result was not only that Britain escaped the revolutions of 1848 but also that the British electorate was largely united during the Victorian period (1837–1901) in its support for British imperialism around the globe.

Romanticism and Realism: Philosophical and Artistic Expression to 1850

Parallel to the evolution of the patterns of constitutionalism and ethnic nationalism, the two movements of romanticism and realism patterned the evolution of culture on both sides of the Atlantic. Romanticism was an outgrowth of strains in the Enlightenment in which the independence of the mind from matter was emphasized. Taking their cue from Rousseau and Kant, romantics emphasized unrestrained individual creativity and spontaneity for the expression of their feelings. As industrialization progressed, however, a growing sense of realism concerning material conditions set in, expressing itself in the arts by greater social awareness.

Romanticism

Inspired by the Enlightenment and the revolutions, a number of philosophers, writers, composers, and painters of the period of **romanticism** in the early 1800s drew the conclusion that humans possessed a fullness of freedom to remake themselves. To them, the mind was entirely independent, creating new aesthetic categories out of its own powers. Not all thinkers and artists went this far, but for romantics creativity became absolute. Indeed, the stereotype of the bohemian creative "genius" crossing new imaginative thresholds became firmly implanted in the public imagination during this time.

Romanticism: Intellectual and artistic movement that emphasized emotion and imagination over reason and sought the sublime in nature.

Philosophers and Artists   The one philosopher who, building on Kant, postulated the freedom of mind or spirit was Georg Wilhelm Friedrich Hegel (1770–1831). The most systematic of the so-called idealist philosophers in Germany, Hegel asserted that all thought proceeded dialectically from the "transcendental ego" to its opposite, matter, and from there to the spiritualized synthesis of nature. This **dialectic** permeates his entire system of philosophy.

Even more than philosophy, music became the medium for expressing the creative genius. The German Ludwig van Beethoven (1770–1827) and the Frenchman Hector Berlioz (1803–1869) pioneered the new genre of program music, with the *Pastoral Symphony* (Symphony no. 6) and the *Symphonie phantastique*, respectively, emphasizing passion and emotional intensity and the freedom of the musical spirit over traditional form. From among the emerging middle class, eager to develop their romantic sensibilities and play music at home, a veritable explosion of composers erupted during the first half of the 1800s. Often composing at a furious rate, these musicians were also virtuosi on the violin or piano, playing their own new musical forms and traveling on concert circuits all across Europe.

The medium of painting also lent itself to the expression of romantic feelings of passion and the mind's overflowing imaginative aesthetics. Not surprisingly, the

Dialectic: The investigation of truth by discussion; in Hegel's thought, the belief that a higher truth is comprehended by a continuous unification of opposites.

proliferation of romantic painters numbered in the hundreds. The common feature of these painters was that they departed from the established academic practices and styles. They either let nature dictate the direction and extent of their absorption into it or expressed their personal impressions forcefully with new, dramatic topics.

As in the other art forms, romanticism in literature appears in heroines or heroes and their passions and sentiments. In the still late-Enlightenment-informed prose of the British author Jane Austen (1775–1817), witty and educated urbane society shapes the character and sensibilities of young women and prepares them for their reward, namely the love of the proper gentleman and marriage to him. A generation later, also in Britain, the three Brontë sisters, Charlotte (1816–1855), Emily (1818–1848), and Anne (1820–1849), published novels with equally complex plots but much greater emphasis on romantic passion on one hand and character flaws or social ills on the other. The novels also contain mysterious, seemingly inexplicable happenings—artistic devices which the American Edgar Allan Poe (1809–1849) used more explicitly in his thematic Gothic stories and tales, such as "The Fall of the House of Usher" (1839).

Realism

Realism: The belief that material reality exists independently of the people who observe it.

Toward the middle of the 1800s, many artists and writers shifted their focus from the romanticism of the self and its aesthetic or moral sentiments to the **realism** of the middle classes whose constitutionalist dreams had been smothered by the repression of the revolutions of 1848. In philosophy, thinkers identified stages leading progressively to the rise of middle classes and industrialism. And in literature, the complex and tangled relationships that characterized the plots of the romantics continued, but were now set in the more prosaic urban world of factories and working classes.

Positivism: A philosophy advocated by Auguste Comte that favors the careful empirical observation of natural phenomena and human behavior over metaphysics.

Philosophy of History   Toward the middle of the 1800s, the French thinker Auguste Comte (1798–1857) composed a six-volume work titled *The Positive Philosophy* (1830–1842). In it he arranged world history into the three successive stages of the theological, metaphysical, and scientific. In his view, the scientific advances of the sciences had all but eclipsed the metaphysical stage and had ushered in the last, scientific era. For Comte this was a sign of Europe's progress and a "positive" stage. His philosophy, labeled **positivism**, exerted a major influence in Europe as well as in Latin America. Comte further argued that the only sure way of arriving at truth was based on scientific facts and knowledge of the world acquired through the senses. In Comte's view, the laws governing human behavior could be ascertained with the same degree of precision as the laws of nature: a utopian ideology still with us today.

Prose Literature   Realistic writers of fiction moved away from personal sentiments to realistic scenes as they were encountered in middle-class society. New aesthetic experimentations ensued so that the ordinary could be a heightened reflection of the new "reality" of life in the industrial age. William Makepeace Thackeray (1811–1863) in England, for example, was a supreme satirist, as displayed in *Vanity Fair*, a book on bourgeois human foibles and peccadilloes. His compatriot Charles Dickens (1812–1870) had a similar focus but centered on working-class and lower-middle-class characters in his many novels. The Englishwoman George Eliot, born Mary Ann Evans (1819–1880), was politically oriented, placing small-town social relations within the context of concrete political events in Great Britain, as in *Middlemarch* (1874). Gustave Flaubert (1821–1880) in France experimented with a

Charles Dickens, excerpt from *Hard Times* (1854)

(a)

(b)

Romantic Art. Romantic painters expressed an absorbing, encompassing nature in their art. Note the barely recognizable steam-powered train in this painting by J. M. W. Turner, *Rain, Steam, and Speed: The Great Western Railway* (1844) (*a*). Romantic painters also depicted dramatic or exotic scenes relating to revolutions or foreign lands, such as the languid harem in *The Women of Algiers in Their Apartment* (1834) by Eugène Delacroix (*b*).

ASSASSINAT DES OTAGES À LA PRISON DE LA ROQUETTE LE 24 MAI 1871
Mᵗ Darboy   Bonjean   Duguerry   Ducoudray   Clerc   Allard

Realism. The documentary power of photography spurred the new impulses of realism that emerged around 1850. The photograph here shows a reenactment of the execution of six hostages by the government of the Commune of Paris on May 24, 1871. This chilling scene was staged several weeks after the collapse of the Commune on May 28 by the photographer Eugène Appert to serve the provisional French government in Versailles in its efforts to expose the crimes of the Commune.

variety of styles, among which those featuring extremely precise and unadorned descriptions of objects and situations are perhaps the most important (*Madame Bovary*, 1857). Henry James (1843–1916), an American living in Britain, in his self-declared masterpiece, *The Ambassadors* (1903), explored the psychological complexities of individuals whose entwined lives crossed both sides of the Atlantic. In the end, realism, with its individuals firmly anchored in the new class society of the 1800s, moved far from the freedom and exuberance celebrated by the romantics.

Putting It All Together

interactive concept map

Though the pattern of nation-state building in Europe and North America was relatively slow and, in places, painful, it has become the dominant mode of political organization in the world today. As we will see in subsequent chapters, the aftermath of World War I and the decolonization movement following World War II gave a tremendous boost to the process of nation-state formation around the world. Here, the legacy of European colonialism both planted these ideas among the colonized and, by supplying the Enlightenment ideas of revolution and the radical remaking of society, gave them the ideological means of achieving their own liberation from foreign rule. In both cases, the aspirations of peoples to "nationhood" followed older European models as the colonies were either granted independence or fought to gain it from declining empires. But, in many respects, their efforts mirrored the difficulties of the first constitutional and ethnic nation-states.

Take the example of the United States. Though it achieved world economic leadership by 1914, it had faced an early constitutional crisis, endured a prolonged sectional struggle in which slavery marred the constitutional order for almost three-quarters of a century, fought a bloody civil war for national unification that very nearly destroyed it, and remained united in part by acquiescing in practices of overt segregation and discrimination against the 10 percent of its population that was of African descent. Or take the case of France. Its people adopted constitutional nationalism in 1789, but the monarchy it seemingly replaced bounced back three times. Thus, even in the later nineteenth century, Abraham Lincoln's resolution that "government of the people, by the people, for the people shall not perish from the earth" was still far from guaranteed.

Yet another example is the case of Germany, where linguistic nationalism diluted the straightforward enthusiasm for the constitution and the symbols accompanying it. Historians continue to argue over whether Germany, and by extension other central and eastern European nations, took a special route (*Sonderweg*) to constitutional normality or whether the path was the same except that the pace slowed at critical times. In retrospect, it is impossible to say which of the speed bumps on the way toward the nation-state—slavery/racism, residual monarchism, or the twentieth-century experiments of communism and supremacist nationalism—were responsible for the longest delay. In Part 6 we will consider all of these developments in more detail.

Review and Relate

Thinking Through Patterns

Examine the ways historians approach the big questions of this chapter.

Constitutionalism emerged as a result of the success of American and French revolutionaries in overthrowing absolute rule. The constitutional revolutionaries replaced the loyalty of subjects to a monarch with that of free and equal citizens to the national constitution. This form of republican constitutionalism called for unity among the citizens regardless of ethnic, linguistic, or religious identity. In the United States, this republicanism had to overcome a conservative adherence to slavery in the South before it gained general recognition after the end of the Civil War. In France, republican constitutionalists battled conservative monarchists for nearly a century before they were able to finally defeat them in the Third Republic.

Constitutionalists emphasized the principles of freedom, equality, constitution, rule of law, elections, and representative assembly regardless of ethnicity, language, or religion. By contrast, ethnic nationalists in areas of Europe lacking centralized monarchies sought to first unify what they identified as dispersed members of their nation through ideologies that emphasized common origin, centuries of collective history, and shared literary, artistic, and religious traditions. In these ethnic (and sometimes in addition religious) ideologies constitutional principles were secondary. Only once unification in a nation-state was achieved would the form of government—monarchist, constitutional–monarchist, or republican—then be chosen.

> How did the pattern of constitutionalism, emerging from the American and French Revolutions, affect the course of events in the Western world during the first half of the nineteenth century?

> In what ways did ethnic nationalism differ from constitutionalism, and what was its influence on the formation of nation-states in the second half of the nineteenth century?

» **What were the reactions among thinkers and artists to the developing pattern of nation-state formation? How did they define the intellectual–artistic movements of romanticism and realism?**

Philosophers and artists in the romantic period put a strong emphasis on individual creativity. They either viewed this creativity as an upwelling of impulses and sentiments pouring forth with little intellectual control or, conversely, considered their creativity to be the result of an absolute or transcendent mind working through them as individuals. By the 1850s, with the rise of the middle class, individual creativity gave way to a greater awareness, called "realism," of the social and political environment with its class structures and industrial characteristics.

| Against the Grain

Consider this as a counterpoint to the main patterns examined in this chapter.

Defying the Third Republic

- Did the members of the Commune of Paris opposition run counter to the pattern of nation-state formation in the nineteenth century, and if so, how did they want to replace it?

- Did the ideas of small communities and opposition to centralized national governments retain their attraction in the twentieth and twenty-first centuries? If yes, which examples come to mind and for which reasons?

Socialist Parisians despised the government and parliament of the new conservative Third Republic of France (February 1871), headquartered in Versailles and dominated by two monarchist factions. They considered it defeatist against the Prussians who had been victorious in the war of 1870. After two failed protests, the final trigger for an outright revolution was the government's attempt in March 1871 to collect some 400 guns left over from the war and under the command of the Parisian National Guard. The attempt turned into a fiasco. The number of horses sent from Versailles to pull the hundreds of cannons away was insufficient, and the government troops fraternized with the Parisian crowds who swarmed around the cannons, offering flowers and food to the soldiers. In the melee, however, several soldiers and two generals were killed (the latter probably by army deserters in Paris, not guardsmen). Seizing the opportunity, the central committee of the National Guard declared its independence and held elections on the basis of male suffrage for a communal council on March 26 (Commune of Paris: March 18 to May 28, 1871).

The council of mostly workers and craftsmen plus a strong contingent of professionals issued a flurry of new laws. All deputies were under binding mandates and could be recalled anytime. As a commune of a desired universal republic, Paris considered all foreigners as equals. France itself was to become a federation of communes. Abandoned factories and workshops were to be directed by workers' councils. Church properties were confiscated, and the separation of church and state was declared. Under the auspices of the women-run Union of Women for the Defense of Paris and the Care of the Injured, measures for equal pay and pensions for retired survivors, regardless of marital status, were envisaged. The official symbol of the Commune was the red flag of the radical French Revolution of 1792, not the republican tricolor. In short, as Haiti had done in 1794, the Commune pushed equality much further than the American and French Revolutions had ever done, frightening the middle classes to their core.

The Commune had no chance of survival against the superior troops of the Third Republic. It was bloodily repressed, although with far fewer victims, according to new documentation analyzed in 2012. The total of communards killed is now estimated to be at most 7,400. The symbolical significance of the Commune, however, was immense: Socialists and Communists made it the mythical dawn of world revolution, working-class dictatorship, and the eventual withering away of the (national) state in the utopia of a classless society.

Key Terms

audio flashcards

Dialectic 681	Realism 682	Romanticism 681
Enlightenment 667	Positivism 682	

For additional resources, please go to
www.oup.com/us/vonsivers.
Please see the Further Resources section at the back of the book for additional readings and suggested websites.

SOURCE 22.1

Declaration of the Rights of Man and of the Citizen

August 26, 1789

When the Third Estate reconstituted itself as the National Assembly in June 1789, among the first measures it considered was a universal declaration of the rights and duties of individual French citizens. A proposal was made by the Marquis de Lafayette to this effect in July, but swift-moving events in Paris, such as the fall of the Bastille on July 14, moved the Revolution in new directions. Undaunted, a subcommittee continued to debate the document, editing a draft proposal of 24 articles down to 17. Like the Declaration of Independence in the American colonies (1776), this document was a compromise statement, drawn up and edited by committee; and yet, like the American Declaration, it is a stirring statement of Enlightenment principles concerning both the individual's role in the state and the ultimate source of all government.

The representatives of the French people, constituted as a National Assembly, and considering that ignorance, neglect, or contempt of the rights of man are the sole causes of public misfortunes and governmental corruption, have resolved to set forth in a solemn declaration the natural, inalienable, and sacred rights of man: so that by being constantly present to all the members of the social body this declaration may always remind them of their rights and duties; so that by being liable at every moment to comparison with the aim of any and all political institutions the acts of the legislative and executive powers may be the more fully respected; and so that by being founded henceforward on simple and incontestable principles the demands of the citizens may always tend toward maintaining the constitution and the general welfare.

In consequence, the National Assembly recognizes and declares, in the presence and under the auspices of the Supreme Being, the following rights of man and the citizen:

1. Men are born and remain free and equal in rights. Social distinctions may be based only on common utility.

Source: Lynn Hunt, ed. and trans., *The French Revolution and Human Rights: A Brief Documentary History* (Boston: Bedford St. Martin's, 1996), 77–79.

2. The purpose of all political association is the preservation of the natural and imprescriptible rights of man. These rights are liberty, property, security, and resistance to oppression.

3. The principle of all sovereignty rests essentially in the nation. No body and no individual may exercise authority which does not emanate expressly from the nation.

4. Liberty consists in the ability to do whatever does not harm another; hence the exercise of the natural rights of each man has no other limits than those which assure to other members of society the enjoyment of the same rights. These limits can only be determined by the law.

5. The law only has the right to prohibit those actions which are injurious to society. No hindrance should be put in the way of anything not prohibited by the law, nor may any one be forced to do what the law does not require.

6. The law is the expression of the general will. All citizens have the right to take part, in person or by their representatives, in its formation. It must be the same for everyone whether it protects or penalizes. All citizens being equal in its eyes are equally admissible to all public dignities, offices, and employments, according to their ability, and with no other distinction than that of their virtues and talents.

. . .

11. The free communication of thoughts and opinions is one of the most precious of the rights of man. Every citizen may therefore speak, write, and print freely, if he accepts his own responsibility for any abuse of this liberty in the cases set by the law.

12. The safeguard of the rights of man and the citizen requires public powers. These powers are therefore instituted for the advantage of all, and not for the private benefit of those to whom they are entrusted.

13. For maintenance of public authority and for expenses of administration, common taxation is indispensable. It should be apportioned equally among all the citizens according to their capacity to pay.

14. All citizens have the right, by themselves or through their representatives, to have demonstrated to them the necessity of public taxes, to consent to them freely, to follow the use made of the proceeds, and to determine the means of apportionment, assessment, and collection, and the duration of them.

. . .

17. Property being an inviolable and sacred right, no one may be deprived of it except when public necessity, certified by law, obviously requires it, and on the condition of a just compensation in advance.

» Working with Sources

1. To what extent does the declaration mix specific provisions and general principles of human rights?

2. How does the document aim to uphold the "common utility"? How is the "public necessity" to be determined?

SOURCE 22.2

Olympe de Gouges, *The Declaration of the Rights of Woman*

September 1791

Women were not included among the new office holders of revolutionary France, nor were they members of the National Assembly, which supposedly represented all members of the country's Third Estate. An immediate question arose concerning the extent to which the benefits of the Revolution should be extended to females (as well as to slaves throughout France's global empire). Some men did advocate the extension of these rights and privileges, but women also took action in their own cause. Among these was the "Cercle Social" (Social Circle), a group of female activists who coordinated their publishing activities on behalf of women and their own goals in the developing Revolution.

One of the leaders of this group was Marie Gouze (1748–1793), who, under her pen name "Olympe de Gouges," attacked both the institution of slavery and the oppression of women in 1791. A playwright, pamphleteer, and political activist, de Gouges published this thoughtful meditation on what the National Assembly should declare concerning "the rights of woman" (as opposed merely to "the rights of man"). Members of the Social Circle were arrested as the Revolution entered its radical phase, and Olympe de Gouges was executed by guillotine in November 1793.

To be decreed by the National Assembly in its last sessions or by the next legislature.

Preamble

Mothers, daughters, sisters, female representatives of the nation ask to be constituted as a national assembly. Considering that ignorance, neglect, or contempt for the rights of woman are the sole causes of public misfortunes and governmental corruption, they have resolved to set forth in a solemn declaration the natural, inalienable, and sacred rights of woman: so that by being constantly present to all the members of the social body this declaration may always remind them of their rights and duties; so that by being liable at every moment to comparison with the aim of any and all political institutions the acts of women's and men's powers may be the more fully respected; and so that by being founded henceforward on simple and incontestable principles the demands of the citizenesses may always tend toward maintaining the constitution, good morals, and the general welfare.

In consequence, the sex that is superior in beauty as in courage, needed in maternal sufferings, recognizes and declares, in the presence and under the auspices of the Supreme Being, the following rights of woman and the citizeness.

Source: Lynn Hunt, ed. and trans., *The French Revolution and Human Rights: A Brief Documentary History* (Boston: Bedford St. Martin's, 1996), 124–126.

1. Woman is born free and remains equal to man in rights. Social distinctions may be based only on common utility.

2. The purpose of all political association is the preservation of the natural and imprescriptible rights of woman and man. These rights are liberty, property, security, and especially resistance to oppression.

3. The principle of all sovereignty rests essentially in the nation, which is but the reuniting of woman and man. No body and no individual may exercise authority which does not emanate expressly from the nation.

4. Liberty and justice consist in restoring all that belongs to another; hence the exercise of the natural rights of woman has no other limits than those that the perpetual tyranny of man opposes to them; these limits must be reformed according to the laws of nature and reason.

5. The laws of nature and reason prohibit all actions which are injurious to society. No hindrance should be put in the way of anything not prohibited by these wise and divine laws, nor may anyone be forced to do what they do not require.

6. The law should be the expression of the general will. All citizenesses and citizens should take part, in person or by their representatives, in its formation. It must be the same for everyone. All citizenesses and citizens, being equal in its eyes, should be equally admissible to all public dignities, offices, and employments, according to their ability, and with no other distinction than that of their virtues and talents.

. . .

11. The free communication of thoughts and opinions is one of the most precious of the rights of woman, since this liberty assures the recognition of children by their fathers. Every citizeness may therefore say freely, I am the mother of your child; a barbarous prejudice [against unmarried women having children] should not force her to hide the truth, so long as responsibility is accepted for any abuse of this liberty in cases determined by the law [women are not allowed to lie about the paternity of their children].

12. The safeguard of the rights of woman and citizeness requires public powers. These powers are instituted for the advantage of all and not for the private benefit of those to whom they are entrusted.

13. For maintenance of public authority and for expenses of administration, taxation of women and men is equal; she takes part in all forced labor service, in all painful tasks; she must therefore have the same proportion in the distribution of places, employments, offices, dignities, and in industry.

14. The citizenesses and citizens have the right, by themselves or through their representatives, to have demonstrated to them the necessity of public taxes. The citizenesses can only agree to them upon admission of an equal division, not only in wealth, but also in the public administration, and to determine the means of apportionment, assessment, and collection, and the duration of the taxes.

. . .

17. Property belongs to both sexes whether united or separated; it is for each of them an inviolable and sacred right, and no one may be deprived of it as a true patrimony of nature, except when public necessity, certified by law, obviously requires it, and then on condition of a just compensation in advance.

1. **What does de Gouges consider woman's "natural and reasonable" share in the "common" life of a society?**

2. **To what extent does biology determine the particular roles and sufferings of women? Are women (in de Gouges's context) to be considered the superior element of human society as a result?**

SOURCE 22.3

Voltaire, "Torture," from the *Philosophical Dictionary*

1769

Voltaire (the pen name of François-Marie Arouet) epitomized the Enlightenment. His *Dictionnaire philosophique* (*Philosophical Dictionary*), the first edition of which appeared in 1764, distilled his thought on philosophical matters in what he self-deprecatingly called an "alphabetical abomination." Voltaire invariably found ways to deploy humor in the pursuit of serious moral, religious, and ethical truths, as the continued popularity of his "contes philosophiques" (philosophical tales), including *Candide*, *Zadig*, and *Micromégas*, attests.

In this "dictionary," arranged alphabetically according to the entry's title (in French), Voltaire tackled matters like atheism, fanaticism, the soul, superstition, and tolerance. His tone is always light and witty, despite the weightiness of (and the violence associated with) the subject matter. Inspired by ongoing court cases and interrogation methods, Voltaire added the following miraculous little essay on the use (and, in some countries, disuse) of torture as a legal instrument to the 1769 version of the *Dictionary*. His satirical approach resonates today, as issues of what constitutes torture and how it ought to be applied continue to dominate our political discourse.

Although there are few articles on jurisprudence in these respectable alphabetical reflections, a word must nevertheless be said about torture, otherwise named the question. It is a strange way to question one. Yet it was not invented by the merely curious. It would appear that this part of our legislation owes its first origin to a highwayman. Most of these gentlemen are still in the habit of squeezing thumbs, burning the feet of those who refuse to tell them where they have put their money, and questioning them by means of other torments.

The conquerors, having succeeded these thieves, found this invention of the greatest utility. They put it into practice when they suspected that some vile plot was being hatched against them, as, for instance, that of being free, a crime of divine and human lèse-majesté. The accomplices had to be known; and to arrive at this knowledge those who were suspected were made to suffer a thousand deaths, because according to the jurisprudence of these first heroes anyone suspected of having had so much as a disrespectful thought about them was worthy of death.

Source: Voltaire, *Philosophical Dictionary*, ed. and trans. Theodore Besterman (Harmondsworth, UK: Penguin, 1972), 394–396.

And once a man has thus deserved death it matters little whether appalling torments are added for a few days or even several weeks. All this even had something of the divine about it. Providence sometimes tortures us by means of the stone, gravel, gout, scurvy, leprosy, pox great and small, griping of the bowels, nervous convulsions, and other executants of the vengeance of providence.

Now since the first despots were images of divinity, as all their courtiers freely admitted, they imitated it so far as they could.

. . .

The grave magistrate who has bought for a little money the right to conduct these experiments on his fellow creatures tells his wife at dinner what happened during the morning. The first time her ladyship is revolted, the second time she acquires a taste for it, for after all women are curious, and then the first thing she says to him when he comes home in his robes is: "My angel, did you give anyone the question today?"

The French, who are considered to be a very humane people, I do not know why, are astonished that the English, who have had the inhumanity to take the whole of Canada from us [in 1760 and ratified in 1763, as a result of the Seven Years' War], have renounced the pleasure of applying the question.

. . .

Empress: Catherine the Great.

In 1700 the Russians were regarded as barbarians. We are now only in 1769, and an **empress** has just given this vast state laws that would have done honour to Minor, to Numa, and to Solon if they had had enough intelligence to compose them. The most remarkable of them is universal toleration, the second is the abolition of torture. Justice and humanity guided her pen, she has reformed everything. Woe to a nation which, long civilized, is still led by atrocious ancient practices! "Why should we change our jurisprudence?" it asks. "Europe uses our cooks, our tailors, our wig-makers; therefore our laws are good."

≫ **Working with Sources**

1. **Does Voltaire make a convincing case that the use of torture results from excessive curiosity and a warped desire to inflict suffering?**

2. **How does he ridicule the continuation of "ancient" practices into modern times, and how does this essay reflect the values of the philosophical Enlightenment?**

SOURCE 22.4

Edmund Burke, *Reflections on the Revolution in France*

1790

Born in Dublin to a Protestant father and a Catholic mother, Edmund Burke (1729–1797) struggled to build a political career in Georgian England. Having established a reputation for brilliant thinking and speaking, he entered Parliament in 1766. One of his principal causes in the 1760s and

Source: Edmund Burke, *Reflections on the Revolution in France*, ed. Thomas H. D. Mahoney (Indianapolis, IN: Liberal Arts, 1955), 66, 68–69, 70–71, 73–74.

1770s was the defense of the American colonists in their conflict with the mother country. Burke opposed the English government's position that England was sovereign over the colonies and could tax the colonists as she saw fit. By contrast, Burke insisted that a "right" was not an abstract principle and that policy should be guided by actual circumstances. When the French Revolution began in 1789, Burke surprised some of his political allies by speaking against it, mainly because he believed that "reason" and "rights" were not absolute principles that justified violent change. His statement against the extremes of revolution, published in November 1790, became the basis for a form of political ideology known as conservatism.

It is no wonder, therefore, that with these ideas of everything in their constitution and government at home, either in church or state, as illegitimate and usurped, or at best as a vain mockery, they look abroad with an eager and passionate enthusiasm. Whilst they are possessed by these notions, it is vain to talk to them of the practice of their ancestors, the fundamental laws of their country, the fixed form of a constitution whose merits are confirmed by the solid test of long experience and an increasing public strength and national prosperity. They despise experience as the wisdom of unlettered men; and as for the rest, they have wrought underground a mine that will blow up, at one grand explosion, all examples of antiquity, all precedents, charters, and acts of parliament. They have "the rights of men." Against these there can be no prescription, against these no agreement is binding; these admit no temperament and no compromise; anything withheld from their full demand is so much of fraud and injustice. Against these their rights of men let no government look for security in the length of its continuance, or in the justice and lenity of its administration.

. . .

Government is not made in virtue of natural rights, which may and do exist in total independence of it, and exist in much greater clearness and in a much greater degree of abstract perfection; but their abstract perfection is their practical defect. By having a right to everything they want everything. Government is a contrivance of human wisdom to provide for human wants. Men have a right that these wants should be provided for by this wisdom. Among these wants is to be reckoned the want, out of civil society, of a sufficient restraint upon their passions. Society requires not only that the passions of individuals should be subjected, but that even in the mass and body, as well as in the individuals, the inclinations of men should frequently be thwarted, their will controlled, and their passions brought into subjection. This can only be done *by a power out of themselves*, and not, in the exercise of its function, subject to that will and to those passions which it is its office to bridle and subdue. In this sense the restraints on men, as well as their liberties, are to be reckoned among their rights. But as the liberties and the restrictions vary with times and circumstances and admit to infinite modifications, they cannot be settled upon any abstract rule; and nothing is so foolish as to discuss them upon that principle.

. . .

The pretended rights of these theorists are all extremes; and in proportion as they are metaphysically true, they are morally and politically false. The rights of men are in a sort of *middle*, incapable of definition, but not impossible to be discerned. The rights of men in governments are their advantages; and these are often in balances between differences of good, in compromises sometimes between good and evil, and sometimes between evil and evil. Political reason is a computing principle: adding, subtracting, multiplying, and dividing, morally and not metaphysically, or mathematically, true moral denominations.

. . .

In France, you are now in the crisis of a revolution and in the transit from one form of government to another—you cannot see that character of men exactly in the same situation in which we see it in this country. With us it is militant; with you it is triumphant; and you know how it can act when its power is commensurate to its will. I would not be supposed to confine these observations to any description of men or to comprehend all men of any description within them—No! far from it. I am as incapable of that injustice as I am of keeping terms with those who profess principles of extremities and who, under the name of religion, teach little else than wild and dangerous politics. The worst of these politics of revolution is this: they temper and harden the breast in order to prepare it for the desperate strokes which are sometimes used in extreme occasions. But as these occasions may never arrive, the mind receives a gratuitous taint; and the moral sentiments suffer not a little when no political purpose is served by the depravation. This sort of people are so taken up with their theories about the rights of man that they have totally forgotten his nature. Without opening one new avenue to the understanding, they have succeeded in stopping up those that lead to the heart. They have perverted in themselves, and in those that attend to them, all the well-placed sympathies of the human breast.

≫ **Working with Sources**

1. Is Burke's protest against the Revolution merely the result of his estimation of its "extremist" nature?

2. Is Burke justified in drawing a connection between metaphysical theorizing and physical violence? Did he provide an accurate prediction of "the Terror," still to come?

SOURCE 22.5   Thomas Paine, *Rights of Man*

1791

As a young man in England, Thomas Paine worked a series of low-paying, menial jobs, most of which he was quickly fired from, being perceived as an uncooperative "troublemaker." In 1774, at the age of 37, seeming to be a total failure in every profession he had attempted, he hired passage on a ship to the American colonies. Fortunately, Paine possessed a letter of

Source: Philip S. Foner, ed., *The Life and Major Writings of Thomas Paine* (New York: Citadel, 1945), 316–317, 340–341.

recommendation from Benjamin Franklin, whom he had met after a scientific lecture in London. On the strength of this letter, Paine found employment as a printer and writer in Philadelphia, and soon became the editor of a journal called the *Pennsylvania Magazine*. Incensed by the abuses to which the colonists were subject, he encouraged his fellow Americans to make a formal break with Britain. He also wrote and published a series of editorials protesting the American institution of slavery, castigating those who were agitating for their own "liberty" while denying it so cruelly to others.

Paine published his thoughts on independence in pamphlet form in January 1776 under the title *Common Sense*. So popular was the document that General Washington ordered that it be read aloud to his troops as they froze along the Delaware River on Christmas Eve 1776. Declaring, "These are the times that try men's souls," Paine continued to offer encouragement to the soldiers in pamphlets later published as *The American Crisis*, and his efforts on behalf of the American cause were recognized by many of the founding fathers of the country during the Revolution.

When he heard about the storming of the Bastille in Paris in July 1789, Paine rushed to France to be a part of this new revolution. Soon afterward, he had the honor of delivering the key to the Bastille from the Marquis de Lafayette to Washington, at which time, he declared, his heart "leaped with joy." When Burke's *Reflections* on the Revolution were published in 1790, Paine felt he had been betrayed by his former friend, with whom he had had many conversations and a meeting of minds in the American cause. As a result, he published *The Rights of Man*, a strong rebuke of Burke's philosophy and commentary, in February 1791. The work was dedicated to the first president of the United States, George Washington.

The three first articles [of the Declaration of the Rights of Man and of the Citizen] are the basis of liberty, as well individual as national; nor can any country be called free, whose government does not take its beginning from the principles they contain, and continue to preserve them pure; and the whole of the Declaration of Rights is of more value to the world, and will do more good, than all the laws and statutes that have yet been promulgated.

In the declaratory exordium which prefaces the Declaration of Rights, we see the solemn and majestic spectacle of a nation opening its commission, under the auspices of its Creator, to establish a Government; a scene so new, and so transcendently unequalled by any thing in the European world, that the name of a revolution is diminutive of its character, and it rises into a regeneration of man.

What are the present governments of Europe, but a scene of iniquity and oppression? What is that of England? Do not its own inhabitants say, It is a market where every man has his price, and where corruption is common traffic, at the expense of a deluded people? No wonder, then, that the French Revolution is traduced.

Had it confined itself merely to the destruction of flagrant despotism, perhaps Mr. Burke and some others had been silent. Their cry now is, "It is gone too far": that is, it has gone too far for them. It stares corruption in the face, and the venal tribe are all alarmed. Their fear discovers itself in their outrage, and they are but publishing the groans of a wounded vice.

But from such opposition, the French Revolution, instead of suffering, receives an homage. The more it is struck, the more sparks it will emit; and the fear is, it will not be struck enough. It has nothing to dread from attacks: Truth has given it an establishment; and Time will record it with a name as lasting as its own.

Having now traced the progress of the French Revolution through most of its principal stages, from its commencement, to the taking of the Bastille, and its establishment by the Declaration of Rights, I will close the subject with the energetic apostrophe of M. de Lafayette—May this great monument, raised to Liberty, serve as a lesson to the oppressor, and an example to the oppressed!

. . .

From the Revolutions of America and France, and the symptoms that have appeared in other countries, it is evident that the opinion of the world is changed with respect to systems of government, and that revolutions are not within the compass of political calculations. The progress of time and circumstances, which men assign to the accomplishment of great changes, is too mechanical to measure the force of the mind, and the rapidity of reflection, by which revolutions are generated. All the old governments have received a shock from those that already appear, and which were once more improbable, and are a greater subject of wonder, than a general revolution in Europe would be now.

When we survey the wretched condition of man under the monarchical and hereditary systems of government, dragged from his home by one power, or driven by another, and impoverished by taxes more than by enemies, it becomes evident that those systems are bad, and that a general revolution in the principle and construction of governments is necessary.

What is government more than the management of the affairs of a nation? It is not, and from its nature cannot be, the property of any particular man or family, but of the whole community, at whose expense it is supported; and though by force or contrivance it has been usurped into an inheritance, the usurpation cannot alter the right of things. Sovereignty, as a matter of right, appertains to the nation only, and not to any individual; and a nation has at all times an inherent indefeasible right to abolish any form of government it finds inconvenient, and establish such as accords with its interest, disposition, and happiness. The romantic and barbarous distinction of [making] men into kings and subjects, though it may suit the condition of courtiers, cannot that of citizens; and is exploded by the principle upon which governments are now founded. Every citizen is a member of the sovereignty, and, as such, can acknowledge no personal subjection; and his obedience can be only to the laws.

>> Working with Sources

1. How does Paine defend the Revolution against the charge of "extremism," as levied by Burke and others?

2. Why does Paine think it dangerous to romanticize kings and queens?

Creoles and Caudillos

LATIN AMERICA IN THE NINETEENTH CENTURY

Among the leaders of the Latin American wars of independence (1810–1826) from Spain, a woman named Juana Azurduy de Padilla (1781–1862) stands out for her bravery. Azurduy [asoor-DOO-ee] was a mestiza military commander in what are today the countries of Bolivia and Argentina. Her father was a Creole landowner near the city of Chuquisaca [choo-kee-SA-ca], and her mother was a Quechua-speaking Amerindian. Sent by her parents to a convent for her education and perhaps the life of a nun, Azurduy preferred the stories of heroic women warrior saints to a more sedate life of contemplation. After she completed her schooling, she married Manuel Ascencio Padilla, the son of a Creole landowner in Upper Peru, a military man in his youth and a law student after that. Together, the two enthusiastically joined the cause of independence in 1810, creating a mini republic (*republiquita*) in the mountains.

Here, Azurduy learned swordsmanship, firearms handling, and logistics for fighting guerilla wars. Well versed in Quechua and Aymara, Azurduy and Ascencio recruited some 6,000 locals, armed with the traditional Inca arms of clubs and slings. Azurduy, adored by these locals as Mother Earth (*pachamama*), and Ascencio with their men joined in 1813 an expeditionary force of independence fighters from Buenos Aires. This force suffered

Mexico
Central America
ATLANTIC OCEAN
SOUTH AMERICA
PACIFIC OCEAN

LATIN AMERICA AND THE CARIBBEAN

ABOVE: Carts loaded high with sugarcane arrive at a sugar mill in Cuba, late nineteenth century.

a crushing defeat, however, at the hands of Spanish royal troops sent by the vice-regent of Peru. In an effort to recover, Azurduy borrowed a training manual and drilled what she called her "Loyal Battalion" for ambushes and quick retreats. But under the relentless pressure of the viceregal troops, the battalion suffered a constant loss of men, including her husband in 1816. Azurduy had no choice but to retreat to what is today northwestern Argentina, where she was incorporated as a lieutenant colonel in the regular independence army, in recognition of her bravery.

In 1824 Upper Peru finally gained its independence, under the name of Bolivia (in honor of the Venezuelan independence leader Simón Bolívar). Azurduy returned from Argentina to retire in her birthplace, renamed Sucre, after the first president of Bolivia. Four of her children had died of malaria, and only her daughter Lisa remained of her family. When Azurduy died in 1862 she was largely forgotten, but in the early 1900s Bolivians remembered her and named a town near her birthplace after her.

T he story of Juana Azurduy highlights important elements in the wars of independence in Latin America. Much more than in the United States, these wars as well as the subsequent creation of republican constitutions were the work not only of European American settlers but also of Amerindians, mestizos, black freedmen, and black slaves. In the United States, only a smattering of Native and African Americans participated in the wars, while independence in Mexico, Colombia, Bolivia, Peru, and Chile would be unthinkable without the prominent participation of Native and/or African Americans. Finally, the fact that a woman was able to buck patriarchal conventions in the early 1800s and rise in the ranks of the military demonstrates the power of the revolutionary ideas of liberty and of the republican and constitutional nation-state (see Chapter 22)—a power that still inspires today.

Independence, Constitutionalism, and Landed Elites

In Latin America, the eighteenth-century Enlightenment was far less an intellectual incubator of independence and republican constitutionalism than in North America. In a few places, notably New Granada (today Colombia, Venezuela, Ecuador, and Panama), there was actually some limited awareness of the New Sciences and social contract theories. But the American and French Revolutions had a limited intellectual impact, and the Haitian slave revolution raised apprehension among Creoles. The Latin American struggle for independence was clearly another chapter in the history of the revolutionary wars of independence since 1776, as discussed in Chapter 22, but its prehistory was much shorter. The real catalyst for the majority of Latin Americans to declare independence and introduce republican constitutions was Napoleon's occupation of the Iberian Peninsula (1807–1814). This occupation confronted the Spanish-speaking Creoles with the choice of continued loyalty to the

Seeing Patterns

❯ Which factors in the complex ethnic and social structures of Latin America were responsible for the emergence of authoritarian politicians, or caudillos?

❯ After achieving independence, why did Latin American countries opt for a continuation of mineral and agricultural commodity exports?

❯ How do the social and economic structures of this period continue to affect the course of Latin America today?

Southern Cone: Geographical term denoting the southern half of South America, with the countries of Brazil, Paraguay, Uruguay, and Argentina.

deposed absolutist Bourbon dynasty, recognition of Napoleon, or full republican independence. In the end, when Napoleon's regime proved to be short-lived and the restored Bourbon king refused constitutional reforms, the choice was clear: Latin America fought for its full republican independence.

After independence, the four regions governed previously by Spanish viceroys—Rio de la Plata in the south, Peru in the west, New Granada in the center, and New Spain in the north—followed their own political trajectories, with comparatively little interaction among themselves. The pattern of republican state formation, with states sometimes in fierce competition with each other, unfolded for the most part *within* each of the four regions.

Independence in the Southern Cone: State Formation in Argentina

Independence movements in the the Viceroyalty of the Río de la Plata formed in June 1810. Under the guise of loyalty to the deposed Fernando VII of Spain, Creoles in the capital, Buenos Aires, seized the initiative to establish a junta rejecting the viceregal Spanish authorities. Outright independence from Spain was declared in 1816, and even though by this time Spanish loyalists in the south had been defeated, their brethren in the far northwest were still strong. Several efforts by troops from Buenos Aires to defeat the loyalists of Upper Peru, part of the Viceroyalty of Río de la Plata, had failed. The figure who finally broke the logjam was one of the heroes of Latin American independence, José de San Martín (1778–1850). After a difficult crossing of the narrow Andes passes in 1816, San Martín was able to liberate Chile (1818) and the Viceroyalty of Peru (1821), but not the Argentinian province of Upper Peru.

Independence in Argentina   The Viceroyalty of La Plata, comprising the modern countries of Argentina, Uruguay, Paraguay, and Bolivia, was the youngest of Spain's colonial units. In the course of the Bourbon reforms, Spain had separated it in 1776 from the Viceroyalty of Peru, where declining silver exports had diminished the importance of the port of Lima. La Plata, with the rising port of Buenos Aires as its capital, had grown through contraband trade with Great Britain, and the Bourbon reformers wanted to redirect its trade more firmly back to Spain. Buenos Aires was so important to the British, however, that they occupied the city in 1806–1807, until Spanish colonial forces drove them out.

Creoles in La Plata had far fewer Amerindians, African slaves, mestizos, and mulattoes to deal with—or fear—than in any of the other viceroyalties. But in 1810, when the first independence movements formed, there was a clear distinction between the pro-independence Creoles of Buenos Aires, or *porteños*, and the Creoles of the *pampas* (grasslands of the temperate interior of Argentina and Uruguay) and the subtropical plains and hills of Paraguay, who favored continued colonialism. The latter were either royalists or strove for independence separate from La Plata.

Uruguay, furthermore, was initially claimed by Brazil and eventually achieved its own independence only in 1828. Upper Peru, or modern Bolivia, with its high-elevation plains, lowland Amazon basin rain forest, large Native American population, and Potosí silver mines, was heavily defended by colonial and Spanish troops. Given these various urban–rural and geographical circumstances, the porteño independence fighters achieved only a standstill during the initial period of 1810–1816, as mentioned in the vignette at the beginning of the chapter.

The breakthrough for independence eventually came via an experienced military figure, the highly popular José de San Martín (ca. 1778–1850). San Martín was a Creole from northeastern Argentina. His father, an immigrant from Spain, was a military officer and administrator of a Jesuit-founded Native American mission district. The son, educated from an early age in a Spanish military academy, began service in the porteño independence movement in 1812, where he distinguished himself in the Argentine struggle for independence.

During his service, San Martín realized that ultimate success in the struggle for independence would require the liberation of the Viceroyalty of Peru. Accordingly, he trained the Army of the Andes, which included large numbers of mulatto and black volunteers. With this army, he crossed the mountains to Chile in 1818, liberating the country from royalist forces. With the help of a newly established navy composed of ships acquired from the United States and Britain, he conquered Lima in Peru. However, San Martín was defied by the local Creoles when he sought to introduce social reforms, such as an end to the Native American tribute system, the *mit'a*, and the emancipation of the children of African slaves. When he was also unable to dislodge Spanish troops from Upper Peru and come to terms about the future of Latin America with Simón Bolívar, the liberation hero of central Latin America, he resigned from the army in 1822, to live mostly in Belgium and France for the remainder of his life.

painting commemorating Chilean independence (1818)

Slow State Formation   After independence, the ruling junta in Buenos Aires solidified into an oligarchy of the city's landowning Creole elite. In the interior, the vast, largely undeveloped areas of the pampas with their small floating population of Amerindians and Creole *gauchos*, or cowboys, remained largely outside the new state. But even the core provinces and the port city of Buenos Aires were unable to come to terms. The provinces cherished their autonomy and resented the city's economic superiority and pretensions to political dominance. Uruguay, one of the provinces of the former Spanish Viceroyalty of La Plata, strove for independence from the start, but was thwarted by both Argentina, the self-declared heir of the Viceroyalty's territories, and Brazil, which claimed it for itself on the grounds of its sizable Portuguese-speaking minority (one fifth of the population). The independence of Uruguay was recognized by its much more powerful neighbors only in 1828, but even then meddling in its internal affairs continued, since the search for territorial consolidation of the states in the southern cone continued.

Political Instability in the Southern Cone   An Argentine constituent assembly finally drew up a definitive federal constitution in 1853 (with amendments still in force today), but state formation and territorial consolidation remained in flux.

interactive timeline

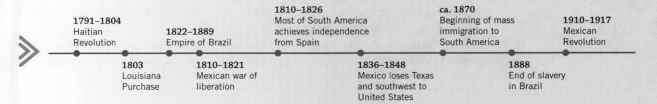

1791–1804 Haitian Revolution

1803 Louisiana Purchase

1822–1889 Empire of Brazil

1810–1821 Mexican war of liberation

1810–1826 Most of South America achieves independence from Spain

1836–1848 Mexico loses Texas and southwest to United States

ca. 1870 Beginning of mass immigration to South America

1888 End of slavery in Brazil

1910–1917 Mexican Revolution

Fiercely Independent Gauchos, around 1900. Gauchos, shown here sharpening their long knives (*facónes*), were recognizable by their ponchos or wool blankets which doubled as winter coats and saddlecloths. As in North America, they were expert riders, calf ropers, and—with their dogs shown in front—cattle herders.

Buenos Aires refused to subscribe to the constitution until 1861 when it finally gave up its resistance to federalism. While the constitutional order was settled at this time, the process of territorial consolidation was not and contributed to continued tensions among Paraguay, Uruguay, Argentina, and Brazil.

Tensions among the four countries reached their fever pitch during the Paraguayan War of 1864–1870, which proved to be the most devastating in the history of nineteenth-century Latin America. In this war, Paraguay was pitted against a triple alliance among Brazil, Argentina, and Uruguay. The ambitious Paraguayan president Francisco Solano López (r. 1862–1870) miscalculated that Argentina would support his idea of a "third force," formed by an alliance between Paraguay and Uruguay, to block Brazil's territorial ambitions. But in spite of their diverging interests, Argentina and Brazil agreed to maintain the traditional policy of keeping Paraguay and Uruguay weak. Paraguay lost the war and suffered terrible destruction by losing more than half of its population and one-third of its territory. Similar to its two better-known companions, the Crimean War (1854) and the US Civil War (1861–1865), the War of Paraguay contributed to the industrialization and professionalization of modern warfare. In particular, it greatly strengthened the political role of the Brazilian military, which culminated in the army overthrow of the monarchy (1889). About the only positive outcome was that it finally settled the state formation and territorial consolidation process of Argentina.

Argentine Demographic Growth   In the years after 1870, many of the same forces that were shaping the North American West were also actively transforming the pampas of Argentina. Encouraged by the government, European immigrants streamed into the country. The land was opened to settlement, driving the gauchos from their independent existence into becoming hired hands. The railroad was spurring settlement, and the remaining Amerindians were driven south to Patagonia or exterminated. In contrast to the homesteading policies in the United States, however, the pampas were divided up into huge estates (*estancias*) of tens of thousands of acres, aided by the introduction of barbed wire to fence in the ranges. The old system of rounding up essentially wild livestock and driving it to market now gave way to the ranching of cattle, sheep, and goats. As in other areas of South America, the new landed Creole elite dominated politics and the economy long into the twentieth century.

While landed interests continued to prevail, the urban center of Buenos Aires, expanding through waves of Spanish and Italian immigrants, grew restless under the rotating presidency that characterized the period of 1880–1900. Spurred by the development of radical politics in Europe, especially versions of Marxism and Socialism, two major urban opposition parties took shape in the 1890s: the Radical Party and the Socialists. As the influence of these parties grew, electoral reforms were forced on an unwilling landed oligarchy. In 1912, universal male suffrage was passed, and voting by secret ballot was established. By 1916, the closed oligarchy was at last cracked open by the arrival of a new president, Hipólito Yrigoyen (1916–1922, 1928–1930), a former schoolteacher. He relied for support mostly on an urban constituency, which dominated politics in the early twentieth century.

Brazil: From Kingdom to Republic

During the late colonial period, Brazil underwent the same centralizing administrative, fiscal, and trade reforms as the Spanish possessions. These reforms were resented as much by the Brazilian planters and urban Creoles (Portuguese *crioulos*) as by their Spanish counterparts. But their fear of rebellion by the huge population of black slaves held them back from openly demanding independence. As it happened, independence arrived without bloody internecine wars through the relocation of the monarchy from Portugal to Brazil in the wake of Napoleon's invasion of Iberia in 1807. Brazil became a monarchically governed empire, striving for expansion into Spanish-speaking territories. When Brazil, under pressure from Britain, finally abolished slavery in 1888, the politically abandoned plantation oligarchy and allied military avenged itself by deposing the emperor, switching to a republican regime under the military in 1889. Given the enormous size of the country, as well as the split of the Creole oligarchy into groups with diverging mining, sugar, and coffee interests, the regime became solidly federal, making it difficult for authoritarian rulers to succeed.

Relocation of the Dynasty   Portugal's royal family fled the country in advance of Napoleon's armies in 1807. Escorted by British ships, it took refuge in Brazil and elevated the colony to the status of a coequal kingdom in union with Portugal but governed from Brazil after Napoleon's defeat in 1815. The arrival of some 15,000 Portuguese together with the dynasty, however, created resentment among the Brazilian Creoles, sharpening the traditional tension between Creoles and Portuguese-born reformers. A crisis point was reached in 1820 when rebels in Portugal adopted a liberal constitution, which demanded the return of Brazil to colonial status as well as the transfer of the dynasty back to Portugal. The reigning king went back but left his son, Pedro I (r. 1822–1831), behind in Brazil. Thereupon, Pedro uttered in 1822 his famous "*Fico*" ("I remain"), and proclaimed "independence or death!" thereby making Brazil an independent state.

Pedro I's Authoritarianism   On acceding to the throne, Pedro declared Brazil an empire because of its size and diversity. His rule at the head of the Creole landowner ruling class, however, shared many of the same characteristics as that of the early caudillos in the Spanish-speaking South American countries. In addition, like the restoration monarchs of Europe in the early 1800s, he firmly adhered to his belief in divine right, which was incompatible with more than token constitutionalism. Consequently, he rejected an attempt by the landed oligarchy to limit monarchical rule. Instead, he issued his own constitution in 1823, which concentrated most powers in his hands, as well as a council of state, with a weak lifetime senate and a legislative chamber based on severely limited voting rights. Since he also reserved for himself the nomination and dismissal of ministers, the dissolution of the chamber, and, above all, the appointment of provincial governors, his rule was far too authoritarian even for the conservative planter elite.

In reaction, in 1824, six northeastern provinces attempted to secede. They proclaimed the republican Federation of the Equator and, somewhat illogically, demanded more central government support for the traditional northern sugar and cotton plantations, neglected by a rising emphasis on south-central coffee plantations. Increased British patrols in the Atlantic to suppress the slave trade had increased the price for slaves. The sugar planters could ill afford the increased prices, but the expanding coffee market enabled its planters to pay (see "Patterns Up Close").

Given the close ties between Britain and Brazil, Pedro found it difficult to resist the British demands for the abolition of slavery. As a result, early signs of alienation between the crown and the Creole planter elite crept in. It also did not help that Pedro supported the open immigration to Brazil of skilled foreigners from Europe, as well as foreign loans and investments for development. As the sources document, Pedro's policy was directed at increasing the number of whites in order to decrease the proportion of blacks and Amerindians.

By contrast, the plantation elites were primarily interested in acquiring servile labor and control of the courts to ensure severe punishments for infractions by slaves. They voiced their opposition to internal improvements, like railroads, for fear of disrupting the stability of the plantation system. Ultimately, a succession crisis in Portugal in 1830 led to a conservative revolt against Pedro. In 1831, he lost his nerve and abdicated, sailing back to Portugal. He left the throne to his 5-year-old son, Pedro II (r. 1831–1889), who required a regent. The landowning elite exploited the opportunity of the temporarily weak monarchy by renewing its demands for federalism.

The Federalist Interlude After lengthy debates, in 1834 the government granted the provinces their own legislative assemblies with strong tax and budget powers, effectively strengthening the provincial landholding elites with their various regional interests. It also abolished the council of state but created a national guard to suppress slave revolts and urban mobs. This mixed bag of reforms was too much for some provinces. The most dangerous revolt against the reforms was that of 1835 in Rio Grande do Sul, a southern province dominated by cattle owners who did not own many slaves and commanded military forces composed of gauchos. These owners established an independent republic that attracted many domestic and foreign radicals opposed to slavery, including Giuseppe Garibaldi, the Italian nationalist who played a crucial role in the unification of Italy (see Chapter 22). In reaction to the coexistence of a now weak and decentralized monarchy and an antislavery republic offering refuge to runaways on Brazilian soil, the centralists reasserted themselves. In 1840 they proclaimed the 14-year-old Pedro II emperor and curbed the powers of the provincial assemblies. In 1845 they negotiated a return of Rio Grande do Sul to Brazil.

images from the
Ragamuffin War
(1835)

The End of Slavery The 1830s and 1840s coincided with a transition in Brazil from sugar to coffee as a major export commodity on the world market. The old sugar plantation elite lost clout, and a newer coffee planter oligarchy ascended to prominence. Both needed slaves, and as long as the crown did not seriously seek to fulfill its promises of 1831 to the British to curb the importation of slaves, there was no more than unease about the mutual dependence of the crown and the oligarchy on the continued existence of slave labor. But when the British in 1849 authorized warships to enter Brazilian waters to intercept slave ships, the importation of slaves

virtually ceased, causing a serious labor shortage. Sugar, cotton, and coffee plantation owners began to think of ridding themselves of a monarchy that was unable to
maintain the flow of slaves from overseas.

In the 1860s and 1870s, antimonarchy agitation gathered speed. Brazilians, especially professionals and intellectuals in the cities, became sensitive to their country
being isolated in the world on the issue of slavery. After the United States emanci-
pated slaves in 1863, the Spanish colonies of Puerto Rico and Cuba followed suit by
ending slavery for all elderly slaves and newborn children. Brazil was now left as the
only unreformed slaveholding country in the Western Hemisphere.

In the following decade and a half, the antislavery chorus increased in volume.
While the government introduced a few cosmetic changes, it fell to the provinces to
take more serious steps. Planters, who began to see the demise of the system on the ho-
rizon, encouraged their provinces to increase the flow of foreign immigrants, to be employed as wage labor on the coffee plantations. The political situation neared the point
of anarchy in 1885, with mass flights of slaves from plantations and armed clashes to
keep them there. Only in 1888 did the central government finally end slavery.

painting showing a
white Brazilian couple
being served by black
slaves (1839)

The Coffee Boom   Predictably, given the grip of the planter elite on the labor force,
little changed in social relations after the abolition of slavery. The coffee growers,
enjoying high international coffee prices and the benefits of infrastructure improvements through railroads and telegraph lines since the 1850s, could afford low-wage
hired labor. The now-free blacks received no land, education, or urban jobs, scraping
by with low wages on the coffee and sugar plantations. Economically, however, after
freeing itself from the burdens of slavery, Brazil expanded its economy in the 5 years
following 1888 as much as in the 70 years of slavery since independence.

The monarchy, having dragged its feet for half a century on the slavery issue, was
thoroughly discredited among the landowners and their military offshoot, the officer corps. During the War of Paraguay (1865–1870, see p. 692), the military had
transformed itself into a well-equipped, professional body, with its own sense of mission. By the 1880s, officers were also drawn from professional and intellectual urban
circles. Increasingly, these officers subscribed to the ideology of *positivism* coming
from France, which celebrated the idea of secular scientific and technological progress (see Chapter 22). Positivists, almost by definition, were liberal and republican
in political orientation. In 1889, a revolt in the military supported by the Creole
plantation oligarchy resulted in the abolition of the monarchy and proclamation of a
republic, with practically no resistance from any quarter.

Two political tendencies emerged in the constituent assembly 2 years after the
proclamation of the republic. The coffee interests of the south-central states favored
federalism, with the right of the provinces to collect export taxes and maintain militias. The urban professional and intellectual interests, especially lawyers, supported
a strong presidency with control over tariffs and import taxes as well as powers to
use the federal military against provinces in cases of national emergency. The two
tendencies resulted in a compromise with a tilt toward federalism, which produced
provincial authoritarian rulers on the one hand but also regularly elected presidents
on the other.

Following this tilt, in the 1890s the government was strongly supportive of agricultural commodity exports. Coffee, rubber, and sugar exports yielded high profits
and taxes until 1896, when overproduction of coffee resulted in diminishing returns.

Slave Rebellions in Cuba and Brazil

Blacks had gained little from the American and French Revolutions, and the pattern of brutal exploitation continued in many parts of the Americas. Not surprisingly, therefore, blacks sought to emulate the example of Haiti's successful slave revolt during the first half of the 1800s. However, none of the subsequent Haiti-inspired revolts were any more successful against the well-prepared authorities than previous revolts had been in the 1700s, as a look at rebellions in Cuba and Brazil during the first half of the nineteenth century shows.

In Cuba, the decline of sugar production in Haiti during the Revolution encouraged a rapid expansion of plantations and the importation of African slaves. As previously in Haiti, a relatively diversified eighteenth-century society of whites, free mulattoes, and blacks, as well as urban and rural black slaves, was transformed into a heavily African-born plantation slave society, forming a large majority in many rural districts. The black freedman José Antonio Aponte (ca. 1756–1812), a militiaman

Slave Revolt Aboard Ship. Rebellions aboard ship, such as the famous 1839 mutiny aboard the *Amistad* shown here, were common occurrences. The *Amistad* was engaged in intra-American slave trafficking, and the slaves overpowered the crew shortly after embarkation in Cuba. After protracted legal negotiations, the slaves were eventually freed and returned to Africa.

Import-substitution industrialization: The practice by which countries protect their economies by setting high tariffs and construct factories for the production of consumer goods (textiles, furniture, shoes, followed later by appliances, automobiles, electronics) and/or capital goods (steel, chemicals, machinery).

The state of São Paulo then regulated the sale of coffee on the world market through a state purchase scheme, which brought some stabilization to coffee production. At the same time and continuing into the early twentieth century (and without much state or central government support), immigrants and foreign investors laid the foundation for **import-substitution industrialization**, beginning with textile and food-processing factories. The comparative advantage afforded by commodity exports had run its course by the late 1800s and early 1900s and now had to be supplemented with industrialization.

Independence and State Formation in Western and Northern South America

Compared to the Viceroyalty of La Plata in the south, the Spanish Viceroyalty of New Granada in northern South America, with today's countries of Venezuela,

and head of the Yoruba confraternity (*cabilde*) in Havana, led an abortive revolt in 1812 that drew support from both sectors. In the subsequent revolts of 1825, 1835, and 1843, the urban element was less evident. Authorities and planters, heavily invested in new industrial equipment for sugar production and railroads, and exhausted by the unending sequence of uprisings, unleashed a campaign of sweeping arrests of free blacks and mulattoes that cut the urban–rural link once and for all.

Brazil, like Cuba, also benefited from the collapse of sugar production on Haiti in the 1790s and the first half of the 1800s. It expanded its plantation sector, particularly in the province of Bahia, and imported large numbers of slaves from Africa. But here distrust divided those born in Africa from Brazilian-born slaves, freedmen, and mulattoes. Many freedmen and mulattoes served in the militias that the authorities used to suppress the revolts. Furthermore, in contrast to the narrow island of Cuba, plantation slaves could run away more easily to independent settlements (called *quilombos*) in the wide-open Brazilian interior, from where revolts were more easily organized than in cities or on plantations. In fact, no fewer than a dozen quilombo revolts extending into plantations occurred in Bahia during 1807–1828, revolts which the militias found difficult to crush, having to march into often remote areas.

Two urban revolts of the period were remarkable for their exceptional mix of insurgents, unparalleled in Cuba or elsewhere in Latin America. The first was the Tailor's Rebellion of 1798 in Salvador, Bahía's capital. Freedmen, mulattoes, and white craftspeople cooperated in the name of freedom and equality against the Creole oligarchy. The second was the Muslim uprising of 1835, also in Bahía, organized by African-born freedmen as well as slaves with Islamic clerical educations that they had received in West Africa before their enslavement.

Questions

- Do the slave rebellions in Cuba and Brazil in the early nineteenth century confirm or complicate the pattern of slave revolutions that was manifested first in Haiti?

- What role did geography play in the success or failure of a revolution?

Colombia, Ecuador, and Panama, had far fewer Creoles. For its struggle for independence to succeed, leaders had to seek support from the *pardos*, as the majority population of free black and mulatto craftspeople in the cities was called. Independence eventually came through the building of strong armies from these diverse elements, mostly by Simón Bolívar, the liberator of northern South America. After independence, however, the Creoles quickly moved to dissolve their coalitions with the lower classes and embraced the caudillo politics that were also practiced in other parts of South America.

Creoles and Pardos In contrast to Mexico, with its relatively large Creole and mestizo populations in the cities and countryside, New Granada's Creole population was small in relation to mestizos and pardos. The latter constituted over half of the urban and two-thirds of the rural people. In 1810, the New Granadans created *juntas*, or committees, among which the junta of Cartagena was the most important,

Liberation of the Slaves in Colombia. As a Creole growing up on his father's cacao plantation, worked by slaves, Bolívar was intimately familiar with slavery. But his exile in postrevolutionary Haiti 1814–1816 demonstrated to him that slavery was incompatible not only with the principles of the American and French Revolutions but also with the revolutions in Spanish America, of which he was one of the main leaders.

and drove the colonial Spaniards from their administrative positions. Initially, the Creole-led juntas agreed on the equality of all ethnicities and worked on constitutions that provided for elections by all free men. But they were also suspicious of each other, denouncing their allegedly aristocratic, nondemocratic aspirations.

In 1811, cooperation broke down and the pardos assumed power in a coup. The Creoles struck back a year later when they declared the First Republic of Cartagena. Their power was limited by the pardo-dominated militias, however, and in a compromise they agreed on the continuation of full voting rights. In the long run, during the 1800s, this revolutionary achievement did not last, and the Creoles established oligarchic rule.

Bolívar the Liberator   The junta of Cartagena, together with other juntas, formed the federation of the United Provinces of New Granada in 1811, with a weak executive unable to prevent squabbling among the juntas or even defend their independence. The Spanish king, Fernando VII, after returning to the throne in 1813, was determined to reestablish colonial control by dispatching armies to Latin America. The largest forces, comprising some 10,000 troops, landed in the United Provinces in 1814, took Cartagena after a siege, and resurrected the viceroyalty of New Granada.

The eventual liberator of northern South America from renewed Spanish rule in 1819 was Simón Bolívar (1783–1830). Bolívar was born in Venezuela, into a wealthy Creole family; it owned cacao plantations worked by African slaves and was engaged in colonial trade. Although lacking a formal education, thanks to his tutor Bolívar was familiar with Enlightenment literature. In 1799, he visited Spain, where he met his future wife, and later returned to Europe after her death. In 1804, he was deeply impressed when he watched the lavish spectacle of Napoleon crowning himself emperor in Paris. These European visits instilled in Bolívar a lasting admiration for European ideals of liberty and popular sovereignty, and he longed to create a constitutional republic in his homeland.

In 1810, similar to Cartagena, Venezuelan cities formed Creole-led juntas with pardo participation. In 1814, of course, when the Viceroyalty returned to power, the juntas were squashed. But in 1816 Bolívar returned from exile to Venezuela with a military force, partly supplied by Haiti. After some initial difficulties, he succeeded in defeating the Spanish troops. In 1822, he assumed the presidency of "Gran Colombia," an independent republic comprising the later states of Colombia, Venezuela, Ecuador, and Panama.

The Bolívar–San Martín Encounter   After their defeat in Gran Colombia, Spanish troops continued to hold Upper Peru in the Andes, where an independence movement supported by Argentina—including Juana Azurduy, discussed in the opening vignette of this chapter—was active but had made little progress against Spanish and royalist Creole troops. In the face of this situation, the Argentinean liberator José de San Martín (previously discussed) and Bolívar met in 1822 to deliberate on how to drive the Spanish from Peru and to shape the future of an independent Latin America.

As for fighting Spain, they agreed that Bolívar was in a better geographical position than San Martín to send military forces to Peru. But even with these forces Bolívar's task of attacking the Spanish was daunting. The troops were unaccustomed to high-altitude fighting and were hindered as much by mountain sickness as by enemy resistance. After two years of fighting, one of Bolívar's lieutenants finally got the better of the fiercely resisting Spanish. Two years later, in 1826, Spanish colonialism in Latin America finally ended when the last troops surrendered on an island off the Chilean coast.

The content of the discussion for the future of Latin America between San Martín and Bolívar never became public and has remained a bone of contention among historians. San Martín, bitterly disappointed by endless disputes among liberal constitutionalists and royalists, federalists and centralists, as well as Creole elitists and mestizo, pardo, and mulatto populists, apparently favored monarchical rule to bring stability to Latin America. Bolívar, so it is believed, preferred republicanism and Creole oligarchical rule. Both sought limited mestizo and pardo collaboration, especially in their armies. Apart from their awareness of the need for ethnic and racial integration, there was not much common ground between the two independence leaders.

San Martín's sudden withdrawal from the Andes after the meeting and his subsequent resignation from politics, however, can be taken as an indication of his realization that the chances for a South American monarchy were small indeed. Bolívar, also acutely aware of the multiple cleavages in Latin American politics, more realistically envisioned the future of Latin America as that of relatively small independent republics, held together by strong, lifelong presidencies and hereditary senates. He actually implemented this vision in the 1825 constitution of independent Upper Peru, renamed Bolivia after him.

Ironically, in his own country of Gran Colombia Bolívar was denied the role of strong president. Although he made himself a caudillo, he was unable to coax recalcitrant politicians into an agreement on a constitution for Gran Colombia similar to that of Bolivia. Eventually, in 1830 Bolívar resigned, dying shortly afterward of tuberculosis. In 1831 Gran Colombia divided into its component parts of Colombia, Venezuela, Ecuador, and (later) Panama.

Caudillo Rule Independent Venezuela, as perhaps the poorest and most underpopulated of northern South America's newly independent countries, became the politically most turbulent Latin American republic. In Carácas, the capital, caudillos from the landowning Creole families displaced each other at a rapid rate. By one estimate, there were 41 presidencies and 30 insurrections in the period of 1830–1899. Although many of the presidents sought foreign financial support for development, little was accomplished and much of the money went into the private coffers of the leaders. The main issue that kept rival factions at odds was federalism versus tighter central control, with at least one all-out war being fought over the issue during the 1860s.

Venezuela's neighboring countries followed a similar pattern of caudillo politics. Though enjoying longer periods of stability, Colombia—the name adopted in 1861

Simon Bolivar, Letter to General Juan Jose Flores, November 9, 1830 ("Ploughing the Sea")

Caudillo: Term referring to authoritarian Latin American rulers who disregard the constitutional limits to their powers. Derived from Latin *capitellum* (little head). Authoritarianism was most pronounced in northern South America.

to replace that of New Granada—also saw a continuing struggle between federalists and centralizers, with each side seeking the support of the Catholic Church. From 1899 until 1902, the two sides fought the War of a Thousand Days, leaving the country sufficiently weak for Panamanian rebels to establish an independent state of Panama in 1903, supported by the United States.

After independence, the administration of Theodore Roosevelt (1901–1909) swiftly concluded a treaty with the new country. In this treaty, the United States was to take control of a 10-mile-wide strip bisecting the narrow isthmus for the completion of the construction of the Panama Canal. A French consortium had begun gigantic earthmoving work in 1879 but was constantly behind schedule, as a result of landslides, flooding, tropical diseases, and engineering disputes, and went bankrupt in 1888. The government-sponsored construction took only seven years (1904–1911), but at the cost of appalling conditions for the Caribbean (African American) and European (Spanish) workers, who received half of the wages of their American counterparts.

The Andean States   As with the other new states in South America, it took decades for Peru, Bolivia, and Chile to work out territorial conflicts and complete their respective patterns of state formation. One of these conflicts was the War of the Pacific from 1879 to 1884, resulting in a victorious Chile annexing Peruvian and Bolivian lands. Most devastating for Peru was the destruction that Chilean troops wrought in southern Peru. The economy, which had made modest progress by using nitrate exports in the form of guano to fund railroad building and mining, was only painfully rebuilt after the destructions of war.

Political stability for several decades returned under the presidency of Nicolás de Piérola, who introduced a few belated reforms during his terms (1879–1881 and 1895–1899). The two most important ones were the stabilization of the monetary system and the professionalization of the army. As the presidency from this time until the 1920s was held by men from the upper landowning Creole class, this Peruvian period is often called the period of the "Aristocratic Republic."

Independence and Political Development in the North: Mexico

In contrast to the central Spanish colony of New Granada with its substantial black and mulatto populations and relatively few Amerindians, the Viceroyalty of New Spain (Mexico and Mesoamerica) had few inhabitants of African descent and large numbers of indigenous Americans. Therefore, from the beginning of the independence struggle, mestizos and Amerindians had prominent and ongoing roles in the political development of the nineteenth century. As in the other Viceroyalties, however, conservative landowning Creoles were for most of the time dominant in the political process. Only toward the end of the 1800s did urban white, mestizo, and Amerindian residents acquire a voice. Landless rural laborers entered the political stage in the early twentieth century, during the Mexican Revolution.

The Mexican Uprising   In 1810, Miguel Hidalgo y Costilla (1753–1811), the son of a Creole hacienda estate administrator and his Creole wife, declared its loyalty to the deposed king of Spain, Fernando VII, and launched a movement in opposition to the Viceroyalty and its colonial military. A churchman since his youth,

Hidalgo was broadly educated, well versed in Enlightenment literature, conversant in Nahuatl, and on the margins of strict Catholicism. As a young adult, he became a parish priest and devoted himself to creating employment opportunities for Amerindians in a province southeast of Mexico City.

Under the leadership of Hidalgo, tens of thousands of poor Creoles, mestizos, and Amerindians, who had suffered in a recent drought, marched on Guanajuato (in south-central Mexico), indiscriminately looting and killing both Spaniards and Creoles. Initially, they were successful in defeating the Spanish troops marching against them. When Hidalgo, shocked by the violence, called off an attack on Mexico City, however, the rebellion began to sputter and was eventually defeated in 1811. Colonial Spanish forces ultimately captured and executed Hidalgo.

War of Independence   After the defeat, associates of Hidalgo carried on in several southwestern provinces of Mexico but failed to make a comeback in the heartland around Mexico City. Here, royalists intent on preserving the union between Spain and Mexico after the return of Fernando VII to power in 1813 remained supreme. In 1813, Hidalgist nationalist rebels adopted a program for independence that envisioned a constitutional government, abolished slavery, and declared all native-born inhabitants of New Spain "Americans," without regard to ethnic differences. A year later they promulgated a constitution providing for a strong legislature and a weak executive. Both program and constitution, however, still awaited the conclusion of the civil war between nationalists and royalists for their implementation.

The war ended in 1821 with Mexico's independence, based on a compromise between the nationalist Vicente Guerrero (1782–1831) and the royalist Agustín de Iturbide (1783–1824). Both leaders came from wealthy landowning families, although the Guerreros also owned transportation enterprises and gunsmithies. Guerrero's father was a mestizo, his mother an African slave; Iturbide was a Creole of Basque gentry descent who insisted—against some doubts—that his mother was also Creole. According to the compromise, Mexico was to become an independent constitutional "empire" (in view of New Spain extending to Mesoamerica), give full citizenship rights to all inhabitants regardless of race and ethnicity, and adhere to Catholicism.

Iturbide became Mexico's first ruler, with the title "emperor," but abdicated in 1823 when his pro-landowner policies and continued tolerance of slavery provoked a military uprising. By that time, Mexico was no longer an empire; already in 1821, El Salvador, Nicaragua, Costa Rica, and Honduras had declared their independence. With a new constitution in 1824, Mexico became a republic. For eight months in 1829, the liberation hero Guerrero was the republic's second president. During his short tenure he officially abolished slavery, before losing both his office

Land and Liberty. This enormous mural by Diego Rivera (1886–1957), in the National Palace in Mexico City, shows Father Hidalgo above the Mexican eagle, flanked by other independence fighters. Above them are Emiliano Zapata, Pancho Villa, and other heroes of the Revolution of 1910. The other parts of the mural show historical scenes from the Spanish conquest to the twentieth century.

image analysis

Revolutionary Women.
Women, such as these *soldaderas* taking rifle practice, played many significant roles in the Mexican Revolution, 1910–1920.

and his life in another military uprising. As in other parts of Latin America during the period of early independence, politics remained unstable, pitting federalists and centralists against each other. Centralists eventually triumphed and, for a long period under the caudillo Antonio López de Santa Anna (in office 1833–1836 and 1839–1845), maintained authoritarian rule until 1855.

Northern Mexico and the Comanches
Initially, Mexico had a number of advantages as an independent nation. It had abundant natural resources, and its nominal northern territories—Texas, New Mexico, and California—contained much valuable pasture and farmland. These territories were inhabited by numerous Native American peoples, among whom the Comanches were the most powerful. Originally from the Great Basin, they had migrated to the Colorado plains around the Arkansas River in the 1600s. Here, they acquired horses during the Pueblo Revolt (1680) against Spain. As migrants, they adapted more readily to the opportunities offered through horse-breeding and contraband firearms than other, more settled Native American peoples.

In the course of the mid-1700s, they built a 400-mile-wide empire from the Arkansas River to just north of San Antonio. They raided regularly into New Mexico and maintained a flourishing trade of horses, cattle, bison hides, and enslaved war captives, including blacks, on their borders. In the last decades of Spanish rule, colonial reformers, intent on creating a northern buffer zone to protect their silver mines, dispatched troops to check the Comanche expansion. But during the war of Mexican independence, Comanche raids resumed and wiped out the recent gains.

Highly Mobile Comanches. The Comanches, having acquired horses and muskets, became the most efficient bison hunters prior to white Americans moving in with modern breechloaders. Living in tents, as shown here in a late nineteenth-century photograph, the highly mobile Comanches maintained a militarily powerful trading and raiding empire on the southwestern plains (1700–1875).

Northern Immigration To diminish the endemic insecurity in the northern borderlands resulting from the Comanches, beginning in the early 1820s Mexico supported immigration from the United States. It sold land to settlers on generous terms and allowed them to be largely self-governing as long as taxes were duly paid. At the same time, the United States entered a protracted period of growth. Settlement of the rich agricultural areas of the formerly French Ohio and Mississippi valleys moved with astonishing speed. The new demand for American cotton in British and American factories drove a frenetic expansion into Alabama, Mississippi, Louisiana, and Arkansas. Cotton exhausted the soil quickly, and the availability of cheap land made it more efficient to abandon the depleted lands and keep pushing the realm of "King Cotton" ever westward.

Many US citizens emigrated to Mexico to take advantage of its generous land policy and autonomy. The Mexican province of Texas was particularly attractive, especially to southerners, because of its nearness to the settled southern states and its suitability for cotton cultivation. While Mexico had outlawed slavery, most slave owners who migrated to Texas ignored these restrictions. The increasingly blatant violation of the antislavery laws and the swelling numbers of immigrants seeking opportunity in Texas came to alarm the Mexican national government by the 1830s.

The US–Mexico War In 1836, the Mexican president Santa Anna led some 4,000 troops against the militias maintained by the Texans. At first, these troops were successful, decimating Texan militiamen and US volunteers defending the Alamo, a fort near San Antonio. But then Texan forces defeated Santa Anna, and the state declared its independence (1836). Mexico refused to recognize Texas, and nine years later Texas opted for the security of union with the United States. It also settled in 1844

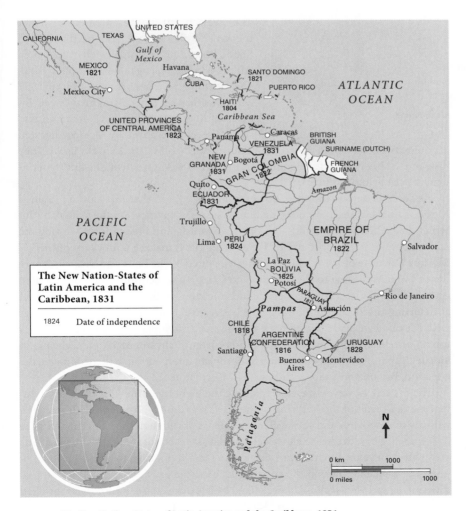

MAP **23.1** **The New Nation-States of Latin America and the Caribbean, 1831.**

MAP **23.2** **Mexico's Loss of Territory to the United States, 1824–1854.**

Mexico, 1824–1854

— Boundary of Mexico, 1824

Texas, independent republic 1836–45, 1845 to US

Ceded 1845, 1850

Ceded by Treaty of Guadalupe Hidalgo, 1848

Ceded 1853 (Gadsden Purchase)

Mexico, 1854

with the Comanches for an end to the raiding which had wrought havoc in western Texas.

The other northern territories of Mexico had also suffered debilitating devastations from Comanche raids. As a result, the government found it impossible to defend itself effectively in 1846 when the United States declared war on Mexico over a Texas border dispute. Within two years, Santa Anna's troops were defeated and Mexico was forced to give up over half of its territory (everything north of the Rio Grande and Gila Rivers), in return for 18 million dollars as part of a previous purchase offer and the Mexican state debt, as well as a promise of protection from future Comanche raids (see Map 23.2).

The French Interlude in Mexico   After the crushing losses of land to the United States, Santa Anna eventually fell from power, and in 1855 liberals gained the upper hand. They introduced a new constitution in 1857 which reaffirmed federalism, guaranteed individual liberties, and separated church and state. The conservatives in Mexico detested this new constitution and waged the "Reform War" (1857–1861) to abolish it. They lost, and the liberals elected Benito Juárez (1861–1864) president, the first Amerindian to accede to the office.

As soon as he was in office, however, he discovered that the war had drained Mexico's financial reserves, obliging him to suspend payment on the state debt. International reaction was swift, with British, Spanish, and French forces seizing the customs house in the port city of Veracruz in 1861, making a mockery of the US Monroe Doctrine of 1823, which had been inspired by the Latin American independence wars. According to the doctrine, no foreign intervention would be tolerated again in the Americas. For four decades the doctrine had been remarkably successful at deterring the European powers, largely because it suited British trade policy as well. Mexico had easily beaten back two invasion attempts by small expeditionary forces, one from Spain in 1829 and another from France in 1838. Not wishing to violate the pan-American opposition to European intervention with a prolonged occupation, Britain and Spain withdrew their forces quickly.

The French, however, stayed, exploiting the inability of the United States to intervene as a result of the outbreak of the Civil War. Louis-Napoleon III Bonaparte, nephew of Napoleon and self-declared emperor, was determined to return France to imperial glory overseas. He seized on the issue of suspended debt payments and, with an eye on the Mexican silver mines, set in motion an ambitious plan of imposing a pliable ruler on the country. In 1862, he provided military backing to the Austrian prince Maximilian, well liked by Mexican conservatives, who installed himself as the emperor of Mexico (1864–1867).

With the defeat of the Confederate states in the US Civil War in April 1865, however, Maximilian's position became precarious. The Union army was ballooning to over a million men, many of whom had just been sent to Texas to suppress the last Confederate holdouts. In 1866, after some discreet aid from the US government, an uprising broke out in Mexico. With Maximilian cut off from any hope of quick support from France, liberal forces defeated and captured him, executing him by firing squad in 1867.

Díaz's Long Peace A period of relative peace arrived at last with the withdrawal of most US government troops from Texas at the end of Reconstruction—ending the potential threat of invasion or border incursions—and the rise of Mexico's next caudillo, Porfirio Díaz (in office 1876–1880 and 1884–1911). Díaz's lengthy hold on power allowed a degree of conservative stability to settle over Mexico's turbulent politics. Moreover, the period also coincided with the defeat of the last Amerindians north of the border and the settlement and development of the American West.

In addition, Díaz, like his contemporary President José Balmaceda (1886–1891) of Chile, was the first to favor infrastructural and industrial development. The two realized that mineral and agricultural exports made their countries too dependent on the world market with its periodic depressions, such as the Long Depression of 1873–1896. The basic infrastructure of Mexico's rail, telegraph, and telephone systems were laid during this time; textile factories and some basic heavy industries were set up; oil was produced in quantity; and modest agricultural improvements were made. Overall, the economy expanded by 6 percent annually during the Porfiriato, as the period of Díaz's government was called.

The Execution of Emperor Maximilian of Mexico, June 19, 1867. Édouard Manet has been characterized as the "inventor of modernity," not only for his technique but for the way he portrayed events, even significant political events, in a calm and composed manner. The soldiers who dispatch the hapless emperor come across as cool and professional—what they are doing is all in a day's work.

Much of Díaz's conservative stability was built on the faction of Creole landowners with whom Díaz had come to power. This faction had grown through the addition of groups of technocrat administrators (*científicos*), financiers, land speculators, and industrialists. As in all ruling classes, personal connections and mutual promotions provided the glue for cohesiveness; but what characterized the Porfiriato regime in addition was the undisguised desire for self-enrichment while disregarding the law and even resorting to physical violence. Critics of the regime were arrested, beaten, and sent to exile on the Yucatán Peninsula as the Porfiriato became increasingly repressive.

The number of critics rose steadily, however, in tandem with the growth of cities and the urban middle classes of professionals (journalists, lawyers, doctors, teachers, small businessmen, accountants, etc.). They found themselves excluded from economic or even political participation. Meeting in liberal clubs, they demanded a return to the constitution of 1857. Critics also arose among the working classes (miners, railroad and streetcar workers, textile and steel workers, and some craftsmen) who found themselves prohibited from forming trade unions and carrying out strikes, although there were nevertheless frequent strikes in the textile factories. In the early 1900s, an aging Díaz and his septuagenarian *científicos* faced an increasingly restless urban population.

photograph of two *hacendado* (late 19th century)

The countryside, where the large majority of Mexicans still lived and worked, was just as restless. Ever since colonial times, there was a profound division between Creole estate (*hacienda*) owners, as well as mestizo and Amerindian rurals (that is, people farming or working on the estates and peasants in their own villages). For most of the 1800s, the economy of the countryside had been typified by self-sufficiency: Nearly everything was produced and consumed there, as transportation costs were prohibitive.

But with the construction of the railroad system under Díaz, the transportation costs of sending a ton of cotton from the provinces to Mexico City sank from $63 to $3. Now the hacienda landlords could produce crops for the market and, accordingly, gobbled up acres of farmland by the millions from Amerindian villagers who could not show legal titles to the land. Even if villagers did legally own the land, corrupt lawyers outmaneuvered them. The wealthiest landlord was Luis Terrazas, with 50 haciendas totaling nearly 7 million acres, mostly in the northern state of Chihuahua. Asked whether he was *from* Chihuahua, Terrazas was reported to have said, "*I am* Chihuahua!"

The Early Mexican Revolution   Middle-class discontent was the first to manifest itself in the elections of 1910, which Díaz had to hold according to the constitution. As before, this election had once more been manipulated in favor of Díaz. But the president, currying the favor of a fawning US journalist, had declared in 1908 that he would like to have an opposition party in Mexico. For a short time, liberals in the country were greatly encouraged, and they found a surprisingly popular candidate.

This candidate was Francisco Madero (1873–1913), the dissident son of a wealthy Creole landowner family who was deeply committed to the social justice proclaimed in the 1857 constitution. Madero refused to recognize the election and called on the middle classes, working classes, and peasants to rise up against the tyrant Díaz. The call was couched in cautious terms, making the case for a return to the constitutional revolution of the early 1800s. But by mentioning also the right of workers to organize in trade unions and of peasants to receive their own plots of land, he opened the floodgates for a full social and economic revolution.

Among the first to respond was Pancho Villa (1878–1923), a muleteer-cum-cattle-rustler asked by a motley group of miners, ranch hands, cowboys, and military colonists to lead them in their rebellion in the northern state of Chihuahua. Another rebel leader was Emiliano Zapata (1879–1919), head of a village in the state of Morelos in south-central Mexico, who had begun with his *campesinos* (tenant farmers, laborers, and village peasants) to occupy sugar plantations and distribute plantation land to them. Victories of Villa in the north and Zapata as close as 20 miles from Mexico City against federal troops persuaded Díaz to step down in May 1911 and leave for exile in France.

Madero was sworn in as the new president. But soon into his tenure it became clear that his vision for a constitutional revolution was incompatible with the social and economic revolutions pursued by Zapata and Villa. Madero sent federal troops against Zapata to force an end to his land distributions. Compromising and pacific, Madero was increasingly driven into the arms of Porfiriato officers who, supported by the US government, were nervous about the events in Mexico. The officers had no use for Madero, however, and deposed and executed him in February 1913.

The Later Revolution   During the subsequent 15 months, power in Mexico was disputed between Porfiriato reactionaries in Mexico City and the constitutionalists (those faithful to the liberal constitution of 1857) in the wealthy states of the north, along the US border. Many of the constitutionalists were from the urban middle classes whose ambitions had been thwarted during Díaz's regime. They were opposed to land distribution, but they needed more troops to overthrow the reactionaries. Constitutionalists, Pancho Villa, and Emiliano Zapata, therefore, forged an alliance that made Venustiano Carranza (1859–1920), from a wealthy but liberal Creole family, their leader. Together, they ended the reactionary regime in Mexico City in July 1914.

Once in power, the constitutionalists dissolved the reactionary federal army but then broke apart over the issue of land reform. The antireform minority left Mexico City and retreated to Veracruz on the east coast to reorganize itself. Villa and Zapata, at the head of the pro-reform majority, entered Mexico City. But they were too committed to the continuing land reforms in their respective northern and south-central states to form a functional central government. By default, the working classes and their union representatives began to assume their own role in the revolution. They decided to support Álvaro Obregón (1880–1928), a rising commander among the constitutionalists from the northern state of Sonora, where he had been a commercial farmer and businessman opposed to Díaz. After the departure of Villa and Zapata for their home states, Obregón entered Mexico City in February 1915.

Emiliano Zapata and Fellow Revolutionaries in Mexico City, June 4, 1911. Shortly after the fall of Díaz, his opponents Madero, Villa, and Zapata (seated, second from left) entered Mexico City in triumph, to celebrate the end of the regime of Díaz. But already by June 8, Zapata and Madero disagreed on the issue of land reform. The moderate Madero wanted to halt it; Zapata wanted to continue it in his state of Morelos. This disagreement, among other internal rifts in the revolutionary camp, was responsible for the revolution dragging on to 1920.

Platform of the "Socio Political Reform Program of the Revolution," Cuernavaca, Mexico, October 26, 1915

Although the constitutionalists had overcome the reactionary Creole landowner interests, they were deeply divided between a policy of a constitutional revolution under a strong central government with a modest land and labor reform program and a policy of agrarian revolutions in autonomous states. The supporters of the constitutional revolution gained the initiative when Obregón succeeded in driving Villa in the north from power. Carranza followed by having Zapata eliminated by treachery.

Carranza, in office as president of Mexico from 1915 to 1920, systematically removed a host of minor agrarian revolutionaries from their states and villages and ended all land distributions. But Obregón, more sympathetic to labor and land reform (albeit guided from the top and carried out in moderation), successfully challenged Carranza for the presidency in the next elections. With the support of the Constitutional army he forced Carranza to surrender and ended the Mexican Revolution late in 1920.

All constitutional revolutions of 1776–1826 in Europe and the Americas were works in progress, because they proclaimed universal liberty, equality, and brotherhood without initially granting it to all inhabitants of the nation. In Mexico, as in the other Latin American nation-states, only the estate-owning Creole oligarchy embodied the nation in the years after 1826. The Mexican Revolution expanded the constitutional process to the urban middle class, workers, farmers, and villagers. It did so because it also brought about real social and economic gains for men and women other than the landowners. All this happened at the tremendous human cost of 1 million victims, but as complex as the events of 1910–1920 were, they made the Mexican nation much more cohesive than it had been a century earlier.

Latin American Society and Economy in the Nineteenth Century

Independence meant both disruptions and continuities in the economy just as much as in politics (discussed in the first half of this chapter). In Spanish and Portuguese America, five colonial regions broke apart into what were eventually 21 independent republics, organized around the pattern of constitutional nationalism. Trade with Europe was thus radically altered. What continued were deep divisions between the small landowning elites and the urban masses of officials, professionals, craftspeople, and laborers. Although many members of the elites and urban middle and lower classes had collaborated in the drive for independence, afterward the Creole landowning elite made participation of the urban classes in the constitutional process increasingly difficult. Correspondingly, when trade with Europe resumed, this elite was primarily interested in the export of mineral and agricultural commodities, from which it reaped the most benefits (see Map 23.3).

Rebuilding Societies and Economies

Reconstruction in the independent Spanish-speaking republics and the Brazilian monarchy took several decades. Mercantilist trade was gone, replaced by free trade on the world market. Production in the mines and on the estates had to be restarted with fresh capital. All this took time, and it was only by mid-century that Latin America had overcome the aftereffects of the wars of independence.

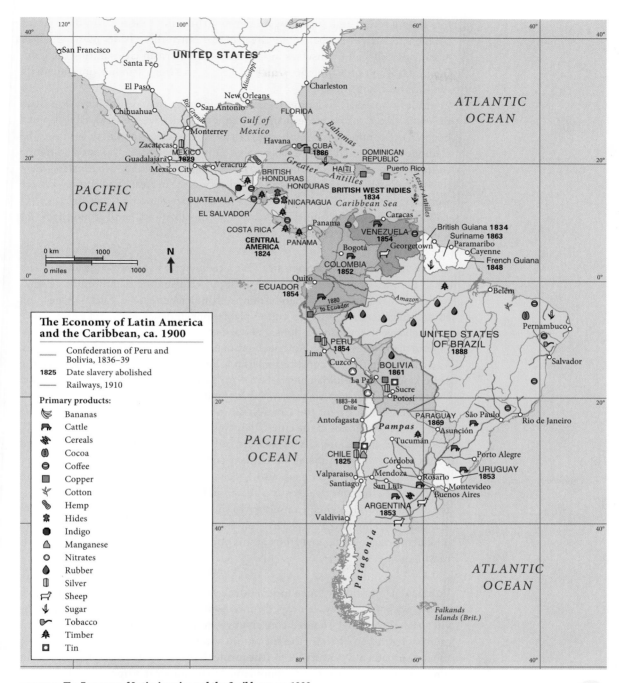

MAP **23.3** **The Economy of Latin America and the Caribbean, ca. 1900.**

map analysis

After Independence The achievement of independence in the 1820s, after lengthy struggles with Spain and local and internal conflicts, had a number of far-reaching consequences. The most important result was the end of Spain's mercantilist monopoly, weak as it had been. The Latin American republics were free to buy or sell and to borrow money anywhere in the world. Among trading partners, this freedom benefited Great Britain most directly. Its merchants had already established themselves in several Latin American cities during the Continental boycott of Napoleon, which had shut out Great Britain from trade with the European continent.

Initially, however, for Latin Americans the freedom to trade was more hope than reality. Dislocations from the struggle of independence were considerable. Capital had fled the continent and left behind uncultivated estates and flooded mines. The Catholic Church held huge, uncollectable debts. In many areas taxes could not be collected. Troops helped themselves to payment through plunder. In Mexico, where the struggle between republicans and royalists was the fiercest, the disruptions were worst and reconstruction took longest. Chile also experienced violent struggles but stabilized itself relatively quickly. On average, though, it took until around 1850 for Latin America to fully recover.

Constitutionalism and Society   The Creoles were in many countries the leaders in the wars of independence. The most powerful among them were large landowners—that is, owners of grain-farming self-sufficiency estates, cattle ranches, and sugar, indigo, cacao, coffee, or cotton plantations. Independence did not produce much change in agrarian relations: Landowners of self-sufficient estates and plantations in many parts of Latin America continued to employ tenant farmers and slaves. Their interpretation of constitutionalism tended toward *caudillismo*—that is, the same kind of authoritarian and paternalistic form of action that they practiced on their estates. They were the conservatives of independence.

Contrasting worlds: photographs of a cholo family, Mexico, and the Rambla at Mar del Plata, Argentina (early twentieth century)

The large majority of the Creoles, however, were not landowners but people who made their money in the cities. They were urban administrators, professionals, craftspeople, and laborers. Their leaders, ardent constitutionalists, tended toward political and economic liberalism. In many countries they were joined by mestizos, mulattoes, and black freedmen, also largely craftspeople and laborers. The main issue dividing the conservatives and liberals in the early years of independence was the extent of voting rights: Conservatives sought to limit the vote to a minority of males through literacy and property requirements, while liberals wanted to extend it to all males. No influential group at this point considered extending voting rights to women.

Political Divisions   Once independence was won, distrust between the two groups with very different property interests set in, and the political consensus fell apart. Accordingly, landed conservatives restricted voting rights, to the detriment of the urban liberals. The exceptions were Argentina and, for a time during the mid-nineteenth century, Peru: The former had few mestizos and mulattoes but a relatively large urban Creole population that gained the upper hand, and the latter had large numbers of urban mestizos and Amerindians who could not be ignored. Nevertheless, even if liberal constitutionalism was submerged for periods of time under caudillo authoritarianism in the mid-1800s, the expansion of constitutionalism from the landowning oligarchy to larger segments of the population remained a permanent fixture in the minds of many, especially intellectuals and political activists in cities. It was this early presence of constitutionalism in the wider population which distinguished Latin America from the Ottoman Empire,

Russia, China, and Japan and made its constitutional process similar to those of the United States and France.

Split over State–Church Relations

Among the many issues over which conservatives and liberals split, the relationship between state and church was the deepest. Initially, given the more or less close collaboration between conservatives and liberals during the struggle for independence, Catholicism remained the national religion for all. Accordingly, education and extensive property remained under church control, as guaranteed by the constitutions.

But the new republics ended the powers of the Inquisition and claimed the right of *patronato*—that is, of naming bishops. At the behest of Spain, however, the pope left bishoprics empty rather than agreeing to this new form of lay investiture. In fact, Rome would not even recognize the independence of the Latin American nations until the mid-1830s. The conflict was aggravated by the church's focus on its institutional rather than pastoral role. The Catholic clergy provided little guidance later on during the 1800s when rapid urbanization and industrial modernity were crying out for spiritual reorientation. At the same time, papal pronouncements made plain the church's hostility toward the developing capitalist industrial order.

religious procession, Mexico, early twentieth century

This hostility of the church was thus one of the factors that in the mid-1800s contributed to a swing back to liberalism, beginning with Colombia in 1849. Many countries adopted a formal separation between church and state and introduced secular educational systems. But the state–church issue remained bitter, especially in Mexico, Guatemala, Ecuador, and Venezuela, where it was often at the center of political shifts between liberals and conservatives. In Colombia, for example, it even led to a complete reversal of liberal trends in the mid-1880s, with the reintroduction of Catholicism as the state religion.

Economic Recovery

Given the shifts of leadership between conservatives and liberals during the period of recovery after independence (ca. 1820–1850), the reconstruction of a coherent fiscal system to support the governments was difficult to accomplish. For example, governments often resorted to taxation of trade, even if this interfered with declared policies of free trade. The yields on tariffs and export taxes, however, were inevitably low and made the financing of strong central governments difficult. Consequently, maneuvering for the most productive mix of the two taxes trumped official pronouncements in favor of free trade and often eroded confidence among trade partners.

This maneuvering had little effect on the domestic economy—self-sufficiency agriculture and urban crafts production—which represented the great bulk of economic activities in Latin America. Grain production on large estates and small farms, especially in Brazil, where gold production had declined in late colonial times, had escaped the turbulence of the independence war and recovery periods relatively unscathed. Land remained plentiful, and the main bottleneck continued to be labor. The distribution of marketable surpluses declined, however, given the new internal borders in Latin America with their accompanying tariffs and export taxes. Self-sufficiency agriculture, and local economies relying on it, thus remained largely unchanged throughout the 1800s.

The crafts workshops, especially for textiles, suffered from the arrival of cheap British factory-produced cottons, which represented the majority of imports by the mid-1800s. Their impact, however, remained relatively limited, mostly to the coasts, since in the absence of railroads transportation costs to the interior were prohibitively expensive. Only Mexico encouraged the financing of machine-driven textile factories, but the failure of its state bank in 1842—from issuing too many loans—ended this policy for a number of decades. On one hand, there was a definite awareness in most countries of the benefits of factories, using domestic resources, and linking the self-sufficiency agricultural sector to modern industrial development. On the other hand, industry's necessity in the face of traditional opposition was not demonstrated until later in the nineteenth century.

Export-Led Growth

The pursuit of a policy of commodity exports—export-led growth—from about 1850 led to rises in the standard of living for many Latin Americans. The industrializing countries in Europe and North America were voracious consumers of the minerals that Latin America had in abundance, as well as of its tropical agricultural products. More could have been sold, had there not been a chronic labor shortage.

Raw Materials and Cash Crops   Mining and agricultural cash crop production recovered gradually, so that by the 1850s nearly all Latin American governments had adopted export-led economic growth as their basic policy. This was about all the conservatives and liberals were able to agree on, since land distribution to poor farmers and a system of income taxes were beyond any consensus. Mexican and Peruvian silver production, once the mainstay of the colonial mercantilist economy, became strong again, although the British adoption of the gold standard in 1821 imposed limits on silver exports. Peru found a partial replacement for silver with guano, which was mined and exported for use as an organic fertilizer and as a source of nitrates for explosives. Chile hit the jackpot with guano, nitrate, and copper exports, of crucial importance during the chemical- and electricity-driven second Industrial Revolution in Germany and the United States.

In other Latin American countries, tropical and subtropical cash crops defined export-led economic growth during the mid-1800s. In Brazil, Colombia, and Costa Rica, labor-intensive coffee growing redefined the agricultural sector. In Argentina, the production of jerked (dried) beef, similarly labor intensive, refashioned the ranching economy. The main importers of this beef were regions in the Americas where plantation slavery continued into the second half of the 1800s, especially the United States, Brazil, and Cuba. The latter, which remained a Spanish colony until 1898, profited from the relocation of sugarcane plantations from the mainland and Caribbean islands after the British outlawing of the slave trade (1807) and slavery itself (1834) as well as the Latin American wars of independence (1810–1826).

In the long run, however, like silver, cane sugar had a limited future, given the rise of beet sugar production in Europe. Minerals and cash crops were excellent for export-led economic growth, especially if they required secondary activities such as the processing of meat or the use of mining machinery. But competition on the world market increased during the 1800s, and thus there was ultimately a ceiling, which was reached in the 1890s.

Broadening of Exports   With their eyes increasingly focused on mineral and agricultural exports, Latin American governments responded quickly to the

meatpacking plant, Uruguay, early twentieth century

increased market opportunities resulting from the Industrial Revolution in Great Britain, the European continent, and the United States. Peru broadened its mineral exports with copper, Bolivia with tin, and Chile with nitrates. Brazil and Peru added rubber, Argentina and Uruguay wool, and Mexico *henequen* (a fiber for ropes and sacks) to its traditional exports. Luxuries from tropical Latin America, like coffee, cacao (for chocolate bars, invented in 1847), vanilla, and bananas, joined sugar after 1850 in becoming affordable mass consumer items in the industrialized countries. Argentina, with investments in refrigeration made by Britain, added frozen meat to this list in 1883. This commodity diversification met not only the broadened demand of the second Industrial Revolution, with its need for chemicals and electricity, but also the demand for consumer goods among the newly affluent middle classes.

Since the choice among minerals and crops was limited, however, most nations remained wedded to one commodity only (50 percent of exports or more). Only two, Argentina and Peru, were able to diversify (exports of less than 25 percent for the leading commodity). They were more successful at distributing their exports over the four main industrial markets of Great Britain, Germany, France, and the United States. On the eve of World War I the United States had grown to be the most important trading partner in 11 of the 21 Latin American countries. Given its own endowments and under the conditions of world trade in the second half of the nineteenth century, the continent's trade was relatively well diversified.

The prices of all Latin American commodities fluctuated substantially during the second half of the nineteenth century, in contrast to the imported manufactured goods (primarily textiles, metal utensils, and implements), which became cheaper over time. In fact, Brazil's government was so concerned about fluctuating coffee prices in the 1890s that it introduced the Taubaté coffee valorization scheme in 1906. As the largest producer, it regulated the amount of coffee offered on the world market, carefully adjusting production to keep market prices relatively stable in much the same way that oil-producing countries would later do with petroleum.

Since coffee trees need 5 years to mature, Brazil was largely successful with its scheme until World War I, when global conditions changed. An American oligopoly (the United and Standard Fruit Companies) in control of banana production in Central America from the 1890s controlled prices similarly. A careful investigation of commodity prices by economic historians has resulted in the conclusion that, in spite of all fluctuations, commodity prices rose overall during 1850–1914.

Rising Living Standards From all evidence, in the period from the middle of the 1800s to the eve of World War I, Latin American governments can be judged as having been successful with their choice of export-led growth as their consensus policy. Living standards rose, as measured in gross domestic product (GDP). At various times during 1850–1900, between five and eight Latin American countries kept pace with the living standards in the industrialized countries. Argentina and Chile were the most consistent leaders throughout the period. Thus, although many politicians were aware that at some point their countries would have to industrialize in addition to relying on commodity export growth, they can perhaps be forgiven for keeping their faith in exports as the engine for improved living standards right up to World War I.

late nineteenth-century photos of Brazilian coffee pickers and farmhands on a Costa Rican banana plantation

Labor and Immigrants   As in the industrialized countries, the profitability of exports was achieved through low wages. Together with the rest of the world, Latin America experienced high population increases during the 1800s. The population grew sevenfold, to 74 million, although it remained small in comparison to the populations of Europe, which doubled to 408 million, and Africa and Asia, which each grew by one-third to 113 and 947 million, respectively. The increases were not large enough to alter the favorable land–person ratio, so it is not surprising that the high demand for labor continued during the 1800s. This demand, of course, was the reason why the institution of forced labor—revolving labor duties (*mit'a*) among Amerindians in the Andes and slavery—had come into existence in the first place.

Not surprisingly, *mit'a* and slavery continued during the 1800s, liberal constitutionalism notwithstanding, in a number of countries. Even where forced labor was abolished early, moreover, low wages continued. One would have expected wages to rise rapidly, given the continuing conditions of labor shortage and land availability. Mine operators and landowners, however, were reluctant to raise wages because they feared for the competitiveness of their commodities on the world market. They could get away with low wages because of ethnic discrimination: Racism trumped market conditions. Nevertheless, on occasion labor shortages were so severe and European immigration so insufficient that governments resorted to measures of selective mass immigration, in order to enlarge the labor pool.

Typical examples of selective immigration were *coolies* (from Urdu *kuli*, hireling)—that is, indentured laborers recruited from India and China on 5- or 10-year contracts working off the costs of their transportation. During 1847–1874, nearly half a million East Indians traveled to various European colonies in the Caribbean. Similarly, 235,000 Chinese came to Peru, Cuba, and Costa Rica, working in guano pits and silver mines, on sugar and cotton plantations, and later on

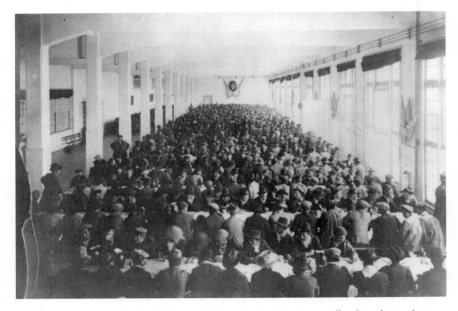

Dining Hall for Recently Arrived Immigrants, Buenos Aires. Immigrants, all male, and more than likely all Spanish and Italian, rub shoulders sometime around 1900 in a dining hall in Buenos Aires set up for newly arrived immigrants. By 1914, 20 percent each of the population of Argentina had been born in Spain and Italy.

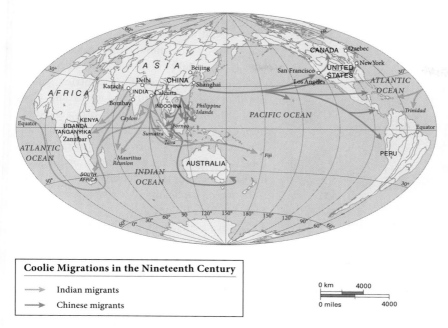

Coolie Migrations in the Nineteenth Century

→ Indian migrants

→ Chinese migrants

0 km   4000

0 miles   4000

MAP **23.4 Non-Western Migrations in the Nineteenth Century.**

railroads. If the experience of five Caribbean islands can be taken as a guide, only about 10 percent of the coolies returned home. Coolie migration to Latin America, therefore, can be described as a major part of the pattern of massive migration streams across the world that typified the nineteenth century (see Map 23.4).

Immigration to Latin America from Europe was less controlled, more regular, and on a much bigger scale. In Argentina, Uruguay, Brazil, and Chile, Italians and Spaniards settled in large numbers from around 1870 on. In Argentina, nearly one-third of the population consisted of immigrants, a share much higher than at any time in the United States. The Italian population of Argentina numbered close to 1 million by the turn of the century. Most immigrants settled in cities, and Buenos Aires became the first city on the continent with more than a million people. Only here did a semiregular labor market develop, with rising urban and rural wages prior to World War I. Elsewhere in Latin America, governments, beholden to large landowners, feared the rise of cities with immigrant laborers who did not share their interests. They, therefore, opposed mass immigration.

Self-Sufficiency Agriculture   Except for Argentina, Chile, and Uruguay, the levels of commodity exports did not rise sufficiently to reduce the size of the rural labor force engaged in self-sufficiency farming—a major condition for improved living standards. On the eve of World War I, between two-thirds and half of the laborers in most Latin American countries were still employed as tenant farmers or farmhands on large estates. Smaller numbers of these laborers were indigenous village farmers who owned their small farmsteads. Their contribution to the national GDP in Brazil and Mexico, for example, was less than one-quarter. Toward the end of the century, observers began to realize that export-led growth—even though it looked like an effective economic driver—did not have much of a transformative effect on the rural masses in most countries.

Mexican Textile Factory.
Cocolapam in the state of
Veracruz was the site of the first
Mexican cotton textile factory,
founded in 1836 by Lucas
Alamán, a Mexican government
minister and investment banker.
Its machinery, imported from
Great Britain, was water driven.
The textiles it produced re-
mained inferior to imports, but
they were cheap and satisfied the
needs of most Mexicans.

The absence of such transformative effects was especially visible in the high levels of illiteracy among rural inhabitants. Adult illiteracy rates of up to 80 percent were not uncommon, even in relatively diversified countries, such as Brazil and Mexico. Only Argentina and Chile after 1860 invested heavily in primary education, on levels similar to the United States and Britain, followed by Costa Rica in the 1890s. Literate self-sufficiency farmers, knowledgeable in plant and animal selection as well as fertilizers, were practically nonexistent prior to the Mexican Revolution.

Governments paid greater attention to the improvement of rural infrastructures from about 1870 onward, with the development of railroads. Almost everywhere, they looked to direct foreign investment, given the low-yielding and highly regressive trade taxes on which the relatively slim central domestic revenues depended. The foreign investors or consortiums built these railroads primarily for the transportation of commodities to ports. Many self-sufficiency farmers and even landlords, therefore, received little encouragement to produce more food staples for urban markets inland. Argentina and Chile, followed by Costa Rica and Uruguay, built the most railroads. Correspondingly, with fertilizers and better implements available via railroads, corn yields quintupled in Argentina. Conversely, these yields changed little in Mexico outside the railroad corridors concentrated in the north and center. Overall, the Latin American railroad network represented only about one-fifth to one-third of that in other Western developing settler countries, such as Australia, Canada, and New Zealand.

Factories   Until about 1870, the handicrafts sector met the demands of the rural and low-earning urban populations. It produced cheap, low-quality textiles, shoes, soap, candles, tools, implements, cutlery, and horse tack. As is well known, this sector failed in most parts of the world during the 1800s or 1900s to mechanize itself and establish a modern factory system. Latin America was no exception. Most crafts shops were based on family labor, with a high degree of self-exploitation, unconnected to the landowning elite and deemed too small by lending banks. There was no path from workshops to factories.

However, even entrepreneurial investors interested in building factories for the manufacture of yarn or textiles were hampered in their efforts. They had little chance of success prior to the appearance of public utilities in the 1880s, providing water during the dry season and electricity as an energy source, in the absence of high-quality coal in most parts of Latin America. Even then, the risk of engaging in manufacturing, requiring long-term strategies with no or low profits, was so great that the typical founders of factories were not Creoles but European immigrants.

In Argentina and Chile these immigrants labored hard during their first years after arrival and saved the start-up capital necessary to launch small but modern textile, food-processing, and beverage factories. Argentina, Chile, Mexico, and Peru made the greatest advances toward factory industrialization, producing import-substituting consumer goods to the tune of 50–80 percent. Prior to World War I, the only country that took the step from consumer goods to capital goods (goods for building and equipping factories) was Mexico. This occurred with the foundation of the Fundidora Iron and Steel Mill in 1910 in Monterrey, which, however, was unprofitable for a long time. Full capital goods industrialization had to await the postwar period.

Culture, Family, and the Status of Women

Economic growth and urbanization added considerably to the growth of constitutional-nationalist modernity in Latin America. But the absence of industrialization until the end of the nineteenth century slowed the transformation of society and its cultural institutions. The law and custom represented by the Catholic Church remained pervasive. In the second half of the nineteenth century, however, with the diversification of the urban population, the idea of separating church and state gained adherents, with some major legal consequences for social institutions.

Role of the Church   In most countries, repeated attempts by governments after independence to reduce the role of the Catholic Church in society remained unsuccessful. The church resisted the efforts of the constitutional nationalists to carry out land expropriations and to separate state and church in social legislation. In a number of civil codes women's rights in inheritance and property control improved, but overall husbands retained their patriarchal rights over their families. Typically, they were entitled to the control over the family budget, contractual engagements, choice of husbands for their daughters (up to age 25 in some countries), or residence of unmarried daughters (at home, up to age 30). Only from the middle of the nineteenth century did the influence of the Catholic Church diminish sufficiently to allow legislation for secular marriages and divorce in a number of countries. Catholicism remained doctrinally unchanged.

Family Relations   As it also developed in the Euro-American Victorian world, on the cultural level there was a popular ideal in nineteenth-century Latin America of nuclear-family domesticity. But, as research has also shown, in both places this was often honored more in the breach than the observance. That is to say, in Mexico and South America, despite the long-standing proverb *El hombre en la calle, la mujer en la casa* ("Men in the street, women in the home"), it was often the case that the two spheres were intermingled. In urban areas, women frequently ran shops, managed markets, were proprietors of *cantinas*, and performed a host of skilled and unskilled jobs, particularly in the textile and food trades. In rural areas, farm work on small holdings and peonages was often shared by men and women, though a number of individual tasks—plowing, for example—were most frequently done by men.

As in Europe and North America, too, there was a remarkably high level of widowhood and spinsterhood. In areas where the predominant form of employment was dangerous—mining, for example—the incidence of widowhood was very high. Widows often could not or chose not to remarry, especially if they had relatives to fall back on or were left an income. The stereotype of the stern patriarchal husband was also pervasive enough so that many middle-class women, often to the consternation of their families, chose not to marry at all.

Mexican woman making tortillas, Mexico, ca. 1900

Both of these conditions were common enough so that by one estimate one-third of all the households in Mexico City in the early nineteenth century were headed by women. Widows were entitled to their dowries and half of the community property, while boys and girls received equal portions of the inheritance. Thus, despite society's pressures to marry and raise children, many women did not marry or, after becoming widowed, remained single. In this sense, they achieved a considerable degree of autonomy in a male-dominated society. Thus social realities and legal rights diverged in early independent Latin America, even before legal reform.

The Visual and Literary Arts   To try to encapsulate the culture and arts of more than a continent—and one so vast and diverse as Latin America—is far beyond the scope of this textbook. Suffice it to say that the trend in nineteenth-century culture under the aegis of Spanish and Portuguese influences after independence was toward "indigenization": Much like the way the United States attempted during this time to break away from European art and literary influences, a similar movement pervaded the Latin American world. Along with attempts to form national and regional styles of their own, many countries also engaged in art as a nation-building exercise—artistic and literary celebrations of new national heroes or famous historic events through portraiture and landscape painting. Finally, there were also periodic engagements with the popular or folk arts of Amerindian peoples, mulattoes, mestizos, and Africans in celebration of regional uniqueness.

Literature to some extent paralleled the trajectory of the other arts. In the later eighteenth and early nineteenth centuries, an indigenous style developed, called *criollo*, for its inception and popularity in the Creole class. Literature often turned to themes befitting countries trying to establish themselves as nations with distinct historic pasts and great future potential. In some cases, critique of the present was the order of the day. Artists had a keen eye for a society caught between the specific kind of preindustrial tradition and modernity that characterized the Spanish- and Portuguese-speaking countries of the Americas during the nineteenth century.

❯ Putting It All Together

interactive concept map

The term "banana republic" appeared for the first time in 1904. The American humorist O. Henry (1862–1910) coined it to represent politically unstable and economically poor Latin American countries, governed by small elites and relying on tropical exports, such as bananas. O. Henry had spent several years at the end of the nineteenth century in Honduras, hiding from US authorities. Thus, he knew whereof he spoke.

Today, political stability is much greater; but many parts of Latin America are still poor and underindustrialized. Consequently, the expression banana republic still resonates. Were Latin American elites, therefore, wrong to engage in a pattern of export-led growth through mineral and agricultural commodities? And did they collude with elites in the industrial countries to maneuver the continent into permanent dependence on the latter? Indeed, an entire generation of scholars in the second half of the twentieth century answered the question in the affirmative and wrote the history of the 1800s in gloomy and condemnatory tones. They called their analysis "dependency theory."

Contemporary historians are less certain about many of these conclusions. They compare Latin America not with the United States or Western Europe but with the settler colonies of South Africa, Australia, and New Zealand or the old empires of the Middle East and Asia. In these comparisons, Latin America did very well and was not any more dependent on the industrializing countries than the latter were on Latin America.

Dependence increased only at the very end of the 1800s when industrial countries like the United States and Britain began to make significant capital investments. It was then that foreign companies, such as those that owned railroads in Nicaragua and Honduras, succeeded in exploiting and controlling production and export. The question we may need to ask then is not why Latin America failed to industrialize in the 1800s but, rather, whether Latin America, selecting from the available choices, made the right decision when it opted for export-led growth up to about 1890. Did such a choice represent a "third way" toward economic growth, separate from industrial capitalism and tenacious attempts to keep economies closed off from the vagaries of world trade? Perhaps it did.

Review and Relate

| Thinking Through Patterns

Examine the ways historians approach the big questions of this chapter.

Similar to those of the United States and France, which also underwent revolutions in the late 1700s and early 1800s, Latin America's independence movements (1810–1824) did not extend the constitutional revolution beyond a small number of property owners who inhabited the highest levels of the social strata. The dominant class of large landlords and plantation owners was conservative and did not favor land reform for the benefit of small farmers. Urban professionals and craftspeople, divided in many places by ethnicity, did not share common interests that allowed them to provide an effective opposition to the landed class. Landowning and plantation interests thus protected themselves through authoritarian caudillo politics and sought to keep the opposition weak.

>> **Which factors in the complex ethnic and social structures of Latin America were responsible for the emergence of authoritarian politicians?**

In colonial times, Latin America was the warm-weather extension of Europe, sending its mineral and agricultural commodities to Europe. When it acquired its independence and Europe industrialized during the 1800s, these commodities became even more important, and the continent opted for a pattern of export-led development. This meant the systematic increase of mineral and agricultural commodity exports, with rising living standards not only for those who profited directly from the exports but also for many in the urban centers. Even with rising living standards it became clear by the turn of the century that a supplementary policy of industrialization had to be pursued.

>> **Why did Latin American countries, after achieving independence, opt for a continuation of mineral and agricultural commodity exports?**

> ≫ **How do the social and economic structures of this period continue to affect the course of Latin America today?**

Many countries in Latin America are barely richer than they were in the 1800s. Even though industry, mineral and commodity exports, and services expanded in urban centers in the early part of the twentieth century, poor farmers with low incomes continued to be a drag on development. This phenomenon still characterizes many parts of Latin America today.

| Against the Grain

Consider this as a counterpoint to the main patterns examined in this chapter.

Early Industrialization in Chile?

- Why and how does rapid urbanization create the demand for industrialization?

- Was Balmaceda too progressive for the Chilean Creole class? Should he have attempted a different course?

In the early 1880s, Chilean businessmen began to discuss the idea of moving away from exclusive reliance on the export of coal and copper, as world market prices for those commodities fluctuated widely, and encouraging the turn to industrialization. They founded the Society for the Stimulation of Manufacturing in 1883, with the purpose of building factories for the transformation of raw materials into finished goods. Their ideas turned into a concrete governmental program under the presidency of José Manuel Balmaceda Fernández (1886–1891), who in 1888 created a ministry for industry and public works. Balmaceda, a black sheep of Chile's conservative Creole class, had strong liberal-constitutionalist convictions and was acutely aware of Chile's changing economic and social conditions in the last quarter of the century.

Chile had experienced a substantial population increase, from 2 to 2.5 million during 1875–1885. The urban population had grown even faster, rising from half to two-thirds the size of the rural population during the same time. Farmers and farmhands were particularly drawn to the mining cities in the newly acquired north (as the result of Chile winning the War of the Pacific during 1879–1884 against Peru and Bolivia), with its nitrate deposits. Other cities had grown near the existing coal and copper mines further south. Santiago, Valparaíso, and Concepción had evolved into major urban centers. Although farming still supported the majority of Chileans, urban employments had risen greatly in numbers and importance.

Balmaceda's new ministry for industry and public works engaged in a massive investment program in education, railroads, ports, armaments, and naval ships, financed with the revenue from mining exports, including the northern nitrates. Keeping at least a portion of these nitrates in the country and making them the foundation for a chemical industry became a newly envisaged option. The second Industrial Revolution had begun during the 1860s in Germany and the United States on the basis of nitrates, crucial for the production of sulfuric acid, which, in turn, was used for the production of glass, soap, bleach, paper, dyes, pottery, and nitroglycerin—all transformative industries absorbing large numbers of the urban population of unskilled and skilled laborers.

Unfortunately, Balmaceda's energetic program of import-substitution industrialization fell apart as soon as 1891, without any outside imperialist British or other foreign intervention. Perhaps Balmaceda's investment program was too much, introduced too fast. Favoritism in appointments and corruption among office holders aroused opposition not only among the conservative Creole landowners but also among dissident liberals who disliked Balmaceda's imperious style. The opposition unleashed a civil war, in which Balmaceda was deposed. With Balmaceda's suicide the incipient indigenous industrialization program ended, apparently still too weak against the dominant policy of export-led economic growth based on mineral extraction.

Key Terms

audio flashcards

Caudillo　699

Import-substitution
industrialization　696

Southern Cone　690

For additional resources, please go to
www.oup.com/us/vonsivers.
Please see the Further Resources section at the back of the book for additional readings and suggested websites.

Sources for Chapter 23

| SOURCE 23.1 | Memoirs of General Antonio López de Santa Anna |

1872

Santa Anna (1794–1876) is recognized today by Americans, and especially by Texans, primarily for his successful siege of the Alamo in March 1836. However, he also epitomized the caudillo type in nineteenth-century Mexico, dominating his country's political life and weathering a series of highs and lows throughout his long career. Although he served as president for 11 nonconsecutive terms (some of only a few months) over a period of 22 years, Santa Anna is more famous for his military achievements and losses—including some extraordinary adventures. For example, in an 1838 battle against the French at Veracruz, Santa Anna's leg was shattered during a cannon volley. The leg was amputated and buried with full military honors. Exiled multiple times, to Cuba, Jamaica, Colombia, and even the United States, Santa Anna devoted his final years to compiling his memoirs, an excerpt of which is translated below. This passage details his turbulent political career—at least from his perspective—in the early 1840s.

Sixty-two days after my foot had been amputated, Gen. Guadalupe Victoria called on me at the instigation of the government. He informed me that a revolution was threatening, and that the government desired me to take [Anastasio] Bustamante's place as temporary president in this time of trial. How well the people knew me! They knew I would never desert my principles and would always be on hand when my country needed me!

I was carried to the capital on a litter. Although my trip was made with extreme care, the hardships of the journey and the change of climate weakened me. However, despite my poor health, I assumed the office of president immediately. The tasks involved completely overwhelmed me, but I pulled through. The government forces triumphed throughout the country. Gen. Gabriel Valencia captured and executed the hope of the revolution, José A. Mejia, in

Source: Antonio López de Santa Anna, *The Eagle: The Autobiography of Santa Anna*, ed. and trans. Ann Fears Crawford (Austin, TX: Pemberton, 1967), 65–69, as excerpted in James A. Wood and John Charles Chasteen, *Problems in Modern Latin American History: Sources and Interpretations*, 3rd ed. (Lanham, MD: Rowman & Littlefield, 2009), 79–81.

the vicinity of the town of Acajeta. The dreaded threat of revolution died, and peace was restored.

Bustamante once again took up the reins of government, and I retired to [my estate] to complete my recovery. However, Bustamante's loss of prestige with the people caused his government to fail. In the town of Guadalajara, in the early months of 1841, arrangements were made for Bustamante to abdicate and for the reform of the Constitution of 1824. In Tacubaya, a council of generals agreed upon basic ground rules to help bring about these reforms, and once again I assumed the office of provisional president. . . .

In order to conform to public opinion, I called together a group of prominent citizens from all states in the nation to instigate needed reforms. This group drew up *The Principles of Political Organization* on June 12, 1844. This constitution was circulated by the government, and each of the states accepted and ratified it without dissension.

In September 1844, my beloved wife died. Greater sorrow I had never known! General of Division Valentín Canalizo substituted for me while I devoted myself to family matters.

During the first session under our new Constitution, I was duly elected president and called to the capital to administer the customary oath. The election saddened me even more. My deep melancholy drove me to abhor the glamorous life of the capital and to prefer a life of solitude. I resigned the noble office to which I had been called, but the public intruded upon my privacy, pleading that I return. My friends, with the greatest of good faith, also begged me to resume my office. Their pleas led me to sacrifice myself to the public good. I withdrew my resignation.

Near the end of October, General [Mariano] Paredes rebelled against the government in Guadalajara. When the news was communicated to me by the government, they ordered me to take the troops quartered in Jalapa and march to the capital. I instantly obeyed the orders. Paredes had been relieved of his command of the Capital District due to excesses of intoxication while he was commanding his troops. He bore a grudge and was determined to take revenge. In our country one spark was sufficient to set aflame a revolution.

I was marching toward Guadalajara under orders, when I received the news of an upheaval in the capital. The situation seemed serious, and I halted my advance. Details of the revolt in the capital arrived soon after my halt. The messenger read me the following infamous words:

> The majority of Congress openly favor the Paredes revolution. The government, in self-defense or wishing to avoid revolution, has issued a decree by which the sessions of Congress have been suspended. This decree has served as a pretext for General José J. Herrera to join the revolt. Rioters have torn down the bronze bust of President Santa Anna that stood in the Plaza del Mercado. They have also taken his amputated foot from the cemetery of Santa Paula and proceeded to drag it through the streets to the sounds of savage laughter.

I interrupted the narrator, exclaiming "Stop! I don't wish to hear any more! Almighty God! A member of my body, lost in the service of my country, dragged from the funeral urn, broken into bits to be made sport of in such a barbaric manner!" In that moment of grief and frenzy, I decided to leave my native country, object of my dreams and of my illusions, for all time.

> ## » Working with Sources

1. How were Santa Anna's personal setbacks interwoven with his political career in this period, at least in his recollection?

2. What does Santa Anna's memoir reveal about the presumed indispensability of the caudillo, and the connection between his physical body and his political power?

SOURCE 23.2 Simón Bolívar, "The Jamaica Letter"

September 6, 1815

Simón Bolívar (1783–1830), the eventual liberator of northern South America from Spanish control, was born in Venezuela but profoundly influenced by the culture of peninsular Spain and the European Enlightenment. He visited Spain in 1799, and traveled to Paris to witness Napoleon's coronation as emperor in 1804. Bolívar aspired to bring the values of the Enlightenment, and particularly the notions of liberty and popular sovereignty, to his homeland. Having declared an independent Venezuela in 1812, he was driven into exile in British Jamaica with the landing of a Spanish expeditionary force in 1815. In 1816, he returned with a military force and assumed the presidency of "Gran Colombia" in 1822. The following letter is renowned for its expression of Bolívar's ambitions, at a time when the outcome of "liberation" from Spain seemed uncertain.

Kingston, Jamaica, September 6, 1815.
My dear Sir:
I hasten to reply to the letter of the 29th ultimo which you had the honor of sending me and which I received with the greatest satisfaction.

· · ·

With what a feeling of gratitude I read that passage in your letter in which you say to me: "I hope that the success which then followed Spanish arms may now turn in favor of their adversaries, the badly oppressed people of South America." I take this hope as a prediction, if it is justice that determines man's contests. Success will crown our efforts, because the destiny of America has been irrevocably decided; the tie that bound her to Spain has been severed.

Source: *Selected Writings of Bolivar*, trans. Lewis Bertrand (New York: Colonial, 1951), as edited in: http://faculty.smu.edu/bakewell/BAKEWELL/texts/jamaica-letter.html.

Only a concept maintained that tie and kept the parts of that immense monarchy together. That which formerly bound them now divides them. The hatred that the Peninsula has inspired in us is greater than the ocean between us. It would be easier to have the two continents meet than to reconcile the spirits of the two countries. The habit of obedience; a community of interest, of understanding, of religion; mutual goodwill; a tender regard for the birthplace and good name of our forefathers; in short, all that gave rise to our hopes, came to us from Spain. As a result there was a born principle of affinity that seemed eternal, notwithstanding the misbehavior of our rulers which weakened that sympathy, or, rather, that bond enforced by the domination of their rule. At present the contrary attitude persists: we are threatened with the fear of death, dishonor, and every harm; there is nothing we have not suffered at the hands of that unnatural stepmother—Spain. The veil has been torn asunder. We have already seen the light, and it is not our desire to be thrust back into darkness. The chains have been broken; we have been freed, and now our enemies seek to enslave us anew. For this reason America fights desperately, and seldom has desperation failed to achieve victory.

Because successes have been partial and spasmodic, we must not lose faith. In some regions the Independents triumph, while in others the tyrants have the advantage. What is the end result? Is not the entire New World in motion, armed for defense? We have but to look around us on this hemisphere to witness a simultaneous struggle at every point.

. . .

This picture represents, on a military map, an area of 2,000 longitudinal and 900 latitudinal leagues at its greatest point, wherein 16,000,000 Americans either defend their rights or suffer repression at the hands of Spain, which, although once the world's greatest empire, is now too weak, with what little is left her, to rule the new hemisphere or even to maintain herself in the old. And shall Europe, the civilized, the merchant, the lover of liberty allow an aged serpent, bent only on satisfying its venomous rage, devour the fairest part of our globe? What! Is Europe deaf to the clamor of her own interests? Has she no eyes to see justice? Has she grown so hardened as to become insensible? The more I ponder these questions, the more I am confused. I am led to think that America's disappearance is desired; but this is impossible because all Europe is not Spain. What madness for our enemy to hope to reconquer America when she has no navy, no funds, and almost no soldiers! Those troops which she has are scarcely adequate to keep her own people in a state of forced obedience and to defend herself from her neighbors. On the other hand, can that nation carry on the exclusive commerce of one-half the world when it lacks manufactures, agricultural products, crafts and sciences, and even a policy? Assume that this mad venture were successful, and further assume that pacification ensued, would not the sons of the Americans of today, together with the sons of the European *reconquistadores* twenty years hence, conceive the same patriotic designs that are now being fought for?

. . .

More than anyone, I desire to see America fashioned into the greatest nation in the world, greatest not so much by virtue of her area and wealth as by her freedom and glory. Although I seek perfection for the government of my country, I cannot persuade myself that the New World can, at the moment, be organized as a great republic. Since it is impossible, I dare not desire it; yet much less do I desire to have all America a monarchy because this plan is not only impracticable but also impossible. Wrongs now existing could not be righted, and our emancipation would be fruitless. The American states need the care of paternal governments to heal the sores and wounds of despotism and war. The parent country, for example, might be Mexico, the only country fitted for the position by her intrinsic strength, and without such power there can be no parent country. Let us assume it were to be the Isthmus of Panamá, the most central point of this vast continent. Would not all parts continue in their lethargy and even in their present disorder? For a single government to infuse life into the New World; to put into use all the resources for public prosperity; to improve, educate, and perfect the New World, that government would have to possess the authority of a god, much less the knowledge and virtues of mankind.

. . .

It is a grandiose idea to think of consolidating the New World into a single nation, united by pacts into a single bond. It is reasoned that, as these parts have a common origin, language, customs, and religion, they ought to have a single government to permit the newly formed states to unite in a confederation. But this is not possible. Actually, America is separated by climatic differences, geographic diversity, conflicting interests, and dissimilar characteristics. How beautiful it would be if the Isthmus of Panamá could be for us what the Isthmus of Corinth was for the Greeks! Would to God that some day we may have the good fortune to convene there an august assembly of representatives of republics, kingdoms, and empires to deliberate upon the high interests of peace and war with the nations of the other three-quarters of the globe. This type of organization may come to pass in some happier period of our regeneration. But any other plan, such as that of Abbé St. Pierre, who in laudable delirium conceived the idea of assembling a European congress to decide the fate and interests of those nations, would be meaningless.

Among the popular and representative systems, I do not favor the federal system. It is over-perfect, and it demands political virtues and talents far superior to our own. For the same reason I reject a monarchy that is part aristocracy and part democracy, although with such a government England has achieved much fortune and splendor. Since it is not possible for us to select the most perfect and complete form of government, let us avoid falling into demagogic anarchy or monocratic tyranny. These opposite extremes would only wreck us on similar reefs of misfortune and dishonor; hence, we must seek a mean between them. I say: Do not adopt the best system of government, but the one that is most likely to succeed.

» **Working with Sources**

1. How does Bolívar's advice combine practical suggestions with idealistic principles?

2. To what extent does Bolívar believe the revolt to have been triggered by Spain's refusal to live up to its own best principles?

SOURCE 23.3 Domingo Faustino Sarmiento,
Travels in the United States in 1847

1849

The journalist and eventual Argentine president Sarmiento (1811–1888) is most famous today for his novel *Facundo: Civilization and Barbarism* (1845), a sharp and daring satire of the caudillo Juán Manuel de Rosas. His indictment of Rosas, thinly disguised as the biography of another brutal dictator (called Juán Facundo Quiroga), was written while Sarmiento was an exile from the regime. Representing the government of Chile, Sarmiento traveled throughout Europe, North Africa, and North America, observing local political and social conditions closely and comparing them with what he knew of Argentine society. The result is a fascinating travelogue of his impressions of and reactions to the people of the United States, with vivid descriptions of many of its man-made and natural wonders. Nevertheless, his hopes for his native Argentina were never very far from the foreground, as this excerpt reveals.

The fatal error of the Spanish colonization of South America, the deep wound which has condemned present generations to inertia and backwardness, was in the system of land distribution. In Chile, great concessions of land, measuring from one hill to another and from the side of a river to the banks of an arroyo, were given to the conquistadors. The captains established earldoms for themselves, while their soldiers, fathers of the sharecropper, that worker without land who multiplies without increasing the number of his buildings, sheltered themselves in the shade of their improvised roofs. The passion to occupy lands in the name of the king drove men to dominion over entire districts, which put great distances between landowners so that after three centuries the intervening land still has not been cleared. The city, for this reason, has been suppressed in this vast design, and the few villages which have been created since the conquest have been *decreed* by presidents. I know of at least five villages which were created in Chile in this official and contrived manner. But see how the American, recently called in the nineteenth century to conquer his piece of the world, does it. There the government has been careful to set aside land for all the coming generations. The young men aspiring to property each year crowd around the auction rooms in which public lands are sold, and, with the numbers of their lots in hand, they leave to take possession of their property, expecting to receive their titles later on from the offices in Washington. The most energetic Yankees, the misanthropes, the rustics, the SQUATTERS, in short, work in a manner which is more romantic, more

Source: Domingo Faustino Sarmiento, *Travels in the United States in 1847*, trans. Michael Aaron Rockland (Princeton, NJ: Princeton University Press, 1970), 164–166.

poetic, and more primitive. Armed with their rifles, they immerse themselves in the virgin wilderness. For a pastime they kill the squirrels that unceasingly romp among the branches of the trees. A well-aimed bullet heads up into the sky to connect with an eagle which soars with majestic wings over the dark green surface formed by the boughs of the trees. The axe is the faithful companion of such a man, though he uses it for nothing more than to flex his muscles by throwing cedars and oaks to the ground. During his vagabond excursions this independent farmer looks for fertile land, a picturesque spot, something beside a navigable river; and when he has made up his mind, as in the most primitive times in the world's history, he says, "This is mine!" and without further ado takes possession of the land in name of the kings of the world: Work and Good Will. If one day the surveyor of the state's lands should arrive at the border of the land which he has laid out as his own, the auction will only serve to tell him what he owes for the land he has under cultivation, which will be the same sum as the adjacent uncultivated lands are going for. It is not unusual for this indomitable and unsociable character, overtaken by populations advancing through the wilderness, to sell his place and move away with his family, his oxen, and his horses searching for the desired solitude of the forests. The Yankee is a born proprietor. If he does not have anything and never has had anything he does not say that he is poor but that he is poor right now, or that he has been unlucky, or that times are bad. And then, in his imagination he sees the primitive, dark, solitary, isolated forests and in the midst of them the mansion he means to have on the bank of some unknown river, with smoke rising from the chimney and oxen returning home with slow step to his property as the sun goes down. From that moment he talks of nothing else but going out to occupy and settle new lands. His evenings are spent over the map, computing the stages of the journey, tracing a route for his wagon. And in the newspaper he does not look for anything except announcements of sales of state lands, or word of the new city that is being built on the shores of Lake Superior.

Alexander the Great, upon destroying Tyre, had to give world commerce a new distribution center for the spices of the Orient, one from which they could be sent at once to the Mediterranean coasts. The founding of Alexandria was an example of Alexander's renowned cleverness, even though the commercial routes were known and the Isthmus of Suez the indispensable trading ground between the waters of the India, Europe, and Africa of those days. This work is accomplished every day by American Alexanders, who wander through the wilds looking for points that a profound study of the future indicates will be centers of commerce.

≫ Working with Sources

1. **In what respects, and with what degree of conviction, does Sarmiento compare the acquisition of land in Latin America with land ownership in the United States?**

2. **Is Sarmiento convinced that this degree of cultivation and building of commerce cannot happen in Argentina? Why or why not?**

SOURCE 23.4   Amulet containing passages from the Qur'an, worn by Muslim slaves who rioted in Bahia, Brazil

1835

Although slavery was not abolished in Brazil until 1888, slave revolts were frequent and remarkable for their ambitions, success, and diversity of participating elements. Two urban revolts of the nineteenth century were especially significant. First, the Tailor's Rebellion of 1798, in Salvador, the capital of the Brazilian state of Bahia, drew on the assistance of freedmen, people of mixed race, and even craftspeople of Portuguese descent. The second was a Muslim-inspired and Muslim-directed uprising of slaves in Bahia in 1835, organized by African-born freedmen and slaves who had attained an Islamic education in West Africa before enslavement. This Muslim revolt is particularly fascinating because of the role of written documents, here deployed as protective amulets, among the members of the slave resistance. This excerpt from a book by a Brazilian scholar attempts to demonstrate the role of the written word in this rebellion, illustrating another, and less frequently recognized, "power" within historical documents.

The written word, which the Malês used, had a great seductive power over Africans whose roots belonged in oral cultures. The amulets consisted of pieces of paper containing passages from the *Koran* and powerful prayers. The paper was carefully folded in an operation that had its own magical dimension. It was then placed in a small leather pouch, which was sewn shut. In many cases, besides the paper, other ingredients appeared in those charms. A police scribe described the contents of one amulet as follows:

> Little bundles or leather pouches were opened at this time by cutting them at the seams with a penknife. Inside were found several pieces of insignificant things such as cotton wrapped in a little powder [*sic*], others with tiny scraps of garbage, and little sacks with some seashells inside. Inside one of the leather pouches was a piece of paper with Arabic letters written on it.

The "insignificant" substances referred to here likely included sand moistened beforehand in some sort of holy water, perhaps water used by some renowned and pious alufá or water used to wash the tablets on which Malês wrote their religious texts. In the latter case, this water could also be drunk, since the ink was made of burnt rice; such a drink was believed to seal the body against outside

Source: João José Reis, *Slave Rebellion in Brazil: The Muslim Uprising of 1835 in Bahia*, trans. Arthur Brakel (Baltimore: Johns Hopkins University Press, 1993), 99–103.

harm. Some of the amulets were made of West African fabric; leather was used more often, since it provided better protection for both the sacred words and the other charms. There is a remarkable similarity between the Bahian Malê talismans and those still in use in black Africa, although the Bahian amulet seems to have had more "pagan" ingredients. According to Vincent Monteil, "In general the Islamic Talisman is a leather case, sewn together and containing a piece of stiff cardboard . . . and inside this is a folded piece of paper on which are written phrases in praise of God and cabalistic symbols—that is, Arabic letters, pentacles, and the like." Kabbalistic drawings such as the ones mentioned here were found in several amulets confiscated in 1835.

The Magrebian Arabic in the Malê amulets found on the bodies of dead rebels or in Muslims' houses has been studied and translated by Vincent Monteil and Rolf Reichert. Reichert took stock of twelve amulets, some of which contained kabbalistic shapes. . . .

The magic in the Islamic texts and drawings worked as protection against various threats. The Africans arrested in 1835 said little about their magic, and when they did say something, they avoided linking it to the revolt. However, besides their obvious political function, these amulets were especially designed to control daily life. A freedman named Silvestre José Antônio, a merchant, was arrested with five amulets in his case. He declared they "were prayers to save [him] from any unfortunate happenstance in his travels through the Recôncavo." Whether in Africa or in Brazil, a good Muslim merchant never traveled without a considerable number of protecting charms. A booklet of Islamic prayers could also work to protect its holder against evil spells. It was for that reason that a freedman named Pedro Pinto asked a literate Malê to make one for him, so he could "be free from wagging tongues." Pedro, by the way, was not a Malê.

. . .

Even so, one Malê fisherman made a good living from amulet making. According to one witness, Antônio, a Hausa slave residing in Itapagipe, "wrote prayers in his language and sold them to his partners making 4 *patacas* [1,280 réis] a day doing that." When he was arrested, a writing quill was found in his room: "Asked . . . by the justice [of the peace] why he kept such a quill, the same slave answered that he kept it so as to write things having to do with his Nation. He was then asked to write and he made a few scribbles with the phoney quill and the justice asked . . . what he had written. He answered that what he had written was the name of the 'Hail Mary.'" This Islamic-Christian melding does not seem to have impressed the justice of the peace. Antônio calmly went on telling his questioners that "when he was a young boy in his homeland, he went to school," and there he had learned Arabic so as to write "prayers according to the schism of his homeland."

» Working with Sources

1. How did the Malês use the written word to resist authority, and why did they use the Arabic language?

2. What do the documents created by the slaveholders and their supporting institutions reveal about the power of written sources as well?

SOURCE 23.5 Photograph of a Chinese coolie, Peru

1881

Chinese migration to Latin America was a major part of the pattern of mass migration streams across the world that typified the nineteenth century. "Coolies" (from the Urdu word *kuli*, or "hireling") were indentured laborers recruited from India and China on 5- or 10-year contracts, who were forced to work to pay off the cost of their transportation. Roughly 235,000 Chinese came to Peru, Cuba, and Costa Rica, working in guano pits and silver mines, on sugar and cotton plantations, and later on railroads. Such work contracts were little better than slavery, and oftentimes were accompanied by institutions familiar from enslavement itself. This photograph, published in a Chilean army newspaper, depicts a Chinese coolie who is being liberated by an invading Chilean army in 1881.

>> **Working with Sources**

1. Look closely at the man's feet and ankles. What might have been attached to him, and why?

2. How might this image have been deployed for propaganda purposes by the invading Chilean army?

Source: http://commons.wikimedia.org/wiki/File:Enslaved_Chinese_coolie_in_Peru_1881.jpg.

Credits

Chapter 1: Reprinted by permission from Macmillan Publishers Ltd: Nature 521, 310–315 (21 May 2015), copyright 2015, p. 6; Bettman/Getty Images, p.7; (top left) akg-images / CDA/Guillemot; p. 12 (top right) akg-images /CDA/Guillemot; p. 12 (bottom) National Museum of Tanzania, Dar es Salaam, (c) 1985 David L. Brill, p.9; © Kenneth Garrett Photography, p. 13; CC-by-SA-2.0 Bradshaw Art, TimJN1 via Wikicommons, p. 17; (top) INTERFOTO/Alamy Stock Photo; (bottom) Foto: Hilde Jensen, copyright University Tübingen, p. 18; Walter Geiersperger/Getty Images, p. 19; Philippe Psaila/Science Source, p. 20; DEA/C. SAPPA/Getty Images, p. 22; James Chatters/ASSOCIATED PRESS, p. 27.

Chapter 2: The Trustees of The British Museum/Art Resource, NY, p. 30; DEA PICTURE LIBRARY/Getty Images, p. 37; Erich Lessing/Art Resource, N.Y, p. 39; Réunion des Musées Nationaux-Grand Palais/Art Resource, NY, p. 43; (top) © Copyright Alfred Molon, p. 44; (bottom) pius99/iStock Photo, p. 44; Werner Forman/Art Resource, NY, p. 49; SOTK2011/ Alamy Stock Photo, p. 50; Ivy Close Images/Alamy Stock Photo, p. 57; (right) akg-images/John Hios. (left, nude) Egyptian Museum, Cairo, p. 59.

Chapter 3: © DeA Picture Library/Art Resource, NY, p. 64; Photo courtesy of National Museum of Pakistan, Karachi, p. 71; © Doranne Jacobson/International Images, p. 73; Firmin Didot, ~ 1810, Copyright: ImagesofAsia.com, p. 77; bpk, Bildagenteur/Museum fuer Asiatische Kunst, Staatliche Museen /Iris Papadopoulos/ Art Resource, NY, p. 81; © Doranne Jacobson/International Images, p. 85; © Doranne Jacobson/International Images, p. 86.

Chapter 4: Xiaoyang Liu/Getty Images, p. 90; (top and middle) © by Liu Liquin/ChinaStock, p. 95; Martha Avery/Getty Images, p. 96; V&A Images, London/Art Resource, NY, p. 100; © Gary Lee Todd, p. 101; Lowell Georgia/Getty Images, p. 111; joannawnuk/Shutterstock Photo, p. 112; Martha Avery/Getty Images, p. 114.

Chapter 5: ERNESTO BENAVIDES/AFP/Getty Images, p. 118; The Witte Museum, p. 126; H. John Maier Jr./The LIFE Images Collection/Getty Images, p. 127; Adapted from Greger Larson and Dorian Fuller/The Evolution of Animal Domestication/The Annual Review of Ecology, Evolution and Systematics, 45:115–36, 2014, p. 128; © Sean Sprague/The Image Works, p. 130; Insights/UIG via Getty Images, p. 133; akg/Bildarchiv Steffens AKG603103, p. 134; "From MA. DEL CARMEN RODRÍGUEZ MARTÍNEZ, PONCIANO ORTÍZ CEBALLOS, MICHAEL D. COE, RICHARD A. DIEHL, STEPHEN D. HOUSTON, KARL A. TAUBE, ALFREDO DELGADO CALDERÓN "THE OLDEST WRITING IN THE WORD" SCIENCE, 15 SEPT. 2006 : 1610–1614. Reprinted with permission from AAAS, p. 137; © Caroline Penn/Alamy Stock Photo, p. 141; Keystone/Getty Images, p. 142.

Chapter 6: Kazuyoshi Nomachi/Getty Images, p. 148; Werner Forman/Art Resource, NY, p. 155; The Metropolitan Museum of Art, New York. Purchase, Buckeye Trust and Mr. and Mrs. Milton F. Rosenthal Gifts, Joseph Pulitzer Bequest and Harris Brisbane Dick and Rogers Funds, 1981, p. 156; Werner Forman/Art Resource, NY, p. 160; Gardel Bertrand/Hemis/Alamy Stock Photo, p. 163; bpk, Bildagentur/Ethnologisches Museum, Staatliche Museen/Art Resource, NY, p. 167; Photograph K2803© Justin Kerr, p. 168; DEA/G. DAGLI Orti/Getty Images, p. 171; DEA/G. DAGLI ORTI/De Agostini/Getty Images, p. 172; Keren Su/Getty Images, p. 173.

Chapter 7: Vanni Archive/Art Resource, NY, p. 178; SEF/Art Resource, NY, p. 182; 205 Louis and Nancy Hatch Dupree Collection, Williams Afghan Media Project Archive, p. 186; Vanni Archive/Art Resource, NY, p. 189; © Vanni Archive/Art Resource, NY, p. 190; Wolfgang Kaehler/Getty Images, p. 199; © Zev Radovan/Bridgeman Images, p. 203; akg-images/Gerard Degeorge, p. 206; Image copyright © The Metropolitan Museum of Art. Image source: Art Resource, NY, p. 208; (top) MS Vat. lat. 3867 (Romanus), folio 106 recto (5th c CE), p. 209; (bottom) Erich Lessing/Art Resource, NY, p. 209.

Chapter 8: Courtesy of the Library of Congress, p. 214; Borromeo/Art Resource, NY, p. 220; Coins of the Northwest, Second Century BCE and Late First Century CE, p. 222; JeremyRichards/iStock Photo, p. 223; R. u. S. Michaud/akg-images, p. 226; akg-images/A.F.Kersting, p. 228; © The Trustees of the British Museum, p. 234; Image copyright © The Metropolitan Museum of Art/Art Resource, NY, p. 237.

Chapter 9: © The Trustees of the British Museum/Art Resource, NY, p. 242; © Glow Asia RF/Alamy, p. 246; akg-images/Laurent Lecat, p. 250; photo by Gary Lee Todd, p. 254; Researched by Liu Liqin/ChinaStock, 256; Courtesy of ChinaStock, p. 259; Photograph © 2014 Museum of Fine Arts, Boston, p. 264; SSPL/Getty Images, p. 266.

Chapter 10: Courtesy of the Library of Congress, p. 272; The Trustees of the British Museum/Art Resource, NY, p. 275; ALIMDI.NET/Fabian von Poser, p. 281; John Hicks/Getty Images, p. 283; Album/Art Resource, NY, p. 286; Paris, Bibliotheque Nat., p. 288; © British Library Board. All Rights Reserved./Bridgeman Images, p. 292; Scala/White Images/Art Resource, NY, p. 294; bpk, Bildagentur/Bibliotheque Nationale /Gérard Le Gall/Art Resource, NY, p. 299.

© British Library Board/Robana /Art Resource, NY, p. 597; © The Metropolitan Museum of Art. Image source: Art Resource, NY, p. 598; Joana Kruse/Alamy Stock Photo, p. 599; Akbar and the Jesuits, The Book of Akbar (In 03.263), © The Trustees of the Chester Beatty Library, Dublin, p. 602; FineArt/Alamy Stock Photo, p. 605; Digital Image ©2009 Museum Associates/LACMA . Licensed by Art Resource, NY, p. 610; Erich Lessing/Art Resource, NY, p. 615.

Chapter 21: John C. Weber Collection. Photo: John Bigelow Taylor, p. 620; Metropolitan Museum of Art, Rogers Fund, 1917, p. 626; Image copyright © The Metropolitan Museum of Art. Image source: Art Resource, NY, p. 627; © by Qi Wen/ChinaStock, p. 629; Bettmann/Getty Images, p. 631; Roy Miles Fine Paintings/Bridgeman Images, p. 632; © Chinese Commercial Enterprises, p. 634; Courtesy of the Library of Congress, p. 635; Réunion des Musées Nationaux-Grand Palais/Art Resource, NY, p. 637; © The Granger Collection, New York, p. 639; Courtesy of the Library of Congress, p. 642; University of British Columbia Library, Rare Books and Special Collections, p.643; akg-images, p. 646; V&A Images, London/Art Resource, NY, p. 648.

Chapter 22: HIP/Art Resource, NY, p. 654; (a) (top left) © Bettmann/Getty Images, (b) (bottom left) Classic Image/Alamy Stock Photo, (c) (right) Niday Picture Library/Alamy Stock Photo, p. 661; Print Collector/Getty Images, p. 662; © RMN-Grand Palais/Art Resource, NY, p. 664; Wellcome Images/Science Source, p. 669; bpk, Bildagentur/Art Resource, NY, p. 670; Culture Club/Getty Images, p. 673; Artokoloro Quint Lox Limited/Alamy Stock Photo, p. 679; (a) National Gallery, London/Art Resource, NY, (b) Erich Lessing/Art Resource, NY, p. 683; Hulton-Deutsch Collection/Getty Images, p. 684.

Chapter 23: Courtesy of the Library of Congress, p. 688; Library of Congress Reproduction Number: LC-USZ62-99485, p. 692; The Granger Collection, New York, p. 696; Gianni Dagli Orti/Topkapi Museum Istanbul/The Art Archive/Art Resource, NY, p. 698; Schalkwijk/Art Resource, NY. © 2017 Banco de Mexico Diego Rivera Frida Kahlo Museums Trust, Mexico, D.F./Artists Rights Society (ARS), New York, p. 701; Library of Congress/Getty Images, p. 702; Library of Congress reproduction number LC-USZ62-125988, p. 702; Erich Lessing/Art Resource, NY, p. 705; Library of Congress reproduction number LC-USZ62-73425, p. 707; Courtesy of the Library of Congress, LC-USZ62-26047, p. 714.

Chapter 24: Collection of Museum of Fine Arts, Boston via Wikipedia Commons, p. 722; The Art Archive at Art Resource, NY, p. 727; Courtesy of the Library of Congress, p. 727; Hirarchivum Press/Alamy Stock Photo, p. 728; (a) National Palace Museum, (b) The Print Collector/Print Collector/Getty Images, p.731; (a) akg-images/British Library, (b)

© Peter NEWark Pictures/Bridgeman Images, p. 732; (a) © Philadelphia Museum of Art, (b) British Library via Wikicommons, p. 735; Heritage Images/Getty Images, p.736; Private Collection/Bridgeman Images, p. 737; IAM /akg/NA, p. 739; John Thomson, (1874). Illustrations of China and Its People, Vol 4. MIT Libraries, p. 743; Courtesy of the Library of Congress, p. 747.

Chapter 25: Bettmann/Getty Images, p. 761; Bettmann/Getty Images, p. 763; SEF/Art Resource, NY, p. 766; Michael Kappeler/AP Photo, p. 768; Print Collector/Getty Images, p. 773; North Wind Picture Archives/Alamy Stock Photo, p. 775; RussiaSputnik/Bridgeman Images, p. 780.

Chapter 26: SSPL/Science Museum/Art Resource, NY, p. 784; Science & Society Picture Library/Getty Images, p. 792; Robert Hunt Library/Chronicle/Alamy Stock Photo, p. 796; The Print Collector/Alamy Stock Photo, p. 801; The Stapleton Collection/Bridgeman Images, p. 802; Bettmann/Getty Images, p. 803; Archives Charmet/Bridgeman Images, p. 804; © Peter NEWark Pictures/Bridgeman Images, p.807; Natural History Museum, London, UK/Bridgeman Images, p. 810.

Chapter 27: Chronicle/Alamy Stock Photo, p. 816; (a) Peter Horree/Alamy Stock Photo, (b) Granger Historical Picture Archive/Alamy Stock Photo, p. 819; Bettman Images/Getty Images, p. 822; Réunion des Musées Nationaux-Grand Palais/Art Resource, NY, p. 826; Archives Charmet/Bridgeman Images, p. 827; Hulton-Deutsch Collection/Getty Images, p. 830; Timewatch Images/Alamy Stock Photo, p. 835; Panos Pictures ASL00010DRC, p. 836; Courtesy of the Library of Congress, p. 841.

Chapter 28: Courtesy of the Library of Congress, p. 850; Hulton-Deutsch/Getty Images, p. 852; Photograph, World War One, Western Front, (1914–1918), 1916. Imperial War Museum, UK, p. 855; Courtesy of the Library of Congress, p. 858; Hulton Archives/Getty Images, p. 859; Library of Congress LC-USW3-001543-D, p. 860; Kurt Hutton/Getty Images, p. 863; Fotosearch/Getty Images, p. 866; Bettman Images /Getty Images, p. 867; Heritage Image Partnership Ltd/Alamy Stock Photo, p. 870; World History Archive/Alamy Stock Photo, p. 873; Courtesy of the Library of Congress, p. 877; Hulton Archives/Getty Images, p. 880; Bettman/Getty Images, p. 882.

Chapter 29: Keystone/Getty Images, p. 888; Alfred Eisenstaedt/Getty Images, p. 890; Associated Press, p. 893; Bettmann/Getty Images, p. 896; Rykoff Collection/Getty Images, p. 898; Library of Congress/Getty Images, p. 900; (a) © The Museum of Modern Art/Licensed by SCALA/Art Resource, NY. With permission of the Renate, Hans & Maria Hoffman Trust/Artists Rights Society (ARS), New York, (b) © 2009 Museum Associates/LACMA/Art Resource, NY. © 2017

Source Index

Page numbers of the form S8-7–S8-8 indicate, in this case, a source document in chapter 8 on pages 7–8 in the source documents at the end of chapter 8. If the page number for the source document is followed by (d) this indicates a text source document. If the page number for the source document is followed by (v) this indicates a visual source document.

Subject Index

Page numbers followed by f denote a figure or illustration. Page numbers followed by m denote a map.